The

GREEK DIALECTS

The
GREEK DIALECTS

Grammar
Selected Inscriptions
Glossary

By

Carl Darling Buck

THE UNIVERSITY OF CHICAGO PRESS

CHICAGO & LONDON

The present volume is a complete revision and expansion of
Introduction to the Study of the Greek Dialects, published by
Ginn and Co., Copyright 1928.

THE UNIVERSITY OF CHICAGO PRESS, CHICAGO 60637

The University of Chicago Press, Ltd., London W.C.1

*Copyright 1955 under the International Copyright Union. All
rights reserved. Published 1955. Fourth Impression (corrected)
1968. Printed in the United States of America*

Midway Reprint 1973

PREFACE

The changes from the previous editions of the *Introduction to the Study of the Greek Dialects* have been so great that the old plates could not be used, and this is virtually a new book.

I have changed the title to *The Greek Dialects*, as both simpler and in a measure also appropriate. For it is fair to claim that the book is, for the time being, the most up-to-date treatment of the subject. Bechtel's monumental work (3 vols; 1,781 pp.) is a storehouse containing many items of detail not noticed here. But there is a deal of repetition incident to the arrangement adopted, and, more important, much new material has become available since its date.

The new material furnishes significant additions to our knowledge of several dialects, as Thessalian, Boeotian, and notably that of Cyrene. But I have hoped in vain for the greatest desiderata—early inscriptions of some extent from Lesbos and from East Locris.

I am more than ever convinced that the arrangement adopted here is not only more economical of space, but also more illuminating, than the separate treatment of the several dialects followed in other works.

I am indebted to the University of Chicago Press, to which the copyright has been transferred from the previous publishers, for undertaking the new publication and for the competent services in its execution; and to Dr. D. Georgacas for painstaking proofreading and other assistance.

CONTENTS

vii

PART II: SELECTED INSCRIPTIONS

APPENDIX

PART I

GRAMMAR OF THE DIALECTS

ABBREVIATIONS

The following abbreviations are employed for languages, dialects, and local sources of the forms quoted.

Acarn. = Acarnanian
Ach. = Achaean
Aegin. = Aeginetan
Aetol. = Aetolian
Agrig. = of Agrigentum
Amorg. = of Amorgos
Amphiss. = Amphissan
And. = of Andania
Arc. = Arcadian
Arc.-Cypr. = Arcado-Cyprian
Arg. = Argive (of Argos)
Argol. = Argolic (of Argolis, outside of or including Argos; but mostly marked Epid., Troez., etc.)
Astyp. = of Astypalaea
Att. = Attic
Att.-Ion. = Attic-Ionic
Avest. = Avestan
Boeot. = Boeotian
Calymn. = of Calymna
Carpath. = of Carpathos
Chalced. = of Chalcedon
Chalcid. = Chalcidian
Cleon. = of Cleonae
Cnid. = Cnidian
Corinth. = Corinthian
Corcyr. = Corcyraean
Cret. = Cretan
Cypr. = Cyprian
Cyren. = Cyrenaean
Delph. = Delphian
Dodon. = of Dodona
Dor. = Doric
El. = Elean
Eng. = English
Ephes. = Ephesian
Epid. = Epidaurian
Epir. = Epirotan
Eretr. = Eretrian

Eub. = Euboean
Germ. = German
Gortyn. = Gortynian
Heracl. = Heraclean
Herm. = of Hermione
IE = Indo-European
Ion. = Ionic
Lac. = Laconian
Lat. = Latin
Lesb. = Lesbian
Locr. = Locrian
Mant. = Mantinean
Meg. = Megarian
Mel. = of Melos
Mess. = Messenian
Mil. = of Miletus
Mycen. = of Mycenæ
Nisyr. = of Nisyros
N.W.Grk. = Northwest Greek
Olynth. = of Olynthus
Orop. = of Oropus
Pamph. = Pamphylian
Phlias. = Phliasian (of Phlius)
Phoc. = Phocian
Rheg. = of Rhegium
Rhod. = Rhodian
Selin. = of Selinus
Sicil. = Sicilian
Sicyon. = Sicyonian
Skt. = Sanskrit
Stir. = of Stiris
Styr. = of Styra
Sybar. = of Sybaris
Syrac. = Syracusan
Teg. = Tegean
Thas. = of Thasos
Ther. = Theran
Thess. = Thessalian
Troez. = of Troezen

For abbreviations of modern works of reference see pp. 337 ff. Those used for the names of Greek authors are familiar. Likewise those used for grammatical terms, as adj., adv., sb. (= substantive, noun), vb., cpd., sg., pl., masc., fem., gen., dat., act., mid., pass., subj., opt., infin., imv., pple., etc. Note also gram. = grammarians or grammatical (with reference to forms quoted from the ancient grammarians), and lit. = literary (with reference to forms quoted from the literary dialects without mention of the individual authors).

INTRODUCTION

CLASSIFICATION AND INTERRELATION OF THE DIALECTS

1. When the ancient grammarians spoke of the four dialects of Greece—Attic, Ionic, Aeolic, and Doric, to which some added the κοινή as a fifth—they had in mind solely the literary dialects, which furnished the occasion and object of their study. But these literary dialects represent only a few of the many forms of speech current in Greece, most of which play no part whatever in literature, and, apart from some scattered glosses, would be entirely unknown to us were it not for the wealth of inscriptions which the soil of Greece has yielded in modern times.

The existence of Ionic, Aeolic, and Doric elements in the people and speech of Greece is an undoubted fact of Greek history, and one of the first importance to an understanding of the dialect relations. But there is no warrant, either in the earlier Greek tradition or in the linguistic evidence, for making this an all-inclusive classification. These three elements were precipitated, as it were, on the coast of Asia Minor, where their juxtaposition gave rise to the historical recognition of the distinction. And as the Ionians, Aeolians, and Dorians of Asia Minor were colonists from Greece proper, it was a natural and proper inference of the historians that they reflected ethnic divisions which also existed, or had once existed, in the mother country.

As to who were the Dorians of Greece proper there was of course no mystery. They formed a well-defined group throughout the historical period, and the tradition that they came originally from the Northwest is completely borne out by the close relationship of the Doric and Northwest Greek dialects (see below).

That the Ionians were akin to the inhabitants of Attica was an accepted fact in Greek history, and the Athenians are called Ionic both in Herodotus (e.g., 1.56) and Thucydides (6.82, 7.57). The linguistic evidence is equally unmistakable. The only un-

3

certainty here is as to the extent of territory which was once Ionic. There are various accounts according to which Ionians once occupied the southern shore of the Corinthian gulf, the later Achaea (e.g., Hdt. 1.145-46, 7.94), Megara (e.g., Strabo 9.392), Epidaurus (e.g., Paus. 2.26.2), and Cynuria (Hdt. 8.73). If these accounts in themselves are of questionable value, yet we cannot doubt that the Ionians before the migration were not confined to Attica. The close relations of Epidaurus and Troezen with Athens, in cult and legend, are significant for the Argolic Acte, and it is reasonable to assume that at least the entire shore of the Saronic gulf was once Ionic. Indeed it is now a widely favored view, uncertain yet not unlikely, that the ancestors of the Ionians (the name of course is later) constituted the first wave of Greek migration and once occupied much of the territory which, with the next waves of migration, was held by speakers of Aeolic and the dialect which later survived as Arcado-Cyprian.

The affinities of the Aeolians were more obscure, for theirs was the earliest migration to Asia Minor, the most remote from the historical period. But Thessaly was the scene of their favorite legends, the home of Achilles, as also of their eponymous hero Aeolus, and many of their place-names had their counterpart in Thessaly. In Herodotus we find the tradition that the Thessalians of the historical period were invaders from the west who occupied what had hitherto been an Aeolic land [1], and with this the linguistic evidence is in perfect accord. For Thessalian is of all dialects the most closely related to Lesbian, and at the same time shares in some of the characteristics of the West Greek dialects, this admixture of West Greek elements being somewhat stronger in Thessaliotis than in Pelasgiotis. See **201, 202, 210**, and Charts I, II. The Boeotians also are called Aeolians by Thucydides, [2] and the Boeotian dialect is, next to Thessalian, the most closely related to Lesbian. These three have several notable characteristics in common (see **201** and Charts I, II),

---

[1] Hdt. 7.176: ἐπεὶ Θεσσαλοὶ ἦλθον ἐκ Θεσπρωτῶν οἰκήσοντες γῆν τὴν Αἰολίδα, τὴν περ νῦν ἐκτέαται.

[2] Thuc. 7.57: οὗτοι δὲ Αἰολῆς Αἰολεῦσι τοῖς κτίσασι Βοιωτοῖς τοῖς μετὰ Συρακοσίων κατ' ἀνάγκην ἐμάχοντο, i.e., the Aeolians of Methymna, Tenedos, etc., were compelled to fight against the Aeolians who founded these cities, namely, the Boeotians; id. 3.2: Βοιωτῶν ξυγγενῶν ὄντων (of the Lesbians)

and are known as the Aeolic dialects. But in Boeotian there is
an even stronger admixture of West Greek elements than in
Thessalian (see **217** and Charts I, II), the historical explanation
of which must be the same. If we credit the statement of Thucydides that the Boeotian invaders were from Arne, whence they
had been driven by the Thessalians, [3] we should recognize in
these Boeotians not a part of the old Aeolic population of Thessaly, but a tribe of West Greek invaders from Epirus (cf. Mt.
Boeon), like the Thessalians who forced them onward. The
Aeolic element is to be ascribed rather to the tribes, or some of
them, comprising the early stratum, as, for example, the Minyans
of Orchomenos. However obscure such details may be, the
evidence is perfectly clear that both Boeotia and Thessaly
were once Aeolic, but were overrun by West Greek tribes which
adopted the speech of the earlier inhabitants in greater or less
degree.

It is a natural presumption, of which there are some specific
indications, that not only Thessaly and Boeotia but the intermediate lands of Phocis and Locris, and even southern Aetolia—
in fact, all that portion of Greece north of Attica which plays
a role in the legends of early Greece—was once Aeolic. Phocaea
in Asia Minor, which, though later Ionic, surely belonged originally to the strip of Aeolic colonies, was believed to be a colony
of Phocis and in the dialect of Phocis there are actually some
relics of Aeolic speech as the dative plural of consonant stems in
-εσσι, which is also found in Locris (**107**.3). As for southern
Aetolia, the region of Calydon and Pleuron was once called
Aeolis according to Thucydides, [4] and the probability is that
the Aetolians of the Homeric period were Aeolic, though their
name was taken by the later, West Greek, invaders. The Aetolian
occupation of Elis was an accepted tradition, and the existence
of an Aeolic element in the dialect of Elis, like the dative plural
in -εσσι, may be brought into connection with this if we assume
that while the invaders were Aetolians in the later sense, that is,
West Greek, as Elean is distinctly a West Greek dialect, they

---

[3] Thuc. 1.12: Βοιωτοί τε γὰρ οἱ νῦν ἑξηκοστῷ ἔτει μετὰ Ἰλίου ἅλωσιν ἐξ
Ἄρνης ἀναστάντες ὑπὸ Θεσσαλῶν τὴν νῦν Βοιωτίαν, πρότερον δὲ Καδμηίδα γῆν
καλουμένην ᾤκησαν.
[4] Thuc. 3.102: ἐς τὴν Αἰολίδα τὴν νῦν καλουμένην Καλυδῶνα καὶ Πλευρῶνα.

had nevertheless adopted certain characteristics of the earlier Aeolic Aetolian and brought them to Elis.

Corinth was also once occupied by Aeolians according to Thucydides, [5] and it is a noteworthy fact that the dative plural in -εσσι, which is unknown in other Doric dialects, is found in various Corinthian colonies (107.3).

But we have passed beyond the limits within which the term Aeolic, or in general the division into Ionic, Doric, and Aeolic, can with any propriety be applied to the peoples and dialects of the historical period. It is only in Strabo that these three groups are made into an all-inclusive system of classification, by means of an unwarranted extension of Aeolic to include everything that is not Ionic or Doric. And yet it is, unfortunately, this statement of Strabo's, [6] the error of which has long since been recognized, that has often been taken as representative of ancient tradition and still colors, in the literal sense, our maps of ancient Greece. The historical Phocians, Locrians, Aetolians, etc., were not, as Strabo's statement implies, called Aeolic. Neither in Herodotus, Thucydides, nor any early writer are they ever brought under any one of the three groups. Their dialects, with that of Elis, which Strabo also calls Aeolic, all of which may be conveniently designated the Northwest Greek dialects, are, in spite of some few traces of Aeolic as mentioned above, most closely related to the Doric dialects. There is scarcely one of the general characteristics common to the Doric dialects in which they do not share, though they also have certain peculiarities of their own (see 223, 226, and Charts I, II). If we were to classify them under any one of the three groups, it is unquestionably Doric to which they have the best claim, and if Strabo and our maps so classed them there would be no very

---

[5] Thuc. 4.42: ὑπὲρ οὗ ὁ Σολύγειος λόφος ἐστίν, ἐφ' ὃν Δωριῆς τὸ πάλαι ἱδρυθέντες τοῖς ἐν τῇ πόλει Κορινθίοις ἐπολέμουν, οὖσιν Αἰολεῦσι.

[6] Strabo 8.333: πάντες γὰρ οἱ ἐκτὸς Ἰσθμοῦ πλὴν Ἀθηναίων καὶ Μεγαρέων καὶ τῶν περὶ τὸν Παρνασσὸν Δωριέων καὶ νῦν ἔτι Αἰολεῖς καλοῦνται... καὶ οἱ ἐντὸς (sc. Ἰσθμοῦ) Αἰολεῖς πρότερον ἦσαν, εἶτ' ἐμίχθησαν, Ἰώνων μὲν ἐκ τῆς Ἀττικῆς τὸν Αἰγιαλὸν κατασχόντων, τῶν δ' Ἡρακλειδῶν τοὺς Δωριέας καταγαγόντων... οἱ μὲν οὖν Ἴωνες ἐξέπεσον πάλιν ταχέως ὑπὸ Ἀχαιῶν, Αἰολικοῦ ἔθνους· ἐλείφθη δ' ἐν τῇ Πελοποννήσῳ τὰ δύο ἔθνη, τό τε Αἰολικὸν καὶ τὸ Δωρικόν. ὅσοι μὲν οὖν ἧττον τοῖς Δωριεῦσιν ἐπεπλέκοντο, καθάπερ συνέβη τοῖς τε Ἀρκάσι καὶ τοῖς Ἠλείοις, ..., οὗτοι αἰολιστὶ διελέχθησαν, οἱ δ' ἄλλοι μικτῇ τινι ἐχρήσαντο ἐξ ἀμφοῖν, οἱ μὲν μᾶλλον οἱ δ' ἧττον αἰολίζοντες.

serious objection. Indeed, modern scholars do often class them under "Doric in the wider sense," calling them specifically "North Doric". But on the whole it seems preferable to retain the term Doric in its historical application and employ West Greek as the comprehensive term to include the Northwest Greek dialects and the Doric proper. As to the Arcadians too, calling them Aeolic is without warrant in earlier usage. For example, Thucydides in describing the forces engaged at Syracuse (7.57) makes the most of the distinction between Ionic, Doric, and Aeolic elements, but does not class the Arcadians with any of these.

The most fundamental division of the Greek dialects is that into the West Greek and the East Greek dialects, the terms referring to their location prior to the great migrations. The East Greek are the "Old Hellenic" dialects, that is, those employed by the peoples who held the stage almost exclusively in the period represented by the Homeric poems, when the West Greek peoples remained in obscurity in the northwest. To the East Greek division belong the Ionic and Aeolic groups, though, of the latter, Thessalian and Boeotian, as explained above, are mixed dialects belonging in part also in the West Greek division. And to East Greek belongs also the Arcado-Cyprian.

No two dialects, not even Attic and Ionic, belong together more obviously than do those of Arcadia and the distant Cyprus. They share in a number of notable peculiarities which are unknown elsewhere. See **189** and Chart I. This is to be accounted for by the fact that Cyprus was colonized, not necessarily or probably from Arcadia itself, as tradition states, but from the Peloponnesian coast, at a time when its speech was like that which in Arcadia survived the Doric migration. This group represents, beyond question, the pre-Doric speech of most of the Peloponnesus, whatever we choose to call it. The term Arcado-Cyprian, while describing accurately what is left of the group in historical times, is strikingly infelicitous when applied to the prehistoric period. But it is difficult to find a substitute which is not arbitrary or ambiguous. [7]

[7] Both, in the case of "Achaean," a term used in this sense by some and so in the previous editions of this book, but now discarded. Its

This group is by several scholars combined with the Aeolic under the head of "Achaean" ("North Achaean" = Aeolic, "South Achaean" = Arcado-Cyprian) or "Central Greek." There are in fact notable points of agreement between Arcado-Cyprian and Aeolic (see **190**.3-6 and Chart I), which cannot be accidental. On the other hand, many of the common Aeolic characteristics are lacking, and there are certain points of agreement with Attic-Ionic (see **190, 193**.1, 2), as well as many quite special features (see **189**). It is probable that the connections with Aeolic reflect a remote period of geographical contiguity with Aeolic peoples in northern Greece or even before the migration into Greece, with a subsequent quite independent development. If, then, we classify the dialects, not according to supposed prehistoric relations, but as we actually know them, it is only proper to class Arcado-Cyprian as a distinct group coordinate with others of the East Greek division. [8]

Just as in the Northwest Greek dialects some traces of the former Aeolic speech have survived, as noted above, so there are also some traces of pre-Doric speech (either Aeolic or of the Arcado-Cyprian type) in the Doric dialects. Thus Lac. Ποhοιδάν and Ποhοίδαια unmistakably represent (with Lac. *h* from σ) a form of the name which is attested in Arc. Ποσοιδᾶν, and is in contrast to the genuine Dor. ΠοτειδάϜων, Ποτειδάν. And the Ποσειδάν which also occurs in inscriptions of many Doric lands may represent another pre-Doric form. But see **61**.4. The ἰν = ἐν, regular in Arcado-Cyprian and Pamphylian, occurs also in two Cretan towns and the Achaean colony of Metapontum (see **10a**). The occurrence of the Aeolic dat. pl. -εσσι in consonant stems

specific application to this group does not conform to any of the accepted uses of Ἀχαιοί, namely, (1) those of Achaea Phthiotis, (2) those of the Peloponnesian Achaea, (3) in Homer a generic term for the Greeks before Troy by no means restricted to the southern group; and furthermore stands in rivalry with various other modern and partly visionary applications of the same term.

[8] The partial decipherment of the tablets in Cretan script (Linear B) from Pylos, Mycenae, and Cnossus, dating from about 1400-1200 B.C. (Pylos) and earlier, has revealed an early Greek dialect, one that must be a precursor of Arcado-Cyprian. In view of the incomplete state of decipherment, it would be premature to attempt a detailed description of this dialect. But a notable feature is the preservation of the old labiovelar voiceless stop with a value like that of Lat. *qu*, as in *quetro-*=Att. Τετρα- (for *ro* cf. Thess. πετρο-, etc., 6). This lines up with the fact that in Arcado-Cyprian labiovelars show a special development different from that in other dialects (see **68**. 3).

in Corinthian colonies, as well as in the Northwest Greek dialects, has already been noted.

The peculiar development of secondary νσ as seen in Lesb. παῖσα from πάνσα, etc. is now fully attested for Cyrene, with traces in Thera (see **77**.3). The agreement is such a striking innovation that it is surely not accidental. True, any direct connection with the Asiatic Aeolians is unlikely. For the missing link we must assume that a continental mother dialect of the Asiatic Aeolic, one containing forms like παῖσα though such are unknown in the actual Thessalian and Boeotian dialects, once existed in a part of this once Aeolic territory before the West Greek overlay. We may then credit the accounts of Minyan participation in the colonization of Thera (e.g., Hdt. 4.145 ff.) with reflecting some genuine tradition.

There are some other alleged, and possible, but more dubious, examples of pre-Doric survival. The question of survival versus accidental agreement or historical borrowing is often difficult.

The classification of the dialects is then, in outline, as follows:

West Greek	East Greek
NORTHWEST GREEK	ATTIC-IONIC
Phocian	Attic
Locrian	Ionic
Elean	AEOLIC
Northwest Greek	Lesbian
κοινή	
	Thessalian
	Boeotian
DORIC	ARCADO-CYPRIAN
Laconian	Arcadian
Heraclean	Cyprian
Megarian	
Argolic	
Rhodian	
Coan	
Theran, Cyrenaean	
Cretan, etc.	
Pamphylian	

2. The Greek dialects, classified in accordance with the preceding scheme, and with their important subdivisions noted, are the following. For summaries of the characteristics of each, see **180-273**.

East Greek

I. THE ATTIC-IONIC GROUP

1. **Attic.**
2. **Ionic.**

A. **East Ionic,** or Ionic of Asia Minor. The Ionic cities of the coast of Asia Minor and the adjacent islands, Samos, Chios, etc., together with their colonies, mostly on the Hellespont, Propontis, and Euxine. There are some local varieties, of which the most marked is Chian, containing some Lesbian features.

B. **Central Ionic,** or Ionic of the Cyclades. The Ionic Cyclades, Naxos, Amorgos, Paros with its colony Thasos, Delos, Tenos, Andros, Ceos, etc.

C. **West Ionic,** or **Euboean.** Chalcis (with its colonies in Italy, Sicily, and the Chalcidian peninsula) and the other cities of Euboea. A local dialect with marked characteristics is the Eretrian, seen in the inscriptions of Eretria and Oropus.

II. THE ARCADO-CYPRIAN GROUP

1. **Arcadian.** The material is now considerable, owing to the increasing number of newly found inscriptions.
2. **Cyprian.** There are numerous short inscriptions, and one of considerable length, the bronze of Idalium. All are in the Cyprian syllabary. Inscriptions in the Greek Alphabet, beginning in the Macedonian period, are all in the κοινή.
3. **Pamphylian.** The only inscription of any extent (Schwyzer 686), though the interpretation is in many parts doubtful, contains plenty of clearly identifiable words. The dialect shows many notable characteristics of this group, combined with others which are West Greek or reminders of Cretan. See **200**. The earliest colonists were doubtless pre-Doric Peloponnesians, as in Cyprus, followed by Dorians. The mixture is then somewhat similar to that of Aeolic and West Greek in Thessaly and Boeotia.

III. THE AEOLIC GROUP

1. **Lesbian**, or Asiatic Aeolic. [9] The inscriptional material is fairly extensive, but late. There is nothing approaching the time of the poems of Alcaeus and Sappho, and very little that is older than the Macedonian period. Most of the inscriptions are from the cities of Lesbos, but a few are from other islands and towns of the Aeolic mainland.

2. **Thessalian.** [10] Two subdivisions with marked differences are formed by the dialect of Pelasgiotis and that of Thessaliotis. For these and for other parts of Thessaly, see **214**.

3. **Boeotian.** [10] The material is very extensive, and representative of all the important Boeotian towns, but is meager for the early period.

West Greek

IV. THE NORTHWEST GREEK GROUP

1. **Phocian.** A large part of the material, including nearly all that is of an early date, is from Delphi, and is quoted specifically as **Delphian**.

2. **Locrian.** The two early inscriptions long known, to which a third is now added, are from Western Locris, but one of these is presumably based on an East Locrian draft. Most of the other material is much later and with more or less mixture. See **236**.

3. **Elean.** Numerous very early inscriptions from Olympia, with a few later ones that are still in dialect with some mixture. See **241**.

4. The **Northwest Greek** κοινή. Employed in Aetolia and other regions under the domination of the Aetolian league. See **279**.

NOTE. Only Phocian, Locrian, and Elean are known to us as distinct dialects of this group. Of others which presumably belong here we have almost no material from a time when they retained their individuality. In Aetolia, except for a few very short inscriptions, the material is from the time of the Aetolian league, and in the mixed Northwest Greek κοινή.

[9] Sometimes simply called Aeolic. But, to avoid confusion with Aeolic in its wider sense, the designation Lesbian is to be preferred in spite of the formal impropriety of applying it to a dialect not restricted to Lesbos. Most of the material is actually from Lesbos.

[10] That Thessalian and Boeotian are only in part Aeolic, in part West Greek, has been explained above.

Of the speech of Aeniania and Malis previous to the Aetolian domination we have no remains. It is natural to suppose that Northwest Greek dialects were once spoken also in Acarnania and Epirus. But here the influence of the Corinthian colonies was strong from an early period, as shown by the use of the Corinthian alphabet in the few early inscriptions; and in later times, from which nearly all the material dates, the language employed is not the Northwest Greek κοινή, but the Doric κοινή, like that of the contemporaneous inscriptions of Corcyra. See **279**. Hence the actual material from Acarnania and Epirus is more properly classified with Corinthian. From Cephallenia and Ithaca we have decrees in the Northwest Greek κοινή from the Aetolian period (see **279**), but from earlier times not enough to show whether the dialect was Northwest Greek or Doric. From Zacynthus there is almost nothing. The dialect of Achaea (i.e., Peloponnesian Achaea in the historical period) is generally believed to belong to this group. This is probable on general grounds, but there is as yet no adequate linguistic evidence of it. For, apart from the inscriptions of Achaean colonies in Magna Graecia, which, on account of both their meagerness and the mixed elements in the colonization, are indecisive, nearly all the material is from the time of the Achaean league, and this is not in the Northwest Greek κοινή, but in the same Doric κοινή that was used in Corinth and Sicyon.

V. THE DORIC GROUP

1. **Laconian** and **Heraclean**. Laconia and its colonies Tarentum and Heraclea. Heraclean, well known from the Heraclean Tables, has peculiarities of its own, and is treated as a distinct dialect.

2. **Messenian**. Most of the material is late and with considerable κοινή mixture, as the famous cult inscription of Andania (nearly 200 lines).

3. **Megarian**. Megara, and its colonies in Sicily (especially Selinus) and on the Propontis and Bosporus (as Byzantium, Chalcedon, etc.). Except from Selinus the material is late.

4. **Corinthian**. Corinth, Sicyon, Cleonae, Phlius, and the Corinthian colonies Corcyra (with its own colonies Apollonia and Dyrrhachium), Leucas, Anactorium, Ambracia, etc. For Syracusan, etc., see below, 10. Material from places other than Corinth, though coming under the general head of Corinthian, is generally quoted specifically as Sicyonian, Corcyraean, etc.

5. **Argolic**. Argos, Mycenae, etc., and the cities of the Acte, as Hermione, Troezen, and Epidaurus, together with Aegina.

Argolic (Argol.) is used as the general term, while Argive (Arg.) refers more specifically to the material from Argos (with the Argive Heraeum), as Epidaurian to that from Epidaurus. From Aegina there is not much material from the period before the Athenian occupation, but enough to show that the dialect was Argolic.

Argos (or in some sources one of the other Argolic cities) was the reputed mother city of Crete, Rhodes, Cos, etc., and in historical times Argos was often chosen as arbitrator in their local disputes (cf., e.g., nos. 85, 86). There are in fact some, but not too impressive, points of agreement (besides the general Doric) in the dialects.

6. **Rhodian**. Rhodes with the adjacent small islands and the mainland settlements (the Rhodian Peraea), Phaselis in Pamphylia, Cnidus, Syme, Telos, Nisyros, Carpathos, Casos, the Sicilian colonies of Gela and Agrigentum. An inscription of Rhegium, though not a Rhodian colony, is in the same dialect and there are other signs of the spread of Rhodian influence, notably the infin. -μειν (**154**.5). The material is extensive, but little of it early. The inclusion of Cnidus and some of the islands named, in which examples of distinctive features like the infin. -μειν are lacking, is at least convenient and probably justified (cf. now IG XII. Suppl., p. 1).

7. **Coan**. Cos and Calymna. The material is considerable, but not early.

8. **Theran** and **Cyrenaean**. Thera, with Melos, Cimolos, Pholegandros, Sicinos, probably Anaphe, and perhaps Astypalaea.— Cyrene. There are archaic inscriptions in the same type of alphabet from Thera, Melos, Sicinos, and Anaphe. Those of Sicinos (IG XII. Suppl. pp. 178, 180), which was formerly classed among the Ionic islands, indicate that it was, at least in the early period, Doric. For, though metrical to be sure, they show regular Doric forms like σᾶμα and μνᾶμα and the loss of Ϝ as in the earliest Theran.

The dialect of Cyrene, a colony of Thera, is now by far the best known, owing to the discoveries of the last decades.

9. **Cretan**. This is now the best known of all the Doric dialects, owing to the very extensive early material, especially from

Gortyn. The dialect of Gortyn and other cities of the great central portion of the island is also known more specifically as Central Cretan, to exclude the divergent type seen in the inscriptions, mostly late, from the eastern and western extremities of the island. See **273**. But the term Cretan alone is to be understood as referring to this Central Cretan, unless otherwise stated.

10. **Sicilian Doric.** Owing to the mixture of population it is the exception that the dialect of Sicilian cities can be clearly grouped with that of their mother cities. That of Selinus and Megara Hybla may be classed as Megarian, and that of Gela and Agrigentum as Rhodian. But in Syracuse Gelon's wholesale transplantation of population from Gela and other cities must have left the old Corinthian element in a minority. There are (at least, as yet) no inscriptions written in the Corinthian alphabet or with the typical early OV for secondary ō (**25d**), and there is nothing distinctively Corinthian in the dialect of either the inscriptions or the works of the Syracusan writers. With but few exceptions, the inscriptions of Syracuse and the other cities are late. The longest, those of Halaesa and Tauromenium, are in a mixture of Doric and Attic κοινή, with some local features in vocabulary. A noteworthy spread of Rhodian influence is seen in the typical infin. -μειν used by Epicharmus and occurring in several places in Sicily and Magna Graecia (**154.**5).

The Dialects in Literature

3. Of the numerous dialects of Greece a few attained the rank of literary dialects, though for the most part in a mixed and artificial form not corresponding to anything actually spoken at a given time and place. Moreover, in the course of literary development these dialects came to be characteristic of certain classes of literature, and, their role once established, the choice of one or the other usually depended upon this factor rather than upon the native dialect of the author.

The literary development of epic songs began with the Aeolians of Asia Minor, whence it passed into the hands of the neighboring Ionians, and the language of Homer, which became the norm of all epic poetry and strongly affected subsequent poetry of all

classes, is a mixture of Aeolic and Ionic—in the main Old Ionic
but with the retention of many Aeolic forms, such as ἄμμες beside ἡμεῖς, genitive singular in -ᾱο beside -εω, etc. The language
of Hesiod is substantially the same, but with some Aeolic forms
not used in Homer, also some Boeotian and Doric peculiarities.
The elegiac and iambic poets also use the epic dialect with some
modifications, not only Ionians like Archilochus, but the Athenian Solon, the Spartan Tyrtaeus, the Megarian Theognis, etc.

Of the melic poets, Alcaeus and Sappho followed very closely
their native Lesbian dialect, though not entirely unaffected by
epic influence. The language of these and other Lesbian poets
was directly imitated by some later writers, notably by Theocritus
in three of his idyls, and contributed an important element to
the language of many more, e.g., Anacreon of Teos, who in the
main employed his native Ionic (New Ionic), and, in general,
to the choral lyric, which was mainly Doric.

The choral lyric was developed among Doric peoples, though
under the impulse of Lesbian poets, who we know were welcomed
in Sparta, for example, in the seventh century. Its language is
Doric, with an admixture of Lesbian and epic forms, no matter
whether the poet is a Dorian, or a Boeotian like Pindar, or an
Ionian like Simonides and Bacchylides. This Doric, however,
is not identical with any specific Doric dialect, but is an artificial
composite, showing many of the general Doric characteristics,
but with the elimination of local peculiarities. An exception
is to be made in the case of Alcman, whose Doric is of a severer
type and evidently based upon the Laconian, though also mixed
with Lesbian and epic forms.

The earliest prose writers were the Ionic philosophers and
historians of the sixth century, and in the fifth century not only
Herodotus, but Hippocrates of Cos, a Dorian, wrote in Ionic.
In the meantime, with the political and intellectual supremacy
of Athens, Attic had become the recognized language of the
drama, and before the end of the fifth century was employed
in prose also, though the earlier prose writers as Thucydides,
like the tragedians, avoided certain Attic peculiarities which
were still felt as provincialisms (e.g., ττ = σσ, ρρ = ρσ). Henceforth Attic was the language of literary prose.   .

The dialects mentioned are the only literary dialects known and cultivated throughout the Greek world. But some few others were employed locally. Epicharmus and Sophron wrote in their native Syracusan Doric, as did later, but in a more mixed form, Archimedes and Theocritus. A form of Doric prose was developed among the Pythagoreans of Magna Graecia, seen in some fragments of Archytas of Tarentum, Philolaus of Croton, and others, though the greater part of the writings of this class are spurious. The comic poet Rhinthon, from whom the grammarians sometimes quote, used the Doric of Tarentum. The fragments of Corinna of Tanagra, whose fame was scarcely more than local, are in Boeotian, and the Boeotian dialect, as well as Megarian and Laconian, are caricatured by Aristophanes. But the great majority of the dialects play no role whatever in literature.

Even for those dialects which are represented, the literary remains must for the most part be regarded as secondary sources, not only because of their artificial character but also because of the corruptions which they have suffered in transmission. Exceptional importance, however, attaches to the language of Homer because of its antiquity, and to the Lesbian of Alcaeus and Sappho because it is relatively pure and much older than the inscriptional material.

NOTE. In the following exposition, dialectal forms from literary and grammatical sources are not infrequently quoted, especially where the inscriptional evidence is slight, as it is, for example, quite naturally, for the personal pronouns. Such forms are sometimes quoted with their specific sources, sometimes simply as literary Doric (lit. Dor.), literary Lesbian (lit. Lesb.), literary Ionic (lit. Ion.), or grammatical (gram.). But a detailed treatment of the dialectal peculiarities observed in our literary texts is so bound up with questions of literary tradition and textual criticism that it is best left to the critical editions of the various authors. It would be impracticable in a work of the present scope, and would, moreover, tend to obscure that more trustworthy picture of the dialects which is gained from inscriptions, and which is so important as a basis for the critical study of the mixed literary forms. However, see the Appendix, pp. 342 ff.

PHONOLOGY

THE ALPHABET

4. The numerous differences in the local alphabets, so far as they consist merely in variations of the forms of the letters, need not be discussed here, important as they are to the epigraphist in deciding the age and source of inscriptions. But certain points in the use of the alphabet and its development as a means of expressing the Greek sounds should be noted.

1. In the most primitive type of the Greek alphabet, as it is seen in the earliest inscriptions of Crete, Thera, and Melos, the non Phoenician signs Φ, Χ, Υ have not yet been introduced, and the Ξ is not in use. The sounds of φ, χ are represented by πh, χh (or Ϙh), or, as in Crete, where Β (H) when used is η not h, are not distinguished from π, κ; those of ψ, ξ by πσ, κσ.

2. In the next stage of development, after the introduction of Φ, Χ, Υ, the alphabets fall into two classes, according to the values attached to these signs. The eastern division, to which Ionic belongs, employs them as φ, χ, ψ, and also uses the Ξ as ξ, though a subdivision of this group, represented mainly by the Attic alphabet, uses only the first two and expresses ψ, ξ by φσ, χσ. The western division, [1] to which belong the majority of the alphabets of Greece proper as well as that of Euboea, and which became the source of the Latin alphabet, employs Φ, Χ, Υ as φ, ξ, χ, not using Ξ at all, and generally expressing ψ by πσ or, oftener, φσ (but a special sign for ψ in Locris and Mantinea, another rarely in Elis and Laconia).

3. In the earliest inscriptions nearly all the alphabets have the

---

[1] This distinction of Eastern and Western alphabets, the distribution of which is clearly shown in the map in Kirchhoff's Studien zur Geschichte des griechischen Alphabets (which, however, now needs some corrections; see Appendix), has no connection with that of East and West Greek dialects and is anything but coincident with it. From the coloring of Kirchhoff's map the convenient short terms, "red", "blue," and "green" alphabets, have come into use.

Ϝ (vau or digamma); and many the Ϙ (koppa), which is used before ο or υ, and that too even if a liquid intervenes, e.g., Ϙορινθόθεν, hόρϘος, ΛοϘρός, ἐϘρότε͞, ΠάτροϘλος, λέϘυθος, Ϙλύτος (in other positions it is very rare).

4. The four Phoenician signs for sibilants were taken over, but with varying distribution or values. Both the ϲ or Ʂ (sigma) an Ϻ (san) were used for σ, but, with few exceptions (e.g., once Ϻ beside Ʂ in the Locrian no. 59), only one or the other at the same place and time. A sign И, a simplified form of Ϻ is used in an Arcadian inscription for a sibilant of special origin, as Иις = τίς, Cypr. σις (no. 17; see **68**.3). T, occurring also in the Carian alphabet and perhaps ultimately another modification of the san, is used for usual σσ = Att. ττ at Halicarnassus ('ΑλικαρναΤέ(ω)ν beside 'Αλικαρνασσέων), Teos (θαλάΤης beside θάλασσαν), Ephesus (τέΤαρες, etc.) and elsewhere (see p. 348). This is the source of the numeral sign for 900, namely ⅀, known by the late name "sampi" (σὰν πῖ 'like πῖ', from its form).

Ξ and I were adopted, but for a time without full stabilization in value. Ξ = ξ in the Ionic, Corinthian, and (ⱈ) Argive alphabets, but lacking in the majority of alphabets (not only where X = ξ, but also in Attic where φσ = ξ, and occurring = I in Theran Ξεύς, Ξηύς, Corinth. ΞΒΥϺ = Ζεύς. Conversely I for Ξ in Epid. Ἄναιις. I in earliest Cretan, precise phonetic value uncertain, = later ττ; Att. σ, as ὅΙος, etc. (**82**).

5. In Boeotian Ⱶ, a compromise between E and I, is sometimes used for the close ε, later ι (**9**.4). At Corinth with Corcyra, Sicyon, Cleonae, and Megara there were two characters for the e-sounds, namely, Corinth. ß, Sicyon, ꟻ = ε or η, but ß or (Corcyr.) ßꟅ = original ει or secondary ε͞ (but ß in an archaic Meg. inscription = ε only, not η, and at Cleonae = η only. Cf. nos. 91–97.

6. In most of the alphabets the ⱨ (early ß) is the sign of the spiritus asper, and neither η and ω nor the secondary ε͞ and ō (**25**) are distinguished from the short ε and ο. But in East Ionic, where the sound of the spiritus asper was lost at a very early period, the ⱨ, which was thus left free, was turned to account as a vowel sign, not so much to show a difference in quantity (in the case of ᾱ, ῑ, ῡ no such need was felt) as one of quality. It was probably used first only for the extremely open ē coming

from ᾱ, that is, for the specifically Attic-Ionic η (**8**), which for a time was more open than the sound of the inherited ē, though this was also open as compared with the short ε, and both soon became identical and were denoted in the same way. To be sure, no such distinction is to be observed in East Ionic inscriptions, but it is seen in some of the Cyclades, to which the use of the H has passed from East Ionic, e.g., from Naxos (no. 6) Νικάνδρη, Ϙόρη, etc. but ἀνέθε̄κεν (with E in the penult). Similar examples from Andros and Ceoṣ (nos. 7, 8), also Amorgos.

The use of B = η extended not only to the Ionic but also to the Doric islands, Rhodes, Thera, Melos, and Crete, where it is found in the earliest inscriptions, though in Crete it went out of use for a time, not appearing, for example, in the Law Code. In Central Ionic, where the sound of the spiritus asper still survived, as also in Rhodes, Thera, and Melos, the sign was used both as η and as *h*. It occurs also with syllabic value = *h*ε or *h*ε̄, as Bκηβόλο̄ι (Naxos, no. 6), Hσπέρης (Oropus, no. 14.46), Hλλε̄ν (Paros), Ther. Hρμοκρέ(ο̄ν), Arg. (no. 85) Hραι beside HEραι, Boeot. (no. 39) Hνδεκα, Hξ, Hμιττα, even late Aetol. Hτέων (= hετέων, cf. ἔτος **58***c*).

The Ionic alphabet is also characterized by its distinction of the o-vowels through differentiated forms of O, usually Ω = ω, which became universal, but in archaic inscriptions of Delos, Paros, Thasos, and Siphnos Ω = ο and O or ⊙ = ω; of Thera O = ο, ⊙ = ω; of Melos and Cnidus C = ο, O = ω.

7. In 403 B.C. the Ionic alphabet was officially introduced at Athens, and not much later replaced the native or "epichoric" alphabets in other parts of Greece. Inscriptions of the end of the fifth or the beginning of the fourth century often show a transitional form of the alphabet, partly epichoric, partly Ionic. Even with the full Ionic alphabet, F was generally retained where it was still sounded, and sometimes a form of H was used for the spiritus asper, as ⊢ in the Heraclean Tables and occasionally elsewhere (Elis, Cumae, Sicyon, Epidaurus). The Delphian Labyadae inscription (no. 52) has B = *h*, H = η; likewise an Argive inscription.

For the Cyprian syllabary, see p. 210.

Vowels

α

5. o for α before or after liquids. Examples are most numerous in Lesbian, mainly from literary and grammatical sources, as στρότος = στρατός, βροχέως = βραχέως, χόλαισι = χαλῶσι; etc. (see p. 342). So ἀμβρ[ό]την (no. 25) = ἁμαρτεῖν, like Hom. ἤμβροτον = ἤμαρτον (μβρ from μρ, as regularly). Both στρόταγος and στράταγος occur in inscriptions; likewise in Boeotian στροτός in numerous proper names, στροτιώτας, ἐστροτεύαθη, but also στρατός in proper names, στραταγίοντος. The στρατ-forms, which are the only ones so far attested for Thessalian, are to be attributed to κοινή influence. Boeot., Thess. ἐροτός = ἐρατός, βροχύς = βραχύς, attested by proper names, Boeot., Lesb. πόρνοψ = πάρνοψ, whence Lesb. Πορνοπία, Thess. πετρο- = τετρα-.

In Arcado-Cyprian also we find Arc. ἐφθορκώς = ἐφθαρκώς, πανάγορσις belonging with West Ion. ἄγαρρις (**49**.2) τέτορτος, Βρόχυς, στορπάος = ἀστραπαῖος (also Arc. στορπά, Cypr. στροπά in Hesych.), Cypr. κορζία (Hesych.) = καρδία, κατέϝοργον = *κατεϝαργον aorist of *κατ-εϝέργω (κατείργω) with the weak grade of the root as in ἔδρακον from δέρκομαι (**49**.2).

Here perhaps also, as an Aeolic survival, Aetol. Λόφριον beside usual epithets Λάφριος, Λάφρια. But for the widespread γροφεύς, etc. see **49**.2.

6. o for α in other cases. ὀν = ἀνά in Lesbian, Thessalian (Pelasgiotis), and Arcado-Cyprian (also ὐν-, see **22**). Cf. also Thess. ὀστροφά, from *ὀνστροφά=ἀναστροφή. Lesb., Arc. δέκοτος = δέκατος, also Arc. δέκο = δέκα, ἑκοτόν = ἑκατόν, and Lesb. ἔνοτος = ἔνατος. Thess. ἐξόμεινvον = ἐξάμηνον. Delph. ἐντοφήια 'burial rites,' Cyren. ἐντόφιον 'burial gift,' Heracl. τοφιών 'burial place' (cf. τάφος). κοθαρός = καθαρός in Heraclea, Sybaris, Locris (Περ-ϙοθαριᾶν), Lesbos, Elean κόθαρσις.

a. The explanation is uncertain, and not necessarily the same for all the forms cited here. For example, it is possible that the o of δέκοτος, etc. is to be viewed in the some light as that of εἴκοσι = West Greek ϝίκατι. See **116***a*. But the preference for o appears to be, here as in 5, an Aeolic-Arc.-Cypr. characteristic.

7. ε for α. For forms with ε beside α which fall within the regular system of vowel-gradation, see **49**.2-4.

An actual change of final α to ε is seen in Thess. διέ = διά. Cf.
Thess. -ει=-αι (27).

ᾱ

8. Attic-Ionic η from ᾱ. Original ᾱ, which remains unchanged
in all other dialects, becomes η in Attic-Ionic. Thus τιμή, φημί,
ἵστημι, but in other dialects τιμά̄ (ᾱ-stem), φᾱμί (Lat. *fārī*),
ἵστᾱμι (Lat. *stāre*). For the contrast between this η and that
which represents an inherited ē-sound and is common to the
other dialects also, note Att.-Ion. μήτηρ, elsewhere μά̄τηρ (Lat.
māter).

But Attic differs from Ionic, in that it has ᾱ, not η, after ε, ι,
and ρ, as γενεά̄, οἰκίᾱ, χώρᾱ = Ion. γενεή, οἰκία, χώρη.

a. In some Central Ionic inscriptions, as noted in **4.**6, only this η from
ᾱ was written Ꙟ, Н, vs. E for η = original *ē*. This distinction was probably
once general Attic-Ionic, the sound resulting from ᾱ being still somewhat
more open than that representing original *ē*.

b. It is a widely held, but also disputed, view that the change of ᾱ to
η, or rather to the sound close to but not quite identical with η = original *ē*
(above, a) was general Attic-Ionic and that the ᾱ of Att. γενεά̄, etc., was
a reversion rather than an uninterrupted retention of ᾱ in such cases. The
evidence is complicated and open to more than one interpretation.
As the problem is a purely Attic one, it need not concern us further.

c. In Att. κόρη, δέρη the η after ρ is explained by the fact that it was
originally preceded by ϝ (**54**). But Att. εἰρήνη, κρήνη vs. Dor. ἰρά̄νᾱ, κρά̄νᾱ
are anomalous and variously explained.

d. The ᾱ arising from lengthening of α in connection with original
intervocalic, νσ, σν, etc., undergoes the same change, e.g., Att.-Ion.
ἔφηνα from ἔφᾱνα, original *ἔφανσα. See **76**, **77.**1. But in τά̄ς from τάνς and
πᾶσα from πάνσα, original *πάντι̯α, the ᾱ was of later origin and was unaffected. See **77.**3, **78**.

ε

9. ι from ε before (mostly α- and ο-) vowels.

1. Even in Attic an ε before another vowel had a closer sound
than in other positions, and was frequently written ει, as θειός =
θεός, νειώς = νεώς. So, sometimes, in Ionic, as εἴως = ἔως,
δειόμενος (Oropus) = δεόμενος.

In several dialects the ε progressed so far in the direction of ι
that it was frequently, or even regularly, written ι. Thus:

2. Lesbian. Spelling ε in θεός, ἐών, etc. But χρύσιος, χάλκιος,

συκία, κυνία, ὅστιον, etc., show the same phonetic tendency as in other dialects, although the uniform spelling here may be due to the favoring influence of parallel suffixes. So also τίωι, τίοισι (cf. Hom. τέω, ὁτέοισιν) in which the ι may have been reinforced by that of τίς.

3. **Thessalian.** Frequently ι, as θιός, λίθιος, Λίοντα, etc., but also ε in ηυλόρέοντος, παρέοντος, τοίνεος, etc.

4. **Boeotian.** The spelling is usually ι, but sometimes ε, ει, or ͱ (see **4**.5), as θιός, θειός = θεός, ἀνέθιαν, ἀνέθειαν, beside ἀνέθεαν, Πολυκλͱ῁῁ς = Πολυκλέης, ἰόντος = ἐόντος, ῥίοντος = ῥέοντος.

a. Boeotian ε in general had a relatively close sound, and the spelling ει occurs occasionally even before a consonant, as Ξενκρείτω = Ξεναρέτου, Θιόφειστος = *Θεόθεστος (**68**.2), πεποιόντεισσι = -εσσι. In ἐν Θεισπιῆς, Θεισπιεύς, etc., the spelling ει is so constant that it perhaps stands for original η (**16**), which in other dialects was shortened as if the name of the town were connected with θέσπις, etc.

5. **Arcadian.** Regularly ε before a back vowel, as θεός, Ϝέτεα, ἐόντος, etc. But ι before a front vowel in ἀπυδίει = ἀποδέει, Αὐκλίεια = Εὐκλέεια (?); so also -εϊ to -ιϊ, whence -ῑ in dat. sg. πλήθι, ἔτι, ἱερῖ, etc. A somewhat different, but related, case is ἀπυλιῶναι (no. 22.20), from an elsewhere attested ἀπολειόω (162.1ὸ).

6. **Cyprian.** At Idalium the spelling is regularly ι, as θιός, ἰό(ν)τα = ἐόντα, Ϝέπιϳα = ἔπεα. So Pamph. Ϝέτιια, ἀνδριῶνα.

7. **Cretan.** We find ι regularly, except where the ε was once followed by Ϝ. That is, the change was prior to the loss of intervocalic Ϝ; and the ε which later, with the loss of Ϝ, came to stand before another vowel, was unaffected. Thus ἰόντος = ἐόντος, καλίων = καλέων, πλίες = Hom. πλέες,—but υἱέος, Ϝοικέος, δρομέōν.

8. **Laconian.** We find ι, with the same restriction as in Cretan, in early inscription (also in Alcman and Ar. Lysist.), e.g. θιός, ἀνιοχίōν = ἡνιοχέων. In later inscriptions the spelling is usually ε.

9. **Heraclean.** Verbal forms show ι, with the same restriction as in Cretan, e.g., ἀδικίων, ἐμετρίωμες, ἀναγγελίοντι, but ῥέοντα, δεόμενα. In other words, Τιμοκράτιος, τοφιῶν, but usually ε, as Ϝέτεος, owing to κοινή influence.

10. **Argolic.** Frequently θιός, Θίων, etc., in Argos and Epidaurus, but otherwise usually ε.

11. Corinthian. Usually ε, but θιαρός in two late decrees of Corcyra and Epidamnus.

10. ι from ε before ν in Arcado-Cyprian. Here ἰν = ἐν is the regular form (cf. also Pamph. ἰ πόλιι and ἰς from *ἰνς = ἐνς, εἰς), also in compounds as Arc. ἰνάγω, ἰμφαίνω, ἰνφορβίω, ἰγκεχηρήκοι, ἴνδικος, ἴνπασις, ἰνπολά, ἴγγυος, ἰνμενφής and ἴνμονφος 'blameworthy' (opp. to ἀμεμφής, ἄμομφος), Cypr. ἰναλίνω (ἰναλαλισμένα). Cf. also Arc. μίνονσαι = μένουσαι, Ἐρχομίνιοι = Ὀρχομένιοι, ἀπεχομίνος, ἀπυσεδομίνος, διαβωλευσαμίνος = -μένους, etc., but in such forms the later inscriptions have εν. There are a few examples in other positions, as Arc. Τιλείας, Cypr. Μιγαλαθέδ, indicating that in general ε had a relatively close sound (as also in Boeotian, 9.4a). The foreign names appearing as Ἐδάλιον, Κέτιον in the Cyprian texts were usually rendered Ἰδάλιον, Κίτιον.

a. ἰν = ἐν is found also, probably a pre-Doric survival, in some inscriptions of the Cretan towns of Eleutherna and Vaxus, and the Achaean colony of Metapontum.

11. ι beside ε in other cases. The interchange is occasionally seen among dialectal forms of the same word, as in Hom. πίσυρες = πέσσυρες, τέσσερες. Att. ἑστία appears with ι in all other dialects, so far as quotable, e.g., Ion. ἱστίη, Lesb. ἱστία, Thess. Ἰσστιαίειος, Boet. Ἱστιήω, Delph. Ἱστιώ (but ὁμέστιος), Locr. ἱστία, Heracl. Ἱστίειος, Syrac. Ἱστία, Rhod. ἱστιατόριον, Coan ἱστία, Cret. Ἱστία, Arc. Ϝιστίαν. Here the ι may be due to the influence of ἵστημι.

12. α from ε before ρ in Northwest Greek. Locr. φάρειν, πατάρα, ἀμάρα, ἀνφόταρος, Ϝεσπάριος (but μέρος no. 57, περί, ἐνφέροι, Ϝερρέτō no. 59). Here also ἡαρέσται (no. 57; but ἡελέσται no. 58) = ἑλέσθαι, with ρ for λ after the analogy of the present αἱρέω (as, conversely, Cret. αἱλέω = αἱρέω, with λ from the aorist). El. φάρεν, Ϝάργον, Ϝάρρēν, πάρ (= περί), ὁπόταρος, ἐλεύθαρος, ὕσταριν, but the spelling αρ is not quite uniform even in the early inscriptions, and later gives way to ερ (see 241). Delph. φάρεν, ματάρα, Ϝαργάναι, δάρματα, πενταμαριτεύων, but in the later inscriptions the spelling is ερ (φέρεν even in no. 52) Cf. also Ach. Ζεὺς Ἀμάριος, Pamph. ὕπαρ = ὕπερ, Thess. Κιάριον = Κιέριον.

a. Elean has α also after ρ, as λατραι[όμενον] beside λατρειόμενον, μαστράαι from *μαστρεία (31), κατιαραίων, κατιαραύσειε in contrast to φυγαδείην, φυγαδεύαντι (see **161**.1); also before final ν, as μάν = μέν, γνῶμαν = γνῶμεν, 3 pl. opt. ἀποτίνοιαν, ἐπιθεῖαν, συνέαν, etc.; occasionally elsewhere, as εὐσαβέοι = εὐσεβέοι, σκευάŏν = -έων, showing that Elean ε in general had a very open sound. Cf. El. ᾱ = η (**15**).

b. A similar change before λ in Delphian appears in Δαλφοῖς of an inscription and in Δα, Δαλ, Δαλφικόν of the earliest coins.

c. Epid. κραμάσαι = κρεμάσαι and μάντοι = μέντοι, though more isolated, and open to other possible explanations (μάντοι blend with μάν = μήν, κραμάσαι weak grade or assimilation), are perhaps to be viewed in the same light as the Elean forms under α.

13. West Greek α = East Greek ε. Besides the examples of dialectal interchange of α and ε cited under the head of vowel gradation (**49**.2-4), in which the distribution of the α and ε forms is various (e.g., ἄρσην, ἔρσην,—βάλλω, δέλλω), there is a group of parallel forms in which the preference for the α forms is a marked West Greek characteristic.

1. ἱαρός (or ἰαρός) is the regular form in early inscriptions of all West Greek dialects, Pamphylian (ηιαρύ), and Boeotian, ἱερός occurring only later and plainly due to κοινή influence. The situation is probably the same in Thessalian, though the occurrences of both forms are late. ἱερός (or ἰερός) is Attic-Ionic and Arcado-Cyprian, while a third form is seen in Lesb. ἶρος, (likewise ἶρευς, ἴρεια, ἰρητεύω, late κατείρων with ει = ῑ), Ion. ἱρός, ἰρός beside ἱερός, ἰερός. There are many other words with variation between -ερός and -αρός, as μιερός, μιαρός (likewise πύελος, πύαλος, etc.), but with widely different dialectal distribution.

2. Ἄρταμις, so far as the name is quotable from early inscriptions, is the form of all West Greek dialects except Cretan, and of Boeotian. In later Doric and Delphian inscriptions this is usually replaced by Ἄρτεμις. Thessalian has both forms.

3. κα = κε (ἄν) is the form of all West Greek dialects and Boeotian, while Thessalian has κε, like Lesbian and Cyprian. See **134**.2. West Greek and Boeotian ὅκα, etc. = Att.-Ion., Arc.-Cypr. ὅτε, etc. (but Lesb. ὅτα, etc.). See **132**.11. -γα = -γε is likewise West Greek and Boeotian. Adverbs in -(σ)θα = -(σ)θεν, -(σ)θε are usual in West Greek (προσθα- also Arc.). See **133**.1.

a. ἅτερος = ἕτερος is not confined to West Greek dialects, but is also quotable from Arcadian, Boeotian, and Lesbian, and even for Attic is implied by ἄτερος with crasis. So far as we know, ἕτερος belongs to Attic-Ionic only, all examples in other dialects being late.

η

14. Original η, that is, η representing original ē, remains unchanged in nearly all dialects. Contrast the special Attic-Ionic η from ᾱ (8), both being seen in Attic-Ionic μήτηρ = μάτηρ of other dialects. On the introduction of the character Η, see 4.6.

15. ᾱ from η in Elean. The sound of η was so open in Elean that it approximated that of ᾱ, and was frequently, though by no means consistently, denoted by α. Thus μά (but also μέ, μή) = μή, Ϝράτρα = ῥήτρα, βασιλᾶες = ἦες, ἔα (but also εἴε) = εἴη, δαμοσιοία = -οίη πλαθύοντα beside πλεθύοντι, 3 sg. subj. ἐκπέμπᾱ (149). Cf. α for ε (12a).

a. An isolated case outside of Elis is ποίασε on a vase from Ithaca.

16. ει from η in Thessalian and Boeotian. In these dialects the sound was so close that with the introduction of the Ionic alphabet it was uniformly denoted not by η but by ει, which at that time represented a close ē. Thess., Boeot. μεί = μή, ἀνέθεικε = ἀνέθηκε, μεινός = μηνός, Thess. βασιλεῖος, Boeot. γραμματεῖος = -ῆος, Thess., Boeot. στατεῖρας, Boeot. μάτειρ, πατείρ = -τηρ.

a. The spelling ι also occurs in Cypr. ἴ = ἤ 'or' (no.23.24), perhaps ὄπι (no. 23.29) = ὄπη (132.7), in Pamph. Μάνιτους beside Μάνειτυς (gen. sg. = -ητος), and some late Boeot. forms, as παρῖς beside παρεῖς (εἷς = ἧς, Att. ἤν. 163.3).

17. Lesb. αἰμισέων (no. 25), αἰμιθέων (Alc.), αἰμιόνοις (Sappho), all = ἡμι-. The explanation is difficult, since in all other cases η remains unchanged in Lesbian. Perhaps η was more open initially than in other positions, and this, in connection with an epenthetic vowel (but see 47), led to αι.

ι

18. ε from ι after ρ in the Aeolic dialects. An open pronunciation of ι after ρ is indicated by occasional spellings such as Lesb. Δαμοκρέτω = Δημοκρίτου (but κρίννω, κρίτων), Thess. χρεννέμεν (Lesb. κρίννω), Ὑβρέστας beside Ὑβρίστας, ἀπελευθερεσθένσα from ἀπελευθερίζω, Boeot. Διοχρένες = -κρίνης, τρέπεδδα, τρεπεδδίτας (Hesych. τρίπεζαν· τὴν τράπεζαν. Βοιωτοί).

a. Cf. also Lesb. ερ = ρι (probably through the medium of a syllabic ρ) in τέρτος (in glosses and proper names) = τρίτος, and in forms cited in **19**.2; also Lesb. ερ = ιρ in κέρναν = κιρνάναι (influence of ἐκέρασα, etc. ?). *b*. There are scattered examples of ε for ι elsewhere, as El. πόλερ beside πόλιρ = πόλις, βενέοι = *βινέοι (Att. βῖνέω), Ach. ἐρανεσταί = ἐρανισταί, Sicil. Dor. περιωρεσία = *περιωρισία.

19. Consonantal ι (ι̯) from antevocalic ι in Lesbian and Thessalian. The consonantal pronunciation of antevocalic ι might occur anywhere in rapid speech, but was especially characteristic of Aeolic, as indicated by the following related phenomena in Lesbian and Thessalian.

1. Lesb. ζ from δι in ζά, κάρζα, Ζόννυσος, from glosses or late inscriptions, the usual inscriptional spelling being διά, etc. Cf. also Ζιονύ(σιος) on an early coin of Phocaea, Cypr. κορζία · καρδία (Hesych.). Compounds with ζα- = δια- are frequent in the Lesbian poets, as ζάβαις, ζάδηλος, etc., and occur elsewhere, as Hom. ζάθεος (Boeot. δάθιος Corinna), etc.

2. Lesb. μετέρρος, ἀλλότερρος, Πέρραμος, Πέραμος = μέτριος, ἀλλότριος, Πρίαμος, the development being ρι, ρι̯, ερι̯, ερρ.

3. Thessalian doubling of consonants before ι, which may then be retained or omitted in the spelling, as ἰδδίαν, ἰτδίαν, πόλλιος, προξεννιοῦν, ἐξακάττιοι, ἐκκλησσία, κῦρρον beside κύριον, ἀργύρροι gen. sg. = ἀργυρίου beside Μνασσᾶ = Μνασία. Cf. Att. βορρᾶς from βορέας.

4. Omission of ι, as Lesb. ἄργυρα = ἀργύρια, Thess. τρακάδι = τριακάδι, etc. (see also under 3.)

20. Interchange of ι and υ. Assimilation of ι to υ of the following syllable is seen in ἥμυσυ = ἥμισυ, which appears in an Ionic inscription of the fifth century B.C. (τώμυσυ), also in Attic and elsewhere; the opposite assimilation in βιβλίον beside βυβλίον. Influence of the preceding ευ, or of the suffix -σύνη, in Lac. Ἐλευhύνια = Ἐλευσίνια (also Olynth. Ἐλευσύνιος, name of a month). Other by-forms, the relation of which is uncertain, are Ἀμφικτίονες and Ἀμφικτύονες, Meg. αἰσιμνάτας, αἰσιμνάω = Ion. αἰσυμνήτης, αἰσυμνάω, μόλυβδος beside μόλιβος, βόλιμος, etc. (**88**).

a. A secondary ι before σ + consonant appears in sporadic spellings, as Boeot. αἴστεα = ἄστεα, Lesb. παλαίστα = Att. παλαστή (but also παλαιστή Aristot., papyri), Argol. Αἰσκλαπιός (cf. also Corinth. Αἰσχλαβίος and Lat. *Aesculapius* from a similar source) = usual Ἀσκλαπιός, Τροιζάνιος (in a fourth-century inscription of Hermione, otherwise only late) = usual Τροζάνιος, beside Τροζάν, the usual spelling until Roman times. But for Lesb. είκοστος, etc., commonly cited in this connection, the uniform spelling (seven occurrences) favors a different and more special explanation, for which see **77**.2, **116***a*. For Thess. πρεισβεία, etc., see **86**.3.

ι

21. ι remains unchanged everywhere. But in late inscriptions it is sometimes denoted by ει, which had come to have the sound ī, as τειμά or τειμή = τῑμή.

o

22. υ from o, especially in Arcado-Cyprian. In both Arcadian and Cyprian, final o nearly always appears as υ. Gen. sg. -āυ = -āο, as Arc. Καλλίαυ, Cypr. 'Ονασιγόραυ. Middle endings -τυ, -ντυ = -το, -ντο, as Arc. διωρθώσατυ, ἐγάμαντυ (but also -το, from Attic), Cypr. γένοιτυ, ἐϜρἔτάσατυ. Arc., Cypr. (also Lesb., Thess.) ἀπύ = ἀπό, Arc. ὀπύ = ὑπό, also κατύ by analogy, ἄλλυ = ἄλλο. Cf. also ὐν for ὀν = ἀνά (**6**) in Cypr. ὐνέθἔκε (once) beside ὀνέθἔκε, and Arc. ὐνέθυσε, ὐνιερόσει beside ὄνδικα (later ἀν- due to Attic influence).

a. In Pamphylian, υ for o not only when final, but also in final syllables ending in a consonant and once medially in composition, e.g., gen. sg. Πυλώραυ, 3 sg. mid. ἐβōλάσετυ, nom. sg. ὐ βōλἔμενυς (= ὁ βουλόμενος), gen. sg. Μάνἔτυς, cpd. νοικυπολίς (= *Ϝοικοπολίς).

b. In Lesbian there are several examples (beside ἀπύ) of υ = o, especially before μ, as ὐμοίως, ὐμολογία, and (lit.) ὔμοι, ὐπίσσω, ὔσδων. Also Arc. ὐμοίοις, στυμέον.

c. ὄνυμα = ὄνομα is common to nearly all, perhaps all, dialects except Attic-Ionic. Cf. the compounds ἀνώνυμος etc., which are universal.

d. In Chalcid. hυπύ = ὑπό, and Ϙύϙνυς, the second υ is due to assimilation to the first.

ω

23. ου from ω in Thessalian. Long ō in Thessalian, whether original or secondary (**25**), became a close ō, then ū, and, after the introduction of the Ionic alphabet, was regularly denoted by ου. χούρα = χώρα, φιλάνθρουπα = φιλάνθρωπα, τοῦν ταγοῦν πάντουν = τῶν ταγῶν πάντων. Cf. ει from η (**16**).

υ and ῡ

24. Instead of becoming a sound like German *ü*, French *u*, as it did in Attic at an early period, the original *u*-sound (English *oo* in *food*) was retained in several, perhaps the majority of, dialects. This is most obvious where, the Attic values of the letters being taken as a basis, the spelling υ was replaced by ου. In Boeotian, ου begins to appear in the early fourth century B.C. (no. 39), and is frequent after 300 B.C., though υ is not uncommon until the last quarter of the century. Thus οὑπέρ, κούριος, ἀργούριον, τούχα, ὄνουμα, (**22***c*), etc. In the third century the spelling ιου (pronounced like English *u* in *cube*?) is also employed, though never consistently, after τ, δ, θ, ν, and λ, as τιούχα, διού = δύο, 'Ιθιούδικος, ὄνιουμα, Διωνιούσιος, Λιουκίσκω, etc.; also once after σ (Σιούνεσις) and once initially (ἰουιῶ = υἱοῦ). Another spelling is ο, as Boeot. ὁπέρ=ὑπέρ, θοσίης=θυσίαις, also (no. 39) δοώδεκα, σκόφος, and perhaps κόρτον, κότος, Arc. ὀπύ, ὀπέρ.

a. Except in Boeotian, the spelling υ is generally retained in inscriptions. So in Laconian, for which the retention of the *u*-sound is amply attested by the numerous glosses spelled with ου in accordance with Attic values, and by the pronunciation of the modern Tsakonian. In various other dialects, as Arcadian, Cyprian, Thessalian, Lesbian, Cretan, Euboean, there are indications, of one kind or another, of the same pronunciation, such as the occasional spelling ου or ο for υ, or υ for ο (**22***a*), use of ϙ before υ (Chalcid. ϙύϙνυς, λήϙυθος, etc.) and occasional ϝ for υ (**52***c*).

Secondary ē̦ and ō̦. „Spurious Diphthongs"

25. In many dialects, as in Attic, ε and ο differed in quality from η and ω, being close vowels (*ẹ̄, ọ̄*). Consequently the long vowels which came from them by contraction or compensative lengthening, since they retained the same quality, were not identical with η and ω, but were *ē̦* and *ō̦*, the latter becoming *ū*, and eventually came to be designated by ει and ου after these original diphthongs had become monophthongs in pronunciation (**28, 34**). But in other dialects they became identical with η and ω, and were so written. Hence such dialectal variations as τρεῖς—τρῆς from *τρέιες (**42**.3), (ἐ)κεῖνος—κῆνος (-ε-ενος), εἰμί—ἠμί from *ἐσμί (**76**), φθείρω—φθήρω from *φθέρι̯ω (**74**), ξεῖνος—

ξῆνος from ξένϜος (54), χείλιοι—χήλιοι from *χέσλιοι (76), χείρ—
χήρ from *χεσρ (76), βουλή—βωλά (75), κούρη—κώρᾱ from κόρϜᾱ
(54), gen. sg. -ου—ω from -οιο (106.1), acc. pl. -ους—ως
from -ονς (78).

The dialects which regularly have η and ω in such forms are
Arcadian (and presumably Cyprian, though the spelling of course
is indeterminate), Lesbian, Elean, Laconian, Heraclean, and
Cretan. Boeotian and Thessalian properly belong to this group,
since Boeotian has ω, and ει is the same as for original η (16),
and Thess. ει, ου are the same as for original η, ω (16, 23).

In several dialects there is some evidence of a qualitative
difference between the vowels resulting from lengthening and
those resulting from contraction.

a. Cretan. The earliest Cretan inscriptions which have the letter Ｂ
show this for the vowel resulting from the early lengthenings (before
original σμ, etc. as ＢμΕν), but E for that before original νϜ, as κσΕνιος =
later ξήνιος, and usually for the result of contraction, as ἀναιρΕσθαι,
μōλΕν (= later μωλῆν, κοσμΕν, ἀποδόμΕν, ＢμΕν, etc. (rarely -μＢν; ἀπο-
στάμＢν, and ＢμΕν and ＢμＢν in the same inscription, no. 116). After the
introduction of ω there are a few cases of O for the contracted vowel,
as gen. sg. κόσμΟ. In later times regularly η, ω for both lengthened and
contracted vowels.

b. Theran and Cyrenaean. Regularly η, ω for the lengthened vowels,
as δήλομαι, ἦμεν, βωλά (in proper names), Cyren. χήλιοι. Before original
νϜ, etc., Cyren. ἤνατος but Ther. οὖροι. For contraction archaic Theran E
(vs. Ｂ) in ἐποίΕ, etc., later ει, rarely η as τρῆς. Cyren. 3 sg. mid. Dor.
future δησῆται and παισεῖται in the same inscriptions. Ther. gen. sg.
archaic -O (vs. Θ == ω); similarly in Melos gen. sg. -Ｃ (vs. Θ = ω), later
-ου. Cyren. gen. sg. -O in a fifth-century inscription which has ω, later
always -ω; also ω from οε in λωσάμενος.

Somewhat similar situation in Rhodes, Cos, etc. Rhod. ἤμειν, Rhod.,
Coan δήλομαι, βωλά (in proper names), κῆνος, but more commonly ει, ου.

c. Argolic. By lengthening, ἡμί, χηρός, χῆρα, ἤνατος, βωλά, ὧρος, etc.,
but frequently and especially later, ει, ου. By contraction η in augmented
forms, ἦρπε, ἦχον, ἤλετο (beside εἴλετο), but in forms of verbs in -εω usually
ει and at Argos even ι in τελίτō, ἀφαιρῖσθαι (no. 85, about 450 B.C.) and
later καλῖσθαι. Also, strangely, ι for genuine ει in the thrice recurring hῑ,
ῑ = εῑ (132.2). By contraction ω in λωτήριον gen. sg. and acc. pl. of
σ-stems, -ω,-ως at Hermione, but usually -ου and -ονς, -ος.

d. It is to be remembered that in the inscriptions of most dialects
before the introduction of the Ionic alphabet, and except for the early
vowel use of Ｂ, H in Crete, Rhodes, etc., or the use of different signs for

o and ω in some of the islands, the spelling was simply E, O, which we transcribe ē,ō, whether the later spelling is ει, ου or η, ω.

In Corinthian the identity of secondary ē, ō and original ει, ου belongs to the earliest period, owing to the very early monophthongization of the diphthongs (28, 34). The spelling is E at Corinth and Sicyon (vs. Corinth. Ⱥ, Sicyon Ⅹ = ε, η), Ɓ⁊ at Corcyra, and OV in all three places. It is possible that the situation was similar in Megarian, where there is some indication of early monophthongization of ει (28).

In early Locrian, no. 58, 59 have only E, O, while no. 57 has EI (φάρΕΙν, etc.) and OV in the acc. pl. (τΟVς) but O in the gen. sg. (δάμΟ). Later regularly ει, ου.

In Attic-Ionic, E, O are common until after 400 B.C. and occasionally much later, while EI, OV in general begin to appear in the fifth century B.c. But remarkable is the exceptionally early appearance of EI in EIμί, of which there is one example from the eighth (Hesperia 5.33) and several from the sixth century B.c. in Attic (e.g., no. 1 in the Attic, vs. Εμί in the Ionic version), Eretrian, etc. Conversely, there are a few very early examples of E = original ει, as 3 sg. ἄρχΕ, etc.

e. An early change of ē to ī occurs in Att. χίλιοι vs. Ion. χείλιοι, etc. (76), and ἱμάτιον vs. εἱμάτιον in other dialects, like εἷμα.

f. The lengthening of o before σ + nasal (76), gives Att.-Ion. ω not ου, as in ὦμος (cf. Goth. *ams,* Skt. *aṅsa-,* Lat. *umerus,* and Lesb. ἐπομμαδίαις), ὠνή (cf. Skt. *vasna-* 'price,' Lat. *vēnum* 'sale,' and Lesb. ὄννα), Hom. Διώνυσος. The relation of Att. οὖν to ὦν of other dialects is obscure; likewise the history of Att.-Ion. δοῦλος vs. Dor. (Cret., Lac., etc.) δῶλος.

DIPHTHONGS

αι

26. η from αι in Boeotian. The diphthong is retained in the earliest inscriptions, sometimes as αι, sometimes as αε, especially at Tanagra, e.g., Αἐσχόνδας, Ὀκίβαε. But it came to be pronounced as a monophthong, an open ē, and with the introduction of the Ionic alphabet was regularly denoted by η, e.g., κή = καί; ἡ = αἱ; Θειβῆος = Θηβαῖος; dat. sg. and nom. pl. -η = -αι; dat. pl. -ης = -αις; infin. -ση, -σθη = -σαι, -σθαι. In very late inscriptions even ει is found, as Θειβεῖος.

a. An alleged Cret. κή = καί in an early inscription (SEG 2.509, Inscr. Cret. 1, p. 90) is at variance with all other evidence and is surely to be rejected. The first occurrence has already been eliminated by a corrected reading. Namely, αἰ δέ κα κὴ ῥίς ῥοοσει is to be read αἰ δέ κα κηρί (= χηρί) τρόοσει. The second occurrence, which still stands in the latest edition, namely, αἰ δὲ κὴ ῥινὸς αἷμα ῥυῆι, may be read αἰ δέ κ' with elision (and so corresponding to αἱ δέ κα of the previous clause), followed by ἡ ῥινὸς αἷμα from ἐς (=ἐκ) ῥινός with the development as in medial σρ (76).

27. ει from αι in Thessalian. In general αι remains, but at Larissa we find ει for final αι; e.g., ἐψάφιστει = ἐψήφισται, βέλλειτει = βούληται, γινύειτει = γίγνηται; and with added ν (139.2, 156) πεπεῖστειν = πεπεῖσθαι, ὀνγράψειν = ἀναγράψαι, ἐφάνγρενθειν = ἐφαιροῦνται, βέλλουνθειν = βούλωνται. Also Εἰμούνειος (Αἴμων).

ει

28. Sooner or later ει became everywhere a monophthong, a close ε̄ (ẹ̄), though the spelling was retained and in certain dialects extended to the secondary ε̄ (25). In Corinthian this had taken place at the time of the earliest inscriptions, and, while at Corcyra the spelling was Βʔ (25d), at Corinth the sound was nearly always denoted by a single sign, though generally differentiated from ε or η, e.g., ΔϜΕνία = Δεινίου, ΠοτΕδάν (rarely with ΕϹ or Βϵ), but ἀνΒθΒχΒ = ἀνέθηκε. From Megara there are a few examples of Ε = ει, as names in -χλΕδας.

a. At a late period the ẹ̄ progressed still further to an ῑ, usually with retention of the old spelling ει, which then came to be used also for original ῑ (21), but sometimes with phonetic spelling ι. In some words this late spelling with ι became fixed in our texts, e.g., τίσω, ἔτισα, ἔκτισις, of which the proper spelling, as shown by inscriptions and papyri, is τείσω, ἔτεισα, ἔκτεισις.

b. But before vowels it remained ẹ̄ for some time after it had become ῑ elsewhere, and to distinguish it from ει = ῑ, was often written η, e.g., πολιτήαν, ἱέρηα, etc., especially in the Augustan period.

c. For Elean αι from ει after ρ, see 12a.

29. ι from ει in Boeotian. The change in pronunciation which took place everywhere at a late period (28a) occurred very early in Boeotian, and here showed itself in the spelling, which in the fifth century varies between ει, Ⱶ (4.5), and ι, but later is regularly ι, e.g., ΤⰊσιμένες = Τεισιμένης, ἐπί = ἐπεί, ἐπιδεί = ἐπειδή (cf. also 16), ἔχι = ἔχει, χιμένας = χειμένας. For Arg. hῑ = εἶ, see 25c.

οι

30. υ from οι in Boeotian. The diphthong οι was retained much longer than αι (**26**) or ει (**29**), appearing as οι, but also, in some of the earliest inscriptions especially of Tanagra, as οε, e.g. Χοερίλος, Ϝηεκαδάμοε. But in the third century it became a monophthong, probably similar to the German ö, to denote which, approximately, the υ, with its Attic value of ü as a basis, was employed with increasing frequency from about 250 B.C. on, though not uniformly until the end of the century, e.g., Ϝυχία = οἰκία, datϝ sg. and nom. pl. -υ = -οι, dat. pl. -υς = -οις. Where οι is followed by a vowel, it is usually retained (in contrast to αι, **26**), as Βοιωτῦς, though Βυωτῶν occurs once.

In some late inscriptions of Lebadea and Chaeronea the spelling ει is also found, indicating the further progress of the sound to ῑ (see **28**a), e.g., αὐτεῖς = αὐτοῖς.

a. Late Cret. Ποίτιος (no. 120.24) = Πύτιος illustrates the confusion of οι and υ which later prevailed in the κοινή (hence, with still later change in sound to ι, their identity in Modern Greek).

αι, ει, οι before Vowels

31. In the case of αι, ει, οι, also υι, before vowels the omission of ι, consequent upon its consonantal pronunciation with the following vowel, is to be observed in various dialects, though the spelling is anything but constant, and it is impossible to make any general statement as to the conditions of the loss. Thus, as in Attic Ἀθηναία, later Ἀθηνάα, Ἀθηνᾶ, δωρεά beside earlier δωρειά, εὔνοα beside εὔνοια, ὑς beside υἱός, υἱύς, so, e.g., Ion. ἀτελέη beside ἀτελείη, ποιήσεαν = ποιήσειαν, Lesb. δικάως = δικαίως, εὔνοαν = εὔνοιαν, Thess. Γεννάοι = Γενναίου, Arc. στορπάος = ἀστραπαῖος, El. ἔα beside εἴε = εἴη, μαστράα = *μαστρεία (**12**a), Cret. ἀγελάοι = ἀγελαῖοι, Delph. φαωτός = *φαιωτός (φαιός). So especially in forms of ποιέω, as Att. ποεῖ,ποέσω (but ποιῶν), Lesb. πόησαι, etc., Boeot. ἐπόεισε, Arc. ποέντω, El. ἐπι-ποέντων, Coan ναποᾶν beside ναποιάς. Contraction, as in Ἀθηνᾶ, in Lesb. Φώκαι = Φωκαίαι.

a. Owing to the variation in forms like the above, the diphthongal spelling sometimes appears in words where it has no etymological justi-fication, as late ὀγδοίης, ὀγδοικοντα, βοιηθέω.

αυ, ευ, ου

32. In αυ, ευ,ου, the υ remained an *u*-sound, not becoming *ü*
as it did in Attic when not part of a diphthong. This is shown
not only by Ionic αο, εο (33), but by occasional varieties of spelling such as Corinth. 'Αχιλλεούς, Corcyr. ἀϜυτάν, Att. ἀϜυτάρ,
Ion. ἀϜυτō, Cret. ἀμεϜύσασθαι, where Ϝ indicates the natural
glide before the *u*-sound, and Locr. ΝαϜπακτίōν, Cret. σποϜδδάν,
etc.

33. αο, εο from αυ, ευ appear in East Ionic inscriptions (εο also
in Amphipolis and Thasos) of the fourth century and later,
e.g., αὸτός, ταōτα, εὄνοια, εὀεργέτης, φεόγειν. This spelling is
frequent even in κοινή inscriptions of this region.

a. Cretan inscriptions show several examples of ου beside usual ευ,
as early 'Ελτυνιοῦσι, τιτοϜτός, τιτουϜέσθō (from *τιτεύομαι 'impose a fine'),
later ἐλούθερος, ἐπιτάδουμα, etc. For El. αυ from ευ after ρ, see 12*a*.
Sporadic cases of αυ = ευ elsewhere, as late Delph. ἐλαύθερος, ἱεραύς,
βουλαυόντων, Arc. Αὐκλίεια (= Εὐκλέεια?), Ther. αὐνοίας, αὐεργέταν, Αὐήμερος,
Pholeg. ψαυδῆ, late πέταυρον v.l. of πέτευρον (hence *petaurum* in Lucil., etc.).

34. ου became, in most dialects, a monophthong (first ọ̄, later
ü), though the spelling ου was generally retained and eventually
extended in certain dialects to the secondary ō. In Corinthian
this had taken place at the time of the earliest inscriptions.
See **25***d*.

a. Occasionally words which contain genuine ου are found with the
spelling O in early inscriptions when O for secondary ō was usual, e.g.,
ὂκ = οὐκ, βõν = βοῦν (or = βῶν? See **37**.1). In forms of οὗτος, which in
general have genuine ου (e.g., Cret. τούτō etc.), this spelling is so frequent
in early Attic, e.g., τõτο, τότόν (τōτο also in Thasos; cf. also Orop. ἐντōθα,
i.e. ἐντοῦθη = ἐνταῦθα), as to point to some special cause. Possibly, as has
been suggested, there existed beside the usual forms with genuine ου
(e.g. τοῦτο from *το-υ-το), a gen. sg. τότō (τούτου,), formed by doubling of
τō (τοῦ), which then influenced the other forms.

35. Certain words show a υ diphthong only, or mainly, in
Lesbian. So αὔως = Dor. ἀϜώς (Arg. ποτ' ἀϜώ, Lac. ἀβιώρ
Hesych.), ἀώς, Hom. ἠώς, Att. ἕως, from *αὐσώς (cf. Lat. *aurōra*
from *ausōs-ā*); παραύα = Dor. παραά (implied by εὐπάραος), Ion.
παρηή (implied by καλλιπάρηος, παρήιον), Att. παρεά, from *παρ-
αυσ-ā (cf. Lat. *auris*); ναῦος = Dor. etc., νᾱ(Ϝ)ός (cf. Lac. ναϜōν),

Hom. νηός, Att. νεώς, probably from *νασϝός (54d); δεύω (also Thess., no. 33.27 and Hom.), from *δεύσω(?); αὐάδης (Sappho) = Att. ἀηδής, from *ἀ-σϝᾱδής. Cf. also Hom. εὔαδε from *ἔσϝαδε, and αὐερύω from *ἀϝϝερύω, *ἀν-ϝερύω.

a. In such forms υ comes from a combination containing υ or ϝ, not from simple intervocalic ϝ, which in Lesbian, as elsewhere, regularly drops out without affecting the preceding vowel. Forms like αὐάτα (Alcaeus, Pindar) = ἀϝάτα (cf. 53), ε[ὔ]ιδε (Balbilla), etc. (several forms in glosses, presumably from the Lesbian poets; some also in Homer) are poetical only, and represent an artificial doubling or shift in syllabification, perhaps in imitation of cases like the above, coming from a combination. The consonant-doubling in hypocoristic proper names (89.5) accounts for the diphthong in Thess. Κλεύας, from *Κλέϝᾱς, Calymn. Κλεύαντος, Cret. Φαῦος, Νεύαντος.

36. In words with regular antevocalic ευ the natural glide between υ and the following vowel is often expressed by ϝ, as Boeot. Βακεύϝαι, Cypr. κατεσκεύϝασε, Lac. Εὐβάλκης (β = ϝ, **51**), Locr. Εὔϝανδρος.

In late inscriptions υ is sometimes omitted, especially in derivatives of σκεῦος, as Att. παρεσκεασμένων, Lesb. ἐπισκεάσαντα, Corcyr. ἐπισκεάζειν, σκεοθήκας, Delph. κατασκεώσηται.

Long Diphthongs

37. 1. The original long diphthongs āi, āu, ēi, ēu, ōi, ōu, except when final, were regularly shortened in prehistoric times to ai, au, ei, eu, oi, ou, or, in some cases, lost the second element. Hence such by-forms as βοῦς from *βῶυς (cf. Skt. gāus), acc. βοῦν, but Arg., Epid., Cret., Syrac. βῶς, βῶν (cf. Lat. bōs, Skt. acc. sg. gām), Ζεύς from *Ζηύς (cf. Skt. dyāus) but acc. Ζῆν (cf. Lat. diēs), whence, with transfer to consonant declension, Ζῆνα, Ζηνός, etc., Cret. Δῆνα, Τῆνα (**84**).

2. The Greek long diphthongs may be original when final, but otherwise are of secondary origin. Most of the latter arose by loss of an intervening consonant, as κλᾱΐς, κληΐς, from *κλᾱϝίς (cf. Lat. clāvis), and in the earlier period these were not diphthongs but were pronounced in two syllables. So κληΐς, χρηΐζω, πολεμήϊος, πατρώϊος, etc., regularly in Homer, and often in the later Ionic poets. This pronunciation is also indicated by occasional

spellings such as Τήιοι, θωιιήν, ἱερήιια, χρηιίζω, in inscriptions.
On the other hand the change of ηι to ει (**39**) or the loss of the ι
(**38**) presupposes the diphthongal pronunciation; and where we
find, e.g., χρήζω, ἱερῆον, and χρηιζω, ἱερηιον, side by side, the latter
must be understood as χρήιζω, ἱερῆιον. But in general it is impossible to determine just when the change from dissyllabic
to diphthongal pronunciation took place, and hence it is often
uncertain whether we should accent, e.g., κλῄς (κλῃίς) or κλῆις
(κλῆς), χρῄζω or χρήιζω, οἰκήιος, οἰκηίου or οἰκῆιος, οἰκῆιου, and
editors of the same texts differ in their practice. We employ
the accentuation which goes with the earlier pronunciation,
though without the mark of diaeresis, for the early Ionic inscriptions; and likewise in general, simply as a matter of convention,
in citing forms of this kind in the grammar.

38. ᾱ, η, ω from ᾱι, ηι, ωι. In Attic the ι ceased to be pronounced in the second century B.C., and the spelling without ι (the
iota subscript is a medieval device; in inscriptions ι is written
like other letters or omitted entirely) became more and more
frequent, and may be found in late inscriptions from all parts
of Greece. But in some dialects this dates from an earlier period.

East Ionic has occasional examples of dat. sg. -η = -ηι from
the sixth century B.C. on, though -ηι is the usual spelling.

Lesbian has τῶ Νικιαίōι in a fifth-century inscription (no. 24),
the earliest loss of ι in the article. No. 25 (first half fourth century) and no. 26 (324 B.C.) have uniformly dat. sg. -ᾱι, -ωι
(3 sg. subj. -ηι in no. 25, -η in no. 26), while no. 27 (319/7) has
3 sg. subj. -η, dat. sg. -ω, but -ᾱι, a difference observed in some
other texts (also, though anachronistic, in some texts of the
Lesbian poets; see pp. 342 f.). After the fourth century the forms
in ᾱ, -ω, -η predominate.

Thessalian has from the fifth century dat. sg. τᾱφροδίται τᾱ,
and ταγᾶ beside ἀταγίαι (in no. 35), and in inscriptions in the
Ionic alphabet we find regularly dat. sg. -ᾱ, -ου (=ω, **23**), 3 sg.
subj. -ει (= η, **16**).

Cyprian has dat. sg. -ᾱ, -ō, beside -ᾱι, -ōι, but in the Idalium
bronze (no. 23) only in the case of the article when followed
by ι, as τᾶ ἰ(ν).

a. The loss of ι probably began in the article, which was proclitic.

b. The fluctuation between the historical and the phonetic spelling in late inscriptions introduced confusion in the spelling of forms with original η, ω; hence such spellings as nom. sg. βουλήι, gen. sg. τῶι δάμωι, imv. ἐχέτωι. Such imperative forms in -τωι and -σθωι, where this spelling was favored by the subj. in -ηι, are especially frequent.

39. ει from ηι. The history of ηι differs in some dialects from that of ᾱι, ωι,—especially in Attic, where it became ει (i.e., ē̆) some two centuries before ᾱι, ωι became ᾱ, ω.

In the case of ηι of secondary origin (37.2) the spelling ει is frequent in the fourth century and from about 300 B.C. is almost universal, e.g., κλείς from κλῇς, λειστής from λῃστής, λειτουργέω from λῃτουργέω.

In inflectional endings ει is also frequent in the fourth century and predominates in the third and second, e.g., dat. sg. βουλεῖ, 3 sg. subj. εἴπει. But here, owing to the analogy of other forms with η of the same system, as βουλῆς, βουλήν, εἴπητε, ηι was never given up and eventually was fully restored, so that the normal spelling in imperial times was ηι or η (38).

The spelling ει beside ηι, partly at least due to Attic influence, is also frequent in third- and second-century inscriptions of other dialects, or even earlier as in the Heraclean Tables, where we find 3 sg. subj. νέμει, φέρει, etc. (so usually, but twice -ηι, once -η).

a. The change of ηι to ει is also Euboean, where it was accompanied by a change of ωι to οι. In Eretrian this was effected about 400 B.C. Somewhat later ει occurs beside ηι at Amphipolis, and οι beside ωι at Olynthus. Dat. sg. ει is found also in an inscription from Naples.

NON-DIPHTHONGAL COMBINATIONS OF VOWELS
(CONTRACTION, ETC.)

40. Owing to the proethnic loss of intervocalic ι and σ, a large number of new vowel combinations arose, and these were subsequently augmented by the dialectal loss of intervocalic ϝ (53). An exhaustive treatment of their history in the several dialects would require not merely that each of the numerous combinations should be considered by itself, but that further distinctions should be made according to the character of the consonant which was lost, that of the sound which preceded the combina-

tion, the accent, the number of syllables in the word, etc.
See 45. Only some of the most important facts can be stated here.

α or ᾱ + Vowel

41. 1. α + ε, ε̄ (secondary ε̄), or η. Att.-Ionic ᾱ, but η in West
Greek and Boeotian. Similarly ᾱι or ηι from α + ει, ηι. Examples
are forms of verbs in -αω, as Att.-Ion. νικᾱι(αει), νικᾱτε (αε),
νικᾶν (αε̄), etc., but η in West Greek and Boeotian, e.g., Cret.,
Arg. νικῆν, Lac. ἐνίκε̄, Rhod. θοινῆται, Meg. φοιτήτω, Corcyr.
τιμῆν, Locr. συλε̄ν, Delph. συλῆν, Boeot. φυσῆτε (Ar.), etc.

a. For Lesbian, Thessalian, and Arcado-Cyprian direct evidence is
lacking but η is probable in view of the η in crasis (**94**.6). Lesb.
τίμαι, βόαι (gram.; βόα text of Sappho), Thess. ἐρουτᾱι, probably belong
to the -ᾱω type (**159**)?

2. α + ο or ω. When contracted, the result is ω in all dialects.
So regularly in forms of verbs in -αω, as Att. τιμῶ, τιμῶμεν, Meg.
(Selinus) νικο̄μες, νικῶντι, Locr. συλο̄ντα, Boeot. σουλῶντες, Lac.
hε̄βο̄ντι (subj.), ἐνhε̄βόhαις (ἡβώσαις from ἡβαώσαις), but also,
rarely, uncontracted as Boeot. ἰαόντυς. Cf. also Heracl. τέτρωρον
'group of four boundary-stones' from *τετρα-ορον, παμῶχος
(παμωχέω) from *παμα-οχος. αο from αϝο is uncontracted in
Boeotian (as in Homer), but in most dialects yields ω, as φῶς
from φάος (*φαϝος, cf. Hesych. φαυοφόρος), Boeot. Καλλιφάων,
etc., ᾿Αγλω- from ἀγλαο- (*ἀγλαϝο-), Boeot. ᾿Αγλαόδωρος, etc.
(᾿Αγλαο- also Thess., Coan, etc.), σῶς, σω-, Σω-, from σάϝος (cf.
Cypr. ΣαϝοκλέϜες). Boeot. περίσαος, Σαυκράτεις, Σαυγένεις, etc.
Arc., Σακρέτης, Σάδαμος, Σακλῆς (beside Σαοκλῆς), Σάανδρος,
Boeot. Σακράτης, etc., are to be read Σᾰ-, this from Σαο-, or
parallel to Meg. Θέδωρος, etc. (**42**.5*f*)?

3. ᾱ + ε. Attic-Ionic η, elsewhere ᾱ. Att.-Ion. ἥλιος (Hom.
ἠέλιος) from ἀϝέλιος (Cret. gloss ἀβέλιος), ᾱ̓έλιος (Pind., etc.,
Arc.), Dor. ἅλιος, Lesb. ἄλιος.

4. ᾱ + ο or ω. Attic-Ionic εω or ω, elsewhere ᾱ or uncontracted. In Attic-Ionic first ηο, ηω (cf. **8**), often preserved in
Homer, whence εω (with shortening of the first vowel and, in
the case of ηο, lengthening of the second; cf. **43**), which may be
further contracted to ω (in Ionic mostly after vowels, cf. **45**.2;

in Attic not so restricted, but the conditions are complicated
and not wholly clear). In the other dialects the uncontracted
forms are most general in Boeotian.

Gen. sg. masc. ᾱ-stems, Ion. -εω, -ω (also -ηο in no. 6), from -ᾱο
as in Homer (here Aeolic, beside Ion. -εω) and Boeotian (rare in
Thessalian), Arc.-Cypr. -ᾱυ (22), Lesb., Thess., West Greek -ᾱ.
Att.-Ion. ἕως (Hom. εἶος, i.e. ἧος) from *ἆϝος (Skt. yāvat),
Lesb. ἇς, Boeot., West Greek ἇς (late Boeot. also hybrid ἇως).
Att.-Ion. λεώς, νεώς, ἕως (Hom. νηός, ἠώς), ληός (in Eub. Ἀγασιλέϝō) from λᾱϝός (seen in personal names of several dialects),
νᾱϝός, ἆϝώς (but see 35, 54d), in most dialects λᾱός, νᾱός, ἀώς
but λᾱ-, νᾱ-, in compounds as Λᾱκρίνης, νᾱκόρος νᾱποῖαι, also -λᾱς
frequent for -λᾱος, etc., in personal names, as the widespread
Ἀρκεσίλας (Cyrene sixth century, etc.) beside the rare Ἀρκεσί-
λαϝος (on an Apulian vase).

Gen. pl. ᾱ-stems, Ion. -έων, -ῶν (also -ηον in no. 6), Att. -ῶν,
from -ᾱων (*-āsōm, Skt. -āsām) as in Homer (Aeolic), Boeotian
(but always τᾶν, see 45.4), Thessalian (τᾶν κοινάουν, etc. at
Crannon, but otherwise -ᾶν), Lesb. -ᾶν, Arc., West Greek -ᾶν.
Att.-Ion. θεωρός, Lesb. θέᾱρος, West Greek θεᾱρός, beside
uncontracted Arc. θεᾱορός, from *θεᾱ-ϝορός (or-hορός, cf.
φρουρός from *προ-hορός; both from -hϝορος). Boeot. θιαωρία
could be from a parallel form with ω-grade in the second part,
but more likely is a hybrid, influenced by Att. θεωρία.

Att. κοινών, ξυνών, Ion. ξυνεών (Hes. ξυνήονας) from *-ᾱϝων,
*-ᾱϝονος, ξυνᾱονες Pindar, Arc., West Greek κοινᾱν. So Epid.
κυκᾱν = κυκεών.

Att. Ποσειδῶν, Ion. Ποσειδέων, Hom. Ποσειδᾱων (-ᾱωνος), Co-
rinth. ΠοτΕδᾶϝονι, ΠοτΕδᾶνι, ΠοτΕδᾶν, Boeot. Ποτειδᾶονι, Cret.,
Rhod., Delph. Ποτειδᾶν (-ᾶνος), Lesb. Ποσείδᾶν, Arc. Ποσοιδᾶνος,
Lac. Ποhοιδᾶν (-ᾶνι).

Arc. Πᾱονι beside Πᾶνός, Πᾶνί. Here the native Arcadian form
was adopted in Attic-Ionic.

a. In Ionic, beside usual εω, there are some examples of εο or ευ (cf. 33),
as θεορός, θευρός (Paros, Thasos), gen. sg. -ευ (Erythrae, etc.).

b. In Ionic some of the older forms with unshortened η, as in Homer,
are employed also by later writers, as νηός, etc. So ἠώς in Herodotus and
in an inscription of Oropus (gen. sg. ἠῶς).

c. Homer has the non-Ion. λᾱός, which also displaced λεώς in the κοινή and Modern Greek. Similarly νᾱός instead of νεώς in the κοινή and Modern Greek.

d. In Thessalian there are some examples of ō, ου (from ω, **23**), where we expect ᾱ, as gen. pl. προξεννιοῦν, Γομφιτοῦν, θεουρός, Ποτείδουνι, hυλōρέοντος (cf. ὑληωρός, ὑλωρός). But the first four are probably κοινή forms with dialectal coloring (for such hybrids, see **280**), and hυλōρέοντος is from ὑλο- beside ὑλᾱ- (see **167**).

ε + Vowel

42.1. ε + α. Uncontracted εα in most dialects, contracted η in some. Acc. pl. neut. of σ-stems, Arc., Locr., Lac. Ϝέτεα, Boeot. Ϝέτια, Pamph. Ϝέτεια, Ion., Delph. ἔτεα, Cret. μέρεα, Lesb. μέλεα—Heracl. Ϝέτη (but δένδρεα), Att., Argol., Rhod. ἔτη, Coan μέρη, θύη, etc., also Ion. θύη (no. 8), σκέλη, etc. beside ἔτεα, etc. Acc. sg. masc. σ-stems, mostly εα, but η in Attic, also Rhod. λειόλη (no. 100, sixth century B.C.), Lac. Θιοκλε͞ (sixth century B.C.), Κλεογένε͞, Ion. ἐξώλη (but earlier ἀφανέα, no. 4.11), Troez. ἐπιαλε͞, Delph. ἐνδογενῆ, Ἀγαθοκλῆ, etc. Acc. pl. masc. fem. -εας, but Cyren. τριήρης. Cf. also Coan ηὐτῶν = ἑαυτῶν. Att.-Ion. ἔαρ, gen. ἦρος, but ἦρ in Alcman, Delph. ἠρινός.

Even εα from εϝα, which is uncontracted in Attic, sometimes becomes η in West Greek, as Delph., Rhod., Coan, Cyren. ἐννῆ = ἐννέα, Ther. ἡμίση = ἡμίσεα, Κληγόρας = Κλεαγόρας, Rhod. Ἀγῆναξ = Ἀγεαναξ, Dor. κρῆς (Theocr., etc.) = κρέας, Sicil. (Acrae) φρήτιον =φρεάτιον (cf. φρητί Callim.). Dor. βλῆρ (Alcman) = Att. δέλεαρ (cf. dat. sg. δέλητι Hesych., δελήτιον Sophron).

2. ε + ᾱ. Personal names in -εας, as Τιμέας, Δημέας, usually remain uncontracted in Attic (Ἑρμῆς is the Ionic form) and most dialects, though in late times partly replaced by -ᾱς, as Δημᾶς, Δαμᾶς. But -ῆς regularly in Ionic (from -έης), as Δημῆς, Ἀπελλῆς, and sometimes elsewhere, as Rhod. Ἀριστῆς, Ther. Κυδρῆς, Θαρῆς (archaic). Cf. Rhod. Χαλκῆ from Χαλκέᾱ.

3. ε + ε. Regularly contracted to ē (ει) or η (see **25**), as Att. τρεῖς, Ther. τρῆς, from *τρέι̯ες (Skt. *trayas*). But uncontracted forms also occur, as Cret. τρέες, δρομέες, Arg. γροφέες, Boeot. ϜικατιϜέτιες. See **45**.5.

4. ε + ει, ηι, or η. Regularly contracted to ει, ηι, η, as φιλεῖ, φιλῆι, φιλῆται. Uncontracted forms, like Locr. δοκέ͞ει, ἀνχōρέ͞ει,

λιποτελέει (but read -εει by some, as belonging to type -ηω, **159**), Delph. ἀδικέη, ποιέη, Lesb. ἔη, Boeot. ἵει, δοκίει (**9**, **16**), are rare. See **45**.5. But forms like δέηι, δέηται (from εϝη, see **45**.1) are usually uncontracted. Names in -κλέης occur in some dialects, though most have only -κλῆς. See **108**.1*a*.

5. ε + ο. The contraction to secondary ō (ου), as in γένους from *γενεσος,φιλοῦμεν from *φιλέ̣ιομεν (but πλέομεν, ἡδέος, etc., see **45**.1), is Attic only. Most dialects have εο or ιο (**9**), as γένεος (-ιος), φιλέομεν (-ίομεν).

In Ionic εο often has the value of one syllable in poetry, and this diphthongal pronunciation came to be represented by ευ (cf. εο = original ευ, **33**). This spelling, though found in our texts of earlier authors (sometimes even in Homer, as μευ, φιλεῦντας), does not appear in Ionic inscriptions until the fourth century B.C. But it occurs also in Rhodes, Cos, Thera, Cyrene, Megara, Delphi, Corcyra, etc., mostly late but an exceptionally early example is Corinth. Θευγένēς of the sixth century B.C.

Also from ε + secondary ō (Att. ου) spelling εο or ευ, Coan κυεōσα, κυεῦσα, τελεῦσα, παρεῦσα.

a. Boeotian has some examples of ιυ, ιου, beside ιο (both original and from εο), but mostly after dentals, where it was supported by the prevalence of the spelling ιου = υ (**24**). Thus Νιουμείνιος and Νιυμείνιος, νιουμεινίη, Θιουτίμυ, Διουκλεῖς, but once also Βιούτη.

b. Change to εω in Cyren. ἐπαρεώμενοι, παρβεῶντας (with transfer from -αω to -εω type, **161**.2), and (with ι from ε, **9**.8, 9) Lac. ὁμιώμεθα, Heracl. ἐμετρίωμες, μετριώμεναι (before single consonant, vs. ιο in ἀναγγελίοντι, etc.). Cf. also Tarentine pron. gen. sg. (gram.) ἐμίω(ς), τίω(ς) = ἐμεο(ς), τεο(ς).

c. Contraction to ω in some towns of East and West Crete, mostly in open syllables, as ἐπαινῶμεν, εὐχαριστῶμες, ὠνώμενος, etc., but also παρακαλῶντι, διατηρῶντες. Likewise ἐξαιρῶντες in an inscription of Phaselis.

d. Change to ο before ντ or final ν. East Cret. (especially Hierapytna; but some examples also in the west) κοσμόντες, κρατόντες, ἐπιορκόντι, ἐπεστάτον, etc., Arg. διατελόντι, κοινανόντι, ἐμφανιξόντας, δαμιοργόντōν, ἐπῶλον, (here also probably Heracl. fut. κοψοντι, etc., but disputed; see **141***b*), Delph. θεαρόντōν, ποιόντων (beside ποιέοντα in the same inscription), Heracl. ποιόντασσι, ἐξεποίον, Mess. ποιόντι, Chian ποιόντος. In these last examples, from ποιέω, the fact that a vowel preceded the original εο is a special factor, and the similar loss of ε is seen in other forms of the same verb, as Delph. ποιῶντι, ποιοῖ, El. ἐνποιō̄ν, ἐνποιον (beside ἐξαγρέōν, ἐξαγρέοι in the same inscription), Troez. ποιōν.

e. Change to ε before ντ in Cyren. ἐκτιμασέντι (3 pl. Dor. fut.), δαμιεργέντων, Λέντιχος, τελεσφορέντες, etc. (thus showing that the old view of τελεσφορέντες as an unthematic form was mistaken).

f. Personal names compounded of θεός show forms in Θε- and Θο-. Though found elsewhere, these are most common in Megarian and nearly always with θε- before a simple consonant, Θο- before two, as Θέδωρος, Θέτιμος, but Θοκρίνης, Θοκλείδας. Cf. also Ion. Θόκλος, Κλόδεινος, ὁρτή = ἑορτή, νοσσιή, late Att. νοσσιά, νοσσίον, etc. for earlier νεοττία, etc.

g. More isolated is Arc. πλός from *πλέος = πλέον (113.2).

6. ε + ω or οι. In Attic regularly contracted, as φιλῶ, φιλοῖ, but πλέω, ἡδέων, etc., see 45.1). In other dialects regularly uncontracted εω, εοι, or ιω, ιοι (9), but sometimes ω, οι, mostly after a vowel (see 45.2). Ion. εἰδέωσιν but ποιῶσιν, ἀνωθεοίη but ποιοῖ, Lesb. ἀνατεθέωσι, Delph. ἐνκαλέοι, εὐδοκέωντι but ποιῶντι, Locr. ἔοντι, προξενέοι. El. ἐξαγρέον, δοκέοι but ποιον, ἐνποιοῖ, ποιοῖτο (also ποιέοι), Heracl. ἀδικίων, ἐγϜηληθίωντι, but ποιῶν, ποιῶντι, Cret. ἐνθίωμεν, πōνίοι(φωνέοι), Arg. (early) δαμιιοργοῖ, ἀφικνοῖτο.

η + Vowel

43. In the declension of nouns in -ευς the η of the stem is retained, as in Homer, in the Aeolic dialects, Arcado-Cyprian, and Elean, but shortened in most West Greek dialects and Attic-Ionic; in Attic this is accompanied by lengthening of the second vowel, if ο or α (βασιλέως, βασιλέᾱ). See 111. This "quantitative metathesis" seen in Attic is in many other words Ionic also (as usually from ηο = ᾱο, 41.4), e.g., ἵλεως (Herodas—Hdt. ἵλεως or ἵλεος?) from ἵληος (49.5), πόλεως (109.2), Mil. ἱέρεως (111.5), also τέλεως (Herodas, and, borrowed from Ionic, in Coan) = Cret. τέληος, though the usual Ionic form is τέλειος, τέλεος.

Cret., Arc. χρῆος (Hom. χρεῖος), Att. χρέως and χρέος; χρέος in most dialects (for verbal forms, see 162.13).

Cf. also the subjunctives with η retained in Hom. θήομεν (θείομεν), Boeot. κουρουθείει, etc., but shortened in most dialects, as Ion. θέωμεν (Att. θῶμεν), Cret. ἐνθίωμεν, etc. See 151.2.

Contraction of ηα to η (but probably through εα, cf. 42.1) is seen in Eub. 3 pl. εἰρῆται from *εἰρήαται (cf. Hom. βεβλήαται), εἰρέαται (Hdt.), and in βασιλῆ, etc. of Delphian and most Doric dialects (111.3).

o + Vowel

44. 1. o + α. When contracted, the result is ω in all dialects (cf. ω from α + o, **41.**2), e.g., Att. ἡδίω, Heracl. μείω from -o(σ)α, Τιμῶναξ, Ἱππῶναξ, etc. in West as well as East Greek dialects, from -o-(F)αναξ (for Rhod. Τιμᾶναξ, see **167**). Cf. also ω in crasis, as Corinth. τώγαθόν = τὸ ἀγαθόν, etc. (**94**).

a. The older view that o + α gives Dor. ᾱ rests on a false derivation of Dor. πρᾶτος (see **114**.1a).

2. o + ᾱ. Usually uncontracted (Att. οη), but in Ionic regularly ω, in other dialects sometimes ᾱ, e.g., Rhod. βοᾱθέω, Cret. βοᾱθίω, Aetol. βοᾱθοέω, Att. βοηθέω, but Ion. βωθέω, Lesb. βᾱθοέω, Att. βοηδρομιών, but Coan, Rhod. Βᾱδρόμιος, Att. dat. sg. ὀγδόηι, Coan, Rhod. ὀγδᾶι. For Ionic ω from οη, no matter whether η is from ᾱ or original η, cf. also ὀγδῶι (once) = ὀγδόηι, and ὀγδώκοντα from ὀγδοήκοντα (with original η), and Hdt. βῶσαι, νῶσαι, ἀλλογνῶσας.

3. o + o. Regularly contracted to secondary ō(ου) or ω (see **25**), as gen. sg. -ου or -ω from -οιο (**106**.1).

4. o + ε. When contracted, the result is the same as from o + o (3), e.g., Att. ἐλάττους (nom. pl., from -o(σ)ες), but Lac. ἐλάσσως, Att. λουτρόν (Hom. λοετρόν), Arg., Heracl. λωτήριον, Cyren. λωσάμενος. So Heracl. πρώγγυος from *προέγγυος. Cf. also the crasis in Att. τοῦτος, Lesb. ὠνίαυτος, etc. (**94**.2). But we also find uncontracted οε, mainly from οFε, and, before two consonants, sometimes o, e.g., Lesb. ὁμονόεντες, λοεσσάμενος, Μαλόεντι, Arc. Σινόεντι, Locr. Ὀπόεντι and in the same inscription Ὀποντίους, Meg. Σελινόεντι but Σελινόντιοι, Cret. Βολόεντα, Βολοεντίων, later Ὀλόντι, Ὀλοντίοις, all from -ο-Fεντ- (**164**.2). For δαμιοργός, δαμιεργός, etc., see **167**.

45. Notes to **41-44**. Besides the so-called "hyphaeresis" in ε or o from εο (**42**.5d, e, f, g), o from οε (**44**.4), and ε from εε as in the widespread gen. sg. -κλέος in proper names, there are also scattered examples of o from oo. So late Cret. βοᾱθός, Att.-Ion. βοηθός (Hdt., Thuc.) beside -θόος (Hom.), as in several dialects βοᾱθέω instead of βοᾱθοέω. Arc. βουσός 'cattle-run' from *βουσόος like μᾱλοσόᾱ, μηλοσόη 'sheep-run' (Hesych.). Here apparently gen. sg. Cyren. λεχός, etc. (**111**.5a) from -οος. Some of the

factors which help to account for divergence in the development
of the same combination of vowels are the following.

1. A combination which arises by the loss of Ϝ, being of later
origin than that arising from the loss of ι or σ, may remain uncontracted, or be contracted only later. So Att. πλέομεν, ἡδέος,
ἡδέα, ἡδέων, in contrast to φιλοῦμεν, γένους, γένη, γενῶν, Locr.
'Οπόεντι, later 'Οποῦντι.

2. A combination which is otherwise uncontracted may be
contracted after a vowel, Att. βασιλέως but ἁλιῶς, Ion. Μεγαβάτεω
but Παναμύω (-ω sometimes after consonants also, but not
usually), ἀνωθεοίη but ποιοῖ, El. δοκέοι but ποιοῖτο, etc. (see
42.6).

3. A combination which is otherwise contracted may remain
uncontracted in dissyllabic words. Att. πέος, θεός, ζέω, and likewise, though belonging also under 1, Att. νέος and νεώς, λεώς,
Dor. νᾱός, λᾱός. Such words may be contracted in compounds,
as Att. Θούτιμος, νουμηνία, Dor. νᾱκόρος, Λᾱκρίνης, 'Αρκεσίλᾱς.
Cf. also Meg. Θέδωρος, Θοκρίνης (**42**.5ƒ).

4. The article, as proclitic, is often the first form to show
contraction. Cf. Boet. τᾱν μωσᾱων, Thess. τᾱν κοινᾱουν (Crannon;
elsewhere -ᾱν in nouns also), Eub. τῶν δραχμέων.

5. The analogical influence of grammatically related forms in
which the vowel, either of stem or ending, is not subject to contraction often counteracts the normal phonetic development.
So Cret. τρέες, etc., with -ες after forms like πόδες, Ion. βασιλέος,
etc. (not -εως), after ποδός etc., Locr. δοκέει, etc., after δοκέομεν etc.

6. A late contraction of ιο to ι is indicated by the frequent
spelling ι or ει in Hellenistic times, e.g., in proper names Διονύσις,
etc. = -ιος, nom. - acc. sg. neut. ἀργύριν, παιδείν, etc. = -ιον
(hence modern παιδί, etc.). So late Lac. κασσηρατόριν beside
-τοριον, likewise (for ιο from εο) Σίδαμος = Θεόδαμος, acc. sg.
θίν = θεόν, gen. sg. Καλλικράτις, 'Αριστοτέληρ.

Assimilation and Dissimilation of Vowels

46. 1. The assimilation of vowels is comparatively rare in
Greek, and not characteristic of any particular dialect. Here
may be mentioned 'Ορχομενός from 'Ερχομενός, the regular

native form of the name of both the Boeotian and the Arcadian town, Τροφώνιος from Τρεφώνιος, name of the Boeotian local hero, Chian Ἑρμώνοσσα = -ασσα, Thess. Ϝεκέδαμος = Boeot. Ϝhεκάδα-μος, Delph. Φανατεύς beside Φανοτεύς. Cyren. βάβᾱλος = usual Dor. βέβαλος, Att. βέβηλος, late Cret. θαραπεύσαντες, Ἀπταραῖος, etc. For examples of ι and υ, see 20. For Boeot. τρέπεδδα, see 18. For Ποσοιδάν, Ἀπόλλων, ὀβολός, in which assimilation is a possible but not necessary assumption, see 49.1, 3.

2. Prehistoric dissimilation of Ϝευ- to Ϝε:- in εἶπον, ἔϝειπον (cf. Cret. Ϝεῖπαι) from *εϝευπον (= Skt. avocam) and probably (though disputed) in ἀ(ϝ)είδω. Dissimilation of -αια to -εια is generally assumed for Mess. αὐλεία = αὐλαία, Heracl. προτερεία = Att. προτεραία (ἡμέρα), Att. Ῥήνεια beside Ῥηναιεύς, Thess. Μελίτεια beside Μελιταιεύς, Arc. Αὐκλίεια (if = *Εὐκλέεια). But possibly these are cases of suffix-interchange rather than phonetic change.

Epenthetic Vowels

47. Lesb. γέλαιμι, etc. quoted by grammarians, are of doubtful authenticity. (3 sg. φαῖσι, Sappho, may be due to 3 pl. φαῖσι, 77.3). For epenthesis in the case of original νι, ρι, λι, see 74a, b.

Anaptyctic Vowels

48. ἕβδομος and ἕβδεμος (114.7) from *ἕβδμο-, *ἕπτμο-. Other examples are of only exceptional occurrence, as Att. Ἐρεμῆς = Ἑρμῆς, El. Σαλαμόνᾱ = Σαλμώνη, Thess. Ἀσκαλαπιός = Ἀσκλαπιός, Delph. Τολοφώνιος = Τολφώνιος. The widely attested πέλεθρον = πλέθρον (Cret., Delph., Thess., etc., as in Homer) is perhaps an inherited by-form.

Vowel-Gradation

49. In the system of inherited vowel-gradation (or "ablaut," to use the widely adopted German term) the dialects generally agree in the grade shown by corresponding forms, e.g., λείπω, λέλοιπα, ἔλιπον, in all dialects alike. But there are some examples of dialectal differences, of which the following may be mentioned.[2]

---

[2] Some cases where the variation is quite possibly not inherited, but which fall into the same system, are included for convenience.

1. Series, ει, οι, ι (λείπω, λέλοιπα, ἔλιπον). Cret. δίκνυμι (προ-
δίκνυτι) = Att. δείκνυμι (cf. δίκη, etc.). Ion. δέκνυμι is perhaps due
to a blend of δεικ- and δικ-. Lesb. ὀείγω (*ὀϜειγ-) = Att. οἴγω
(*ὀϜιγ-). ἤνεικα and ἤνικα in various dialects (144a). Ποσειδῶν,
Ποτειδάν, etc. (41.4) with ει (Ποτιδάν very rare), but usually ι
in derivatives, as Att. Ποσίδειος, Ion. Ποσιδήιος, Carpath. Ποτίδαιον
(but the famous Potidaea was Ποτείδαια), also οι (assimilation?)
in Arc. Ποσοιδᾶν, Lac. Ποhοιδᾶν, Ποhοίδαια, and Π]οτοιδᾶνι
of uncertain dialect (Schwyzer 642).

2. Series ερ, ορ, αρ or ρα (δέρκομαι, δέδορκα, ἔδρακον). τέσσερες,
τέτορες, τέτταρες, etc. (114.4). Ion. (Hdt.), Lesb., Cret., Mess.,
Epid., Coan, Cyren., El. ἔρσην, but Ion. (Miletus, Thasos) ἄρσην
(also in the κοινή and hence in late Arcadian, Theran), Lac.
ἄρσης, Att. ἄρρην, Arc. ἀρρέντερος, etc. (80). θέρσος = θάρσος
in Aeolic (gram.; Lesb. θέρσεισ' in Theocritus), and in proper
names most frequently in Lesbian, Thessalian, Boeotian, and
Arcadian, as Lesb. Θέρσιππος, Thess. Θερσίτας, Θέρσουν, Boeot.
Θερσάνδριχος, Arc. Θερσίας, etc. κρέτος = κράτος in Lesbian
(poet.), and in proper names also frequent in Arcado-Cyprian,
as Τιμοκρέτης, Σωκρέτης, etc. Ion. κρέσσων (in κρείσσων, κρείττων, the ει is not original), but Cret. κάρτων (cf. καρτερός, κρατερός), Cret. τράπω = τρέπω, as sometimes in Herodotus, Cret.,
Meg. τράφω = τρέφω, as in Pindar, etc., Delph. ἀποστράψαι = ἀποστρέψαι. East Ionic ἄγερσις 'assembly' (ἀγείρω, ἀγορά), West
Ion. ἄγαρρις (Naples), Arc. πανάγορσις (see 5) = πανήγυρις (with
obscure υ). Beside usual γράφω, etc., also (like -τροφος beside
τρέφω, τράφω) Mel. γρόπhōν, γρόφων 'carving,' Arg., Mycen.,
Epid., Sicyon., Cyren., El. γροφεύς, in Argolis also γροφά,
γροφίς, γροφεύω, ἀγγροφά, ἐγγροφά, σύγγροφος (the last also
Delph.), Heracl. ἀνεπίγροφος, Cret. ἀντίγροφον, ἔγγροφος. Here
probably Delph. σταρέστω, from aor. of στέρομαι (rather than
pres. with α from ε).

a. The weak grade varies between αρ and ρα, as in Hom. κράτος and
κάρτος, κρατερός and καρτερός, etc. So Cret. κάρτος, καρταῖπος, καρτερός,
κάρτων, likewise σταρτός = στρατός, Arc., Cypr., Boeot., Corcyr., El.
δαρχμά, Cret. δαρκνά = δραχμή, Epid. φάρχμα, φάρξις = φράγμα, *φράξις,
Boeot. πέτρατος (Hom. τέτρατος) = τέταρτος, Lesb. ἀμβρ[ό]την (5) =
ἁμαρτεῖν. This variation is in part due to transposition, and clearly so
in Cretan, which has αρ uniformly, as it also has πορτί = προτί. See 70.1.

3. Series ελ, ολ, αλ or λα (στέλλω, στόλος, ἐστάλην), Arc. δέλλω = βάλλω (cf. βέλος, etc.). West Greek and Arc. ὀδελός, Boeot. ὀβελός (rarely early Attic), Thess. ὀβελλός (**89.**4)=ὀβολός (assimilation?). West Greek δείλομαι, δήλομαι, Boeot. βείλομαι, Thess. βέλλομαι, all from a grade in ελ, = βούλομαι (see **75**). Cypr. δάλτος = δέλτος (but this is a Semitic loanword). Coan ἔτελον, Lesb. ἔταλον 'yearling' (cf. Lat. *vitulus*). Cret., Lac., Mess., Corinth., Pamph. Ἀπέλλων, Cypr. Ἀπείλōν (cf. **74**b) = Att.-Ion., Delph., Locr., Cyren., Ἀπόλλων (also Lac., Corinth. beside Ἀπέλλων), Thess. Ἄπλουν (with weak grade πλ). Coan, Calymn. Δολφοί = Δελφοί (cf. δολφός = δελφύς Hesych.). Epid., Cret. καταλοβεύς 'support' = *καταλαβεύς. Cret. ἀβλοπής (Hesych.), ἀβλοπία = ἀβλαβής, etc.

4. Series εν (εμ), ον (ομ), α or αν (αμ) (τείνω from *τενϳω, τόνος, τατός), Ion., Dor. τάμνω = Att. τέμνω (εμ from ἔτεμον). For Ϝίκατι = εἴκοσι, etc., see **116**a. For participles with ατ beside εντ and οντ, as ἔασσα, ἴαττα = οὖσα, and ἔντες = ὄντες, see **163**.8.

5. Series η, ω, α (ῥήγνυμι, ἔρρωγα, ἐρράγην), ἴλ̄ηος (Lac. hίλēϝος), whence Att.-Ion. ἵλεως, Cret. ἵλεος, but Arc. ἵλαος like Hom. ἵλαος, Ion. γλάσσα = γλῶσσα. For Heracl. ἐρρηγεῖα = ἐρρωγυῖα, Dor. ἔωκα = εἶκα, see **146**.3.

CONSONANTS

Ϝ

50. In Attic-Ionic the Ϝ was lost at a very early period. In East Ionic there is no trace of it even in the earliest inscriptions; it is very rare in Central and West Ionic; and in Attic the only evidence of its existence is its occasional use to express the glide sound before υ, as ἀϝυτάρ (**32**). In Thera, too, it is absent from the earliest inscriptions; likewise at Rhodes, Cos, etc., though here early material is scanty. In Lesbian it was already on the wane in the time of Alcaeus and Sappho, and is not found in inscriptions, of which, however, none of any extent is earlier than the fourth century.

But in most dialects it is of frequent occurrence initially, where it survives till the fourth century, and in some much later (especially as β; see **51**). Between vowels it occurs in the earliest inscriptions of many dialects, after consonants in several, and before consonants in a very few.

a. In some cases the disappearance of Ϝ from inscriptions is due to κοινή influence rather than to an organic loss of the sound within the dialect. So evidently in Laconian, as shown not only by its reappearance in the spelling β (**51**), but by its survival in some words in Tsakonian, the modern representative of Laconian, e.g., βάννε (*vanne*) 'lamb' (Ϝαρν-).

b. Even where there is no reason to doubt the actual loss of the sound, the spelling, as is natural in such cases, only gradually adapted itself to the pronunciation, and often there is an interval of considerable length in which the older spelling with Ϝ and the later spelling without Ϝ occur promiscuously, even in the same inscription. In the Heraclean Tables the presence or omission of initial Ϝ is constant for certain words, e.g., always Ϝ in Ϝέξ, Ϝίκατι and derivatives, also Ϝέτος, Ϝίδιος, ἐγϜηληθίωντι, but οἶκος, ἐργάζομαι, ἕκαστος, ἴσος and ἴσος, etc.

51. β for Ϝ. Ϝ is represented by β, which we must understand in its later value of a spirant (Eng. *v*), in numerous glosses and in the later inscriptions of several dialects. So frequently in Laconian from the fourth century B.C. to the second century A.D., e.g. βίδεοι, βίδυοι, title of officials (Ϝιδ-), Βωρθέα, Βωρσέα beside Ϝωρθέα (cf. nos. 75-78) = ᾿Ορθία, προβειπάηας = προϜειπάσας, διαβέτης = διαϜέτης, ὠβά from *ὠϜά (cf. Hesych. ὤας· τὰς κώμας, ὠγή· κώμη, and οὐαί· φυλαί), etc.; and in Cretan, e.g. Βόρθιος, Βολόεντα, βέρδηι, βεκάτεροι, διαβειπάμενος, ὑπόβοικοι, etc. Cf. also Arg. Βορθαγόρας, Πυρβαλίων = older ΠυρϜαλίον, Corcyr. ὄρβος = earlier ὄρϜος, El. βοικίαρ = Ϝοικίας (no. 66, in the stereotyped phrase γᾶρ καὶ βοικίαρ, otherwise Ϝ lost). For initial βρ = Ϝρ, see **55**.

a. Conversely, Ϝ is used in place of β in ἀμοιϜά = ἀμοιβά of an early Corinthian inscription. The name of the Cretan town Ϝάξος was sometimes represented by ῎Οαξος, as Lat. *Nerva* by Νέροα. Cf. κοάξ of the quacking of frogs. Ϝ is also represented by υ in Cret. ὑέργων once = Ϝέργων, as conversely Ϝ for υ (**52c**). In the lexicographers Ϝ is represented by β, or from graphic confusion by γ (likeness of Γ and Ϝ), and other letters.

b. Pamphylian has Ϝ in some words (Ϝέτιια, etc.), but in others a sign Ͷ (e.g. Ͷοικυπολίς = *οἰκοπολίς), which is used also for β (e.g., ἐφιιεͶόται), and for υ in the αυ, ευ diphthongs (e.g., ἀͶταῖσι) and the glide (e.g., ΣελύͶιιυς). A similar sign occurs in the Cretan towns of Eleutherna and Vaxus with the value of Ϝ, and at Selinus and Melos for β. It presumably represented a fricative pronunciation like that of English *v* and so is best transcribed as *v* (*w* in German publications). Also once φίκατι = Ϝίκατι.

52. Ϝ initially before a vowel. Examples are numerous in inscriptions of most dialects, e.g., Ϝέτος (cf. Lat. *vetus*), Ϝοῖκος (cf. Lat. *vīcus*), Ϝίχατι (cf. Lat. *vīgintī*), Ϝάναξ, Ϝαρήν, Ϝαστός, Ϝέπος, Ϝειπ-, Ϝέργον, Ϝέρρω, Ϝίδιος, Ϝίσος, Ϝοῖνος, and many others, especially in proper names.

a. In several dialects which otherwise preserve Ϝ it is lost before ο and ω (but not before οι), as in Homer, e.g., in Gortynian forms of ὠνή, ὠθέω, etc., without Ϝ beside Ϝίχατι, Ϝέχαστος, Ϝοιχεύς, etc. (Ϝόν, Ϝὅν by analogy of Ϝά, Ϝίν, etc.). But the precise dialectal scope of this phenomenon is not yet determined, and Ϝο is by no means unknown, e.g., Arc. Ϝōφλἔκόσι (no. 17, fifth century; in no. 18, fourth century, ὀφλέν beside Ϝαστόν, Ϝέχαστον, etc.), Ϝορθασία, Cret. Βόρθιος, Lac. Βωρθέα, etc. (see 51).

b. Initial σϜ yields hϜ, occasionally written Ϝh (cf. Eng. *which*) but usually simply Ϝ, which, however, was pronounced as hϜ (or a voiceless Ϝ), as shown by the fact that after the loss of Ϝ such words have the spiritus asper. Thus Pamph. Ϝhέ = ἕ (cf. Cypr. Ϝοι, etc.), Boeot. Ϝhεχα-δάμοε, Thess. Ϝεχέ-δαμος, Cret., Locr. Delph., El., Arc. Ϝέχαστος, later ἕχαστος, Arg. Ϝhεδιέστας = ἰδιώτης (cf. Arg. hίδιος = ἴδιος). In some dialects this Ϝ was lost earlier than Ϝ in general, e.g., in Boeotian, where ἔξ (from Ϝέξ, i.e., Ϝhέξ, from *sweks) and ἔχαστος are frequent in inscriptions which otherwise have initial Ϝ, as Ϝιχαστῆ χὴ ἔχτη (no. 43.8).

c. The unique Ϝhιός = υἱός (no. 97) represents a dissyllabic pronunciation tion of the word, with Ϝh = hϜ as usual (above) and Ϝ for consonantal *u*, as in Arg. Ϝαχίνθια = Ὑαχίνθια (no. 85.17) and Cret. Ϝαχίνθιος name of a month.

d. There are also some words with initial Ϝ and ' in their later forms for which there is no trace of an initial *s* in cognates (a hypothetical initial "laryngeal" is now assumed by some), e.g., Att. ἴστωρ, ἰστορία (cf. Boeot. Ϝίστωρ, from Ϝιδ-, Lat. *vid*-), ἔννυμι, εἶμα (cf. Cret. Ϝῆμα, Lat. *ves-tis*), ἔσπερος (cf. Locr. Ϝεσπάριος, Lat. *vesper*), ἑχών (cf. Locr. Ϝεϙόντας, Skt. *vac*-), ἁλίσχομαι (cf. Thess. Ϝαλίσχεται, Goth. *wilwan*).

53. Intervocalic Ϝ. This was lost sooner than initial Ϝ, hence is found in fewer dialects, and in most of these only in the earliest inscriptions. Often we find forms with and without Ϝ from the same period or the same inscription, showing that it was either weakly sounded or wholly lost in pronunciation and retained only in the spelling. This inconstancy is much greater than in the case of initial Ϝ. The spelling with Ϝ often persists in proper names, and sometimes in certain conventional or solemn expressions, longer than elsewhere.

Examples are most frequent in Cyprian, where it appears almost uniformly except in some later inscriptions, e.g., αἰϜεί, οἶϜος, ῥόϜος, δοϜέναι, βασιλἔϜος, etc. (but always παῖς, παιδός, with loss of Ϝ). Eub. ἈγασιλέϜō with Ϝ in the proper name

beside ἐποίεσεν (no. 9). Thess. ΔάϜōν, but otherwise lost, as in
ἔσōσε (no. 35). Boeot. ΠτōιεϜι, ἐποίϜεσε, χαρίϜετταν, ΚαρυκεϜίō,
γαϜεργείσει, also late διϜύκισις, τραγαϜυδία, τραγαϜυδός, κωμαϜυδός,
etc. (these last probably archaistic). Phoc. κλέϜος, αἰϜεί, Delph.
ΛαϜόσοϜος, Ach. ᾿ΑρκεσίλαϜος. Locr. καταιϜεί (also ἐπίϜοικος,
μεταϜοικέοι, ϜεϜαδēκότα, but see a) beside παῖς, ᾿Οπόεντι, δαμιορ-
γούς. El. [πο]ιϜέοι once (also ἀποϜēλέοι, but see a), but usually
ποιέοι, even in the same inscription, βασιλᾶες, etc. Lac. ἱιλέϜōι,
ναϜōν, ΓαιαϜόχō (cf. Cypr., Pamph. Ϝέχω, Lat. vehō), ἀϜάταται
(cf. Lesb. αὐάτα, El. ἀνάατορ, elsewhere contracted as in Att.-Ion.
ἄτη, Cret. ἄτα, ἄπατος, etc.), late ὠβά (51). Arg. ΔιϜός, ὄϜινς,
ποιϜέματα, ἐϜεργάσατο. Corinth. ΠοτΕδάϜōνι beside ΠοτΕδᾱνι,
ΑἴϜας, ΛαϜοπτόλεμος, etc. Corcyr. phoϜαῖσι, στονόϜεσαν, etc.
There are no examples of intervocalic Ϝ in even the earliest
Cretan (cf. αἰεί, ναός, Ϝοικέος, etc.) except for the gloss ἀβέλιος
(Cret. in Hesych.) and in compounds or augmented forms (a);
nor in Arcadian (cf. ἐποίες, ἵλαος, Παδόεσσα vs. init. Ϝ, ρϜ, Ϝρ),
except ἄ]Ϝεθλα(?) in an archaic inscription.

a. Even where intervocalic Ϝ is regularly lost, it may appear in compounds or in augmented or reduplicated forms, owing to the influence of
the simplex or of the forms without augment or reduplication, where Ϝ
has survived as initial, e.g., Cret. προϜειπάτō, ἔραδε, and late διαϜειπάμενος.
Hence such forms are not necessarily evidence of the survival of true
intervocalic Ϝ.

b. Ϝ is often used to indicate the natural glide before or after υ. So
before or after the υ of diphthongs, as already noted (32, 36), and Chalcid.
δύϜο, Eretr., Aetol. δύϜε, Sicyon. ΣεϟυϜόνιος, Pamphyl. Σελύνιυς.

54. Postconsonantal Ϝ. The combinations νϜ, ρϜ, λϜ, and
(secondary) σϜ are preserved in the earliest inscriptions of some
dialects. The loss of Ϝ was accompanied by lengthening of the
preceding vowel in East Ionic, Central Ionic (in part; see a),
Doric of Argolis, Crete, Thera, Cos, Rhodes and colonies, while
in other dialects, as in Attic, the vowel was not affected.

Corinth. ΞένϜōν, Corcyr.	Ion. ξεῖνος, Cret. πρό-	Att., etc. ξένος,
πρόξενϜος, El. Ξεν-	ξηνος, Cyren. Φιλό-	πρόξενος
Ϝάρεορ	ξηνος, Rhod. Ξην-,	
	Ξειν-	

*ἐνϜατος	Ion. εἴνατος, Arg.,	ἔνατος
	Cyren., Cret. ἤνατος	
*ἐνϜεκα, *μόνϜος	Ion. εἴνεκα, μοῦνος	ἕνεκα, μόνος
Arc., Corinth. κόρϜα	Ion. κούρη, Cret. κώρα	κόρα (κόρη)
Corcyr. ὄρϜος, Arc.	Ion. οὖρος, Arg., Cret.	ὅρος
εὐθυορϜία	ὦρος, Ther. οὖρος	
Arc. κάταρϜος	Ion. ἀρή	ἀρά
Boeot. καλϜός	Ion. κᾱλός	καλός
*ὅλϜος	Ion. οὖλος	ὅλος
Boeot., Arc., Cret.,	Ion. ἴσος	ἴσος
Sicyon. ϜίσϜος		
Arc. δέρϜα	Ion. δειρή	δέρα (δέρη)
*ὀδϜός	Ion. οὐδός, Cyren. ὠδός	ὀδός

a. To the lengthening in East Ionic there are possibly some local exceptions, but, in general, forms like ξένος, and especially πρόξενος, are due to Attic influence. Similarly in Rhodian, etc., where ξεῖνος has survived only in proper names, and in late Cretan where πρόξενος is far more common than πρόξηνος. In Central Ionic the lengthening is attested for Paros and Thasos, but it is uncertain how far west this extended. From many of the islands, both Ionic and Doric, decisive material is lacking.

b. Lesb. ξέννος, ἔννεκα, in grammarians and late inscriptions (ἔννεκα also codd. Alcaeus, Theocr.), are probably hyper-Aeolic, due to the frequency of νν from νι̯, σν, etc. (74, 76, 77.1). Cf. also ἰσσοθέοισι in an inscription of A.D. 2-14. For Thess. προξεννιοῦν see 19.3.

c. In Arcadian there is fluctuation in the same inscription, e.g., no. 18 κάταρϜος but ξένος, no. 20 δέρϜα, εὐθυορϜία, but ὅριον, ὥρισαν, δίωρος (this last with ω by composition lengthening, 167a).

d. In Cretan the Ϝ of σϜ survives longer than that of νϜ, etc. So in the Law-Code ϜισϜόμοιρον beside κσενίō and καλōς. This is a secondary σϜ (ϜίσϜος probably from *ϜιτσϜος cognate with εἶδος 'form'). The development of original σϜ, somewhat similar to that of σλ, etc. (76), is seen in Lesb. ναῦος, Dor. νᾱ(Ϝ)ός, Ion. νηός, probably from *νασϜός, also ἰός 'arrow' from *ισϜός (cf. Skt. iṣu- 'arrow').

e. Different from ὄρϜος, etc., is Corinth. ΠύρϜος (cf. Argol. ΠυρϜίας, ΠυρϜαλίōν), probably for *ΠύρρϜος (from *ΠυρσϜος with assimilation of ρσ before Ϝ), whence the Πύρρος of most dialects.

f. Preservation of Ϝ after a stop is rare. There are a few examples of δϜ in archaic inscriptions, as Corinth. ΔϜΕνιᾱ = Δεινίου (cf. the indirect evidence of Hom. ἔδδεισεν, etc.), Aetol. ΧελιδϜόν (IG IX².i.86.1). But τϜ was changed in prehistoric times, becoming σσ or ττ (see 81). Likewise κϜ (IE k̑w), becoming ππ, as in ἵππος (Skt. aςvas).

55. Ϝ before consonants. Corresponding to Att. ῥήτρα, ἐρρήθην, etc. (from Ϝρη- beside Ϝερ- in ἐρέω, cf. Lat. *verbum*), we have El. Ϝράτρα (**15**), Cypr. Ϝρῆτα (**70**.3) with its denominative Ϝρητάω (ἐϜρητάσατυ, also spelled εὐϜρητάσατυ, indicating an anticipation of the Ϝ. Cf. *a* and **35**. So also κενευϜόν from κενεϜόν), Arg. ϜεϜρεμένα, ἀϜρέτευε, later ἀρήτευε 'was spokesman, presided,' Arc. Ϝρῆσις. El. ἀϜλανέος 'wholly' (cf. Hesych. ἀλανέως· ὁλοσχερῶς, also ἀλλανής· ἀσφαλής and ἀλανές· ἀληθές), is from ἀ-Ϝλα-, and related to ἀελλής (ἀ-Ϝελ-), ἀολλής (ἀ-Ϝαλ- with Aeolic ο, cf. **5**), ἀλής, Dor., Delph. ἀλία 'assembly,' Ion. (Hdt.) ἀλίη (also from ἀϜαλ-, with Ion. ᾱ from αϜα as in ἄτη, ἀνᾱλίσκω), Cleon. Ϝρέξαντα (= Att. ῥέξαντα, ἔρξαντα, cf. Cret. Ϝέρχσαι, etc.).

Ϝρ appears as βρ, indicating a pronunciation *vr*, in Lesbian words quoted by grammarians and in our texts of the Lesbian poets (βρήτωρ, βρόδον, etc.), though this has become simply ρ at the time of our earliest inscriptions. Cf. also Boeot. Βρανίδας beside Ϝάρνων.

In most dialects Ϝ was lost before the time of our earliest inscriptions, and we find, as in Attic, ῥ, medial ρρ or ρ. See *a*.

a. In the case of medial Ϝρ, the Ϝ unites with the preceding vowel to form a diphthong in Lesb. εὐράγη, αὔρηκτος (Herodian) from *ἐ-Ϝράγη, *α-Ϝρηκτος (Att. ἐρράγη, ἄρρηκτος), Hom. ταλαύρινος, καλαῦροψ, ἀπούρας, from *ταλά-Ϝρινος, etc. But generally the syllabification of the simplex (or form without augment or reduplication) was retained (i.e., Ϝρ with the following vowel), and later this Ϝρ became ρρ or sometimes ρ, e.g., Arg. ϜεϜρεμένα, ἀϜρέτευε, later ἀρήτευε. In Attic and most dialects augmented and reduplicated forms have ρρ, as Att. ἐρρήθην (εἴρηκα is formed after the analogy of forms like εἴληφα, **76**), ἐρράγην, ἔρρωγα, Heracl. ἔρρηγα, while compounds also usually have ρρ but sometimes ρ under the continued influence of the simplex, as Att. ἀναρρηθείς but also ἀναρηθείς, Delph. hεμιρρήνιον (from *ἡμί-Ϝρην, like ἡμί-ονος, cf. Hom. πολύ-ρρην). Cf. ρρ and ρ from σρ, **76**. For medial Ϝλ, cf. El. ἀϜλανέος (above), but diphthongization in αὔλαξ (from *ἀϜλακ- beside *ἀϜολκ-, *ἀϜλοκ- in Hom. ὦλξ, Att. ἄλοξ), Dor. αὔληρα (Epich.; ἄβληρα Hesych.).

b. The much discussed Arg. ἀϜρέτευε, ἀρήτευε is best taken as from a compound of ἀν- = ἀνα- (perhaps first in an agent noun *αν-Ϝρέτας) with assimilation of νϜ and further simplification, as in Arc. συϜοικία = συνοικία (see **96**.5). Cf. also Hom. αὐερύω from *αϜϜερύω, *αν-Ϝερύω. The view that α stands for the augment (no present forms occur) cannot be made plausible by reference to the cases of αυ = ευ, which are all only sporadic spellings and none of them Argive (**33**α), whereas in this

word the α is constant (examples, including the abbreviations ἀρ, α,
very numerous) vs. the regular ἐ in ἐϝεργάσατο, etc.

Consonantal ι (ι̯)

56. Original consonantal ι (IE *y* with the value of *y* in Eng.
yet; for Greek we use the symbol ι̯) almost wholly disappeared
from Greek in prehistoric times, giving ' or, rarely, ζ initially,
as in ὅς (Skt. *yas*), ἧπαρ (Lat. *iecur*), ζυγόν (Skt. *yugam*), etc.,
yielding various results in combinations with a preceding consonant (**74, 81, 82, 84**), and being dropped between vowels,
as in τρεῖς from *τρέι̯ες (Skt. *trayas*), etc. But between ι and a
following vowel, as in ἵππιος, it always existed as a natural
glide in pronunciation, and in a few dialects this is expressed
in the spelling. So, by the repetition of ι, in Pamphylian, as διά,
ἱιαροῖσι, etc., frequently in early Argive as Πολιιάδι, Σιχελίιας,
θιιοῖν, δαμιιοργοῖ, and occasionally elsewhere, as Ion. (Priene)
Διιοφάνης, Sicyon. Σεϙυϝόνιιος. Cf. also Ion. Τήιιοι, etc. (**37**.2),
Arg. Ἀθαναίιας, Καρνείιας, Ἐράτυιιος. In Cyprian a special
character, which we transcribe *ϳ*, is generally employed, though
not uniformly, as in the Idalium bronze (no. 23) regularly before α,
but not before ε or ο, e.g. ἰϳατῆραν but ἰερεϝίϳαν, ϝέπιϳα but θιόν.

The Spiritus Asper. Psilosis

57. The spiritus asper generally represents an IE initial *s*
(**59**) or *y* (**56**), but in some words is of secondary, and sometimes
obscure, origin, e.g., ἵππος (cf. Lat. *equus*; ἵππος regularly as the
second part of compounds, Ἄλκιππος, Ἄντιππος, etc., rarely
Ἄνθιππος), ἡμεῖς, ἁμές (cf. Skt. *asmān*) with ' after the analogy
of ὑμεῖς (with ' from *y*). The sound was denoted by Η (earlier Β)
until the introduction of the Ionic η = η, after which it was
generally left undesignated. [3] But see **4**.7.

---

[3] In quoting forms from inscriptions, wherever the sign for the spiritus
asper appears in the original it is transcribed *h*, to be distinguished from ',
which is supplied as a purely diacritical sign, like accent marks, and the
employment of which is, in many special cases, of doubtful propriety.
That is, the evidence is often insufficient to determine whether the omission of the sign of the asper is merely graphic, in which case we should
transcribe the form with ', or due to an actual loss of the sound, in which
case we should transcribe with '. As a working rule we employ the lenis

Psilosis, or the loss of the spiritus asper, is characteristic of
East Ionic (whence the sign was left free for use as η; see 4.6),
Lesbian, Elean, Cyprian, and Cretan.

a. Psilosis is shown, not only by the absence of Η = h, but by the
presence of phrases and compounds in which a preceding stop is not
changed to the aspirate, e.g., East Ion. ἀπ' ἑκάστου, ἀπ' οὗ, κατάπερ, El.
κατισταίε̄, Cret. κατιστάμεν But psilosis is no bar to the retention of aspirated stops in phrases and compounds which were formed prior to the loss
of the asper. For they would be affected, if at all, only by the analogical
influence of the simplex, as Cret. κατιστάμεν by ἱστάμεν. Hence East. Ion.
κάθοδος, El. ποθελόμενος, etc. Cf. Mod. Grk. καθίσταμαι (of the written
puristic language), ἀφοῦ, etc., in spite of the loss of the spiritus asper.

b. The denial, by some, of Cretan psilosis is unwarranted, certainly
for Central Cretan. In the early inscriptions the letter Β, Η is used only
for a vowel, never also = h as was the case at Rhodes, Thera, and Melos.
Examples of aspiration, as χἱρήνα, ἀφ' ἅς are late and may be due to
external influence, which is evident in other matters. The late inscriptions
of Hierapytna and Drerus (as nos. 119, 120) are generally edited with
supplied (οἱ, ὅτι, etc.).

c. Even in Central and West Ionic, where Β, Β for the spiritus asper is
frequent in archaic inscriptions, it ceased to be so used at an early period.
So in no. 7 (Andros) only once (hελέσθō) vs. 26 cases of omission in no. 8
(Ceos) not at all, in no. 14 (Oropus) only once Η = hε vs. over 30 cases of
omission. Even the archaic Βύβων inscription at Olympia (Ditt. Syll.
1071), which the combined evidence of forms and script shows to be
based on a West-Ionic dialect (cf. also Eub. names Βύβα, Βύσαλκος), has
psilosis, and in the case of τὲτέρε̄ι with the attendant crasis it is impossible to attribute this to an Elean engraver.

58. Even in those dialects which generally preserve the spiritus
asper, and which, in distinction from those with psilosis, we may
call the h-dialects, there are many irregularities, partly in special
words, where by-forms evidently existed, partly due to the weak
pronunciation of the sound in general (cf. the variations in Latin
spelling).

a. In several dialects the forms of the article, ὁ, ἁ etc., appear regularly
or frequently without h, showing that in these proclitic forms it was
either wholly lost or more weakly sounded than elsewhere. So in Locrian
(nos. 57-59) always ὁ, never ho (cf. also κ' ὁ), also ὅδε, fem. twice ἁ, once
hα; in Delphian (no. 52) ὁ as article (A 30, 38, C 19), but demonstrative
ho (B 53); Thess. κοί = καὶ οἱ; ὁ likewise in some early inscriptions of

in quoting forms without h from inscriptions which have the character or
are of a period when it was certainly in common use.

Boeotia, Pamphylia, Syracuse, Metapontum, and Sybaris. Cf. also Boeot. ὅς = ὥς (no. 38.5) and Delph. ἄς (ʰo. 52 A 28) beside usual ʰō, ʰόστις, etc.

b. Other forms which regularly have the spiritus asper, but for which by-forms with the lenis are to be recognized, are: ἡμέρα, but even in Attic inscriptions frequently ἐμέρα, and Argol., Lac., Mess., Ther. ἀμέρα, Delph., Locr. ἀμάρα. ἱερός (ʰιερός, ʰιαρός, in numerous dialects), but with lenis in Rhodian and Argolic, as Rhod. ἐπ' ἱερέως, Arg. ἰαρομνάμονες (nos. 81, 82, with ʰo, etc.), Epid. ἰαρομμνάμονες (no. 89, with ʰομονάοις, etc.), Aegin. ἰαρέος (beside ʰοῖκος = ὁ οἶκος, χō = καὶ ὁ). So ἐπ' ἰαρεῦς in the Megarian inscription no. 99, in contrast to ʰιαρόν at Selinus, is probably due to the Epidaurian engraver. ἡμεῖς (see 57), in Doric dialects ἀμές (Lac. ποθ' ἀμέ, Heracl. ʰαμές), but also ἀμές (Coan μετ' ἀμῶν, etc.), Att. ἕστηκα, but also Thess. ἐπεστάκοντα, Mess. κατεσταμένοι.

c. Conversely, several words which regularly have the lenis show secondary forms with the asper in various dialects. Thus ἔτος (from Ϝέτος), but Heracl. πεντα-ʰετηρίδα (beside Ϝέτος), Aetol. Ητέων = ʰετέων, Epid. πενθ' ἔτη, and frequently καθ' ἔτος,, etc., in the κοινή (cf. Mod. Grk. ἐφέτος). ἴσος (from ϜίσϜος), but Heracl. ʰίσος beside ἴσος, and ἐφ' ἴσης in the κοινή. Locr. ἔντε (cf. ἔστε), but Delph. ʰέντε. Heracl. ʰοκτώ, ʰοκτακάτιοι, ʰεννέα, Delph. Ther. ʰένατος, all after ἑπτά. Ther. ʰικάδι = εἰκάδι. ἄκρος, but Corcyr. καθ' ἄκρον, Heracl. ʰακροσκιρίας. Boeot. ʰιράνα, late Cret. χιρήνα vs. usual ἰράνα, εἰρήνα. Epid. ἐγκαθιδών with θ from present καθοράω. Delph., Locr. ἐφιορκέω, occurring also in κοινή inscriptions, with φ by anticipation of the asper in ὅρκος, like φρουρός from *προ-ʰορός (or blend of ἐπιορκέω and *ἐφορκέω?). In Att. ὅρος (ʰόρος very frequent) the asper is probably secondary vs. Corcyr. ὄρϜος (so, not ʰόρϜος; see IG IX.ii.695), Heracl. ὅρος, Arg. ὅροι (no. 85.26), ὧρος. In Delph. ἐφακείσθων, Arg. ἀφακεσάσθō vs. Att. ἄκος, ἀκέομαι the asper is, by a probable etymology, original. So also in Arg. ʰίδιος (from *swidios; cf. Arg. Ϝʰεδιέστας = ἰδιώτης), Thess. καθ' ἰδδίαν (similar forms in late inscriptions of several dialects, even Attic) vs. usual Ϝίδιος, ἴδιος. In Thess. ἀνγρέω (ἐφανγρένθειν) = Lesb. ἀγρέω, etc. (162.2) the asper, as well as the ν, is probably due to a blend with some other word.

d. Besides such special cases as have been noted above, there are in some dialects irregularities which seem to be due to confusion in spelling consequent upon the asper being weakly sounded or on the verge of disappearance. This is especially noticeable in Arcadian and Locrian, to some extent in Heraclean and Argolic.—In Arcadian the early no. 16 has no ʰ, and no. 17 only once (and this unetymological if Ηέσκλαρος = *Ἐκκληρος), but ἱεροῖ, ὀσέοι, ἵλαον. The somewhat later no. 18 has ʰ uniformly in ʰιερά, ʰιερέν, etc., ʰεβδόμαι, ʰέκοτον, ʰίκοντα, παρʰεταξαμένος, but ἔμισυ three times without ʰ vs. once ʰέμισυ, ὑστέρας, ὅτι, ἄν = ἄν = ἄ ἄν, and conversely ʰάν = ἄν.—The early Locrian inscriptions nos. 57-59 have usually νότι, ʰόστις, ʰοίτινες, ʰόπō, ʰόπōς, (but in no. 59 ὅιτινι beside ʰότι, ʰόστις), ʰυπό, Ηυποκναμίδιος, (but in no. 59 ὑπαπροσθίδιος), ήόρκον, ηορκōμότας, but πεντορκίαν, hιαρός, ιαρός (both in no. 58), hεκατόν (no. 57) but χέκατόν (no. 59); further without *h* (beside ἀ, ὅδε, ἀμάρα, for which see above, *a*, *b*) ἔμισον (no. 59), ὑδρία (vs. hυπó), ιστίαι, κατιϙόμενον; unetymological *h* in hάγεν, ἐφάγεσθαι (vs. ὁπάγōν), Hοποντίōν vs. usual 'Οποντίους, etc.—The Heraclean Tables have more examples of *h* than any other single inscription, and most of them correct. But (besides the cases mentioned above, *c*) unetymological *h* in hοισόντι, hάρνησις.—Argolic has *h* regularly in ho, hα, hᾶι, hῑ, hοιζ(=οῖς), hόπαι, hόπυι, hίδιος, hέμισα, hέπεσθαι (all these in no. 85), etc., but also (besides ιαρομνάμονες, above, *b*) ιχέτας (no. 80), ἄτερον (no. 89, four times beside words with *h*), ἔλοιεν beside hέλōμες (no. 85), and conversely unetymological *h* in hἔ = ἤ 'or' and Hαισκλαπιεῖ.

σ. Loss of Intervocalic σ

59. Original initial *s* became the spiritus asper in proethnic Greek, as in ἕδος (Lat. *sedeō*, Skt. *sad-*), ἕπομαι (Lat. *sequor*, Skt. *sac-*), etc. At the same time intervocalic *s* was changed in the same way and then lost, as in γένεος (Skt. *janasas*, Lat. *generis*), etc. Nevertheless there are many Greek words with intervocalic σ, either retained by analogy as in the aorist, or of secondary origin as σ from τ (61).

This Greek intervocalic σ was subjected to a similar process, namely, became *h* and was later lost, in Laconian, Argolic, Elean, and Cyprian.

1. Laconian. Early ἐποίεhε, νιχάhας, ἐνhēβόhαις, Ποhοιδᾶνι, Λύhιππον, 'Ελευhύνια, etc.; later Παhιφᾶι, προβειπάhας, πᾶhιν, νιχάας, 'Οναιτέλης ('Ονασι-), Πειιχλείδα (Πεισι-), βαιλέος (βασιλέος), etc. Cf. also 97.5*a*. In Aristophanes' Lysistrata occur similar forms with omission of σ (μῶα, πᾶα, etc.), also γερωχία representing γερωhία, which, though not as yet quotable, is the correct native form for which the Attic writers substitute γερουσία or γεροντία (Xen.). This was a characteristic of Laconian speech from the earliest known period, and is faithfully represented in the spelling of most of the early inscriptions. But it was felt as a provincialism and ignored in the spelling of some of the early and the majority of the later inscriptions.

2. Argolic. Mycen. Φραhιαρίδας, Arg. ἐποίϜεhε, 'Αρχεhίλας, etc. Later, mostly in Arg. inscriptions of the third century B.C., numerous examples of total loss (sometimes with σ- forms in

the same inscription), e.g., θηαυρός (= θησαυρός), χρῆις (= χρῆ-
σις), ἔμπαις (= ἔμπασις), ἐμέτρηε (= -ησε), στεφανῶαι (=-ῶσαι),
etc. But several early Arg. inscriptions (as nos. 81, 83, 84, 85, 86)
show only σ-forms, as θἔσαυρός, etc., and so many of the later
ones.

a. The explanation of the fluctuation is the same as that given for
Laconian. See above, 1 and 275. Significant of this is the contemporaneous
appearance of Κνόσιος and Κνōhίαν in different drafts of the same document (see no. 85 with note).

On present evidence this change of intervocalic σ seems to belong only
to Argos and the vicinity, in contrast to the towns of the Acte, where we
find only σ from the earliest times (ποιϜέσανς Methana, sixth century
B.C.). The only apparent exceptions, Νικαhαρίστα and Κτēhίλας in dedications found at Epidaurus, may be names of Argives, like the ᾿Αρχεhίλας
᾿Αργεῖος of the same source (IG IV².i.137, 138, 140).

3. Elean. In no. 65 (middle of fourth century) ἀδεαλτώhαιε,
φυγαδεύαντι (aor. subj.), beside δαμοσιῶμεν, δαμοσιοία. In no. 66
ποιήασσαι (ποιήσασθαι), ποιήαται (aor. subj.), beside ἀναθέσιορ, etc.
In all the earlier inscriptions intervocalic σ is unchanged.

4. Cyprian. φρονέōι (φρονέωσι), ποεχόμενον (ποσ-εχόμενον), also
in sentence combination (cf. 97a), as κὰ ἀ(ν)τί (κὰς ἀντί), τᾶ ὑχἔρōν
(τᾶς ὑχήρων). But generally σ is written in the inscriptions.
Several glosses in Hesychius show loss of intervocalic (and also
initial) σ.

a. In Arcadian the unique πόεστι (no. 22.12) for πόσεστι is probably
a special case of dissimilatory loss of the first σ.

Rhotacism

60. Rhotacism, or change of σ to ρ, is found in Elean, late
Laconian, and Eretrian, rarely elsewhere.

1. Elean. Final ς appears uniformly as ρ in the later inscriptions, nos. 65, 66, e.g. τιρ, αἵματορ, ὅπωρ, πόλιορ. Most of the
earlier inscriptions show -ς and -ρ side by side without any apparent system. Rhotacism of intervocalic σ is unknown (cf. 59.3).

a. In the earlier inscriptions ρ is relatively most frequent in forms of
the article and the indefinite or the relative pronoun, e.g., τοίρ, τιρ, ὅρ,
and possibly the rhotacism began in such enclitic and proclitic forms.
But even here there is great fluctuation in the spelling.

2. Laconian. Rhotacism of final ς is seen in very late inscriptions, e.g., νικάαρ, βουαγόρ, etc. (nos. 75-78), confirmed by numerous glosses, and in the spurious Timotheus decree.

3. Eretrian. Rhotacism of intervocalic σ is frequent in inscriptions of Eretria and Oropus, e.g., Eretr. ἔχουριν, θύωριν, ἐπιδημέωριν, συνελευθερώραντι, παιρίν, σίτηριν, Ἀρτεμίρια, Orop. δημορίων. But there are many exceptions, and the use of ρ is gradually given up under Attic influence. Although Plato, Cratylus 434 C, remarks that the Eretrians say σκληρότηρ for σκληρότης, there is no inscriptional example of ρ for final ς except once ὅπωρ ἄν, for which see **97a**.

4. Rhotacism of σ before a voiced consonant is seen in Eretr. Μίργος = Μίσγος, late Cretan (Gortyn) κόρμοι = κόσμοι, Thess. Θεορδότειος, Lac. Θιοκορμίδας. In most dialects σ in this position was pronounced as a voiced sound (z), and in late times often indicated by ζ, as ψήφιζμα.

Change of τ to σ

61. τ is changed to σ very frequently before ι, and sometimes before υ. The more precise conditions are uncertain, and the change is in part independent of dialectal variation, τ being retained in some words in all dialects, e.g., ἀντί, and in some words becoming σ in all dialects, e.g., most words like βάσις (Skt. ga-ti-s), στάσις, etc.

But in a considerable class of words there is a distinct dialectal distribution of the τ- and σ-forms, the retention of τ being a notable characteristic of the West Greek dialects, in which Boeotian, Thessalian, and Pamphylian also share.

1. Verb forms with the endings -τι, -ντι, as δίδωτι, φέροντι = δίδωσι, φέρουσι (Arc. φέρονσι, Lesb. φέροισι). Examples are plentiful in all the West Greek dialects and Boeotian (-τι, -νθι), and for Thessalian and Pamphylian (in which no 3 sg. μι-forms are yet quotable) the third plural forms are attested. See **138**.2, 4.

2. The numerals for 20 and the hundreds, (ϝ)ίκατι = εἴκοσι, -κάτιοι = -κόσιοι (Arc. -κάσιοι). See **116, 117**.2.

3. Some nouns and adjectives in -τις, -τιος, etc. Att.-Ion. -σις,

etc. Boeot. Εὔτρητις (shown by Εὐτρειτιδεῖες and Εὐτρētίφαντος; see no. 38.5), the native name of the town vs. Εὔτρησις in Homer. Delph., Coan ἐνιαύτιος = ἐνιαύσιος. Arg. ῥύτιον (no. 86.41; cf. Troez. ῥυτιάζω), Boeot. πλατίος, lit. Dor. (Epich.), Epid. πλατίον = πλησίος, πλησίον. 'Αρταμίτιος, 'Αφροδίτιος in many West Greek dialects. Rhod., Thess. ἐναράτιον = ἐνηρόσιον.

4. Corinth. ΠοτΕδᾶϝōνι, ΠοτΕδᾶνι Ποτειδᾶν with similar τ-forms in Cretan, Rhodian, Coan, Delphian, Boeotian, and Thessalian, also Ποτοιδᾶνι of uncertain dialect (Schwyzer 642), all = Hom. Ποσειδάων, Ion. Ποσειδέων, Att. Ποσειδῶν, Lesb. Ποσείδᾶν, Arc. Ποσοιδᾶν (49.1). Lac. Ποhοιδᾶν (cf. also Ποhοίδαια) is plainly from the pre-Doric form represented by Arc. Ποσοιδᾶν. So perhaps from another pre-Doric σ-form the Ποσειδᾶν occurring in Argolic (Argos, no. 86.15; later at Mycenae, Calauria, Epidaurus) and in later inscriptions of various dialects, as Arcadian (no. 22.57), Cretan, Rhodian, etc. But one suspects that in some of the late occurrences it may be merely a hybrid, influenced by the familiar Ποσειδῶν, as conversely Thess. Ποτειδοῦνι with native τ but -ουνι from Att. -ῶνι.

a. The distribution of West Greek προτί, ποτί vs. Att.-Ion., Lesb. πρός, Arc.-Cypr. πός is like that in 1-4 above, except that Homer has πρότι, πότι beside πρός. But here there are no forms in -σι, and it is a question whether the -ς of πρός, πός comes from -σι by elision and apocope or is a different ending, original -ς.

5. Lit. Dor. τύ, Boeot. τού = Att.-Ion., Lesb. σύ. Cret. ἥμιτυς (in ἡμιτυέκτō; cf. also Epid. hēμίτεια) = Att.-Ion., Arc. ἥμισυς, Lesb. αἵμισυς, with suffix -τυ- beside -τϝο- in ἥμισσον, etc. (81).

β, δ, γ

62. In general β, δ, γ remained simple mediae, but in some dialects there are indications of their pronunciation as spirants, which eventually prevailed even in Attic (cf. Mod. Grk. β = Eng. v, δ = Eng. th in then, γ guttural spirant). Such are:

1. The use of β for ϝ in later Laconian, etc. 51.

2. The occasional representation of δ by ζ, as in three of the very earliest Elean inscriptions, e.g., ζέ, ζέκα, ζίκαια, ζίφυιον, ζαμιοργία, Φειζός, also early Rhod. τόζ' = τόδε (no. 100), early Arg. Φισζείē (for σζ see 89.1) = εἰδείη, and Phlias. ζέκα =

δέκα (SEG 11.275).—Cret. ρ from ρδ (86.6). Cret. ἀντρήιον (=
usual ἀνδρήιον) with τ indicating retention of stop after a nasal
(as in Mod. Grk. ἄντρας pronounced andras), perhaps Cret.
σποϜδδάν (89.4).

3. The occasional omission of γ or substitution of ι, as in
Boeot. ἰώ, ἰών (Ar., Corinna) = ἐγώ, Pamph. μhειάλαν, μhειάλ̄ετι,
etc. (μεγάλος), Arc. ἐπιθιάν̄ε (ἐπιθιγγάνῃ) ,Mess., Arc. Φιάλεια
beside Φιγάλεια, and ὀλίος (ὀλίγος) in late inscriptions of various
places. The occasional representation of γ by ζ in Cyprian, as
ζᾶ (γᾶ), ἀζαθός (ἀγαθός).

φ, θ, χ

63. In general, φ, θ, χ remained true aspirated stops, and in
the earliest type of the alphabet, which had a sign for θ but none
for φ or χ, these two were represented by πh and χh, as at Thera,
or, where a sign for h was not in use, simply by π and χ, as in the
Gortyn Law Code (e.g., χρόνος = χρόνος, πυλά = φυλή). Spellings like γέγραπφα, δεδόκχθαι are mostly late, an exceptionally
early example being Delph. λεχοῖ (no. 52 D 13; dat. sg. of λεχώ).

But the pronunciation as spirants (Eng. *f*, *th* in *thin*, Germ. *ch*),
which eventually prevailed even in Attic, existed at a much
earlier period in some dialects. Such a pronunciation of θ is
certainly presupposed by Lac. σ = θ (64), probably by El.
σσ = σθ (85.2), late Cret. θθ = σσ (Ϝέτεθθι), Thess. φεῶν, φύοντες
(68.5), and possibly by some other spellings which, however,
may be variously interpreted.

64. Laconian σ = θ. The use of σ by Aristophanes in the
Lysistrata to indicate the sound of the Laconian θ (and there is
no good reason to doubt that this belongs to the original text)
shows that it had become a spirant which would strike the Athenian ear as σ, even if not yet fully identical with it. The Laconians
themselves retained the spelling θ in all the earlier inscriptions,
but ἀνέσηκε (ἀνέθηκε) and σιῶ (θεοῦ) occur in a fourth century
inscription, and in very late inscriptions ἀνέσηκε, Βωρσέα (Ϝορθία),
κασσηρατόριν beside καθθηρατόριον, etc.

Interchange of Voiceless and Voiced Stops and Aspirates

65. Dissimilation and assimilation of aspirates, or transposi-

tion of the aspiration. The dissimilation seen in τίθημι from *θίθημι, τρέχω from *θρέχω (cf. θρέξομαι), etc., belongs to the proethnic period. But there are some examples of later, dialectal assimilation. So Cret. θιθέμενος = τιθέμενος, θύκα (i.e., θύχα) = τύχη, West Ion. (Cumae) θυφλός = τυφλός, Arc. (also early Att. inscr.) φαρθένος = παρθένος, Thess. Φερσεφόνα = Περσεφόνη, Boeot. φεφύλαχσο = πεφύλαξο, Lac., Epid., Thess. θεθμός, Locr. θέθμιον = τεθμός, τέθμιον, Att. θεσμός, θέσμιον (164.4), Att. (inscr.) ἐνθαῦθα = usual Att. ἐνταῦθα. Ion. ἐνθαῦτα is the more original form (from ἔνθα), whence Att. ἐνταῦθα through transposition of the aspiration and influence of ταῦτα. Cf. also Eub. ἐντοῦθα like τοῦτα (124), El. ἐνταῦτα, Argol. ἐντάδε = ἐνθάδε, intluenced by ταῦτα, τάδε (but cf. also 66). Regular dissimilation in Arc. μεσακόθεν vs. Att. πανταχόθεν, etc., and in Arc. ἐσκεθῆν, Lesb. ὑποσκέθην vs. Hom. σχεθέειν, etc. For transposition cf. also Ion. ἄχαντος = ἄκανθος, Cret. καυχός = χαλκός, Thess. Πετθαλός from Φετταλός (68.2).

66. There are scattered examples of variation between stop and aspirate and between voiceless and voiced stops, especially before a nasal. Locr. τέκνα = τέχνη, Cret. τνατός, τετνακός = θνητός, τεθνηκός (also ἄντρōπος, Pamph. ἄτρōπος), Heracl. διακνόντων beside διαγνόντων, Eretr. ἀποδείγνυσθαι, Ther. ἐνδειγνύμενος to δείκνυμι, Aetol. ἀχνηκότας beside ἀγνηκώς (ἀγνέω = ἄγω). Ion. πρῆχμα = πρῆγμα, μέλιχμα = μείλιγμα, Epid. φάρχμα = φράγμα, πάρδειχμα = παράδειγμα, Arg. ῥηχμός = ῥηγμός (-σμα, -σμος). Cf. τέχνη from *τέκσνᾱ. (So perhaps Delph., Locr., Arg. ἐχθός from *ἐχτός, this from *ἐκσ-τός. Cf. early Att. ἔδοχσε, etc.)

In Pamphylian ντ became regularly νδ (influenced by languages of Asia Minor in which the change of nt to nd is widely attested), with ν not written (69.2), as πέδε = πέντε, ἐξάγōδι = ἐξάγωντι. Cret. ἀβλοπία, καταβλάπεθαι = ἀβλαβία, etc., Mess. κεκλεβώς (κλέπτω), Arg. γεγράβανται = γεγράφαται, are examples of analogical interchange in roots ending in a labial, owing to common forms in ψ. So also Coan στέπτω = στέφω. Locr. φρίν = πρίν and Arc., Cret., Pamph. Πύτιος = Πύθιος, are obscure.

El. πάσκω = πάσχω is probably due to the influence of other verbs in -σκω (but possibly like στ = σθ, cf. 85.1). For Att.-Ion.

δέχομαι other dialects (and Ionic in part) have the original
δέκομαι (cf. Att. δωροδόκος), οὐδείς, μηδείς are replaced by
οὐθείς, μηθείς, with θ from δ + the spiritus asper of εἷς, in later
Attic and elsewhere.

a. Very late inscriptions show numerous examples of confusion, not
confined to any special conditions, as ἀδελπός = ἀδελφός, φρεσβύτερος =
πρεσβύτερος, Lesb. ὑπάρκοισαν = ὑπάρχουσαν, Delph. βρυτανεῖον (also Cretan), βρυτανεύω = πρυτανεῖον, etc., and Βαλλάντιον = Παλλάντιον. Some
such forms as these last, reflecting occasional colloquial pronunciation,
presumably underlie the too sweeping statement of Plutarch (Mor. 292E)
that the Delphians used β in place of π.

Interchange of π and πτ

67. Of the Homeric by-forms of πόλις and πόλεμος, πτόλις is
found also in Cyprian, and in Thess. οἱ ττολίαρχοι, ἀρχιττολιαρχέντος (ττ from πτ, **86**.2) and Arc. Πτόλις (place name), Cret.
Πτολίοικος; πτόλεμος is found in Cyprian (gloss) and in proper
names like the Maced. Πτολεμαῖος and others from various places.

Interchange of Labials, Dentals, and Gutturals

68. 1. Those sounds of the parent speech which are called
labiovelars and are here designated as k^w, g^w, g^wh, appear in
Greek regularly as (1) labials before the back vowels α, o, ω and
before consonants, (2) dentals before the front vowels ι, ε, η,
(3) gutturals before and after υ. Thus ποῦ, πόθεν (Lat. *quod*, cf.
Osc. *pod*), ὁποῖος, but τίς (Lat. *quis*), τε (Lat. *que*), Cret. ὀτεῖος,—
πεμπάς πέμπτος, but πέντε (Lat. *quinque*),—λύκος (Eng. *wolf*),
γυνή (Eng. *queen*) beside Boeot. βανά. But before ι usually β,
φ, e. g. βίος (Lat. *vīvus*), with δ only in Heracl. ἐνδεδιωκότα = ἐμβεβιωκότα. Many exceptions are due to leveling between related
forms, e.g., βέλος after βάλλω, etc. Instead of πρέσβυς, with analogical β, several dialects have forms with γ, which is regular
before υ, e.g., Cret. πρεῖγυς, Boeot. πρισγεῖες, etc. (see **86**.3).
Examples of the normal relation are Arc. δέλλω = βάλλω,
West Greek δήλομαι, δείλομαι (**75**) = βούλομαι, West Greek and
Arc. ὀδελός = ὀβολός (but if from the rare early Att. ὀβελός, β
is analogical, as in ὀβελίσκος. Boeot. ὀβελός, Thess. ὀβελλός may
belong under 2, below), Dor. βλῆρ = δέλεαρ.

2. But it is a notable characteristic of the Aeolic dialects that they very frequently show a labial even before a front vowel, where the dental is regular elsewhere. Thus Lesb., Thess. πέμπε = πέντε. Lesb. πέσσυρες (Hesych., cf. Hom. πίσυρες), Boeot. πέτταρες, πέτρατος, πετραμείννιον, Thess. πετροετηρίς = τέτταρες, etc. Thess. πεῖσαι, ἀππεισάτου, Boeot. ποταποπισάτω = τεῖσαι, etc., Lesb. πήλυι (Sappho), Boeot. Πειλε-στροτίδας to τῆλε. Thess. βέλλομαι, Boeot. βείλομαι = West Greek δήλομαι, δείλομαι. Lesb. Βέλφοι (gloss), Boeot. Βελφοί = Δελφοί, Thess. Βέλφαιον = *Δέλφαιον. Boeot. βέφυρα = Cret. δέφυρα, Att. γέφυρα (for γ see 88), Lesb. φήρ (gloss), Thess. πεφειράκοντες = θήρ, τεθηρακότες (though this is a case of original ĝhw not gʷh). Boeot. Φετταλός, whence Thess. Πετθαλός with transposition of the aspiration (65) = Att. Θετταλός, Ion. Θεσσαλός. Yet some words always have the dental, e.g., τε, τις, τιμά, the reason for this being obscure.

a. An apparently similar case is Lesb. σπέλλω = στέλλω (fut. κασπολέω Sappho 42 Diehl; Hesych. κασπέλη· στορνύει, σπελλάμεναι· στελλάμεναι, σπολεῖσα· σταλεῖσα), with Thess. σπόλος 'stake.' But στέλλω is almost certainly from a root *stel- with original dental (seen also in Lesb. στάλλα), and we have to do with two parallel roots στελ- and σπελ-.

b. Cypr. πείσει = τείσει is in striking agreement with the Aeolic forms quoted above. But if it is the result of the same phonetic change (and not with π by analogy of ποινά, etc.), and so to be reckoned as an Aeolic element in Arcado-Cyprian, it is quite isolated in this development in contrast to that seen in Arc. ἀπυτεισάτω, δέλλω, Cypr. Τὲλεφάνō and in Arc. ϟις, Cypr. σίς, etc. (below, 3).

3. In Arcado-Cyprian there is evidence of a sibilant pronunciation before a front vowel. Cypr. σις = τις (no. 23), σί = τί (Hesych.). Arc. ὄϟις = ὄτις (no. 16), and in no. 17 (written with a special letter, 4.4) ϟις = τις, εἴϟε = εἴτε, ὀϟέοι = ὄτεῳ. Further, τζετρακάτιαι = τετρακάτιαι in no. 70, due to the Arcadian engraver. Cf. also the gloss ζέλλω (Hesych.) beside inscriptional δέλλω = βάλλω, and ζέρεθρον (Strabo) = δέρεθρον, βάραθρον.

a. The σ occurs also for an original dental in ἀπυσεδομένος = ἀπδεδομένος. But this is probably a special case of dissimilation like that in 'Αρκασίδης = 'Αρκαδίδης. Otherwise the dentals appear without change in the same inscription, e.g., δέ, τότε, etc. The

sibilant development is definitely linked with labiovelar origin, and this goes well
with the preservation of the old labiovelar voiceless stop in the pre-Arcado-Cyprian
of Cretan script (p. 8, footnote). The fact that in Arcadian the sibilant appears only
in early inscriptions is like the case of El. ϛ = δ only in the earliest inscriptions, then
replaced by the usual (see 275).

4. There are some pronominal forms with κ in place of the
usual π or τ. Thus Ion. κῶς = πῶς, κότερος, etc. (in texts of
Ionic authors; in inscriptions only once ὁκοῖα, otherwise π),
Thess. κίς, διὲ κί, πὸκ κί = τίς, etc.

  a. Thess., Cypr. δαύχνα in συνδαυχναφόροι, Δαυχναφόριος (cf. δαυχμός in
Nicand., Hesych.) is from *δαυκσνᾱ (cf. **66**) belonging with δαῦκος, δαῦκον,
a plant much like the δάφνη (cf. δαῦκον δαφνοειδές, Theophr.). The form
δαύχνα then served as the equivalent of the similar though unrelated δάφνη.

5. A change of θ to φ, that is, doubtless, of spirant *th* to *f*,
is seen in φεῶν, φύοντες = θεῶν, θύοντες, of an inscription
found at Dodona.

Nasals and Liquids

69. Nasal before consonant. The nasal was always assimilated
to the character of the following consonant, but was less distinctly
sounded than in the intervocalic position. With this are connected
the following facts.

  1. The letter ν is freely used for the guttural and the labial
nasal, as well as for the dental, e.g., Ὀλύνπιος, ἀνφί, λανχάνω.

  2. The nasal is omitted in the spelling, occasionally in all
dialects, and regularly in Cyprian and Pamphylian, as Cypr.
ἀτί = ἀντί, Pamph. πέδε = πέντε.

  3. Complete assimilation to a following stop, though not regular
in any dialect, sometimes occurred in careless pronunciation, as
shown by occasional, and mostly late, spellings, e.g., Att. ξυββάλ-
λεσθαι, Boeot. Ὀλυππίχην (late κοινή inscription), Delph. Ἄθαββος,
σύββολον, λαββάνοντες. From Crete, where in general consonant
assimilation is most extensive (**86**), there are several examples, as ποππάν = πομπάν, ἀφφάνω = ἀμφάνω, and the assimilated
form was usual in the name of the town Lappa, whose coins
show Λαππαίων. In some cases the dissimilative influence of a
preceding or following nasal was probably a factor, e.g., Delph.

ἀνεκκλήτως = ἀνεγκλήτως, ἐπάνακκον (papyr.) = ἐπάναγκον, Locr. ἔκκλημα = ἔγκλημα, ἀνακκάζηι = ἀναγκάζῃ, Thess. ἐξξανακάδεν = ἐξαναγκάζειν.

4. A special case is Boeot. ἔππασις (uniformly so spelled) = ἔμπασις. This is from *ἔμ-ππᾱσις as also Boeot. ἀππασάμενος (Corinna) from *ἀν-ππᾱ-. So also Boeot. τὰ ππάματα. See 162.12.

a. Assimilation of a nasal to the character of the preceding stop is perhaps to be seen in Coan 'Αρίσταιχνος = 'Αρίσταιχμος, and, Cret. δαρκνά = δαρχμά, δραχμή. Cf. Mod. Grk. Πάτνος from Πάτμος, λαχνός from λαχμός.

70. Transposition of a liquid, or loss by dissimilation.

1. Transposition within the same syllable. Cret. πορτί = προτί, 'Αφορδίτα = 'Αφροδίτη, also κάρτος, σταρτός, etc., for which see 49.2a. Pamph. περτ', 'Αφορδίσιυς, Πρείας = Περγαίας, Ther. Καρτι-, Σταρτο-.

2. Transposition between different syllables. Heracl. τράφος, Amorg. τράφη = τάφρος, τάφρη, Syrac. δρίφος = δίφρος (Hesych.).

3. Loss by dissimilation. Cypr. ϝρέτα = ῥήτρα, El. ϝράτρα, Epid. ῥόπτον = ῥόπτρον, φατρία or φάτρα in various dialects = φρατρία, Hom. φρήτρη, conversely φρήταρχος at Naples.

71. Cretan υ from λ. In Cretan the λ was a deep guttural *l* closely resembling *u* (cf. French *autre* from Lat. *alter*, etc.), and the spelling υ is fairly common. So ἀδευπιαί = ἀδελφεαί (once in Law-Code beside usual ἀδελπιός, etc.), ϝευμένας = ϝελμένας, καυχός = καλχός, αὐφίτων = ἀλφίτων, ἐπευθών, πορτῆυθον = ἐπελθών, προσῆλθον (further examples in Hesychius).

a. Cret., Epid. μαίτυρες (hence nom. Cret. μαίτυρς, μαῖτυς) = μάρτυρες, with Sicil. μαιτυρήσηι (SEG 4.31, with p. 141) are apparently to be explained as due to dissimilation of the two ρ's with palatalization of the first.

b. A palatalized λ is indicated by the spelling λε, which is frequent in Cos, and occurs also in Melos, Thasos, and Cnidus. Thus Coan ξύλεα, ξύλεων=ξύλα, ξύλων, κοτύλεαι. = κοτύλαι, Παμφύλεων beside Πάμφυλοι. Φιλεωνίδας, etc., Thas. Φιλεωνίδεος, Mel. Φίλεων, etc.

c. The change of λ to ρ before a consonant, regular in popular Mod. Grk. (ἀδερφός = ἀδελφός, etc.) appears in occasional forms from the second century A.D. on, e.g., Delph. Δερφοί, Att. ἀδερφοί.

72. ντ, νθ from λτ, λθ. Several examples occur in West Greek and Arcadian. Φίντων (Φίλτων) or Φιντίας in many West Greek dialects and Arcadian. Arg. Μίντων (Μίλτων), κέντο (κέλτο) in Alcman, φίντατος (φίλτατος) in Epicharmus, βέντιστος (βέλτιστος) in Theocritus. Cyren. τένται from *τέλται = τέλεται = ἔσεται. ἐνθεῖν (ἐλθεῖν) is most widespread, occurring in Doric wiiters and in Corcyrean, Cyrenaean, Arcadian, late Delphian, late Cretan. Meg. ἐνπίδες = ἐλπίδες stands alone.

Double Liquids and Nasals in Lesbian and Thessalian

73. The combinations discussed in **74-76**, also **77.**1, **79**, have in part a common history, since they all become double liquids and nasals in Lesbian and Thessalian, but in other dialects a single liquid or nasal accompanied by lengthening of the preceding vowel.

a. This doubling is observed regularly only in Lesbian and Thessalian, and is one of the most distinctive Aeolic characteristics, one that is familiar in Lesbian poetry and in some Homeric forms (ἄμμε, ἔμμεν, etc.). But there are scattered examples elsewhere, which are relics of an Aeolic element. Thus from the once Aeolic Chian region (cf. **184**) Πελιινναῖον, Ἄργεννον, Φαννόθεμις, Lac. Φάβεννος, Φαβέννα, Arc. (Orchomenos) ὀφέλλω (vs. ὀφήλω Tegea), ἔκριννα; Ther. ἐλλύτα = Boeot. εἰλύτα 'a kind of cake' (from εἰλύω 'roll').

74. ρ, ν, + ι, when preceded by any other vowel than α or ο. From *φθέρι̯ω, Lesb. φθέρρω (gram.), Att. etc. φθείρω, Arc. φθήρω. From *κρίνι̯ω, Lesb. κρίννω (gram.), Thess. κρέννω (**18**), Att., etc., κρίνω. From *κτένι̯ω, Lesb. κτέννω (gram.), Att., etc. κτείνω.

a. But if α or ο precedes, epenthesis takes place, the result being the same in all dialects, e.g., χαίρω from *χαρι̯ω, μοῖρα from *μόρι̯α, βαίνω from *βάνι̯ω.

b. λι gives λλ in nearly all dialects, e.g., ἄλλος (Lat. *alius*), στέλλω from *στέλι̯ω. But Cyprian has αἶλος (beside ἀλ(λ)ά) and Ἀπείλōν = Ἀπόλλων, and Elean once αἰλότρια (beside ἄλλα, στέλλω).

75. λν or/and λσ. Lesb., Thess. στάλλα, Dor. στάλα, Att.-Ion. στήλη, Lesb. βόλλομαι, βόλλα, Thess. βέλλομαι, Att.-Ion. βουλή, βούλομαι, Boeot. βωλά, βείλομαι, West-Grk. βωλά, βουλά, δήλομαι, δείλομαι, Lesb. ἀπέλλω (gloss), Ion. εἴλω, εἰλέω, Delph. εἰλέσθω, El. ἀποϜελέοι, -έοιαν, Heracl. ἐγϜηληθίωντι (in these forms the meaning is 'shut out' or 'prevent'; cf. also Att. δίκη ἐξούλης 'action of ejectment.' Cret. Ϝευμένας = Ϝελμένας and καταϜελμένōν are

perf. pass. participles, like Hom. ἐελμένος but meaning 'assembled'
(cf. ἀολλής, etc. 55), Lesb., Hom. ὀφέλλω 'owe' (also Arc.,
73a), Att. ὀφείλω, Arg., Cret., Arc. ὀφήλω.

a. The dialectal relations are clear, but whether the original consonant
group was λν or λσ has been a matter of dispute. From the point of view
of word formation a ν-suffix is distinctly the most probable in most cases,
e.g., στάλλᾱ, etc., from *σταλ-νᾱ, εἴλω from *Fέλ-νω. The conflicting λλ
of Att. ὄλλῡμι may be explained as a later treatment of a restored *ὄλνῡμι,
parallel to that in Att. ἕννῡμι vs. Ion. εἵνῡμι with the normal development
of σν. (Some other cases of λλ, apparently from λν, are not so easy.)
But the group βούλομαι, etc. (also Hom., Eretr., Arc.-Cypr. βόλομαι
without suffix), is now generally believed to be based on an λσ (perhaps
an aor. subj.) form, with the same development as in Lesb. ἔστελλα, Att.
ἔστειλα, etc. (79).

76. 1. Medial σ + liquid or nasal. From *χέσλιοι (cf. Skt. *sa-
hasra-*), Lesb., Thess. χέλλιοι, Ion. etc., χείλιοι, Lac. χήλιοι (Att.
χἵλιοι, see 25e). From *χεσρ- (cf. Hitt. *kessar* and *kessras* 'hand'),
Lesb. χέρρας (Alc., Theocr.), elsewhere χείρ or χήρ. From *ἔσμι
(Skt. *asmi*), Lesb. ἔμμι, Thess. ἐμμί, elsewhere εἰμί or ἠμί (25).
From *ἄσμε (cf. Skt. *asmān*), Lesb. ἄμμε, Thess. ἀμμέ, elsewhere
ἀμέ, Att.-Ion. ἡμέας. From *σελάσνᾱ (σέλας), Lesb. σελάννᾱ,
elsewhere σελᾱνᾱ, Att.-Ion. σελήνη.

a. Initial σλ, etc., became ἡλ, etc., later simple λ, etc. The earlier
stage is represented by occasional early spellings with λh, etc. (cf. Fh,
51b, c), e.g., Aegin. λhαβών (cf. εἴληφα, Hom. ἔλλαβε,, below), Corcyr.
ρhοFαῖσι (cf. Skt. *srava* = Eng. *stream*). But also where there is no trace of
an initial s in cognates (some assume an initial "laryngeal"), Corcyr.
Μhείξιος, Meg. Μhεγαρεύς, Pamph. μhειάλαν, Att. μhεγάλō in an early
inscription.

2. Compounds and augmented or reduplicated forms of such
words only rarely show the development proper to intervocalic
σλ, etc., as Att. εἴληφα from *σέσλᾱφα. Usually this was checked
by the analogical influence of the simplex, and the subsequent
development was to λλ, etc., later (under the continued influence
of the simplex and of words with original initial λ, etc.) simply
λ, etc., e.g., Hom. ἔ-λλαβε, ἄ-λληκτος, ἔ-ρρεον, ἔ-ννεον, φιλο-μμει-
δής, later ἔλαβε, etc. Locr., Delph., Cret. ἀμφιλλέγω, Arc. ἀμφίλλογος, from ἀμφισ-λ-, whence Meg. ἀμφέλλεγον as if from ἀμφιλλέγω. But ρρ usually remained, e.g., Att. ἐρρύην beside ἔλαβε,
Dor. -ερρύᾱ, though here there is considerable variation, especial-

ly in compounds (Att. παραρύματα and παραρρύματα, etc.). Cf. ρρ from Ϝρ, **55**a.

νς

77. 1. Original intervocalic νσ. From *μηνσός (cf. Lat. *mēnsis*), Lesb. μῆννος (also μῆνος), Thess. μειννός (also μεινός), Att. etc. μηνός (in this word the vowel was already long). From *ἔκρινσα, Lesb. ἔκριννα, Att., etc., ἔκρῑνα. From *ἔμενσα, Thess. ἔμεννα, Att., etc. ἔμεινα. From *ἔφανσα, Dor., etc., ἔφᾱνα, Att.-Ion. ἔφηνα. Similarly μσ, as, from *ἔνεμσα, Lesb. ἔνεμμα (gram.), Att., etc., ἔνειμα.

a. The dat. pl. of ν-stems, as ποιμέσι, δαίμοσι, is not formed from -ενσι, -ονσι, but from -ασι (cf. φρασί Pindar) with substitution of the vowel of the other cases. But in Arc. ἱερομνάμονσι the ν also is introduced from the other cases, and this secondary νσ is retained (cf. **3**).

2. νσ + consonant lost its ν in proethnic Greek without effect on the preceding vowel, e.g., κεστός from *κενστός (cf. κεντέω), συσκευάζω, etc., from συν-. So also later in Thess. ὀστροφά from *ὀνστροφά = ἀναστροφή. But ν might be restored by analogy, with resulting treatment of νσ as in **3**. Att. ἔσπεισται from *ἔσπενσται, Lesb. εἴκοιστος, etc. (**116** with a), Arg. ποιγραψάνσθω, etc. (**140**.3b).

3. Secondary intervocalic νσ, in which σ comes from τι, dental + σ, or τ before ι, had an entirely different history from that of original νσ, which was changed before the new νσ came into existence. This νσ is retained in Cretan (i.e., Central Cretan, cf. **273**), Argolic (mainly Argive, cf. **251**), Thessalian, and Arcadian, while in other dialects it loses the ν with lengthening, in Lesbian and Cyrenaean with diphthongization, of the preceding vowel. Thus from *πάντια, Cret., Arg., Thess., Arc. πάνσα, Att., etc., πᾶσα, Lesb., Ther., Cyren. παῖσα. From *μόντια, *μόνσα (not yet quotable), Lesb. μοῖσα, elsewhere μοῦσα or μῶσα. From nom. sg. fem. pres. part. -ντ-ια, Cret. ἔχονσα, ἄγονσα, ἐβίονσα, etc. (but ὑπάρχωνσα, etc., in East and West Cretan), Thess. ἔνσα, λειτορεύσανσα, ἀπελευθερεσθένσα, Arc. μίνονσα, etc., Arg. ἀντιτύχονσα, etc., Lesb. ἔχοισα, ἀρμόζοισα, δάμεισα, etc., Cyren. ἐκοῖσα, καθάραισα, etc., elsewhere -ουσα or -ωσα, -ᾱσα, -εισα. From dat. pl. of the ντ-stems, Cret. ἐπιβάλλονσι, ἐλόνσι, νικάσανσι, etc., Arg.

θύονσι, ἅπανσι, Arc. πάνσι, πολιτεύονσι, Cyren. ἐμμένοισι, πλέοισι, etc., elsewhere -ουσι, -ωσι, -ᾱσι, etc. From aor. *ἔσπενδσα, Cret. ἔσπενσα, Att., etc. ἔσπεισα. From 3 pl. -ντι (West Greek φέροντι, etc.), Arc. κρίνωνσι, ποίενσι, etc., Lesb. ἔχοισι, γράφωισι, τίθεισι, etc. (so also Chian λάβωισιν, πρήξοισιν, cf. 184), Att., etc., φέρουσι. Observe that 3 pl. -νσι is exclusively Arcadian, since this is the only dialect which belongs both to the νσ and the σι from τι (61) groups.

a. In derivatives in -σις from verbs in -νω, νσ is kept in all dialects, e.g., not only Cret. ἄνπανσις = ἀνάφανσις, Epid. ἅλινσις, but Att. πρόφανσις, ὕφανσις, etc., owing to the influence of the verbs.

78. Final νς. Since νσ + consonant lost its ν in proethnic Greek (77.2), the same would be true of final νς in close combination with a following word beginning with a consonant. Hence there arose doublets such as (1) before vowel τόνς, τάνς, (2) before consonants τός, τάς. Such doublets are found in Cretan, the Gortyn Law-Code still adhering very closely to the original distribution in the case of the article, e.g., τὸνς ἐλευθέρονς, but τὸς καδεστάνς. But elsewhere the use of one or the other set of forms has ceased to depend at all upon the initial of the following word.

Accusatives in -ος, -ας are the regular forms in Thessalian, Arcadian (so probably Cyprian -ος not -ōς), Theran, Cyrenaean, Coan, and are occasionally found in other Doric dialects and in literary Doric (e.g., frequent in Theocritus). Other dialects have -ονς, -ανς, or forms coming therefrom by the same development as that seen in the case of secondary intervocalic νσ (πάνσα, etc., 77.3), e.g., Argol. -ονς, -ανς, -ινς (less commonly -ος), Lesb. -οίς, -αίς, in most dialects -ούς or -ώς (25), -ᾱς. Only Elean, though medially it has πᾶσα not παῖσα, has here a development similar to the Lesbian, namely, -αις (and presumably -οις, but no o-stem acc. pl. forms occur in the inscriptions which have -αις), and later -αιρ, -οιρ. But there are also early forms in -Aς, -Oς, later -Oρ, of which the proper transcription and relation to the preceding are uncertain (short-vowel forms parallel to Cret. -ος beside -ονς?).

Similarly the preposition ἐνς, whence ἐς or εἰς. Cret., Argol. ἐνς and ἐς. ἐς in most Doric dialects (Lac., Heracl., Rhod., Coan,

Ther., Cyren., but also εἰς in some, mostly from the κοινή). Ion., Att.-Ion. ἐς and εἰς (both in Homer; Ion. mostly ἐς, Att. mostly εἰς), Lesb. εἰς (but here with genuine diphthong like τοῖς). Cf. also the treatment of final νς from -ντ-ς, e.g., nom. sg. part. Cret. νικάσανς, καταθένς, Argol. ποιϜέσανς, Heracl. καταλυμακωθής, Att., etc., τιθείς, Lesb. στοίχεις, Thess. εὐεργετές, Arc. ἱεροθυτές, Ther. αἱρεθές, Cyren. κοιμαθές, πωληθές.

λσ, ρσ

79. From *ἔστελσα, Lesb., Thess. ἔστελλα, Att., etc., ἔστειλα, Cret. ἔστηλα. Cf. also Lesb. βόλλομαι, Att. βούλομαι (**75** with a). From *ἔφθερσα, Att., etc., ἔφθειρα.

80. But in another set of words λσ and ρσ did not have this development, but remained unchanged in most dialects, while in several this ρσ was assimilated to ρρ. Cf. Hom. κέλσαι, ἔχερσεν, ὦρσε, ἄρσην, θάρσος, the widespread ἔρσην (**49**.2), and θάρσος or θέρσος in most dialects (partly in proper names only).

The assimilation to ρρ is Attic as ἄρρην, θάρρος, etc. (so in the earliest inscriptions; ρσ in early Attic writers is Ionic), West Ionic as ἀρρενικός (Cumae), ἄγαρρις (Naples), Θαρριπίδης, etc., Arcadian as φθέραι (for φθέρραι corresponding to φθέρσαι, like φθέρσαντες in Lycophron, not to φθεῖραι, which would be φθῆραι in Arcadian), ἀρρέντερος, Elean as θάρρος, θαρρῆν (ερσ in later ἐρσεναίτερος is due to κοινή influence), Theran as ([ἄ]ρενα dubious), Θαρῆς, Θηαρύμαϙhος, etc. (all archaic; in later ἄρσην, Θάρσων, ρσ is due to κοινή influence). Proper names with ρρ = ρσ occur also in several other dialects, e.g., Delph. Θαρρίκων, Θάρρανδρος, Amphiss. Θάρρυς, Boeot. Θάροψ, Meg. Χερρίας, Ὄρριππος, Corinth. Δαμοθέρρης. Cf. also κάρρων from *κάρσων (Cret. κάρτων, **81**), in Alcman, Epicharmus, Sophron, Plut. Lyc., etc.

a. Even in dialects which regularly have ρρ, ρσ may be retained by analogy, e.g., Att. θηρσί after other datives in -σι, κάθαρσις etc. after other nouns in -σις. So Arc. πανάγορσις. But even in these words there is sometimes assimilation, as Att. δέρρις, West Ion. ἄγαρρις.

σσ, ττ

81. Att. ττ = Ion. σσ comes from κ ι, χ ι, and in the following categories also from τ ι or θ ι (but see **82a**). So in presents like φυλάττω, φυλάσσω (κι̯), κορύττω, κορύσσω (θι̯), in feminines like γλῶττα, γλῶσσα (χι̯), μέλιττα, μέλισσα (τι̯), and in comparatives like ἥττων, ἥσσων (κι̯), κρείττων, κρέσσων (τι̯). τϜ gives the same result. So τέτταρες, τέσσερες (cf. Lat. *quattuor*, Skt. *catvāras*; see **114**.4), and ἥμισσον (also ἥμισον, **89**.6) in many dialects (Arc., Locr., Delph., Arg., Meg., etc.), Boeot. hέμιττα, εἵμιττον (nos. 39 and 42), from *ἥμι-τϜο- beside ἥμι-τυ- in a Cret. compound and Att.-Ion. ἥμισυς (**61**.5). Inscriptions show that Attic had ττ from the earliest times, the σσ of earlier writers being due to Ionic influence. But in the later κοινή, σσ is more common than ττ. Most of the dialects agree with Ionic, but ττ, as in Attic, is also Boeotian (φυλάττω, θάλαττα, πέτταρες, hέμιττα), Cretan (ἵαττα = Arg. ἔασσα, κάρτων from *κάρττων), and Euboean, at least in Styra, Eretria, Oropus (ἐλάττων, πρήττω, Κιττιής).

a. Late Cret. σσ in πράσσω, θάλασσα, ἥμισσον, also in ὅσσος, δασσάσθωσαν belonging under **82**, is due to (Attic-Ionic or Doric) κοινή.

b. Late Cret. θθ in words of this class, as θάλαθθα, ἵαθθα, also in ὀθθάκιν, Ἀρκάθθι belonging under **82**, and even for original σσ in Ϝέτεθθι. For σθ it is earlier and more frequent (**83**).

c. Although the Thessalian inscriptions usually have σσ, there is some evidence that the dialect had ττ originally, or at least in certain localities. Aside from θάλαττα, πίττα, which are quoted as Thessalian, cf. the proper names Κόττυφος, Φαύττιος, etc., and especially Πετθαλός from Φετταλός (**65**).

σ, σσ, ττ

82. τι̯ and θι̯ give Att. σ not ττ, and Ion. σ (early σσ often in poetry, but never in inscriptions) in ὅσος, ὁπόσος (τι̯), μέσος (*μέθι̯ος, cf. Skt. *madhyas*). A dental + σ gives precisely the same result, e.g., ἐκόμισα, ἐδίκασα, etc. In all such cases most dialects have σσ (but σ, as Att.-Ion., in Arcadian, as μέσος, ὅσος, ἐδικάσαμεν, δάσασθαι, elsewhere late), e.g., ὅσσος, τόσσος, Lesb. μέσσος, ἐδίκασσαν, Heracl. μέσσος, ἐδασσάμεθα, Arg. ἠργάσσαντο, ἐδίκασσαν, hίσσατο, ἐσσάμενοι, Cyren. ἵσσαντα, ἰσσάμενος. But Boeotian and Cretan have ττ, e.g., Boeot. μέττος, ὁπόττος, ἐψαφίτατο, ἀπολογίτταστη, Cret. μέττος, ὅττος, ὁπόττος, δάτταθθαι. In some very early Cretan inscriptions we find ζ, as ὄζος, ἀνδάζαθαι.

a. This is to be recognized as the normal development of τι and θι. The different result seen in the classes of words mentioned in **81** is due to the influence of the forms containing gutturals. After a consonant τι gives σ in all dialects; e.g., πάνσα, πᾶσα, from *πάντια.

b. Forms of Dor. ἴσᾱμι (**162**.9) regularly show single σ. Only late Cret. ἴθθαντες, ἴθθᾱντι seem to point to σσ (unless Hom. ἴσᾱσι beside ἴσᾱσι stands for ἴσσᾱσι), and these are not to be taken too seriously.

Original σσ

83. Original σσ, which becomes σ in Attic (ἐτέλεσα, γένεσι), is retained, as in Homer, etc., in most dialects (cf. ὅσσος, etc., **82**), e.g., Lesb. ἔσσονται, Thess. ἔσσεσθειν, Heracl. ἐσσῆται, Ther. ἐσσεῖται, dat. pl. -εσσι in numerous dialects, Heracl. -ασσι (**107**.3). For late Cret. ϝέτεθθι see **81***b*.

ζ, δδ

84. Attic-Ionic ζ, the early pronunciation of which was *zd* and which comes from *zd* (ὄζος, cf. Germ. *Ast*,; 'Αθήναζε from -α(ν)ς-δε) or, more often, from γι (μείζων, μέζων) or δι (πεζός)), is also ζ in the majority of other dialects. Lesb. σδ, found in our literary texts and in a few late inscriptions, is only another spelling of the same sound, adopted perhaps because ζ was used with the value of *z* in ζά = διά, etc. (**19**.1).

But assimilation to δδ, initial δ, is Boeotian, Thessalian, Elean, Cretan, Laconian, and Megarian (?). Boeot. γραμματίδδω, ψαφίδδω, δοκιμάδδω, ἰαρειάδδω, τρέπεδδα, δώω (ζώω), Δεύς, δύγαστρον, μέδδονος (= μέζονος), Thess. ἐξξανακάδεν (no. 35; the only example, so possibly δδ only in Thessaliotis, but there is no evidence against its being general Thessalian). El. δικάδω, χραίδω, Cret. δικάδδω, ψαφίδδω, ἐργάδδομαι, φροντιδδω, δώω, δωός, δυγόν, Δῆνα (Ζῆνα), Lac. γυμνάδδομαι, etc. in Ar. Lys., μιχκιχιδδόμενος, ὀπιδό[μενος], Δεύς in inscriptions. Δεύς occurs also on a vase from Rhodes, and is perhaps genuine Rhodian. Cf. the occasional assimilation of σδ in external combination in Rhodian (**97**.4). Meg. δδ is doubtful (Ar. Ach. μᾶδδα, χρήδδω, but only ζ in inscriptions).

In Cretan and Elean the spelling ττ is also found, as Cret. φροντίττω, ἐσπρεμμίττω (ἐκπρεμνίζω), ἀπολογίττω (but see also below, *a*), Τττῆνα, Τῆνα (Ζῆνα), El. νοστίττω (νοστίζω), ἀττάμιος (ἀζήμιος).

a. There is some interchange between presents in -σσω or -ττω and those in -ζω or -δδω, owing to the identity of their future and aorist forms. Thus Att. σφάττω = Ion. σφάζω, Boeot. σφάδδω, Boeot. φράττω (Corinna) = Att. φράζω, Thess. ἐμφανίσσω = Att. ἐμφανίζω, and, conversely, Cret. πράδδω, συνεσσάδδω = Att. πράττω, -σάττω, Cret. ἀλλάδδω, Locr. ἀλάζω (regular from γι, cf. ἀλλαγή) = Att. ἀλλάττω, Ion. ἀλλάσσω.

σθ

85. 1. στ = σθ. The use of στ for σθ is mainly characteristic of Northwest Greek. It is the regular spelling in Locrian, as hελέσται, hαρέσται, and early Elean, as χρεῆσται, λυσάστō, and occurs with some frequency in Phocian, as Delph. πρόστα, hιλαξάστō, later γινέστω, etc., Stir. θέστων, ἀποπολιτεύσασται. It occurs also in Boeotian, in late inscriptions of Orchomenus (ἀπολογίττασтη, etc.), where it is perhaps due to Aetolian influence, and rarely in Thessalian (πεπεῖστειν, ἐλέστειν, πρόστεν). But there are some early examples in other dialects, as Cret. μιστός, Lac. ἀποστρυθεῆσται, χρῆσται, Arc. (probably) [ἀφάε]σται, and in late times it is found in many parts of Greece, even at Athens.

2. σσ = σθ. This is found in late Elean, as ἀποδόσσαι (no. 65), ποιήασσαι (no. 66).

3. θθ = σθ. This is regular in Central Crete, e.g., πρόθθα, ἀποϜειπάθθō, πράδεθθαι, δατεῆθθαι, etc. (numerous examples in Law-Code, always θθ or θ), also rarely τθ as δέκετθαι, χρῆτθαι (no. 118), ἀπολογιττέτθω. But σθ occurs in some of the earliest inscriptions, and also (here probably from the κοινή) in the late inscriptions from other parts of Crete.

Assimilation, Dissimilation, and Transposition of Consonants

86. Assimilation in consonant groups. Many of the changes belonging under this head have been given already, e.g., under **55a, 69**.3, **74-76, 77**.1, **80, 84, 85**.2, 3. See also under external combination **96-100**. No notice is taken of assimilation which is common to all dialects and presumably proethnic, as δλ to λλ, etc.; nor of the partial assimilation involved in the familiar shift of voiced to voiceless before voiceless or conversely (but ζμ, ζβ, ζγ, ζδ, for σμ, etc., though widespread, are mostly late). This class of phenomena is one in which the difference between colloquial and careful speech is most noticeable, as may readily be observed in English. While some assimilations are so uniformly effected that the unassimilated form is completely displaced and forgotten, others remain colloquial only, the unassimilated form being still preferred in careful speech and writing. This accounts for much of the lack of uniformity in the evidence as regards some of the changes mentioned in this and the other sections. In some cases the spelling varies greatly even in the dialects where the change is best attested. Sometimes the assimilation is uniform in certain dialects, but evidently existed colloquially in others also and only sporadically made its appearance in the spelling. Assimilation is most extensive in Cretan.

1. κτ>ττ in Cretan. νυττί = νυκτί, ἐσπράτται = ἐκπράκται, Λύττος = Λύκτος.

2. πτ>ττ in Cretan and Thessalian. Cret. ἔγρατται = γέγραπται, ἐττά = ἑπτά, πέντος (also Amorg., but here special case) = πέμπτος, Thess. Λεττίναιος (Λεπτίναιος), οἱ ττολίαρχοι, ἀρχιττολιαρχέντος (πτόλις, **67**), also ἀτ τᾶς, etc. in external combination (**99**.2). Cf. also Thess. Ἀτθόνειτος = Ἀφθόνητος.

3. σγ>γγ or γ (with graphic or actual simplification). Cret. πρείγōν, πρείγιστος (both in Law Code), πρεῖγυς, πρειγήια, πρειγευτάς, πρειγευσάντων, Locr. πρείγα (no. 59.10), all from πρεισ-γ- seen in Boeot. (ι from ει, **29**) πρισγῆες, πρισγεῖες (no. 40), πρισγούτερος (Ἀρχ. Δελτ. 14, πίναξ 4a, l. 48), beside πρεισ-β- in Thess. πρεισβεία and πρεσ-γ-, πρεσ-β- in Arg. πρεσγέα (no. 85.39), later πρεσβήα (hybrid form), Att.-Ion. πρέσβυς, etc.

a. The form πρεισ- is not from πρεσ-, but an independent parallel form (cf. Lat. preiscus, priscus, and prīs- in Lat. prīmus, Pael. prismu). For the interchange of γ and β, see **68**.1. Late Cret. πρεισγευτάς and πρεγγευτάς in inscriptions of Teos are hybrid forms. In late Cret. πρήγιστος and late Coan πρηγιστεύω the η is due to the late confusion of ει and η.

b. A parallel change of σκ to κκ is attested for late Laconian by glosses like ἀκκόρ· ἀσκός. Λάκωνες (Hesych.), in this case confirmed by the modern Tsakonian form.

4. στ>ττ. Examples in several dialects, beside usual spelling στ. Cret. μεττ' ἐς beside μέστα, Lac. βεττόν 'dress' (Etym. M.)

74 THE GREEK DIALECTS [88

= *Ϝεστόν, Boeot. ἔττε = ἔστε, ἴττω (Ar., Plato) = ἴστω.

5. ρν>νν. Cret. ἀννίοιτο = ἀρνέοιτο, ὄννιθα = ὄρνιθα, 'Ελευθεν-
ναῖος = 'Ελευθερναῖος.

6. ρδ (through ρρ) >ρ with lengthening of the preceding
vowel. Cret. Ϝέροντι, Ϝηρόντων (Gortyn) beside Ϝέρδηι (Lato),
πῆριξ· πέρδιξ Hesych.

7. μν > μμ. Cret. ἐσπρεμμίττω = ἐκπρεμνίζω.

8. νμ>μμ. Att. (inscriptions) ὕφαμμα, Cyren. ποτιπίαμμα,
Troez. πεπεμμένος (from πένομαι). But usually replaced by analogical σμ, as ὕφασμα, etc.

9. γμ>μμ. Cret. ψάφιμμα = ψάφιγμα (142a).

10. γν>ν. γίγνομαι appears as γίνομαι in most dialects except
Attic (here also, but late), or as γίνυμαι (Thess., Boeot.). γινώσκω
= γιγνώσκω occurs in Lesbian and in Ionic prose writers (Att.
γεινώσκω very late), and in some late Doric inscriptions. This is
not really assimilation, but loss of γ by dissimilation from the
initial γ, supported, in the case of γίνομαι, by the γεν of other
tenses.

87. Transposition in consonant groups. As τίκτω from *τίτκω,
so probably δάκτυλος from *δάτκυλος, to which points Boeot.
δακκύλιος (κκ from τκ as in Thess. πὸκ κί from πὸτ κί, whereas κκ
from κτ would be contrary to all analogy, cf. 86.1). But most examples are of colloquial and transitory character, more or less
frequently repeated slips of the tongue, or sometimes, without
doubt, only graphic. Thus from Attic inscriptions σχυναρχόντων
= χσυν- (ξυν-), εὐσχάμενος = εὐχσάμενος, σφυχή = ψυχή, ἔ-
γρασφεν (often on vases) = usual ἔγραφσεν, μεσόμνη = μεσόδμη
(δμ first to νμ by assimilation); Arg. ξύλλεσθαι = σκύλλεσθαι;
Syrac., Cret. ψέ, ψίν (Cret. ψὲ αὐτόν, ψὶν αὐτοῖς) = σφέ, σφίν.

88. Assimilation, dissimilation, and transposition, between
non-contiguous consonants. Except for the regular dissimilation
of aspirates in proethnic Greek (65), these phenomena are of
the same occasional character as the preceding (87). They are
most frequently observable in the case of aspirates, or of liquids,
for which see 65, 70. A nasal may interchange with an oral
stop of its own class, by assimilation or dissimilation with another nasal, e.g., Cret. νύναμαι = δύναμαι (cf. Mod. Grk. Μεντέλη
beside Πεντέλη, name of Mt. Pentelicus), or, conversely, Att.

τέρβινθος beside τέρμινθος, Att. κυβερνάω from *κυμερνάω beside
Cypr. κυμερênαι and βάρναμαι = μάρναμαι, which occurs in
certain inscriptions in epic style from Athens, Corcyra, etc.
(nos. 94, 95). But Arg. σπάδιον = στάδιον is perhaps the earlier
form, the Att. στ due to influence of στάδιος. Dissimilatory loss
of the labial element in the labiovelars (68), as in ἀρτοκόπος from
-πόπος, Att. γέφυρα (68.2), Dor. γλέπω, γλέφαρον = βλέπω, βλέφαρον, Ion. γλήχων, Dor., Boeot. γλάχων = Att. βλήχων. Transposition,
e.g., Ion. ἀμιθρέω = ἀριθμέω, Arg. φάλυρον = λάφυρον, Delph.,
Epid. βόλιμος = μόλιβος (Att. usually μόλυβδος, βόλυβδος), also with
assimilation Rhod. βόλιβος in περιβολιβῶσαι, Cret. νεμονηία,
Νεμονήιος = νεομηνία, Νεομήνιος.

a. Among the examples of haplology or syllabic loss by dissimilation
(Att. ἀμφορεύς vs. Hom. ἀμφιφορεύς) some are dialectal. Epid. hεμίδιμμνον
from ἡμι(μέ)διμνον, as Att. ἡμέδιμνον from ἡ(μι)μέδιμνον. Cret. νεότας
'body of young men,' gen. νεότας from νεότα(το)ς, acc. νεότα from νεό-
τατα, Lac. ΣαϜάναξ from Σα(ϝο)Ϝάναξ.

b. There are other cases of syllabic loss which do not come under the
head of haplology. Many Thess. proper names in 'Αστο- = 'Αριστο-, as
'Αστοκράτεις, 'Αστόδαμος, etc., Thess. Λασαίοις (no. 32.19), Λασαίοι
(gen. sg.), also Λάσαν· τὴν Λάρισσαν Hesych., beside usual Λαρισαῖος, etc.
(or later σσ).

Doubling of Consonants, Simplification of Double Consonants, and Other Losses of Consonants

89. A single consonant is often written double, this indicating
a syllabic division by which it was heard at the end of one syllable
and the beginning of the next. But not all the examples below
can be understood in this way.

1. σστ, σσκ, σζ, ξσ, ξξ, etc. Such spellings as 'Αρισστο-, ὅσστις,
'Ασσκλαπιός, κόσσμος, γράσσμα are frequent and not confined to
particular dialects. Similarly σζ (= zzd) in Arg. δικάσζω (no. 84,
early), Delph. δουλίσζω, etc.; ξσ (= κσσ) in Corinth. Ϙόραξς,
Rhod. κύλιξς, Πραξσιόδō (no. 101), Ion. ἔξς (no. 4.5), Boeot.
ἀργυροτόξσοι, Naxian Ναξσίō, Φηράξσō, ἔξσοχος (probably; see
no. 6); ξξ in Thess. ἔξξοι, ἐξξανακάδεν, Locr. ψάφιξξιν, δόξξαι,
ἐξξόλλειαν, ἀξξιομάχōς, Arc. Πολυξξένα, etc. Cf. also Locr.
ἐκκπρᾶξαι, Lesb. ἐκκτός, Ion. (Ephesus) ἔκττη, ὀκττώ, ἡμίεκττα
(also ἐκ ττῶν, etc.).

2. μμν, ττρ. Epid. μέδιμμνον, hēμίδιμμνον, ἱαρομμνάμονες (no. 89), Arg. γυμμνικός, πέττρινον, Cret. ἀλλόττριος.

3. Doubling before consonantal ι in Thessalian. See 19.3.

4. Doubling between vowels (besides ξξ, for which see above, 1), mainly of nasals or liquids. Thess. μναμμεῖον, Δαμμάτρειος, ὀβελλός, δούρραντα, Lesb. πραγρημμένω, φίλημμι, δίννηντες, διννάεις, ἀρότρωμμεν, etc., Rhod. εἴμμειν, Dodon. ἄμμεινον, Boeot. θάλλατταν, Delph. ἐλλευθερία. Likewise in external combination (101.1). But also El. ἀνταποδιδῶσσα, Cret. σποϜδδάν (spirant δ?).

a. The frequency of such forms in Lesbian and Thessalian was promoted by the numerous cases of regular μμ, etc., from combinations (74-76).

b. Single σ is the correct early spelling of Cret. Κνωσός (single σ also confirmed by Arg. Κνόhιοι = Κνόσιοι), and the Thessalian and Argive Λάρισα. The forms with σσ are late.

5. Doubling in hypocoristic proper names, where it originates in the vocative and is due to the emphatic utterance in calling. Examples, though found elsewhere, are by far most frequent in Boeotian, e.g., Ἀγαθθώ, Βίοττος, Μέννει, etc.

a. Similar to this "expressive" doubling in hypocoristic names is that in nursery words like πάππα, ἄττα, etc., and in some colloquial words like γύννις (from γυνή), Lat. gibbus, lippus, etc. Here lies the probable explanation of the widespread μικκός (Dor., Boeot., etc.; proper names Μίκκος, Μικκιάδης) formed from the μικ- of μικρός. Hence also with diminutive suffixes μικκύλος and Lac. *μικκιχός implied by μι(κ)κιχιδδόμενος (cf. nos. 75-78, note).

6. The simplification of double consonants is in part only graphic. For the writing of single for double consonants is common in early inscriptions, with varying degrees of frequency. Thus in the earliest Attic inscriptions it is the usual practice. In the Gortyn Law-Code, in case of the infinitives from -σθαι the proportion of -θαι to -θθαι is roughly 3 : 1, while in external combination the double consonants resulting from assimilation are so written in the majority of cases (97.3, 4, 5; 98). Graphic simplification is of course to be assumed in all cases of θάλασα = θάλασσα, feminine adjectives in εσα = -εσσα (for στονόϜεσσαν, no. 94, there is the added metrical evidence), and many others. So for early examples of ἥμισον = usual ἥμισσον (e.g., Locr. no.

59.17, Arg. no. 85.7), in spite of the frequency in later times of ἥμισον, which was probably influenced by Att. ἥμισυς.

7. But actual simplification occurs in Att.-Ion., Arc. σ from σσ in forms like μέσος, aor. ἐδίκασα, dat. pl. γένεσι, etc. (82, 83), more exceptionally in Arc. φθέραι, Boeot. Θάροψ, etc. (80). It is also probable in external combination and composition in the numerous cases like κὰ τόν, πὸ τόν from κὰτ τόν, πὸτ τόν, El. καδαλέοιτο, καθυτάς, Arc. κακρίνε̄, κακριθέε̄, κακειμέναυ, ἰνηάταν, ἰμέσουν, ἰμέσος, (= ιν- ιμ-), τὰ Ϝάδω (= τὰν Ϝάδω), συϜοικία, κὰ Ϝοικίας τὰ δέ, (96.5, 97.2), Lac. τᾶ σιῶ (= τᾶς σιῶ), Locr. ἐ τᾶς, ἐ δάμō, ἐ λιμένος, etc., from assimilated ἐκ (100), Locr. also αἴ τι, ἀνάτō, ἀδίκō = αἴ τις, ἀνάτος, ἀδίκος, all before συλō̃ι, etc.

a. In many editions of texts it is the practice to expand the spellings, e.g., θάλα(σ)σα, πὸ(τ) τόν, etc. But in this book, with occasional exceptions to save comment, the simple consonants are left as in the original.

8. The loss ot a consonant in groups of three is mainly prehistoric and general Greek, as in γεγράφθαι from *γεγράφσθαι. But there are some cases of loss in a secondary group of special dialectal forms. Att.-Ion., Delph., Epid. παστάς from *παρστάς, παραστάς, Thess. πεστάντες from *περστάντες (= περι-), Arc. θύσθεν from *θυρσθεν (133.1), Lesb. ἔσλος, Ion. (Chios), lit. Dor. (Pindar) ἐσλός, also ἡεσλός (Olympia, dialect uncertain) = ἐσθλός, Lesb. μάσλης = μάσθλης.

9. The loss of final ν, frequent in inscriptions and papyri of Hellenistic times, is also seen in Pamph. πόλι beside πόλιν, ἰ = ἰν. Some alleged early anticipations of this tendency are of uncertain significance, in part perhaps only graphic errors, e.g., Arg. τελαμό (no. 82) = τελαμών, and Arg. gen. dual τοῖ Ϝανάκοι (the τοῖ could be from τοιν by assimilation and simplification, like that in Arc. τὰ Ϝάδω, συϜοικία, 96.5).

CHANGES IN EXTERNAL COMBINATION [4]

90. The phenomena of external combination, or sentence phonetics, such as elision, crasis, consonant assimilation, etc., are found in all dialects. But in Greek, as in most other languages,

---

[4] Some matters which strictly belong under this head have been discussed elsewhere, as the rhotacism of final ς, treatment of final νς, etc.

there is a tendency to limit more and more the scope of such changes, and to prefer, in formal speech and its written form, the uncombined forms. The inscriptions, Attic as well as those of other dialects, differ greatly in this respect according to their time and character. The following general observations may be made.

1. The changes occur mainly between words standing in close logical relation. Thus oftenest in prepositional phrases, or between the article, adjective, or particle and the noun with which it agrees; frequently between particles like καί, δέ, μέν, etc., and the preceding or following word; less often between the subject or object and the following verb; and very rarely in looser combinations.

2. While the less radical changes, such as the elision of a short vowel or the simpler forms of consonant assimilation, are least restricted in scope and survive the longest, the more violent forms of crasis and of consonant assimilation are the most infrequent and the soonest given up. Thus, in the matter of consonant assimilation, the partial assimilation of a nasal to a following stop, especially a labial, as in τὰμ πόλιν, is very common in all dialects down to a late period and sometimes observed even in loose combinations (cf. **96**.1), but examples like τὸλ λόγον, τοὺν νόμους, etc., are comparatively infrequent and practically restricted to early inscriptions.

3. Although the dialects differ in the extent to which they exhibit these phenomena and in some details (e.g., Cretan shows the most extensive and radical series of consonant assimilations), the differences depend more upon the time and character of the inscription, the degree to which the language has been formalized.

4. There is no consistency in the spelling, even as regards the milder changes, combined and uncombined forms often standing side by side in the same inscription.

Elision

91. Elision is common to all dialects, but, as in Attic, subject to great inconsistency as regards the written form, which even in metrical inscriptions is very often not in accord with the demands of the meter. In general, elision is most frequent in the conjunctions and particles such as δέ (ὅδε, οὐδέ, etc.), τε, κα, ἀλλά, etc., the prepositions, and, among case-forms, in stereotyped phrases like πόλλ' ἀγαθά, etc. The elision of a diphthong, e.g., Locr. δείλετ' ἀνχōρεῖν, is comparatively rare. For elision in place of usual crasis, see 94.

a. Elision in περί (Attic only before ι), as in Doric poetry, in Cypr. περ' Ἐδάλιον, and in compounds Delph., Lesb., Boeot. (also in Pindar) πέροδος, Locr. Περόχθεος, Boeot. περαγείς (Corinna). Cf. πέρ by apocope (95).

Aphaeresis

92. Examples of aphaeresis occur in various dialects. Ion. ἤ 'ς, μὴ 'λάσσονες (Chios, no. 4), Locr. ἒ 'δελφιόν, ἒ 'χεπάμōν, μὲ 'ποστᾶμεν, ἒ 'ν πόλι, ἒ 'ν ἀποκλēσίαι, El. μὲ 'νπōι, μὲ 'πιποεόντōν, μὲ 'πιθεῖαν, Lesb. σ[τάλλ]α 'πι, Cret. ἤ 'ν, ἤ 'πί.

Shortening of a Final Long Vowel

93. The shortening of a final long vowel before an initial vowel, so well known in poetry, may occasionally show itself in the spelling of inscriptions, e.g., Cret. μὲ ἔκηι (μὴ ἔχη), μὲ ἔνδικον, etc., Meg. ἐπειδὲ Ἱκέσιος.

Crasis

94. Crasis, mostly of καί or forms of the article with the following word, is found in the early inscriptions of all dialects, though the uncombined forms are more frequent. As between the "phonetic principle", where the result of crasis is in accordance with the regular laws of contraction, and the "etymological principle," with lengthening of the vowel as in Att. ἁνήρ = ὁ ἀνήρ, the former is almost, if not wholly, predominant outside of Attic.

1. o, secondary ō (ου), ω, + α (cf. 44.1). Ion. ὡνήρ, τὠγῶνος (τοῦ ἀγῶνος), with the regular contraction to ω, where Attic has ἁνήρ, τἀγῶνος. Similarly Lesb. (lit.) ὤνηρ, Arc. κὰ τόρρέντερον (κατὰ τὸ ἀρρέντερον), Delph. τὠπελλαίου (τοῦ Ἀπελλαίου), τὠπόλλωνι (τῶι Ἀπόλλωνι), Boeot. τὀπόλλōνι (τοῖ Ἀπόλλωνι), Corinth. τὀπέλōνι (τῶι Ἀπέλλωνι), τὠγαθόν (τὸ ἀγαθόν), Meg. ὀρχέδαμε (ὦ

'Αρχέδαμε), and so regularly in literary Doric. Elision, rather than crasis, according to the "etymological principle", is probably to be assumed in Arc. τἀπόλλωνι [5] (τοῖ 'Απ-), Corinth. τἀριστερόν (τὸ ἀριστερόν), Arg. τἀργεῖοι (τοὶ 'Αργεῖοι), τἀργείō (τοῦ 'Αργείου), Locr. τἀπόλογοι (τοὶ ἀπόλογοι).

2. o + o, ε or η (cf. 44.2, 3, 4). Att.-Ion. τοὖνομα, Lesb. ὠνίαυτος (ὁ ἐνίαυτος), Locr. ὀπάγōν (ὁ ἐπάγων). Ion. τώμισυ (τὸ ἤμισυ).

3. α + o (cf. 41.2). Att., Dor. χώ (καὶ ὁ), Ion., Cret. κώ (καὶ ὁ), Lesb. (lit.) κώττι (καὶ ὅττι), El. κōπόταροι (καὶ ὁπόταροι). Cf. Aegin. χōλέφας (καὶ ὁ ἐλέφας) with double crasis, like χῶκ (καὶ ὁ ἐκ) in Theocritus.

4. ᾱ + o (cf. 41.4). Meg. ἀλυνπιάς (ἁ 'Ολυνπιάς).

5. ᾱ + ε (cf. 41.3). Locr. hαπιϜοικία (ἁ ἐπιϜοικία).

6. α + ε (cf. 41.1). Att.-Ion. κἀγώ (καὶ ἐγώ), καπί (καὶ ἐπί), τᾱν (τὰ ἐν), etc., West Greek κήν, κήκ, κηπί (καὶ ἐν, καὶ ἐκ, καὶ ἐπί), Boeot. κηπιχάρitται (Ar.), etc. So also in Thessalian (no. 35) κεν and τες (τὰ ἐς). Lesbian has κεμέ (καὶ ἐμέ) in an early inscription, while the texts of the Aeolic poets vary between α and η (see p. 343); and Arcadian has κεπί. Elision before ε plus two consonants, Cret. κέρσενος, Epid. κένκαύσιος, etc.

7. With words beginning with a diphthong. Delph. κηὔκλεια (καὶ Εὔκλεια), κ]ωῦτε (καὶ οὖτε), Rhod. ōὐδάμō (ὁ Εὐδάμου), Ion. ὠισυμνήτης (ὁ αἰσυμνήτης), like lit. ωὑτός (ὁ αὐτος) in Homer, etc., κωὐδέν (καὶ οὐδέν) in Epicharmus, ὡπόλος (ὁ αἰπόλος), τωὐβούλοιο (τῶ Εὐβ-) in Theocritus. But also with diphthong unchanged, that is, with what is really elision, as commonly in lit. Attic and Ionic (κοὐ, κοὖτε, χοἰ= καὶ οἰ, κεὐ- = καὶ εὐ-), Thess. κοἰ (καὶ οἰ), Ion. τοικόπεδον (τὸ οἰκό-), κοινοπίδης (καὶ Οἰνο-), Arc. κευορκέντι (καὶ εὐ-). The proper transcription of forms in the pre-Ionic alphabet is sometimes uncertain, but, in general, crasis is most common in early inscriptions, and it is probable that we should transcribe Thess. κεὐϜεργέταν (no. 35), Boeot. τεὐτρετιφάντō (no. 38.5), and Aegin. hōικος (ὁ οἰκος).

---

[5] We continue, as a matter of convention, to transcribe in the form of crasis when the combination belongs to those which commonly suffer crasis, even in cases where we believe the phenomenon is elision. For it is impossible to draw the line between crasis and elision with certainty. See also here under 7, 8, 9.

8. With words beginning with ι or υ. Cret. κυιέες (καὶ υἱέες), El. κυπαδυκίοι (καὶ ὑπα-), Delph. κίδιῶται (καὶ ἰδιῶται).

In such cases there is of course no evidence as to whether the υ or ι was lengthened, as usually in Attic-Ionic, but probably we have here simply elision.

9. In Elean in the forms of the article the final vowel or diphthong disappears, sometimes even the vowel with final consonant. Thus τἱαρόν (τὸ ἱαρόν), τἱαρō̄ (τῶ ἱαρῶ), τἱαροῖ (τοῖ ἱαροῖ), τἐπιάροι (τοῖ ἐπιάροι), and even τὸρ ἱαρομάορ τόλυνπίαι (τὸρ Ὀλυνπίαι). This is clearly not crasis proper, but an extension of the principle of elision. Cf. θυιῶι (τῶι υἰῶι) in an Attic inscription and Locr. (Halae) τὸαροί = τοὶ ἱαροί.

Apocope

95. Apocope of prepositions, while very rare in Attic-Ionic prose, is common in other dialects, with differences in frequency, chronology, and especially in the range of prepositions affected. Most widespread are ἄν (or ὀν-, ὑν-, 6, 22) and πάρ. — κάτ and (in the ποτί-dialects) πότ are common, in the West Greek dialects mostly before a dental (in Heraclean only so), and frequently with simplification of the double consonants (89.6), κὰ τὸν, πὸ τόν, etc. But also before other consonants (like Hom. κὰκ κεφαλῆς, κὰγ γόνυ, κὰν νόμον, etc.), as Boeot. κὰγ γᾶν, πὸκ κατόπτας, Thess. κἀπ παντός, πὸκ κί, Lac. καββαλικός, Καβάτα, Lesb. κάλλιπεν, etc. Regularly κά, κα- in the early Arcadian and Elean inscriptions, as Arc. κὰ μῆνα, κακρίνē̄, El. καδαλέοιτο, καθυτάς, etc.—Arc. also πέ from πεδά in πὲ τοῖς Φοικιάταις.— πέρ from περί occurs in Delphian, Elean (πάρ), Thessalian, lit. Lesbian, and in proper names in Locrian (Περϟοθαριᾶν), Laconian, Messenian and Cretan. — ἄπ, ἔπ, ὑπ are (except for a few cases in compounds before a labial, as Hom. ἀππέμψει, ὑββάλλειν, Lesb. ἄπ πατέρων (Alcaeus) only Thessalian, which in general has more extensive apocope than any other dialect, namely ἄν, πάρ, πέρ, κάτ, πότ, ἄπ (ἀτ τᾶς), ἔπ (ἐτ τᾶ, ἐτ τοῖ), ὑπ- (ὑππρό). Cf. also Thess. gen. sg. -οι from -οιο, doubtless first in the proclitic article.

a. There is an unimportant difference of practice in regard to the apocopated forms beginning with a vowel. In some editions of literary texts and inscriptions they are given without accent, on the analogy of ἐκ, ἐν, etc., e.g., Lesb. ἀπ πατέρων, Thess. ἀτ τᾶς. But consistently with the prevailing reading of Hom. ἀμ πεδίον, etc., we read ἀτ τᾶς, etc.

Consonant Assimilation

(in part with further simplification of· the double consonants. **89**.6)

96. Assimilation of final ν.

1. To the class of a following labial or guttural. Cases like τὴμ πόλιν, τὸγ κήρυκα, νῦμ μέν, are frequent in Attic inscriptions, and likewise in the other dialects. So also between object and verb as Delph. τόκιομ φερέτω, Arc. πόσοδομ ποέντω, and in looser combinations as Att. ἐστὶμ περί, Arc. ἰν ἐπίκρισιγ κατάπερ, Arg. ποιοῖεγ κατά.

2. To σ. Att. ἐς Σάμωι, ἐᾶ Σαλαμίνι (= ἐᾶν Σ-), Ion. τῶς συμπάντων, Epid. τὸς σακόν. Cf. Ion. πασσυδίηι beside πανσυδίηι, and Lesb. πασσυδιάσαντος.

Before σ + consonant. Att. ἐσ στήληι but oftener ἐ στήληι, also τὲ στέλεν. So Rhod., Cret. ἐ στάλαι, El. τὰ στάλαν. These do not arise by assimilation but by regular loss of ν. See **77**.2, **78**.

3. To λ. Att. ἐλ λίμναις, τὸλ λόγον, Ion. ἐλ Λαρυσσῶι, Delph. τῶλ Λαβυαδᾶν, Lac. ἐλ Λακεδαίμονι, Epid. τὸλ λίθον, τῶλ λίθων. Cf. συλλέγω, ἀλλύω = ἀναλύω, etc.

4. To ρ. Att. ἐρ Ῥόδωι, τὸρ Ῥόδιον. Cf. συρρίπτω, etc.

5. To Ϝ. Arc. συϜοικία, τὰ Ϝάδω = τὰν Ϝάδω.

a. In Cyprian, where ν before a consonant is always omitted in the interior of a word, it is also frequently omitted in sentence combination as τὰ (ν) πτόλιν.

97. Assimilation of final ς.

1. To ν. Delph. τοὺν νόμους. Cf. Πελοπόννησος (Πέλοπος νῆσος), Arc. ταῖννυ, ταιννί (ταῖς-νυ, -νί), ταννί (τασ-νί, acc. pl.), τανί (gen. sg.).

2. To μ and Ϝ. Cypr. Ϝέπο μέγα = Ϝέπος μέγα, τᾶ Ϝανάσας = τᾶς Ϝανάσσας. In the same way arose κά = κάς (καί) in Cypr. κὰ μέν, Arc. κὰ Ϝοικίας.

3. To λ. Att. τὸλ λίθος, Cret. τοῖλ λείονσι, τὶλ λἐῖ, Lac. ἐλ Λακεδαίμονα (ἐλ = ἐς), τοῖ Λακεδαιμονίοις, Cyren. ἐλ Λιβύαν, Arg. κὲλ Λευκόπορον (καὶ ἐλ Λ-).

4. To δ. So regularly in Cretan, e.g., τᾶδ δαίσιος, τᾶδ δέ, ἐδ δικαστέριον, πατρὸδ δόντος τᾶ δίκας, τὸδ δ' ὀδελόνς. Rarely else-

where, but cf. Rhod. Ζεὺ δέ (no. 100), ματρὸ δέ, τὰ δευτέρας, Arc. τὰ δέ = τὰς δέ. Assimilation in the opposite direction is seen in Arg. βωλᾶς σευτέρας (no. 86). Partial assimilation in early Arg. τοῖζ δε. Cf. late Arg. πρεζβευτῶν, etc.

5. To θ. Cretan only, as τὰθ θυγατέρας. Cf. Cret. θθ = σθ medially (**85**.3).

a. Before a word beginning with a vowel final ς may be treated as intervocalic, e.g., Lac. Διοhικέτα, Διōλευθερίō = Διὸς hικέτου, Διὸς ἐλευθερίου (cf. **59**.1), Cypr. κὰ ἀ(ν)τί, τᾶ ὑχέρον (**59**.4), Eretr. ὅπωρ ἄν (**60**.3).

98. Assimilation of final ρ to δ. So regularly in Cretan, e.g., ἀνὲδ δōι, πατὲδ δόει, and πατὲ δόει. Cf. Cnid. πὰ Δάματρα = παρὰ Δ-.

99. Assimilation of a final stop.

1. Final τ. The apocopated forms of κατά and ποτί, so far as they occur otherwise than before τ (cf. **95**), are generally assimilated (sometimes with further simplification; see **89**.7), e.g., Thess. κὰπ παντός, πὸκ κί (πὸτ κί = πρὸς τί), Boeot. πὸδ Δάφνη, πὸκ κατόπτας, Lesb. κὰκ κεφάλας (Alcaeus), κὰμ μέν (Sappho), etc. So in compounds, e.g., El. καδαλέοιτο, καθυτάς, Lesb. κάββαλλε (Alcaeus), καλλύοντος, Arc. κακειμέναυ, κακρίνε̄, Lac. Καβάτα (Καταβάτου), καβαίνων (Alcman), etc. But -τ θ- is often unassimilated.

2. Final π. Thess. ἄπ, ἔπ = ἀπό, ἐπί are assimilated in ἀτ τᾶς, ἐτ τοῖ. Cf. **86**.2.

3. Final κ. See **100**.

100. ἐξ. In most dialects, as in Attic, ἐξ becomes ἐκ before a consonant, thus appearing often as ἐχ before an aspirate, and ἐγ before voiced stops and λ, μ, ν, Ϝ, until late times, when ἐκ is usual before all consonants. The general rule is, then, ἐξ before vowels, and ἐκ (ἐχ, ἐγ) before consonants. But the antevocalic form ἐξ occasionally appears before consonants in various dialects (so regularly in Cyprian, as ἐξ τōι, etc.).

In Locrian it is fully assimilated to all consonants, whence, with the simplification of double consonants, it appears simply as ἐ, e.g., ἐ τᾶς, ἐ δάμō, ἐ Ϝοινάνōν, ἐ θαλάσας, ἐ λιμένος, ἐ Ναυπάκτō. Cf. also Mess. ἐ Φιαλείας.

In Thessalian, Boeotian, Arcadian, and Cretan the regular form before consonants is ἐς, e.g., Thess. ἐς τᾶν, ἐσδόμεν, Boeot. ἐς τῶν, ἐσλιήνω (cf. also ἐσκηδεκάτη from ἔξ), Arc. ἐς τοῖ, ἐσδέλλοντες,

ἑσπερᾶσαι, Cret. ἐς τὸν, ἐσκλησία, Thess., Boeot., Cret. ἔσγονος =
ἔκγονος. All these dialects have ἐξ before vowels except Boeotian,
where ἐχς appears in an early inscription, but usually ἐσς, as
ἐσς ἐφείβων, ἔσσειμεν. This is probably a transfer or the ante-
consonantal form in an intermediate stage of its development
(ἐξ, ἐσς, ἐς).

a. There are some traces of ἐς in other dialects which generally have
ἐκ or ἐξ, e.g. Cypr. ἐς πόθ' ἕρπες· πόθεν ἥκεις (Hesych.), Arg. ἐ Σικελίιας,
ἐς πόλιος, Rheg. ἔσκλητος (no. 107, note), Delph. ἐς τοῦ δρόμου (no. 50),
ἔσγονος (no. 52 C 45).

Consonant Doubling

101. 1. Before vowels. Cret. τὰνν ἐμίναν, συνν-ε̃ι, Boeot., Corinth. ἀνν-έθηκε, Att. ξυνν-όντι, lit. Lesb. ὀνν-ώρινε, ἀσύννετος,
Delph. ἐλεύθεροvν εἶμεν.

2. With ὅσστις etc. (**89.**1), compare Att. εἰσς τήν, Epid. ἐσς τό,
etc., or Epid. τὸ σσκέλος, Coan τοῦ σστεφάνου. Ion. ἐξς (no. 4)
like ψάφιξξις, Ion. ἐκ ττῶν like ὀκττώ (**89.**1), ἐκκ τοῦ in Attic
inscriptions, etc.

ν Movable

102. The ν movable in the dative plural in -σι(ν) and in the
verb forms in -σι(ν) and ε(ν) is a marked characteristic of Attic-
Ionic, where it appears from the earliest inscriptions on with
increasing frequency and before both vowels and consonants.
(In Attic its use becomes gradually more and more uniform
before vowels, and it is also somewhat more common before a
pause in the sense than elsewhere.) In verb forms it is wholly
unknown in the older inscriptions of other dialects, and where
found is a sure sign of κοινή influence. But in the dative plural
(where the ν is due to the analogy of pronominal datives like
Att. ἡμῖν, Dor. ἁμίν, Lesb. ἄμμιν beside ἄμμι in which the ν is
inherited) it appears outside of Attic-Ionic at an early period.
Thus Thess. χρέμασιν (no. 35), Locr. ἀνδράσιν, γονεῦσιν, παμάτε-
σιν (no. 59), Sicyon. φέρουσιν, Ϝοικέουσιν (no. 96); and so the later
Lac. πᾶhιν, Heracl. ἔντασσιν, etc., Arc. χρήμασιν, ἀναλώμασιν,
need not necessarily be charged to the κοινή.

103. Of the dialects outside of Attic-Ionic, Lesbian is the only one of whose accentual peculiarities we have any adequate knowledge. This was characterized by the recessive accent, e.g., πόταμος, σόφος, βασίλευς, λεῦκος,

The Doric accent is said by the grammarians to be processive in certain classes of forms, e.g., ἐλάβον, στάσαι, αἴγες = Att. ἔλαβον, στῆσαι, αἶγες. But the statements are too meager to admit of generalization as to the system as a whole, nor is it known whether all Doric dialects had these peculiarities. Hence the practice now frequently adopted, and followed in this book, of giving Doric forms with the ordinary Attic accent, except in a few well-established forms like Ποτιδάν. In general our accentuation of dialect forms can be little more than a matter of convenience. [6]

a. A question of detail, touching which there is considerable difference of practice among editors of dialect texts, is whether, in the case of inflectional forms which differ in their quantitative relations from the corresponding Attic forms, to adopt the actual accent of the Attic forms or to change the accent to accord with the Attic system, e.g., infin. κρίνεν like κρίνειν, or κρῖνεν, acc. pl. φερομένος like φερομένους, or φερόμενος, Cret. κάρτονανς, στατῆρανς like κρείττονας, στατῆρας, or καρτόνανς, στατῆρανς. The question of the true accentuation is a complicated one, differing in each class of forms, and impossible of any certain answer. But practical convenience favors the use of the Attic accent in some cases, as in the accusative plural to distinguish it from the nominative, and we adopt this alternative in all the cases mentioned.

b. The pronominal adverbs in -ει, -αι, and -ω we accent as perispomena, following here what the grammarians laid down as the Doric accent, since this affords a convenient working rule, and serves to distinguish, e.g., τουτῶ from gen. τούτω. But it is far from certain that the accent was uniform, and that we should write, e.g., ἀλλεῖ, ἀλλᾶι, πανταῖ, as we do, and not, with some, ἄλλει like Att. οἴκει, and ἄλλαι, πάνται like Att. ἄλλη, πάντῃ. And as between ὁπεῖ and ὅπει, etc., about which the grammarians were in doubt, we definitely prefer ὅπει, ὅπαι, ὅπυι, ὅπη, ὅπω (cf. Att. ὅπου beside ποῦ, in spite of αὐτοῦ, etc.). We accent ἔνδοι, ἔξοι, ἦχοι, etc., like οἴκοι, though ἐνδοῖ etc. (cf. ἐνταυθοῖ) may also be defended.

---

[6] It has been urged that dialect forms and texts should be printed without accents. But, our ignorance being once for all admitted, the current practice is justified by its greater convenience for the reader,

INFLECTION

NOUNS AND ADJECTIVES

Feminine ᾱ-Stems

104. 1. NOM. SG. -ᾱ, Att.-Ion. -η.

2. GEN. SG. -ᾱς, Att.-Ion. -ης.—Arc. -ᾱυ after the masculine, as οἰκίαυ, ζαμίαυ, but only at Tegea, and here -ᾱς beside -ᾱυ in early inscriptions, and always τᾶς.

3. DAT. SG. -ᾱι, Att.-Ion. -ηι, whence also -ᾱ, -η, -ει. See **38**, **39**.—Boeot. -αι (-αε, -η, **26**), and this is to be assumed in the other dialects which have -οι (**106**.2)

4. ACC. SG. -ᾱν, Att.-Ion. -ην.

5. NOM. PL. -αι (Boeot. -αε, -η, **26**).

6. GEN. PL. -άων, -έων, -ῶν, -ᾶν. See **41**.4.

7. DAT. PL. In early Attic -ᾱσι(ν), -ησι(ν), sometimes -ᾱισι(ν), -ηισι(ν), after 420 B.C. -αις .—In Ionic usually -ηισι(ν), rarely -ηις, -ησι(ν), also -αις.— -ᾱσι rarely elsewhere, as early Troez. Θέβᾱσσι, Cret. (Drerus) πύλᾱσι, ἀγέλᾱσι (BCH 70.590, 597).— -ᾱισι or -αισι in Lesbian (but ταῖς), Pamphylian also Corcyrean (ῥhοϜαῖσι poet.), and rarely in Cretan (beside rare -ᾱσι and usual -αις). The majority of dialects have -αις from the earliest times.

8. ACC. PL. -ανς, with the same development as has -ονς from o-stems, namely (see also **78**):

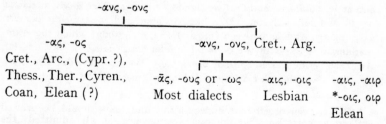

9. NOM.-ACC. DUAL. Att. -ᾱ formed on the analogy of -ω in o-stems, but in pronouns usually τώ, etc., with o-stem form used

also for feminine. Examples in other dialects are rare, but Corinth. πύκτᾶ, and Boeot. δαρχμάω δύο, a blend of the two types.

10. GEN.-DAT. DUAL. Att. -αιν, examples in other dialects rare. Locr. τοῖν κόραιν (with o-stem in the article, as in Attic), Arc. τοῖς Κράναιυν (with pl. o-stem in article), and (AJA 1939, 196) Τυδαριδίαιυς. Cf. Arc. -οιυν, **106.**7.

11. The dual in general. The dual, which in Attic disappeared in the course of the fourth century B.C., and eventually everywhere, was lost at a still earlier period in some dialects. It is lacking in Ionic and Cretan inscriptions (cf. Cret. δύο στατε̄ρανς). But dual forms are quotable from several dialects, as Arc. -ω, -αιυν, -οιυν (no. 20), Boeot. Fαγάνω, δραχμάω, λέβε̄τε, all reinforced by δύο (no. 39), Locr. τοῖν κόραιν (no. 60), El. καταστατό̄, δυοίοις, αὐτοίοιρ (also dual verbal forms), Delph. δύο ὀδελώ, φρυκτώ (no. 53; but δύ' ὀδελός in the earlier no. 51), Lac. ἐπάκω, ἐπάκοε (nos. 72, 73), Corinth. πύκτᾶ, Arg. ἰλάρχω, Coan οἶε τέλεω.

Masculine ᾱ-Stems

105. 1. NOM. SG. -ᾱς (with secondary ς, after the analogy of -ος), Att.-Ion. -ης.

a. Forms without ς also occur, several in Boeotian, as Καλλία, Μογέα, etc., and a few from other parts of Northwest Greece, as Σϙόπα (Halae), Φιλοκλέδα (Dodona), etc. El. τελεστά is a form in -τᾱ like Hom. ἱππότα.

2. GEN. SG. -ᾱο (with o, in place of ς, after that of o-stems), whence Arc.-Cypr. -ᾱυ (**22**), elsewhere -ᾱ, Ion. -εω, -ω. See **41.**4. Att. -ου is not from -ᾱο, but the o-stem form taken over as a whole.

a. There are a few Cypr. examples of -ᾱ, beside usual -ᾱυ, as 'Αμενίjα no. 23.19 vs. 'Ονασιγόραυ ll.1/2, 22.

b. -ᾱFο, in ΤλασίαFο, ΠασιάδαFο, of two metrical inscriptions from Corcyra and Gela (nos. 93, 105), is a reminiscence of the epic -ᾱο (the spoken form was already -ᾱ, which appears in other equally early inscriptions, as 'Αρνιάδα no. 94, ΔFενία no. 91) with the introduction of a non-etymological F, either representing a glide sound before the following o (cf. ἀFυτάν, no. 94; see **32**), or due to a false extension from forms with etymological F, as λᾱFός = Hom. λᾱός (cf. Ion. 'ΑγασιλέFō, no. 9).

c. Forms in -ᾱς, with the old ending unchanged and belonging with the nominatives in -ᾱ (above, 1*a*) occur in scattered examples in Megarian as Φάγας, etc. (no. 99) and from various parts of Northwest Greece, as Προκλείδας (no. 95).

d. Att.-Ion. proper names in -ης, from the fourth century on, frequently form the genitive after the analogy of σ-stems, e.g., Att. Καλλιάδους (after Δημοσθένους, etc.), Ion. Λεάδεος, ᾿Αριστείδευς. This type spreads to other dialects, e.g., Rhod. Μυωνίδευς.

o-Stems

106. 1. GEN. SG. -οιο (from *-οσιο, cf. Skt. -*asya*) as in Homer, whence, with apocope, Thess. (Pelasgiotis) -οι, as τοῖ, χρόνοι, etc. Elsewhere, with loss of ι and contraction, -ου or -ω (**25**).—In Cyprian -ον beside -ō (at Idalium μισθō̄ν, ἀργύρō̄ν, Φιλοκύπρō̄ν, etc., and so usually -ον in nouns, whether vowel or consonant follows; but also ἀργύρō̄, ἄλϜō̄, before a consonant, and always τō̄).

a. -οιο is often employed in metrical inscriptions, in imitation of the epic, e.g., nos. 93, 94. But in Thessalian it also occurs in a few prose inscriptions, and the grammarians often refer to the Thessalian genitive in -οιο. This, together with the fact that apocope is more extensive in Thessalian than in any other dialect (see **95**), makes obvious the derivation of the usual Thess. -οι from -οιο, probably starting in the article, which was of course proclitic like the prepositions. For the added ν in Cyprian no explanation that has been offered is adequate.

2. DAT. SG. -ωι in most dialects, whence also -ω (**38**; Thess. ου, **23**).—οι in Arcadian (usually, but in no. 20 τῶι, τωινί, τῶινυ beside βουσοῖ, etc.), Elean, Boeotian (-οε, -υ, -ει, **30**), and in later inscriptions from various parts of Northern Greece (Delphi, Aetolia, Acarnania, Epirus, Cierium in Thessaly, Euboea).

a. In Euboea -οι replaces earlier -ωι and may be derived from it, like -ει from -ηι (see **39**). But in general -οι is rather the original locative (cf. οἴκοι) in use as the dative. In some dialects the history of the dative is obscure, owing to the lack of early material or the ambiguity of -OI in the pre-Ionic alphabets.

3. NOM. PL. -οι (Boeot. -οε, -υ, **30**).

4. DAT. PL. -οισι(ν), as in Homer, in early Attic, Ionic, where it lasts somewhat longer than in Attic (but some early examples of -οις, especially in West Ionic), Lesbian (but here always τοῖς), Pamphylian, and sometimes Cretan (but rare vs. -οις), Argive (only early), and Syracusan.—Elsewhere only -οις (Boeot. -υς, -εις, Elean -οιρ).

5. Acc. Pl. -ονς, with the same development as -ανς. See **78**, **104**.8.

6. Nom.-Acc. Dual. -ω. This is by far the most frequently attested dual form.

7. Gen.-Dat. Dual. -οιιν as in Homer, whence -οιν in most dialects in which the form occurs. But El. -οιοις, -οιοιρ. Arc. (no. 20) ἰμέσουν τοῖς Διδύμοιυν (cf. the preceding τὼ Διδύμω), like the -αιυν in ā-stems (**104**.10).

a. The unique Arcadian forms seem to contain an inherited *u* connected with the *u*-diphthong to which the Sanskrit and Slavic dual forms point (Skt. *tayos*, ChSl. *toju*), but the detailed analysis is highly uncertain.

Consonant Stems in General

107. 1. Acc. Sg. -αν in place of the usual -α, with ν added after the analogy of vowel stems, occurs in Cypr. ἰjατε͂ραν, ἀ(ν)δριjά(ν)ταν, Thess. κίοναν, El. ἀγαλματοφῶραν (but possibly -φώρᾱν from nom. -φώρᾱς), and among late inscriptions of various dialects.

2. Nom. Pl. -εν for usual -ες occurs in late Cretan, having originated in pronominal forms. See **119**.2a.

3. Dat. Pl. -εσσι, as in Hom. πόδεσσι (either based on the -εσ-σι of σ stems or, as many prefer, formed to nom. pl. -ες after the analogy of -αισι, -οισι to -αι, -οι) is characteristic of the Aeolic dialects, Lesbian, Thessalian (but also χρέμασιν, ὑπάρχονσι), and Boeotian, also Pamphylian, Delphian, Locrian (no. 59 πα[μάτεσιν beside ἀνδράσιν, etc.; East Locr. χρημάτεσσι, etc.; but -οις in nos. 57, 58, 60), Elean (φυγάδεσσι no. 65; elsewhere -οις), with occasional forms in Cyrenaean (Εὐεσπερίδεσσι), and Corinthian colonies.—Heraclean has -ασσι in pres. pple. ἔντασσιν (a blend of ἐντ- with ἄσσι = Skt. *satsu*, see **163**.8), πρασσόντασσι, etc.— -οις, as πάντοις, etc., after the analogy of o-stems, is characteristic of Locrian (otherwise no. 59, see above), Elean, and the Northwest Greek κοινή, whence it finds its way into various dialects in later times. So in late inscriptions of Messenia, Laconia, Crete, and Tauromenium.

4. Acc. Pl. -ες in place of -ας, i.e., the nom. for the acc., perhaps first used in the numeral τέτορες owing to the influence

of the indeclinable πέντε, etc., is seen in Delph. δεκατέτορες, τέτορες, Δελφίδες (nos. 49, 51), and regularly in Elean ([τέτορ]ες, sixth century, πλείονερ, χάριτερ, no. 66, etc.) and Achaean (ἐλάσσονες, δαμοσιοφύλακες, etc.), also in the very late inscriptions of various dialects, even Attic. Cret. -ανς beside -ας, e.g. θυγατέρανς, δρομέανς, κύνανς, after the analogy of -ανς, -ας from ᾱ-stems (104.8).

σ-Stems

108. 1. All dialects except Attic have the uncontracted forms. Gen. sg. in most dialects -εος, whence -ιος in Boeotian, Cretan, etc. (9), -ευς in later Ionic, Rhodian, etc. (42.5). Acc. sg. masc. and acc. pl. neut. -εα, or contracted η (42.1). Acc. pl. masc. fem. -εας in most dialects (Cyren. τριήρης, 42.1), Att. -εις (nom. used as acc.), also late in other dialects.

a. Proper names in -κλέης, -κλῆς. Cypr. -κλέϝες, whence -κλέης in Attic (beside -κλῆς), Boeotian (-κλέες, -κλίες) till about 400 B.C., and regularly in Euboean (gen. -κλέω, 2), but in the other dialects regularly -κλῆς. Gen. sg. Cypr. -κλέϝεος, Boeot. -κλεῖος (= Hom. -κλῆος, cf. **16**), Att. -κλέους, but in most dialects -κλέος.
For names in -κλέᾱς instead of -κλέης, see **166**.1.

2. Proper names often have forms which are modeled after the analogy of the masc. ᾱ-stems, and this not only in Attic-Ionic (e.g., Att. Σωκράτην, Σωκράτου, Eretr. gen. Εὐκράτω, Τιμοκλέω), where the agreement in the nom. -ης was especially favorable to this, but also in other dialects. Thus acc. sg. in -ην (-ην : -ης = -ᾱν : -ᾱς), e.g., Boeot. Δαμοτέλειν, Arc. Ἐπιτέλην, and even in appellatives, e.g., Lesb. δαμοτέλην, Cypr. ἀτελέν.—Dat. sg. in -ηι, Lesb. Καλλίκληι, Cret. Δαμοκούδηι.—Gen. sg. in -η (like -ᾱ) in Lesb. Θεογένη, Thess. Φιλόκλει, Cret. Ἀλκιμένη, etc.; also, perhaps, -ης (like -ᾱς, **105**.2*b*) in Thess. Ἱπποκράτεις, Φερεκράτες (no. 35; or Φερεκράτε(ο)ς?).—Voc. sg. in -η (like -ᾱ) in Arc. Ἀτέλη, etc., Delph. Πολυκράτη; in -ε (like -ᾰ in Δίκα) in Lesb. μελλιχόμειδε.

The numerous Boeotian hypocoristic names in -ει as Μέννει, Φίλλει, Θάλλει, Ξέννει, are also best understood as vocatives of this type used as nominatives. They correspond to names in -ης,

-ητος, in other dialects, but in Boeotian follow the analogy
of σ-stems (gen. sg. -ιος, acc. sg. -ειν).

ι-Stems

109. 1. In all dialects except Attic-Ionic, and, for the most
part, in Ionic too, the regular type of declension is that with
ι throughout, namely, -ις, -ιος, -ῑ, -ιν, -ιες, -ιων, -ισι, -ῑς (Arg.
Cret. -ινς) or -ιας (rare).

2. The type in -ις, -εως (from -ηος, as in Homer), -ει, pl. -εις,
etc., is almost exclusively Attic. In Ionic πόλεως occurs in
early inscriptions of Chios (no. 4) and Thasos, and Δυνάμει in
Teos (no. 3). But otherwise in Ionic, and always in other dialects,
forms of this type are late and to be attributed to Attic influence.
In general, the Attic datives, -ει and -εσι, are the first to be
adopted, next the nom.-acc. pl. -εις, and lastly the gen. sg. -εως.
Thus in the later inscriptions of many dialects it is common
to find gen. sg. -ιος, but dat. sg. -ει.

The nom. pl., originally -ε‍ιες whence Att. -εις, in other dialects
only in the numeral Cret. τρέες, Ther. τρῆς, etc.

A gen. sg. πόλεος is found in the κοινή and in later inscriptions
of various dialects.

3. Lesbian has a nom. pl. -ῑς (πόλις, no. 25), perhaps the accusative used as nominative.

4. Cyprian has such forms as gen. sg. ΤιμοχάριϜος, dat. sg.
πτόλιϜι. The Ϝ is certainly not original here, and is perhaps due
to the analogy of υ- and ηυ-stems (gen. -υϜος, -ēϜος).

5. A transfer to the type -ις, -ιδος, as frequently in Attic, is
characteristic of Euboean proper names in -ις, as Δημοχάριδος.

υ-Stems

110. Nearly all the inscriptional forms occurring are the usual
ones of the type -ῠς, -υος. Boeot. [Ϝ]άστιος (ι from ε, **9**) agrees
with the ἄστεος of non-Attic literature. For υἱύς see **112**.2.

Nouns in -ευς

111. The stem is ηυ, ηϜ throughout, nom. sg. -ευς (from -ηυς,
37.1), gen. sg. -ηϜος, etc.

1. The original forms in -ηϝος, -ηϝι, etc., are preserved, with or without the ϝ, in Cyprian (βασιλῆϝος, 'Εδαλιῆϝι, 'Εδαλιῆϝες), Lesbian (βασίληος, etc.), Boeotian (Πτōιῆϝι, γραμματεῖος, etc.), Thessalian (βασιλεῖος, etc.), and Elean (βασιλᾶες), as also in Homer.

2. Attic only are βασιλέως, βασιλέᾱ, with quantitative metathesis. But from the beginning of κοινή influence, βασιλέως is one of the Attic forms most widely adopted by other dialects.

3. Most dialects, namely, Ionic and the West Greek dialects except Elean, have βασιλέος, βασιλεῖ, etc., with shortening of the η. Generally these are the forms of even the earliest inscriptions (Cret. ϝοικέος, etc.), but we find Coan ἱερῆι, Πολιῆι, etc. (no. 108; later always ἱερεῖ, etc.), and once Rhod. 'Ιδαμενῆος (cf. Ποντωρηίδος). Beside -εος sometimes -ευς (cf. 42.5), as Meg. ἱαρεῦς, but owing to the confusion with the nominative, this spelling is far less common than in the genitive of σ-stems.

Acc. Sg. -έα in Ionic, Locrian, Cretan. But in Delphian and most of the Doric dialects -ῆ is the regular form, e.g., Delph. ἱερῆ, βασιλῆ, Lac. βασιλῆ, Mess. ἱερῆ, Meg. ἱερῆ, Mycen. Περσῆ (no. 81, fifth century B.C.), Arg. βασιλῆ, Rhod. βασιλῆ, γραμματῆ, Coan βασιλῆ, etc. In these dialects -εα is of later occurrence, and due to κοινή influence.

Nom. Pl. -έες in Cretan (e.g., δρομέες) and elsewhere, but usually contracted to -εῖς. Also -ῆς (in part at least directly from -ῆες) in early Attic, Coan (τεταρτῆς), Laconian (Μεγαρῆς, etc., no. 69), and Arcadian (Μαντινῆς). At Cyrene occurs nom. and acc. pl. ἱαρές, and dat. pl. Μεγαρέσσι, etc. (cf. δρομέσι Callim.).

Acc. Pl. -έας in Ionic and Doric (Cret. δρομέανς, cf. 107.4), when not replaced by -εῖς of the κοινή.

4. Arcadian has nom. sg. in -ής, as ἱερής, γραφής, φονές (Cyprian also once ἰjερές, but usually -εύς), acc. sg. ἱιερέν (cf. 108.2), nom. pl. Μαντινῆς, gen. pl. Τορθυνήων, Μετιδριήων. Some proper names in -ής = -εύς are also found elsewhere.

5. In Miletus and colonies occurs nom. sg. ἱέρεως, gen. sg. ἱέρεω, likewise at Ephesus gen. sg. Φλέω belonging to Φλεύς.

a. The feminine OI-stems, most widely attested in proper names. Nom. sg. mostly -ω, but also -ωι, as Cyren. λεχώι, Corinth. Συϙόι, Φιλόι, etc. (OI regularly on old Corinthian vases; -ῳ beside -ω in grammarians).

Gen. sg. -οος, -ους, -ως (Cret. Λατῶς), but Cyren. λεχός (no. 115.109), Rhod. Φιλτός (IG XII.i.719), Delph. Λατός (so probably, not Λατος, Schwyzer 325.8). Dat. sg. Delph. λεχχοῖ, Cret. Λατοῖ, Λατῶι. Acc. sg. -οα, -ώ. Also inflection with ω throughout, parallel to ᾱ-stems, as Boeot., Cret. -ώ, -ῶς, -ῶι, -ών.

Some Irregular Nouns

112. 1. Ζεύς. Ζεύς or Δεύς (**84**). Δι(F)ός, Δι(F)ί, Δί(F)α in most dialects. An old dative Διεί (cf. Oscan *Diúveí*) occurs alone, but rarely, and in Att. Διειτρέφης, Cypr. ΔιFείθεμις, ΔιFείφιλος (Hom. διΐφιλος). Also in various dialects (attested for East Ion., Coan, Ther., Cret., El.), as in Homer, Ζηνός, Ζηνί, Ζῆνα (Cret. Δῆνα, Τῆνα, etc., **84**). See **37**.1. There are some unexplained forms with α (or ᾱ?), as Ion. Ζάς, gen. Ζανός.

2. υἱός, υἱύς. Aside from the o-stem forms, the inscriptional occurrences are as follows, mostly from a stem υἱυ-:

Νομ. Sg. υἱύς Cret., Lac., Att. (Att. also ὑύς, ὕς).
Gen. Sg. υἱέος Cret., Att.; Thess. hυῖος (no. 35).
Dat. Sg. υἱεῖ Argol., Phoc., Att.
Acc. Sg. υἱύν Arc., Cret., Locr., etc.
Νομ. Pl. υἱέες Cret. (as in Hom.); Att. υἱεῖς.
Dat. Pl. υἱάσι Cret. (as in Hom.), after analogy of πατράσι, etc.
Acc. Pl. υἱύνς Arg., Cret.; Att. υἱεῖς.

3. μήν. Stem *μηνσ- (cf. Lat. *mēnsis*), whence (**77**.1) Lesb. μῆννος, Thess. μειννός, Att. etc. μηνός. The nom. *μήνς became *μένς (vowel-shortening before ν + cons., but later than the assimilation of medial νσ), whence regularly (**78**) Ion., Corcyr., Meg. μείς, Epid., Heracl. μής. In Attic, μείς was replaced by μήν formed after the analogy of original ν-stems in -ην, -ηνος. Elean μεύς is perhaps due to the analogy of Ζεύς, Ζηνός (above, 1).

4. λᾶς, Hom. λᾶας. Originally a neuter σ-stem τὸ λᾶας, becoming ὁ λᾶας, ὁ λᾶς, after the analogy of ὁ λίθος etc. Hence in genitive beside λᾶος also Att. λᾶου (Soph.), Cret. λᾶ͂ο.

5. Cret. Fῆμα nom.-acc. sg. = εἷμα, but gen. sg. τᾶς Fήμᾱς from a stem in -μᾱ. So also Cret. *ἀμφίδημα 'ornament' (cf. διάδημα), but gen. sg. ἀμπιδήμᾱς.

6. χοῦς, which in Attic is declined as a consonant stem (gen. sg. χοός), is properly a contracted o-stem (from χόFο-) like πλοῦς,

and remains so in Ionic, e.g., acc. sg. χοῦν, gen. pl. χῶν. 7. χείρ, χήρ. See **25, 76**.

Comparison of Adjectives

113. 1. Beside μείζων and κρείττων, both with anomalous ει, we find the normal μέζων (from *μέγιων) in Ionic and Arcadian, and κρέσσων (from *κρέτι̯ων) in Ionic. For Dor. κάρρων, Cret. κάρτων (both from *κάρτι̯ων) see **49**.2 with *a*, **80, 81**.

2. Beside πλέων, pl. πλέονες, σ-stem forms, like Hom. πλέες, πλέας, occur in Lesbian (πλέας no. 25) and Cretan (e.g., Gortyn. πλίες, πλίανς, πλία, beside πλίονος, πλίονα, πλίον. πλίασιν, Drerus, is in origin a ν-stem form, cf. **77**.1*a*). Cf. also Arc. πλός (from *πλέος, **42**.5*g*) adv. = πλέον.

Heracl. πόλιστος = πλεῖστος is formed directly from πολύς. The rare μεῖστος, superlative of μείων and parallel to πλεῖστος, is now confirmed by the Locr. adv. μεῖστον (no. 59.9).

3. El., Lac. ἄσιστα (ἄσσιστα also in Aesch.) = ἄγχιστα, is formed from the compar. ἆσσον (this regularly from *ἄγχι̯ον).

NUMERALS

Cardinals and Ordinals

114.1-10. 1. Nom. sg. masc. Att., etc. εἷς, Heracl. ἧς (cf. Lac. οὐδές), Cret. ἔνς (ἔνδ δ- = ἔνς δ-, Law-Code IX.50; see **97**.4), from *ἕνς. Cf. **78**.—Fem. μία, but, of other origin, Lesb., Thess., Boeot. ἴα, as in Homer (so Lesb. μηδεία = μηδεμία). Also ἰός in Hom. dat. sg. neut. ἰῷ and Mess. (probable reading) τόν γ' ἰὸν ἐνιαυτόν 'the one (= same) year,' and in Cretan, but here with pronominal force 'that one' = ἐκεῖνος.

Att.-Ion., Arc.-Cypr., Lesb. πρῶτος, Thess. προῦτος, West Greek and Boeot. πρᾶτος. Cf. also Att.-Ion. πρώτιστος, Cret., Coan, Ther., Cyren. πράτιστος.

a. The still frequently stated derivation from a *πρόατος or *πρόϝατος is untenable. Apart from the fact that such uncontracted forms do not exist, the supposed contraction of ο + α > Dor. ᾱ is contrary to the other evidence (**44**.1). πρῶτος and πρᾶτος are parallel forms from πρω- and πρᾱ-, the latter probably a weak grade, such as is seen in Skt. *pūrvas* and Lith. *pìrmas*. For such parallel forms, cf. Lat. *prīmus*, Pael. *prismu* vs. Umbr. *promom*, from *prīs-* and *pro-* respectively.

2. δύο in most dialects, δύω beside δύο in Homer, etc. Chalcid. δύϜο (with glide, 53b). Boeot. δύο, δούο, and διού (24) attested before consonant as well as before vowel. Eretr., Aetol. δύϜε, Lac. δύε, with the third declension ending. Gen.-dat. Att.-Ion. δυοῖν, late Att. δυεῖν, El. δυοίοις. Plural forms in various dialects, as Ion. (Hdt. and Chios), Cret., Heracl. δυῶν, Thess. δύας, Cret. δυοῖς, late Att. δυσί(ν).

δεύτερος in all dialects so far as known, and quotable in many.

3. τρεῖς, Cret. τρέες, Ther. τρῆς (also Lesb., gram.), from *τρέιες. See 25, 45.5.—Acc. τρῖς, Cret. τρίινς (for τρίνς with ι introduced anew from τριῶν, etc.). Under the influence of the indeclinable numerals, the nominative or the accusative is used for both cases in some dialects, namely, nom. τρεῖς in Attic and elsewhere, and acc. τρῖς in Heraclean, Delphian, and Troezenian.

τρίτος, Lesb. τέρτος (18a).

4. Att. τέτταρες, Ion., Arc. τέσσερες (also τέσσαρες in Ionic and κοινή), Boeot. πέτταρες, Lesb. πέσσυρες (Hom. πίσυρες), Thess. πετροετηρίς = τετρο-, West Greek τέτορες. From kʷetwer- (cf. Lat. quattuor, Skt. catvāras), the differences being due to inherited variations in the second syllable (twer, twor, tur, twr̥), and to the divergent development of kʷ (68) and tw (54f, 81)

τέταρτος, Hom. τέτρατος, Boeot. πέτρατος, Arc. τέτορτος (49.2a, 5).

5. πέντε, Lesb., Thess. πέμπε (68.3), Pamph. πέδε (66, 69.2). πέμπτος, Cret., Amorg. πέντος (86.2). Arc. πέμποτος after δέκοτος.

6. ἕξ, Cret., Delph., Heracl. Ϝέξ. See 52b. Boeot. ἐσκηδέκατος, like ἐς from ἐξ (100).

ἕκτος, Cret. once Ϝέκτος.

7. ἑπτά, Cret. once ἐττά (86.2). Att.-Ion. ἕβδομος, West Greek ἕβδεμος (attested directly in Delph., Cyren., Aetol., by derivatives in Heracl., Epid.).

8. ὀκτώ, Lesb. ὄκτο, Boeot. ὀκτό (like δύο), Heracl. hοκτώ (58c), El. ὀπτό (with π from ἑπτά).

ὄγδοος, from ὄγδοϜος now attested in Aetol. [ὀγ]δόϜα (IG IX². i.152).

9. ἐννέα, Delph., Rhod., Coan, Cyren. ἐννῆ (42.1), Heracl.
hεννέα (58c).

Att. ἔνατος, Ion. εἴνατος, Arg., Cret., Cyren. ἤνατος, from
*ἐνϜατος (54), Delph., Ther. hένατος (58c), Lesb. ἔνοτος (6,
116a).

10. δέκα, Arc. δέκο.
δέκατος, Arc., Lesb. δέκοτος (6, 116a).

115.11-19. ἔνδεκα, rarely δέκα εἷς (e.g., Heracl. δέκα hέν).—
Att. and Hom. δώδεκα, but in most dialects δυώδεκα, rarely
δυόδεκα (e.g., Boeot. δυοδέκατος), Delph., Heracl. δέκα δύο (also
late Attic.)—τρεῖς καὶ δέκα, also indecl. τρεισκαίδεκα (Attic after
300 B.C.) and τρισκαίδεκα (Boeotian, etc.; cf. 114.3); also δέκα
τρεῖς, especially when the substantive precedes (so Attic even in
fifth century).—Similar variations for 14-19.

ἑνδέκατος, δωδέκατος, δυωδέκατος, δυοδέκατος (see above —
13th-19th, Att. τρίτος καὶ δέκατος, etc., but τρεισκαιδέκατος or
τρισκαιδέκατος, etc., in East Ionic, Boeotian, and Lesbian
(-δέκοτος).

116.20-90. εἴκοσι (from *ἐ-Ϝίκοσι) in Attic, Ionic, Lesbian,
Arcadian (no occurrence in Cyprian), but Ϝίκατι, ἴκατι (cf. Ther.
hικάδι, Thess. ἰκάδι) in West Greek, Boeotian, Thessalian and
Pamphylian (φίκατι), with ι not ει, and τ retained (61.2). The
ει of Heracl. Ϝείκατι beside Ϝίκατι is due to the influence of Att.
εἴκοσι.—Att. etc. τριάκοντα, Ion. τριήκοντα.—τετταράκοντα,
τεσσεράκοντα, τεσσαράκοντα, πετταράκοντα (see 114.4), Sicil.
West Ion. τετράϟοντα (SEG 4.64), Dor., Delph. τετρώκοντα (so
doubtless in all West Greek dialects previous to Attic influence).
—πεντήκοντα, ἑξήκοντα (Ϝεξήκοντα), etc., with η in all dialects
(Ion. ὀγδώκοντα, 44.2).—Delph., Heracl. hεβδεμήκοντα, Heracl.
hογδοήκοντα, hενενήκοντα. See 114.7-9.—Gen. τεσσ[ερ]ακόντων,
πεντηκόντων, etc. in Chios, where the use of such inflected
genitives (also δέκων) is one of the Aeolic features of the dialect
(cf. πέμπων, δέκων in Alcaeus, also τριηκόντων in Hesiod).

Att., Ion. εἰκοστός etc., Boeot. Ϝικαστός (-καστός doubtless in
all West Greek dialects also; but Thess. ἰκοστός), Lesb. εἴκοιστος,
τριάκοιστος, ἑξήκοιστος).

a. The earliest form of the ordinals is that in -καστος (from -k̥mt-to-, cf.
Skt. triṅçat-tama-, etc.). Under the influence of the cardinals in -κοντα

this became -κοστος in Attic, etc. Under the same influence also *-κονστος, the probable source of Lesb. -κοιστος, with the regular Lesbian development of secondary νσ (77.3, 78). For a different view of the Lesbian forms, see 20a. To the same analogy is due the ο of εἴκοσι, and of the hundreds in -κόσιοι (e.g., τριακόσιοι after τριάκοντα), instead of the more original α in ϝίκατι (Skt. viṅçati-, Lat. vigintī), -κάτιοι, -κάσιοι (cf. ἑκατόν, Skt. çatam, Lat. centum). It is possible that a still further extension of this analogical ο is to be assumed in explanation of Arc. ἡεκοτόν, Arc., Lesb. δέκοτος, Arc. δέκο, Lesb. ἔνοτος.

117. 1. 100. Att. etc. ἑκατόν, Arc. ἡεκοτόν, See **6, 116a.**

2. 200-900. Att.-Ion., Lesb. -κόσιοι, West Greek, Boeot., Thess. -κάτιοι (Thess. ἐξεικάττιοι, SEG 2.264), Arc. -κάσιοι (with East Greek σ, but West Greek α). See **61.2, 116a.**

The ᾱ of τριᾱκόσιοι (Ion. τριηκόσιοι) is extended to διᾱκόσιοι (Ion. διηκόσιοι), and the α of τετρακόσιοι, ἑπτακόσιοι, ἐνακόσιοι to πεντακόσιοι, ἑξακόσιοι, ὀκτακόσιοι. But Thess. ἐξεικάττιοι with (ει=) η as in ἑξήκοντα. Lesb. ὀκτωκόσιοι.

3. 1000. Att. χῑλιοι (**25e**), Ion. χείλιοι, Lac., Cyren. χήλιοι, Lesb., Thess. χέλλιοι, from *χέσλιοι. See **76.1.**

PRONOUNS

Personal Pronouns [1]

118. SINGULAR. 1. The stems, except in the nominative, begin with: 1. ἐμ- or μ-.—2. Original *tw-*, whence East Greek σ-, West Greek τ- (τέος, τίν, τέ). But enclitic τοι is from a form without *w* (cf. Skt. *te*), and occurs also in Ionic (Hom., Hdt., etc.). Hom. τεοῖο and τείν are from the possessive stem *tewo-* (**120.2**).—3. Original *sw-*, whence ϝ- in some dialects (ϝέος, ϝοι, ϝίν), otherwise ʼ.

2. NOM. ἐγώ, ἐγών (Boeot. ἰώ, ἰών, **62.3**).—Att.-Ion., Lesb., Arc. σύ, Dor. τύ, Boeot. τού. See **61.5.**

3. GEN. *a.* -ειο (Hom. ἐμεῖο, etc., like τοῖο), whence -εο, later Ion. -ευ, Att. -ου.—*b.* -εος in West Greek, as lit. Dor. ἐμέος, τέος, Locr. ϝέος.—*c.* -θεν in lit. Lesb. ἔμεθεν, σέθεν, ϝέθεν, Hom. ἐμέθεν, σέθεν, ἔθεν, Epid. ἔθεν, Syrac. μεθέν (Sophron).

---

[1] As the personal pronouns, especially in the singular, are of comparatively rare occurrence in inscriptions, some forms are added which are quotable only from literary sources, but only a few out of the great variety, for which see Kühner-Blass I, pp. 580 ff.

4. DAT. *a.* -οι, as ἐμοί, μοι, σοί, σοι (lit. Dor. τοί, τοι, lit. Ion. τοι), οἶ, οἱ (Arg., Cret., Delph., Cypr., Lesb. Ϝοι).—*b.* -ιν in West Greek (where also -οι, but mostly in the enclitic forms, as μοι, never ἐμοί, Ϝοι, οἱ, and τοι, though also τοί), as Cret., Calymn., Rhod., Delph., and lit. Dor. ἐμίν, lit. Dor. τίν, Cret. Ϝίν.

5. ACC. 1. ἐμέ, με.—2. Att.-Ion., Lesb. σέ, lit. Dor. τέ (Cret. τϜέ, written τρέ, in Hesych.); also lit. Dor. and Epid. τύ (nom. used as acc.)—3. ἔ (Ϝέ); also lit. Dor. and Epid. νίν.

119. PLURAL. 1. The forms of the first and second persons contain, apart from the endings, ἀσμ- (cf. Skt. *asmān*, etc.) and ὐσμ- (cf. Skt. *yuṣmān*, etc.), whence Lesb., Thess. ἀμμ-, Lesb. ὐμμ-, elsewhere ἀμ- (Att.-Ion. ἡμ-) or ἀμ-, ὐμ-. See **76**.1, and, for the spiritus asper or lenis in the first person, **57**, **58***b*.

2. NOM. -ες in all dialects except Attic-Ionic, where it was replaced by -εις. Lesb. ἄμμες, ὔμμες, Dor. etc. ἀμές, ὑμές.

a. In late Cretan ἀμές was frequently replaced by ἀμέν under the influence of 1 pl. verbal forms in which Dor. -μες was often replaced by the κοινή -μεν. That is, ἀμέν for ἀμές after φέρομεν for φέρομες. From ἀμέν, -εν was extended to other pronouns and to participles, as ὐμέν, τινέν, ἀκούσαντεν, etc.

3. GEN. -ειων (Hom. ἡμείων), whence -εων, -ιων (**9**), -ῶν. Lesb. ἀμμέων, Thess. ἀμμέουν, El. ἀμέων, Dor. ἀμέων, ἀμίων (Cret.), later ἀμῶν.

4. DAT. -ι(ν), Lesb. ἄμμιν, ἄμμι, etc., Dor. ἀμίν, ὑμίν, Att.-Ion. ἡμῖν, ὑμῖν. So Dor. σφιν, σφι, Cret., Syrac. ψιν (**87**), but Att.-Ion. σφίσι, Arc. σφεις, the latter not satisfactorily explained.

5. ACC. -ε in all dialects except Attic-Ionic, where it was replaced by -εας, -ᾶς. Lesb. ἄμμε, ὔμμε, Thess. ἀμμέ, Dor., etc. ἀμέ, ὐμέ, Dor., etc. σφέ, Cret., Syrac. ψέ (**87**).

Possessives

120. 1. ἐμός.—Pl. Dor., etc., ἀμός (Lesb. ἄμμος) and ἀμέτερος (Lesb. ἀμμέτερος, Att.-Ion. ἡμέτερος).

2. *a.* *two-*, Att., etc., σός. *b.* **tewo-*, Dor., Lesb. τεός, Boeot. τιός (all in literature only). Both forms in Homer.—Pl. ὑμός and ὑμέτερος.

3. *a.* **swo-*, Att., etc., ὅς, Cret. Ϝός. *b.* **sewo-*, Dor. (lit.), Thess. ἑός. Both forms in Homer.—Pl. σφός and σφέτερος.

Reflexive Pronouns

121. Aside from the reflexive use of the forms of the personal
pronouns as given in **118, 119,** especially that of the third person,
which is itself a reflexive in origin, various forms of expression
are employed, as follows:

1. Combinations of the personal pronouns with αὐτός, each
keeping its own inflection, as in Homer (σοὶ αὐτῷ, etc.). So Epid.
αὐτοῦ ἔθεν, Cret. Ϝὶν αὐτοῖ, ψὲ αὐτόνς, πσὶν αὐτοῖς. Cf. also, with
the possessive, Cret. τὰ Ϝὰ αὐτᾶς= τὰ ἑαυτῆς.

2. Compounds of the same elements, with only the second
part declined. Att. ἐμαυτοῦ, σεαυτοῦ or σαυτοῦ, ἑαυτοῦ or αὐτοῦ
(also late ἑατοῦ, ἀτῶν, with ᾱ from ᾱυ); Coan ἡύτῶν with η from
εα; Thess. εὑτοῖ, εὑτοῦ, εὑτάς; Cret. Ϝιαυτο͂; Ion. (lit.) ἐμεωυτοῦ
etc. The forms found in Ionic inscriptions are like the Attic.

3. αὐτός alone, as sometimes in Homer. Thus Delph. αὐτοῦ
= ἐμαυτοῦ, El. αὐτὰρ = ἑαυτῆς (no. 66.17), Lac. αὐτο͂ = ἑαυτοῦ
(no. 71.7, 16 ff.), Corinth. περὶ τᾶς αὐτοῦ γᾶς (no. 95), Thess.
αὐτᾶ = ἑαυτῇ, Boeot. αὐτάν = ἑαυτήν.

4. αὐτὸς αὐτός, either with each declined separately, or, oftener
merged into compounds of somewhat varying form.

This combination is comparatively late, replacing the earlier
types mentioned under 1-3. It is most frequent in Delphian
and Boeotian, but is found in several of the other West Greek
dialects, and probably even in Attic (Kühner-Blass I, p. 600,
anm. 5).

a. αὐτὸς αὐτός. Delph. αὐτοὶ ποτὶ αὐτούς, Boeot. κατ' αὐτὺ (= αὐτοὶ)
αὐτῶν.

b. αὐτοσαυτός. Delph. αὐτοσαυτοῦ, etc., Boeot. ὑπὲρ αὐτοσαυτῶ, Heracl.
μετ' αὐτοσαυτῶν, Cret. αὐτοσαυτοῖς, etc., Corcyr. αὐτοσαυτόν.

c. αὐσαυτός. Delph. αὐσαυτοῦ, etc., Cret., Argol. (Calauria) αὐσαυτᾶς,
Arc. ὑπὲρ αὐσαυτόν.

d. ἀσαυτός. Boeot. ἀσαυτῦ.

e. αὐσωτός. Delph. αὐσωτᾶς, etc.

f. αὐταυτός. Heracl. αὐταυτᾶς (as in Sophron and Epicharmus), Aegin.
αὐταυτόν.

g. Sicil. gen. sg. αὐτοῦτα (Segesta), gen. pl. αὐτῶντα (Thermae). Probably from αὐτατοῦ, αὐτατῶν (cf. late ἑατοῦ, above, 2), with transposition
of the last two syllables.

Demonstrative Pronouns

122. The article. Nom. pl. τοί, ταί, as in Homer, in the West Greek dialects except Cretan, and in Boeotian. Att. etc. οἱ, αἱ, after the analogy of ὁ, ἡ. For ὁ, ἁ̄ in some dialects which in general have ΄, see **58**a. Thess. οἱ, but τοί at Pharsalus (Schwyzer 566). Forms with added ι, used like ὅδε, are found in Elean (το-ί̆, τα-ί̆) and Boeotian (ταν-ί; τοι-ί̆, τυ-ί̆). For the relative use, see **126**.

a. Just as in Homer the use as article is less frequent than the demonstrative and the article is often lacking where it is obligatory or usual in later times, so (apart from certain categories in which the absence of the article is usual) in inscriptions of some dialects. So frequently in headings, like that of no. 67, Συνθήκα καὶ Συμμαχία (but El. ἁ Ϝράτρα nos. 61-63, etc.). With names of official bodies or officials, e.g., Cret. ἀδ᾽ ἔϝαδε πόλι (no. 116), Arg. (no. 85) βōλὰ ἐπαγέτō, ἁ(Ϝρέτευε) βōλᾶς, ἀλιαίαι ἔδοξε, ἐπὶ κόσμος, Epid. ἔδοξε βουλᾶι καὶ δάμωι, κατάλογος βουλᾶς, Locr. (no. 59.10/11) ἐν πρείγαι ἐν πόλι ε̄̓ 'ν ἀποκλε̄σίαι. (In Att. fifth century inscriptions there are a few examples of βōλέ̄ without article, but much more commonly with the article).

123. Thess. ὅ-νε, Arc. ὁ-νί, Arc.-Cypr. ὅ-νυ = ὅδε. Thess. τόνε, τάνε, and, with both parts inflected (cf. Hom. τοῖσδεσι), gen. sg. τοῖνεος, gen. pl. τοῦννεουν.᾽—Arc. τωνί (gen. sg.), τωινί, ταιννί (dat. pl. fem.), ταννί, τανί (gen. sg., gen. pl., and acc. pl. fem.). Cf. also Boeot. προτηνί (**136**.1).—Cypr. ὄνυ, τόνυ, Arc. τάνυ (acc. pl. neut.), τῶννι (gen. pl.), τῶινυ (11 times in no. 20 vs. once τωινί), also by an alien engraver τάννυν, τόσνυν. Cf. Hom., Boeot., Cypr. νυ.

From ὅδε, cf. also Arg. τōνδεōνέν, ταδέν with addition of emphatic -ην (ἤν, Lat. ēn).

124. οὗτος. Nom. pl. τοῦτοι, ταῦται, like τοί, ταί, in West Greek (examples from Cos, Delphi, Rhodes, Selinus). Att. etc. οὗτοι, αὗται, after οὗτος, etc. Boeotian, with τ replaced by ΄ throughout, οὗτον, οὗτων, etc.—Interchange of αυ and ου. Att. gen. pl. fem. τούτων after masc.-neut.; conversely El. neut. ταύτων, due to influence of ταῦτα. ου throughout is Boeotian (οὗτο, οὗτα) and Euboean (τοῦτα, τούτεῖ, also ἐντοῦθα = ἐν-ταῦθα), also οὗτα = ταῦτα in Sophron. So also Delph. τοῦτα, τούτας (but also ταῦται). For the spelling with O instead of OV, see **34**a.

125. 1. ἐκεῖνος. Ion. κεῖνος, Lesb., Cret., Rhod., Coan κῆνος, both from *κε-ενος. Cf. **25.**—τῆνος, of different origin (cf. Hom. τῆ), in Delphian, Heraclean, Argolic (Aegina), Megarian, as well as in Sicilian Doric writers (Theocr., Sophron, Epicharmus). 2. αὐτός. Neut. αὐτόν in Cretan, as sometimes in Attic inscriptions.

Relative, Interrogative, and Indefinite Pronouns

126. The relative ὅς occurs in all dialects. But the relative use of forms of the article, frequent in Homer and Herodotus, is usual in Lesbian (so always in the earlier inscriptions and nearly always in Alcaeus and Sappho; ὅς in later inscriptions is due to κοινή influence, as shown by the spiritus asper, καθ' ὅν, etc.), Thessalian (τά, καττάπερ; ἐν τοῦ 'in which', no. 33.27, but also ὅς in an early metrical inscription), and Arcado-Cyprian (Arc.ὅπερ, ταῖ, τοῖς, etc., Cypr. ὁ, τόν, etc., but also Arc. ἄν, Cypr. ὂι, οἴ). So also in Boeotian in a fourth-century inscription (no. 40), but later only ὅς (cf. Lesbian). It is also Heraclean (τόν, τά, etc.; so often in Epicharmus), and Cyrenaean (ὁ, τό, τά), but in most West Greek dialects it occurs, if at all, only in later inscriptions (so in late Delphian, Elean, and Cretan, never in the earlier period).

For the demonstrative use of ὅς, cf. Heracl. hᾶι μὲν... hᾶι δὲ (no. 79.82).

127. Cret. ὅτερος 'which of two' is the true relative correlative of πότερος (cf. Skt. yataras beside kataras), and so related to the usual ὁπότερος as οἷος to ὁποῖος, ὅτε to ὁπότε.

128. τίς, τις. Cypr. σις, Arc. σις, ὅζις, see **68.**3. Thess. κίς, κις, κινες, see **68.**4. The inflection with ν, gen. sg. τινός, etc., presumably based on the original acc. sg. *τίν, is widespread. But forms of the earlier type, without ν, like Hom. τεο, ὅττεο, τεω, ὀτέοισιν, Att. του, τω, ὅτοις, are seen also in Lesb. τίωι, τίοισι (**9.**2), Arc. ὀσέοι (**68.**3), gen. sg. Lesb. ὅττω, Boeot. ὅττω, Meg. σά (from *τϳα), Att.-Ion. ἄττα, ἄσσα (from *άτϳα), Cret. dat. sg. τῖμι in ὅτιμι, from *τι-σμι with the same pronominal sm as in Skt. kasmin, Umbr. pusme, etc.

129. The indefinite relative ὅστις, ὅτις.

1. ὅστις, with both parts declined, Att.-Ion., also in various dialects, e.g., Locr. hoίτινες, Cret. οἵτινες, Boeot. ὥστινας.

2. ὅτις, with only the second part declined, Att.-Ion., also in various dialects, e.g., Arc. ὅτις, ὅζις, ὀσέοι (68.3), Cret. ὅτιμι (128), Delph. ὅτινος, ὅτινι.—Further, with ττ spread from the neut. ὅττι (*ὅδ-τι), Lesb. ὅττις, ὅττινας, ὅττω, etc. (cf. also ὅππα, ὅππως, etc.), Boeot. ὅττω, Arg. ὅττινες.

a. Locr. Fότι (no. 58.6), at variance with all other evidence, is almost certainly an error for hότι (so nos. 57, 59, as in other dialects).

3. Neuter forms in -τι, with only the first part declined, in Cretan, e.g., ἄτι = ἄτινα, ὅτι = οὕτινος.

130. Cret. ὀτεῖος = ὁποῖος, but used like adjectival ὅστις, as ὀτεῖος δέ κα κόσμος μὴ βέρδηι, γυνὰ ὀτεία κρέματα μὲ ἔκει, ὀτείαι δὲ (sc. γυναικὶ) πρόθθ᾽ ἔδωκε. Here also Boeot. dat. sg. fem. μηδοτίη (= μηδοτείαι). For the form (also Hesych. τεῖον ·· ποῖον, Κρῆτες), cf. Hom. τέο, τέῳ, etc., and Lesb. (lit.) τέουτος τοιοῦτος (with loss of ι 31).

131. Interrogative pronouns used as indefinite relatives. So regularly in Thessalian, e.g., κίς κε γινύειτει = ὅστις ἂν γίγνηται, διὲ κί (in form διὰ τί) = διότι, πὸκ κί (in form πρὸς τί) = ὅτι, φυλᾶς ποίας κε βέλλειτει = φυλῆς ὁποίας (ἦστινος) ἂν βούληται. Elsewhere the use of τίς = ὅστις is, with some rare exceptions in literature, found only in late Greek.

ADVERBS AND CONJUNCTIONS

Pronominal Adverbs and Conjunctions of Place, Time, and Manner

132. 1. -ου. Place 'where.' Att.-Ion. ποῦ, ὅπου, αὐτοῦ, ὁμοῦ, etc. These are of genitive origin, and are specifically Attic-Ionic.

2. -ει. Place 'where.' These are the usual equivalents of Att.-Ion. -ου, occurring in West Greek dialects and Boeotian, e.g., εῖ, πεῖ, πει (Cret. αἴ πει = Att. εἴ που), ὅπει, τεῖδε, τουτεῖ, τηνεῖ, αὐτεῖ (Boeot. αὐτῖ), ἀλλεῖ, ἀμεῖ, μηδαμεῖ. Here also Arg. hῖ, ῖ (25c) 'where' and 'when.' By analogy, Locr. παντεῖ 'everywhere,' Heracl., Arg. ποτεχεῖ = προσεχῶς, Delph. ἐπεχεῖ = ἐφεξῆς (beside Arg. ἐπεχές, Ach. ποτεχές, etc.), Cret., Heracl. διπλεῖ 'doubly.'

3. -οι. Place 'where' and (so usually in Attic) 'whither.' οῖ,

ποῖ, ὅποι in many dialects, and with -ς, Delph. οἷς. Cf. Lesb. αἴ
ποι = Att. εἴ που. By analogy Lesb. ὔψοι or ἴψοι (cf. ὑψί),
Orop. ἤχοι (from ἤχι, below, 6), also (133.3-5) ἔνδοι, ἔχθοι, ἔξοι.

4. -υι. Place 'where' and 'whither.' Cret. υἶ 'where' (Hierapytna, e.g., no. 119.16, 22), Cret. ὅπυι, Arg., Cyren. ὅπυι (Arg.
'for whatever purpose'); in -υις or -υς, Rhod. υἷς 'as far as' (no.
104.3), Arg. ὖς (IG IV.498.4 'whither', 'to whom'), Rhod. ὅπυς,
lit. Dor. (Syrac.) ὖς, πῦς. Cf. also Cret. πλίυι (to πλίες, 113.2),
lit. Lesb. τυῖδε, ἄλλυι, πήλυι.

5. -ᾱι (Att.-Ion. -ηι). Place 'where' or (mostly Delph.) 'whither,'
and especially manner. Thus ἄι, ὅπαι in many West Greek dialects
and Boeotian (ὅπη). In Cretan used also as final, and (ἄι) temporal
conjunctions. Cret., Corcyr. ἀλλᾶι 'otherwise,' Heracl. παντᾶι 'in
all directions,' Lesb. πάνται. The indefinite παι (cf. Corcyr. ἀλλᾶι
παι 'in any other way') is used in Cyprian as a strengthening
particle (κάς παι 'and indeed,' ἰδέ παι 'then indeed,' no. 23.4, 12).

6. -ᾱ (Att.-Ion. -η). Uses as in the preceding. Delph., Cyren.
ἇδε, Cret. ἇδε (no. 116) 'in this way,' Lac. ταυτᾶ hᾶτ' 'in such a
way as,' haμᾶ 'likewise,' Locr. ταὐτᾶ 'in the same way.' Locr.,
Cyren. ἆ κα 'in case that' (nos. 60.19; 115.93), lit. Dor. ἆχι = Hom.
ἤχι 'where.' Lesb. ὅππα 'where,' ἄλλα 'elsewhere' (no. 27.49 beside
dat. sg. -αι, and so better here than under 5, above).

7. -η. Place 'where,' time 'when,' etc. Cret. ἐ̄, Heracl., Cyren. ἦ
(this accent preferred here, vs. ἤ 'or, than' but practice varies),
'when' (so Heracl., Cyren., Cret.; Cret. also 'where', 'in case
that') Cret. ὅπε̄, Cyren. ὅπη 'where,' Lac. hόπε̄ 'in such a way as,'
Thess. ὅπει (ει=η) 'when' (no. 33.26; cf. ὀπειδεί, ibid. l. 12, in
form a blend of ὅπει and ἐπειδεί, in sense = ἐπειδή). Lac. πέποκα =
πώποτε. El., Meg., Ther., Eretr. τε̄δε 'here,' El. ταὐτε̄ 'here.' Meg.
ἄ(λ)λε̄, Cyren. ἄλλη πη 'elsewhere,' Cret. ϝεκατέρη 'in each place.'

8. -ω. Place 'whence.' Lit. Dor. ὤ, πῶ, ὅπω, Cret. ὀ̄, ὅπο̄, Locr.
hο̄, hόπο̄, Cret. τῶδε, Cret., Coan τουτῶ. Syrac. τηνῶ, τηνῶθε,
Meg. τηνῶθεν. Similarly Delph. ϝοίκω 'from the house.'

a. These adverbs are not to be confounded with another class, mostly
from prepositions, meaning place 'where' or 'whither' and occurring in
Attic-Ionic also, as ἄνω, κάτω, ἔξω, etc. Here belong Delph. ἔνδω 'within,'
Coan ἑκατέρω 'on each side of.'

9. -θεν. Place 'whence.' Att.-Ion. ὅθεν, πόθεν, etc. This -θεν,

which though formally related must be distinguished from the
-(σ)θεν, -(σ)θε of adverbs like ἄνωθε(ν), πρόσθε(ν) without the
'whence' sense (133.1), is mainly Attic-Ionic in pronominal
adverbs (such forms in Doric, in place of the usual -ω, are rare).
But in adverbs derived from place names it is also West Greek,
as Ϙορινθόθεν, Κνωσόθεν, Μυκανέᾱθεν, Θήρᾱθεν, Γορτύνᾱθεν, Φλει-
Ϝόντᾱθεν.

10. -ως. Manner. ὡς, πῶς, ὅπως, etc. in all dialects. ὡς also
'when' and in some dialects 'where.'

a. ὡς and ὅπως are also the most widespread final conjunctions. The
final use of ἵνα, originally 'where,' developed in Attic-Ionic, but spread
to other dialects (appearing mostly in late inscriptions; in the early Rhod.
no. 100 clearly due to epic influence. Early Cretan had none of these,
but only ὅπαι or ἄι in final sense (above, 5).

11. -τε, -τα, -κα. Temporal, ὅτε, τότε, πότε in Attic-Ionic and
Arcado-Cyprian (Arc. τότε, ὁπότε, οὔποτε, Cypr. ὅτε μέποτε) but
Att. εἶτα, ἔπειτα, Ion. εἶτεν, ἔπειτε, ἔπειτεν.—ὅτα, πότα, ἄλλοτα
in Lesbian.—ὅκα, etc., in West Greek and Boeotian, as Boeot.
πόκα, Cret. ὅκα, τόκα, ποκα, Cyren. ὅκα, τόκα, ὁπόκα, Rhod. ὅκα,
Lac. πέποκα, El. τόκα, Delph. ὅκα, οὐδέποκα, μηδέποκα. The form
ὅκκα (from ὅκα κα) occurs in Laconian, Megarian, Rhodian,
Coan, and literary Doric.

12. Other temporal conjunctions. Besides ὅτε, etc. (above, 11),
ἐπεί, and the occasional temporal use of forms in -ει, -αι, -η, -ως
(above 2, 5, 6, 8), there are various words for 'so long as, while,'
and 'until' (conjunction and preposition). ἕως, ἆς (41.4)—ἔστε,
Boeot. ἔττε, Locr. ἔντε, Delph. ἥντε (135.4) — μέχρι, ἄχρι —
Cret., Cyren. μέστα (Cret. also μέττ' ἐς), Arc. [μέ]στε (probable,
-τε as in ὅτε, etc.), μέστ', Thess. μέσποδι, Hom. μέσφα, all having
in common μές now attested in Thess. preposition μές (no. 33.6)—
εἰς(ἐς) ὅ—Boeot. ἐν τάν (sc. ἀμέραν), 136.1.

Prepositional and Other Adverbs

133. 1. -(σ)θεν, -(σ)θε, -(σ)θα. Att.-Ion. ἄνωθεν, ἄνωθε, ὕπερθεν,
ὕπερθε, etc., Arc. μεσακόθεν (65), Heracl. ἄνωθα. With -σθεν,
etc. Att.-Ion. πρόσθεν, πρόσθε, Lesb. πρόσθε (so in inscriptions,
in lyric also πρόσθεν), Thess. πρόστεν (85.1), Dor. πρόσθα (gram.),
Heracl., Arg. ἔμπροσθα (but also Troez. ἔμπροσθε, ὄπισθε, and

once Meg. πρόσθε), Cret. πρόθθα (85.3), Delph. πρόστα (85.1), Arc. προσθαγενές. Arc. θύσθεν 'outside of' from *θυρ-σθεν (cf. θύρδα, 2).

a. Also -θι, as in Hom., etc. So Arc. ὅθι, ὁπόθι, μηδεπόθι, ἰσόθι, αὖθι.

2. -δε (-ζε), -δα. Arc. -δα is seen in θύρδα ἔξω = Hom. θύραζε.

3. For Delph., Locr., Arg. ἐχθός = ἐκτός, see 66. Hence, after the analogy of other adverbs in -ω (132.8) and -οι (132.3), Delph., Epid. ἔχθω, Epid. ἔχθοι.

4. From ἔνδον are formed—besides Att.-Ion. ἔνδοθεν, ἔνδοθι, Ion. ἐνδόσε (Ceos)—Cret., Delph., Meg., Syrac., ἐνδός (after ἐντός), Delph. ἔνδω, Lesb., Epid., Syrac., Cyren. ἔνδοι.

5. Beside ἔξω (132.8a) are formed, after the analogy of other adverbs, Lac. ἔξει, Thess., Cret., Syrac., Cyren. ἔξοι, Dor., Delph. ἔξος (after ἐκτός, etc., cf. ἐνδός).

6. -ις, -ιν, -ι. Forms with adverbial -ς or -ν sometimes interchange with each other and with forms without either -ς or -ν, as the numeral adverbs in -κις, -κιν, -κι. Thus in most dialects -κις, sometimes -κι, but -κιν in Lac. τετράκιν, ἑπτάκιν, ὀκτάκιν, Cret. ὀθθάκιν = ὁσάκις. Likewise -ιν in other adverbs of time (cf. Att. πάλιν), as Cret. αὖτιν, Rheg. αὖθιν = Ion., Arc. αὖτις, Att. αὖθις. Cret. αὐταμέριν = Att. αὐθημερόν, Lesb., Coan αὐταμερόν, Locr. αὐταμαρόν (accents uncertain), El. ὕσταριν = ὕστερον. Here also Thess. ἀίν, Arc. ἀί, Lesb. ἄι (also αἶιν Hdn.), Ion. αἰί (also ἀίδασμος 'under perpetual lease') = usual αἰές, αἰεί, αἰέν (all from *αἰϝί, *αἰϝίν, *αἰϝές, etc., cf. Cypr., Phoc. αἰϝεί), while a corresponding form in -ις is to be seen in Cypr. ὐϝαίς 'forever,' a combination like Att. εἰς ἀεί, containing ὐ = ἐπί and ἀίς from *αἰϝίς (omission of ϝ peculiar, but cf. παῖς, 53).

Cf. also Epid. ἄνευν, El. ἄνευς = ἄνευ (Meg. ἄνις, also at Tauromeniun, in late poets, is formed after χωρίς), Dor. ἔμπᾶν (Pindar) beside ἔμπᾶς = ἔμπης, Coan, Rhod., Ther. ἐξάν = ἐξῆς.

7. A combination of -ιν with -δην, -δᾶν (cf. -δα, -δον, etc.). Att. ἀριστίνδην, πλουτίνδην, ἀγχιστίνδην, Locr. ἀριστίνδαν, πλουτίνδαν, but ἀγχιστέδαν, formed from the stem ἀγχιστη- of ἀγχιστεύς.

134. 1. The conditional conjunction. εἰ in Attic-Ionic and Arcadian; αἰ in Lesbian, Thessalian, Boeotian (ἠ), and all the West Greek dialects; ἐ (ἠ) in Cyprian.

2. ἄν, κε, κα. ἄν is only Attic-Ionic and Arcadian. In all other

dialects the unrelated κε, κα is used—κε in Lesbian (also κεν), Thessalian, and Cyprian, κα in the West Greek dialects and Boeotian.

a. Arcadian once had κε, like Cyprian, and a relic of this is to be seen in the κ which appears, where there would otherwise be hiatus, between εἰ and a following ἄν, which had regularly replaced κε as a significant element (probably through prehistoric Ionic influence, cf. p. 4). Thus regularly εἴ κ' ἄν, or better εἰκ ἄν, since εἰκ has become a mere by-form of εἰ (like οὐκ beside οὐ), but εἰ δ' ἄν. Once, without ἄν, εἰκ ἐπὶ δõμα πῦρ ἐποίσε, where some assume a significant κ', in place of usual ἄν, but best classed with the subjunctive clauses without ἄν (**174**).

b. In Attic-Ionic, εἰ combines with ἄν—in Attic to ἐάν or ἄν, in Ionic to ἤν.

c. The substitution of εἰ for αἰ belongs to the earliest stage of Attic (κοινή) influence in the West Greek dialects, but that of ἄν for κα only to the latest, being rarely found except where the dialect is almost wholly κοινή. Hence the hybrid combination εἴ κα is the rule in the later inscriptions of most West Greek dialects.

3. καί. Arc.-Cypr. κάς (also κά, for which see **97**.2), the relation of which to καί is obscure (antevocalic κα(ι) + ς ?). In Arcadian this occurs only in the early Mantinean inscription, no. 17, elsewhere καί. See **275**.

4. δέ. Thessalian uses μά, related to μέν, for δέ, e.g. τὸ μὰ ψάφισμα, τὰμ μὲν ἴαν ... τὰμ μὰ ἄλλαν (no. 32.22; τὰν δὲ ἄλλαν l. 45 is due to κοινή influence).

5. νυ, identical with -νυ in Arc.-Cypr. ὄνυ = ὅδε (**123**), and with Hom. νυν, νυ occurs as an independent particle in Cyprian and Boeotian, e.g., Cypr. δυϝάνοι νυ, δόκοι νυ, Boeot. ἄκουρύ νυ ἔνθω.

Cf. νι in Arc. τωνί, etc. (**123**), Boeot. προτηνί (**136**.1), Pamph. καί νι.

6. ἰδέ, in form = Hom. ἰδέ, occurs in Cyprian introducing the conclusion of a condition (ἰδέ παι 'then indeed,' ἰδέ 'then,' no. 23.12, 25), or a new sentence (ἰδέ 'and' no. 23.26).

7. ναί, νή. Arc. νεί (νεὶ τὸν Δία). Cf. εἰ, αἰ, ἤ, above, 1.

PREPOSITIONS

Peculiarities in Form

135. 1. For apocope of the final vowel, see **95**.

2. For assimilation of final consonants, see **96, 97, 99**.—ἐς =

ἐκ, **100**. For ὸν = ἀνά, see **6**.—ἰν = ἐν, **10**.—ἀπύ = ἀπό, **22**.—
κατύ = κατά, **22**.

3. ὑπά, ὐπά = ὑπό, formed after the analogy of κατά, in Lesbian, Boeotian, and (quotable examples only compounds) Locrian (ὐπαπροσθιδίōν no. 59 vs. Ηυποκναμιδίōν no. 57) and Elean (ὑπαδυγίοις, ὑπαδυκιοίοις).

4. ἐν, εἰς. The inherited use of ἐν with the accusative (cf. the use of Lat. *in*) is retained in the Northwest Greek dialects (and in the Northwest Greek κοινή, **279**) together with Boeotian and Thessalian, and in Arcado-Cyprian (ἰν). Elsewhere this was replaced by an extended form ἐν-ς, whence εἰς, ἐς or (from *ἰν-ς) ἰς in Pamphylian and at Vaxus. See **78**.

Similarly ἔντε = ἔστε in Locrian, Delphian (ηέντε, **58c**) and the Northwest Greek κοινή. But Boeotian, in spite of ἐν, has ἔττε = ἔστε.

5. μετά, πεδά. πεδά, unrelated to μετά in origin, is used in its place in Lesbian, Boeotian (probably in Thessalian too, though not yet quotable), Arcadian (πέ, **95**), Argolic, Cretan, and Theran. (Most of these dialects show also μετά, but at a time when κοινή influence is probable.) So also in compounds, as Lesb., Cret., Cyren. πεδέχω, Arg. πεδάγαγον, πεδάϝοικοι = μέτοικοι, Epid. πεδαφορᾶς, and proper names, as Boeot. Πεδάκων, Arg. Πεδάκριτος. The name of the month Πεδαγείτνυος or (by blend with μετα-) Πεταγείτνυος (or -ιος) = Att. Μεταγειτνιών occurs in Rhodes, Cos, Calymna, Megara, Sicily, and Magna Graecia, where πεδά alone is not attested.

a. The same blend of πεδα- and μετα- as in the month-name is also to be recognized in Del., Orop. πέτευρον 'notice-board, tablet' (so πετεύριον at Erythrae), elsewhere (with v.l. πέταυρον) 'roosting-perch, springboard,' etc., cpd. like Lesb. πεδάορος, Att. μετέωρος (ευ as in Thas. θευρός = θεωρός, **41**.4*a*).

6. πρός. There are two independent series of forms, one with and one without the ρ, each with variation between final -ς and -τι (**61**.4*a*)—1. προτί (= Skt. *prati*) in Homer (beside ποτί and usual πρός), quoted as Doric (Apoll. Dysc.), restored in Alcman, and almost certainly attested for Argive (πρὸτ' Schwyzer 84.3) Cret. πορτί (**70**.1), Pamph. περτ'—Att.-Ion., Lesb. πρός.

2. ποτί (= Avest. *pa'ti*) with πότ, πό (95) in the West Greek dialects with Thessalian and Boeotian.— Arc.-Cypr. πός.

Still another form, ποί, occurring mostly, though not exclusively, before dentals (hence possibly to be explained as coming from ποτί by dissimilatory loss of τ) is frequent in Argive and Delphian, with scattered examples in Locrian (no. 58.14) and elsewhere. Numerous examples before dentals, as ποὶ τόν, etc. But also Arg. ποιγραψάνσθō, Epid. ποὶ ῥόπτον, Delph. ποικεφάλαιον, ποὶ γᾶν, and a few others before non-dentals.

a. πός occurs also several times in inscriptions of Phrygia and Pamphylia, where it has been plausibly explained as introduced from Pamphylia (though a Pamph. πός is not actually attested) and so ultimately belonging with the Arc.-Cypr. πός.

7. σύν, ξύν. ξύν, as in Homer, in early Attic, elsewhere σύν. But Ion. ξῡνός from *ξυν-ι̯ός. Cypr. ὕγγεμος· συλλαβή (Hesych.).

8. Cypr. ὐ = ἐπί, e.g., ὐ τύχα = ἐπὶ τύχη, ὐχέρōν = ἐπιχείρου. Probably cognate with Skt. *ud*, Eng. *out* (cf. ὕσ-τερος = Skt. *uttaras*). There are traces of the same prefix in a few Rhodian and Boeotian proper names.

Peculiarities in Meaning and Construction

136. 1. Dative instead of the usual genitive construction in Arcado-Cyprian. (1) ἀπύ. Arc. ἀπὺ ταῖ (sc. ἀμέραι). Cypr. ἀπὺ ταῖ ζᾶι.—(2) ἐξ. Arc. ἐς τοῖ ἔργοι, Cypr. ἐξ ταῖ ζᾶι.—(3) περί. Arc. περὶ τοι-νί, Cypr. περὶ παιδί.—(4) ὑπέρ. Arc. ὑπέρ ταῖ τᾶς πόλιος ἐλευθερίαι.—(5) ὑπό. Arc. ὑπὸ πάντων τῶν γεγονότων ὑπὸ ταῖ πόλι.—(6) παρά. Arc. παρὰ ταῖ ἰδίαι πόλι 'from their own city.'—(7) πεδά. Arc. πὲ τοῖς Ϝοικιάται[ς].—(8) ἐπί. Arc. ἐπὶ ἱε[ρομνάμοσι το]ῖς.

ἐξ with dative occurs also in Pamph. ἐξ δὲ φυσελαι; πρό with dative in Boeot. προτηνί 'formerly,' i.e., πρὸ ται-νί (sc. ἀμέραι.) Cf. Thess. ὑππρὸ τᾶς (sc. ἀμέρας) 'just previously,' and Boeot. ἐν τάν (sc. ἀμέραν) 'until,' no. 43.49).

a. This growth, at the expense of the genitive, of the dative (locative) construction, which in the case of most of the above-mentioned prepositions was also an inherited one (cf. περί, ὑπό, etc., with dative), and its extension even to ἀπύ and ἐξ, was probably furthered by the influence of the most frequent locative construction, that with ἐν (ἰν).

2. παρά 'at, with,' with accusative instead of dative. Though

occasional even in Attic writers and elsewhere, this is especially
common in the Northwest Greek dialects, including Thessalian
and Boeotian, e.g., Thess. τοῖ παρ' ἀμμὲ πολιτεύματος (no. 32;
corresponding to τοῦ παρ' ὑμῖν πολιτεύματος of Philip's letter in
the κοινή), Boeot. ἁ σούγγραφος πὰρ Ϝιφιάδαν, Delph. παραμεινάτω
δὲ Νικὼ παρὰ Μνασίξενον, El. πεπολιτευκὼρ παρ' ἀμέ.

a. Much later, and rarely seen in dialect inscriptions, is the more
general confusion between the dative with verbs of rest and the accusative
with verbs of motion, and the final supremacy of the accusative construction, as ἔμειναν εἰς τὸν οἶκον.

3. πρός 'by, in the sight of,' with accusative instead of genitive,
in Elean πό (= ποτί). ὀμόσαντες πὸ τὸν θεὸν τὸν 'Ολύνπιον,—ὅτι
δοκέοι καλιτέρōς ἔχε͂ν πὸ τὸν θεόν,—Ϝέρε͂ν αὐτὸν πὸ τὸν Δία 'he
shall be judged guilty in the eyes of Zeus.' In a later Elean
inscription (no. 65) the same idea is expressed by φευγέτω πὸτ
τῶ Διόρ τὠλυμπίω αἵματορ where both the genitive construction
and the use of φεύγω instead of the genuine Elean Ϝέρρω are
concessions to Attic usage. This Elean use is only a step removed
from that of πρός 'in relation to' with accusative.

4. El. ἄνευς = ἄνευ, with accusative instead of genitive, as
ἄνευς βōλάν.

5. κατά 'according to' with genitive instead of accusative,
in Locrian. καθ' ὧν = καθ' ἅ,—κὰ τō͂νδε = κατὰ τάδε,—κὰ τᾶς
συνβολᾶς, κατὰ ξενίας.

6. ἐπί with the dative of the deceased person, in epitaphs. This
occurs in a few early epitaphs in Lesbian, Phocian, and Locrian,
but is especially common in Boeotian, e.g., ἐπὶ Ϝhεκαδάμοε ἐμί,
ἐπὶ 'Ὀκίβαε. In most dialects the name of the deceased appears
in the nominative.

7. ἀμφί. In most dialects ἀμφί is obsolete. In the phrase ἀμφί
τινα, which survives also in Attic prose, it occurs in Argive and
Rhodian; in Argive also once in purely local force. In Cretan
it is used freely in the meaning 'about, concerning' (as in Homer),
with dative or accusative, e.g., αἰ δέ κ' ἀντὶ δόλōι μōλίοντι 'if they
contend about a slave.'—ἀνπὶ τὰν δαῖσιν 'about the division.'

8. ἀντί. The original local meaning 'in the face of, in front of,
before' (cf. Lat. ante) is preserved in Cret. ἀντὶ μαιτύρōν 'before
witnesses', Locr. ἀντὶ τō͂ ἀρχō͂ 'before the magistrate' (no. 59.19),

Att. ἀντὶ τοῦ Μινωταύρου, and a few other Att. examples. Hence the sense 'in return for' and the early and usual 'instead of.' This is sometimes weakened to denote mere equivalence ('in place of' = 'as, for'), e.g., Hom.ἀντὶ ... ἱκετάο 'as a suppliant'. From 'in return for' arose a freer distributive use seen in Arc. τρῖς ὀδελὸς ὀφλὲν ἀντὶ ϝεκάσταυ 'shall pay a fine of three obols for each (wagon).' Further, Delph. ἀντὶ ϝέτεος (no. 52 A 45), Arc. ἀντ' ἐνιαυτοῦ (IG V.ii.266), Boeot. ἀντ' ἐνιαυτῶ (cf. BCH 60.183), all meaning 'by the year, yearly,' and even Coan ἀντὶ νυκτός 'by night' (no. 108.42). Cf. Hesych. ἀντέτους · τοῦ αὐτοῦ ἔτους. Λάκωνες, ἀντὶ μῆνα · κατὰ μῆνα, and ἀνθ' ἡμέρας · δι' ὅλης τῆς ἡμέρας.

9. ἐξ. An extension of the regular use of ἐξ (or ἀπό) with the genitive to denote material and source, is seen in certain expressions of amount or value, e.g., Att. στεφάνωι ἀπὸ χιλίων δραχμῶν 'with a crown worth 1000 drachmas'.—Ion. στεφανῶσαι Μαύσσωλον μὲν ἐκ δαρεικῶν πεντήκοντα, 'Αρτεμισίην δὲ ἐκ τριήκοντα δαρεικῶν 'crown Maussolus with a crown worth fifty darics, Artemisia with one worth thirty.'—Att. κριθῶν...πραθεισῶν ἐκ τριῶν δραχμῶν τὸν μέδιμνον ἕκαστον 'barley purchased at three drachmas a medimnus,' and even more freely Ther. πυρῶν ἐγ μεδίμνου καὶ κριθῶν ἐγ δύο μεδίμνων 'a medimnus of wheat and two of barley.'

10. ὑπέρ 'in behalf of' with accusative instead of genitive, in late Locrian, Delphian, Epidaurian, Arcadian, Rhodian, e.g., Delph. ὑπὲρ τὰν πόλιν. Cf. above, 2 with a.

11. ὑπό instead of usual ἐπί with genitive in expressions of dating occurs with genitive in Elean (no. 66.2), and with accusative in Laconian (no. 71.66).

12. Noteworthy combinations are Thess. ὑππρό 'just before', and Arc. ἐπές from ἐπί and ἐς = ἐξ (cf. ὑπέκ, διέκ, παρέκ), meaning 'for and on occasion of, with reference to.'

Verbs

Augment and Reduplication

137. Most peculiarities are such as are due to divergence in the form of contraction where a consonant has been lost (εἶχον or ἦχον, cf. 25), or in the treatment of consonant groups, as Att. εἴληφα, Phoc. εἰλάφει, from *σέσλᾱφα (76.2), but Ion., Epid., Arc. λελάβηκα after λέλοιπα, etc., with original initial λ, Arg. ϝεϝρεμένα, but Att.-Ion. εἴρηκα after forms like εἴληφα (55a), Cret., El. ἔγραμμαι = γέγραμμαι, like Ion. ἔκτημαι = Att. κέκτημαι, ἔγνωκα in all dialects. Note also Cret. ἤγραμμαι, with which compare ἤθελον, ἠβουλόμην.

Active Personal Endings

138. 1. Second singular. The original primary ending -si (Skt. -si) is preserved in Hom., Syrac. ἐσσί, also in Epid. συντίθησι, and so perhaps regularly in West Greek dialects (inscriptional examples of the second singular are, naturally, very rare), the retention of intervocalic σ being due to the analogy of ἐσσί. But in the East Greek dialects, where 3 sg. τίθητι became τίθησι (61.1), τίθης, etc., with secondary ending, were employed.

Thematic primary -εις (with genuine ει) in nearly all dialects, but Cypr. ἔρπες, etc. (Hesych.), Dor. συρίσδες, etc. (Theocr.).

Also -σθα, starting from οἶσθα, ἦσθα, with the original perfect ending -θα, is widely used in literary Lesbian and Doric, as in Homer (τίθησθα, βάλοισθα, etc.).

a. Occasional examples of -ης (also -ηις) in literary Lesbian and Doric texts, beside the normal -εις, are almost certainly corruptions, due to the grammarians' false extension of η = secondary ει.

2. Third singular. The original primary ending -ti (Skt. -ti) is preserved in West Greek, Boeot. τίθητι, δίδωτι, etc., whence East Greek τίθησι, δίδωσι. See 61.1. Thematic primary -ει (with genuine ει), secondary -ε in all dialects.

a. Herodian quotes as Aeolic τίθη, δίδω, ζεύγνυ, that is, with secondary ending as in ἐτίθη, etc. There is some confirmation of such forms, e.g., δείκνῡ in Hesiod, δάμνᾱ (correction of the impossible δάμνησι) in Alcaeus.

3. First plural. West Greek -μες (cf. Skt. -mas, Lat. -mus from -mos), originally the primary ending,—East Greek -μεν, originally the secondary ending. See 223a.

4. Third plural, primary. West Greek -ντι (Skt. -nti), East Greek -(ν)σι. Thus, in thematic verbs, West Greek φέροντι, Pamph. ἐξάγōδι (= ἐξάγωντι, see 66), Arc. φέρονσι, Lesb. (and Chian) φέροισι, Att.-Ion. φέρουσι. See 61.1, 77.3.

So also in μι-verbs, West Greek ἐντί, φαντί, τίθεντι, δίδοντι, whence Att.-Ion. εἰσί, φᾶσί, Ion. (with the accent of contract forms, see **160**) τιθεῖσι, διδοῦσι. But Att. τιθέᾶσι, διδόᾶσι, etc., represent a later formation, with -αντι (-ᾶσι) added to the final vowel of the stem, as also in Boeot. perf. δεδόανθι. Cf. Boeot. ἔθεαν, etc., below, 5.

In the perfect the earliest type is that in -ᾰτι (-ηti, Skt. -ati in redupl. pres. *dadhati*), whence also -ᾱσι. Thus Phoc. ἱερητεύκατι, Delph. καθεστάκατι, Aetol. γεγόνατι, Rhod. ἀνατεθήκατι, Hom. πεφύκασι, Arc. [Ϝō]φλέᾱσι, ἐσλελοίπασι. But this is commonly replaced by -αντι, as Dor. κεχάναντι (Sophron), Phoc. ἀνατεθέκαντι, Delph. ἐπιτετελέκαντι, Arg. ἐπιμεμηνάκαντι, Rhod. ἀπεστάλκαντι, etc., Att.-Ion. -ᾶσι. Late inscriptions of various dialects have also the secondary -αν, as Cret. ἔσταλκαν.

Boeotian and Thessalian have -νθι, as Boeot. οἴσονθι, ἴωνθι, δώωνθι, ἀποδεδόανθι, etc., Thess. ὑπάρχονθι, κατοικείουνθι (but also -ουντι at Phalanna). Similarly imv. -νθω in Boeot. ἔνθω, δαμιώνθω, etc., and θ in middle endings (**139**.2). Two different explanations have been suggested, (1) that the type started with a *ἐνθί derived from *ἐντί (**163**.2) by transposition of the aspiration, (2) that the θ started in the middle endings under the influence of -μεθα, -σθε.

5. Third plural, secondary. -ν (from -*nt*) in ἔφερον, etc. So also in the μι-forms, as ἔθεν, ἔδον, which are retained in most dialects, as in Homer. Likewise pass. ἐλύθεν, ἐλέγεν (from -ηντ, with regular shortening), but also sometimes -ην (with η from the other persons), as Hom. μιάνθην, Cret., Epir. διελέγην, Corcyr. ἐστεφανώθην, Delph. ἀπελύθην.

But Attic-Ionic has ἔθεσαν, ἔδοσαν, ἐλύθησαν, etc., with -σαν taken over from the σ-aorist, as also ἦσαν, where most dialects have ἦν (**163**.3, 4). Similarly -ν is replaced by -αν (also, mainly after aorist forms like ἔλυσαν or ἤνικαν) in Boeot. ἀνέθεαν, ἀνέθειαν, ἀνέθιαν (**9**.4), παρεῖαν, Locr. ἀνέθεαν, Arc. συνέθεαν, Cypr. κατέθιjαν (**9**.6); and in Thessalian by -εν (an inherited ending seen in Hom. ἦεν, or perhaps from -αν, cf. **7**, **27**), as ἐδούκαεμ (ἔδωκαν), ὀνεθείκαεν (beside ὀνέθεικαν), and, with diphthongal αι from αε, ἐτάξαιν (similarly ἐδώκαιν, probably due to Thessalian influence, in a Delphian inscription), also once even in a thematic form, ἐνεφανίσσοεν = ἐνεφάνιζον.

a. In the κοινή the ending -σαν spread even to thematic forms and to the optative, a nd such forms occur in late inscriptions of various dialects, e.g., Delph. ἐλέγοσαν, ἔχοισαν, etc. Similar forms in LXX and NT.

6. Third dual, secondary. Att.-Ion. -την, elsewhere -τᾱν, e.g., Arc., Boeot., Epid. ἀνεθέταν, El. λεοίταν. Similarly 1 sg. mid. Att.-Ion. -μην, elsewhere -μᾱν.

Middle Personal Endings

139. 1. Third singular. Primary -ται, Boeot. -τη (**26**), Thess. -τει (**27**). Arcadian has -τοι (perhaps also Cyprian, but not quotable), due to the influence of the secondary -το (before its change to -τυ), e.g., γένητοι, δέατοι, βόλετοι. Cf. also 2 sg. κεῖοι = κεῖσαι, and 3 pl. διαδικάσωντοι.

Secondary -το, Arc.-Cypr. -τυ.

2. Third plural. Usually -νται, -ντο (Arc. -ντυ). But also -αται, -ατο, mostly in the perfect and pluperfect after a consonant (e.g., γεγράφαται), but also after a vowel in Boeotian (-αθη, see below); and so regularly in Ionic in the perfect (e.g., Hom. βεβλήαται, later εἰρέαται, contracted εἰρῆται), pluperfect, and optative, and even in unthematic presents and imperfects, e.g., τιθέαται and also δυνέαται, κιρνέαται, to δύνημι, κίρνημι (with suffix νᾱ, weak να), after the analogy of τιθέαται to τίθημι. Arg. γεγράβανται has -ανται for -αται like -αντι for -ατι (**138.**4).

Boeotian and Thessalian have θ in these, as in the active, endings. Boeot. ἀδικίωνθη (-νται), ἐστροτεύαθη, μεμισθώαθη (-αται), ἐποιείσανθο, ἀπεγράψανθο, etc. Thess. ἔλκονθαι, ἐπαγγέλουνθαι (subj.), ἐγένονθο, εἴλονθο, also ἐφάγρενθειν = ἐφαιροῦνται, βέλλουνθειν = βούλωνται, with ει from αι (**27**) and an added ν (perhaps the active secondary ending; cf. the double pluralization in the imv. -ντων).

Imperative Active and Middle

140. In the third plural the dialects exhibit the following types.
1. The same form as the third singular. Rare, and only in the

middle. Corcyr. κρινέσθω, ἐκδανειζέσθω, Calymn. ἐπισαμαινέσθω, Coan αἱρείσθω, Thas. θέσθω, Rhod. ἐπιμελέσθω.

2. *a.* -των, formed from the third singular by the addition of the secondary ending -ν. ἔστων, as in Homer, in Ionic only. A corresponding thematic φερέτων is unknown.

b. -σθων, similarly formed from the third singular. φερέσθων, τιθέσθων, etc., the usual form in most dialects.

3. *a.* -ντω, formed after the analogy of 3 pl. indic. -ντι. φερόντω, τιθέντω, etc., in Arcadian, Boeotian (-νθω, 139.2), Locrian, and the Doric dialects except Cretan, Theran, Cyrenaean. Later Doric inscriptions often show the Att. -ντων beside -ντω. Conversely the later Delphian inscriptions often have the general Doric -ντω beside -ντων, which is the form of the earliest Delphian (likewise later Cret. -ντω vs. earlier -ντων.)

b. -νσθω, formed to act. -ντω and with the treatment of secondary νσ (77.2). Arg. ποιγραψάνσθō, χρόνσθō, Corcyr. ἐκλογιζούσθω, and so to be read with long vowel Epid. φερόσθō, Lac. ἀνελόσθō, Heracl. ἐπελάσθω (159) (-ᾱ-όνσθω). Similarly -ōσθōν in type 4*b.*

4. *a.* -ντων, with double pluralization, a combination of types 2 and 3. φερόντων, τιθέντων, as in Homer, in Attic-Ionic, Delphian, Cretan, Theran, Cyrenaean.

b. -(ν)σθων, formed to act. -ντων. Early Att. ἐπιμελόσθōν, χρόσθōν, etc., Locr. δαμευόσθōν, El. τιμόστōν.

c. The coexistence of act. -ντω, but mid. -σθων (where the pluralizing final ν was more essential) is found in several dialects (Arc., Locr., Aetol., Meg., Coan, Rhod.).

5. -ντον, -σθον. This is the regular type in Lesbian, e.g., φέροντον, κάλεντον, ἐπιμέλεσθον, and Pamphylian (e.g., ὄδυ = ὄντον), and also appears, probably through Pamphylian influence, in an inscription of Phaselis which is otherwise in the Rhodian dialect, and in a Rhodian decree at Seleucia in Cilicia.

6. -τωσαν, -σθωσαν, with -ν replaced by -σαν (cf. 138.5). Att. ἔστωσαν, φερέτωσαν (more rarely φερόντωσαν), ἐπιμελέσθωσαν, etc., after abuot 300 B.C., hence in later inscriptions of various dialects.

Future and Aorist

141. "Doric future" in -σεω. Except for a few middle forms
in Attic-Ionic (Hom. ἐσσεῖται, Att. πλευσοῦμαι, etc.), this type
is confined to the West Greek dialects (examples in most of the
Doric dialects and in Delphian; in Locrian and Elean no futures
occur). Thus, from the very numerous examples, Delph. ταγευσέω,
κλεψέω, Cret. σπευσίω (ι from ε, **9**), πραξίομεν, βοαθησίοντι, τεισῆται,
πραξῆται, Epid. βλαψεῖσθαι, Coan, Cnid. ποιησεῖται, Rhod. ἀπο-
δωσεῦντι, Cyren. δησῆται, παισεῖται, ἐκτιμασέντι (**42**.5*e*). Ther.
θησέοντι, πραξοῦντι (with Att. ου, as often in the Doric κοινή, see
278), Arg. ἐμφανιξόντας (cf. **42**.5*d*).

a. The 3 sg. forms in -σει, though in themselves ambiguous, are rightly
assumed to belong here and accented -σεῖ in dialects which show unam-
biguous forms of this type.

b. Heraclean shows the -σέω type unmistakably in ἐργαξῆται, καρπευσῆται, ἐσσῆται, etc., and so presumably the 3 sg. act. κοψεῖ, etc., is to be
so accented. But the 3 pl. forms are act. κοψοντι, ποισοντι, etc., mid.
ἐργαξονται, ἐσσονται, etc. According to the current view, these belong
to the -σω future and are accented κόψοντι, ἔσσονται, etc. But co-existence
of the two types (barring the frequent intrusion of κοινή forms) with
such a precise distribution is unknown elsewhere, and is difficult to credit.
It now seems preferable to revert to the older view (Ahrens, Meister,
IG XIV. 645) and assume that, despite the ιο for εο after liquids (ἀναγγελίοντι, etc.), we have here the same change of εο to ο before ντ that was
formerly known only in parts of Crete but is now so well attested by Arg.
κοινανόντι, etc., including the fut. pple. ἐμφανιξόντας (**42**.5*d*).

142. ξ in the future and aorist of verbs in -ζω. The extension
of ξ, which is regular in the case of guttural stems, to other verbs
in -ζω, which regularly have σσ, σ (δικάσω, ἐδίκασα), is seen in some
isolated examples even in Homer (πολεμίξομεν, as, conversely,
ἥρπασε beside ἥρπαξε) and Hesiod (φημίξωσι). But as a general
phenomenon it is characteristic of the West Greek dialects,
together with Thessalian and (in part) Boeotian, and Arcado-
Cyprian. Thus, from the countless examples, Cret. δικάκσει,
Rhod. διωρίξαντο, Coan ἐργάξασθαι, Ther. δείπνιξεν, Meg. ἐτερμό-
νιξαν, Corcyr. ἀπολογίξασθαι, Heracl. ἐτέρμαξαν (ξ in forms of
12 verbs, but also κατεσώισαμες, probably influenced by ἔσωσα
from σώω), El. ποταρμόξαιτο, (Locr. ψάφιξξις, see below, *a*),

116   THE GREEK DIALECTS   [144

Delph. ἀγωνίξατο, Thess. ψαφίξασθειν, ἐργάξατο, Arc. παρετάξωνσι, ποινίξασθαι, Cypr. ἐξορύξε.

But in Argolic the ξ formation is avoided when a guttural preceded, e.g., Arg. ἐδίκασσαν, ἐργάσσαντο, Epid. ἐργάσασθαι, ἀνσχίσσαι, beside ἀγωνίξασθαι, προσεφάνιξε, ἐμφανιξόντας. Similarly Arc. ἐδικάσαμεν, δικάσασθαι, ἀναγκάσαι (but also ὤρισαν) beside παρετάξωνσι, etc. Boeotian has, from different localities, both ξ and ττ (= Att. σ, 82), e.g., ἐκομιξάμεθα, ἐπεσκεύαξε, ἐμέριξε, ἰαρειάξασα, and κομιττάμενοι, κατασκευάττη, ἐψαφίττατο, ἀπολογίττατη, καταδουλίττατη.

a. A similar extension of guttural stems is sometimes seen in other forms, e.g., Heracl. ποτικλαίγω = προσκλείω, Argol., Mess. κλάιξ (as in Theocr.), κλαικτός, Lac. κέλεξ = κέλης, Dor. ὄρνιξ, gen. ὄρνιχος (lit. Dor., Coan, Cyren.) = ὄρνις, ὄρνιθος, Cret. ψάφιγμα (also ψάφιμμα) = ψήφισμα, Lesb. ψάφιγγι = ψηφῖδι, and especially the frequent abstracts in -ξις = -σις, as Aetol. ψάφιξις, Locr. ψάφιξξις (89.1), Corcyr. χείριξις, Cret. ἀπολάγαξις, χρημάτιξις.

143. σσ in the future and aorist of verb stems ending in a short vowel. The Homeric extension of σσ from ἐτέλεσ-σα to ἐκάλε-σσα is an Aeolic characteristic. Lesb. [καλε]σσάτωσαν, ὁμόσσαντες, Boeot. σουνκαλέσσαντες. Other dialects may have σσ from stems ending in σ or a dental, as ἐτέλεσσα or ἐδίκασσα (Boeot. ττ), ἐδασσάμην (Cret. ττ), later with one σ (82, 83), but always ἐκάλεσα, ὤμοσα.

144. Aorist in -α. εἶπα and ἤνεγκα, ἤνεικα, or ἤνικα in various dialects. Arc. pple. ἀπυδόας=ἀποδούς, Lesb. ἔχευα, elsewhere ἔχεα (e.g., Ion. συγχέαι, no. 2). In late times this type is extended to many other verbs, e.g., ἦλθα, γενάμενος.

a. ἤνεικα or ἤνικα, not ἤνεγκα, is the form of most dialects except Attic, e.g., Ion. ἤνεικα (Hom., Hdt.), ἐνεικάντων (Chios), also ἐξενιχθῆι (Ceos); Lesb., Delph., Argol., Calymn. ἤνικα, Boeot. ἐνενιχθείει (ι probably original, not = ει) and 3 pl. εἴνιξαν, the latter a blend with the σ-aorist.
b. Aorist in -ᾱ (beside the familiar ἔδρᾱν, etc.). Epid. ἐξερρύᾱ, Lac. ἀπεσσούᾱ, 3 sg. subj. Calymn. ἐγρυᾶι, Cyren. μιᾶι, ἴσᾱι.
c. Aorist of ἵζω. Corcyr. ἵσατο, Arg. ἴσσατο, Cyren. ἴσσαντα, ἰσσάμενος vs. Hom. καθεῖσα, ἐφέσσαι, Arg. ἥσσαντο, ἐσσάμενος, from ἕζω.
d. σ-aorist forms with thematic vowel instead of the usual α by extension. Like Hom. ἐβήσετο, etc., are Pamph. ἐβōλάσετυ and 3 pl. imv. κατε-Ϝερξόδυ.

145. Future passive with active endings. Rhod. ἐπιμεληθη-σεῦντι, ἀποσταλησεῖ, σταθησεῖ, Ther. συναχθησοῦντι, Cret., Carpath. ἀναγραφησ[εῖ], Astyp. ἐπιμεληθησεῖ, and φανησεῖν, δειχθη-σοῦντι in Archimedes. Although the inscriptional examples are, as yet, confined to the Doric islands, it is not improbable that this was a general Doric or West Greek characteristic. Forms with middle endings, like Ther. ἀνατεθησεῦνται, are from the κοινή with local coloring.

Perfect

146. 1. κ-perfect. This is usual for vowel stems in all dialects. But there are some few forms without κ, outside the indicative singular, like Hom. βεβάασι beside βέβηκας, κεκμηώς beside κέκμη-κας, etc., e.g., Boeot. ἀποδεδόανθι, καταβεβάων, δεδώωση = δεδω-κυῖαι, ϜεϜυκονομειόντων = ῳκονομηκότων, πεπιτευόντεσσι, πεποι-όντεισσι, καταβεβλειώσας, ἀπειλθείοντες, Arc. [Ϝō]φλέασι (but pple. Ϝōφλēκόσι).

The gradual extension of the κ-type to other than original vowel stems is by no means confined to Attic (cf., e.g., Arc. ἐφθορκώς; Att. ἔφθαρκα but also ἔφθορα), and some verbs which usually have the strong perfect show dialect forms with a vowel stem and κ. So ἀνδάνω, λαμβάνω, with usual ἔᾱδα, εἴληφα (εἴλᾱφα), but Locr. ϜεϜαδēκότα, Ion. ἄδηκε (Hippon.), Arc., Ion., Epid. λελάβηκα, from the vowel stem which is present in many verbs in -άνω (cf. τετύχηκα, μεμάθηκα, etc.). Usual ἐλήλυθα, but ἤλθηκα in Boeot. διεσσείθεικε (pple. ἀπειλθείοντες without κ, see above), Arc. κατηνθηκότι. Similarly from a secondary ᾱ-stem, Lesb. ὑπαδεδρόμᾱκε (Sappho), Arg. ἐπιμεμηνάκαντι (η from aor.; cf. μεμενᾱκός Archim., Att. μεμένηκα). For secondary forms in -ωκα, see **162**.3.

2. Aspirated perfect. This is mainly an Attic-Ionic development. But there are some examples of aspirated forms of the κ-perfect, which even in Attic are only late (εἴρηχα, etc., in papyri), Syrac. ἐκρατερίχημες (Sophron), Arg. δέδωχε, Arc. ἱερίτευχε.

3. Dialectal variations in the grade of the root (**49**) are not infrequent, as Cret. ἀμπεληλεύθεν, Cyren. κατεληλευθυῖα (vs.

Hom. εἰλήλουθα, εἰληλουθώς), Heracl. ἐρρηγεῖα = Att. ἐρρωγυῖα,
Dor. ἔωκα = Att. εἶκα from ἵημι (cf. ἔρρωγα from ῥήγνυμι), also
in the middle, Heracl. ἀνhεῶσθαι, Arc. ἀφεώσθω (so ἀνέωνται
Hdt., ἀφέωνται NT).

4. For the reduplication, see **137**; for the 3 pl. ending, see
138.4.

5. Heracl. γεγράψαται (no. 79.121) and subj. μεμισθωσῶνται
(no. 79.106) have generally been taken as perfect forms, with
difficult explanation. But they are rather future perfect forms,
suitable to the context and much easier to explain. γεγράψαται
has simply taken over the ending of the perfect γεγράφαται.
μεμισθωσῶνται is precisely the form to be expected as subj. of
3 pl. indic. fut. perf. μεμισθωσόνται (on the accent, which would
be the same as in the future, see **141**b). To be sure, our grammars
give an optative but no subjunctive for the future perfect, but
both were given in the old τύπτω paradigm (cf. Uhlig,
Dionysius Thrax, p. 125 ff., where the 3 pl. mid. fut. perf. subj.
τετύψωνται is (apart our assumption of -σέω type and consequent
accentuation) just what we assume for μεμισθωσῶνται.

147. Thematic forms in the perfect. Aside from the subjunctive, optative, and imperative, which regularly have thematic
inflection, we find:

1. Indicative. Forms inflected like presents are often employed
by the Sicilian Doric writers, e.g., Theocr. δεδοίκω, πεπόνθεις,
πεφύκει, Epich. γεγάθει, Archim. τετμάκει, and occur in some
inscriptions of Rhodes, Cnidus, and Carpathus, e.g., τετιμάκει,
γεγόνει, ἑστάκει, and occasionally elsewhere, as Phoc. εἰλάφει.

2. Infinitive. Forms in -ειν (-εν, -ην) instead of -εναι (-εμεν, etc.)
are found in Lesbian and in some West Greek dialects, e.g., Lesb.
τεθνάκην, τεθεωρήκην, Delph. ἀποτετείχεν, Cret. ἀμπεληλεύθεν,
Calymn., Nisyr. δεδώκεν, Rhod. γεγόνειν, Epid. λελαβήκειν.
So Pindar κεχλάδειν, Theocr. δεδύκειν.

Cf. also Heracl. πεφυτευκῆμεν, etc., from -ε-εμεν instead of
simply -εμεν.

3. Participle. The thematic inflection is regular in the Aeolic
dialects, e.g., Lesb. κατεληλύθοντος, κατεστακόντων, Thess.
πεφειράκοντες, ἐπεστάκοντα, Boeot. ϜεϜυκονομειόντων, δεδώωση
(**146**.1). Cf. Hom. κεκλήγοντες.

a. There are some feminine forms in -ουσα in later Delphian (e.g., δεδωκούσας), and elsewhere, but these represent a more restricted phenomenon, quite independent of the preceding. Cf. also Ion. ἑστεῶσα, Att. ἑστῶσα.

148. The participle in its regular (unthematic) form usually has the feminine in -υῖα. But forms in -εῖα are found in late Attic and elsewhere, e.g., Heracl. ἐρρηγεῖα, Ther. ἑστακεῖα.

Subjunctive

149. The subjunctive of thematic forms. The mood sign is η/ω, to which the personal endings were added directly. So originally the second and third singular in -ης, -η, but replaced in the majority of dialects by -ηις, -ηι on the analogy of the indicative -εις, -ει. Thus 3 sg. -ηι from the earliest times in Attic-Ionic, Phocian (φάρει, ἄγηι, etc.), Locrian (ἀποθάνει, etc.), Cretan (πάθηι, φέρηι, etc.) and so generally in the Doric dialects (or later -ει).

But the earlier type with 3 sg. -η prevails in Arcadian (Cyprian examples lacking) and is also attested elsewhere. Thus Arc. λέγε̄, νέμε̄, ἔχη, etc. (so uniformly), Thess. θέλε̄, Boeot. πίε̄ (and so later Thess., Boeot. -ει probably = η, **16**, though could also = ηι), El. ἐκπέμπᾱ (ᾱ = η, **15**), Lac. ζόε̄ (no. 70, due to the Arcadian engraver? cf. ἀποθάνει in the same inscription and usual Lac. -ηι). Other scattered examples of -η, beside usual -ηι or -ει, may be merely graphic variants of the latter and are dubious representatives of the early type. Thus Lesb. ἐμμένη (no. 26, but -ηι in the earlier no. 25), Heracl. ἀμμισθωθῆ (once beside -ηι or usual -ει), Mess. ἐξάγη (beside χρήζηι in the same inscription), Corcyr. λίπη, Epid. πέτη, Coan λάθη, and many others.

Arc. 1 sg. ἀψευδήων (no. 21) is unique and variously explained. Probably -ω with addition of secondary ending, like Hom. subj. ἐθέλωμι, etc., with addition of the primary ending.

150. The subjunctive of the σ-aorist. As in the case of other unthematic formations (cf. Hom. ἴομεν to indic. ἴμεν), this was originally a short-vowel subjunctive in ε/ο, and only later came to follow the more common long-vowel type in η/ω. Besides Hom. βήσομεν (cf. βάσομεν Pindar), etc., the old short-vowel forms are widely attested for the σ-aorist and occur also in the α-aorist.

East Ion. ποιήσει, κατάξει, ἐκκόψει (no. 3, Teos), ἀποκρύψει, ἐξομόσει, ἐπάρει, κατείπει, κατακτείνōσιν (that is, -ουσιν, not -ωσιν), Chian πρήξοισιν (no. 4; with Lesb. οισ from ονσ, 77.3). Lesb. ἀποτείσει, κωλύσει, ἀποπεράσσει, χαλάσσομεν, and (with extension to the thematic aorist) τέκοισι. Cret. δείκσει, ἀδικήσει, etc. (hence the forms of the Law-Code are to be transcribed -ει, not -ēι), ἐκσαννήσεται, ὁμόσοντι, etc., Coan ὑποκύψει, Astyp. δόξει. Cyren. ἄρξεται, καταγγήλει, ἐνίκει.

a. Heracl. ἀρτύσει, πράξει, etc., do not belong here, but have -ει from -ηι as in the thematic forms ἀποθάνει, λάβει (with pres. subj. φέρει, νέμει, etc.). The long-vowel type is shown clearly in 3 pl. ἀρτύσωντι, etc.

b. The early Locr. forms ἀποτείσΕι, διαφθείσΕι, φυτεύσΕται, though ambiguous, may well belong here, being much earlier than the Delph. forms, which show only the long-vowel type, ἀποτείσηι, κωλύσωντι, etc.

c. A still earlier type, with the ending added directly to the short vowel without the secondary ι of the usual forms (and so agreeing with the type Skt. -sas, -sat) is seen in Cyren. 2 sg. ποιῆσες and [ἐ]ρείσες (nos. 115.9, 119). In view of this positive evidence we should probably transcribe Aegin. στασΕς (IG IV.177) as στάσες (for Argol. -ης would be anomalous). But Cypr. Ϝείσες (Schwyzer 685), is more probable than Ϝεῖσες (cf. meter, and Arc. -στάση, etc.). There is no similar evidence of a corresponding 3 sg. -σε (parallel to Skt. -sat). It is only a possibility that the Cypr. forms which are usually transcribed λύσē, ἐξορύξē, and the early Arc. forms with E, should be read with ε, in spite of the later Arc. -στάσης, -βλάψης, etc.

151. The subjunctive of unthematic vowel stems. There are two distinct types.

1. The endings are added directly to the long vowel of the stem. This type is found mostly in those forms of which the corresponding indicative has the short vowel. So especially in the middle, e.g., Cret. δύναμαι, νύναται, νύνανται, Lesb., Cyren. δύνανται beside indic. δύναμαι, Arc. ἐπισυνίστάται beside indic. ἵστάται, δέατοι (cf. Hon. δέᾱτο). But also, when the indicative also has a long vowel, Cret. πέπᾱται, ἐστετέκνōται, Ther. πέπρᾱται. Further, in the active, Mess. τίθηντι beside indic. τίθεντι (hence also, beside ἐντί, Mess. ἦνται = ὦσι, Delph. ἦται = ᾖ), γράφηντι beside indic. ἔγραφεν, Cret. ἵσαντι, Cyren. ἵσᾱι, also (beside indic. ᾱ) Cyren. μιᾶι, Calymn. ἐγρυᾶι (cf. 144b).

After the relation of ἵστᾱται to ἵστᾶται there arose also an aor.

subj. σᾶ beside indic. σᾰ, e.g., Cret. παρθύσᾱται, Arc. βωλεύσᾱνται, likewise in Elean, with loss of σ (59.3), φυγαδεύᾱντι (no. 65), ποιήᾱται (no. 66).

2. The usual type is that in which the long vowel of the stem was followed by the short vowel subjunctive sign ε/ο, this being generally replaced by the more usual η/ω (cf. 150). Further change is due to the shortening, in the majority of dialects, of the long stem vowel before the following vowel (43). Hom. θήομεν (θείομεν), θήης, δώομεν, δώῃ, Boeot. καθιστάει, ἀποδώει, Delph. δώῃ, ἀντιπριάηται, Heracl. φᾶντι (from *φᾱωντι), Thess. δυνᾱ̆εται, but with shortening Ion. θέωμεν, Att. θῶμεν, Cret. ἐνθίωμεν (ι from ε), etc. Similarly in the aorist passive, Hom. δαμήῃς, μιγήῃς, Boeot. κουρωθείει, ἐπιμελειθείει, κατασκευασθείει, ἐνενιχθείει, Arc. κακριθέ̄ε, but with shortening Ion. λυθέωμεν, Att. λυθῶμεν, Cret. πειθθίωντι (cf. ἐνθίωμεν), Heracl. ἐγϜηληθίωντι, Rhod. ἐργασθέωντι, etc.

3. Subjunctive of εἰμι. Att.-Ion. ἴω, etc., with weak grade of the root. But Cret. εἴε̄ι, ἐνσ-είε̄ι, Cyren. ἐπείηι, Syrac. εἴω (Sophron).

Optative

152. 1. Arc. 1 sg. ἐξελαύνοια represents a form long since assumed by comparative grammar (*-oi-m̥, whence -οια with ι retained under the influence of -οις, etc.), but generally replaced by -οιμι.

2. In the third plural *-οιαν (cf. 1) was replaced by -οιεν (after εἶεν, etc.), for which sometimes late -οιν, e.g., Delphian θέλοιν.

3. Unthematic type in contract verbs. See **157b**.

4. σ-aorist. Most dialects show the secondary type with αι (α spread from the indicative). But the old unthematic mood sign seen in present εἴην, etc., appears in Cret. 3 sg. κοσμησίε̄, δικακσίε̄, 3 pl. Ϝέρκσιεν. The type -ειας, -ειε (perhaps starting in a 1 sg. -εια parallel to Arc. ἐξελαύνοια), more common than the αι-forms in Homer and early Attic writers, is also attested in Tean ἀ[ποκ]τένει[ε] (no. 3.10, probable reading), Lesb. [δ]ιαδέξειε (IG XII.ii.527.57), El. κατιαραύσειε, ἀδεαλτώhαιε. Arc. διακωλύσει (no. 19.6/7) and ὑνιερόσει (no. 16) would be variants of this type.

Infinitive

153. The infinitive of thematic forms.

1. -ειν or -ην, according as the dialect has ει or η from ε + ε
(25). So Att.-Ion., Thess. (Thessaliotis), Locr., Corinth., Meg.,
Rhod. -ειν, but Lesb., El., Lac. -ην.

2. -εν. So in Arcadian (but -ην at Lycosura, Orchomenos)
Cyprian (or -εν?), Delphian, and many of the Doric dialects
(Heracl., Argol., Cret., Ther., Cyren., Coan, etc.), also once in
a late East Locr. inscription (IG IX.i.267).

3. Some of these dialects have -εν even from verbs in -εω, e.g.,
Ther. διοικέν, Cyren. πλέν, εὐτυχέν (cf. also mid. δωρέσθαι, ὠνέσθαι),
Coan δειπνέν, Calymn. μαρτυρέν, Arg. πωλέν, Delph. ψαφοφορέν,
ἐνοικέν (but usually -εῖν).

154. The infinitive of unthematic forms.

1. -ναι. So in Attic-Ionic and Arcado-Cyprian, e.g., Att.-Ion.
εἶναι, δοῦναι, Cypr. δοϝέναι (-ϝεναι, like -μεναι; or δοϝ-έναι going
with δυϝάνω, 162.5?), κυμερῆναι, Arc. ἦναι.

2. -μεναι. So in Lesbian, as in Homer, e.g., ἔμμεναι, θέμεναι,
δόμεναι. But see 155.2, 3.

3. -μεν. εἶμεν, etc., in Thessalian, Boeotian, and most of the
West Greek dialects.

4. -μην. Cret. ἤμην, etc.

5. -μειν. εἴμειν, etc. in Rhodes and vicinity (Carpathus, Telos)
and the Rhodian colonies (Phaselis in Pamphylia; Gela and
Agrigentum in Sicily; also at Tauromenium, Rhegium, Croton,
and in Epicharmus).

a. Cret. -μην, Rhod. -μειν are probably formed from -μεν with the vowel
influenced by the thematic type, Cret. *-ην (before it was replaced by -εν),
Rhod. -ειν.

155. Interchange of thematic and unthematic types of infinitive.

1. -μεν is extended to thematic forms in Boeotian and Thessalian (Pelasgiotis), as sometimes in Homer (cf. εἰπέμεν, and εἰπέ-
μεναι), e.g., Boeot. φερέμεν, Thess. ὑπαρχέμεν. Cf. also Cret.
προϝειπέμεν in an early inscription of Lyttus.

2. The aorist passive infinitive, which is regularly unthematic
(Att. γραφῆναι, Dor. γραφῆμεν), follows the thematic type in

Lesbian, e.g., ἐπιμελήθην, ὀντέθην, etc. This belongs with the following.

3. In Lesbian the present infinitive of unthematic vowel stems, as well as of the contract verbs, which otherwise follow the unthematic type (**157**), ends in -ν, not -μεναι, e.g., δίδων, κέρνᾱν, ὄμνῡν, κάλην, στεφάνων, κατείρων (καθιεροῦν). Once also aor. infin. πρόστᾱν (but usually -μεναι, as θέμεναι, δόμεναι).

4. For thematic forms of the perfect infinitive in various dialects see **147**.2.

5. For Euboean τιθεῖν, etc., and even εἶν beside εἶναι, see **160**.

156. The infinitives in -σαι and -σθαι. Thessalian (Larissa) has ὀνγράψειν, δεδόσθειν, ἔσσεσθειν, πεπεῖστειν, ἐλέστειν, etc., with -ει from -αι (**27**), and ν added after the analogy of other infinitives. Boeot. -σθη, -στη with η from αι (**26**), and στ = σθ (**85**.1).

Unthematic Inflection of Contract Verbs

157. The μι-inflection of contract verbs, sometimes known as the Aeolic inflection, is characteristic of Lesbian, Thessalian, and Arcado-Cyprian, e.g., Lesb. κάλημμι, φίλημμι, κάλεντον, κατάγρεντον, εὐεργετέντεσσι, [ὀ]μονόεντες, προσμέτρεις, στοίχεις (**78**), Thess. ἐφάνγρενθειν = ἐφαιροῦνται, εὐεργετές (**78**), στραταγέν-τος, Arc. ποίενσι, ποέντω, ἀδικέντα, κυένσαν, ἱεροθυτές (**78**), ζαμιόντω, καταφρονῆναι, Cypr. κυμερῆναι. μι-forms are also quoted as Boeotian by the grammarians, but the inscriptions show only the usual type (στραταγίοντος, etc.).

a. The stem ends in a long vowel, which is regularly shortened before ντ (though also, with analogical η, Lesb. κατοικήντων in contrast to usual εὐεργετέντεσσι, etc., and προνόηνται, διασάφηνται, δίννηντες, like Att. δίζην-ται, in contrast to Thess. ἐφάνγρενθειν), but is otherwise retained through-out, e.g., Lesb. αἴτηται, κάλησθαι, ἐπιμελήσθω, ζαμιώσθω, ποιήμενος, προ-αγρημμένω, Thess. ἀπελευθερούσθειν, διεσαφείμενος, Arc. ἀδικήμενος, ζα-μιώσθω. This type, then, follows the analogy of that seen in ἔβλην, βλῆτο, βλήμενος, δίζημαι, etc., rather than that of τίθημι, τίθεμεν, τιθέμενος, with vowel-gradation. But even the latter sometimes shows an extension of the long vowel from the singular active, e.g., Lesb. [προστί]θησ[θον], δίδωσθαι, like Hom. τιθήμεναι, τιθήμενος.

b. But also thematic forms. Thess. ἐρουτᾶι, ηὐλόρεοντος (no. 35), Lesb. ποτέονται, ὀγκαλέοντες, 2 sg. ὄπταις, χαύνοις, 3 sg. ἄγρει, τίμαι, βόαι (also γέλαι, νίκαι gram.).

c. The more limited extension of the μι-inflection to the optative of contract verbs, as in Att. φιλοίην, μισθοίην, etc., is occasionally found elsewhere. Ion. ἀνωθεοίη beside ποιοῖ, El. συλαίε̄, δαμοσιοία (= -οίη) beside δοκέοι, ποιέοι, ἐνπο̄ι, Arg. οἰκείη. Cf. also the infinitives El. δαμοσιῶμεν, Cret. δαμιόμε̄ν.

Middle Participle in -ειμενος

158. The middle participle in -ειμενος (or -ημενος) from verbs in -εω, as if from -ε-εμενος instead of -ε-ομενος, is characteristic of the Northwest Greek dialects and Boeotian, e.g., Locr. ἐνκαλείμενος, Delph. καλείμενος, ποιείμενος, χρείμενος, etc., Boeot. δείμενος (and so under Boeotian influence ἀφικνε̄μένων at Oropus), El. καδαλέμενος. But also Cret. χρήμενος, Cyren. χρείμενος (no 115.8; or here the Delph. form ͻ). This is due to the analogy of forms which regularly had ει (or η) from ε-ε, as the infinitive καλεῖσθαι. Cf. Phoc. ποιεῖνται = ποιοῦνται, formed after ποιεῖσθε, Delph. συντελείντω.

a. Lesb. καλήμενος, Arc. ἀδικήμενος, Thess. διεσαφείμενος probably do not belong here, but among the other μι-forms of these dialects. See **157a**.

Type -ήω, -ώω, also -ᾱ́ω

159. Forms in -ηω, -ωω, with the long-vowel stem of the other tenses extended to the present, are found in various dialects. Lesb. ἀδικήει, ποθήω, Arc. ἀψευδήων, Thess. κατοικείουνθι (3 pl. subj.), Delph. στεφανωέτω, δουλώηι, ποιήουσα, Phoc. κλαρώειν, Boeot. δαμιωέμεν, δαμιώοντες, στεφανωέμεν (only in late inscriptions, and perhaps due to Aetolian influence).

A parallel type in -ᾱω is to be recognized in certain forms with ᾱ from ᾱο or ᾱε (vs. Dor. ω or η from the -αω type). Syrac. ὀπτᾱντες (Epich.), ἐπεγγυᾱμενοι (Sophron), γελᾱντι, παρελᾱντα (Theocr.), and so to be read with ᾱ Epid. διεγέλᾱ, καταγελᾱμενος, and (ἐλᾱω vs. Hom. ἐλάω = ἐλαύνω) Coan ἐλᾱντι, ἐλᾱντω, Arg. ποτελᾱτο̄, Locr. ἀπελᾱο̄νται, Heracl. ἐπελᾱσθω. Here also τιμᾱντι (dat. sg. pple.) in an inscription of Dodona, and probably Thess. ἐρουτᾱι, Lesb. τίμαι, βόαι.

a. Further probable, though less certain, examples of the -ωω type are Coan καρπῶντι, ἱερώσθω, Calymn. ἐξορκώντω, ἀξιῶι, Astyp. στεφανῶι, στεφανῶν (στεφανῶι also at Gela and Thera), since in these dialects the contraction of ο + ο or ε usually appears as ου (cf., e.g., Coan ἀξιοῦντι, ζαμιούντω). Heracl. πριῶι (subj.) may belong here, but there is nothing against its derivation from -οει or -οηι (cf. ω from ο + ε in λωτήριον, **44**.4). The forms attributed above to γελάω, ἐλάω are taken by some as formed directly from unthematic stems γελα-, ἐλα-, in that case to be read with short α.

Transfer of μι-Verbs to the Type of Contract Verbs

160. The transfer of certain forms of μι-verbs to the inflection of contract verbs is found in various dialects, as Att. ἐτίθει, ἐδίδου, Delph. ἀποκαθιστάοντες, διδέουσα, but is most widespread in Ionic. With τιθεῖ, etc. in Homer and Herodotus, compare διδοῖ (Miletus) and the Euboean infinitives τιθεῖν, διδοῦν, καθιστᾶν, and even εἶν beside εἶναι. εἶν is also Chian. Cyren. καττιθέν, διδών, beside θέμεν, δόμεν.

Some Other Interchanges in the Present System

161. 1. Verbs in -ευω form their present in -ειω in Elean, as φυγαδείην = φυγαδεύειν, beside aor. φυγαδεύαντι, also (with α after ρ, **12**α) κατιαραίων = καθιερεύων, beside aor. κατιαραύσειε, and λατραι[όμενον], λατρειόμενον = λατρευόμενον. So also μαστείει = μαστεύει, in an inscription of Dodona. This represents the normal phonetic development from -εϝιω, the usual -ευω being due to the influence of the other tenses.

2. Verbs in -αω show forms in -εω in various dialects, but, with few exceptions, only where the ε is followed by an ο-vowel, e.g., aside from literary examples (as Hom. μενοίνεον, Alcm. ὀρέων, Theocr. ὀρεῦσα), Delph. συλέοι, συλέοντες (but συλῆν, συλήτω), ἐπιτιμέοντες, θωεόντων (Att. θῶᾶν, Locr. θοιέστō), Aetol. νικεόντοις, Rhod. τιμοῦντες and also τιμεῖν (Agrig.), Boeot. τιμίωσα, El. ἐνεβέοι, Cret. (with ι from ε, **9**.7) ἐβίōν, ἐπαριόμενον, μοικίōν (μοιχάω). Cyren. παρβεῶντας, ἐπαρεώμενοι (cf. **42**.5 b), σιγέν. According to many, this rests upon an actual phonetic change of αο to εο, the αο (ω) in Attic and elsewhere being a restoration due to leveling with the αε forms. But we may have to do simply with a trasfer to the -εω type, which was mainly favored where it offered uncontracted forms (in most dialects εο was uncontracted until late, but εε contracted; in all forms like Rhod. τιμοῦντες the ου is an Attic substitution for εο).

a. Conversely -αω = usual -εω. πονάω in Sappho, Pind., Theocr., πτοάω in Sappho, etc., φωνάω in Pind. Thess. δούρραντα from *δωράω =

δωρέω. Pamph. 3 sg. aor. ἐβōλάσετυ, from βōλάομαι, denominative of βωλά, but pres. pple. βōλέμενυς, like Cret. χρήμενος (158).

3. Spread of -οω type, especially in non-present forms. Boeot. ἐπίθωσε = ἔπεισε (Boeot. pres. not quotable; πίθω = πείθω, or πιθόω?), Heracl. 3 sg. subj. πριῶι, fut. πριωσεῖ (cf. πεπριωμένος Hippoc., πρίωμα Hesych.) vs. usual πρίω, El. τετίμōνται, τιμόστōν, Att. ἠτίμωσα, Ion. δοκιμῶσαι, Lesb. δοκίμωμι, δοκίμοι (= usual δοκιμάζω), Meg., Cret. ἐπεσκεύωσαν, Delph. κατεσκεύωται, Ther. κατεσκεύωκε, etc. (such forms, as if from σκευόω =σκευάζω, are widespread), Cyren. ἐφορευωκότων, ἱαριτευωκότων, from usual -ευω presents.

4. -ίζω = -οω, especially in West Greek. Boeot., Phoc. δουλίζω (Delph. δουλόω intrans. = Att. δουλεύω), Delph., Thess. ἀπελευθερίζω, Delph., Rhod., Mess., Cret. ὁρκίζω (but also Ionic and Attic sometimes), Dor. στεφανίζω (ἐστεφάνιξα Ar.). Cf. also -ίζω = usual -εύω in late Mess. γραμματίζω, Boeot. γραμματίδδω beside Ach., Boeot., Delph., Epir. γραμματιστάς (also -τής Hdt.) = usual γραμματεύς.

5. -αω = -οω. Lesb. ἀξιάω (ἀξιάσει), Thess., Dor. κοινάω, Heracl. ἀράω (ἀράσοντι) = ἀρόω. Cf. Cret. ἄρατρον = ἄροτρον.

162. Other more individual peculiarities in form or use (others in Glossary).

1. ἀγνέω = ἄγω in perfect foims. Aetol. ἀγνηκώς, ἀχνηκότας (66), Lac. ἄγνηκε (Hesych. emend.), διεξαγνηκέναι. Cf. also ἀγνεῖν· ἄγειν. Κρῆτες, Hesych.

2. Lesb., El. ἀγρέω, Thess. ἀνγρέω (58c) = αἱρέω. Cf. also Lesb. ἄγρεσις, Thess. ἄνγρεσις, Coan ἀγρεταί, Hom. ἄγρει, αὐτάγρετος, etc. Pamph. ἀνhαγλέσθō (blend with a form like Cret. αἰλέω?).

3. ἀνδάνω = δοκέω 'be approved, voted.' Cret. ἔϝαδε, Ion. ἔαδε, Locr. ϝεϝαδεκότα. Cf. Ion. ἄδος 'decree,' and Hesych. ἄδμα, ἄδημα, ἄδισμα defined by ψήφισμα, δόγμα, also ϝάδιξις (γάδιξις), Tarent. ἄδιξις. ὁμολογία (cf. ψάφιξις, 142a).

4. Boeot., Thess. γίνυμαι = γίνομαι.

5. Cypr. δυϝάνω (cf. Lat. duim) and δώκω (from ἔδωκα, cf. στήκω in NT) =δίδωμι.

6. ἔρπω 'go, come' (as sometimes in Att. poetry) in many dialects, Arc., Cypr. (Hesych.), Epid., Cret., etc.

7. El. Ƒάρρω, Ƒέρρω, Locr. Ƒέρρω (Att.-Ion. ἔρρω; cf. ἔρρε 'begone!') used as a legal term like Att. φεύγω. Cf. the similar use of Arg. τρέω (no. 85.5).

8. For Att. ζῶ, 3 sg. ζῇ (from *ζήει) most dialects have ζώω (Boeot., Cret. δώω), as in Homer.

9. Dor. ἴσᾱμι = οἶδα and formed from its 3 pl. ἴσαντι, Hom. ἴσᾱσι (this with σ from forms like ἴστε). Attested in Cret. Ƒισάμην, ἴσαντι (subj.), ἴθθαντες (82b), Cyren. ἴσᾱι (subj.), and in literary Doric (Pind., Epich., Theocr.).

10. Compounds of λεαίνω, λειαίνω, or λειόω 'make smooth' (from λεῖος 'smooth') used as financial terms. Boeot. ἀπο-, δια-, ἐσ-λιήνω, act. 'cancel,' mid. 'have cancelled,' Arc. ἀπυλιῶναι probably 'discharge, settle' (no. 22.20). Cf. ἀπολειόω 'erase'.

11. West Grk. λείω, λέω = θέλω. Cret. λείοι, λείοντι, etc., also λέοι, subj. λῆι, Cyren. λέων, subj. λῆι, El. 3 dual. opt. λεοίταν. Contracted forms λῶ, λῶμες, subj. λῆι, λῶντι, etc., attested in most Doric dialects and in Doric writers (Epich., Theocr., etc.).

12. πάομαι in sense = κτάομαι, aor. ἐπᾱσάμην, perf. πέπᾱμαι. Verb forms or derivatives in many West Greek dialects, also Arcadian, Lesbian, Boeotian, and probably common to all non-Att.-Ion. dialects (in Attic poetical, rarely in prose). Cret. perf. subj. πέπᾱται, aor. subj. πάσεται, πᾶμα = κτῆμα (also Arg., Boeot., Arc.), πάστας 'owner,' Heracl. πᾱμωχεῖ, Locr. ἐχεπάμον, πᾱματοφαγεῖσται 'be confiscated' (cpd. with the root of ἔφαγον, originally 'share in,' whence 'partake of, eat'), El. πεπᾱστō, Delph. πεπᾶσθαι, Arg. ἐνιπᾱσκομαι 'acquire,' Lesb. (in Homer) πολυπάμων, Delph., Meg. ἔμπᾱσις, Arc. ἴμπᾱσις, Boeot. ἔππᾱσις. Root πᾱ- from ππᾱ- (this probably from an IE k̑wā- with ππ from k̑w as in ἵππος), seen in Boeot. τὰ ππάματα, Τυνό-ππαστος, Θιόππαστος, ἔππᾱσις, from *ἔμ-ππᾱσις, ἀππᾱσάμενος (Corinna) from *ἀν-ππᾱσάμενος.

a. The ἔγκτησις which occurs in late inscriptions of Crete, Sparta, etc., is from the κοινή. Late Corcyr., Epir., Troez. ἔγκτασις, Thess. ἔντασις is probably to be read with ᾱ (not α as weak grade of η) and explained as a blend of ἔγκτησις with native ἔμπᾱσις.

13. χρηέομαι, forms of Chalced. χρηείσθω, El. χρεῖσθαι, Boeot. χρειεῖσθη, Arc. χρέεσθαι, Att.-Ion., Heracl. χρῆσθαι, Cret. χρῆτθαι (85.3), Locr. χρεῖστō, χρεῖσται, Lac. χρῆσται, Arg. χρόνσθō (140.3b).

Ion. χρεώμενος, Att. χρώμενος, Dodon. χρεόμενος, Cret. χρήμενος.
Delph., Cyren. χρείμενος (158).

14. χρηίζω, χρήιζω, χρήζω (37.2) often simply 'wish' = θέλω or
βούλομαι, so even in Attic (ἴθ' ὅποι χρήζεις Ar., etc.) and in inscriptions of Delphi (no. 52 A 38), Argos (no. 86.24), Troezen,
Rhodes, Cos, Cnidus, Nisyros, Thera, etc.

15. Το πεύθομαι, ὠνέομαι, ἐλεύσομαι Cretan has the active
forms πεύθω 'inform,' ὠνέω (ὀνῆν, ὀνίοι) 'sell,' ἐπελευσεῖ 'will
bring' (cf. Hesych. ἐλευσίω·οἴσω), aor. ἐπελεῦσαι, etc.

The Verb εἰμί

163. 1. First singular present indicative. *ἐσμί, whence Lesb.
ἔμμι, Thess. ἐμμί, elsewhere εἰμί or ἠμί. See 76.

2. Third plural present indicative. *ἐντί (cf. Skt. santi, Osc.-
Umbr. sent), whence, with substitution of ἐ after the analogy
of the other forms, West Greek ἐντί, Att.-Ion. εἰσί. See 61.1, 77.3.

3. Third singular imperfect. ἦς (from *ἦσ-τ, cf. Ved. Skt. ās)
is attested for various West Greek dialects (Acarn., Corcyr.,
Delph., Epid., lit. Doric), Boeotian, Lesbian, Arcadian, and
Cyprian, and is probably the form in all dialects (for Locr. ἔν,
see no. 57.9, note) except Attic-Ionic, where it was replaced by
ἦν (Hom. ἦεν), the old third plural (from *ἦσεν, cf. Skt. āsan).

4. Third plural imperfect. Most dialects had ἦν (see above, 3),
examples of which are found in literary Doric, Delphian, and
Locrian. For Boeot. παρεῖαν, Att.-Ion. ἦσαν, see 138.5.

5. Third singular imperative. ἔστω in most dialects. But late
ἤτω, with ἠ of ἦν etc. after the analogy of, e.g., στήτω to ἔστην.
El. ἤστω, also with analogical η but with retention of σ.

6. Third plural imperative. Arg. ἔντō, Boeot. ἔνθω (138.4),
Cret. ἔντων, formed from 3 pl. indic. ἐντί. Also thematic ἐόντω,
ἐόντων, e.g., in Delphian. Ion. ἔστων, Attic ὄντων, and late
ἔστωσαν.

7. Present infinitive. The difference in the form of the ending
(154) and also in the development of σ + nasal (76) explains
the great variety of forms, Attic-Ionic εἶναι (also Eub. εἶν, 160),
Arc. ἦναι, Lesb. ἔμμεναι, Thess. ἔμμεν, West Greek and Boeotian
εἶμεν or ἦμεν (25), Rhod. ἤμειν, Cret. ἤμην.

8. Present participle. ἐών in most dialects, Att. ὤν. But also unthematic forms. Heracl. ἔντες, dat. pl. ἔντασσιν (blend with *ἄσσι = Skt. *satsu*), Arg., Lac. (Alcman) παρέντων, Thess. ἔνσα (*ἔντι̯α, **77**.3), all with ἐντ- for ἐντ- as in ἐντί (above, 2). Lesb., Epid., Troez. ἔσσα (also in some Doric writers; cf. ἐσσία = οὐσία Plato, Crat. 401 C), Arc., Mess. ἔασσα, Cret. ἴαττα, ἴαθθα, all from *ἄτι̯α = Skt. *satī*, with the substitution or prefixing of ε after the analogy of the other forms.

   a. Other similar unthematic feminine forms are ἴεσσα (Hesych.), ἴασσα in Ἐπίασσα, Cyren. κατίασσα = ἰοῦσα, and Cyren. ἔκασσα (beside ἐκοῖσα) = ἐκοῦσα, and in Hesych. ἀέκασσα, γέκαθα, the last presumably for a Cret. ϝέκαθθα.

9. Middle forms, as imperf. ἤμην etc., are late. Cf. 3 sg. subj. ἦται at Delphi, 3 pl. subj. ἦνται at Andania, ἤμην in the κοινή, ἤμεθα in NT.

   a. The middle inflection spread until, in Modern Greek, all the present and imperfect forms are of this type, except 3 sg., pl. pres. εἶναι, which is from ἔνι = ἔνεστι, with vowels after the other forms.

10. Confusion between third singular and third plural present (favored by expressions corresponding to Eng. *there are*, Fr. *il y a*). ἐντι as third singular in Rhodian (no. 103.10) and later Doric inscriptions and literature (frequent in Archimedes). ἐστι as third plural in late Lesbian, as ἔτοιμοί ἐστι, ἐψαφίσμενοί ἐστι (cf. also διαδεδίκασται αἰ δίκαι).

WORD-FORMATION

ON THE FORM AND USE OF CERTAIN SUFFIXES AND CERTAIN PECULIARITIES OF COMPOSITION

164. 1. -ειος, -ηιος. The Att. adjectives in -εῖος, -ειος and the nouns in -εῖον, -ειον, and -εία are in many cases from earlier -ήιος (three syllables, also written -ηιος, but later sometimes -ηος; see **37.**2), etc., these again in part from -ήϜιος, etc. (cf. Boeot. ΚαρυκεϜίō, Cypr. ἱερεϜίjαν). The earlier forms with η, besides the many in Homer, etc., are widely attested, e.g., ἱερήιον, ἱαρήιον in many dialects, Ion., Lesb., Cret. πρυτανήιον, Ion. βασιλήιος, φοινικήια, Delph. παιδήια, ἐντοφήια, Cret. οἰκήιος, ἀνδρήιον, ἀρχηία, πρειγηία, νυμφήιον, ἀγνηία, πολιτηία. Forms with ι lost, e.g., Ion. ἱερήον, Delph. ἀνδρῆος, Cyren. ἑταιρήα, Arg. μαντῆον, μαντήα, στρατήα, πρεσγέα, πρεσβήα.

2. Adjectives of the type χαρίεις are from -Ϝεντ- (Skt. *-vant-*). The feminine was originally -Ϝατια (like Skt. *-vatī*, from the weak stem *-wn̥t-*; cf. ἕασσα **163.**8), whence, with the substitution of ε for α from the analogy of the forms in -Ϝεντ-, arose -Ϝετια, this yielding -(Ϝ)εσσα or -(Ϝ)εττα (**81**). Cf. Boeot. χαρίϜετταν, Corcyr. στονόϜε(σ)σαν, Pamph. τιμάϜε(σ)σα (for Ϝ cf. also ΦλειϜόντᾱθεν). The genuine Attic forms have ττ, as μελιτοῦττα (Ar.), Μυρρινοῦττα (inscr.), those with σσ being poetical and in origin Ionic. Most adjectives of this type are poetical only, except in substantive use, especially the numerous place-names in -όεις, for which see also **44.**4.

3. -τις, -σις. See **61.**3. For -ξις see **142a**. We find -σσις instead of usual -σις in Arg. ἁλιάσσιος, Epid. στεγάσσιος, Troez. ἑρμάσσιος, Boeot. ἀγόρασσιν. Probably *-ασ-τις, normal from dental stems (cf. πίστις), became -ασ-σις, with -σις after the analogy of the common type. Similarly Troez. ἱμασσία.

4. -σμος, -σμα. In most words σ has replaced, by analogy, an earlier dental, which is sometimes preserved, as in Hom. ὀδμή = Att. ὀσμή. So for Att. θεσμός, θέσμιος we find West Greek τεθμός,

Locr. also τετθμός, Lac., Epid., Thess. θεθμός, El. θεθτμός,
Boeot. τέθμιον, Locr. θέθμιον (65). Locr., Sicil., Naxian δαιθμός
(from δαίω) = usual δασμός (from δατέομαι). Other variations of
-μα forms, partly unexplained, are Lesb. ὄππα (Sappho) = ὄμμα,
γρόππα (Balbilla) = γράμμα. Also θμ in ὄθμα (Aeolic in Hesych.;
also in Call. and Nic.) = ὄμμα, στέθμα (Hesych.) = στέμμα, Arg.
γράθμα but also γράσσμα (after ψάφισμα) = γράμμα. For Cret.
ψάφιγμα, ψάφιμμα = ψάφισμα see 86.9, 142a.
Also from v-stems usually -σμα, as ὕφασμα, μίασμα, πίασμα. But
Att. also (inscriptions) ὕφαμμα, Cyren. ποτιπίαμμα. Analogical
-σμος in Arc. ἀπυδοσμός = ἀπόδοσις.

5. -τηρ = -της(-τᾱς). As a productive suffix of nouns of agency
the older -τηρ has been very largely displaced by -της (-τᾱς), but
most fully in Attic prose. As forms with -τηρ = usual -της (-τᾱς)
are not infrequent in poetry, e.g., Hom. ἐθελοντήρ, Hes. αὐλητήρ,
so they occur also frequently in the dialects, e.g., Locr., Delph.,
Pamph. δικαστήρ, Argol. κριτήρ, τελεστήρ, ἐγδοτήρ, Lac. ἐγδοτήρ,
Arc. ἐσδοτήρ, Locr., Delph., Aetol. βεβαιωτήρ, Corcyr. διορθωτήρ,
Cyren. οἰκιστήρ, τιματήρ. Cf. also Cypr. ἰjατήρ like Hom. ἰητήρ =
usual ἰατρός. But Cretan has -τᾱς from the earliest period, as
δικαστάς, πάστας, τίτας, etc., the few examples of -τηρ (κοσμητήρ,
νικατήρ) being late.

6. -ιος = -εος. In adjectives of material Lesbian and Thessalian
have -ιος (phonetic change supported by parallel suffix; cf.
9.2), as Lesb. χρύσιος, χάλκιος, ἀργύριος, Thess. λίθιος (cf.
Hom. λίθεος, in most dialects λίθινος; conversely Boeot. λίνινος
= λίνεος).

7. -ήν = -ων. Personal names in -ήν (short names, hypocoristic
in origin) instead of usual -ων, e.g., 'Αρχήν, Τιμήν vs. usual
"Αρχων, Τίμων, occur occasionally in Delphi, Megara, Epidaurus,
Corinth, etc., but are conspicuously frequent in the Corinthian colonies of Apollonia and Epidamnus.

8. -ώνδας, -όνδας. Beside the usual (originally patronymic)
personal names in -ίδης etc., forms in -ώνδας, or less commonly
-όνδας, are most frequent in Boeotian, like the familiar 'Επαμει-
νώνδας, but occur also in Thessalian, Phocian, Megarian, and
(-ώνδης) Euboean, rarely elsewhere.

9. The diminutive -ιχος, as in ὀρτάλιχος, ὄσσιχος and names

like Σίμμιχος, is to be recognized in Lac. παιδιχός beside usual παιδικός, δαριχίς, and μικχιχός implied by μικκιγιδδόμενος.

10. Individual cases of dialectal variation in suffix are of course frequent. So, for example, Thess. λίθιος = λίθινος (cf. above, 6), Ion. νόμαιος, Locr. νόμιος = νόμιμος, Thess. ὀνάλα (but also ὀνάλουμα) = ἀνάλωμα (cf. also Boeot. ἄλωμα), Boeot., Epir. ποθόδωμα (after ἀνάλωμα) = πρόσοδος, Delph., Mess. κεφάλωμα = κεφαλαῖον, Heracl. ἐπιζαμίωμα beside ἐπιζάμιον, Thess. συνκλείς (stem -κλη-τ-, cf. προβλής, etc.) = σύγκλητος ἐκκλησία, Cret. ἡμίνα (also Cypr. gloss) = τὸ ἥμισυ (also Sicil. ἡμίνα, used, like Epid. hεμίτεια, in the sense of ἡμίεκτον), Cret. θῖνος (from *θίινος formed from θιός after the analogy of ἀνθρώπ-ινος), ἔνθῖνος = θεῖος, ἔνθεος, Att. ἀδελφός but ἀδελφεός in other dialects, Delph. γάμελα (cf. γαμέτης) = γαμήλια. Arc. γνōσία, τιμασία, παναγορία = γνῶσις, etc.

11. Nouns in -ιος, -ιον appear frequently as -ις, -ιν in late inscriptions. See 45.6.

165. 1. -τερος. Noteworthy examples of the use of this suffix to denote contrasted relations (not merely those of degree as in the comparatives), as in δεξιτερός, ἀριστερός, are Arc. ἀρρέντερος, El. ἐρσεναίτερος (for αι cf. γεραίτερος, παλαίτερος), θηλύτερος.

2. -ιδιος forming adjectives from adverbs or adverbial phrases, as ἀίδιος, ἐπιθαλασσίδιος. So El. προσθίδιος (προστιζίōν), Locr. ὑπαπροσθίδιος, Cret. ἐνδοθίδιος (ἐνδοθιδίαν δόλαν 'household slave'), Epid. ἐνδοσθίδιος (ἐνδοσθίδια 'entrails'; so ἐντοσθίδια Arist., Hipp.), Cret. ἐξαρχίδιος = ἐξ ἀρχῆς γιγνόμενος.

3. -τρον. From words like λύτρον 'means of release,' hence 'ransom,' the suffix came to be used freely in words denoting reward or amount paid, as νίκαστρον 'reward of victory,' Epid. ἴατρα 'perquisites for healing,' Ion., Coan τέλεστρα 'expenses of inauguration' (of the priest. Cf. Coan τελέω 'inaugurate'), Cret. κόμιστρα 'gifts' (more specific?), and, even from a numeral, Cret. τρίτρα 'the threefold amount.'

4. -εων, -ων in nouns denoting place, as ἀνδρών (Ion. ἀνδρεών, Pamph. ἀ(ν)δριιόν), ἀμπελών, νεκρών, ὀρνιθών. To this large class belong Heracl. τοφιών (6, 9.9) = ταφεών 'burial place,' γαιών 'mound of earth' (cf. γαεών from Halaesa), βοών 'cow-shed,' Ion. στεφών 'ridge.'

This class is not to be confused with nouns of agency in Ion.
-εών but Dor. etc., -άων, -άν, as Ion. ξυνεών, Dor. κοινάν. See **41**.4.

166. 1. Personal names in -κλέᾱς, instead of -κλέης, -κλῆς, as
Ἱπποκλέας, are most common in Thessalian, but also occur in
Boeotian, Locrian, Phocian, Aetolian, and Megarian (here in
the form -χλίας). -κλέᾱς is a modification of -κλέης under the
influence of hypocoristics in -έᾱς.

2. Διόζοτος (i.e., Διόσ-δοτος, cf. Διόσ-κουροι) and Θειόσδοτος
Θεόσζοτος, Θεόζοτος, Θιόζοτος (formed after Διόσ-δοτος, cf.
θεόσδοτος in Hesiod), instead of usual Διόδοτος, Θεόδοτος, are
frequent in Boeotian, and Thessalian also has Θεόζοτος, Θιόζοτος,
and Θεορδότειος (**60**.4). Elsewhere such forms are rare and
doubtless imported.

167. The interchange of different vowel stems in the first
member of a compound, or before a derivative suffix, is sometimes
dialectal. Thus Τιμοκλῆς, Τιμοκράτης, etc., in most dialects, but
Ion. Τιμηκλῆς, Τιμηκράτης, Cnid. Τιμᾱκλῆς, Rhod. Τιμᾱκράτης,
Τιμάπολις, likewise Rhod. Τιμᾱναξ (*Τιμᾱ-(F)αναξ) instead of usual
Τιμῶναξ (*Τιμό-(F)αναξ). Thess. ὑλōρός (hυλōρέοντος) from *ὑλο-
Fορός and so related to Att. ὑλωρός (late poet. ὑληωρός) from ὑλᾱ-
as ὑλοτόμος to ὑλᾱτόμος.

Arc., Locr., Thess. οἰκιάτᾱς (or Fοικιάτᾱς) from οἰκίᾱ, for usual
οἰκέτης from οἶκος (Fοικεύς, fem. Fοικέα, are the forms used in
Cretan). Ion. πολιήτης, Cret., Epid. πολιάτᾱς (also Pindar), Cret.
πολιᾱτεύω, Arc. πολιᾶτις, for usual πολίτης, etc.; cf. Heracl.
πολιᾱνόμος, Ion. πολιήοχος (Epic), Lac. πολιᾶχος (but Att.
πολιοῦχος with -οῦχος from κληροῦχος etc.). Cret. ὀφέλōμα after
ἀνάλωμα.

Late Att. ἱερᾱτεύω, Locr., Phoc. ἱερητεύω (also in some κοινή
inscriptions), Lesb. ἱρητεύω, Cret., Cyren. ἱαριτεύω, Mess. ἱεριτεύω,
Chalced. ἱερωτεύω, ἱερωτεία (cf. Att. ἱερωσύνη).

Carpath. δαμέτᾱς, like οἰκέτης, for usual δαμότᾱς, δημότης, as
conversely οἰκότης in an Attic inscription. So Cret. βίετος (cf.
Astyp. Βίεττος) = βίοτος, Arg. κωμέτᾱς, Rhod. κτοινέτᾱς, beside
κτοινάτᾱς, after φυλέτᾱς. Dor. ἀνδρεφόνος (Hdn.), Locr. ἀνδρεφονικός for usual ἀνδρο-, Rhod. Ἱππέδαμος = Ἱππόδαμος, but Rhod.
Ἀρχοκράτης = Ἀρχεκράτης, Cret. Μενοκράτης = Μενεκράτης.

After the analogy of names containing inherited ι-stems arose also forms like 'Αρχίλοχος, 'Αρχίδαμος, etc. (cf. ἀρχιτέκτων), in various dialects, Rhod. Μενίδαμος, El. Σαίχλαρος, Coan, Nisyr., Mel. Λαίστρατος, Nisyr. Λαισθένης. Parallel forms *δᾱμιο-Fεργός and *δᾱμιο-Fοργός (attested by the verbal Arc. δαμιοFοργε͂, no. 16). From the former, Hom. δημιοεργός, and with contraction Att. δημιουργός (though of course this could equally well come from the second form), with elision δαμιεργός, occurring at Cyrene, Astypalaea, and Nisyros. The much more common δημιοργός (Ion.), δᾱμιοργός (Arc., El., Locr., Delph. and most Doric dialects), could come also from *δᾱμιοFεργός (cf. Locr. 'Οπόντιοι, Meg. Σελινόντιοι, from -ο-Fεντ, 44.4), but more easily with elision from *δᾱμιοFοργός.—Other compounds in this group, Boeot. γᾱFεργός (cf. 3 sg. fut. γαFεργείσι, no. 42.11), Lac. γαFεργόρ (Hesych.), frequently -εργός, rarely -οργός (ἀλοργός Sicil., Hesych., cf. Ion. ἀλοργής, ἀλοργίη), most commonly contracted -ουργός, also -ωργός; cf. Heracl. ἀμπελωργικός). Att. γεωργός from *γᾱ-(F)οργός (cf. Thess. γαοργεῖμεν) or γᾱο-F- (as in γεωγραφία, etc.)?

a. The well-known lengthening of the initial vowel of the second member of compounds, as in ἀνώνυμος, πανήγυρις, is seen in Ion. ἀνηρίθευτος = Att. ἀνερίθευτος, Att., Cret. εὐθυωρία, Heracl. εὐθυωρεία (vs. Arc. εὐθυορFία), Arc. δίωρος (like δι-ώβολος). To the analogy of forms like ἐπάκοος, ἐπήκοος, which are of the same kind, is due to the ἐπᾱ- of Cret., Boeot. ἐπᾱβολά 'share' (cf. Hesych. ἐπηβολή · μέρος) and Att.-Ion. ἐπήβολος. Cf. κατηβολή in Euripides.

168. Use of a patronymic adjective instead of the genitive singular of the father's name. Though occasionally found in literature, as in Hom. Τελαμώνιος Αἴας, this is the regular practice in prose only in the three Aeolic dialects. Thus Lesb. Μέλανχρος Πιθώνειος, 'Αρχίππα 'Αθανάεια, Thess. Σύχουν 'Αντιγόνειος, Νικόλαος 'Αγεισίαιος, Boeot. Θιόπομπος 'Ολυμπίχιος, 'Ερμάιος Νικιῆος. Examples in other dialects are rare.

a. When the father's name is itself a patronymic form in -δας or -ιος, the genitive is regularly employed in Boeotian; so also in early Thessalian, but later the adjective forms like 'Επικρατίδαιος, Τιμουνίδαιος are usual.

b. Under κοινή influence the use of the adjective was given up in favor of the ordinary genitive construction. Thus in Boeotian the genitive is usual after about 250 B.C. and occasionally found earlier. There is some evidence that the Plataeans adopted the Attic usage at an early date. See no. 41, note.

c. There are also examples in Thessalian and Boeotian of adjectives in agreement with appellatives, in place of a genitive of possession. Thess. Πολυξεναία ἐμμί (sc. ἀ στάλλα), etc. See the following.

d. A genitive may be used in apposition to that implied by the adjective, as in Hom. Γοργείη κεφαλὴ δεινοῖο πελώρου. Boeot. Καλιαία ἐμὶ (sc. ἀ κύλιξ) τõ Κέντρõνος, Γοργίνιός ἐμι ὁ κότυλος καλὸς κ[αλ]õ, Lesb. σ[τάλλ]α 'πὶ Σθενείαι ἔμμι τõ Νικιαίōι (dat.) τõ Γαυκίō (gen.) 'the son of Nicias, the son of Glaucus,' where Γαυκίō is also a patronymic adjective, but in apposition with the genitive implied in Νικιαίōι. Thess. ᾽Ανφιονεία στάλα τõὐφρόνετος (τοῦ Εὐφρόνητος).

SYNTAX

169. Although the syntax of the dialects deserves fuller investigation than it has received, yet syntactical differences between the dialects are much less striking than those of phonology and inflection. To a considerable extent they consist merely in the conservation in some dialects of early forms of expression which have become rare or obsolete in literary Greek, and in a less strict formalization of usage. Some peculiarities have already been mentioned in connection with the forms, e.g., in the use of certain pronouns (**121-31**), adverbs and conjunctions (**132-34**), and in the meaning and construction of prepositions (**136**). It is necessary to add here only a few comments on certain uses of the cases and the moods. Some other, more isolated, peculiarities are observed in the notes to the inscriptions.

CASES

The Genitive

170. Genitive of time. The genitive of the 'time within which' is especially frequent in the early Cretan inscriptions, although ἐν with the dative is already the more usual expression. Cf. Law Code, I.25 λαγάσαι τᾶν πέντ' ἀμερᾶν 'release within five days'; but I.6 ἐν ταῖς τρισὶ ἀμέραις, in another Gortyn inscription τὸ ἐνιαυτõ 'within the year.' So also, but without the article, as in early Attic inscriptions, Cret. δέκα ϝετίõν (no. 116), Locr. τριõν μενõν beside ἐν τριάϟοντα ἀμάραις, Boeot. τριῶν ἀμεράων (no. 42.16).

Aside from the adverbial phrases νυκτός, etc., the use of the genitive of time is most persistent in dating, as μηνὸς ἑβδόμου, etc., the usual expression in most dialects. More noteworthy is the phrase καὶ πολέμου (-ω) καὶ εἰρήνης(-ας) which is common in the proxeny decrees of various dialects, though eventually replaced in many by ἐν πολέμωι κτλ.

The genitive of time is used distributively in various dialects, as also in Attic, e.g., τᾶς ἀμέρας or τᾶς ἀμέρας Ϝεκάστας 'daily,' beside κατ' ἀμέραν.

171. Genitive of the matter or person involved. Besides the familiar genitive of the charge or penalty, the genitive is also used more broadly to denote the matter or person involved, e.g., Cret. καταδικακσάτō τō ἐλευθέρō δέκα στατῆρανς, τō δόλō πέντε 'shall condemn him to a fine of ten staters in the case of a freeman, five staters in the case of a slave,' ἀι Ϝεκάστō ἔγρατται 'as is prescribed for each case.' Such genitives may serve as headings, like 'Ικεσίων no. 115.110. In the long cult-inscription of Andania most of the headings are in the simple genitive, beside a few cases of περί with genitive.

The Dative

172. The adnominal dative is more common than in literary Greek, and is especially frequent in the introduction to inscriptions or their separate sections, e.g., El. ἀ Ϝράτρα τοῖς Ϝαλείοις, Locr. τὸ τέθμιον τοῖς Ηυποκναμιδίοις Λοϟροῖς, Phoc. ὁμολογία τᾶ πόλει Στειρίων καὶ τᾶ πόλει Μεδεωνίων, Boeot. διαγραφὰ Νικαρέτη, Att. ἀπαρχὲ τἀθεναίαι, γραμματεὺς τῆι βουλῆι καὶ τῶι δάμωι.

For the dative instead of the genitive construction with various prepositions in Arcado-Cyprian, see **136**.1.

The Accusative

173. The accusative absolute of participles is common enough in literature (Hdt. +), but mostly in impersonal constructions. Examples of personal construction in the dialects are worth noting. Thus Arc. εἰ μὲ παρhεταξαμένος τὸς πεντέκοντα ἒ τὸς τριακοσίος 'unless the Fifty or the Three Hundred approve.' This is an extension from instances where the participle agrees with the accusative of a preceding clause, as Arc. μὲ νέμεν μέτε ξένον μέτε Ϝαστόν, εἰ μὲ ἐπὶ θοίναν hίκοντα. Cf. also Arc. κατάπερ τὸς ἐπισυνισταμένος...γέγραπτοι 'as is prescribed in the case of those who conspire,' Coan αἱρεθέντας ἑκατέρων δέκα 'ten of each being chosen.' Such use is increasingly common in late Greek and led to the modern indeclinable participle in -οντα(ς).

THE MOODS

The Subjunctive

174. The subjunctive without ἄν or κα in conditional, relative, and temporal clauses, where the particle is regularly employed in Attic prose, though frequently omitted in Homer and sometimes elsewhere (Kühner-Gerth II, pp. 426, 449, 474), is attested for several dialects, though always as the less common construction. Locr. αἰ δείλητ' ἀνχōρεῖν, αἴ τις ἀνχōρέēι (no. 57.7, 26; ten examples with κα in the same inscription), Arc. εἰ δέ τις ἐπιθιγάνē, εἰκ ἐπὶ δōμα πῦρ ἐποίσē (no. 18.21; other probable examples in no. 16) in contrast to usual εἰκ ἄν (see **134**.2*a*), Cypr. ὁ ἐξορύξē, οἰ...ἴōσι (no. 23.25, 31), Cret. θυγατρὶ ē διδōι 'in case one gives it to the daughter' (Law-Code VI.1). Examples are not infrequent in later Locrian, Phocian, and Delphian inscriptions.

The Optative

175. In Elean the optative with κα is the usual form of prescriptions, e.g., συνμαχία κ' ἔα ἑκατὸν Ϝέτεα 'let there be alliance for a hundred years,' ζέκα μναίς κα ἀποτίνοι Ϝέκαστος 'let each pay a fine of ten minae.' Similarly, but without the particle, Arc. ἐξόλοιτυ 'shall be put to death' (no. 16), Cypr. δόκοι νυ βασιλεύς 'the king shall give.'

The subjunctive without κα is used in the same sense in a late Elean inscription (66.32, 36).

176. 1 The optative in conditional clauses survives in several dialects, although, except in Elean, it is much less frequent than the subjunctive, and indeed is almost wholly eliminated in favor of the subjunctive in Attic-Ionic inscriptions, and in the majority of dialects. Where the optative survives, it is sometimes used with a still recognizable differentiation from the subjunctive, but oftener without such. In the Gortyn Law Code which offers the fullest material, there are in conditional clauses about 50 optatives to about 80 subjunctives. Some of these occur where the contingency is obviously one more remotely anticipated (e.g., VII.9 'but if there should not be any free persons,' as contemplated in the preceding subjunctive clauses; I.11 'but if

one should deny'), others as mere variants of the subjunctive
for parallel or even identical contingencies (e.g., opt. IX.18 =
subj. VI.25). In Locrian nos. 57 and 58B have the subjunctive
only, but nos. 58A and 59 the optative only. In Delphian, no.
52 has the subjunctive usually, but αἰ δ᾽ ἐφιορκέοιμι A17, also
αἰ δ᾽ ἐφιορκέοι C6, in an oath, where Attic also would have the
optative, and αἰ δέ τι τούτων παρβάλλοιτο C25, C50, D17; and in
the numerous Phocian and Delphian manumission decrees the
optative is of very frequent occurrence. The optative, beside the
subjunctive, occurs also in Corcyraean, Achaean, and in the
Northwest Greek κοινή (e.g., no. 67). In Argolic, the archaic nos.
83 and 85 have the optative only, and this occurs in some of
the later inscriptions. In Arcadian, nos. 17 and 18 have the
subjunctive only, but in no. 19 there are some examples of the
optative. Even in the same clause the alternation of subjunctive
and optative is not infrequent, e.g., Delph. εἰ δέ κα μὴ ποιῇ ἢ μὴ
παραμένοι or εἰ δὲ μὴ ποιέοι ἢ μὴ παραμένη.

2. In relative and temporal clauses of future time, the pre-
dominance of the subjunctive is even more marked. Noteworthy
is the Tean curse, no. 3, where ὅστις with the optative is used in
the curse proper, ll. 1-34, while in the postscript warning against
harming the stele on which the curse is inscribed, ll. 35-40, we
find ὃς ἄν with the subjunctive. There are a few examples of
the optative in Cretan (Law Code IV.14/15, and a few others),
Locrian (ϝότι συλάσαι no. 58.5, hόσστις δὲ δαιθμὸν ἐνφέροι no.
59.10 vs. hότι δέ κα φυτεύσεται l.6), Delphian, and elsewhere
(see also 177).

3. But in Elean the optative is regularly employed in conditional, relative, and temporal clauses. For examples in conditional
and relative clauses, see nos 61-64. In the later no. 65 the subjunctive occurs once in a conditional clause with future perfect
force, and in relative clauses.

4. In final clauses the optative occurs, e.g., Heracl. Tab.
I.53 ff. ἐστάσαμες ... ἀνχωρίξαντες ..., hως μὴ καταλυμακωθῆς
ἀδηλωθείη, Lesb. no. 26.13 ff. ἐπιμέλεσθαι ..., κατάγρεντον ...,
ὥς κε ... ἐμμένοιεν. But it is very rare, and most dialects have
only the subjunctive with or without ἄν (κα, κε), or sometimes
the future indicative.

177. There are some examples of κα with the optative in conditional and other clauses as sometimes with κε or κα in Homer, Pindar, etc., e.g., Locr. αἴ κ' ἀδίκō συλōι (no. 58.4), Cret. αἴ κα ... μὴ νυνατὸς εἴη, Epid. αἴ κα ὑγιῆ νιν ποιήσαι (no. 90.60), Delph. εἰ δέ [τίς] κα ἐφάπτοιτο, ἐπεί κά τι πάθοι, Corcyr. ἀφ' οὖ κ' ἀρχὰ γένοιτο, Ach. ἔστε κα ἀποδοῖεν, Arg. αἴ κα δικάσσαιεν.

The Imperative and the Infinitive

178. Both the imperative and the infinitive are freely used in prescriptions, often side by side in the same inscription. In general the infinitive is more frequent in early, the imperative in later, inscriptions. For the use of the optative with the same force, see **175.**

WORD ORDER

179. A peculiarity of word order which is worthy of mention is the position of τις before κα in the phrase αἴ τίς κα, αἰ δέ τίς κα. This is the regular order in the West Greek dialects, as contrasted not only with Att.-Ion. ἐάν τις, ἤν τις, but with Arc. εἰ δ' ἄν τις, Cypr. ἔ κέ σις, Lesb. αἴ κέ τις, Thess. αἰ μά κέ κις, Boeot. ἠ δέ κα τις. Boeot. has also, though less frequently, the West Greek order ἠ τίς κα.

SUMMARIES OF THE CHARACTERISTICS OF THE SEVERAL GROUPS AND DIALECTS

180. The following summaries, while not exhaustive, are intended to call attention to the most important characteristics of each group and dialect. These are indicated in the briefest manner, sometimes by a mere example, sufficient to identify, but not always to define, the phenomenon in question, and these brief indications are always to be interpreted in the light of the sections to which reference is made in each case. Several features that are only occasional or late, though noted in the main texts, are ignored here.

To avoid needless repetition, many phenomena which are peculiar from the standpoint of Attic or Attic-Ionic, but are common to all or most of the other dialects, are usually omitted, e.g.:

1. Originial ᾱ unchanged. **8**
2. ᾱ from ᾱο, ᾱω. **41**.4
3. η from α + ε. **41**.1
4. σσ = Att., Cret., Boeot., Eub. ττ in φυλάττω, etc. **81**
5. σσ = Att. σ, Cret., Boeot. ττ in Att. ὅσος, μέσος, ἐδίκασα. **82**
6. σσ = original σσ, Att. σ. **83**
7. πόλις, πόλιος, etc. **109**.1
8. ἀμές, ὑμές, acc. ἀμέ, ὑμέ = ἡμεῖς, etc. **119**.2, 5

9. 3 pl. ἔθεν, ἔδον, etc. **138**.5
10. ἧς = ἦν. **163**.3
11. ἐών = ὤν **163**.8
12. αἰ = εἰ. **134**.1
13. ἅτερος = ἕτερος. **13a**
14. ἱστία = ἑστία. **11**
15. γίνομαι = γίγνομαι **86**.10
16. δέκομαι = δέχομαι. **66**
17. ὄνυμα = ὄνομα. **22b**
18. ἤνεικα, ἤνικα = ἤνεγκα. **144a**
19. πᾶμα = κτῆμα. **162**.12
20. ἵκω = ἥκω. Glossary

EAST GREEK

ATTIC-IONIC

181. Important characteristics of Attic-Ionic (1-7 specific Att.-Ion., 8-9 in common with Arc., 10 with Arc.-Cypr.):

141

1. η from ᾱ. 8
2. Quantitative metathesis (λεώς, etc.). 41.4, 43
3. ν-movable. 102
4. ἡμεῖς, acc. -έας, -ᾱς. 119.2, 5
5. ποῦ, ὅπου, etc. 132.1

6. ἔθεσαν, ἔδοσαν, etc. 138.5
7. ἦν 3 sg. imperf. of εἰμί. 163.3
8. Conjunction εἰ. 134.1
9. Particle ἄν. 134.2
10. Infin. -ναι. 154.1
11. Very early loss of ϝ. 50

Ionic

182. The chief characteristics of Ionic, as compared with Attic, are as follows. Some few of these are Ionic only (notably 1, also 8, 9, 14, 20, 22), but most are common to various other dialects, some indeed to all except Attic, being repeated here from **180** to bring out the contrast with Attic more fully. A few peculiarities which are not general Ionic, but are common to all branches except West Ionic, are included.

1. η from ᾱ even after ε, ι, ρ. 8
2. εα, εο, εω, εοι usually uncontracted. 42.1, 5, 6
3. ευ = εο, from fourth century on. 42.5
4. Crasis of ο, ō (οι), ω, + α = ω, as τὠγῶνος. 94.1
5. ω from οη. 44.2
6. ξεῖνος, κούρη, etc. 54 with a
7. σσ = Att. ττ. 81
8. ρσ = Att. ρρ. 80
9. ἤν = Att. ἐάν, ἄν. 134.1b
10. ᾱ-stems, gen. sg. m. -εω, -ω, gen. pl. -εων, -ῶν, dat. pl. -ῃσι (ν). 41.4, 104.7
11. πόλις, πόλιος, etc. 109.1, 2
12. βασιλεύς, -έος, etc. 111.3
13. -κλῆς, -κλέος. 108.1a
14. μι-verbs inflected like contracts, as τιθεῖ, τιθεῖν. 160

15. 3 pl. τιθέαται, etc. 139.2
16. ἐών = Att. ὤν. 163.8
17. Suffix -ηιος = Att. -ειος. 164.1
18. βόλομαι = βούλομαι. 75b
19. ἱρός (ἱρός) beside ἱερός. 13.1
20. μέζων = Att. μείζων. 113.1
21. δέκνῡμι = Att. δείκνῡμι. 49.1
22. κεῖνος = Att. ἐκεῖνος. 125.1
23. ξυνός = Att. κοινός. 135.7
24. καρτερός = Att. κρατερός, in meaning = κύριος. 49. 2a, Glossary
25. δημιοργός = Att. -ουργός. 167
26. ἱστίη (ἱστία)=Att. ἑστία. 11
27. ἤνεικα, ἤνικα = Att. ἤνεγκα. 144a
28. ἰθύς = Att. εὐθύς. Glossary

183. East Ionic is further characterized by:

1. Psilosis. **57.** 2. αο, εο = αυ, ευ from fourth century B.C. on. **33.** 3. Short-vowel subj. of σ aorist. **150.**

184. Chian. The dialect of Chios contains a few special characteristics, which are of Aeolic origin:

1. 3 pl. λάβωισιν, πρήξοισιν, etc., with ισ from νσ. **77.**3.

2. Inflected cardinals, δέκων, πεντηκόντων, etc. **116.**

Note also γεγωνέω 'call aloud,' as in Homer.

a. The Aeolic doubling of nasals (**73** ff.) is seen in the names of the mountain Πελινναῖον in Chios and the promontory Ἄργεννον opposite Chios, also in the personal name Φαννόθεμις in an inscription of Erythrae. Likewise Aeolic is the Phocaean Ζιονύ(σιος), **19.**1. All these features are relics of a time when the line between the Aeolic and the Ionic colonies was farther south than in the historical period.

185. Central Ionic differs from East Ionic in having the spiritus asper in early inscriptions. **57**c. Note also the restricted use of H as a vowel, i.e., only η from ᾱ, in the early inscriptions of some of the islands. **4.6.**

186. West Ionic, or Euboean, differs from the other divisions of Ionic as follows.

1. ττ as in Attic, not σσ. **81**

2. ρρ as in Attic, not ρσ. **80**

3. ξένος, etc. as in Attic, not ξεῖνος. **54**

4. -ει, -οι from -ηι, -ωι (in Eretria about 400 B.C.). **39**a

5. τοῦτα, τούτει, ἐντοῦθα = ταῦτα, ταύτηι, ἐνταῦθα. **124**

6. -κλέης, gen. -κλέω. **108.**1a

7. Proper names in -ις, gen. -ιδος, as often in Attic (East and Central Ion. -ιος). **109.5**

8. εἶν beside εἶναι. **160**

187. Eretrian. In addition to the other Euboean peculiarities, the dialect of Eretria, seen in inscriptions of Eretria and Oropus, is specifically characterized by the rhotacism of intervocalic σ, as ἔχουριν = ἔχουσιν, **60.**3. The use of ἄν (Oropus), ἐάν (Eretria) is due to Attic influence.

188. Attic influence. Ionic was the first of all dialects to yield to Attic influence, and after the fifth century B.C. there are few inscriptions that are wholly free from Attic forms. See **277.**

ARCADO-CYPRIAN [1]

189. Special characteristics of Arcado-Cyprian. [2]

1. ἰν = ἐν. **10**
2. Gen sg. -αυ. **22**
3. πός = πρός. **135**.6
4. κάς = καί (but Arc. usually καί). **134**.3

5. σις, ϲις = τις. **68**.3
6. Mid. endings -τυ, -ντυ. **22**
7. ὄνυ = ὅδε. **123**
8. Dat. with ἀπό, ἐξ, etc. **136**.1
9. -κρέτης = -κράτης. **49**.2

190. Common to Arcado-Cyprian and various other dialects (1 Att.-Ion., 2 Ion., 3-6 Aeol., 7 N.W. Grk.).

1. Infin. in -ναι. **154**.1
2. βόλομαι = βούλομαι. **75**b
3. ἀπύ = ἀπό. **22**
4. ὄν (ὐν) = ἀνά. **6, 22**
5. op = αρ. **5**
6. μι -inflect. of contract vbs. **157**
7. ἐν (ἰν) = εἰς. **135**.4
8. η, ω = secondary ε̄, ō. **25**
9. ἐς = ἐξ before cons. (but Cypr. also ἐξ). **100**

10. Masc. σ-stems, acc. sg. -ην (Arc. also voc. sg. -η). **108**.2
11. ἱερής = ἱερεύς, etc. (but usual only in Arc.). **111**.4
12. Subj. -ης, -η. **149**
13. Article as relative. **126**
14. Opt. in prescriptions. **175**
15. πτόλις. **67**

191. Noteworthy is the considerable number of words or meanings which are otherwise known only, or with rare exceptions, as poetical, mainly Homeric. Some of the most striking examples are

1. In Arcadian and Cyprian, αἶσα 'share' (also Arg.), οἶ(ϝ)ος 'alone,' εὐχωλά 'prayer' or 'imprecation.'

2. In Arcadian. δέαμαι, ἀπύω 'summon,' κέλευθος 'road,' δῶμα 'temple,' ἆμαρ (but see no. 17.22, note), λεύσσω 'behold.'

3. In Cyprian. ϝάναξ, ἀνώγω, αὐτάρ, ἕλος 'meadow,' ἰjατήρ, κασίγνητος (also Lesb.; Thess. κατίγν[ειτος]), χραύομαι 'border on' (Hom. χραύω 'graze'), ἰδέ, νυ (also Boeot. **134**.5).

---

[1] Several of the characteristics cited below under the head of Arcadian or of Cyprian, for which corresponding forms are lacking or ambiguous in the other dialect, probably are also Arcado-Cyprian. See also **199**.

[2] In this and similar captions "special" is not to be taken too rigorously. Some few peculiarities of which occasional examples are found elsewhere are included, e.g., in this section, ἰν = ἐν, which is regularly found only in Arcado-Cyprian, but of which there are a few examples elsewhere.

Arcadian

192. Arcado-Cyprian characteristics. See **189/91**.

193. In common with various other dialects (1, 2 Att.-Ion., 3 Lesb., 5 Aeol., etc., 6, 16 West Greek).

1. Conjunction εἰ. **134**.1
2. Particle ἄν. **134**.2
3. δέκοτος = δέκατος. **6**
4. ἦνθον = ἦλθον. **72**
5. πεδά (πέ) = μετά. **135**.5
6. παρετάξωνσι, etc. **142**
7. ρρ = ρσ. **80**
8. πάνσα, etc. **77**.3
9. Acc. pl. -ος, nom. sg. pple. ἱεροθυτές. **78**
10. ἥμισσον. **81**
11. Dat. sg. -οι. **106**.2
12. Subj. δέᾱτοι, etc. **151**.1
13. Infin. -εν and -ην. **153**.2

14. 3 pl. imv. -ντω. **140**.3a; mid. -σθων **140**.2b
15. Adverbs in -θι place 'where,' as ὁπόθι, etc. **132**.9a
16. ὀδελός = ὀβολός. **49**.3
17. μέστ' 'until.' **132**.10
18. Peculiarities in the use of the spiritus asper. **58**d
19. ϝ in early inscr. initially and after cons., but lost between vowels; initially till about 300 B.C. **52, 53, 54**

194. Special Arcadian.

1. Gen. sg. fem. -ᾱυ (Tegea). **104**.2
2. 3 pl. -νσι. **77**.3
3. 3 sg. mid. -τοι = -ται. **139**.1
4. δέκο, ἑηκοτόν = δέκα, ἑκατόν. **6**
5. Numerals in -κάσιοι = -κό- σιοι. **117**.2
6. ι from ε before front vowels, and ῑ from ει. **9**.5

7. ὀνί = ὅδε. **123**
8. κατύ = κατά. **22, 95**
9. πλός = πλέον. **113**.2
10. εἰκ ἄν. **134**.2a
11. ἀπυδόας = ἀποδούς. **144**
12. τείω = τίνω. **162**.14
13. δέλλω = βάλλω. **68**.1
14. Ποσοιδᾶν = Ποσειδῶν. **49**.1, **61**.5
15. Dual forms in -αιυν, -οιυν. **106**.6

195. External influence in the dialect. The fact that κάς and σις, ὄζις, agreeing with Cyprian, are found only in the early inscriptions (nos. 16, 17), while all others have καί and τις, is probably due to external influence, though not specifically Attic. See **275**. The Tegean building inscription (no. 19) of the fourth century B.C. shows some few Attic κοινή forms, as πλέον instead of πλός, once gen. sg. -ου, etc. From the latter part of the third century on, when the chief Arcadian cities belonged to the Achaean League, or in some cases were controlled by the Aetolian League, most of the inscriptions are in the Doric or the Northwest Greek κοινή, e.g., one from Stymphalus (IG V.ii.359) with forms like κα, ὅκα, τετρώκοντα, πότ, τοῦ, τούς, δόντω and ἐν = εἰς. But a decree of Megalopolis (Ditt. Syll. 559), of about 200 B.C. in the time of a temporary revival of the Arcadian League, is mainly in the native dialect (ἰν, acc. pl. -ος, ποίενσι, τοσνύν). Curious is the occasional late occurrence of the Lac. σ = θ (68), as Σιοῦ = Θεοῦ, Σίπομπος = Θεόπομπος, etc.

Cyprian

196. Arcado-Cyprian characteristics. See **189-91**.

197. In common with various other dialects.

1. ι from ε before vowels. **9.**6
2. Glide sound after ι expressed, as ἰjατἔραν. **56**
3. αἶλος = ἄλλος. **74**b
4. Psilosis. **57**
5. πείσει = τείσει. **68.**2a
6. F in all positions. **52-55**
7. Occasional omission of intervoc. and final σ. **59.**4

8. Dat. sg. -ō, -ᾱ beside -ōι, -ᾱι. **38**
9. Acc. sg. ἰjατἔραν, etc. **107.**1
10. βασιλεύς, -ἔϝος. **111.**1
11. 3 pl. κατέθιjαν. **138.**5
12. κε = ἄν. **134.**2
13. ἕρπω 'go, come.' **162.**6
14. ἡμίνα. **164.**10
15. See also in Glossary, ἀκεύω, λιμήν, παῖς.

198. Special Cyprian.

1. Gen. sg. -ōν. **106.**1
2. πτόλιϝι, etc. **109.**4
3. ϝρέτα, ϝρετάω. **55, 70.**3
4. ζᾶ = γᾶ, etc. **62.**4
5. ὐ = ἐπί. **135.**8
6. παι 'indeed.' **132.**5

7. ἔ = εἰ. **134.**1
8. δυϝάνω, δώκω = δίδωμι. **162.**5
9. See, in Glossary, ἄλϝον, ἰχμάμενος, ἰναλίνω, οἴρων, ὕγγεμος.

199. It is uncertain whether the infinitive should be transcribed with -εν or -ἔν, the accusative with -ος, -ōς or -ο(ν)ς. In the absence of any evidence to the contrary, we assume -εν and -ος in agreement with Arcadian. But the dative singular is to be transcribed -ōι, in spite of Arc. -οι, on account of the frequent omission of the final ι (**38**); and the third plural ending is transcribed with -σι, not -(ν)σι, in spite of Arc. -νσι, on account of φρονέōι (**59**.4).

Pamphylian

200. 1 (in part)-8 in common with Arcado-Cyprian, or Aeolic, 9-15 with West Greek or Cretan..

1. ἰν (written ί) = ἐν. ἰς from *ἰνς = εἰς. **10**, **135**.4
2. υ from ο. **22**a
3. Dative with ἐξ. **136**.1
4. Particle νι. **134**.5
5. Spelling διά, etc. **56**
6. Omission of ν before consonants. **69**.2
7. Dat. pl. of cons. stems -εσσι. **107**.3
8. 3 pl. imv. -ντον (-δυ). **140**.5
9. ἰαρός. **13**.1
10. Retention of τι. **61**.1, 2. **138**.4
11. φίκατι = εἴκοσι. **51**b, **61**.2, **116**
12. ὄκα. **132**.9
13. τ for θ in ἄτρōπος, Πύτιος. **63**

14. Ἀπέλλων Πύτιος. **49**.3, **63**
15. Ἀφορδίσιυς. **70**.1
16. ι from ε before vowels. **9**.6
17. Secondary ō, by lengthening ω, by contraction ου. **25**d
18. μhειάλαν, etc. **62**.3, **76**b
19. ὔπαρ = ὔπερ. **12**
20. Ϝ preserved, expressed by two different letters. **51**b
21. περτί = πρός. **61**.4, **70**.1, **135**.6
22. ἐβōλάσετυ, βολέμενυς. **22**a, **25**d, **142**c, **161**b
23. Change of ντ to νδ, with ν not written. **66**, **69**.2
24. Final ν usually omitted. **89**.9

AEOLIC

201. Aeolic characteristics, common to Lesbian, Thessalian, [3] and Boeotian (6 also Delph., etc., 7 also Arc.-Cypr., 8 also Arc.).

1. Labial instead of dental in πέμπε = πέντε, etc. **68**.2
2. Perf. act. pple. -ων, -οντος. **147**.3
3. Patron. adj. instead of gen. sg. of father's name. **168**

4. ἴα = μία. **114**.1
5. ρε = ρι. **18**
6. Dat. pl. πόδεσσι, etc. **107**.3
7. ρο = ρα, etc. **5**
8. Θερσ- = Θαρσ-. **49**.2

---

[3] In some cases only East Thessalian (Pelasgiotis). See **214**.

202. Aeolic characteristics, common to Lesbian and Thessalian (4-7 also Arc.-Cypr.).

1. Double liquids and nasals in ἐμμί, στάλλα, etc. **74-76, 77.**1, **79**
2. ἀγρέω (ἀνγρέω) = αἱρέω. **162.**2
3. ṛ from ι before vowels. **19**

4. μι-inflection of contract verbs. **157**
5. ὄν = ἀνά. **6**
6. ἀπύ =· ἀπό. **22**
7. κε = ἄν. **134.**2

203. Characteristics common to Lesbian and Boeotian (2 also Arc., Cret., etc.).

1. ἐκάλε-σσα, etc. **143**
2. πεδά = μετά. **135.**5

204. Characteristics common to Thessalian and Boeotian only (of which, however, only 1, which is Homeric, belongs to the Aeolic elements of these dialects).

1. Infin. φερέμεν, etc. **155.**1
2. 3 pl. -νθι, etc. **139.**2
3. ει = η. **16**
4. γίνυμαι = γίγνομαι. **162.**4
5. Θεόζοτος. **166.**2

6. ἔλεξε = εἶπε in the official language of decrees (but also Argive).
7. ὑστερομει(ν)νία. Glossary.

Lesbian

205. Characteristics in common with one or both of the other Aeolic dialects. See **201-3.**

206. In common with various other dialects.

1. η, ω = secondary ē, ō. **25**
2. Final -ᾱ, -η, -ω = ᾱι, ηι, ωι, from end of fourth century on. **38**
3. Psilosis. **57**
4. Early loss of ϝ. **50**
5. δέχοτος = δέχατος. **6**
6. Dat. pl. -αισι, -οισι. **104.**7, **106.**4

7. βασίλευς, -ηος, etc. **111.**1
8. Masc. σ-stems, acc. sg. -ην, gen. sg. -η, etc. **108.**2
9. Article as relative. **126**
10. ὑπά = ὑπό. **135.**3
11. Infin. -ην. **153.**1
12. Perf. infin. -ην. **147.**2
13. Pass. infin. -ην. **155.**2
14. παῖς 'son.' Glossary

207. Special Lesbian (1 in part Elean and in part Cyrenaean).

1. ισ from νς, as παῖσα, etc. (also Cyren.), acc. pl. ταίς, τοίς (also El.), 3 pl. φέροισι. **77.**3, **78**

2. αἴμισυς = ἤμισυς, etc. **17**

3. αὔως, ναῦος, etc. **35**

4. ὅτα = ὅτε. **132.**11

5. ὅττι, ὅππως, etc. **129.**2

6. Infin. ἔμμεναι, etc. **154.**2

7. Infin. δίδων, κέρνᾱν, etc. **155.**3

8. 3 pl. imv. -ντον, -σθον. **140.**5

9. Recessive accent. **103**

10. εὔκοιστος, etc. = Att. -κοσ- τος. **116**

11. σπέλλω = στέλλω. **68.**2a

12. ἔταλον 'yearling.' **49.**3

13. ἀρνηάς 'ewe,' ἔπερος 'sheep', δικάσκοποι, official title. Glossary

14. πρότανις (rarely Attic) = πρύτανις. Glossary

208. External influence in the dialect. From the Macedonian period on—and very few of the inscriptions are earlier—there is usually some admixture of κοινή forms, as ἀνά beside ὀν, μετά beside πεδά, ὅτε beside ὅτα, etc. But in the main the dialect is employed in inscriptions till about the middle of the second century B.C. Its use in inscriptions of Roman imperial times (cf. no. 27) represents an artificial revival. See **280**.

Thessalian

209. Aeolic characteristics in common with one or both of the Aeolic dialects. See **201, 202**.

210. West Greek and Northwest Greek characteristics (cf. **223.**1, 2, 3, 4, 6, and **226.**1, 4).

1. Retention of τ in 3 pl. -ντι -νθι **61, 138.**4

2. ἴκατι = εἴκοσι. **116**

3. -κάτιοι (ἐξεικάττιοι). **117**

4. ψαφίξασθειν, etc. **142**

5. ἰαρός beside ἱερός. **13.**1

6. ἐν = εἰς. **135.**4

7. στ = σθ (rare). **85.**1

211. In common with various other dialects.

1. ι from ε before vowels (but oftener ε). **9.**3

2. ει, ου (but from η, ω) = secondary ε̄, ō. **25**

3. Final -ᾱ, -ου (from ω), -ει (from η) = -ᾱι, -ωι, -ηι. **38**

4. ἐς = ἐξ before cons. **100**

5. πάνσα, etc. **77.**3

6. Acc. pl. -ος. **78**

7. ττ = ππ. **86.**2

8. πτόλις beside πόλις. **67**

9. δδ = ζ. **84**

10. Doubling of ξ. **89**.1
11. Psilosis in article. **58***a*
12. Ϝ init. till about 400 B.C.
13. Gen. sg. -αο, usually ᾱ. **41**.4
14. Gen. pl. -άουν, usually -ᾶν. **41**.4
15. βασιλεύς, -εῖος, etc. **111**.1

16. Plural inflection of δύω, as δύας. **114**.2
17. Article as relative. **126**
18. παρά 'at, with,' with acc. **136**.2
19. Names in -κλέᾱς. **166**.1
20. Ϝοικιάτας = οἰκέτης. **167**

212. In common with Boeotian only. See **204.**
213. Special Thessalian.

1. ου = ω. **23**
2. Gen. sg. -οι (but see **214**). **106**.1
3. κίς = τίς (but see **214**). **68**.4
4. More extensive apocope than in any other dialect, namely in κάτ, πότ, πάρ, πέρ, ὀν, ἀπ, ἐπ, ὑπ. **95**
5. Consonant-doubling in πόλλιος, ἰδδίαν, κῦρρον = κύριον, etc. **19**.3
6. διέ = διά. **7**
7. βέλλομαι = βούλομαι. **75**
8. ὀστροφά = ἀναστροφή. **77**.2
9. ὄνε (τόνε, τοίνεος, etc.) = ὅδε. **123**
10. Relative use of κίς, ποῖος. **131**
11. ὅπει, ὀπειδεί = ἐπεί, ἐπειδή. **132**.7
12. μές, μέσποδι 'until.' **132**.12
13. μά = δέ. **134**.4
14. τᾶμον 'of the present time.' Glossary
15. 3 pl. ἐνεφανίσσοεν, ἐδούκαεμ, etc. **138**.5

16. 3 sg. mid. ἐψάφιστει, etc. (Larissa). **27**
17. 3 pl. mid. ἐφάνγρενθειν, etc. (Larissa). **27, 139**.2
18. Infin. δεδόσθειν, etc. (Larissa). **27, 156**
19. ἔνσα = οὖσα. **163**.8
20. πεστάντες = περιστάντες. **89**.7
21. Λασαῖος = Λαρισαῖος. **89***b*
22. Ἄπλουν = Ἀπόλλων. **49**.3
23. Πετθαλός = Θεσσαλός. **65, 68**.2
24. λίθιος = λίθινος. **164**.6, 9
25. δαύχνα = δάφνη. **68**.4*a*
26. ὀνάλα = ἀνάλωμα. **164**.9
27. λιμήν = ἀγορά 'market-place' (ἀγορά being = ἐκκλησία)
28. κίων often used in place of στάλλα (στήλη)
29. ταγός as title of a state or municipal official
30. σπόλος 'stake.' **68**.2*a*
31. συνκλείς. **164**.9
32. λειτορεύω. Glossary

214. Differences within Thessalian. The form of Thessalian which is best known is that of Pelasgiotis, represented mainly by inscriptions of Larisa, which show some special local peculiarities (**213**.8-10), Crannon, and Phalanna. [4] The dialect of Thessaliotis, represented mainly by inscriptions of Pharsalus and Cierium, differs from that of Pelasgiotis in two important respects, (1) gen. sg. of o-stems in -ō, -ου, not -οι, (2) pres. infin. of thematic verbs in -ēν, -ειν, not -εμεν. The early inscription, no. 35, from Thetonium in the neighborhood of Cierium, shows, in addition to these two points of difference, τις not κις, dat. pl. of consonant stems in -σιν (χρέμασιν) not -εσσι (as at Pharsalus as well as in Pelasgiotis), hυλōρέοντος not -έντος, uncontracted gen. sg. in -αο, gen. sg. of father's name instead of patronymic adjective (? see no. 35.11, note). Late inscriptions of Cierium have dat. sg. -οι, -αι, though at Pharsalus we find -ου, -α, just as in Pelasgiotis, and in no. 35 ἐν ταγᾶ beside ἐν ἀταγίαι points to -ᾶι, -ōι. On δδ = ζ in ἐξξανακάδεν, no. 35, see **84**; on ττ beside σσ, see **81**c.

From Histiaeotis and Perrhaebia the material is very scanty. From Magnesia there are a few fragmentary archaic inscriptions, but most are late and in the Attic κοινή. An early inscription of Phthiotis (Μεθίστας Πιθούνειος Ἄπλουνι IG IX.ii.199) shows conclusively, what was only natural to expect, that its dialect was also Thessalian. But nearly all the inscriptions date from the period of Aetolian domination and are in the Northwest Greek κοινή (**279**.)

Many of the characteristics cited in the preceding sections are as yet attested only in the inscriptions of Pelasgiotis, but, except where there is evidence to the contrary as stated, it is to be assumed provisionally that they are general Thessalian. For the points of agreement are more pronounced than the differences.

215. External influence in the dialect. Occasional κοινή forms appear in the inscriptions of the third and second centuries B.C., especially ἀνά, ἀπό, περί, κατά, δέ, gen. sg. instead of patronymic adjective, η (not ει), γίνομαι (not γίνυμαι), etc. But the dialect as a whole is employed in inscriptions until about the end of the second century B.C. and occasionally later.

---

[4] Really in Perrhaebia, so far as this was recognized as a distinct division of Thessaly, but in the part near Pelasgiotis.

Boeotian

216. Aeolic characteristics in common with one or both of the other Aeolic dialects. See **201, 203**.

217. West Greek and Northwest Greek characteristics (cf. **223**.1-10, and **226**.1, 2, 4).

1. δίδωτι, etc., **61**
2. Ϝίκατι = είκοσι. **116**
3. πεντακάτιοι, etc. **116**a, **117**
4. ἐπεσκεύαξε, etc. (but oftener ττ). **142**
5. τοί, ταί = οἱ, αἱ. **122**
6. ἱαρός = ἱερός. **13**.1
7. Ἄρταμις = Ἄρτεμις. **13**.2

8. κα = κε, ἄν. **134**.2
9. πόκα. **132**.11
10. πρᾶτος = πρῶτος. **114**.1
11. αὐτῖ, i.e. αὐτεῖ = αὐτοῦ. **132**.2
12. ἐν = εἰς. **135**.4
13. δείμενος = δεόμενος. **158**
14. παρά 'at, with,' with acc. **136**.2

218. In common with various other dialects.

1. ει (from η), ω = secondary ε̄, ō. **25**
2. ι from ε before vowels. **9**.4
3. ττ in θάλαττα, εἴμιττον, etc. **81**
4. ττ in μέττος, ἐψαφίττατο, etc. **82**
5. δδ, initial δ = ζ. **84**
6. ἐς = ἐξ before cons. (see also **220**.1). **100**
7. πρισγεύς = πρεσβεύς. **68**.1, **86**.3
8. Ϝ initial and intervocalic frequently (but not consistently) until nearly 200 B.C. **50, 53**
9. Nom. sg. m. -ᾱ beside -ᾱς. **105**.1a
10. Gen. sg. m. and gen. pl. in -ᾱο, -ᾱων (but τᾶν). **41**.4

11. Dat. sg. -αι(-η), -οι (-υ), **104**.3, **106**.2
12. -ευς, -εῖος, -έϜι. **111**.1
13. αὐτοσαυτός, αὐσαυτός, etc. **121**.4
14. ταν-ί, etc. **122**
15. ὑπά = ὑπό. **135**.3
16. ἀντί 'during.' **136**.8
17. Article as relative (rare). **126**
18. 3 pl. ἀνέθεαν, ἀνέθιαν, etc. **138**.5
19. 3 pl. imv. -ντω (-νθω). **140**.3a
20. Perf. ἀποδεδόανθι, etc., without κ. **146**.1
21. ἔντω (ἔνθω) = ὄντων. **163**.6
22. Διοκλέας, etc. **166**.1
23. Consonant-doubling in hypocoristics. **89**.5
24. Names in -ώνδας. **164**.8
25. γραμματιστάς. **161**.4

26. ποθόδωμα. **164**.10

27. λάζομαι (λάδδουσθη) = λαμβάνω. Glossary

28. παῖς 'son.' Glossary

29. εἰλύτα 'a kind of cake' =
Ther. ἐλλύτα. **73**a

219. In common with Thessalian only. See **204**.

220. Special Boeotian. Most of the peculiarities of the vowel
system (**221**) also belong here.

1. ἐσς = ἐξ before vowels. **100**
2. ἔππασις = ἔμπασις. **69**.4
3. οὗτος, οὗτα, etc. **124**
4. εἴνιξαν = ἤνεγκαν. **144**a
5. βείλομαι = βούλομαι. **75**
6. Hypocoristics in ει. **108**.2
7. ἄλωμα = ἀνάλωμα. **164**.10
8. γαεργός, 3 sg. fut. γαϜερ-
γείσι = γεωργός, etc. **167**
9. ἐπίθωσε = ἔπεισε. **161**.3

10. -λιηνω 'cancel.' **162**.10
11. Ϝίστωρ 'witness.' **52**d
12. ἀφεδριατεύω. No. 41, note
13. προτηνί 'formerly.' **123**,
136.1
14. πιτεύω 'irrigate.' Glossary
15. περίσαος 'left over, remaining.' Glossary
16. Several new words for
utensils in no. 39

221. The Boeotian vowel-system. The most striking and
obvious characteristic of Boeotian lies in its vowel-system. One
peculiarity consists merely in the retention of the original sound,
namely, that of υ as *u*. But even this led to a change in spelling
to ου, while on the other hand the υ with its Attic value of *ü* as a
basis was used to indicate approximately the sound, probably *ö*,
which the diphthong οι had come to have. See **24**, **30**. The other
peculiarities consist in changes of diphthongs to monophthongs
and of more open to closer vowels, such as eventually prevailed
everywhere and led to the Modern Greek pronunciation.

The chief orthographical peculiarities, with the approximate
date of their introduction, are as follows:

ι = ε before vowels. **9**.4. Fifth century B.C. (in the epichoric
alphabet ι, ε, ει, Ⱶ)

ι = ει. **29**. Fifth century B.C. (in the epichoric alphabet
ι, ει, Ⱶ)

η = αι. **26**. Early fourth century B.C.

ει = η. **16**.

ου = υ. **24**. Early fourth century B.C., common after 300 B.C.
(but great inconsistency is the spelling. υ = υ and οι
= οι also frequent till near end of the third century),

ιου = υ.   **24.** About 300 B.C.

υ = οι.   **30.** About 250 B.C.

ει = οι.   **30.** Second century B.C. (rare)

222. External influence. Although Boeotia was for a short time in the Aetolian League, there are no Boeotian inscriptions in the Northwest Greek κοινή. But there are some scattered examples of the dative plural of consonant stems in -οις, as ἤγυς (αἴγοις), etc., and the appearance of στ = σθ (**85**.1) and δαμιωέμεν, δαμιώοντες (**159**) in some late inscriptions of Orchomenos is also probably due to Aetolian influence. The influence of the Attic κοινή becomes considerable toward the end of the third century B.C, and some inscriptions or portions of inscriptions are wholly in κοινή, e.g. the formal contract in the Nicareta inscription (no. 43.VI). But most of the inscriptions are substantially dialectal until the second half of the second century B.C.

WEST GREEK

223. General West Greek characteristics:

1. δίδωτι, etc. with retention of τ. **61**.
2. (F)ίκατι = εἴκοσι. **116** with a
3. -κάτιοι = -κόσιοι. **116**a, **117**.2
4. ἐδίκαξα, etc. But restricted in Argolic. **142**
5. τοί, ταί = οἱ, αἱ. But Cret. οἱ, αἱ. **122**
6. ἱαρός (ἱαρός) = ἱερός. **13**.1
7. Ἄρταμις = Ἄρτεμις. But Cret. Ἄρτεμις. **13**.2
8. κα, τόκα, πόκα, ὄκα, γα. **132**.11, **134**.2
9. πρᾶτος = πρῶτος. **114**.1

10. ὅπει, etc. **132**.2
11. ὅπη, etc. **132**.7
12. ὅπω, etc. **132**.8
13. φέρομες, etc. **138**.3
14. Fut. -σέω. **141**
15. τέτορες = τέτταρες. **114**.4
16. τετρώκοντα = τετταράκοντα. **116**
17. ἔβδεμος = ἔβδομος. **114**.7
18. ἐμίν = ἐμοί, etc. **118**.4b
19. ἐμέος = ἐμοῦ, etc. **118**.3b
20. ὀδελός = ὀβολός. **49**.3
21. δήλομαι, δείλομαι. **68**.1, **75**
22. λείω, λέω = θέλω. **162**.11
23. Word-order αἴ τίς κα. **179**

a. Although only a part of these characteristics are actually quotable from every one of the West Greek dialects, some indeed from only a few, it is probable that, except for the divergence of Cretan in 5 and 7, they were common to all, and that the absence of examples in any dialect is accidental. Thus, forms like φέρομες are attested for Phocian and most of the Doric dialects, but there is no occurrence of a first plural form in Locrian and Elean, and in Rhodian only from the time when -μεν had been introduced from the κοινή, just as it was at Delphi before the end of the fourth century B.C. The early substitution of the κοινή forms of the numerals and the rare occurrence of the personal pronouns in inscriptions, account for the incomplete representation of 2, 3, 15-19.

b. The first ten of these characteristics are also Boeotian (**217**), several also Thessalian (**220**), and a few also Arcadian.

224. There are various other phenomena which are common to the West Greek dialects, but are not confined to them even in the widest application of the term. Several of those mentioned in **180** are often casually referred to as "Doric," e.g., αἰ = εἰ, ἦς = ἦν, ἀμές, ἔθεν, πᾶμα, ἴκω, but none of them has any claim to be regarded as specifically West Greek, with the possible exception of η from αε (**41**.1 with *a*).

a. Even of the peculiarities cited in **223** some consist merely in the retention of the original forms which must have been universal at one time; and that τοί, ταί or pron. datives like ἐμίν still existed in East Greek in the historical period is shown by their appearance in Homer. Some others also may prove to be of wider scope, e.g., ὅπει, since ὅπου is, so far as we know, only Attic-Ionic. But so far as the present evidence of inscriptions goes, the peculiarities given in **223** are distinctly characteristic of West Greek.

225. The declension of nouns in -εύς with gen. sg. -έος, acc. sg. -ῆ is common to Delphian and the majority, but not all, of the Doric dialects. See **111**.5. The 3 pl. imv. -ντω is common to all the Doric dialects except Cretan, Theran, Cyrenaean, but the distribution of -ντω and -ντων does not coincide at all with the East and West Greek divisions. See **140**.3, 4. There are various peculiarities which are West Greek in a limited sense, but demonstrably not general West Greek, e.g., τῆνος = ἐκεῖνος (**125**.1), αὐτοσαυτός (**121**.4), πρόσθα = πρόσθε (**133**.1), Ἀπέλλων (**49**.3), ντ, νθ = λτ, λθ (**72**).

NORTHWEST GREEK

226. The chief characteristics of Northwest Greek as distinguished from Doric, including however some which are not common to all the dialects of this group and some which are not strictly confined to them, are:

1. ἐν = εἰς. Also Thess., Boet., and Arc.-Cypr. (ἰν), 135.4
2. καλείμενος, etc. (El. -ημε-νος). Also Boeot., etc. 158
3. φάρω, etc. But rare in Delph. 12
4. στ = σθ 85.1
5. ἔντε, Delph. hέντε = ἔστε. No example in El. 135.4

6. πάντοις, etc., dat. pl. But in Delph. only late and due to Aetolian influence, and in Locr. also other forms. 107.3
7. τέτορες, etc., acc. pl. El., Ach., but not Locr., and rare in Delph. 107.4

a. There are various other peculiarities the scope of which coincides even less definitely with the Northwest Greek dialects proper, but the spread of which in the northern part of Greece is noticeable, e.g., masc. ā-stems with nom. sg. -ā, gen. sg. -ᾱς (105.1a, 2e), personal names in -ώνδας or -όνδας (164.8), and in -κλέας (166.1).

Phocian (Mostly Delphian)

227. West Greek characteristics. See **223-25**.

228. Northwest Greek characteristics. See **226**.

229. Aeolic elements: πάντεσσι, etc. in all the earlier inscriptions. **107.3**. Here also, perhaps, the words ταγός (also Thess., Cypr., and poetical), κεραίω (also Hom.) = κεράννυμι, δίδημι (also Boeot. and Hom.) == δέω 'bind'.

230. Characteristics mostly in common with various other dialects.

1. ει, ου = secondary ē, ō. 25
2. ϝ initial till about 400 B.C. Intervocalic only in a sixth century inscription.
3. Peculiarities in the use of the spiritus asper. 58a, b, c
4. ἐντοφήια. 6
5. η from εα, in part. 42.1
6. ἀποστράψαι. 49.2
7. hēμιρρήνιον. 55a

8. φατρία (Stiris) = φρατρία. 70.3
9. ἀμφιλλέγω. 76
10. ρρ=ρσ in Θαρρίκων, etc. 80
11. ἥμισσον. 81
12. Crasis in κήν, κηὔκλεια, κωὒτε, etc. 94.6,7
13. Apocope in κάτ, πότ, πάρ, πέρ, and in compounds ἀν (ἀμμόνιον). 95 Elision in πέροδος. 91a.

14. τῶλ Λαβυαδᾶν, τοὺν νό-
    μους, etc. **96, 97**
15. αὐτός as reflexive. **121**.3
16. αὐτοσαυτός, αὐσαυτός.
    121.4
17. τοῦτοι = οὗτοι, τοῦτα = ταῦ-
    τα. **124**
18. τῆνος (in τηνεῖ) = ἐκεῖνος.
    125 ι
19. ἄδε. **132**.6
20. Ϝοίκω = οἰκόθεν. **132**.8
21. ἐχθός, ἔχθω. **133**.3
22. ἐνδός, ἔνδω. **133**.4
23. ποί (beside πότ) = πρός.
    135.6
24. 3 pl. perf. -ατι. **138**.4
25. 3 pl. imv. -ντων. **140**.4*a*
26. Infin. -εν. **153**.2
27. στεφανώω, etc. = -όω. **159**
28. συλέω = συλάω. **161**.2
29. ποιῶντι, ποιόντων, θεαρόν-
    τον. **42**.5*d*

30. ποεῖνται. **158**
31. ἦται (late). **163**.9
32. παρά 'at, with,' with acc.
    136.2
33. ἀντί 'during.' **136**.8
34. ὑπέρ 'in behalf of' with acc.
    136.10
35. χρήζω 'wish.' **162**.14
36. γραμματιστάς. **161**.4
37. κεφάλωμα = κεφαλαῖον.
    164.10
38. πενταμαριτεύω. **12**, no. 52
    D 16, note
39. ἀζετόω 'convict.' No. 55.17
    note
40. δαράται and γάμελα. No.
    52 A 24, note
41. πατρία 'gens.' No. 52 A 25,
    note
42. See also, in Glossary, αἶνος,
    ἀλία, ἀμμόνιον, ἀρέσμιον,
    προτεράσιος, τέλειος.

231. External influence in the dialect. The temple accounts of 353-325 B.C. show plain evidences of Attic influence. With the Aetolian domination (278-178 B.C.) a new element is added, that of the Northwest Greek κοινή (see **279**), resulting in the striking mixture (e.g., dat. pl. πάντεσσι, πάντοις, πᾶσι) seen in the numerous proxeny and manumission decrees, some of them as late as the first and second centuries A.D. There are even some few traces of Boeotian influence, as in ἱστάνθω, θέλωνθι, κλαρωσῖ (ῑ = εῖ) from Stiris, near the Boeotian boundary, and the spellings κή (= καί), ἄσουλον in a decree of the Phocians. The Amphictionic decrees immediately following the Aetolian conquest are in the pure Attic κοινή, but the dialect was gradually resumed, in the mixed form which it shows in the other classes of inscriptions.

Locrian

232. West Greek characteristics. See **223-25**.

233. Northwest Greek characteristics. See **226.**

234. In common with various other dialects.

1. Ε, ΕΙ, Ο, OV, later ει, ου = secondary ē, ō. **25d**
2. κοθαρός (Περϙοθαριᾶν) = καθαρός. **6**
3. 'Οπόεντι, 'Οποντίους. **44.4**
4. Ϝ initial, rarely intervocalic. **52, 53**
5. Peculiarities in the use of the spiritus asper. **58a, d**
6. ἔμισον. **58d, 81, 89.6**
7. Doubling of ξ. **89.1**
8. τόαροί = τοὶ ἱαροί. (Halae). **94.9**
9. Apocope, assimilation, and simplification in κὰ τᾶς, κὰ τῶνδε, πὸ τούς. **89.7, 95**
10. ἀμφιλλέγω. **76**
11. μεῖστον. **113.2**
12. ταὐτᾶ, ἅ. **132.6**

13. ἀριστίνδαν, πλουτίνδαν, ἀγχιστέδαν. **133.7**
14. ἐχθός = ἐκτός. **133.3**
15. ὑπα- = ὑπο-. **135.3**
16. ποί (once) = πρός. **135.6b**
17. 3 pl. imv. -ντō; mid. -ōσθōν. **140.3a, 4b**
18. ἐλᾶ- in ἀπελᾶōνται. **159**
19. Ϝέρρω = φεύγω. **162.7**
20. τεθμός, τετθμός, θέθμιον = θεσμός, and δαιθμός = δασμός. **164.4**
21. δικαστήρ. **164.5**
22. οἰκιάτας = οἰκέτης. **167**
23. τέλειος = κύριος 'valid.' Glossary
24. παῖς 'son,' κόρα 'daughter.' Glossary
25. πλέθα 'assembly.' Glossary

235. Special Locrian.

1. ἐ from ἐκ in ἐ δάμō, ἐ λιμένος, etc. **89.7, 100**
2. αἴ τι συλōι, etc. = αἴ τις. **89.7**
3. hαρέσται = ἑλέσθαι. **12**
4. φρίν = πρίν. **66**
5. ἀλάζω = ἀλλάσσω. **84a**
6. κατά 'according to' with gen. **136.5**
7. ἀνδρεφονικός. **167**

8. ἐχεπάμōν 'heir,' παματοφαγεῖσται 'be confiscated.' **162.12**
9. λιποτελέω. Glossary
10. πρείγα 'council.' **86.3**, no. **59.10**
11. πεντάμεροι, title of officials. Glossary
12. ἀξιοδότας. No. **59b**, note

236. The important inscriptions (nos. 57-59) are from the early fifth century B.C., and are from Western Locris. But one of these is presumably a copy of an original draft made at Opus. The other material, except for a few short inscriptions, is from a much later period and in mixed dialect. The view that East and West Locrian were materially different in the early period is without adequate foundation and must be given up.

Elean

237. West Greek characteristics. See **223-25**.

238. Northwest Greek characteristics. See **226**.

239. In common with various other dialects.

1. η, ω = secondary ε̄, ō. **25**
2. Psilosis. **57**
3. δδ (also ττ) = ζ. **84**
4. ρρ = ρσ. **80**
5. Rhotacism of final ς. **60**.1
6. Intervocalic σ > h or lost (late). **59**.3
7. ϝ init. even before consonants, rarely intervoc.; late βοικίαρ = οἰκίας. **51,55**
8. αἰλότρια = ἀλλότρια .**74**b
9. Omission of ι in ἔα = εἴη, etc. **31**
10. γροφεύς = γραφεύς. **49**.2
11. Apocope in κά, πό, πάρ = παρά, and πάρ = περί. **95**
12. Nom. sg. τελεστά. **105**.1a
13. Dat. sg. -οι. **106**.2
14. Acc. pl. -αις, -αιρ, -οιρ. **78**
15. Dat. pl. φυγάδεσσι (but usually -οις). **107**.3
16. βασιλεύς, -ῆος. **111**.1
17. ἄσιστα = ἄγχιστα. **113**.3

18. αὐτός reflexive. **121**.3
19. τοί, ταί = τόδε, τάδε. **122**
20. ταὐτόν = τούτων. **124**
21. Article as relative (late). **126**
22. ὑπα- = ὑπο-. **135**.3
23. παρά 'at, with' with acc. **136**.2
24. ὑπό with gen. in dating. **136**.11
25. ἐγραμένος = γεγραμμένος. **137**
26. 3 pl. imv. -ντōν; mid. -ōστōν. **140**.4a, 4b
72. 3 sg. subj. -ā = -η. **149**
28. Aor. subj. in ā (φυγαδεύαντι, ποιήαται). **151**.1
29. 3 sg. aor. opt. -σειε, -hαιε. **152**.4
30. Infin. -ην. **153**.1
31. μι-forms συλαίē, δαμοσιοία, δαμοσιῶμεν. **157**c
32. ϝάρρω, ϝέρρω = φεύγω. **162**.7

240. Special Elean.

1. ā = η. **15**
2. α = ε, not only before ρ, but after ρ, before final ν, etc. **12** with a

3. πόλερ, βενέοι. **18**b
4. ζ = δ (only in earliest inscr.). **62**.2
5. πάσκω = πάσχω. **66**

6. σσ = σθ (late). **85**.2
7. Extreme elision in article. **94**.9
8. Gen.-dat. dual -οιοις, -οιοιρ. **106**.7
9. μεύς = μήν. **112**.3
10. ὀπτό = ὀκτώ. **114**.8
11. ὕσταριν = ὕστερον. **133**.6
12. ἄνευς = ἄνευ, and used with acc. **133**.6, **136**.4
13. Verbs in -ειω (-αιω) = -ευω. **161**.1

14. ἤστω = ἔστω. **163**.5
15. Opt. with κα in commands; also subj. (late). **175**
16. Opt. regularly in conditions etc. **176**.3
17. For peculiar words and meanings, see, in Glossary, γράφος, δίκαια, δίφυιος, Ϝράτρα, ἐπεμπάω, ἰαρόμαος, κατιαραίω, ἰμάσκω, θηλύτερος, ἐρσεναίτερος.

241. κοινή influence. In the amnesty decree (no. 65), from the second half of the fourth century B.C., αρ from ερ is, with one exception (ὕσταριν), given up, as in θηλυτέραν, ἐρσεναιτέραν (note also ἐρσ- vs. earlier ρρ. **80**), and περί (earlier πάρ, with apocope), though ρα from ρε is seen in κατιαραίων; πάσχω has its usual form (earlier πάσκω); the characteristic Elean words Ϝάρρω, Ϝέρρω = φεύγω in its technical sense, δίφυιον (ζίφυιον), and γράφος have given place to the usual φεύγω, διπλάσιον, and γράμμα. The Damocrates decree (no. 66), from the first half of the third century B.C., has ερ, never αρ, ὑπό not ὑπά, and shows considerable κοινή influence in the vocabulary, e.g., καθώρ (καθώς), ἔγκτησις.

On the other hand most of the characteristics of the dialect persist, and, in contrast to earlier inscriptions, the rhotacism of final ς is uniformly observed. Some of the differences between these two inscriptions and the earlier ones are due to chronological and local variation within the dialect, e.g., in both σσ, not στ, = σθ, loss of intervocalic σ; in no. 65 ττ, not δδ, = ζ, dat. pl. φυγάδεσσι (not -οις); in no. 66 subj. in prescriptions. Even in the earlier inscriptions there are some indications of local differences, but it is impossible with the present material to define their scope.

The definite substitution of the Attic κοινή in public inscriptions of Elis belongs to the end of the third century B.C.

DORIC

Laconian

242. West Greek characteristics. See **223-25**.

243. Partly in common with various other dialects.

1. η, ω = secondary ε̄, ō. **25**
2. ι from ε before vowels. **9**.8
3. η from ε + α, in part. **42**.1
4. Intervocal σ > h or lost. **59**.1
5. Rhotacism of final ς (late). **60**.2
6. σ = θ (late in inscr.). **64**
7. Ποhοιδᾶν=Ποσειδῶν. **49**.1, **61**.4
8. 'Απέλλων = 'Απόλλων. **49**.3
9. ϝ initial till about 400 B.C.; intervocalic in early inscriptions; later sometimes β. **50-53**
10. Apocope in κάτ, κά, πότ, πό, πάρ, πέρ. **95**

11. αὐτός reflex. **121**.3
12. τετράκιν, etc. **133**.6
13. ταυτᾶ, hᾶτ', πέποκα. **132**.6, 7, 11
14. ἄσιστα = ἄγχιστα. **113**.3
15. 3 pl. imv. -ντω; mid. -ōσθō. **140**.3a, 3b
16. Infin. -ην, -μεν. **153**.1, **154**.3
17. ἀγνέω = ἄγω. **162**.1
18. βοῦαι, βουαγόρ, πρατοπάμπαις, ἀτροπάμπαις, μιχιχιδόμενος, εἴρην, κελῦα, κασσηρατόριν. Nos. 75-78, note.
19. See also, in Glossary, ἀπέλλα, βίδεοι, ὠβά.

244. κοινή influence. Inscriptions from the second century B.C. (from the fourth and the third there is very little material) and later are not even in the Doric κοινή (**278**), but substantially in the Attic κοινή, with but slight dialectal coloring. On the revival of the use of the dialect in some inscriptions of the second century A.D., probably representing crudely what still survived as a patois, see note to nos. 75-78.

Heraclean

245. West Greek characteristics. See **223-25**.

246. In common with various other dialects.

1. η, ω = secondary ε̄, ō. **25**
2. ἀνεπίγροφος. **49**.2
3. κοθαρός, τοφιών **6**

4. ι from ε before vowels. **9**.9
5. η from ε + α. **42**.1
6. εω (ιω) from εο. **42**.5b

7. τάμνω = τέμνω. **49**.4
8. Ϝ initial, with some irregularities. **50**b
9. Spiritus asper frequent, but with some irregularities. **58**d
10. ἐγϜηληθίωντι. **75, 151**.2
11. Apocope in ἄν, πάρ, κάτ, πότ. **95**
12. μής = μήν. **112**.3
13. hῆς = εἷς. **114**.1
14. τρῖς as nom. pl. **114**.3

15. αὐτοσαυτός, αὐταυτός. **121**.4
16. τῆνος = ἐκεῖνος. **125**.1
17. Article as relative. **126**
18. ποτεχεῖ. **132**.2
19. ἄνωθα, ἔμπροσθα. **133**.1
20. 3 pl. imv. -ντω, mid. -σθω. **140**.3a, 3b
21. ἀνhεῶσθαι. **146**.3
22. Infin. -εν, -μεν. **153**.2, **154**.3
23. ἐλᾱ- in ἐπελᾱ́σθω. **159**
24. πριῶι, πριωσεῖ. **161**.3
25. ἔντες = ὄντες. **163**.8

247. Special Heraclean.

1. προτερεία. **46**.2
2. ἐνδεδιωκότα. **68**.1
3. ἔντασσι, ποιόντασσι. **107**.3
4. πόλιστος = πλεῖστος. **113**.2
5. ποτικλαίγω. **142**a
6. γεγράψαται, μεμισθωσῶνται. **146**.5
7. πεφυτευκῆμεν. **147**.2

8. ἐρρηγεῖα = ἐρρωγυῖα. **146. 3, 148**
9. Special words or meanings, see, in Glossary, ἀμπώλημα ἄντομος, ἄρρηκτος, ἄφωνος, ἀρτύω, κάδδιξ, μασχάλα, μυχός, ὄρεγμα, πλάγος, ῥήτρα, ῥογός, σαρμεύω.

248. κοινή influence. κοινή forms appear now and then in the Heraclean Tables, especially in the numerals. Thus τρεῖς beside τρῖς — τέσσαρες, τεσσαράκοντα beside τέτορες, τετρώκοντα —-κόσιοι beside -κάτιοι — χίλιοι for χήλιοι — Ϝείκατι, with ει from εἴκοσι, beside Ϝίκατι — εἰ beside αἰ — hοι beside τοί.

Argolic

249. West Greek characteristics. See **223-25**. But δικάσσαι, not δικάξαι, **142**.

250. Mostly in common with various other dialects (but several special features included here, notably 59).

1. η, ω in part, but also ει, ῑ, and ου = secondary ē, ō. **25**c

2. ι from ε before vowels, sometimes. **9**.10
3. βῶν = βοῦν. **37**.1

4. η from ε + α. **42**.1

5. o from εο before ντ. **42**.5*d*

6. γροφεύς, etc. **49**.2

7. φάρχμα, φάρξις. **49**.2*a*, **66**

8. καταλοβεύς = καταλαβεύς. **49**.3

9. τάμνω = τέμνω. **49**.4

10. Ϝ in all positions in earliest inscriptions; initial till *ca.* 400 B.C. **52-55**

11. ἅλιιος, δαμιιοργοῖ, etc. **56**

12. Spiritus asper with some irregularities. **58***d*

13. Intervocalic σ>h or lost. **59**.2

14. ἐντάδε = ἐνθάδε. **65**

15. ῥόπτον, θύρωτον, φάτρα. **70**.3

16. Μίντων = Μίλτων. **72**

17. πάνσα, ἐνς, -ονς, etc. **77**.3, **78**

18. ἥμισσον. **81**

19. πεπεμμένος. **86**.8

20. ξύλλεσθαι = σκύλλεσθαι. **87**

21. βόλιμος, σπάδιον, φάλυρον. **88**

22. ἡμίδιμμνον. **88***a*, **89**.2

23. γυμμνικός, πέττρινον. **89**.2

24. Apocope in ἄν, πάρ, πό, κάτ, κά. **95**

25. ἐς = ἐκ. **100***a*

26. Acc. pl. ανς, -ονς, -ινς (but also -ας, -ος, rarely -ως). **78**, **104**.8

27. μής = μήν. **112**.3

28. ἔθεν, gen. sg. **118**.3

29. τύ, acc. sg., νίν acc. sg. **118**.5

30. αὐτοῦ ἔθεν, reflexive. **121**.1

31. αὐσαυτός, αὐταυτός. **121**. **4***c, f*

32. τῆνος = ἐκεῖνος. **125**.1

33. ποτεχεῖ, hĪ. **132**.2

34. ἔχθω, ἔχθοι, ἔνδοι, ἄνευν. **133**.3, 4, 6

35. πεδά = μετά. **135**.5

36. ποί = πρός. **135**.6

37. ὑπέρ 'in behalf of' with acc. **136**.10

38. 2 sg. συντίθησι. **138**.1

39. γεγράβανται. **66**, **139**.2

40. 3 pl. imv. -ντω; mid. -νσθō. **140**.3*a*, 3*b*

41. κλάιξ, κλαικτός. **142***a*

42. ἔγεντο = ἐγένετο. No. 80, note

43. ἐξερρύα, aor. **144***b*

44. λελάβηκα, ἐπιμεμηνάκαντι. **146**.1

45. στᾶσες, 2 sg. aor. subj. **150***c*

46. Infin. -εν, -μεν. **153**.2, **154**. 3

47. οἰκείη, opt. **157***c*

48. διεγέλᾱ, ποτελάτō. **159**

49. ἔρπω 'go,' ἐνπιπᾱσκομαι 'acquire,' χρηίζω 'wish.' **162**.6, 12, 14

50. ἐντō = ὄντων, ἔντες = ὄντες, ἔσσα = οὖσα. **163**.6, 8

51. μαντήα, πρεσγήα. **164**.1

52. ἀλίασσις, etc. **164**.3

53. θεθμός (**65**), γράσσμα, γράθμα. **164**.4

54. ἡμίτεια. **164**.10

55. ἐνδοσθίδια. **165**.2

56. ἰατρα. **165**.3

57. κωμέτας. **167**

58. Opt. with κα. **177**
59. ἀϜρέτευε, ἀρήτευε 'presided.' **55***b*
60. ἔλεξε = εἶπε 'made the motion.' Glossary
61. Other special words or

meanings, see, in Glossary, ἀλιαία, ἀμβόλιμος, ἀνεπιβασία, ἀρτῦναι, δεμελεῖς, δενδρύω, **δόκημα, Ϝhεδιέστας,** ἐπιπῆν, καλαῖς, ὀπτίλλος, τέλειος, τέλλω, τρέω.

251. There are some differences between the dialect of Argos and vicinity and that which appears in the inscriptions of Epidaurus and other places in the Acte. So the absence in the latter region of the typical Arg. term ἀρήτευε, of the Argive change of intervocalic σ (see **59**.2 with *a*), the rarity of νσ (**77**.3, **78**; only early ποιϜέσανς Methana) which is usual in Argive inscriptions till within the second century B.C.; the infrequency of η, ω for secondary ε̄, ō (**25***c*; only Epid. χηρός, χῆρα, ἀφήλετο, and gen. sg. -ω, acc. pl. -ως at Hermione). Some features are due to the fact that Attic influence was earlier and stronger in the East. Definite Attic forms are frequent in Epidaurian inscriptions of the early fourth century B.C. (see no. 90, note).

But more extensive early material from the Acte may alter the picture.

Corinthian

252. West Greek characteristics. See **223-25.**

253. In common with various other dialects.

1. ευ from εο. **42**.5
2. γροφεύς. **49**.2
3. Ἀπέλλων. **49**.3
4. Ϝ early in all positions. **52-55**
5. ντ, νθ = λτ, λθ. **72**
6. ρh, Μh. **76***a*
7. Apocope in ἄν, πάρ, πότ, πό (but more often full forms). **95**
8. ΦιλοκλέϜδα, nom. sg. **105.1***a*
9. ΤλασίαϜο, gen. sg. **105.2***b*
10. Προκλείδας, gen. sg. **105.2***c*

11. Dat. pl. of consonant stems in -εσσι. **107.3**
12. Διεί, dat. sg. **112.1**
13. μείς = μήν. **112.3**
14. αὐτός, reflex. **121.3**
15. αὐτοσαυτός. **121.4***b*
16. ποί = πρός. **135.6**
17. 3 pl. imv. -ντω; mid. -σθω. **140.3***a, b*
18. hίσατο, aor. of ἵζω. **144***c*
19. Infin. -ειν, -μεν. **153.1, 154.3**
20. Personal names in -ήν frequent. **164.7**

254. Special Corinthian. Very early monophthongization of ει and ου and representation of both original ει and secondary ε̄ by E or EI (vs. ʙ, Sicyon Ɛ = ε or η) and of original ου and secondary ō by OV. **25d, 28, 34.**

255. After the early but brief inscriptions in the epichoric alphabet, there is but scanty material until the third and second centuries B.C., when the admixture of κοινή forms is considerable.

Megarian

256. West Greek characteristics. See **223-25.**

257. In common with various other dialects.

1. E, ει, O, ου = secondary ε̄, ō. **25**
2. E = original ει, rare. **28**
3. ευ = εο, late. **42.5**
4. τράφω = τρέφω. **49.2**
5. Ϝ init. in fifth century B.C., otherwise lost.
6. Φίντων = Φίλτων. **72**
7. Mh in Mhεγαρεύς. **76a**
8. ρρ = ρσ in Ὄρριππος. **80**
9. ἥμισσον. **81**
10. ἀμφιλλέγω. **76**
11. Apocope in ἄν, πάρ, κάτ, πότ. **95**
12. Gen. sg. masc. Φάγας, etc. **105.2c**
13. μείς = μήν. **112.3**
14. τοῦτοι = οὖτοι. **124**

15. τῆνος = ἐκεῖνος. **125.** τηνῶθεν. **132.8**
16. τε̃δε, ἄ(λ)λε̃. **132.7**
17. ὅκκα. **132.11**
18. ἐνδός. **133.4**
19. ἄνις. **133.6**
20. 3 pl. imv. -ντω; mid. -σθων. **140.3a, 2b**
21. Infin. -ειν, -μεν. **153.1, 154.3**
22. ἐπεσκεύωσαν. **161.3**
23. Names in -κλίας, as Εὐκλίας. **166.1**
24. λάζομαι = λαμβάνω. Glossary
25. τελαμών = στήλη. No. 82, note

258. Special Megarian.

1. Θέδωρος, Θοκλείδας, etc. most frequent. **42.5f**
2. ἐνπίδες = ἐλπίδες. **72**
3. σά = τινα. **128**
4. αἰσιμνάτας, αἰσιμνάω = αἰσ-

υμνήτης, etc. **20.** Apart from the difference of vowel, the words are peculiar to Megarian and Ionic.

259. Except for the early inscriptions of Selinus and a few others, the material is from the end of the fourth century or later, and shows κοινή influence.

Rhodian

260. West Greek characteristics. See **223-25**.

261. In common with various other dialects.

1. η, ω and ει, ου = secondary
   ε̄, ō. **25**b
2. Ἀγλου- beside Ἀγλω- from
   Ἀγλαο-. **41**.2
3. η from ε + α. **42**.1
4. ευ = εο. **42**.5
5. ᾱ from ο + ᾱ in ὀγδᾶι, Βᾱδρόμιος. **44**.2
6. Early loss of ϝ. **50**
7. Ξην-, Ξειν-. **54**
8. ἱαρός, ἱερός with lenis. **58**b
9. τόζε = τόδε. **62**.2
10. Φιντίας = Φιλτίας **72**
11. Ζεὺ δέ = Ζεὺς δέ, etc. **97**.4
12. περιβολιβῶσαι. **88**
13. Πασιάδαϝο, gen. sg. **105**.2b
14. Ἰδαμενῆος, gen. sg. **111**.3
15. ἐννῆ. **114**.9
16. τοῦτοι = οὗτοι. **124**
17. κῆνος. **125**.1
18. ὅπυς, υἷς. **132**.4
19. ὅκκα. **132**.11
20. ἐξάν. **133**.6
21. Πεδα- in month name.
    135.5
22. 3 pl. perf. ἀπεστάλκαντι, etc.
    138.4
23. 3 pl. imv. -ντω; mid. -σθων,
    -σθω. **140**.3a, 1, 2b
24. Fut. pass. with active en-
    dings. **145**
25. Perf. 3 sg. τετιμάκει, etc.,
    infin. γεγόνειν. **147**.1, 2
26. τιμέω = τιμάω. **161**.2
27. χρήιζω 'wish.' **162**.14
28. ἐντί as 3 sg. **163**.10
29. Τιμᾱκράτης, Ἱππέδαμος,
    Ἀρχοκράτης, κτοινέτας.
    167

262. Special Rhodian. Infinitive in -μειν. **154**.5. κτοίνα, de-noting a territorial division like the Attic deme, is found only in Rhodes and Carpathos. The μαστροί are known as financial in-vestigators at Delphi and Pallene, but as the chief local officers are peculiar to Rhodes (cf. no. 103), λέσχα in the sense of 'grave' (no. 101) is Rhodian only.

263. κοινή influence shows itself to a slight extent in the fourth century B.C. Most of the material is from the third century or later, and is in the Doric κοινή (**278**), though with frequent retention of the characteristic infinitive in -μειν. In this mixed form the dialect is one of the longest to survive, many peculiarities still appearing in inscriptions of the first and second centuries A.D.

Coan

264. West Greek characteristics. See **223-25**.

265. In common with various other dialects.

1. η, ω and ει, ου = secondary ε̄, ō. **25b**
2. η from ε + α, and special ηὑτῶν = ἑαυτῶν. **42.1**
3. ευ=εο, also from ε + secondary ō in κυεῦσα, etc. **42.5**
4. ᾱ from οᾱ in ὀγδᾱι, Βᾱδρό-μιος. **44.2**
5. Δολφοί, ἔτελον. **49.3**
6. τάμνω = τέμνω. **49.4**
7. Early loss of ϝ. **50**
8. στέπτω = στέφω. **66**
9. Palatalized λ, spelling λε, as ξύλεα = ξύλα. **71b**
10. Acc. pl. of o-stems -ος, also ἐς = εἰς. **78**
11. ἥμισσον. **81**
12. πρηγιστεύω. **86.3a**
13. πράτιστος. **114.1**
14. τοῦτοι = οὗτοι. **124**
15. τουτῶ, ἑκατέρω. **132.8** with a

16. ὄκκα. **132.11**
17. ἐξᾶν. **133.6**
18. 3 pl. imv. -ντω; mid. -σθω, -σθων. **140.3a, 1, 2b**
19. Short-vowel aor. subj. **150**
20. ἐγρυᾶι, aor. subj. (Calymn.) **144b, 151.1**
21. Infin. -εν, also in contract verbs; -μεν. **153.2, 3, 154.3**
22. ἐλάντω, etc.
23. καρπῶντι, ἱερώσθω, ἐξορκώντω, ἀξιῶι. **159a**
24. ἀγρεταί. **162.2**
25. ἔρπω 'go.' **162.6**
26. Other special words or meanings, see, in Glossary, αἱμάτιον, ἀμφεικάς, ἄποτος, γερεαφόρος, δίκρεας, ἔνδορα, ἐπίποκος, ἔτελον, θηκαῖον, καρπόω, ναῦσσον, προσπερμεία, σπυρός, τρικώλιος, χέλυος.

266. There are no very early inscriptions, and only a few even from the fourth century B.C. The most important of these, the sacrificial calendar (cf. no. 108), already shows some κοινή forms, as ἱερεύς beside ἱαρεύς, εἰκάς beside ἰκάς, acc. pl. τρεῖς, ἑστία beside ἱστία, etc., but preserves some forms which are never found later as ἱερῆι, τεταρτῆς (later always -ει, -εις, etc.). Ionic influence is shown in τέλεως, the hybrid ἱαρεωσύνα, and many women's names like 'Αλίη, 'Αρισταγόρη, etc. Most of the material is of the third and second centuries, and in the Doric κοινή as described in **278**.

Theran and Cyrenaean

267. West Greek characteristics. See **223-25**.

268. In common with various other dialects.

1. η, ω = secondary ε̄, ō, but also sometimes ει and (T.) ου. **25***b*
2. αυ from ευ sometimes (T.). **33***a*
3. η from ε + α. **42**.1
4. ευ from εο. **42**.5
5. εω (C.) from εο. **42**.5*b*
6. ὡδός (C.) = Att. ὁδός. **54**
7. ϝ lost in earliest times. **50**
8. ντ, νθ (C.) from λτ, λθ. **72**
9. Type παῖσα (C., traces in T.). **77**.3.
10. Final νς, loss of ν without change of preceding vowel. **78**
11. ρρ = ρσ (early T., later C. ρσ). **80**
12. Crasis of ο + α to ω. **94**.1
13. Assimilation of final ν to following initial λ (C.). **96**.3
14. Assimilation of final σ to following initial λ. **97**.3
15. Article as relative (C.). **126**
16. μέστα 'until.' **132**.12
17. Pron. advs. αὐτεῖ (C.), ὅπυι (C.), ἆδε (C.), ὅπη (C.), ὅκα (C.). **132**.2, 4, 5, 6, 7, 11
18. ἔνδοι, ἔξοι (C.), ἐξᾶν (T.). **133**.4, 5, 6
19. 3 pl. imv. -ντων. **140**.4*a*; mid. -σθων. **140**.2*b*

20. Aorist of ἵζω (vs. ἕζω) ἵσαντα, ἱσσάμενος. **144***c*
21. Aorist in -ᾱ, 3 sg. subj. μιᾶι, ἵσᾱι (Cyren.). **144***b*, **151**.1
22. Fut. pass. with act. endings (T.). **145**
23. Perfect forms as if from -ευόω, ἐφορευωκότων (C), κατεσκεύωκε (T)., **161**.3
24. Perf. act. pple. fem. -υῖα (C.) vs. -εῖα (T.). **148**
25. Short vowel subj. of σ- and α-aor. (C.) **150**
26. Long vowel subj. of unthematic vowel stems, δύνᾱνται, etc. (C.) **151**.1
27. Pres. subj. of εἶμι, ἐπείηι (C.). **151**.3
28. Infin. of thematic forms, -εν. **153**.2, 3
29. Mid, pple. χρείμενος (C.). **158**
30. Transfer of -αω to -εω type (C.). **161**.2
31. Pres. pple. fem. in unthematic form (C.) **163**.8*a*
32. ἵσᾱμι. **162**.9
33. -ηιο- = Att. -ειο- (C.). **164**.1
34. -τηρ in agent nouns = Att. -της. **164**.5
35. δαμιεργός (C.) vs. more common δαμιοργός. **167**

269. Special Cyrenaean.

1. ε from εο before ντ. **42**.5*e*
2. βάβᾱλος = βέβᾱλος. **46**.1
3. Nom. pl. and acc. pl. ἱαρές, dat. pl. Μεγαρέσσι, etc. **111**.3
4. λεχός gen. sg. of λεχώι (C.). **45, 111**.5*a*
5. ἐς νέω = εἰς νέωτα (C.)
6. Forms of μιαίνω, 3 sg. fut. μιανεῖ (trans.), μιασεῖ (pass.), aor. subj. μιᾶι (pass.)
7. παισεῖται = Att. πείσεται,

fut. mid. of πάσχω (with α apparently from that of πάσχω, ἔπαθον).
8. ποτιπίαμμα. **164**.4
9. Some other special words or meanings (C.) ἀδηίζων 'protecting,' δεκατός 'subject to a tithe,' ἴκνυς 'ashes' (?), οἰκισία 'settlement,' κοιτᾱτήριον = κοιμητήριον, ὄροφος 'house,' κολοσός 'plastic figure,' ἔκαμε 'died'

Cretan

270. West Greek characteristics. See **223-25.** But οἱ, αἱ, not τοί, ταί, and Ἄρτεμις not Ἄρταμις.

271. In common with various other dialects.

1. η, ω = secondary ε̄, ō. **25** with *a*
2. ι from ε before vowel. **9**.7
3. β̄ς, β̄ν = βοῦς, βοῦν. **37**.1
4. ο from εο before ντ (not Central Cretan). **42**.5*d*
5. τράπω, τράφω. **49**.2
6. χάρτος, στάρτος, etc. **49**.2*a*
7. Ἀπέλλων. **49**.3
8. ἀντίγροφον, ἔγγροφον. **48**.4
9. Ϝ initial till second century B.C.; sometimes β; intervocalic only in compounds or augmented forms. **50-54**
10. ξῆνος, ὦρος from ξένϜος, etc., but ϜίσϜος. **54** with *d*
11. Psilosis. **57** with *b*
12. μαίτυρες = μάρτυρες. **71***a*

13. ἀμφιλλέγω. **76***a*
14. πάνσα, ἐνς, -ονς, etc. (but also ἐς, -ος). **77**.3, **78**
15. ττ in ἴαττα ὀπόττος, μέττος, δάτταθθαι, etc. **81, 82**
16. δδ (sometimes ττ) = ζ. **84**
17. ττ = κτ and πτ. **86**.1, 2
18. γγ, γ = σγ. **86**.3
19. ττ = στ (rare). **86**.4
20. ψ = σφ. **87**
21. ἀλλόττριος. **89**.4
22. Apocope in ἄν, πάρ (rarely κα(τ), usually κατά). **95**
23. ἐς = ἐξ before consonants. **100**
24. Early loss of dual. **104**.11
25. υἱάσι. **112**.2
26. πλίες. **113**.2

27. Ϝὶν αὐτῶι = ἑαυτῷ, etc.
    121.1
28. αὐτοσαυτός. 121.4b
29. αὐτόν neut. = αὐτό 125.2
30. ὀτεῖος = ὁποῖος, in sense
    adjectival ὅστις. 130
31. ὄπει, ὄπαι, ὄπε̄, ὄπυι. 132.2,
    4, 5, 7
32. μέστα, μεττ' ἐς. 132.12
33. πρόθθα = πρόσθε. 133.1
34. ἐνδός, ἔξοι. 133.4, 5
35. αὖτιν, αὐταμέριν. 133.6
36. πεδά = μετά. 135.5
37. ποί = πρός (rare). 135.6b
38. ἀντί 'in presence of,' ἀμφί
    'concerning.' 136.7, 8
39. ἔγρατται = γέγραπται. 137
40. 3 pl. perf. ἀπεστάλκαντι,
    etc. 138.4
41. 3 pl. imv. -ντων; mid. -σθων.
    140.4a, 1b

42. Fut. pass. with active en-
    dings. 145
43. Short-vowel aor. subj., 3
    sg. δείξει, etc. 150
44. Subj. νύνᾱται, πέπᾱται, etc.
    151.1
45. Infin. -εν; also in contract
    verbs. 153.2, 3
46. χρήμενος. 158
47. Verb-forms in -εω (-ιω) =
    -άω. 161.2
48. -οω type in τρῶσει, 'τρῶ-
    σάντων. 161.3
49. ἔρπω = εἶμι. 162.6
50. ἴσᾱμι. 162.9
51. ἔντων = ὄντων, ἴαττα = οὖ-
    σα. 163.6, 8
52. ἐπᾱβολά. 167a
53. πόλις = δῆμος. Glossary
54. καρτερός = κύριος 'valid.'
    Glossary

272. Special Cretan.

1. ἀβλοπία = ἀβλαβία. 49.3, 66
2. τνατός, τετνακός = θνητός,
   etc. 66
3. δέφυρα = γέφυρα. 68.2
4. θθ = σσ (late). 81a
5. θθ (also τθ) = σθ. 85.3
6. νν = ρν. 86.5
7. μμ = μν. 86.6
8. Ϝήρω = Ϝέρδω. 86.6
9. πρεῖγυς, πρείγων, etc. =
   πρέσβυς, etc. 68.1, 86.3
10. Assimilation in external
    combination more exten-
    sive than elsewhere. 87.4,
    5, 98

11. Acc. pl. of consonant stems
    -ανς. 107.4
12. Ϝῆμα, gen. sg. Ϝήμᾱς. 112.5
13. Acc. pl. τρίινς. 114.3
14. νεότᾱς, gen. sg. νεότᾱς, acc.
    sg. νεότα. 88a
15. ὅτερος = ὁπότερος. 127
16. ὄτις, gen. sg. ὄτι, dat. sg.
    ὄτιμι acc. pl. ἄτι. 128, 129.3
17. ὄπαι as final conj. 132.5,
    10a
18. πορτί = πρός. 135.6
19. 3 pl. opt. Ϝέρχσιεν. 152.4
20. Infin. -μην. 154.4
21. αἰλέω = αἱρέω. 12

22. ἄρατρον = ἄροτρον. **161**.5
23. ἐλευσέω, πεύθω, ὠνέω.
    162.15
24. ἀνδρήιον. **164**.1
25. ψάφιγμα, ψάφιμμα. **164**.4
26. ἐνδοθίδιος, ἐξαρχίδιος.
    165.2
27. κόμιστρα, τρίτρα. **165**.3
28. βίετος, Ϝοικεύς, fem. Ϝοικέα,
    ὀφέλομα. **167**
29. ἐπᾱβολά. **167**a

30. Special words or meanings
    (not all Cretan only), see,
    in Glossary, ἀγέλα, ἄζωστος,
    ἀκεύω, ἀμφαίνομαι, ἄπατος,
    δρομεύς, ἔμμανις, ἔνδικος,
    ἔντιτος, ἐπιβάλλων, κρταῖ-
    πος, καρτερός, κόσμος, λα-
    γαίω, μωλέω, οὐρεῖον, πάσ-
    τας, πατρδιῆχος, περαιόω,
    στέγα, συνεσσάδδω, τέλομαι,
    τίτας, φωνέω

273. Cretan, as commonly understood and as described above, is the dialect of the inscriptions of Gortyn (which is by far the most fully represented), Cnossus, Lyttus, Vaxus, and the other cities of the great central portion of Crete. This is also known more specifically as Central Cretan. Eastward, at Olus, Drerus, Latus, etc., the dialect is much less uniform; and in the inscriptions of cities of the eastern extremity of the island, as Hierapytna, Praesus, and Itanus, and again in those from the cities of the western extremity, as Aptera, Cydonia, etc., many of the most striking Cretan characteristics are wholly lacking. Hence the terms East Cretan, usually reckoned from Hierapytna eastward, and West Cretan, from Lappa westward, are sometimes employed. But there is no sufficient ground for the belief that the East, West, and Central Cretan are fundamental divisions of the dialect, or that they reflect to any degree the various constituent elements in the population. The East and West Cretan inscriptions, the latter very meager, are comparatively late, and show a large degree of obvious κοινή influence, partly Attic, partly the Doric κοινή of the other islands. The absence of many of the Central Cretan characteristics may well be, and probably is, due to external influence, which was felt earlier and more strongly than in Central Crete, where, especially at Gortyn, most of the peculiarities persisted until Roman times. However, an actual divergence of development, for which external causes are not apparent, is to be recognized in the treatment of εο, which, instead of becoming ιο, appears as ο or ω in East and West

Greek (**49***c*, *d*). There are also a few other local variations. But, if we had ample material from the early period, it is highly probable that we should find that in the main the characteristics of Central Cretan were also general Cretan.

SURVIVAL OF THE DIALECTS. GROWTH OF VARIOUS FORMS OF KOINH

274. Not only in early times, but also, in most parts of Greece, long after Attic had become the norm of literary prose, each state employed its own dialect, both in private and public monuments of internal concern, and in those of a more external or interstate character, such as decrees in honor of foreigners, decisions of interstate arbitration, treaties, and, in general, communications between different states. Thus, for example, an honorary decree of a Boeotian city is in the Boeotian dialect, no matter whether the recipient is a citizen of Athens, Delphi, Alexandria, or Tarentum. If the Eleans honor Damocrates of Tenedos, the decree is in the Elean of the time (no. 66). If Mytilene honors Erythrae, the decree is in Lesbian, and a copy in this form is set up at Erythrae. Such is the usual practice, examples of which could be cited by the hundred, and any departure from which is the exception.

A decision of the Argives in a dispute between Melos and Cimolos is in the Argive dialect (no. 87). A treaty between the Cretan cities of Cnossus and Tylissus (no. 86) is in Argive alphabet and dialect, not only the draft deposited at Argos, but also that at Tylissus. And so in general such decisions were regularly rendered in the dialect of the arbitrators, and inscribed in this form by the states involved in the dispute, usually at home, but sometimes also in one of the great religious centers as Delos or Olympia. The extant texts of treaties are, as a rule, in the dialect of that party in whose territory the text was found, and it is to be assumed that the version inscribed by the other party in its home was likewise in its dialect. Thus, for example, the monetary agreement between Mytilene and Phocaea in the Lesbian version found at Mytilene (no. 25), the treaty of alliance between Elis and Heraea (in Arcadia) in the Elean version found at Olympia (no. 62).

In communications between states using different dialects each party employs its own. For example, when Philip V of Macedon sends certain recommendations to the city of Larisa, he writes in the Attic κοινή, which had long been the language of the Macedonian court, but the decrees which the city passes in response are in the Thessalian dialect (no. 32). An inscription of Mytilene contains the text of a decree of the Aetolian league in favor of Mytilene, in its original Aetolian (Northwest Greek κοινή) form, a copy of which had been brought back by the Mytilenaean envoys, followed by a decree of Mytilene in Lesbian, quoting from the former decree and ordering the inscription of both. The regulations of the religious sanctuaries of Greece are drawn up in the dialect of the state which has direct charge of them, no less in the great Hellenic centers than in those of local fame. So, for example, an Amphictionic decree which is known to us only in the copy set up at Athens is in the Delphian dialect.

275. In the period before the rise of Attic as the language of literary prose, no one dialect was in a position even to influence other dialects except within narrow geographical limits. Yet it is probable that even then external influence was not wholly absent. There was no lack of intercourse to awaken consciousness of the peculiarities of one's own dialect as compared with those of others. Some of these peculiarities, especially such as were at variance with the practice of all or nearly all other dialects, might come to be regarded with disfavor as provincialisms, and be avoided in writing, and even in speech, or at least less consistently observed.

For example, the Laconians and the Argives, who were well aware that under certain conditions they omitted, or pronounced as a mere breathing, what was a σ in the speech of most other Greeks, may have felt that this, unlike some of their other peculiarities, was a sort of weakness, which did not deserve to be exploited in writing. This would explain the inconsistency in the treatment of intervocalic σ which is to be observed even in the early inscriptions of Laconia and Argolis, before any specific Attic influence is possible. See **59**.1, 2. The fact that Arcadian σις and κάς, agreeing with Cyprian σις and κάς, are found only in the earliest inscriptions (no. 17; ὄζις also no. 16), while all the later ones have τἰς and καί, may also be ascribed to the combined influence of the other dialects, just as in a later period, when specific Attic influence is more probable, πλός was replaced by the usual πλέον, in spite of the fact that other equally marked peculiarities like ἰν = ἐν were unaffected. The Eleans gave up even in the sixth century their use of ζ for the δ of other dialects, and if, as is likely, this was a concession in spelling only, it is none the less in point.

In fact it is increasingly evident that, more than is commonly recognized, we must reckon with external influence even in very early dialect inscriptions. Some of the disparities between inscriptions of the same dialect, some of those which are commonly attributed to local variation or even to prehistoric dialect mixture are due to nothing more than the elimination by the writer of one or another local peculiarity in favor of what is usual in the majority of dialects and especially in that literary form which was familiar to all, the Homeric.

276. Traces of Ionic influence are seen in the Doric islands, though the earliest evidence of this belongs rather to the history of the alphabet, namely the spread of the Ionic H = η (4.6). It is not accidental that ευ for εο, though occasionally found in continental Greece, is mainly found, outside of Ionic, in Rhodes, Cos, Thera, etc. In Cos occur many Ionic forms, as τέλεως etc. (see **266**a). Even in the fifth century the coins of the Rhodian Ialysus show ᾿Ιελυσίον beside ᾿Ιαλυσίον. Through the medium of the Doric κοινή of the other islands (**278**), some Ionic peculiarities have even spread to Crete, e.g., at Itanus ευ = εο, εο = ευ, and χρεώμεθα.

277. The Attic κοινή. The foundation of the ultimate supremacy of Attic is to be sought in the political conditions of the fifth century B.C. In this we refer to something more than the fact, important as it is, that in this period Athens became the intellectual center of Greece and Attic the recognized language of literary prose. It is within the sphere of influence represented by the confederacy of Delos and the Athenian empire that Attic made its first advance as an ordinary medium of communication. Of all dialects it is Ionic which shows the first signs of Attic influence and is the first to lose its identity as a distinct dialect. Some traces of this influence are seen even in the Ionic inscriptions of the fifth century, especially in the islands, and in the fourth century the majority of inscriptions show at least a mixture of Attic forms, and some, even from the early part of the century, are substantially Attic. After this, Ionic practically ceased to exist as a distinct dialect, though some Ionic peculiarities are occasionally found in much later times, mostly in proper names and certain conventional words or phrases. It is this Attic, already wellnigh established in Ionic territory, and in some respects modified by Ionic, that the Macedonians took up and spread, and which is henceforth termed the κοινή, or, more specifically, the Attic κοινή.

The Macedonian period, indeed, forms the principal landmark in the evolution of a standard language in Greece. For in it the Attic κοινή was spread over a vast territory and permanently established in places which were to become leading centers of Greek life. Yet this is only a stage, marking neither the beginning, as we have seen, nor, still less, the end. Excepting Ionic, and Cyprian, of which we have no later record, the other dialects, though showing more or less κοινή influence, remained in common use in inscriptions from one to upwards of three centuries later. But eventually the κοινή attained complete supremacy both as the written and the spoken language, and from it is descended Modern Greek. The only important exception is the present Tsakonian dialect, spoken in a small portion of Laconia, which is basically the offspring of the ancient Laconian.

278. The Doric κοινή. In most of the Doric dialects Attic influence shows itself, to some extent, even in the fourth century B.C., and there was gradually evolved a type of modified Doric which prevails in the inscriptions of the last three centuries B.C., and is conveniently known as the Doric κοινή. This is substantially Doric, retaining a majority of the general West Greek characteristics, but with a tendency to eliminate local peculiarities, and with a strong admixture of forms from the Attic κοινή. In spite of some variety in the degree of mixture, and the retention of some local peculiarities, e.g., the infinitive in -μειν at Rhodes, there is yet a very considerable unity, amply sufficient to justify us in speaking of a distinct type of κοινή.

That the mixture is not a haphazard one is shown, for example, in the fact that the substitution of εἰ for αἰ, side by side with the retention of κα, resulting in the hybrid εἴ κα, is very general, while the opposite, αἰ ἄν, is unknown. ἰαρός is replaced by ἱερός. The numerals show the forms of the Attic κοινή, e.g., acc. pl. τρεῖς for τρῖς, τέσσερες (or τέσσαρες, τέτταρες) not τέτορες, εἴκοσι for ἴκατι, τεσσεράκοντα (τεσσαράκοντα, τετταράκοντα) for τετρώκοντα, -κόσιοι for -κάτιοι, χίλιοι for χείλιοι or χήλιοι. In ι-stems we usually find πόλιος, πόλιες retained, but πόλει, πόλεσι, acc. pl. πόλεις. Nouns in -εύς follow the Attic type except in the accusative singular, e.g. βασιλέως, nom. acc. pl. βασιλεῖς, but acc. sg. βασιλῆ. So Att. βασιλέως is usual, but Att. πόλεως rare. The substitution of οἰ, αἰ for τοί, ταί is frequent, but there is great variation in this respect, τοί and οἰ occurring not infrequently even in the same inscription. Attic ου from εο is frequent, especially in verbs in -εω. In some places, as far apart as Rhodes and Corcyra, we find inscriptions which have the verb-forms uniformly in ου, but the genitive singular of σ-stems in -εος or -ευς, e.g., Rhod. ἐγκαλοῦντας, etc. but Ἰσοκράτευς, etc. (GDI 3758), Corc. ποιοῦντες, etc. but Ἀριστομένεος etc. (GDI 3206). Attic ω from εω is also more common in verbs than in nouns. In dialects which have ξῆνος or ξεῖνος etc. (54), such forms are often replaced by the Attic, especially in the case of πρόξενος. The first plural ending -μες is generally replaced by -μεν, though it persists in some places.

There are various other Attic forms which are not infrequent, but much less common than the dialect forms, e.g., ὤν beside ἐών, imperative ending -ντων beside -ντω, πρῶτος beside πρᾶτος, πρός beside ποτί, θεωρός beside θεαρός (conversely θεαρός occurs at Andros, no. 7, and Tenos!). Many of the dialectal peculiarities persist with scarcely any intrusion of the corresponding Attic forms, e.g., ᾱ = Att.-Ion. η, κα, verb forms like δίδωτι, φέροντι, Doric future, future and aorist in ξ (142), ἀμές, etc. Att. η, verb forms like δίδωσι, φέρουσι, infinitives in -ναι (also in large measure ἄν and ἄν, but see below, a) are almost unknown except in the very last stages when the Attic κοινή as a whole is practically established. ᾱ is sometimes found as late as the third century A.D., but only as a bit of local color, perhaps artificial, in what is otherwise the Attic κοινή.

a. An interesting example of mixture, though not in all respects typical, is furnished by the long cult inscription of Andania from the early first century B.C. The native Doric features (or in part general non-Attic) persist in ᾱ, ποτί, 3 pl. verb ending -ντι (3 sg. forms like δίδωτι happen to be lacking), 3 pl. imv. act. -ντω (but ἔστωσαν and mid. -σθωσαν), infin. -μεν, ξ in ὀρκιξάτω, etc., also κλάιξ, κλαικτός, ι-stem inflection gen. -ιος (παραδόσιος, παναγύριος, etc., but πόλεος 4 times), nom. pl. ἰδιώτιες (but dat. sg. καταλύσει, παναγύρει, acc. pl. τρεῖς, δέρρεις), κα (beside ἄν, both frequent). Aetolian influence in dat. pl. of cons. stems in -οις (πλεόνοις, etc., 7 examples), and acc. pl. πάντες. Att. κοινή in ου from εο in verb forms (πωλοῦντες, etc.), ἱερός, ρρ in δέρρεις, οἱ, αἱ (never τοί, ταί), numerals εἴκοσι, τεσσαράκοντα, -κόσιοι, χίλιοι, ἕβδομος, some forms of ι-stems (see above), 3 pl. ἔστωσαν, mid. -σθωσαν, ἄν (beside κα) and ἄν (never εἴ κα), ὅταν, ἕως, ὄντων, mid. inflection in 3 pl. subj. ἦνται..

279. The Northwest Greek κοινή. This is very similar to the Doric κοινή, showing about the same mixture of Attic with West Greek forms. But it differs from it in that it retains two of the most characteristic features of the Northwest Greek dialects as compared with Doric, namely ἐν = εἰς, and the dative plural of consonant stems in -οις. The use of this type is closely connected with the political power of the Aetolian league. We find it employed, in the third century B.C. and later, in Aetolia and in all decrees of the Aetolian league, in Western Locris (Naupactus was incorporated in the league in 338 B.C., the rest of Western Locris somewhat later), Phocis (Delphi was in the hands of the Aetolians by at least 290 B.C.), the land of the Aenianes, Malis and Phthiotis, all of which became Aetolian in the course of the third century B.C. Without doubt it was also used in Doris, from which we have no material, and in Eastern Locris. In Boeotia, which was in the Aetolian league but a short time (245-234 B.C.), it was never employed, though there are some few traces of its influence (**222**). The only extant decrees of Cephallenia and Ithaca, of about 200 B.C., are in this same Northwest Greek κοινή, reminding us that Cephallenia, of which Ithaca was a dependency, was allied with the Aetolians (Polyb. 4.6). Parts of the Peloponnesus were also for a time under Aetolian domination, and the characteristic dative plural in -οις is found in Arcadia, Messenia (also ἐν = εἰς), and Laconia. There is one example even so far away as Crete (λιμένοις GDI 4942*b*; 159-138 B.C.), but clearly an importation. Aetolians had taken part in the internal wars of Crete, and Cretans had served in the armies of both the Aetolian and the Achaean leagues (Polyb. 4.53).

The inscriptions of this period from Acarnania, Epirus, and Achaea, including decrees of the Acarnanian, Epirotan, and Achaean leagues, are not in the Northwest Greek κοινή as defined above (they do not have ἐν = εἰς, or the dative plural of consonant stems in -οις), but in the Doric κοινή. At this time at least the speech of Acarnania and Epirus was not essentially different from that of Corcyra, nor that of Achaea from that of Corinth and Sicyon.

In the Arcadian inscriptions of this period the native Arcadian forms are wholly or in part replaced by West Greek forms, and this is probably due in large part to the influence of the Doric κοινή of the Achaean league. But the Aetolians also held parts of Arcadia for a time, and, as noted above, there are some examples of the dative plural in -οις and ἐν = εἰς from the Northwest Greek κοινή.

280. Some more detailed observations upon the time and extent of κοινή influence in the various dialects have been made in connection with the Summaries of Characteristics (**180-273**), and in the notes to some of the late inscriptions.

What has just been noted in the case of the Doric κοινή is true in all dialects, namely, that of the dialectal peculiarities some are given up much earlier than others. Furthermore it is nothing unusual to find hybrid forms, part dialectal, part κοινή, e.g., Doric future with Attic ου, as ποιησοῦντι etc. frequently,—Boeot. ἄως, a contamination of ἄς and ἕως,—Heracl. Ϝείκατι, a contamination of Ϝίκατι and εἴκοσι,—Boeot. ζώωνθι with dialectal present stem and personal ending, but Attic ζ (pure Boeot. δώωνθι), —Boeot. ἐκγόνως with dialectal case-ending, but Attic ἐκ- (pure Boeot. ἐσγόνως),—Thess. acc. pl. γινομένος with dialectal case-ending, but Attic stem (pure Thess. γινυμένος),—Epid. ἐώρη with Doric ending -η from -αε, but Attic stem ἐώρ- from *ἠόρ-.

Besides such hybrids, hyper-Doric or hyper-Aeolic forms are occasionally met with in late inscriptions, though less often than in our literary texts. Thus the Attic term ἔφηβος (with original η, cf. Dor. ἤβα), when adopted in other dialects, was sometimes given the pseudo-dialectal form ἔφαβος, e.g., in some late Doric and Lesbian inscriptions, in imitation of the frequent equivalence of dialectal ᾱ to Attic η. Conversely the Attic form was sometimes retained in opposition to what would be its true dialectal equivalent, as in Boeotian usually ἔφηβος, rarely ἔφειβος. Similarly the Doric ῾Ηρακλῆς and its derivatives keep η in Boeotian.

In Roman imperial times the antiquarian interest in local dialects is reflected in the revival of their use in parts of Greece where for some two centuries previously the Attic κοινή had been in general use, at least in inscriptions. So, for example, in the case of Lesbian (cf. no. 28), Laconian (cf. nos. 75-78) and to some extent in Elean, where examples of rhotacism reappear in the first and second centuries A.D. It is impossible to determine in every case whether this was a wholly artificial revival of a dialect which had long ceased to be spoken, or was an artificial elevation to written use of a dialect which had survived throughout the interval as a patois. The latter is true of Laconian (see **277**, end, and note to nos. 75-78). But for most dialects we have no adequate evidence as to the length of their survival in spoken form.

PART II
SELECTED INSCRIPTIONS

EXPLANATIONS

The brief introductory statement to each inscription gives its provenance and approximate date, with references to several of the most important collections. The extensive bibliographies in these collections make it unnecessary to cite the numerous special discussions in periodicals etc., except in the case of a few recently discovered inscriptions. For the abbreviations employed, see pp. 337 ff. References to the collections are by the numbers of the inscriptions unless otherwise stated, while those to periodicals are by pages.

It has seemed unnecessary to state in the case of every inscription whether the alphabet is the epichoric or the ordinary Ionic, since this is generally obvious from the date given, as well as from the transcription. It may be taken for granted, unless otherwise stated, that inscriptions of the fifth century B.C. or earlier are in the epichoric alphabet, those of the fourth century B.C. or later in the Ionic. Hence comments on the form of the alphabet employed are added only in special cases.

The transcription of texts in the older alphabet is such as to give the student some assistance, without confusing what is in the original and what is a matter of editing. The signs E and O, when representing long vowels, no matter whether the later spelling is η, ω or ει, ου, are transcribed simply ē, ō. The spiritus asper, when expressed in the original, is transcribed *h*, leaving the use of ' as a matter of editing. See p. 52, footnote. The use of the following signs is to be noted.

[ ] for restorations of letters no longer legible.

< > for letters inscribed by mistake, and to be ignored by the reader.

( ) for (1) expansion of abbreviations, (2) letters omitted by mistake, (3) corrected letters. Obvious corrections are given thus, without adding the original reading. Less certain corrections are sometimes commented on in the notes, with citation of the original reading, as are also obscure readings due to the mutilation of the letters. But often this is not done, it being thought unnecessary in a work of this kind to repeat the full critical apparatus of other collections.

- - - for a lacuna, where no restoration is attempted.

. . . . for a similar lacuna where it is desired to show, at least approximately, the number of missing letters, each dot standing for a letter. In general, these are employed only for short lacunae.

| for the beginning of each new line in the original.

|| for the beginning of every fifth line in the original.

183

× ||| for the division between sides or colums, where the text is printed
continuously.
The occasional use of a dot under a letter indicates that it is mutilated.
But this is commonly disregarded if the proper reading is reasonably
certain.

Ionic

East Ionic

1. Sigeum. Early sixth century B.C. GDI 5531. Roberts 42
and pp. 334 ff. Ditt. Syll. 2. Schwyzer 731. Solmsen-Fraenkel 60.
The second version (B) is in Attic.

A 5   Φανοδίκō | ἐμὶ τ̄ρμοκ|ράτεος τ̄ | Προκοννη||σίō · κρητῆρ|α δὲ
10 καὶ ὑποκ|ρητήριον κ|αὶ ἠθμὸν ἐς π|ρυτανήιον || ἔδωκεν Συκεεῦσιν.

B   Φανοδίκō εἰμὶ τ̄ Η|ερμοκράτōς τ̄ Προκο|νε̄σίō κἀγό · κρα-
5 τ̄ρα | κἀπίστατον καὶ hε̄θ||μὸν ἐς πρυτανεῖον ἔ|δōκα μνε̄μα Σι-
γε(ι)|εῦσι, ἐὰν δέ τι πάσχ|ō, μελεδαίνε̄ν με, ō̄ | Σιγειε̄ς. καί μ'
10 ἐπο||(ίε̄)σεν Ηαίσōπος καὶ hἀδελφοί.

Monument of Phanodicus of Proconnesus, recording his gift
of a mixing bowl, a stand for it, and a wine-strainer, to the
Sigean prytaneum. The pillar was prepared and furnished with its
Ionic inscription at Proconnesus, which was a colony of Miletus.
The Attic version was added at Sigeum, which was already at
this time occupied by Athenians.

The divergence between A and the corresponding portion of B
is partly due to the normal differences of dialect, e.g., Ion.
κρητῆρα with η after ρ, πρυτανήιον = Att. πρυτανεῖον, and
τ̄ρμοκράτεος with psilosis and consequent crasis and uncontracted -εος in contrast to Att. τ̄ Ηερμοκράτōς. So ὑποκρητήριον,
in contrast to Att. ἐπίστατον, is an Ionic form found elsewhere.
Other divergencies are due merely to the difference in alphabet
or the early Attic practice of writing single for double consonants
(Προκονε̄σίō)—or are accidental, as dat. pl. in -σιν or -σι. For the
notably early but not unprecedented spelling εἰμί in B, see **25d**.

2. Halicarnassus. Before|454 B.C. GDI 5726. Ditt. Syll. 45.
Roberts 145 and pp. 339 ff. Schwyzer 744. Solmsen-Fraenkel
62. Tod 25. For the character τ, see **4.4**. Letters which, though
now lacking, are found in Lord Charlemont's copy, are printed
without the marks of restoration.

Τάδε ὁ σύλλο[γ]ος ἐβōλεύσατο | ὁ Ἀλικαρνατέ[ω]ν καὶ Σαλμα-
κι|τέων καὶ Λύγδαμις ἐν τῆι ἱερῆ[ι] | ἀγορῆι, μηνὸς Ἑρμαιῶνος
5 πέμ||πτηι ἱσταμένō, ἐπὶ Λέοντος πρυ|ταν[εύον]τος τō Ὀατάτιος
κα|[ὶ] Σα[ρυτ]ώλλō τō Θεκυίλω νε|[ωπ]οί[ō. τ]ὸς μνήμονας μὴ
10 παρα|διδό[ναι] μήτε γῆν μήτε οἰκ[ί||α] τοῖς μνήμοσιν ἐπὶ Ἀπολ-
λω|νίδεω τō Λυγδάμιος μνημονε|ύοντος καὶ Παναμύω τō Κασβώ|λ-
15 λιος καὶ Σαλμακιτέων μνη||μονευόντων Μεγαβάτεω τō Ἀ||φυάσιος
καὶ Φορμίωνος τō Π[α]||νυάτιος. ἢν δέ τις θέληι δικάζε|σθαι περὶ
γῆς ἢ οἰκίων, ἐπικαλ[έ]||τω ἐν ὀκτωκαίδεκα μησὶν ἀπ' ὅτ[εο] | ὁ
20 ἄδος ἐγένετο · νόμωι δὲ κατάπ[ε]||ρ νῦν ὀρκω<ι>σ(α)ι τὸς δικαστάς ·
ὅτ[ι] | ἂν οἱ μνήμονες εἰδέωσιν, τοῦτο | καρτερὸν ε̄ναι. ἢν δέ τις
ὕστερον | ἐπικαλῆι τοῦτō τō χρόνō τῶν | ὀκτωκαίδεκα μηνῶν, ὅρκον
25 ε̄ναι τ||ῶι νεμομένωι τὴγ γῆν ἢ τὰ οἰκ|[ί]α, ὁρκō̄ν δὲ τὸς δικαστὰς
ἡμί|[ε]κτον δεξαμένος · τὸν δὲ ὅρκον εἶ|[ν]αι παρεόντος τō ἐνεστη-
30 κότος · κ|αρτερὸς δ' εἶναι γῆς καὶ οἰκίων οἵτινες || τότ' εἶχον ὅτε
Ἀπολλωνίδης καὶ Παυα|μύης ἐμνημόνευον, εἰ μὴ ὕστερο|ν ἀπεπέ-
ρασαν. τὸν νόμον τοῦτον | ἢν τις θέληι συγχέαι ἢ προθῆτα||[ι]
35 ψῆφον ὥστε μὴ εἶναι τὸν νόμο||ν τοῦτον, τὰ ἐόντα αὐτō̄ πεπρή-
σθω | καὶ τὠπόλλωνος εἶναι ἱερὰ καὶ α|ὐτὸν φεύγēν αἰεί · ἢν δὲ μὴ
ἦι αὐτ|ῶι ἄξια δέκα στατήρων, αὐτὸν [π]||επρῆσθαι ἐπ' ἐξαγωγῆι
40 καὶ μη[δ]||αμὰ κάθοδον εἶναι ἐς Ἀλικαρν|ησσόν. Ἀλικαρνασσέων
δὲ τῶσ σ|υμπάντων τούτωι ἐλεύθερον ε̄|ναι, ὃς ἂν ταῦτα μὴ παρα-
45 βαίνηι, κατό|περ τὰ ὅρκια ἔταμον καὶ ὡς γέγραπτ||αι ἐν τῶι Ἀπολ-
λω[νί]ωι, ἐπικαλε̄ν.

Decree of the council of Halicarnassians and Salmacitians
and Lygdamis regarding disputes over real estate. Lygdamis
is the tyrant who drove Herodotus into exile and whom a re-
volution eventually expelled from the city. It is probable that
this inscription dates from a period when the citizens had arisen
and restored the exiles, but had come to terms temporarily
with Lygdamis. The disputes would then be concerning the
property of the former exiles (cf. no. 22), although this is nowhere stated. Salmacis was a town partially merged with Halicarnassus, and represented with it by a common council, though
still retaining its own officials. Halicarnassus was originally Doric,
but had already become Ionic in speech. Many of the proper
names are of Carian origin.

8 ff. 'The recorders are not to transfer lands or houses to the incoming board consisting of Apollonides and his colleagues.' That is, apparently, property which had been in the hands of the recorders for settlement, or perhaps in sequestration, was now to be turned over to the presumptive owners instead of to the new board, in order to secure an immediate disposal of these matters, even though this might in many cases be only tentative and subject to further litigation. The phrase used in l. 30 'when A. and P. were recorders' has reference to future suits, and is not inconsistent with the view that these men constituted the incoming board at the time of the decree.—16 ff. 'Any one wishing to bring suit must prefer his claim within eighteen months of the time of the decree. The dicasts shall administer the oath (to the one bringing suit) in accordance with the present law. Whatever the recorders have knowledge of (e.g. through their records) shall be valid.'—22 ff. 'If one prefers a claim after the prescribed period, the one in possession of the property shall take the oath (that is, he shall have the preference in taking the oath; cf. the use of ὁρκιότερος in the Gortyn Law-Code). The dicasts shall administer the oath, receiving a twelfth of a stater as fee, and the oath shall be taken in the presence of the claimant. Those who held the property when Apollonides and Panamyes were recorders shall be the legal possessors, unless they have disposed of it later.'—**ἀπεπέρασαν**: ἀποπιπράσκω, a rare compound.—32 ff. 'If any one wishes to annul this law or proposes a vote to this effect, his property shall be sold and dedicated to Apollo, and he himself shall be an exile forever. If his property is not worth ten staters, he himself shall be sold for transportation and never be allowed to return.'—41 ff. 'Of all the Halicarnassians any one who does not transgress these things such as they have sworn to and as is recorded in the temple of Apollo, shall be at liberty to prefer claims.'—**τῶς συμπάν-των**: τῶν συμπάντων. **96**.2.

3. Teos. About 475 B.C. GDI 5632. Roberts 142 and pp. 336 ff. Ditt. Syll. 37, 38. Schwyzer 710. Solmsen-Fraenkel 55. Tod 23.

A   Ὅστις φάρμακα δηλητή|ρια ποιοῖ ἐπὶ Τηίοισι|ν τὸ ξυνὸν ἢ
5 ἐπ' ἰδιώτηι, κ|ἔνον ἀπόλλυσθαι καὶ α||ὐτὸν καὶ γένος τὸ κἔνō. |
   ὅστις ἐς γῆν τὴν Τηίην κ|ωλύοι σῖτον ἐσάγεσθαι | ἢ τέχνηι ἢ μη-

10 χανῆι ἢ κατ|ὰ θάλασσαν ἢ κατ' ἤπειρο||ν ἢ ἐσαχθέντα ἀνωθεοίη,
κἕν|ον ἀπόλλυσθαι καὶ αὐτ|ὸν καὶ γένος τὸ κἕνο.

B [1, 2 fragmentary] ὅστις Τηίων ε[ὐθ]ύνωι | ἢ αἰσυ[μ]νήτηι - - -
5 -ηι ἢ || ἐπανισταῖτο τ[ῶ]ι αἰ[συμ]|νήτηι, ἀπόλλυσθαι καὶ | αὐτὸν
καὶ γένος τὸ κείν|ō. ὅστις τō λοιπō αἰσυμ|νῶν ἐν Τέωι ἢ γῆι τῆι
10 Τη||ίηι [ἀδίκ](ω)ς ἄν(δρ)[α]ς ἀ[ποκ]τ|ένει[ε] ... αρον να [εἰδ]||-
ὡς προδο[ίη ...] τὴ[ν] πό|λ[ιν καὶ γῆν] τὴν Τηί|ων ἢ τō[ς] ἄνδρας
15 [ἐν ν]||ήσωι ἢ θα[λάσσηι] τὸ | μετέ[πειτ' ἢ τὸ] ἐν | Ἀρο[ί]ηι περι-
20 πό[λιον ἢ τō] | λοιπō προδο[ίη ἢ κιξα]||λλεύοι ἢ κιξάλλας ὑπο||δέ-
χοιτο ἢ ληίζοιτο ἢ λ|ηιστὰς ὑποδέχοιτο εἰ|δὼς ἐκ γῆς τῆς Τηίης
25 ἢ [θ]||αλάτης φέροντας ἤ [τι κ]|ακὸν βōλεύοι περὶ Τ[ηί]||ων τō
ξυνō εἰδὼς ἢ π[ρὸς] | Ἕλληνας ἢ πρὸς βαρβάρο|υς, ἀπόλλυσθαι
30 καὶ αὐ|τὸν καὶ γένος τὸ κἕνō. | οἵτινες τιμōχέοντες || τὴν ἐπαρὴν μὴ
ποιήσεα|ν ἐπὶ Δυνάμει καθημέν|ō τὡγῶνος Ἀνθεστηρίο|ισιν καὶ
35 Ἡρακλέοισιν | καὶ Δίοισιν, ἐν τὴπαρῆ||ι ἔχεσθαι. ὃς ἂν τὰ στήλ|ας,
ἐν ἧισιν ἡπαρὴ γέγρ|απται, ἢ κατάξει ἢ φοιν|ικήια ἐκκόψει ἢ ἀφα-
40 νέ|ας ποιήσει, κἕνον ἀπόλ||λυσθαι καὶ αὐτὸν καὶ γ|ένος [τὸ κἕνō].

Imprecations against evil-doers.
A 1 ff. Against those who manufacture poisons.—τὸ ξυνόν:
adv. acc. 'as a community.'—6 ff. Against those who interfere
with the importation of grain, or '(push up =) raise' the price
of what has been imported.—ἀνωθεοίη: contrasted with ποιοῖ
l. 2. See 42.6, 157c.

B 3 ff. Against those who resist the authority of the magistrates. The εὔθυνος must have been a superior official to the
ordinary εὔθυνοι or auditors. The αἰσυμνήτης is often an extraordinary official like the Roman dictator, but possibly a regular
magistrate at Teos.—8 ff. Against unfaithful and treasonable
magistrates. The restoration of ll. 8-18 is uncertain.—29 ff.
Against magistrates who fail to pronounce the imprecations.—
The τιμοῦχοι are probably the regular annual magistrates, like
the archons elsewhere.—ποιήσεαν: ποιήσειαν. 31.—Δυνάμει:
109.2.—καθημένō τὡγῶνος κτλ.: 'during the assembly at the
Anthesteria, etc.'—35 ff. Against those who damage the steles.—
τὰ στήλας: τὰς στήλας 89.7.—κατάξει, etc.: aor. subj. 150, 176.2.
4. Chios. Fifth century B.C. GDI 5653. Roberts 149 and pp.
343 ff. Schwyzer 688. Solmsen-Fraenkel 54.

A -ος· ἀπὸ τούτō μέχρι [τῆς] | τριόδō, ἢ 'ς 'Ερμώνοσσαν [φ]|έρει,
5 τρε͂ς· ἀπὸ τῆς τριόδō ἄ[χ]|ρι 'Ερμωνόσσης ἐς τὴν τρίοδ||ον ἔξς·
ἀπὸ τούτō μέχρι τō | Δηλίō τρε͂ς· σύνπαντες ὄρ|οι ἑβδομήκοντα
10 πέντε. | ὅση τῶν ὄρων τούτων ἔ|σω, πᾶσα Λοφῖτις.

ἢν τίς τ||ινα
τῶν ὄρων τούτων | ἢ ἐξέληι ἢ μεθέληι ἢ ἀ|φανέα ποιήσει ἐπ' ἀδι-
15 κί|ηι τῆς πόλεως, ἑκατὸν σ|τατῆρας ὀφειλέτω κἄτι||μος ἔστω, πρη-
ξάντων δ' ὀ|ροφύλακες· ἢν δὲ μὴ πρή|ξοισιν, αὐτοὶ ὀφειλόντω|ν,
20 πρηξάντων δ' οἱ πεντε|καίδεκα τὸς ὀροφύλακας· || ἢν δὲ μὴ πρήξοι-
σιν, ἐν ἐπ|αρῆι ἔστων.

B1 [οἱ π||ε]ντεκα[ίδεκ]|α ἐς βōλὴ[ν ἐν]|εικάντων [ἐν] | πέντ' ἡμέ-
5 ρη[ι]||σιν· τὸς δὲ κή|ρυκας διαπέ|μψαντες ἐς τ|ὰς χώρας κη[ρ]|υσ-
10 σόντων κα||ὶ διὰ τῆς πόλ|εως ἀδηνέως | γεγωνέοντε|ς, ἀποδεκνύν|-
15 τες τὴν ἡμέρ||ην, ἢν ἂν λάβω|ισιν, καὶ τὸ π|ρῆχμα προσκ|ηρυσσόν-
20 των, | ὅτι ἂμ μέλλη||ι πρήξεσθαι· | κἀγδικασάν|των τριηκοσ|ίων
25 μὴ 'λάσσο|νες ἀνηρίθε|υτοι ἐόντες.

C [ἢν δέ τι|ς τὸς πριαμένōς ἀποκλήι|ηι] ἢ δικά[ζηται, τὸς ἀπο-
κλ|η]ιομένōς ἡ π[ό]λις δεξαμ[έ|ν]η δικαζέσθω κἂν ὄφληι, [ὑ]||περα-
5 ποδότω· τῶι δὲ πρια[μ]||ένωι πρῆχμα ἔστω μηδέν. [ὃ]|ς ἂν τὰς
πρήσις ἀκρατέα[ς] | ποιῆι, ἐπαράσθω κατ' αὐτ[ō] | ὁ βασιλεός,
ἐπὴν τὰς νομ[α]||ίας ἐπαρὰς ποιῆται. ||
10 τὰς γέας καὶ τὰς οἰκί<ε>α[ς] | ἐπρίαντο· τῶν 'Αννικō πα[ί]-|
δων 'Ικέσιος 'Ηγεπόλιος π|εντακισχειλίων τριηκ[ο]|σίων τεσ-
15 σ[ερ]ακόντων, 'Αθ[η]||ναγ[ό]ρ[η]ς 'Η[ροδό]τō χειλί[ω]||ν ἑπτα-
κοσίων· Θαργελέο[ς] | Φιλοκλῆς Ζηνοδότō τὰν [Ε]|υάδησιν δισ-
20 χειλίων ἐ[π]||τακοσίων, Θεόπροπος κο[ὶ]||νοπίδης τὰγ Καμινήηι
χ[ε]||ιλίων καὶ ὀκτακοσίων [ἐπ]||τά· Κήφιος τὰ ἐμ Μελαίνη[ι] |
25 'Ακτῆι τρισχελίων ἑπτακ|οσίων ἐνενηκόντων Βία[ς] || 'Ασιō.

D5 ..ιον ..... | [χ]ειλίων ἐνα|κοσίων· Λεύκ|ιππος Πυθō τ||ὴν
οἰκίην τ[ὴ]|ν 'Ανδρέος π[ε]|ντακοσίων π|εντηκόντων | δυῶν· "Ασ-
10 μιος || Θεόπομπος 'Α|γυαίō τὰν Οἴ|ωι γειλίων τ|ριηκοσίων δ|έκων
15 δυῶν· 'Ι||κεσίō τō Φίλ|ωνος Στράτ[ι|ο]ς Λυσō τοὶκ||[ό]πεδον
διηκ||[ο]σίων ἑνός.

Decree fixing the boundaries of a district called Lophitis,
followed by provisions for its sale and a list of the purchasers.

For the Lesbian elements in the Chian dialect, see **184**. For
πρήξοισιν, short-vowel subj. like ποιήσει, see also **150**. For
πόλεως, see **109**.2. βασιλεός (C 8) is the earliest example of
εο = ευ (**33**).

B 'In the case of a lawsuit (πρῆχμα), the Fifteen are to bring
it before the council within five days and make public announcement of it in the villages and in the city.'

C 1-8. 'If any one excludes the purchasers from possession
or brings suit against them, the city, taking up the cause of those
that are excluded, shall sustain the suit, and, if it loses, reimburse
them. The purchaser shall be free from litigation. Whoever
makes the sales invalid, him shall the βασιλεύς curse, when he
makes the customary imprecations.'—10 ff. 'There purchased
lands and houses: from the sons of Annices, Hicesius, son of
Hegepolis, for 5340 (staters), and Athenagoras, son of Herodotus, for 1700; from Thargeleus, Philocles, son of Zenodotus, the
property in Euadae for 2700'; etc.—20. **κοινοπίδης**: καὶ Οἰ-
νοπίδης. **94**.7.

5. Erythrae. About 357 B.C. GDI 5687. Ditt. Syll. 168.
Schwyzer 703.

Ἔδοξεν τῆι βουλ[ῆι, στρατηγῶν] | γνώμη· Μαύσσωλλο[ν
Ἐ]κατ[όμνω] | Μυλασέα, ἐπεὶ ἀνὴρ ἀγαθὸς [ἐγέ]|νετο περὶ τὴν
5 πόλιν τὴν Ἐρυ||θραίων, εἶναι εοεργέτην τῆς | πόλεως καὶ πρό-
ξενον καὶ πολί|την· καὶ ἔσπλουν καὶ ἔκπλουν | καὶ πολέμō καὶ
10 εἰρήνης ἀσυλε[ὶ] | κα[ὶ] ἀσπονδεί, καὶ ἀτέλειαν κα[ὶ || πρ]οεδρίην·
ταōτα δὲ εἶναι αὀ|[τῶ]ι καὶ ἐκγόνοις. στῆσαι δὲ α[ὀ|τō κ]αὶ εἰκόνα
χαλκῆν ἐν τῆι ἀ|[γορῆ]ι καὶ Ἀρτεμισίης εἰκόνα | [λιθί]νην ἐν τῶι
15 Ἀθηναίωι, καὶ || [στεφ]ανῶσαι Μαύσσωλλον μὲν | [ἐκ δαρ]εικῶν
πεντήκοντα, Ἀρτε|[μισίην] δὲ ἐκ τριήκοντα δαρε[ι|κῶν. γράψ]αι
20 ταōτα ἐ(ς) στήλη[ν | καὶ στῆσα]ι ἐς τὸ Ἀθήναιον, || [ἐπιμελη-
θ](ῆ)ναι [δὲ τοὺς ἐξεταστάς].

Decree in honor of Maussolus, the satrap of Caria, to whose
memory the famous Mausoleum was erected by his widow
Artemisia.—15 ff. See **136**.9.

Central Ionic

6. Naxos. Found at Delos. Seventh or early sixth century B.C.
IG XII.v.2 p. xxiv. GDI 5423. Roberts 25. Schwyzer 758.
Solmsen-Fraenkel 63.

Νικάνδρη μ' ἀνέθēκεν hεκηβόλōι ἰοχεαίρηι,
φόρη Δεινο|δίκηο τō Ναξσίō, ἔξσοχος ἀλήōν,
Δεινομένεος δὲ κασιγνέτη, | Φhράξσō δ' ἄλοχος ν[ῦν].

Inscribed on an archaic statue of Artemis at Delos. Ϙ is used as *h* and *hε*, and for η from ᾱ, but not for original η. See 4.6, 8*a*. In Δεινοδίκηο and ἀλήϙν the endings, as the meter shows, have the value of one syllable, like εω in Homer. See 41.4. The character which appears before σ in Ναϙσίο, etc., is probably a special form of Ξ, the words to be read Ναξσίο, ἔξσοχος, Φηράξσο, parallel to Rhod. κύλιξς, etc. (89.1).

7. Andros, inscribed at Delphi. About 425 B.C. Daux, Hesperia 18.58 ff. The fragmentary first lines of A and B are omitted here.

A 6 τόσδε σῖτ[ο|ν μ]ὲ̄ τιθέναι μεδὲ φρ[υκ]|τός·-ἀρχεθεάρο̄ς τρε͂ς,
10 μ|άντιν, ἄρχοντα, κέρυκα, || αὐλετήν, κυβερνήτεν, κ[ε]||λευστήν,
   π[ρ]ο̄ιρέτεν. Δέ[ρ]||μα δὲ φερέτο̄ κῆρυξ, αὐλε̄|τής, κελευστὴς ἕκασ-
15 τος | τῶν δημοσίον, ἱερέων σῖ||τον παρεχόντων τε͂ι πρό|τει, μᾶζαν,
   κρέα, οἶνον ὁ|πόσ[ο]ν βόλονται καὶ τἆ[λ]λα ἁρμόδια. τὰς δὲ δύο
20 ἡμ|έρας, καίοντος το͂ σίτο̄, τ||ιθέτω ἕκασ(τ)ος καὶ παῖς κ|αὶ ἀνὲρ
   ὀβ[ο]λὸν Α(ἰ)γιναῖον | τῆς ἡμέρ[ε̄]ς ἑκάστης· οἱ δ|ὲ ἀρχεθέαροι
25 καθιερευ|όντο̄ν ὑπὲρ ἕμισυ ἑνί. ὑπ||αρχέτο̄ δὲ τὰ ἐξαίρετα π[ε|λ]α-
   νὸς τέσσαρας, μεταξέν||[ι]α δύο, ἱερεῖ ἐξ ἀπὸ τῆς ἑ[κ|ατ]όμβης
30 ἑκάστ[η]ς. ὁ δὲ ἰδι|[ώτη]ς φερέτω τῶν δερμάτ||[ων ὤ]ν ἂν θύσει
   τὸ τρίτομ μέ|[ρος, π]λὲ̄ν χρε̄στερίων καὶ κ|[αθαρσ]ίων, καὶ ὅσοι
   σὺν τῶ|[ι βασι]λεῖ θεαρέο̄σιν - - -

B 5 Βο̄λὲ̄ δὲ τὸν || πλεόντον ἐς Δελφό[ς) ἑλέσθο̄ πέν|τ' ἄνδρας καὶ
10 ὀρκο̄|σάτο̄. σῖτον δὲ μὲ̄ φερόντο̄ ταύτε̄ς ὀν||εκα τε͂ς ἀρχῆς. οἱ δ|ὲ
   κύριοι ἔστω ζε̄|μιῶσαι τὸν ἀκοσμ|έοντα μέχρι πέν|τε δραχ[μέ̄]ο̄ν
   ἑκάσ|τε̄ς ἑμέρε̄ς· ὃν δ' ἀν||[ζ]ημιόσο̄σι ἀπογρ|αψάντο̄ν ἐν βο̄λε͂ι.

Regulations on the duties of envoys sent to Delphi.

There is great fluctuation in the use of E and H and of O and Ω. H only once = *h* (ἑλέσθο̄, B 6) vs. 26 cases of omission. H and E about equally common for the η from ᾱ, but only E for the original η (μέ̄, μεδέ, ἀνέρ, ἔμισυ, etc.). O always for the secondary ō. Both O and Ω for original ω.

The 3 pl. imv. φερόντο̄ (B 9) vs. the normal Ion. καθιερευόντο̄ν, ἀπογραψάντο̄ν, ἔστων, can hardly be attributed to the Delphian engraver, since even at Delphi at this time the form was -ντων (see 140.3*a*, 4*a*). Still more remarkable is θεᾱρός (in ἀρχεθέαροι three times, and verbal θεαρέο̄σιν) = Att.-Ion. θεωρός. Cf. also θεαροδοκίαν in a late inscription of Tenos (IG XII.v.837).

For the titles A 8 ff. see the editor's commentary.

A 7/8. φρυκτός 'beans' (originally 'roasted'), the religious value of which is widely attested for κύαμος. Cf. also ἐπὶ φρυκτώ no. 53.15/16 with reference to the 'two beans' in drawing lots. A 25 ff. Difficult passage. 'The parts remaining (after the preceding one over half?) shall constitute four pelanoi, two metaxenia (sense here?).' The πελανός is here not a sacrificial libation, but a monetary offering, as clearly in nos. 51, 53, 88, and at Amorgos (IG XII.vii.237.21 f., 241.11). Acc. construction with ὑπαρχέτο is strange.

8. Iulis in Ceos. Last quarter of fifth century B.C. IG XII.v.593. GDI 5398. Ditt. Syll. 1218. Schwyzer 766. Solmsen-Fraenkel 64.

Οἵδε νό[μ]οι περὶ τῶγ καταφθιμ[έ]νω[ν. κατὰ | τ]άδε θά[πτ]ēν
τὸν θανόντα· ἐν ἑματίο[ις τρ|ι]σὶ λευκοῖς, στρώματι καὶ ἐνδύματι
5 [καὶ | ἐ]πιβλέματι, ἐξēναι δὲ καὶ ἐν ἐλάσ[σ]οσ[ι, μ||]ὲ πλέονος ἀξί-
οις τοῖς τρισὶ ἑκατὸν δρ[α|χ]μέων. ἐχφέρēν δὲ ἐγ κλίνηι σφηνό-
πο[δ]ι [κ]|αὶ μὲ καλύπτēν, τὰ δ᾽ ὀλ[ο]σχερ[έ]α τοῖ[ς ἑματ]|ίοις.
φέρēν δὲ οἶνον ἐπὶ τὸ σῆμα [μ]ὲ [πλέον] | τριῶν χῶν καὶ ἔλαιον
10 μὲ πλέο[ν] ἑνό[ς, τὰ δὲ ‖ ἀ]γγεῖα ἀποφέρεσθαι. τὸν θανό[ν]τα
[φέρēν | κ]ατακεκαλυμμένον σιωπῆι μέχρι [ἐπὶ τὸ | σ]ῆμα. προ-
σφαγίωι [χ]ρῆσθαι κατὰ τὰ π[άτρι|α. τ]ὴγ κλίνην ἀπὸ το[ῦ] σή-
[μ]ατο[ς] καὶ τ[ὰ] σ[τρώ]|ματα ἐσφέρēν ἐνδόσε. τῆι δὲ ὑστεραί[ηι
15 ἀ||π]οραίνēν τὴν οἰκίην ἐλεύθερον θαλά[σση|ι] πρῶτον, ἔπειτα δ[ὲ]
ὑσώπωι ο[ἰκ]έτη[ν ἐμβ]|άντα· ἐπὴν δὲ διαρανθῆι, καθαρὴν ἔναι τὴν
οἰκίην καὶ θύη θύēν ἐφί[στι|α.] τὰς γυναῖκας τὰς [ἰ]ούσ[α]ς [ἐ]πὶ
20 τὸ κῆδ[ος] | ἀπιέναι προτέρας τῶν <αν>ἀνδρῶν ἀπὸ [τοῦ] ‖ σήμα-
τος. ἐπὶ τῶι θανόντι τριηκόστ[ια μὲ | π]οιēν. μὲ ὑποτιθέναι κύλικα
ὑπὸ τὴγ [κλί|ν]ην μēδὲ τὸ ὕδωρ ἐκχēν μēδὲ τὰ καλλύ[σμα]|τα
φέρēν ἐπὶ τὸ σῆμα. ὅπου ἂν θάνηι, ἐπὴ]ν ἐ]|ξενιχθēι, μὲ ἰέναι γυναῖ-
25 κας π[ρὸ]ς τ[ὴν οἰ]||κίην ἄλλας ἒ τὰς μιαινομένας· μια[ίνεσθ]|αι
δὲ μητέρα καὶ γυναῖκα καὶ ἀδε[λφεὰς κ|α]ὶ θυγατέρας· πρὸς δὲ
ταύταις μὲ π[λέον π|έ]ντε γυναικῶν, παῖδας δὲ τ[ῶν θ]υγ[ατρῶν
30 κ|ὰ]νεψιῶν, ἄλλον δὲ μ[ε]δένα. τοὺς μια[ινομέ||νους] λουσαμένου[ς]
- - - - - - - - - - - - - - - - ! [ὕδατ]ος [χ]ύσι κα[θαρ]οὺς ἔναι εω
- - - - - - - - .

Burial law directed against extravagance in the funeral rites, like those enacted at Athens under Solon, and at Sparta under Lycurgus.

With two exceptions (θάνηι, διαρανθῆι) H is used only for the η
from ᾱ (or from εα, as ἐπήν, θύη). See 4.6, 8a.

3. **στρώματι** κτλ.: 'a cloth underneath the corpse, one wrapped
about it, and one over it.'—7. **μὲ καλύπτεν** κτλ.: they are not
to use a special covering for the bier, but cover all, the bier and
the corpse, with the cloths before mentioned.—9. **χῶν**: see
112.6.—12. **προσφαγίωι** κτλ.: 'they are to perform the sacrifice
according to the ancestral custom.' By the law of Solon the
sacrifice of an ox was forbidden.—13 f. The bier and the coverings
like the vessels (l. 10), are to be brought home, instead of being
left at the tomb.—15 f. 'The house is to be purified first with
sea-water by a free man, then with hyssop by a slave.' But the
restoration ὁ[ικ]έτη[ν ἐμβ]άντα is uncertain.—20. At Athens cere-
monies in honor of the dead were performed on the third, ninth,
and thirtieth days. The last are expressly forbidden here.—21.
Directed against certain superstitious practices, the significance
of which is not clear.

West Ionic (Euboean)

9. Seventh century B.C. GDI 5292. Rev. Arch. 1902.1.41 ff.

Πύ(ρ)ρος μ' ἐποίεσεν 'Αγασιλέϝō.

On a lecythus, now in the Boston Museum of Fine Arts, the
provenance of which is not stated. Probably manufactured in
Boeotia by a Chalcidian potter, or at least inscribed in the
Chalcidian dialect. Note the retention of intervocalic ϝ in the
proper name 'Αγασιλέϝō (or here secondary ϝ as in Τλασίαϝο
105.2b?), though not in ἐποίεσεν.

10. Cumae in Italy. Sixth century B.C. IG XIV.865, GDI 5267.
Roberts 173. Schwyzer 786.

Ταταίες ἐμὶ λ|έϟυθος· hὸς δ' ἄν με κλέφσ|ει, θυφλὸς ἔσται.

11. Cumae in Italy. Sixth century B.C. IG XIV.871. GDI
5269. Roberts 177a. Schwyzer 791.

hυπὺ τε͂ι κλίνει τούτε͂ι Λε͂νος hύπυ.

'In this niche of the tomb rests Lenos.'—**τούτε͂ι: 124.**—
hύπυ: ὕπεστι.

12. Amphipolis. 357 B.C. GDI 5282. Ditt. Syll. 194. Schwyzer
799. Solmsen-Fraenkel 66. Tod 150.

"Εδοξεν τῶι δήμωι · Φί|λωνα καὶ Στρατοκλέ|α φεόγειν Ἀμφίπο-
5 λι|ν καὶ τὴγ γῆν τὴν Ἀμφ||ιπολιτέων ἀειφυγί|ην καὶ αὐτὸς καὶ τὸς
παῖδας, καὶ ἤμ πō ἀλί|σκωνται, πάσχειν αὐτὸς ὡς πολεμίōς καὶ ||
10 νηποινεὶ τεθνάναι, | τὰ δὲ χρήματ' αὐτῶν δ|ημόσια εἶναι, τὸ δ' ἐπ|ι-
15 δέκατον ἱρὸν τō Ἀ|πόλλωνος καὶ τō Στρ||υμόνος. τὸς δὲ προστ|ά-
τας ἀναγράψαι αὐτ|ὸς ἐστήλην λιθίνην. | ἢν δέ τις τὸ ψήφισμα | ἀνα-
20 ψηφίζει ἢ καταδ||έχηται τούτōς τέχν|ηι ἢ μηχανῆι ὁτεωιōν, τὰ χρή-
ματ' αὐτō δημ|όσια ἔστω καὶ αὐτὸς φεογέτω Ἀμφίπολιν | ἀειφυ-
γίην.

When Philip captured Amphipolis in 357 B.C., he caused the
banishment of his opponents. Cf. Diod. 16.8. Among this number
were the two men against whom this decree was enacted. Amphipolis was a colony of Athens, but the population was mixed.
Cf. Thuc. 4.102 ff. At this time evidently the Chalcidian element
predominated.

3. **φεόγειν**: cf. φεογέτω, l. 24. **33.**—19. **ἀναψηφίζει**: 'proposes
to repeal.' ει for ηι, **39a.**

13. Eretria. (A) End of fifth century B.C., (B) middle of
fourth century B.C. GDI 5308. Ditt. Syll. 105, 106. Schwyzer
804. Tod 82.

A   Θεοί. | "Εδοξεν τεῖ βōλῆι 'Ηγέλοχον | τὸν Ταραντῖνον πρόξενον
5   εἶ|ναι καὶ εὐεργέτην καὶ αὐτὸν || κ[α]ὶ παῖδας καὶ σίτηριν εἶνα|ι καὶ
αὐτῶι καὶ παιρὶν, ὅταν ἐ|[π]ιδημέωριν, καὶ ἀτελέην καὶ | προεδρίην
10 ἐς τὸς ἀγῶνας ὡς σ|υνελευθερώραντι τὴμ πόλιν || ἀπ' Ἀθηνάων.
B   "Εδοξεν τεῖ βουλεῖ καὶ τοῖ δήμοι | 'Ηράκλειτον τὸν Ταραντῖνον |
πρόξενον εἶναι 'Ερετριέων αὐ|τὸν καὶ ἐκγόνους, εἶναι δὲ αὐτοῖ ||
προεδρίην καὶ σίτηριν καὶ αὐ|τοῖ καὶ παιρὶν, ὅσον ἀν χρόνον |
ἐπιδημέωριν, καὶ τὰ ἄλλα, καθ|άπερ τοῖς ἄλλοις προξένοις.

This and no. 14 are in the Eretrian variety of Euboean, for
which see **187.**
A. Ships of Tarentum formed part of the Peloponnesian fleet
which defeated the Athenians off Eretria in 411 B.C. and so led
to the Athenian loss of Eretria. Cf. Thuc. 8.91, 95. It is in gra-
titude for this that Hegelochus of Tarentum and his sons are
honored in this decree.
B. This decree is later than A, but was inscribed on the same

stone, because both recipients of honor are from Tarentum, and possibly relatives.

14. Oropus. 411-402, or 386-377 B.C. IG VII.235. GDI 5339 Ditt. Syll. 1004. Schwyzer 811. Solmsen-Fraenkel 67.

Θεοί. | Τὸν ἱερέα τοῦ Ἀμφιαράου φοιτᾶν εἰς τὸ ἱερό|ν, ἐπειδὰν χειμὼν παρέλθει, μέχρι ἀρότου ὥρ|ης μὴ πλέον διαλείποντα ἢ τρεῖς
5 ἡμέρας καὶ || μένειν ἐν τοῖ ἱεροῖ μὴ ἔλαττον ἢ δέκα ἡμέρα|ς τοῦ μηνὸς ἐκ[ά]στō. καὶ ἐπαναγκάζειν τὸν ν|εωκόρον τοῦ τε ἱεροῦ ἐπιμελεῖσθαι κατὰ τὸ|ν νόμον καὶ τῶν ἀφικνεμένων εἰς τὸ ἱερόν.|
10 ἂν δέ τις ἀδικεῖ ἐν τοῖ ἱεροῖ ἢ ξένος ἢ δημότ||ης, ζημιούτω ὁ ἱερεὺς μέχρι πέντε δραχμέων | κυρίως καὶ ἐνέχυρα λαμβανέτω τοῦ ἐζημιωμ|ένου · ἂν δ' ἐκτίνει τὸ ἀργύριον, παρεόντος τō | ἱερέος ἐμβαλέτω εἰς τὸν θησαυρόν. δικάζει|ν δὲ τὸν ἱερέα, ἄν τις ἰδίει ἀδικηθεῖ
15 ἢ τῶν ξέ||νων ἢ τῶν δημοτέων ἐν τοῖ ἱεροῖ, μέχρι τριῶν | δραχμέων, τὰ δὲ μέζονα, ἧχοι ἑκάστοις αἱ δίκ|αι ἐν τοῖς νόμοις εἰρῆται, ἐντōθα γινέσθων. | προσκαλεῖσθαι δὲ καὶ αὐθημερὸν περὶ τῶν ἐ|ν τοῖ ἱεροῖ
20 ἀδικίων · ἂν δὲ ὁ ἀντίδικος μὴ συνχ||ωρεῖ, εἰς τὴν ὑστέρην ἡ δίκη τελείσθω. ἐπαρ|χὴν δὲ διδοῦν τὸμ μέλλοντα θεραπεύεσθαι ὑ|πὸ τοῦ θεοῦ μὴ ἔλαττον ἐννέ' ὀβολοὺς δοκίμου ἀργ|υρίου καὶ ἐμβάλλειν εἰς τὸν θησαυρὸν παρε|όντος τοῦ νεωκόρου - - - - - - - - - - - - - - ||
25 - - - - - κατεύχεσθαι δὲ τῶν ἱερῶν καὶ ἐπ|ὶ τὸν βωμὸν ἐπιτιθεῖν, ὅταν παρεῖ, τὸν ἱερέα, | ὅταν δὲ μὴ παρεῖ, τὸν θύοντα, καὶ τεῖ θυσίει α|ὐτὸν ἑαυτοῖ κατεύχεσθαι ἕκαστον, τῶν δὲ δη|μορίων τὸν ἱερέα.
30 τῶν δὲ θυομένων ἐν τοῖ ἱε||ροῖ πάντων τὸ δέρμα - - - - - - - -. θύειν δὲ ἐξ|εῖν ἅπαν ὅτι ἂν βόληται ἕκαστος · τῶν δὲ κρεῶ|ν μὴ εἶναι ἐκφορὴν ἔξω τοῦ τεμένεος. τοῖ δὲ | ἱερεῖ διδοῦν τὸς θύοντας ἀπὸ τοῦ ἱερήου ἐκ|άστō τὸν ὦμον, πλὴν ὅταν ἡ ἑορτὴ εἶ · τότε δὲ
35 ἀπ||ὸ τῶν δημορίων λαμβανέτω ὦμον ἀφ' ἑκάστου | τοῦ ἱερήου. ἐγκαθεύδειν δὲ τὸν δειόμενο|ν - | υαυ - - - - - - - - - - - - - - - - - - - πειθόμ|ενον τοῖς νόμοις.
40 τὸ ὄνομα τοῦ ἐγκαθεύδον||τος, ὅταν ἐμβάλλει τὸ ἀργύριον, γράφεσθαι τ|ὸν νεωκόρον καὶ αὐτοῦ καὶ τῆς πόλεος καὶ ἐκ|τιθεῖν ἐν τοῖ ἱεροῖ γράφοντα ἐν πετεύροι σ|κοπεῖν τοῖ βολομένοι. ἐν δὲ τοῖ κοι-
45 μητηρίο|ι καθεύδειν χωρὶς μὲν τὸς ἄνδρας, χωρὶς || δὲ τὰς γυναῖκας, τοὺς μὲν ἄνδρας ἐν τοῖ πρὸ ἠ|ōς τοῦ βωμοῦ, τὰς δὲ γυναῖκας ἐν τοῖ πρὸ ἡεσπέ|[ρης] . . . . τὸ κοιμ]ητήριον τοὺς ἐν|[καθ-εύδοντας . . . .

Regulations of the temple of Amphiaraus at Oropus. Oropus seems to have been an Eretrian possession before it passed into the hands of the Thebans in the sixth century, and preserved the Eretrian dialect throughout the Boeotian and the subsequent Athenian domination. But from the end of the fourth century the inscriptions are in Attic, a few in Boeotian.

1 ff. The priest evidently passed the winters in the town, leaving the temple entirely in the charge of the custodian. But with the end of winter, when visitors became more frequent, he was expected to go to the temple regularly, never missing more than three days at a time and remaining there at least ten days each month. He was to see to it that the custodian took proper care of the temple and its visitors.—8. ἀφικνε͠μένων. 158.— 9 ff. 'If any one commits sacrilege in the temple, the priest shall have the right to impose a fine up to the sum of five drachmas and take pledges of the one penalized. If such a one offers the money, he must deposit it in the treasury in the presence of the priest. If any one suffers a private wrong in the temple, the priest shall decide matters of no more than three drachmas, but the more important cases shall be tried before the proper courts. The summons for wrongs done in the temple shall be made on the same day, but if the opponent does not agree, the case may go over till the next day.'—16. ἐκάστοις: 'for the several persons.'—17. εἰρῆται: 43.—ἐντῦθα: 34a, 124.—19. ἀδικίων: ἀδίκιον=ἀδίκημα.—21 ff. 'The one who is to be treated by the god shall pay a fee of not less than nine obols of current money (no bad coin was to be palmed off) and put it in the treasury in the presence of the custodian.'—ἐννέ' ὀβολούς is crowded into a space where a shorter word had been erased, presumably δραχμήν. Since the law was first inscribed, the amount of the fee had been raised, and at the same time another provision, which followed after νεωκόρου in l. 24, had been abrogated and erased.—25 ff. 'The priest shall make the prayers and place the victims on the altar, if he is present, but, if he is not present, the one who gives the offering. At the festival each shall make his own prayer, but the priest shall make the prayers for the sacrifices in behalf of the state, and he shall receive the skin of all the victims.'—30 ff. θύειν δὲ ἐξεῖν κτλ.: there was no

restriction as to the kind of victims to be offered, such as is often made in temple regulations, but in any case the flesh was not to be carried off.—31. βόληται: so, not βόληται (βούληται), for an Eretrian inscription of later date, which never has ο = ου, reads βόληται, βολόμενον.—32 ff. τοῖ δὲ ἱερεῖ κτλ.: 'the priest is to have the shoulder of each victim, except when there is a festival, and then only from the victims offered for the state.'— 33. ἱερήου: ἱερήιου. 37, 164.1.—36. δειόμενον: δεόμενον. 9.1.— 39 ff. 'The custodian is to inscribe the name of each one who consults the oracle, when he has paid his money, and place it on a tablet in the shrine so that any one who wishes may see it.'— ἐγκαθεύδοντος: as elsewhere, those wishing to consult the oracle went to sleep in a room of the temple assigned for this purpose (see following), and received the oracle in a dream.—πέτευρον: 135.5a.—43 ff. ἐν δὲ τοῖ κοιμητηρίοι κτλ.: 'the men and women are to lie in separate places, the men to the east of the altar, the women to the west.'—46. ἠ̄ς: 41.4b.—ηεσπέρης: he designated by η, as in no. 6, etc. 4.6.

Arcadian

15. Sixth or early fifth century B.C. IG V.ii.554. GDI 373. Ditt. Syll. 1034. Roberts 237a. Schwyzer 676.

Καμὸ̄ ὑνέθυσε ταῖ ΚόρϜαι.

Dedication inscribed on a bronze cymbal, which, according to the more probable of two varying reports, was found near the modern Dimitsana in Arcadia. Formerly read Κάμουν ἔθυσε κτλ. and ascribed to Thessalian, later as Καμὸ̄ ὺν ἔθυσε. But the use of ὑνέθυσε = ἀνέθηκε is confirmed by a later dedication reading Φαυλέας ἀνέθυσε τοῖ Πανί, in which the earlier ὑν- (6, 22) is replaced by ἀνα-.

16. Cleitor or Lusoi? Sixth or early fifth century B.C. D. Robinson, CP 38.191 ff. Beattie, CQ 41.66 ff.

εἰ γυ]νὰ Ϝέσε̄τοι ζτεραῖον λο̄πος, | [ἱερὸ]ν ἔναι ταῖ Δάματρι Θεσμοφόροι. | [εἰ δὲ] μὲ̄ ὑνιερόσει, δῡμενὲς ἔασα ἐπὲ Ϝέργο̄ | 5 [. . . .]ς ζ' ἐξόλοιτυ, κὰ ὅζις τότε δαμιοϜοργε̄ || [ἀφάε]σται δαρχ- μὰς τριάκοντα. εἰ δὲ μὲ̄ ἀφάετοι, | [ὀφλὲν] τὰν ἀσέβειαν. ἔχε̄ ὅδε κῦρος δέκο Ϝέτεα. ἔνα[ι] | [. . . . . .] τόδε.

Bronze tablet, probably the continuation (with the conclusion) of others, constituting a series of temple regulations. There are several serious difficulties, and the following translation is in part only tentative. 'If a woman wears a brightly colored robe, it shall be dedicated to Demeter Thesmophoros. If she does not dedicate it, being ill disposed in respect to the rite (?), let her perish, and whoever is demiurgus at the time shall pay thirty drachmas. If he does not pay, he shall be charged with the impiety. Let this (sc. νόμος) have validity for ten years. - - -'

1. The first (mutilated) letter is just above the second of l. 2, so that five letters may be missing or four with a slight inset,— hardly room for εἰκὰν γυ as read by Beattie.—Ϝέσε̄τοι: 3 sg. aor. subj. without ἄν (150, 174).—ζτεραῖον: with freak spelling (cf. τζετρακάτιαι, no. 70) probably cognate with ζειρόν· ποικίλον and other glosses in Hesych. Cf. the forbidden λωπίον ποικίλον, Schwyzer 429.—3. ὑνιερο̄σει: probably 3 sg. aor. opt. (152.4).— δῡμενές = δυσμενής with normal development of σμ (76) instead of the usual restored δυσ-.—ἔασα: 163.8.—ΕΠΕϜΕΡΓΟ: perhaps to be read ἐπὲ Ϝέργο̄ = ἐπὲς τοῖ ἔργοι, no. 19.54, with assimilation of the final ς and simplification of the double consonant, like Cypr. τᾶ Ϝανάσας = τᾶς Ϝανάσσας (97.2; cf. also Arc. τὰ Ϝάδω = τὰν Ϝάδω) and Ϝέργο̄ with original genitive instead of the usual Arc. dative construction and archaic absence of the article (122a).—4. ζ': could be for τε with ζ as in ὄζις = ὅτις (68.3), but this, though the preceding word to be supplied is quite uncertain, seems to make no sense.—ἐξόλοιτυ: opt. in prescription, like Cypr. δώκοι (175).—δαμιοϜοργε̄: pres. subj. without ἄν (149, 174). Or read τότ' ἐδαμιοϜόργε̄, imperf. indic. ? This is the first example of Ϝ attested in the various forms of this title, for which see 167.—5. ἀφάε]σται: probable restoration in view of the end of the line. στ = σθ though not previously attested in this dialect (85.1).—ἀφάε̄τοι: pres. subj. mid. without ἄν (174) of an otherwise unknown ἀφάομαι, here meaning clearly 'pay', probably compound of ἄομαι 'satiate' (cf. ἄται· πληροῦται Hesych.), with development of 'fill' to 'fulfil' and 'pay,' as in πληρόω.—6. ἔχε̄: 3 sg. subj. in independent use as rarely in Elean (174).—At the end of the line probably ἔνα[ι], but the restoration of the first word in next line is wholly dubious.

17. Mantinea. Fifth century B.C. IG V.ii.262. Schwyzer 661. Solmsen-Fraenkel 5. Comparetti, Annuario 1.1 ff. Buck, CP 20.136 ff. For ϻ, which is transcribed σ, see 4.4, 68.3.

10 [Fō]φλέασι οἴδε ἰν 'Αλέαν · | [ll. 2-9 proper names] || ῎Αδραν-
τος, | 'Αντιλαΐδας, | Βōθις, | Ήέσκλαρος, | Θέμανδρος. | ὀϭέοι ἄν
15 χρēστέριον κακρίνē || ē̄ γνōσίαι κακριθέε̄ τōν χρēμάτōν, | πὲ τοῖς
Fοικιάται(ς) τᾶς θεō̄ ἔναι, κὰ Fοικίας δάσασσθαι τὰς ἄν ὅδ' ἐάσας. |
εἰ τοῖς Fōφλēκόσι ἐπὶ τοῖδ' ἐδικάσαμε[ν], | ἅ τε θεὸς κὰς οἱ δι-
20 κασσταί, ἀπυϭεδομίν[ος] || τōν χρēμάτōν τὸ λάχος, ἀπεχομίνος |
κὰ τόρρέντερον γένος ἔναι | ἄματα πάντα ἀπὺ τοῖ ἱεροῖ, ἵλαον
ἔναι. | εἰ δ' ἄλλα ϭις ἔατοι κὰ τōνν[υ], ἰνμενφὲς ἔναι. | εὐχōλὰ
25 [δ'] ἄδε ἔ[σ]ετοι τοῖ ἀ[- - -]· || εἴ ϭις ἰν το(ῖ) ἱεροῖ τōν τότ[ε
ἀπυθανόντōν] | φονές ἐστι, εἴϭ' αὐτός εἴϭε [τōν ἐσγόνōν] |' ϭις
κὰ τόρρέντερον, εἴϭε τ[ōν ἀνδρōν] εἴϭε τᾶς φαρθένō̄, ἰνμενφ[ὲς
30 ἔναι κὰ] | τὸ χρēστέριον· εἰ δὲ μὲ̄, ἵλαο[ν ἔναι]. || εἰ (Θ)έμανδρος
φονές ἐσστ[ι εἴϭε] | τōν ἀνδρōν εἴϭε τᾶς φαρθέν[ō] | τōν τότε
ἀπυθανόντōν ἰν [τοῖ ἱεροῖ] | κὰς μὲ̄ προσσθαγενὲς τō̄ Fέρ[γō] |
35 τō̄ τότε ἔο[ν]τος, ἰνμονφον θε[οῖ ἔναι]. || εἰ δὲ προσσ(θ)αγενὲς
τō̄ Fέργ[ō], | κὰς μὲ̄ φονές, ἵλαον ἔναι.

Judgment against certain persons guilty of sacrilege toward Athena Alea, whose temple had been made the scene of a bloody fray. Most of the difficulties in the reading and interpretation have been cleared up, but some points are still uncertain.

1. 'The following have been condemned to pay a penalty to the temple of Alea.' Cf., with the aorist, ἑκοτὸν δαρχμὰς ὀφλὲν ἰν δᾱμον, no. 18.4, and for the whole episode οἴδε ὦφλον Δηλίων ἀσεβείας - - - - - , τὸ τίμημα τὸ ἐπιγεγραμμένον καὶ ἀειφυγία, ὅτι ἐκ τοῦ ἱεροῦ τοῦ 'Απόλλωνος τοῦ Δηλίου ἦγον τοὺς 'Αμφικτύονας καὶ ἔτυπτον, IG II².1635.134 ff.—14 ff. 'In the case of any one whom the oracle has condemned or who by judicial process has been condemned to forfeit his property, this together with the serfs shall belong to the goddess, and the houses which he may possess here (?) shall be distributed (i.e., confiscated and disposed of).'— 14. κακρίνē: κατακρίνη. 89.7, 95.—15. γνōσία: Att. γνῶσις in its legal sense.—17. τὰς ἄν ὅδ' ἐάσας: ἄν with pple., Smyth 1846b, Kühner-Gerth 1. 242. Some read ἄνōδ' 'above,' with various interpretations of its significance here.—18 ff. 'Inasmuch as we,

the goddess and the judges, have passed judgment upon the guilty parties as follows, namely that, having given up their inheritance, they shall forever be excluded from the temple, in the male line, it shall be well (propitious). But if any one permits anything else, contrary to these things, it shall be impious.'—22. κὰ τόρρέντερον: κατὰ τὸ ἀρρέντερον. **94**.1, **165**.1.—22. ἄματα πάντα: a formulaic expression, Hom. ἤματα πάντα, retained here in the imprecation, although ἀμέρα is the ordinary prose word for 'day' in Arcadian as elsewhere. Similarly νόμος ἱερὸς ἰν ἄματα πάντα in a Tegean inscription.—24 ff. 'The following shall be the imprecation upon the - -. If any one (present) in the temple is a murderer of those who perished at that time, either himself or any one of his descendants in the male line (that is, if any one of these is present in the temple), (a murderer) of either the men or the maiden, it shall be impious in the eyes of the oracle; if not, it shall be propitious. If Themander is a murderer of either the men or the maiden who perished at that time in the temple, and not (merely, as he claims) present previously to (?) the deed of violence which took place then, he shall be held impious; but if (merely) present previously to (?) the deed, and not a murderer, it shall be propitious.' The reading and interpretation of the last few lines is much disputed.

18. Tegea. About 400 B.C. IG V.ii.3. Schwyzer 654. Solmsen-Fraenkel 1. Vollgraff, BCH 70.617 ff. Alphabet transitional; E = ē, O = ō, ᖰ = h; Ion. Ⱶ = ξ, X = χ.

Τὸν hιερὲν πέντε καὶ εἴκοσι οἷς νέμεν καὶ ζεῦγο|ς καὶ αἶγα· εἰ
δ᾽ ἂν καταλλάσσē, ἰνφορβισμὸν ἔναι· τ|ὸν hιερομνάμονα ἰνφορβίεν·
εἰ δ᾽ ἂν λευτον μὲ ἰνφ|ορβί͡ē, hεκοτὸν δαρχμὰς ὀφλὲν ἰν δᾶμον καὶ
5 κάταρ||Ϝον ἔναι.—τὸν hιεροθύταν νέμεν ἰν Ἀλέαι ὅτι ἂν ἀ|σκ͡ēθὲς
   ͡ē· τὰ δ᾽ ἀνασκ͡ēθέα ἰνφορβίεν· μ͡ēδ᾽ ἐσπερᾶσα|ι πὰρ ἂν λέγ͡ē hιερο-
   θυτές· εἰ δ᾽ ἂν ἐσπεράσē, δυόδεκ|ο δαρχμὰς ὀφλὲν ἰν δᾶμον.—τᾶς
   τριπαναγόρσιος τ|ὰς ὑστέρας τρὶς ἀμέρας νέμεν ὅτι hὰν βόλētοι ὃς
10 μὲ||ἰν τοῖ περιχόροι.· εἰ δ᾽ ἂν ἰν τοῖ περιχόροι, ἰνφο|ρβίεν.—ἰν
   Ἀλέαι μὲ νέμεν μέτε ξένον μέτε Ϝαστὸν | εἰ μὲ ἐπὶ θοίναν hίκοντα·
   τοῖ δὲ ξένοι καταγομέν|οι ἐξ͡ēναι ἀμέραν καὶ νύκτα νέμεν ἐπιζύγιον·
15 εἰ δ᾽ | ἂν πὰρ τάνυ νέμē, τὸ μὲν μέζον πρόβατον δαρχμὰν ὀ||φλέν,

τὸ δὲ μεῖον ἰνφορβίεν.—τὰ hιερὰ πρόβατα μὲ | νέμεν ἰν 'Αλέαι
πλὸς ἀμέραυ καὶ νυκτός, εἰκ ἂν διε|λαυνόμενα τύχε· εἰ δ' ἂν νέμε,
δαρχμὰν ὀφλὲν τὸ πρό|βατον Ϝέκαστον τὸ μέζον, τõν δὲ μειόνõν
20 προβάτõ|ν ὀδελὸν Ϝέκαστον, τᾶν συõν δαρχμὰν Ϝεκάσταυ, ε[ἰ] || μὲ
παρhεταξαμένος τὸς πεντέκοντα ἒ τὸς τριακα|σίος —εἰκ ἐπὶ δõμα
πῦρ ἐποίσε, δυόδεκο δαρχμὰς | ὀφλέν, τὸ μὲν ἔμισυ ταῖ θεοῖ, τὸ
δ' ἔμισυ τοῖς hιερο|μνάμονσι.—εἰκ ἂν παραμαξεύε θύσθεν τᾶς
25 κελε[ύθ]|õ τᾶς κακειμέναυ κὰτ 'Αλέαν, τρὶς ὀδελὸς ὀφλὲ[ν ἂν]||τὶ
Ϝεκάσταυ, τὸ μὲν hέμισυ ταῖ θεοῖ, τὸ δ' ἔμισ[υ τοῖ]|ς hιερομνάμον-
σι.—Ταῖ παναγόρσι τὸς hιερ[ομνάμ]|ονας ἀρτύεν τὰ ἰν ταῖς ἰνπο-
λαῖς πάντα τ[α . . . . —τ]ὸς δαμιοργὸς τὸν κόπρον τὸν ἀπυδόσμ[ιον
30 ἐξάγεν] ταῖ hεβδόμαι τõ Λεσχανασίõ μενός· [εἰ δὲ μέ, δαρχ||μὰ]ν
ὀφλέν. τὸν Παναγόρσιον μēνα [31-35 only a few words left.]

Regulations of the temple of Athena Alea. The first five paragraphs, ll. 1-20, deal with the rights of pasturage in Alea, the
district in which the temple was situated and which was included
in the temple property. The temple officials mentioned are the
hieromnemon, the chief administrator of the affairs of the
temple (also, in the plural, the board of administrators), the
priest, and the hierothytes, a minor official charged with the
technical details of the sacrifice, though in some places this
title came to be one of high rank. The Fifty and the Three
Hundred were, doubtless, civic bodies.

The critical words are ἰνφορβίεν, ἰνφορβισμόν, plainly connected
with φέρβω 'feed,' φορβή 'fodder,' φορβεία 'halter.' The meaning
is not 'seize, seizure,' as the first editor, but 'impose a pasture
tax,' etc. Hesychius has ἐμφόρβιον· τελώνημα, which is parallel
to ἐνοίκιον 'house-rent,' ἐλλιμένιον 'harbor-dues,' etc. From this
would be derived ἰνφορβίεν 'impose a pasture tax,' and from this
again, as if from -ίζω, ἰνφορβισμός 'the imposition of a pasture
tax.' Cf. Solmsen, KZ 34.437 ff.

2. **εἰ δ'ἂν καταλλάσσε**: 'if he makes any change (substitution?).'—3. **λευτον**: meaning and etymology obscure.—5 ff. **τὸν
hιεροθύταν** κτλ.: 'the hierothytes may pasture in Alea animals
without blemish (and so suitable for the sacrifice), but for those
not unblemished (and so suitable only for personal use) one
shall impose a pasture tax. He shall not go beyond what he de-

clares in his function of hierothytes.' That is, his official statement
as to the condition of the animals is final.—7. πὰρ ἄν: πὰρ ἃ ἄν.
58d.—ἱεροθυτές: ἱεροθυτέων. 78, 157.9. hάν: ἄν. 58d.—ὃς μέ:
used like ὅσον μή.—20. 'Unless the Fifty or the Three Hundred
approve.' Acc. abs. construction. 173.—21. δôμα: 'temple.'—
ἐποίσε̄: aor. subj. to fut. οἴσω, cf. Hom. οἰσέμεναι, Hdt. ἀνοῖσαι.
For the absence of ἄν see 174.—23 ff. Meaning uncertain, but
probably 'If one drives in a wagon outside of the high road
leading through Alea, one shall pay a fine of three obols for
each (wagon),' etc.—θύσθεν: adv. from *θύρ-σθεν=θύραζε,
ἔξωθεν. 133.1.—κακειμέναυ: κατακειμένης. 89.7, 95.—26 ff. The
officials are to make all arrangements for the market, which was
held at ancient festivals as at our modern fairs. Cf. Ditt. Syll.
736.99 ff.—28. ἀπυδόσμ[ιον]: adjective derived from a now
quotable ἀπυδοσμός 'payment' (no. 21.39) = ἀπόδοσις, but here
probably meaning 'for sale.'

19. Tegea. Fourth century B.C. IG V.ii.6. GDI 1222. Schwyzer
656. Solmsen-Fraenkel 4. Kalén, Strena phil. Upsal. 1922, 187 ff.
Many smooth breathings are debatable.

πε - - - - - - - - - - - - φι.λο. | εἰκ ἄν τι γίνητοι τοῖς ἐργώναις
τοῖς ἰν τοῖ αὐτοῖ | ἔργοι, ὅσα περὶ τὸ ἔργον· ἀπυέσθω δὲ ὁ ἀδική-
5 μενος | τὸν ἀδικέντα ἰν ἀμέραις τρισὶ ἀπὺ ταῖ ἂν τὸ ἀδί||κημα γένη-
τοι, ὕστερον δὲ μή· καὶ ὅτι ἀγ κρίνωνσι | οἱ ἐσδοτῆρες, κύριον ἔστω.
—εἰ δὲ πόλεμος δια|κωλύσει τι τῶν ἔργων τῶν ἐσδοθέντων ἢ τῶν |
ἠργασμένων τι φθέραι, οἱ τριακάσιοι διαγνόντω | τί δεῖ γίνεσθαι·
10 οἱ δὲ στραταγοὶ πόσοδομ ποέντω, || εἰκ ἂν δέατοί σφεις πόλεμος
ἦναι ὁ κωλύων ἢ ἐ|φθορκὼς τὰ ἔργα, λαφυροπωλίου ἐόντος κατὺ
τᾶς | πόλιος. εἰ δὲ τι(ς) ἐργωνήσας μὴ ἰγκεχηρήκοι τοῖς | ἔργοις, ὁ
δὲ πόλεμος διακωλύοι, ἀπυδόας [τ]ὸ ἀργύριον, | τὸ ἂν λελαβηκὼς
15 τυγχάνη, ἀφεώσθω τῶ ἔργω, || εἰκ ἂν κελεύωνσι οἱ ἐσδοτῆρες.—
εἰ δ' ἄ[ν] τις ἐπι|συνίστατοι ταῖς ἐσδόσεσι τῶν ἔργων ἢ λυμαίνη|τοι
κὰτ εἰ δέ τινα τρόπον φθήρων, ζαμιόντω | οἱ ἐσδοτῆρες, ὅσαι ἂν
δέατοί σφεις ζαμίαι, καὶ | ἀγκαρυσ[σόν]τω ἰν ἐπίκρισιν καὶ ἰνα-
20 γόντω || ἰν δικαστήριον τὸ γινόμενον τοῖ πλήθι τᾶς | ζαμίαυ.—
μὴ ἐξέστω δὲ μηδὲ κοινᾶνας γενέσθαι | πλέον ἢ δύο ἐπὶ μηδενὶ
τῶν ἔργων· εἰ δὲ μή, ὀφλέτω | ἕκαστος πεντήκοντα δαρχμάς,
ἐπελασάσθων | δὲ οἱ ἁλιασταί· ἰμφαῖνεν δὲ τὸμ βολόμενον ἐπὶ
25 τοῖ || ἡμίσσοι τᾶς ζαμίαυ. κὰ τὰ αὐτὰ δὲ καὶ εἰκ ἄν [τ]ις | πλέον

ἢ δύο ἔργα ἔχη τῶν ἱερῶν ἢ τῶν δαμ[ο]σίων | κὰτ εἰ δέ τινα τρό-
πον, ὅτινι ἀμ μὴ οἱ ἀλιαστα[ὶ] | παρετάξωνσι ὁμοθυμαδὸν πάντες,
ζαμιώ[σ]θω | καθ’ ἕκαστον τῶν πλεόνων ἔργων κατὺ μῆνα || πεν- 30
τήκοντα δαρχμαῖς, μέστ’ ἂν ἐπισ[χῆ πάντα] | τὰ ἔργα τὰ πλέονα.
—εἰ δ’ ἄν τι[ς ἰνδ]ίκητοι τῶν | περὶ τὰ ἔργα συ[γγεγραμμένων]
κὰτ εἰ δέ τι, μη|[δὲν δεκέσθω τᾶς τιμα]ῦ· εἰ δὲ μή, μή οἱ ἔστω ἴν-
δικον μηδέποθι ἀλλ’ ἢ ἰν Τεγέαι· εἰ δ’ ἂν ἰνδικάζητοι, || ἀπυτει- 35
σάτω τὸ χρέος διπλάσιον τὸ ἂν δικάζητοι· | ἔστω δὲ καὶ τωνὶ τῶ
ἐπιζαμίω ὁ αὐτὸς ἴγγυος ὅπερ | καὶ τῶ ἔργω ἧς ἰν ἔστεισιν. —εἰ
δ’ ἄν τις ἐργωνήσας | ἔργον τι ποσκατυβλάψη τι ἄλλυ τῶν ὑπαρ-
χόντων | ἔργων εἴτε ἱερὸν εἴτε δαμόσιον εἴτε ἴδιον || πὰρ τὰν 40
σύγγραφον τᾶς ἐσδοκαῦ, ἀπυκαθιστάτω | τὸ κατυβλαφθὲν τοῖς
ἰδίοις ἀναλώμασιν μὴ ἧσσον | ἢ ὑπᾶρχε ἰν τοῖ χρόνοι τᾶς ἐργωνίαυ·
εἰ δ’ ἀμ μὴ | κατυστάση, τὰ ἐπιζάμια ἀπυτειέτω, κὰ τάπερ | ἐπὶ τοῖς
ἄλλοις ἔργοις τοῖς ὑπεραμέροις τέτακτοι. || — εἰ δ’ ἄν τις τῶν 45
ἐργωνᾶν ἢ τῶν ἐργαζομένων | ἐπηρειάζεν δέατοι ἰν τὰ ἔργα ἢ ἀπει-
θῆναι τοῖς | ἐπιμελομένοις ἢ κατυφρονῆναι τῶν ἐπιζαμίων | τῶν
τεταγμένων, κύριοι ἐόντω οἱ ἐσδοτῆρες | τὸμ μὲν ἐργάταν ἐσδέλ-
λοντες ἐς τοῖ ἔργοι, || τὸν δὲ ἐργώναν ζαμιόντες ἰν ἐπίκρισιγ κὰ τά- 50
περ | τὸς ἐπισυνισταμένος ταῖς ἐσδοκαῖς γέγραπ[τ]οι. | — ὅτι δ’
ἂν ἐσδοθῆ ἔργον εἴτε ἱερὸν εἴτε δαμόσι[ον], | ὑπάρχεν τὰγ κοινὰν
σύγγραφον ταν[ν]ὶ κυρί[αν] | πὸς ταῖ ἐπὲς τοῖ ἔργοι γεγραμμέν[αι
συ]γγράφ[οι].

Regulations governing building-contracts.

1 ff. 'if any trouble arises between the contractors on the
same work, as regards the work.'—4. **ἀπὺ ταῖ**: 'from the time
when,' relative use of the article, as in l. 14, etc. See **126**.—6 ff.
'If war should interrupt any of the works contracted for or
should destroy any of those completed.' For διακωλύσει see
152.4.—9 ff. The στραταγοί shall furnish revenue, if it seems
to them that it is war that is hindering or has destroyed the
works, the city having been subjected to a sale of booty.'—
12 ff. 'But if any one who has made a contract has not begun
on the works and war interrupts, he shall return whatever
money he may have received and be excused from the work,
if those giving out the contracts so order.'—15 ff. 'If any one
makes opposition to the allotments of the works or does an injury

in any way,' etc.—**κὰτ εἰ δέ τινα**: εἰ δέ τις, detached from verbal phrases, has come to be used independently in the sense of a simple indefinite, as is sometimes εἴ τις in Attic (e.g., Thuc. 7.21.5) Cf. κὰτ εἰ δέ τι l. 32.—18. **ὅσαι** κτλ.: 'with whatever penalty seems best to them.'—20. 'to the court which is constituted to suit the amount of the penalty.'—**πλήθι**:=πλήθει, like ἔτι = ἔτει, etc., on the reverse side of this same tablet. **9.5.**—21 ff. 'No more than two partners for any one piece of work, and no contractor to have more than two pieces of work without the unanimous consent of the heliasts.'—24. **ἰμφαίνεν** κτλ.: 'any one who wishes may be informer, receiving half the fine as a reward.'—30. 'until all the excess pieces of work cease.'—31 ff. Restorations uncertain, but perhaps 'If any one is a litigant concerning any of the terms of the contract, he shall receive no pay; otherwise he shall not have the right of trial elsewhere than at Tegea; and if suit is brought against him, he shall pay double the amount for which the suit is brought. And the same person who was (the surety) for the work, shall be surety for this fine, for its payment.' ἰν ἔστεισιν refers back to ἐπιζαμίω, not to ἔργω. ἴνδιχος, like Cret. ἔνδιχος, is used impersonally with the dative of the person involved in the suit. For ἰνδιχάζητοι, cf. Aenian. τοῖς ἐνδιχαζομένοις 'the litigants' GDI 1432a, and Delph. ἐνδιχαζόμενοι 'subjected to suit' GDI 1795.—37 ff. 'If a contractor injures any of the existing works contrary to the terms of the contract, he must at his own expense put it in as good condition as it was at the time of the contract. Otherwise he must pay the same penalties that are fixed for other pieces of work overdue.'—43. **κὰ τάπερ**: Att. καθάπερ.—45 ff. 'If a contractor or workman seems to be abusing the works, or disobedient to those in charge, or disregardful of the established fines, the workman may be expelled from the work, and the contractor brought to trial and fined in the same way as is prescribed for those who make opposition to the allotments.'—46. **ἐπηρειάζεν**: this spelling with ει, found also in papyri, is the correct etymological one (cf. ἐπήρεια), while ἐπειρεάζω of our texts is like δωρεά for earlier δωρειά (**31**).—50. **ζαμιόντες ἰν ἐπίκρισιγ**: condensed expression for ζαμιόντες καὶ ἀγκαρύσσοντες κτλ. Cf. ll. 17-19.— 51. **τὸς ἐπισυνισταμένος**: acc. abs. **173**.—**ἐσδοκαῖς**: ἐσδόσεσι in

l. 16. The 'giving out' of the 'contracts' and 'acceptance' of proposals is the same thing.—53 ff. 'This general contract shall be in force in addition to the special contract for the particular piece of work.'

20. Orchomenus. 369 B.C. Schwyzer 664. Solmsen-Fraenkel 2.

- - - - ος | - - - Κ]αλλείδας Τ|[. . . . . .]ων Παρράσιος, ὥρισαν
5 δ|ὲ τὰνγ γᾶν· ἀπὺ τῶι ὁρίοι τῶι πὸς τ||ῶι Μελαμποδέοι τῶι τῶν
'Ορχομ|ενίων καὶ τῶν Τορθυνήων καὶ Μετι|δριήων κοινοῖ ἐπὶ τὸ
Βουφαγέον μεσ|ακόθεν τοῖς κράναιυν· ἀπὺ τωινί | ἰν τὰν πορθιέαν
10 πρώταν· ἀπὺ τωιν||ὶ πὰρ μέσαν τὰν πορθιέαν ἰ νηάτ|αν· ἀπὺ
τῶινυ ἰν τὰν ἅλωνα νηάταν· ἀπὺ τ|ῶινυ ἰν τὸν λόφον τὸν ἰν τῶι
κρόμποι· ἀπὺ τῶι|νυ ἰν τὸν λόφον τὸν συμβολᾶν τὸν τραχύν· δύ|ο
15 ἀπὺ τῶινυ εὐθυορϜίαν πὸς δέρϜαν πὸς λόφο||ν· δύο ἀπὺ τῶινυ ἰν
τὰν δέρϜαν ἰν τᾶι βουσοῖ ὀπ|ὺ τὰ Ϝάδω· ἀπὺ τῶινυ ὁπὲρ τὰμ
Φυλάκω ἰν τῶι κ|ρόμποι· ἀπὺ τῶινυ ἱμέσος Πελειᾶν· ἀπὺ τῶινυ |
ἐπὶ δέρϜαν ἰν τᾶι βουσοῖ τᾶι ἐπὶ Παδόεσσαν· ἁ Παδ|όεσσα κοινὰ
20 ἀμφοτέροις· ἀπὺ Παδοέσσαι ἰν τὸν λ||όφον τὸν δίωρον· καὶ ἀπὺ
τῶινυ ἰν τὰν Τριάγκεια|ν· ἀπὺ τῶινυ ἰν τὸ στυμέον ὀπὺ τὸν ἄκρον·
δύο ἀ|πὺ τῶινυ ἰν τὰμ πέτραν ἰν 'Αρίαν· 'Αρία κοινὰ ἀ|μφοτέροις·
ἀπ' 'Αρίαι τᾶι βουσοῖ ἰν τὰν δρῦν ἰν τὰ|ν δέρϜαν τὰν ἰν τᾶι ἅλωνι·
25 ἀπὺ τῶινυ ὁπὲρ τὼ || Διδύμω· ἀπὺ τῶινυ ἰ μέσουν τοῖς Διδύ-
μοιυν· ἀ|πὺ τῶινυ ἰν τὸ συμβόλικτρον· ἀπὺ συμβολίκτροι || ἰν
ἄκραν Σμαρίαν ἰν τὸ οἱ 'Αρκάδες συνέθε|αν· ἀπὺ τῶινυ ἰγ κοίλαν
εὐθὺ ἰν τὸ Νικαγόρε(ο)ς ἄκρον τὸ οἱ 'Αρκάδες συνέθεαν. 'Ορχομεν-
30 || ίων θεαροὶ οἵδε· Μνασίας, 'Ηραῖος, Κλεόδι|κος, 'Ατέκμαρτος,
Σαιθος· πολέμαρχοι οἵδ|ε· Νικέας, Κάμπος, Εὔδοξος, Φιλόδα-
μος, | Τιμοστρατίδας.

Boundaries between Orchomenus and Methydrium. Μεθύδριον is the usual form, but here Μετιδριήων. 4. τὰνγ γᾶν: merely a careless blend of the two spellings τὰν and τὰγ γᾶν.—4 ff. 'From the boundary (ὅριον, instead of usual ὅρος) near the shrine of Melampous that is common to the Orchomenians, etc., to the shrine of Bouphagus, (passing) between the two springs.' For the duals κράναιυν and ἰ μέσουν τοῖς Διδύμοιυν l. 25, see 105.10, 106.7.—9 ff. 'To the beginning of the πορθιέα ('passage, path'? Cf. πορεία, πορθμός),—along the middle of it to the end of it,—to the end of the plantation,—to the hill in the κρόμπος (meaning?),

—to the rocky hill at the confluence,—two (boundaries) from this point in a straight line to the ridge, to the hill,—two to the ridge in the cattle run below the land of Vadus,—hence above the land of Phylakus in the κρόμπος,—hence (the boundary line is) in the midst of the elms (or the Elms).' For ἱ νηάταν, ἱ μέσουν. ἱμέσος and τὰ Ϝάδω, see 89.7.—νήατος: probably the earliest form = Hom. νείατος, νέατος, Att. νέατος. Cf. νήιστα Hesych.— 16. βουσός: 45.—16. τὰ Ϝάδω: τὰν Ϝάδω. 89.7, 96.5.—21. στυμέον cf. στόμιον. 22b. Here 'cavern'?.—26. συμβόλικτρον: 'junction' of roads?—28. Νικαγόρε(ο)ς: 105.2d.

21. Orchomenus. Middle of fourth century B.C. IG V.ii.343. Schwyzer 665. Solmsen-Fraenkel 3.

Θεός. τύχα ἀγαθ[ά]. συϜοικία Εὐαι|μνίοις Ἐρχομι|νίοις ἐπὶ
5 τοῖς Ϝί||σϜοις καὶ τοῖς ὑμ|οίοις. τὰ δὲ ἱερὰ | τὰ ἐν Εὐαίμονι ἀ|[ι̯
10 κ]ὰ μὴν' αὗθι κὰ [τ|άπε]ρ ἔχει συντ||[ελῆσθαι - - - - a few lines
15 missing] || τὸς δὲ προτέρος [ἱ]|νϜοίκος τᾶς τομ|[ά]δος λαχὴν κὰ
20 τά|[π]ερ ἔδοξε ἀμφο[τ|έ]ροις· τῶν δὲ ἐπὶ || [Χ]αιριάδαι εἴτε [τ|ι]
χωρίον ἀμφίλλ|[ο]γον ἐν ταῖ τομά|[δ]ι, τὸς Ἡραέας δια|[δ]ικάσαι
25 καὶ τὰς δίκα[ς || τ]ὰς προδεδικασμί|νας πάνσας· πομπ[ὰ|ς] δ'
30 ἐπιγενέσθαι δ[ι]|ὰ τρία Ϝέτεα Ἀρ[κά|δω]ν ἐπὶ Ϝρήσι. κ[αὶ || τ]ὰ
χρῆα τὰ δαμόσι|[α] κοιναῖ φέρην ἀ|[μ]φοτέρος. γράφε|α γράψαν-
35 (τ)ας καθ[έ|σ]θ[αι] ὁπόθ' ἄν δεά[σ|η]τοι ἀμφοτέροις. [τ]|οῖς
ἐπὶ Χαιριάδαι, τ|ὰ χρῆα τὰ ὀφέλλον|σι ταῖ θεοῖ, περὶ τὸν ἀ|[π]υ-
40 δοσμὸν αὐτὸς δ[ι]||αβωλευσαμίνος χρό|νον τάξασθαι. καὶ περ[ὶ |
τὰ] μισθώματα τᾶς γᾶς | [τὰν] Μνασιτέλης ἐμί(σ)θ[ω]||σε, κὰ
45 ταῦτά. ὅτις ξέν[αν] || γεγάμηκε, τὸς παῖδας [κ|α]ὶ τὰς γυναῖκας
50 Ἐ[ρ]||χομινίας ἦναι. τὰ ὀρ|[κ]ια πάντα τὸ αὐτὸ [ἀ]|[ι̯ αὗτις. μὴ
ἐσκεθῆ|[ν] μηδ' ἀναγκάσαι μ|[η]δένα. τὰ δὲ δίκ[α|ς] ταννʼ οἱ
55 ξένοι ἔ[κ|ρ]ιννάν τάς τε ἐν Ε|[ὐ]αίμονι καὶ τὰς ἰ[ν || Ἐρχομιν]οῖ
60 [- - - - a few lines missing] || [Ϝε]κατέραι Ἰόλ[λα]ος. ὤμοσαν
οἱ Εὐα[ί]|μνιο(ι) τάδε· ἀψευ[δ]|ίων ἆ τὰν συϜοι[κί]αν τοῖς
65 Ἐρχομιν||[ί]οις πὸς τὰς συνθέ[σ|ι]ς, νεὶ τὸν Δία τὸν Ἄρ[η]|α,
νεὶ τὰν Ἀθάναν τ|ὰν Ἀρείαν. ναὶ τὸν ['Ι]|νυάλιον τὸν Ἄρηα · ||
70 [ο]ὐδ' ἄν ἀνισταίμα|ν ἀπὺ τοῖς Ἐρχομιν|(ί)οις οὔποτε, οὐ τὸν
75 | [Δ]ία τὸν Ἄρηα, οὐ τὰ|ν Ἀθάναν τὰν Ἀρε[ί]||αν, οὐ τὸν
Ἰνυάλιο|ν τὸν Ἄρηα· κεύορ|κέντι μὲν τἀγαθά, | [ἐ]πιορκέντι δὲ
80 ἐξο|[λέ]σθαι αὐτὸγ καὶ γ||ένος. ὤμοσαν Ἐρχ|[ο]μίνιοι τάδε·

ἀψευ|δήων ἂν τὰν συϝο||[ι]κίαν τοῖς Εὐαιμν[ί]|οις πὸς τὰς συνθέ||-
85 [σ]ις, ναὶ τὸν Δία τὸν Ἄ[ρ]ηα, νεὶ τὰν Ἀθάναν | τὰν Ἀρήαν, νεὶ
90 τὸν Ἰν|[υ]άλιον τὸν Ἄρηα· οὐ|δ' ἂν ἐξελαύνοια τ||ὸς Εὐαιμνίος
οὔπο|τε, οὐ τὸν Δία τὸν Ἄ|[ρ]|ηα, οὐ τὰν Ἀθάναν | [τ]ὰν Ἄρηαν,
95 οὐ τὸν Ἰν|υάλιον τὸν Ἄρηα· || κευορ[κέντι] μὲν [τ]||ἀγαθά,
ἐπιορκέντ[ι] | δὲ ἐξολέσθαι κα(ὐ)|τὸν καὶ γένος. | Ἀριστάνωρ ||
100 Ὀνόμαντος | Λαέας | Σαοκλῆς | [- - - - a few lines missing]
108 | .ο ἢ ἀπεόν[τι ...] | ὄνδικα ἦναι.

A joint-citizenship agreement (cf. no. 56) between Orchomenus
and Euaemon, with some matters left to the arbitration of
Heraea. Inscribed on three sides of a column, of which two
pieces were found separately, a small middle piece being missing.
For the purpose of continuous line numbering, the missing
portion is arbitrarily set at five lines.

1. συϝοικία: συνοικία. 89.7.—6 ff. 'The regular monthly sacred
rites at Euaemon shall be held there as is customary.'—15 ff.
'The former inhabitants shall share in the allotment in accordance with the vote of both parties. But as to those of the time
of Chaeriades, if any territory in the allotment is in dispute,
the Heraeans shall decide, and also all the cases in previous
litigation. Missions (of arbitration) shall be established over a
period of three years, upon declaration of the Arcadian league.'—
36 ff. 'For those of the time of Chaeriades, regarding the payment
of the debts which they owe to the goddess, they shall themselves
in consultation fix its time of payment.'—49. αὖτις: emphasizes
the preceding ἀΐ, as in Hom. ἐτ' αὖτις, πάλιν αὖτις, etc.—ἐσκεθῆν:
for ἐσ-σκεθῆν= *ἐκ-σχεθεῖν (cf. 65). The meaning of the sentence
is 'one shall not keep out nor force in anyone,' that is in the matter
of citizenship, which is the subject of the preceding ll. 44-47.—
51. τὰ δὲ=τὰς δὲ.89.7, 97.4.—62-89. For the forms ἀψευδήων and
ἐξελαύνοια, see 149, 159, 152.1. The shift of mood is of interest
in connection with the observation (Smyth 1826a, 1833) that the
use of the optative with ἄν for strong assertions is especially
common after a negative. Here 'I will be faithful and I would
never revolt (expel).'

22. Decree of Tegea, found at Delphi. About 324 B.C. IG V.ii.p.
xxxvi. Plassart, BCH 38.101 ff. Ditt. Syll. 306. Schwyzer 657.
Tod 202. SEG 1.211.

```
·· - - - ση - - - [βασι|λεὺς Ἀλέξ]ανδρος τὸ διάγρ[α]μμα, γρα-
φῆναι κατὺ τὰ ἐ|[πανωρ]θώσατυ ἁ πόλις τὰ ἰν τοῖ διαγράμματι
```
5 ἀντιλ|εγόμενα. (I) τὸς φυγάδας τὸς κατενθόντας τὰ πατρῶια ‖ κο-
μίζεσθαι ἐς τοῖς ἔφευγον, καὶ τὰ ματρῶια, ὅσαι ἀ|νέσδοτοι τὰ
πάματα κατῆχον καὶ οὐκ ἐτύγχανον ἀδ|ελφεὸς πεπαμέναι· εἰ δέ
τινι ἐσδοθένσαι συνέπεσ|ε τὸν ἀδελφεὸν καὶ αὐτὸν καὶ τὰν γενεὰν
ἀπολέσθα|ι, καὶ τανὶ ματρῶια ἦναι, ἀνώτερον δὲ μηκέτι ἦναι.
10 (II) ἐ‖πὲς δὲ ταῖς οἰκίαις μίαν ἕκαστον ἔχεν κατὺ τὸ διά|γραμμα·
εἰ δέ τις ἔχει οἰκία κᾶπον πὸς αὐταῖ, ἄλλον μ|ὴ λαμβανέτω· εἰ δὲ
πὸς ταῖ οἰκίαι μὴ πόεστι κᾶπος, ἐ|ξαντίαι δ᾽ ἔστι ἰσόθι πλέθρω,
λαμβανέτω τὸν κᾶπον· | εἰ δὲ πλέον ἀπέχων ὁ κᾶπός ἐστι πλέθρω,
15 τωνὶ τὸ ἥμι‖σσον λαμβανέτω, ὥσπερ καὶ τῶν ἄλλων χωρίων
γέγρα|πται. τὰν δὲ οἰκιᾶν τιμὰν κομιζέσθω τῶ οἴκω ἑκάστ|ω δύο
μνᾶς, τὰν δὲ τιμασίαν ἦναι τᾶν οἰκιᾶν κὰ τάπε|ρ ἁ πόλις νομίζει·
τῶν δὲ κάπων διπλάσιον τὸ τίμαμ|α κομιζέσθαι ἢ ἐς τοῖ νόμοι. τὰ
20 δὲ χρήματα ἀφεῶσθα|ι τὰν πόλιν καὶ μὴ ἀπυλιῶναι μήτε τοῖς
φυγάσι μήτ|ε τοῖς πρότερον οἴκοι πολιτεύονσι. (III) ἐπὲς δὲ ταῖς
π|αναγορίαις ταῖς ἐσλελοίπασι οἱ φυγάδες, τὰν πόλ|ιν βωλεύσα-
σθαι, ὅτι δ᾽ ἂν βωλεύσητοι ἁ πόλις, κύριο|ν ἔστω. (IV) τὸ δὲ δικα-
25 στήριον τὸ ξενικὸν δικάζεν ἐξήκ‖οντα ἀμερᾶν· ὅσοι δ᾽ ἂν ἰν ταῖς
ἐξήκοντα ἀμέραις μὴ | διαδικάσωνται, μὴ ἦναι αὐτοῖς δικάσασθαι
ἐπὲς τ|οῖς πάμασι ἰν τοῖ ξενικοῖ δικαστηρίοι, ἀλλ᾽ ἰν τοῖ | πολιτικοῖ
ἀτ· εἰ δ᾽ ἄν τι ὕστερον ἐφευρίσκωνσι, ἰν ἁ|μέραις ἐξήκοντα ἀπὺ ταῖ
30 ἂν ἀμέραι τὸ δικαστήριο||ν καθιστᾶ. εἰ δ᾽ ἂν μηδ᾽ ἰν ταῖννυ διαδι-
κάσητοι, μηκέ|τι ἐξέστω αὐτῶι δικάσασθαι· εἰ δ᾽ ἄν τινες
ὕστερον | κατένθωνσι, τῶ δικαστηρίω τῶ ξενικῶ [μ]ηκέτι ἐόντ|ος,
ἀπυγραφέσθω πὸς τὸς στραταγὸς τὰ πάματα ἰν ἀμ|έραις ἐξήκοντα,
35 καὶ εἰκ ἄν τι αὐτοῖς ἐ[π]απύλογον ἦ‖ι, δικαστήριον ἦναι Μαντι-
νέαν· εἰ δ᾽ [ἂν μὴ] διαδικάσ|ητοι ἰν ταιν(νὶ) ταῖς ἀμέραις, μηκέτ[ι]
ἦναι αὐτοῖ δι|κάσασθαι. (V) ἐπὲς δὲ τοῖς ἱεροῖς χρήμασιν .λωι..ν
τοῖς ὀφειλήμασι τὰ μὲμ πὸς τὰν θεὸν ἁ πόλις διωρθώ|σατυ, ὁ ἔχων
40 τὸ πᾶμα ἀπυδότω τῶι κατηνθηκότι τὸ ἥμ‖ισσον κὰ τάπερ οἱ ἄλλοι·
ὅσοι δὲ αὐτοὶ ὤφηλον ταῖ θ|εοῖ συνινγύας ἢ ἄλλως, εἰ μὲν ἂν φαίνη-
τοι ὁ ἔχων τὸ | πᾶμα διωρθωμένος ταῖ θεοῖ τὸ χρέος, ἀπυδότω τὸ
ἥμ|ισσον τῶι κατιόντι, κὰ τάπερ οἱ ἄλλοι, μηδὲν παρέλ|[κ]ων· εἰ δ᾽
45 ἂν μὴ φαίνητοι ἀπυδεδωκὼς ταῖ θεοῖ, ἀπυδό||τω τοῦ κατιόντι τὸ
ἥμισσον τῶ πάματος, ἐς δὲ τοῖ ἡμ|ίσσοι αὐτὸς τὸ χρέος διαλυέτω·
εἰ δ᾽ ἂν μὴ βόλητοι δ|ιαλῦσαι, ἀπυδότω τοῖ κατιόντι τὸ πᾶμα ὅλον,

ὁ δὲ κο|μισάμενος διαλυσάτω τὸ χρέος ταῖ θεοῖ πᾶν. (VI) ὅσαι δ|ὲ
50 γυναῖκες τῶν φυγάδων ἢ θυγατέρες οἴκοι μίνονσ||αι ἐγά[μ]αντυ,
ἢ φυγόνσαι ὕστερον ἐγάμαντυ [ἰ]ν Τεγέ|αν κα[ὶ] ἐπίλυσιν ὠνήσαν-
τυ οἴκοι μίνονσαι, ταννὶ μ|ήτ᾽ ἀ[πυδοκ]ιμάζεσθαι τὰ πατρῶια μήτε
τὰ ματρῶια μ|ηδὲ τὸς ἐσγόνος, ὅσοι μὴ ὕστερον ἔφυγον δι᾽ ἀνάγ-
55 κα|ς καί ἰν τοῖ νῦν ἐόντι καιροῖ καθέρπονσι ἢ αὐταὶ ἢ || παῖδες
ταννί, δοκιμάζεσθαι καὶ αὐτὰς καὶ τὸς ἐς τ|αιννὶ ἐσγόνος τὰ πα-
τρῶια καὶ τὰ ματρῶια κὰ τὸ διά|γραμμα. (VII) ὀμνύω Δία, ᾽Αθά-
ναν, ᾽Απόλλωνα, Ποσειδᾶνα εὐν|οήσω τοῖς κατηνθηκόσι τοῖς
ἔδοξε ταῖ πόλι κατυδ|έχεσθαι, καὶ οὐ μνασικακήσω τῶννυ οὐδεν[ὶ]
60 τ[ὰ] ἂν ἀμ||π[ε]ίση ἀπὺ ταῖ ἀμέραι ταῖ τὸν ὅρκον ὤμοσα, οὐδὲ
δια|κωλύσω τὰν τῶν κατηνθηκότων σωτηρίαν, οὔτε ἰν τα|ῖ
[ll. 62-66 fragmentary.].

Decree regarding the exiles returning under Alexander's edict
of 324 B.C. Cf. no. 26.

1 ff. The city had previously passed certain regulations, some
of which were objected to by Alexander in a special edict and
were now corrected.—4 ff. 'The returning exiles shall recover
the paternal property which they had at the time of their exile,
and likewise the women the maternal property, those who were
unmarried and in possession of the property and had no brothers.
If it happened to a married daughter that her brother and his
offspring died, then she too should share in the maternal property
(ταννί = gen. sg. τασ-νί, 97.1), but it shall never be more' (than
the maternal property ? or 'go beyond this' in line of inheritance ?)
—13. ἐξαντίαι: 'over against, near by.' Cf. ἐκ τῆς ἀντίης (Hdt.).
The true Arcadian form would be ἐσαντίαι. There are some traces
of κοινή influence (cf. also πλέον, ει in ὀφείλημα, ει in Ποσειδᾶνα)
as in no. 19.—ἰσόθι πλέθρω: literally 'in equal place,' but here
clearly 'within the distance of a plethron.'—16 ff. τιμά is the
purchase price, while τιμασία (= Att. τίμησις) is the taxable
valuation, and τίμαμα the assessment. For the cultivated lots
(κᾶποι) the city is to receive double the normal tax.—19 ff. τὰ δὲ
χρήματα κτλ.: difficult passage, but perhaps meaning 'as
to monetary claims (as distinct from real estate) the city shall
be free of responsibility and shall not settle them in favor of
either party,' ἀφεῶσθαι being taken, not (with most editors) as

mid. = act. 'remit,' but (in spite of the crude condensed construction) as pass. as in ἀφεώσθω τῶ ἔργω 'be excused from the work' (no. 19.14) and ἀφεώσθω τᾱς μαρτυρίας 'be excused from testifying' (IG V.ii.357.12). For ἀπυλιῶναι, see **162**.10.— 23 ff. 'with reference to the festivals from which the exiles have been missing, the city shall take counsel,' etc. (probably as to the conditions under which the exiles may resume participation).

24 ff. The ξενικὸν δικαστήριον is a court constituted of judges from other cities, here perhaps Mantinea (cf. l. 35). 'The alien court is to serve for a period of sixty days. Those who do not have their cases settled within this time may not bring suit for property in this court, but only in the regular civic court. If they later discover any additional evidence (or claim), they may present it within sixty days of the time of the constitution of the court. But if any one does not have his case settled within this time, he may not bring action. If any return later, when the alien court is no longer serving, they shall file an inventory of the property with the στραταγοί within sixty days, and if there is anything in defense (against their claims) Mantinea shall serve as the court.—37 ff. Adjustment of debts to the goddess (that is, to the temple, which often served as a banking institution) which were secured by liens on the property.—49 ff. 'The wives of the exiles and the daughters who remained at home and married, or who from exile returned to Tegea and married and bought their release shall not be disqualified for their paternal or maternal inheritance, nor their descendants, except that those who were banished at a later time and are returning at the present time, either the women themselves or their children, they and their descendants shall be subject to investigation as to the paternal or maternal inheritance according to the edict.'—ταννί in l. 51 is acc. pl. (τασ-νί, **97**.1), but gen. pl. in l. 55.—57 ff. The citizens who remained at home take oath to show good will to the returning exiles and not to bear malice against any of them for what he may have plotted (?). ἀμπείση: aor. subj. of ἀναπείθω 'persuade,' used also in a bad sense 'mislead, corrupt, bribe', here perhaps 'plot,' referring to the exiles previous political intrigues.

Cyprian

The Cyprian Syllabary

Nearly all the Cyprian inscriptions are written in a special syllabary. This consists of signs for each of the five vowels— these being used where no consonant immediately precedes, that is initially and for the second element of diphthongs— and signs for each combination of consonant and following vowel, as *ma*, *me*, etc. But there is no distinction between long and short vowels, nor, in the case of stops, between voiceless. voiced, and aspirate. Hence the sign *te* (the transcription with *t* is a matter of convention) may stand for τε, τη, δε, δη, θε, or θη. Nasals before consonants are not written, e.g., *a ti* = ἀ(ν)τί. [1]
For a final consonant the sign containing the vowel *e* is used, e.g., *ka se* = κάς. For groups of consonants the first is indicated by the sign containing the vowel of the syllable to which this consonant belongs. That is, its vowel is determined by the following in the case of initial groups and consonant + liquid; by the preceding in the case of liquid + consonant, and also σ + consonant (cf. **89**.1). Thus *po to li ne* = πτόλιν, *pa ti ri* = πατρί, *e u ve re ta sa tu* = εὐϜρētάσατυ, *a ra ku ro* = ἀργύρō, *e se ta se* = ἔστασε. Examples of other groups are rare. [2]

Words are separated by a special sign, but this is commonly, though not uniformly, omitted after the article, and sometimes in other groups of words. In such groups a final consonant is often treated as medial, hence *ta po to li ne* = τὰ(ν) πτόλιν, etc.

23. Idalium. Probably second half of fifth century B.C. Schwyzer 679. Solmsen-Fraenkel 6. The first five lines only are given in the more exact syllabic transcription. In this | denotes the word separator, not the line division, which is indicated by numerals.

---

[1] In the Greek transcription the stops are distinguished and the nasal before consonants is supplied in parentheses. But ē and ā, not η, ω, are used, in accordance with the practice adopted for other inscriptions where the signs η and ω are not in use. For some uncertainties in regard to the proper transcription, see **199**.
[2] We find *me ma na me no i* = μεμναμένοι, *ka si ke ne to i se* = κασιγνέτοις but *i ki ma me no se* = ἰκμαμένος, *te re ki ni ja* = τέρχνιja, |*ti pe te ra-* = διφθερα-, *va na ko to se* = Ϝάνακτος.

1 o te | ta po to li ne e ta li o ne | ka te vo ro ko ne ma to
i | ka se ke ti e ve se | i to i | pi lo ku po ro ne ve te i to o na
sa ko 2 ra u | pa si le u se | sa ta si ku po ro se | ka se a po to
li se | e ta li e ve se | a no ko ne o na si lo ne | to no na si ku
po 3 ro ne to ni ja te ra ne | ka se | to se | ka si ke ne to se |
i ja sa ta i | to se | a to ro po se | to se | i ta | i | ma ka i | i ki
4 ma me no se | a ne u | mi si to ne | ka sa pa i | e u ve re ta
sa tu | pa si le u se | ka se | a po to li se | o na si 5 lo i | ka
se | to i se | ka si ke ne to i se | a ti to mi si to ne | ka a ti |
ta u ke ro ne | to ve na i | e xe to i | *etc.*

Ὅτε τὰ(ν) πτόλιν Ἐδάλιον κατέϜοργον Μᾶδοι κὰς ΚετιῆϜες
2 ἰ(ν) τῶι Φιλοκύπρōν Ϝέτει τō Ὀνασαγό|ραυ, βασιλεὺς Στασίκυπρος
κὰς ἁ πτόλις ἘδαλιῆϜες ἄνōγον Ὀνάσιλον τὸν Ὀνασικύπ|ρōν
τὸν ἰjατῆραν κὰς τὸς κασιγνέτος ἴjασθαι τὸς ἀ(ν)θρόπος τὸς ἰ(ν)
4 τᾶι μάχαι ἰκ|μαμένος ἄνευ μισθō. κάς παι εὐϜρετάσατυ βασιλεὺς
κὰς ἁ πτόλις Ὀνασί||λōι κὰς τοῖς κασιγνέτοις ἀ(ν)τὶ τō μισθōν κὰ
6 ἀ(ν)τὶ τᾶ ὑχέρōν δοϜέναι ἐξ τōι | Ϝοίκōι τōι βασιλῆϜος κὰς ἐξ τᾶι
πτόλιϜι ἀργύρō τά(λαντον) α΄ τά(λαντον)· ἒ δυϜάνοι νυ ἀ(ν)τὶ τō |
ἀργύρōν τόδε, τō ταλά(ν)τōν, βασιλεὺς κὰς ἁ πτόλις Ὀνασίλōι κὰς
8 τοῖς κασι|γνέτοις ἀπὺ τᾶι ζᾶι τᾶι βασιλῆϜος τᾶ ἰ(ν) τōιρōνι τōι
Ἀλα(μ)πριjάται τὸ(ν) χōρον | τὸν ἰ(ν) τōι ἕλει τὸ(ν) χραυόμενον
10 Ὅ(γ)κα(ν)τος ἄλϜō κὰς τὰ τέρχνιjα τὰ ἐπιό(ν)τα || πά(ν)τα ἔχεν
πανόνιον ὐϜαὶς ζαν ἀτελέν. ἒ κέ σις Ὀνάσιλον ἒ τὸς | κασιγνέτος
ἒ τὸς παῖδας τō(ν) παίδōν τōν Ὀνασικύπρōν ἐξ τōι χόρōι τōιδε | ἐξ-
ορύξē, ἰδέ παι ὁ ἐξορύξē πείσει Ὀνασίλōι κὰς τοῖς κασιγνέτοι|ς ἒ
12 τοῖς παισὶ τὸν ἄργυρον τό(ν)δε, ἀργύρō τά(λαντον) α΄ τά(λαντον). |
14 κὰς Ὀνασίλōι οἴϜōι ἄνευ τō(ν) κασιγνέτōν τōν αἴλōν ἐϜρετάσατυ
βασιλεύ||ς κὰς ἁ πτόλις δοϜέναι ἀ(ν)τὶ τᾶ ὑχέρōν τō μισθōν ἀργύρō
16 πε(λέκεϜα) δ΄ πε(λέκεϜα) | β΄ δι(μναῖα) Ἐ(δάλια)· ἒ δόκοι νυ
βασιλεὺς κὰς ἁ πτόλις Ὀνασί|||λōι ἀ(ν)τὶ τō ἀργύρō τōδε ἀπὺ τᾶι
18 ζᾶι τᾶι βασιλῆϜος τᾶ ἰ(ν) Μαλανίjα|ι τᾶι πεδίjαι τὸ(ν) χōρον τὸ(ν)
χραυζόμενον Ἀμενίjα ἄλϜō κὰς τὰ τέρ|χνιjα τὰ ἐπιό(ν)τα πά(ν)τα,
20 τὸ(ν) ποεχόμενον πὸς τὸ(ν) ῥόϜο(ν) τὸ(ν) Δρύμιον κὰς πὸ||ς τὰν
ἱερῆϜίjαν τᾶς Ἀθάνας, κὰς τὸ(ν) κᾶπον τὸν ἰ(ν) Σίμιδος ἀρούρα|ι,
τό(ν) ΔιϜείθεμις ὁ Ἀρμανεὺς ἔχε ἄλϜο(ν), τὸν ποεχόμενον πὸς
22 Πασαγόρα|ν τὸν Ὀνασαγόραυ κὰς τὰ τέρχνιjα τὰ ἐπιό(ν)τα πά(ν)-
τα ἔχεν πανōνίος ὐ|Ϝαὶς ζαν ἀτελίjα ἰό(ν)τα. ἒ κέ σις Ὀνάσιλον ἒ τὸς
24 παῖδας τὸς Ὀ|νασίλōν ἐξ τᾶι ζᾶι τᾶιδε ἲ ἐξ τōι κάπōι τōιδε ἐξορύξē

ἰ‖δὲ ὁ ἐξορύξε̄ πείσει 'Ονασίλοι ἒ τοῖς παισὶ τὸν ἄργυρον τό(ν)δε,
26 ἀργύρο̄|ν πε(λέκεϜα) δ' πε(λέκεϜα) β' δι(μναῖα) 'Ε(δάλια). ἰδὲ
τὰ(ν) δάλτον τά(ν)δε, τὰ Ϝέπιjα τάδε ἰναλαλισμένα, | βασιλεὺς κὰς
28 ἀ πτόλις κατέθιjαν ἰ(ν) τὰ(ν) θιὸν τὰν 'Αθάναν τά(ν)νε περ' 'Ε|δά-
λιον σὺν ὅρκοις μὲ̄ λῦσαι τὰς Ϝρέτας τάσδε ὐϜαὶς ζαν. | ὅπι σίς κε τὰς
30 Ϝρέτας τάσδε λύσε̄, ἀνοσίjα Ϝοι γένοιτυ. τάς γε ‖ ζᾶς τάσδε κὰς
τὸς κάπος τόσδε ο(ἰ) 'Ονασικύπρον παῖδες κὰς τὸ͂(ν) παίδο̄ν οἰ
πα|ῖδες ἕξο̄σι αἰϜεί, ο(ἰ) ἰ(ν) το̄ιρὸ͂νι το̄ι 'Εδαλιε̄Ϝι ἴο̄σι.

Agreement of the king and city of Idalium with the physician Onasilus and his brothers for the care of the wounded without pay
(that is, for the individual cases) during the siege of the city by
the Persians and the inhabitants of the Phoenician city of Citium.
The king and the city promised to Onasilus and his brothers
instead of (special) pay the sum of a silver talent, or in place
of this a certain tract of land. And they promised to Onasilus
alone the sum of four 'axes' (each = 10 minae) and two double
minae, or another tract of land. Provision is made that, should
they be ousted from the land, the money should be paid.—1.
κατέϜοργον: 5.— 4, 14. εὐϜρε̄τάσατυ, ἐϜρε̄τάσατυ: 55, 70.3.—
5. ἀ(ν)τὶ τὸ͂ μισθνο̄͂ κτλ.: see 136.8.—τᾶ ὐχέρον: 59.4, 135.8.--8.
(ἰ)ν το̄ιρὸ͂νι: 'in the district.' Cf. οἰρῶν 'boundary line' Hesych.
—9. 18, 21. ἄλϜο̄, ἄλϜον: cf. ἄλουα · κῆποι (Cypr.) Hesych., Hom.
ἀλωή, Att., Arc. ἄλων, Sicil. ἄλος, ἀ (GDI 5200 passim). In this
group the meaning is partly the broad 'tract of cultivated land,
plantation,' and partly more specific 'garden,' 'vineyard' or
'orchard.' Here, as shown by ll. 20, 21, the ἄλϜον is more specific
('vineyard'?) than the κᾶπος, which here has the broader sense,
as often elsewhere (e.g., no. 42.10, 22).—10. πανόνιον: 'with all
salable products,' agreeing with τὸ(ν) χὅρον, the intervening τὰ
τέρχνιjα being disregarded as subordinate.—ὐϜαὶς ζαν: ὐϜαίς
'forever' 133.6. ζαν: 'for life' (?). Cf. ζάει · πνεῖ, Κύπριοι. Hesych.
—12, 24. ἐξορύξε̄: 'expropriates,' from *ἐξορϜίζω = Att. ἐξορίζω
(cf. ὅρϜος, 54). For the ending here and in λύσε̄ l. 29 (-ε̄ or -ε?),
see 150c.—15. πε(λέκεϜα) so as neut. pl. in view of the gloss
τὸ γὰρ δεκάμνουν πέλεκυ παρὰ Παφίοις Hesych. s.v. ἡμιπέλεκκον.
πέλεκυς used elsewhere with other values.—29. 'whenever anyone (or whoever?) violates these agreements may impiety rest

upon him,' that is, he shall be guilty of an impious act. ὅπι is
difficult, but possibly ὅπη (132.7). See 16a.

Lesbian

24. Cebrene. Fifth century B.C. Roberts p. 324. Schwyzer 638.
Solmsen-Fraenkel 7.

Σ[τάλλ]α 'πὶ Σθενείαι ἔμμι τῶ Νικιαίδι τῶ Γαυκίδ.

Monument to Stheneias, son of Nicias and grandson of Gaucus.
See 168d, and 38.

25. Mytilene. First half of fourth century B.C. IG XII.ii.1 and
XII Suppl. p. 2. Schwyzer 619. Solmsen-Fraenkel 8. Tod 112.

```
- - - - - - ε - - - - - - - - - - - - - [ὅττι | δέ κε αἰ] πόλις
[ἀ]μφότ[εραι - - - - - - - - - - - | - - - - ] γράφωισι εἰς τὰν [στάλ-
5 λαν ἢ ἐκκ|ολάπ]τωισι, κύ[ρ]ιον ἔστω. τ[ὸν δὲ κέρναν||τα τὸ] χρύ-
σιον ὑπόδικον ἔ[μμεναι ἀμφο|τέρ]αισι ταῖς πολίεσσι. δικ[άσταις
δὲ | ἔμ]μεναι τῶι μὲν ἐμ Μυτιλήναι [κέρναν|τι] ταὶς ἄρχαις παίσαις
10 ταὶς ἐμ Μ[υτιλ|ή]ναι πλέας τῶν αἰμισέων, ἐμ Φώκαι δὲ [τ]||αὶς
ἄρχαις παίσαις ταὶς ἐμ Φώκαι πλ[έ]|ας τῶν αἰμισέω[ν]· τὰν δὲ
δίκαν ἔμμεναι, | ἐπεί κε ὠνίαυτος ἐξέλθηι, ἐν ἐξ μήννεσι. αἰ δέ
κε καταγ[ρ]έθηι τὸ χρύσιον κέρ|ναν ὑδαρέστε[ρ]ο[ν] θέλων, θανά-
15 τωι ζαμι||ώσθω· αἰ δέ κε ἀπυφ[ύ]γηι μ[ὴ] θέλων ἀμβρ[ό]|την,
τιμάτω τ[ὸ] δικαστήριον ὅττι χρῆ α|ὖτ(ο)ν πάθην ἢ κατθέ[μ]εναι,
ἀ δὲ πόλις ἀναί|τιος καὶ ἀζάμιος [ἔσ]τω. ἔλαχον Μυτιλή|ναοι πρό-
20 σθε κόπτην. ἄρχει πρότανις ὁ || πεδὰ Κόλωνον, ἐ[μ Φ]ώκαι δὲ ὁ
πεδὰ Ἀρίσ[τ]|αρχον.
```

Monetary agreement between Mytilene and Phocaea. Coins of
electrum, a compound of gold and silver, were issued by Mytilene
and Phocaea, down to about 350 B.C., and it is to these that the
inscription refers, though the term used of them is χρύσιον.

'Any one debasing the coinage is responsible to both cities.
If at Mytilene, the magistrates of Mytilene are to constitute the
majority of the judges. Similarly at Phocaea. The trial falls
within six months of the expiration of the year. If one is convicted
of intentional adulteration, he is to be punished with death.
But if he is acquitted of intentional wrong-doing, the court
shall decide the penalty or fine. The city is not liable. The

Mytilenians are to issue the coins first (the cities alternating each year.) The agreement goes into effect under the prytanis succeeding Colonus at Mytilene and Aristarchus at Phocaea.'
4-5. τ[ὸν δὲ κέρναντα] : κέρναμι, if correctly supplied here and in ll. 7-8, has the same meaning which is more forcibly expressed by κέρναν ὐδαρέστερον in ll. 13-14. The arrangements for trial immediately following show that the meaning required here is 'debase,' not 'make the alloy,' i.e., simply 'coin,' as often taken. Moreover, the electrum coinage of this time and place was based upon a natural, not an artificial, alloy.—9/10. Φώκαι 31.

26. Mytilene. Soon after 324 B.C. IG XII.ii.6 and XII Suppl. p. 3. Ditt. Orient. 2. Schwyzer 620. Solmsen-Fraenkel 9. Tod 201.

. . . . [καὶ οἰ β]ασί[ληες προστί]θησ[θον τῶι κατελη-
λύθον|τι ὡς τέχναν τεχνα]μέν[ω] τῶ ἐ[ν τᾶι] πόλι πρόσθε [ἔοντος.
αἰ δέ κέ τις | τῶν κατεληλυθόν]των μὴ ἐμμένη ἐν ταῖς διαλυσί[εσ]σι
ταύτ[αισι, | μη . . . . ἐφ]εζέσθω πὰρ τᾶς πόλιος κτήματος
5 μήδενος μη[δὲ στ||ειχέτω ἐπὶ μῆ]δεν τῶμ παρεχώρησαν αὐτωι οἰ
ἐν τᾶι πόλι πρό[σθε | ἔοντες, ἀλλὰ σ]τείχοντον ἐπὶ ταῦτα τὰ κτή-
ματα οἰ παρχωρήσαν[τ|ες αὐτωι ἐκ τῶν] ἐν τᾶι πόλι πρόσθε ἐόντων,
καὶ οἰ στρόταγοι εἰς | [αὖθις ἀποφέρον]τον ἐπὶ τὸν ἐν τᾶι πόλι
πρόσθε ἔοντα τὰ κτήματα | [ὡς μὴ συναλλαγ]μένω τῶ κατεληλύ-
10 θοντος · καὶ οἰ βασίληες προστί||[θησθον τῶι ἐν τ]ᾶι πόλι πρόσθε
ἔοντι ὡς τέχναν τεχναμένω τῶ κα|[τεληλύθοντος ·] μηδ' αἴ κέ τις
δίκαν γράφηται περὶ τ[ο]ύτων, μὴ εἰσά|[γοντον οἰ περί]δρομοι καὶ
οἰ δικάσκοποι μηδὲ ἄ[λλ]α ἄρχα μηδεΐα. | [ἐπιμέλεσθαι δὲ] τοῖς
στροτάγοις καὶ τοῖς β[ασίλ]ηας καὶ τοῖς πε||[ριδρόμοις καὶ τ]οῖς
15 δικασκόποις καὶ ταῖς [ἄλλα]ις ἄρχαις αἴ κε || [μὴ γίνηται ἄπαν]τα
ὡς ἐν τῶι ψ[αφίσματι γέγραπτ]αι, κατάγρεντον | [δὲ τὸν ἀθέτεντά
τι τῶν ἐν τῶι ψαφίσματι γεγρα]μμένων, ὡς κε μῆδ|[εν διάφορον
εἴη τοῖς κατεληλυθόντεσσι π]ρὸς τοῖς ἐν τᾶι πόλι | [πρόσθε ἔον-
τας, ἀλλὰ διάγοιεν οἰ διαλε]λύμενοι πάντες πρὸς ἀλ|[λάλοις ἀνυ-
20 πόπτως καὶ ἀνεπιβουλεύ]τως καὶ ἐμμένοιεν ἐν τᾶι ἀ||[πυκρίσι τᾶι
τῶ βασίληος καὶ ἐν τᾶ]ι διαλύσι τᾶι ἐν τούτωι τῶι ψα|[φίσματι.
διαλλάκταις δ' ἔλεσθ]αι τὸν δᾶμον ἄνδρας εἴκοσι, δέκα | [μὲν ἐκ
τῶν κατελθόντων, δέκα] δὲ ἐκ τῶν ἐν τᾶι πόλι πρόσθε ἐόντων. |
[οὗτοι δὲ πρῶτον μὲν φυλάσσ]οντον καὶ ἐπιμέλεσθον ὡς μῆδεν
ἔσ|[σεται διάφορον τοῖς κατ]ελθόντεσσι καὶ τοῖς ἐν τᾶι πόλι πρό-

25 σ‖[θε ἐόντεσσι. πράξοισι δὲ] καὶ περὶ τῶν ἀμφισβατημένων κτημά-
των | [ὡς οἴ τε κατέλθοντες κ]αὶ πρὸς τοὶς ἐν τᾶι πόλι ἔοντας καὶ
πρὸς | [ἀλλάλοις μάλιστα μ]ὲν διαλυθήσονται, αἰ δὲ μή, ἔσσονται
ὡς δικ|[αιότατοι, καὶ ἐν τα]ῖς διαλυσίεσσι, ταὶς ὀ βασίλευς ἐπέ-
κριννε, | [καὶ ἐν τᾶι συναλλάγ]αι ἐμμενέοισι πάντες καὶ οἰκήσοισι
30 τὰμ πό‖[λιν καὶ τὰγ χώραν ὀ]μονόεντες πρὸς ἀλλάλοις· καὶ περὶ
χρημάτων | [πεδὰ τὸ παραδέδεχ]θαι ταὶς διαλύσις ὡς πλεῖστα καὶ
περὶ ὅρκω | [τὸν κε ἀπομόσσωισι οἰ] | πόλιται, περὶ τούτων πάν-
των ὅσσα κε ὀμο‖[λογέωισι πρὸς ἀλλάλο]ις, οἰ ἀγρέθεντες ἄνδρες
φέροντον ἐπὶ τ‖[ὸν δᾶμον, ὀ δὲ δᾶμος ἀκο]ύσαις ἄι κε ἄγηται συμ-
35 φέρην βολλευέτω. ‖ [αἰ δέ κε ὀ δᾶμος ἄγηται τὰ] ὀμολογήμενα πρὸς
ἀλλάλοις συμφέρον‖[τα, ψαφίσασθαι καὶ τοῖς κα]τελθόντεσσι ἐπὶ
Σμιθίνα προτάνιος | [ὅσσα κε τοῖς λοίποισι ψαφ]ίσθη. αἰ δέ κέ τι
ἐνδεύη τῶ ψαφίσματος, | [περὶ τούτω ἀ κρίσις ἔστω ἐπ]ὶ τᾶι βόλ-
λαι. κυρώθεντος δὲ τῶ ψαφίσ‖[ματος ὑπὸ τῶ δάμω, σύμπαντα] τὸν
40 δᾶμον ἐν τᾶι εἰκοίσται τῶ μῆννος ‖ [πεδὰ τὰν θυσίαν εὔξασθαι] τοῖς
θέοισι ἐπὶ σωτηρίαι καὶ εὐδαι‖[μονίαι τῶμ πολίταν πάντων] γένε-
σθαι τὰν διάλυσιν τοῖς κατελ‖[θόντεσσι καὶ τοῖς πρόσθε] ἐν τᾶι πόλι
ἐόντεσσι· τοὶ[ς δ]ὲ ἴρηας τ‖[οὶς δαμοσίοις ἄπαντας καὶ] ταὶς ἰρείαις
ὀείγην τ[οὶ]ς ναύοις καὶ | [τὸν δᾶμον πρὸς εὔχαν συνέλ]θην. τὰ δὲ
45 ἴρα τὰ ὀ δᾶμος [ε]ὔξατο, ὅτε ἐξ‖[ἐπεμψε τοὶς ἀγγέλοις πρὸς] τὸν
βασίληα, ἀπυδόμεναι τοῖς βασί‖[ληος γενεθλίοισι κὰτ ἐνίαυ]τον·
παρέμμεναι δὲ τᾶι θυσίαι καὶ [τ|οὶς εἴκοσι ἄνδρας καὶ τοὶς ἀ]γγέ-
λοις τοὶς πρὸς τὸν βασίληα πέ[μφ|θεντας τοὶς ἀπὺ τῶν πρόσθε] ἐν
τᾶι πόλι ἐόντων καὶ τοὶς ἀ[πὺ τῶν | κατελθόντων. τὸ δὲ ψάφισμα
τ]οῦτο ἀναγράψαντας τοὶς τ[αμίαις ....

Measures taken for the settlement of disputes arising between
the exiles who returned under Alexander's edict of 324 B.C. and
the remaining citizens of Mytilene.

Most of the restorations adopted are those preferred by Dittenberger l.c. But in many cases others are equally possible.

1 ff. 'The βασίληες shall favor the returned exile on the ground
that the one who remained in residence has been guilty of fraud.
But if any one of the returned exiles does not abide by these terms
of settlement, he shall not receive any property from the city,
nor shall he enter into possession of any of the property which
those who remained in the city have surrendered to him, but

rather those who surrendered it shall enter into possession
of it, and the στρατηγοί shall return the property to the one who
remained in residence, on the ground that the returned exile
has not conformed to the agreement. And the βασίληες shall
favor the one who remained in residence on the ground that the
returned exile has been guilty of fraud. Nor, if any one brings
suit, shall the clerks of the court and inspectors of justice, or any
other magistrate, introduce it.'—13 ff. 'The officials are to in-
tervene if all things prescribed in the decree are not carried out,
and condemn any one who disregards them, so that there may
be no disagreement between the two parties and they may live
amicably and abide by the decision of the king and the settlement reached in this decree.'—21 ff. 'Twenty men are to be
chosen as mediators, ten from each party. They are to see to it
that no disagreement arises, and in the case oi disputed property
they are to bring it about that the parties shall be reconciled,
or, if not, that they shall be as just as possible, and abide by
the terms of settlement which the king decided upon and the
agreement, and dwell in harmony.'—30-31 ff. 'Regarding questions of money, after the terms of settlement have been accepted
as far as possible, and regarding the oath and other matters, the
men selected shall report to the people, who shall take such
measures as seem advantageous. If the people approve the matters agreed upon, they may decree the same privileges for the
exiles returning in the prytany of Smithinas as for the others.'—
38/39 ff. 'When the decree has been confirmed, the people are
to pray that the settlement may be for the general welfare.
The priests and priestesses are to throw open the temples.
The sacrifices which were promised when the messengers were
sent to the king are to be made annually on the anniversary of
the king's birthday in the presence of the twenty men and the
messengers.'—39. For εἰκοίσται, now confirmed by six more
occurrences of -κοιστος at Mytilene (IG XI.1064*b* and XII.ii.82),
see **116a**.

27. Nesos. Between 319 and 317 B.C. IG XII.ii.645.
Ditt. Orient. 4. Schwyzer 634. Solmsen-Fraenkel 10. Only
the text of side A is given here, the more fragmentary B being
omitted.

. . . . κα]ἰ ᾽Αλέξανδρο[ς | . . . . χ]ώρας
τᾶι πόλι καὶ | [. . . . . ὅτα δὲ] ᾽Αλέξανδρος διάλ[λα|ξε τὸμ
5 πὰρ ἀνθρώ]πων βίον, Φίλιππος δὲ [ὁ || Φιλίππω καὶ] ᾽Αλέξανδρος
ὁ ᾽Αλεξάνδρω τ[ὰ|μ βασιλεί]αν παρέλαβον, Θέρσιππος ἔων | [τοῖς
βασ]ιλήεσσι φίλος καὶ τοῖς στροτ[ά|γοισι] καὶ τοῖς ἄλλοισι Μακε-
10 δόνεσσι μ[ε|γάλ]ων ἀγάθων αἴτιος γέγονε τᾶι πόλι. ᾽Α[ν||τιπ]άτρω
γὰρ ἐπιτάξαντος χρήματα εἰς | τὸμ πόλεμον εἰσφέρην πάντων τῶν
ἄλλων |εἰσφερόντων Θέρσιππος παργενόμενος | πρὸς τοὶς βασίληας
καὶ ᾽Αντίπατρον ἐκ[ού]|φισσε τὰμ πόλιν, ἔπραξε δὲ καὶ πρὸς Κλε[ῖ-
15 ||τ]ον περὶ τᾶς εἰς Κύπρον στρατείας καὶ ἐ|[γ] μεγάλας δαπάνας εἰς
μῖκρον συνάγαγε. | [ἐγένετ]ο δὲ καὶ περὶ τὰν σιτοδείαν ἄνη[ρ | ἄγα-
θος] καὶ πὰρ τῶν σαδράπαν εἰσαγώγα[ν | σίτω κα]τεσκεύασσε,
20 ἔδωκε δὲ καὶ τᾶι πόλι || [χρήματ]α εἰς σωτηρίαν καὶ τόκοις ἐλάσ-
[σο|νας αἴτ]ησε τῶγ κατεστακόντων, ἐβαθόη | [δὲ χρη|μάτεσσι καὶ
τοῖς πολίταισι εἰς [σι|τωνία]ν. καὶ Πολυπέρχοντος εἰς τὰν ᾽Ασί[αν|
25 στάλε]ντος διώικησε φίλον αὖτον τᾶι πό||[λι ὑπά]ρχην, παρε-
σκεύασσε δὲ καὶ ᾽Αρράβαι|[ον καὶ] τοὶς ἄλλοις τοὶς ἐπί τινων τε-
τα|[γμένο]ις ὑπὸ τῶν βασιλήων φίλοις τᾶι π[ό|λι κα]ὶ τἆλλα
πράσσει μετ᾽ εὐνοίας πρὸς | [τὸν δ]ᾶμον πάντα· δέδοσθαι αὔτω
30 ἀτέλει[αν || πάντω]ν τὸμ πάντα χρόνον καὶ αὔτω καὶ [ἐκ|γόν]οισι,
στᾶσαι δὲ αὔτω καὶ εἴκονα χαλ[κί|αν], δέδοσθαι δὲ καὶ σίτησιν ἐμ
προτανη[ί|ω, κ]αὶ ὄτα κε ἀ πόλις ἰροπόηται, μέρις δ[ι|δώ]σθω Θερσ-
35 ίππω καὶ τῶν ἐκγόνων ἄι τῶ γ[ε||ραι]τάτω, κάλησθαι δὲ καὶ εἰς
προεδρίαν· | [στε]φανώτω δὲ αὖτον ὁ χοροστάτας ἄι ὁ ἐν[έ|ων ἐ]ν
τῶ ἄγωνι καὶ ὀγκαρυσσέτω ἀνδραγ[α|θί]ας ἔνεκα καὶ εὐνοίας τᾶς
40 πρὸς τὸν δᾶ|[μον], ἴνα γινώσκωισι πάντες ὄτι ὁ δᾶμος ὁ || [Να]σιώ-
ταν τοὶς ἀγάθοις ἄνδρας [κ]αὶ εὐε[ρ|γέ]ταις τί[μαι] καὶ σώθεντος
αὔτω ἐστεφα|[να]φόρησεν ἀμέραις τρῖς καὶ εὐαγγέλια | καὶ σωτήρια
ἔ[θ]υσε καὶ παν[άγυρ]ιν συνά|γαγε δαμοτέ[λ]ην καὶ νῦν τίμαι
45 δικάως. ἀ||νάγραψαι δὲ τοὶς ταμίαις τοὶς μετ᾽ ᾽Ηρα|κλείτω τὸ ψά-
φισμα εἰς στάλλαν λιθίναν | τῶ ἐκ Θέρμας λίθω καὶ στᾶσαι ὄππα
κε Θε[ρ]|σίππω συνα[ρ]έσκη μέχρι Πορνοπίας· ἐξέ[σ]|τω δὲ Θερσ-
50 ί[π]πω καὶ ἄλλα ὄππα κε θέλη τῶ[ν || ἴ]ρων στᾶσα[ι] τὸ ψά-
φισμα, καί κέ τι θέλη π[ρ]|οσγράφην, ἔμμεναι αὔτω, τῶγ κεν
εὐεργέ|τη τὰμ πόλιν.

Decree in honor of Thersippus for using his influence with
the Macedonians in behalf of the city. For the historical references

see Dittenberger, l.c. There are some κοινή forms, as μετά for πεδά,
ἀνάγραψαι beside ὀγκαρυσσέτω.

47. **ἐκ Θέρμας λίθω**: 'of marble from Therma,' a place in
Lesbos near Mytilene.—**μέχρι Πορνοπίας**: site of the temple of
Apollo Parnopius, the epithet being derived from πάρνοψ, Lesb.
Boeot. πόρνοψ (**5**).—48 ff.: 'Thersippus may also have the decree
set up elsewhere in any sanctuary that he chooses and add to it
a statement of any of his other benefactions.'

28. Cyme. Between 2 B.C. and A.D. 19. Schwyzer 647.

- - - [δαμ]οσίαι[ς | - - - ταὶς ὑπαρκοί]σαις αὔτω κτή|[σιας ἐν τῶ
Ζμαραγήω] - - - - η τούτοισι τῶ δά[μω] | - - - - ονια πασσυδιά-
5 σαντος καὶ || [μεγαλο]πρεπεσ(τά)ταις τείμαις δογματίζοντος καὶ
ναύ|ω ἐν τῶ γυμ(ν)ασίω κατείρων προαγρημμένω, ἐν ὧ ταὶς τεί-|
μαις αὔτω κατιδρύσει, κτίσταν τε καὶ εὐεργέταν προσονυ|μάσδεσθαι,
εἰκονάς τε χρυσίαις ὀντέθην, καθὰ τοῖς τὰ μέ|γιστα τὸν δᾶμον εὐερ-
10 γετησάντεσσι νόμιμόν ἐστι, με||τά τε τὰν ἐξ ἀνθρώπων αὔτω μετά-
στασιν καὶ τὰν ἐν|τάφαν καὶ θέσιν τῶ σώματος ἐν τῶ γυμνασίω
γενήθην, | ἀποδεξάμενος ὑπερθύμως τὰν κρίσιν τᾶς πόλιος Λα|βέων,
στοίχεις τοῖς προυπαργμένοισι αὔτω καὶ προσμέ|τρεις τὰν ἑαύτω
15 τύχαν τοῖς ἐφίκτοισιν ἀνθρώπω, τὰν || μὲν ὑπερβάρεα καὶ θέοισι
καὶ τοῖς ἰσσοθέοισι ἁρμόζοι|σαν τᾶς τε τῶ ναύω κατειρώσιος τᾶς
τε τῶ κτίστα | προσονυμασίας τείμαν παρητήσατο, ἀρκέην νομί-|
ζων τὰν κρίσιν τῶ πλάθεος καὶ τὰν εὔνοαν ἐπιτεθε|ωρήκην, ταὶς δὲ
20 τοῖς ἀγάθοισι τῶν ἄνδρων πρεποί||σαις ἀσμενίζοισα χάρα συνεπέ-
νευσε τείμαις· ἐφ' οἷ|σιν πρεπωδέστατόν ἐστι τῶν ἐννόμων ἐόντων |
χρόνων τὰν παντέλεα τῶν εἰς ἀμοίβαν ἀνηκόντων | ἐπαίνων τε
καὶ τειμίων περὶ τᾶς καλοκἀγαθίας αὔτω | μαρτυρίαν ἀπυδέδοσθαι·
25 δι' ἃ καὶ τύχα ἀγάθα δέδοχθαι || τᾶ βόλλα καὶ τῶ δάμω· ἐπαίνην Λα-
βέωνα παίσας ἔοντα τεί|μας ἄξιον καὶ διὰ τὰν λοίπαν μὲν περὶ τὸν
βίον σεμνότατα | καὶ διὰ τὰν φιλοδοξίαν δὲ καὶ τὰν μεγαλοδάπανον
εἰς | τὰν πόλιν διάθεσιν, καὶ ἔχην ἐν τᾶ καλλίστα διαλάμψει τε
καὶ | ἀπυδόχα, καὶ κάλην εἰς προεδρίαν, καὶ στεφάνων ἐν πάν-||
30 τεσσι τοῖς ἀγώνεσσιν, οἷς κεν ἁ πόλις συντελέη, ἐν τᾶ τᾶν | κατεύ-
χαν ἀμέρα ἐπὶ τᾶν σπόνδαν κὰτ τάδε· ὁ δᾶμος στε|φάνοι Λεύκιον
Οὐάκκιον Λευκίω υἱον Αἰμιλία Λαβέωνα, φι|λοκύμαιον εὐεργέταν,
στεφάνω χρυσίω ἀρέτας ἔνεκα | καὶ φιλαγαθίας τᾶς εἰς ἑαυτον· ὀν-
35 τέθην δὲ αὔτω καὶ εἴ||κονας, γράπταν τε ἐν ὅπλω ἐγχρύσω καὶ

χαλκίαν, κὰτ τὰ αὖ|τα δὲ καὶ μαρμαρίαν καὶ χρυσίαν ἐν τῶ γυμνα-
σίω, ἐφ' ἂν ἐπε|γράφην· ὁ δᾶμος ἐτείμασεν Λεύκιον Οὐάκκιον
Λευκίω | υἶον Αἰμιλία Λαβέωνα, φιλοκύμαιον εὐεργέταν, γυμνα-
40 σι|αρχήσαντα κάλως καὶ μεγαλοδόξως, ὄνθεντα δὲ || καὶ τὸ βαλά-
νηον τοῖς νέοισι καὶ πρὸς τὰν εἰς αὖτο κοραγί|αν ταὶς ὑπαρκοίσαις
αὔτω κτήσιας ἐν Ζμαραγήω, καὶ ἐ|πισκεάσαντα τὸ γυμνάσιον,
καὶ ἔκαστα ἐπιτελέσαντα | λάμπρως καὶ μεγαλοψύχως, ἀρέτας
ἔνεκα καὶ εὐνόας | τᾶς εἰς ἔαυτον. καὶ ἐπεί κε δὲ τελευτάση, κατε-
45 νέχθεν||τα αὖτον ὑπὸ τῶν ἐφάβων καὶ τῶν νέων εἰς τὰν ἀγόραν |
στεφανώθην διὰ τῶ τᾶς πόλιος κάρυκος κὰτ τάδε· ὁ δᾶ|μος στεφά-
νοι Λεύκιον Οὐάκκιον Λευκίω υἶον Αἰμιλία Λα|βέωνα, φιλοκύμαιον
εὐεργέταν, στεφάνω χρυσίω ἀρέ|τας ἔνεκα καὶ εὐνόας τᾶς εἰς ἔαυ-
50 τον· εἰσενέχθην δὲ || αὖτον εἰς τὸ γυμνάσιον ὑπό τε τῶν ἐφάβων
καὶ τῶν | νέων, καὶ ἐντάφην ἐν ὧ κ' ἂν εὔθετον ἔμμεναι φαίνηται
τό|πω. τὸ δὲ ψάφισμα τόδε ἀνάγραψαι εἰς στάλαν λίθω λεύ|κω καὶ
ὀνθέμεναι εἰς τὸ γυμνάσιον πὰρ ταὶς δεδο|γματισμέναις αὔτω τεί-
55 μαις. μῆνος Φρατρίω δεκάτα || ἀπίοντος ἐπὶ ἱερέως τᾶς Ῥώμας καὶ
Αὐτοκράτορος | Καίσαρος, θέω υἶω, θέω Σεβάστω, ἀρχίερεος μεγί-
στω καὶ πά|τρος τᾶς πάτριδος Πολέμωνος τῶ Ζήνωνος Λαοδί|κεος,
πρυτάνιος δὲ Λευκίω Οὐακκίω Λευκίω υἶω Αἰμιλί|α Λαβέωνος, φι-
60 λοκυμαίω εὐεργέτα, στεφαναφόρω δὲ || Στράτωνος τῶ Ἡρακλείδα.

Decree in honor of L. Vaccius Labeo. This is a characteristic
example of the artificial revival of the dialect in Roman imperial
times (cf. **280**). With the genuine dialect forms are interspersed
κοινή forms as παρητήσατο, πρύτανις, ἀνα-, μετά, ἱερέως, καθά, ἐφ'
οἶσιν, etc.; hyper-Aeolic forms as ἐφάβων, πλάθεος (words with
original η, not ā); and examples of late spelling as τείμαις, κατείρων
with ει = ι (**21**), ἐπισκεάσαντα (**36**), κοραγίαν, ὑπάρκοισαν with
κ = χ (**66α**). ἀρκέην (infin.), συντελέη beside the normal μι-forms
κάλην, στεφάνων, etc. (**155**.3) are probably artificial. ναύω (l. 5),
if correct, is a blend of ναῦον with Att. νεώ. ἐπεγράφην (l. 36-37)
is an aor. infin. pass., like ὀντέθην, with ε carried over from the
indicative (perhaps only by the engraver). With regard to psilosis,
we find κατείρων, κατιδρύσει, but ἐφίκτοισιν. The forms of the
relative, being borrowed from the κοινή (**126**), are transcribed
with ' throughout (cf. also ἐφ' οἶσιν etc.); and one might also
prefer ἱερέως and ἑαυτόν (instead of ἔαυτον with ' and Lesbian

accent). But it is impossible to determine whether in such cases
the κοινή form was adopted as a whole or only in part (cf.
280), and moreover by this time little, if anything, was left of the
sound of the spiritus asper even in the κοινή. So the transcription
chosen is of small consequence.

15 ff. 'He declined the excessive honor, suitable only to gods
and demi-gods, of dedicating a temple and naming him founder,
thinking it to be enough to have observed the judgment and
good will of the people, but the honors suitable to good men he
accepted with gratification.'—32. Αἰμιλία: name of the tribe,
after the customary Latin abl. sg. (sc. *tribu*).—56 f. 'when Po-
lemon was priest of Rome and Augustus.'

Thessalian

Pelasgiotis

(With Phalanna. See p. 151, footnote)

29. Larisa. Fifth century B.C. IG IX.ii.662-663. Roberts 240.
Schwyzer 584.

a. Πολυξεναία ἐμμί.   *b.* Ϝεκέδαμος.

Πολυξεναία: sc. στάλλα. **168**c.—**Ϝεκέδαμος**: **46**, **52**b.

30. Site of unknown identity, southeast of Larisa. Fifth century B.C. IG IX.ii.1027. Schwyzer 597.

῞Απλōνι Λεσχα[ί]ō[ι] 'Αριστίōν ὀνέθēκε κοὶ συνδαυχναφόροι.
Πρόνος ἐργάξατο.

'Aristion and his fellow δαφνηφόροι set up to Apollo of the Λέσχη.'
δαύχνα: **68**.4*a*.—Λεσχα[ί]ō[ι]: or Λεσχα[ί]ō (see **38**) ? Λεσχηνόριος,
an epithet of Apollo, occurs in Plutarch, and Λεσχανόριος is the
name of a month in Thessalian and Cretan.

31. Phalanna. Fifth century B.C. IG IX.ii.1226. Schwyzer 608.

5 Νόμος. | αἴ κε τὸν | Ϝασστὸν | κις Ϝαλί||οσκϝετα[ι] | κοινὰ χ[ρ]||έ-
10 ματα ἔ[χ]||ον καὶ μ[ὲ] | δυνά̄ετ[α]||ι ἀππε[ῖσ|αι] το - - - -

32. Larisa. About 214 B.C. IG IX.ii.517. Ditt. Syll. 543.
Schwyzer 590. Solmsen-Fraenkel 12.

[Ταγ]ευόντουν 'Αναγκίπποι Πετθαλείοι, 'Αριστονόοι Εὐνομείοι,
2 'Επιγένεος'Ιασονείοι, Εὐδίκο[ι|'Αδα]μαντείοι,'Αλεξία Κλεαρχείοι,
γυμνασιαρχέντος 'Αλεύα Δαμοσθενείοι · Φιλίπποι τοῖ βασιλεῖος

ἐπιστολὰν ἀ|[π]υστέλλαντος πὸτ τὸς ταγὸς καὶ τὰν πόλιν τὰν
ὑπογεγραμμέναν·
4 „Βασιλεὺς Φίλιππος Λαρισαί|ων τοῖς ταγοῖς καὶ τῆι πόλει
χαίρειν. Πετραῖος καὶ Ἀνάγκιππος καὶ Ἀριστόνους ὡς ἀπὸ τῆς
πρεσβείας ἐγένοντο. || ἐνεφάνιζόν μοι ὅτι καὶ ἡ ὑμετέρα πόλις διὰ
τοὺς πολέμους προσδεῖται πλεόνων οἰκητῶν· ἕως ἂν οὖν καὶ ἑτέ-|
6 ρους ἐπινοήσωμεν ἀξίους τοῦ παρ' ὑμῖν πολιτεύματος, ἐπὶ τοῦ παρ-
όντος κρίνω ψηφίσασθαι ὑμᾶς ὅπως τοῖς κατοι|κοῦσιν παρ' ὑμῖν
Θεσσαλῶν ἢ τῶν ἄλλων Ἑλλήνων δοθῆι πολιτεία. τούτου γὰρ
8 συντελεσθέντος καὶ συνμεινάν|των πάντων διὰ τὰ φιλάνθρωπα
πέπεισμαι ἕτερά τε πο[λ]λὰ τῶν χρησίμων ἔσεσθαι καὶ ἐμοὶ καὶ
τῆι πόλει καὶ τὴν | χώραν μᾶλλον ἐξεργασθήσεσθαι. ἔτους β΄
Ὑπερβερεταίου κα΄."
10 ψαφιξαμένας τᾶς πόλιος ψάφισμα || τὸ ὑπογεγραμμένον· „Πα-
νάμμοι τᾶ ἕκτα ἐπ ἰκάδι συνκλεῖτος γενομένας, ἀγορανομέντουν
τοῦν ταγοῦν πάν|τουν· Φιλίπποι τοῖ βασιλεῖος γράμματα πέμψαν-
τος πὸτ τὸς ταγὸς καὶ τὰν πόλιν διὲ κί Πετραῖος καὶ Ἀνάγκιπ-
12 πος καὶ | Ἀριστόνοος, οὓς ἀτ τᾶς πρεισβείας ἐγένονθο, ἐνεφανίσ-
σοεν αὐτοῦ, πὸκ κί καὶ ἀ ἀμμέουν πόλις διὲ τὸς πολέμος πο|τεδέετο
πλειόνουν τοῦν κατοικεισόντουν· μέσποδί κε οὖν καὶ ἕτερος ἐπι-
14 νοείσουμεν ἀξίος τοῖ πὰ[ρ] ἀμμὲ | πολιτεύματος, ἐτ τοῖ παρεόντος
κρεννέμεν ψαφίξασθειν ἀμμὲ ο(ὕ)ς κε τοῖς κατοικέντεσσι πὰρ ἀμμὲ
Πετθ[α]||λοῦν καὶ τοῦν ἄλλουν Ἑλλάνουν δοθεῖ ἀ πολιτεία· τοῖνεος
16 γὰρ συντελεσθέντος καὶ συνμεννάντουν πάν|τουν διὲ τὰ φιλάνθρουπα
πεπεῖστειν ἄλλα τε πολλὰ τοῦν χρεισίμουν ἔσσεσθειν καὶ εὑτοῦ καὶ
τᾶ πόλι καὶ | τὰν χούραν μᾶλλον ἐξεργασθείσεσθειν· ἐψάφιστει τᾶ
18 πολιτεία πρασσέμεν πὲρ τοῦννεουν κὰτ τὰ ὁ βα|σιλεὺς ἔγραψε, καὶ
τοῖς κατοικέντεσσι πὰρ ἀμμὲ Πετθαλοῦν καὶ τοῦν ἄλλουν Ἑλλά-
νουν δεδόσθειν τὰν πολι|τείαν καὶ αὐτοῖς καὶ ἐσγόνοις καὶ τὰ λοιπὰ
τίμια ὑπαρχέμεν αὐτοῖς πάντα ὅσσαπερ Λασαίοις, φυλᾶς ἑλομέ-||
20 νοις ἑκάστου ποίας κε βέλλειτει· τὸ μὰ ψάφισμα τόνε κύρρον
ἔμμεν κὰπ παντὸς χρόνοι καὶ τὸς ταμίας ἐσδό|μεν ὀνγράψειν αὐτὸ
ἐν στάλλας λιθίας δύας καὶ τὰ ὀνύματα τοῦν πολιτογραφειθέντουν
22 καὶ κατθέμεν | τὰμ μὲν ἴαν ἐν τὸ ἱερὸν τοῖ Ἀπλουνος τοῖ Κερδοίοι,
τὰμ μὰ ἄλλαν ἐν τὰν ἀκρόπολιν, καὶ τὰν ὀνάλαν, κίς κε γι|νύειτει
ἐν τάνε, δόμεν·" καὶ ὕστερον Φιλίπποι τοῖ βασιλεῖος ἐπιστολὰν
24 ἄλλαν ἀπυστέλλαντος πὸτ | τὸς ταγὸς καὶ τὰν πόλιν, ταγευόντουν
Ἀριστονόοι Εὐνομείοι, Εὐδίκοι Ἀδαμαντείοι, Ἀλεξίπποι Ἱππολο-

χείοι, ‖ Ἐπιγένεος Ἰασονείοι, Νυμεινίοι Μνασιαίοι, γυμνασιαρχέντος Τιμουνίδα Τιμουνιδαίοι, τὰν ὑπογεγραμμέναν· ‖

26 „Βασιλεὺς Φίλιππος Λαρισαίων τοῖς ταγοῖς καὶ τῆι πόλει χαίρειν. πυνθάνομαι τοὺς πολιτογραφηθέντας κατὰ ‖ τὴν παρ' ἐμοῦ
ἐπιστολὴν καὶ τὸ ψήφισμα τὸ ὑμέτερον καὶ ἀναγραφέντας εἰς τὰς

28 στήλας ἐκκεκολάφθαι· εἴ|περ οὖν ἐγεγόνει τοῦτο, ἠστοχήκεισαν οἱ
συνβουλεύσαντες ὑμῖν καὶ τοῦ συμφέροντος τῆι πατρίδι ‖ καὶ τῆς
ἐμῆς κρίσεως. ὅτι γὰρ πάντων κάλλιστόν ἐστιν ὡς πλείστων μετε-

30 χόντων τοῦ πολιτεύματος ‖ τήν τε πόλιν ἰσχύειν καὶ τὴν χώραν μὴ
ὥσπερ νῦν αἰσχρῶς χερσεύεσθαι, νομίζω μὲν οὐδ' ὑμῶν οὐθένα ἂν
ἀν|τειπεῖν, ἔξεστι δὲ καὶ τοὺς λοιποὺς τοὺς ταῖς ὁμοίαις πολιτο-

32 γραφίαις χρωμένους θεωρεῖν, ὧν καὶ οἱ Ῥωμαῖ|οί εἰσιν, οἳ καὶ τοὺς
οἰκέτας, ὅταν ἐλευθερώσωσιν, προσδεχόμενοι εἰς τὸ πολίτευμα καὶ
τῶν ἀρχαίων με|[ταδι]δόντες καὶ διὰ τοῦ τοιούτου τρόπου οὐ μόνον

34 τὴν ἰδίαν πατρίδα ἐπηυξήκασιν, ἀλλὰ καὶ ἀποικίας (σ)χεδὸν ‖ [εἰς
ἐβ]δομήκοντα τόπους ἐκπεπόμφασιν. πλ[ὴ]ν ἔτι δὲ καὶ νῦν παρα-
καλῶ ὑμᾶς ἀφιλοτίμως προσελθεῖν ‖ [πρὸς τὸ] πρᾶγμα καὶ τοὺς
μὲν κεκριμένους ὑπὸ τῶν πολιτῶν ἀποκαταστῆσαι εἰς τὴν πολι-

36 τείαν, εἰ δέ ‖ [τινες ἀ]νήκεστόν τι πεπράχασιν εἰς τὴν βασιλείαν
ἢ τὴν πόλιν ἢ δι' ἄλλην τινὰ αἰτίαν μὴ ἄξιοί εἰσιν ‖ [μετέχ]ειν
τῆς στήλης ταύτης, περὶ τούτων τὴν ὑπέρθεσιν ποιήσασθαι, ἕως

38 ἂν ἐγὼ ἐπιστρέψας ἀπὸ τῆς ‖ [στρα]τείας διακούσω· τοῖς μέντον
κατηγορεῖν τούτων μέλλουσιν προείπατε ὅπως μὴ φανῶσιν διὰ
φ[ι|λο]τιμίαν τοῦτο ποιοῦντες. ἔτους ζ′ Γορπιαίου ιγ′."

40 ψαφιξαμένας τᾶς πόλιος ψάφισμα τὸ ὑπογε‖|[γ]ραμμένον· „Θε-
μιστίοι τᾶ ὑστερομειννία ἀγορανομέντος Ἀλεξίπποι πὲρ ἱεροῦν,
Ἀλεξίπποι λέξα[ν]|τος ἐψάφιστει τᾶ πολιτεία, ὅσσουν μὲν ἐφάν-
γρενθείν κινες τοῦν πεπολιτογραφειμένουν, τὸς ταγὸς ἐγγρά[ψαν]-|

42 τας ἐν λεύκουμα ἐσθέμεν αὐτὸς ἐν τὸν λιμένα, τοῦ[ν μ]ὰ λοιποῦν
τοῦν πεπολιτογραφειμένουν κὰτ τὰν ἐπιστ[ο]|λὰν τοῖ βασιλεῖος τὰ
ὀνύματα καὶ τὰς ἐπιστολὰς τοῖ βασιλεῖος καὶ τὰ ψαφίσματα τό

44 τε ὑππρὸ [τ]ᾶς γενόμενον ‖ καὶ τὸ τᾶμον ὀγγράψαντας ἐν στάλλας
λιθίας δύας κατθέμεν τὰν μὲν ἴαν ἐν τὸν ναὸν τοῖ Ἀπλουνος τοῖ
Κερδοίοι, ‖ τὰν δὲ ἄλλαν ἐν τὰν ἀκρόπολιν ἐν τὸν ναὸν τᾶς Ἀθάνας,

46 καὶ τὰν ὀνάλαν τὰν ἐν τάνε γινυμέναν τὸς ‖ ταμίας δόμεν ἀτ τᾶν
κοινᾶν ποθόδουν· τὸ μὰ ψάφισμα τόνε κῦρρον ἔμμεν κὰπ παντὸς
χρόνοι." οἱ πεπολιτογραφειμένοι κάτ τε τὰς ἐπιστολὰς τοῖ βασιλεῖος καὶ κὰτ τὰ ψαφίσματα τᾶς πόλιος· ‖

48   Σαμόθρακες· Ἄρχιππος Καλλιφούντειος.
     Κραννούνιοι· Ἀγεισίνοος Λυκίνειος, Φάλα|κρος Σιμίαιος, [κτλ.
     49-78].
79   Γυρτούνιοι· Εὔθοινος Λεττίναιος, Φιλόδαμος Λεττίναιος, Βοί-
     σκος Δαμμάτρειος, [κτλ. 79-92].

Decrees of Larisa made in accordance with recommendations
of the Macedonian king Philip V, whose letters, dated 219 and
214 B.C. and written in the κοινή, are included. The Thessalians
at this time were nominally independent, but actually subject
to Macedonia. Cf. Polyb. 4.76.2.

10. **συνκλεῖτος**: συνκλείς (164.10) is used, like Att. σύγκλητος
ἐκκλησία, of a specially summoned assembly.—16. **εὑτοῦ**: ἑαυτῷ.
So also εὑτοῖ, εὑτῆς in two other inscriptions of Larisa.—19.
Λασαίοις: Λαρισαίοις. 88b.—19 f. **φυλᾶς** κτλ.: 'choosing each the
tribe to which he wishes to belong.' ποίας gen. sg. with ἔμμεν
understood, φυλᾶς gen. sg. by attraction to ποίας. Cf. Att. ἑλέσθαι
δὲ αὐτοὺς φυλὴν καὶ δῆμον καὶ φρατρίαν, ἧς ἂν βούλωνται εἶναι. —28.
ἠστοχήκεισαν: 3 pl. plpf. of ἀστοχέω 'miss the mark, fail.' Both
word and ending are post-classical.—38. **μέντον**: μέντοι. This is
now attested from some half dozen κοινή sources. It is probably
due to the analogy of adverbs like πρῶτον, λοιπόν, etc.—40. **πὲρ
ἱεροῦν**: apparently equivalent, in the language of adulation, to
πὲρ βασιλικῶν.—41. **ὄσσουν** κτλ.: '(the names) of as many of the
enrolled citizens as any accuse.' ἐφάνγρενθειν: **139**.2, **162**.2. In
sense = κατηγοροῦσιν (cf. l. 38).—43. **καὶ τὰ ψαφίσματα** κτλ.:
'and the decrees, both the one just previously passed and the
present one.' ὑππρὸ τᾶς, sc. ἀμέρας. Same phrase in another
inscription of Larisa (IG IX.ii.512.30). **136**.1, 12.

33. Larisa. Second century B.C. Béquignon, BCH **59**.55 ff.
Lejeune, Rev. Ét. Gr. **54**.77 ff.

   Ταγευόντων Κρίτουνος Παυσαναίοι, Κρατει|σίπποι Θερσαν-
   δρείου, Θρασυμάχοι Ἀριστουνεί|οι, Φιλοφείροι Ἀσανδρείοι, Θερσ-
5 άνδροι Πολυξενε|[ί]οι, ταμιευόντουν Λυκίνοι Ἀλ[ε]ξανδρείοι
   καὶ Μενε||κράτεος Εὔστρατ[ι]δαιοι, γυμνασιαρχέντουν | μὲς τᾶς
   πέμπ[τ]ας [τ]οῖ Ὁμολουίοι Πλειστία Ἀσκα|λαπιαδαίοι καὶ Δου-
   ριμαλαίοι Λαμείοι   , ἀτ τᾶ[ς] | μὰ πέμπτας Ἱπποδρομ[ίοι],
10 Αἰσκαναίοι καὶ Φερεκρ[ά]τεος Μενεκρατεί[οι] ||

'Απλουνίοι [ὑ]στέρα, ἀγορᾶς [ἔνσας, ἀ]γορανομέντος Κρίτουνος
Πα[υ]|σανιαίοι, Κρίτουν[ος Παυσα]νιαίοι λέξαντος· ὀπειδεὶ |
[Β]όμβος 'Αλφεί[οι] Α[ἰολεὺς ἀπ' 'Αλεξαν]δρείας, παρεπιδαμεί-|
15 [σ]ας ἐν τᾶ πόλι [ἐπὶ ἀμέρας πλείονα]ς, ἐπιδείξις ἐν τοῦ γ[υ||μ-]
νασί[ου ἐποιείσατο, εὐδοκίμεισε]ν τε τοῖς πεπραγματευμένοις |
αὐτ[οῦ καὶ ἐπεμνάσθει τοῦν γε]γ[ενει]μένουν ἐνδόξουν Λα|ρισαίοις
καὶ [εἴύξεισε τὰν εὐνο]ίαν καὶ φιλίαν ταῖς πολίεσσι π[ὸ]||θ' εὐτὰς,
ὀν[νεουσάμενος] καὶ τὰ φιλάνθρουπα τὰ ὑπάρχοντα | Αἰολείεσσι
20 πὸτ τὰν πόλιν τὰν Λαρισαίουν· ἐποιείσατο μὰ || καὶ τὰν ὀστροφὰν
[εὐσχαμόν]ους καὶ ὂν τρόπον ἐπέβαλλε ἀν|δρὶ καλοῦ καὶ ἀγαθοῦ·
ἔδοξε τοῦ δάμου τοῦ Λαρισαίουν· ἐπα[ι]|νείσειν τε Βόμ[βον] 'Αλ-
[φείοι] Αἰολέα ἀπ' 'Αλεξανδρείας ἔτ τε | τᾶ ὀστροφᾶ καὶ φ[ιλοτιμ]ία
πὲρ τὰν παιδείαν καὶ ἔτ τοῦ τὰ | κάλλιστα τοῦν ἐπιτα[δευ]μάτουν
25 ἐζαλουκέμεν, καὶ δοθέ||μεν αὐτοῦ καὶ ἐσγόνοις πολιτείαν καὶ ἔντασιν
καὶ τὰ λοι|πὰ τίμια ὑπαρχέμεν αὐτ[οῦ] ὅσσα καὶ Λαρισαίοις. καὶ
ὅπεί κε ὁ | [κ]αιρὸς κατενέκει ἐν τοῦ δεύει ἐς τοῦν νόμουν τὰ κὰτ
τᾶς πολ[ι]|τείας οἰκονομείσθειν, φροντίσειν τὸς τάγος οὔστε δοθεῖ
αὐτοῦ | ἀ πολιτεία. τὸ μὰ ψάφισμα τόνε κύριον ἔμμεν κὰ παντὸς
30 χρόνοι || καὶ τὸς ταμίας ἐσδόμεν ὀνγράψει[ν] αὐτὸ ἐν κίονα λιθίαν
καὶ κατα[θέ]|μεν ἐν τὸ ἱερὸν τοῖ "Απλουνος τοῖ Κερδοίοι καὶ τὰν
ὀνάλαν κίς κ[ε| γ]ίνειτει δόμεν.

Decree in honor of Bombus, an Aeolian from Alexandria. The
restorations, with some minor changes, are those of the editor.
6. μές: 'until.' 132.12.—12. ὀπειδεί = ἐπειδή. 132.7.—20.
ὀστροφά: from *ὀνστροφά (6,77.2) = ἀναστροφή, here 'behavior.'
For the whole phrase, ci. πεποίηνται τὰν ἀναστροφὰν καλὰν καὶ
εὐσχήμονα, Ditt. 740.—22 f. καὶ ἔτ τοῦ, κτλ.: 'and for his having
been zealous for the best practices.' Cf. τοῖς τῶν καλλίστων ἐπιταδευ-
μάτων προεστακόσι, Ditt. 721.40.—For ἔτ τοῦ (and ἔτ τε l. 22),
from ἔπ = ἐπί, see 95, 99.2.—26 ff. καὶ ὅπεί κε, κτλ.: 'and when
the time arrives in which it is necessary in accordance with the
laws for matters concerning citizenship to be regulated.'—ὅπει
'when': 132.7.—δεύει: 35.—ll. 32-45, omitted here, contain
another similar decree. The editor's reading Κρατεισίπποιο 'Ερ-
σανδρείοι (ll. 34 f., 39 f.) should be changed to Κρατεισίπποι Θε-
ρσανδρείοι, agreeing with l. 1/2.

34. Crannon. Second century B.C. IG IX.ii.461. Schwyzer 578.

[Στρατα]γέντος τοῦν Πε[τθαλοῦν | Λίοντος] Παυσανιαίοι Μα-
τροπολ[ίτα, | ταγευό]ντουν Σιλάνοι 'Αστο[μαχείοι, | Φίλ]ουνος
5 'Αντιγενείοι, Γεν[νάοι 'Ασ||στον]οείοι, Γεννάοι Αἰσχυλ[είοι, - -]
- - Κ]αλλισθενείοι, ταμιε[υόντουν - - | - - 'Α]ντιγονείοι, Φείδουνος
Εὐ[δοξείοι], | - - ος 'Αντιγενείοι λέξαντο[ς· ἐπει|δεὶ Λί]ουν Παυ-
10 σανίαιο[ς] Ματροπ[ολίτας || διετέ]λει εὐεργετὲς τὸ κοινὸν [τᾶς |
πόλι]ος ἔν τε τοῖς πρότερο[ν χρόνοις | καὶ ἐ]ν τᾶ ἀρχᾶ τᾶ ἑαυτοῖ
καὶ κ[οινᾶ τᾶ | πόλι κ]αὶ καθ' ἰδδίαν ἀὶν τοῦ χρείαν [ἔχο|ντι, ἔδο]ξε
15 τοῦ κοινοῦ τᾶς πόλιος [ἐπαι||νέσαι] Λίοντα ἐτ τᾶ προαυγρέ[σι
τὰν | ἔχει καὶ π]ὸτ τὰν πόλιν καὶ πὸ[θ ἕκαστον | τοῦν] πολιτάουν
καὶ δεδόσ[θαι καὶ αὐ|τοῦ] κα(ὶ) τοῖς ἐσγόνοις ἀτ[έλειαν πάντουν |
20 καὶ] ἀουλίαν καὶ ἰσοτιμίαν καὶ [πάντα || τὰ λοι]πὰ αὐτοῦ ὑπαρχέ-
μεν τίμια [ὅσσα | καὶ] τοῖς λοιποῖς προξένοις, καὶ [φροντίσαι | τὸν]
ταμ[ί]αν Φείδουνα Εὐδόξει[ον οὕς κε | ἀτ τᾶς] τοῦν ταγοῦν γνού-
25 μας [τόνε τὸ | ψάφισμ]α ὀνγραφεῖ ἐν κίονα λιθίν[αν || καὶ τ]ε[θεῖ]
ακρουν ἐν τοῖς ἰαρουτοῖς, [τὸ | μὰ ὀ]νάλουμα τὸ γενόμενον [ἐν
τάνε | ἐγγραφέ]μεν ἐν τοῖς λόγοις τᾶ[ς πόλιος].

Decree in honor of Leon of Matropolis.—25. ακρουν: dubious.

Thessaliotis

35. Thetonium, not far from Cierium. Fifth century B.C.
IG IX.ii.257. Schwyzer 557. Ditt. Syll. 55. Solmsen-Fraenkel 13.

-ἒς ηυλōρέοντος Φιλονίκō ηυῖος. |

Θετōνιοι ἔδōκαν Σōταίρōι τōι Κ|οριντίōι καὐτōι καὶ γένει καὶ
5 Ϝ|οικιάταις καὶ χρḕμασιν ἀσυλί||αν κάτελειαν κεὐϜεργέταν ἐ|ποίē-
σαν κἒν ταγᾶ κἒν ἀταγ|ίαι. αἴ τις παρβαίνοι, τὸ|ν ταγὸν τὸν ἐπε-
10 στάκοντα ἐ|ξξανακάδēν. τὰ χρυσία καὶ τὰ || ἀργύρια τὲς Βελφαίō
ἀπολ]όμενα ἔσōσε 'Ορέσταο Φερεκράτ-

Decree of the Thetonians in honor of Sotaerus the Corinthian,
who had recovered the gold and silver objects that had been
lost from the temple of Apollo. For similar "losses" cf. Ditt.
Syll. 405-6, 416-18.

I, II. It is obvious that the text as it stands is incomplete
both at the beginning and the end, although the bronze tablet
on which it is inscribed is intact. A horizontal line was cut in the
bronze to indicate that l. I did not belong with the following.
It is probable that l.I is the conclusion of the present decree,
and was added at the top when it was found that no space was

left at the bottom. In this case we read 'Ορέσταο Φερεκράτες (cf.
108.2) or, with correction, Φερεκράτε(ο)ς hυλōρέοντος Φιλονίκō hυῖος
'when Orestes, son of Pherecrates of Philonicus, was ὑλωρός.'
The use of the genitive instead of the patronymic adjective
would be only another instance (see **214**) of divergence from the
usual Thessalian. The addition of the grandfather's name is unusual, but not unprecedented (cf., e.g., no. 24), likewise the use
of υἱός instead of the genitive alone (cf., e.g., GDI 1183, Arc.;
Ditt. Syll. 121, Stratus; παῖς often so used in Lesbian and Cyprian).
ὑλωρός occurs in Arist. Pol. 6.8.6 as the title of an official similar
to the ἀγρονόμος, but nowhere else than in this inscription as
an eponymous officer. —5. **χεὐϜεργέταν: 94**.7.—6. **χὲν ταγᾶ χὲν
ἀταγίαι**: 'in war and peace.' The phrase is plainly the equivalent
of the usual καὶ πολέμου καὶ εἰρήνης (or ἐν πολέμωι κτλ.), and is
explained by the fact that in early times, as also later in the time
of Jason of Pherae, the ταγός was the military head of the united
Thessalians, appointed only in time of war. Jason of Pherae, in
boasting of the military strength of the Thessalians on a war
footing, expresses this last by ὅταν ταγεύηται Θετταλία, ὅταν ταγὸς
ἐνθάδε καταστῇ, ὅταν ταγεύηται τὰ κατὰ Θετταλίαν (Xen. Hell.
6.1.8. 9, 12). So ταγά (one would expect ταγία) and ἀταγία (cf.
ἀκοσμία 'time when no κόσμος was in office') were times of war
and peace respectively. But the use of the phrase does not
necessarily show that the institution under which it originated
was in vogue at the time of this inscription; and, in any case, the
ταγός of l. 8 is the municipal official, like the ταγοί of no. 32.

36. Pharsalus. Third century B.C. IG IX.ii.234. Schwyzer
567.

'Α[γαθᾶ τύχα ·] ἁ πόλις Φαρσαλίουν τοῖς καὶ οὓς ἐξ ἀρχᾶς
συμπολιτευομένοις καὶ συμπο|λ[εμεισάντε]σσι πάνσα προθυμία
ἔδουκε τὰν πολιτείαν καττάπερ Φαρσαλίοις τοῖς | ἐ[ξ ἀρχᾶς πο-
λ]ιτευομένοις, ἐδούκαεμ μὰ ἐμ Μακουνίαις τᾶς ἐχομένας τοῦ Λου-
έρχου | (γ)ᾶ[ς μόραν πλέ]θρα ἐξείκοντα ἑκάστου εἰβατᾶ ἔχειν
5 πατρουέαν τὸμ πάντα χρόνον. || τ[αγευόντου]ν Εὐμειλίδα Νικασι-
αίου, Λύκου Δρουπακείου, 'Οιολύκου Μνασιππείου, Λύκου | Φερε-
κρατείου, 'Αντιόχου Δυνατείου. (Four columns of names
follow.)

Pharsalus grants citizenship to those who have assisted it, and gives land to each youth.

1 ff. **τοῖς καὶ οὕς** κτλ.: 'to those who have already from the beginning been politically associated (non-technical use of συμπολιτευομένοις, not 'those who have already enjoyed citizenship'), and to those who have zealously assisted in war, just as to those who have been citizens of Pharsalus from the beginning.' —**καὶ οὕς**: 'even as it is, already.' Cf. GDI 2160 δουλεύων καθὼς καὶ ὡς 'serving just as at present,' GDI 1832.11 μετὰ τῶν καὶ ὡς συνηρημένων 'with those already chosen.'—3. **ἐμ Μακουνίαις**: 'in the district known as the Poppy (μήκων) Fields.'

Boeotian

37. Temple of Apollo Ptous, near Acraephia. Sixth century B.C. Bréal, MSL 7.448. Holleaux, ibid. 8.180. Buck, CP 4.76 ff., 437.

ΚαλϜὸν ἄγαλμα Ϝάνακτι Ϝ[εκαβόλοι 'Απόλōνι
- - -]ορίδας ποίϜεσε μ' 'Εχέστροτος. αὐτὰρ ἔπεμφσαν
[- - - - - - - - - - - - - - - - - - -]ον ΠτōιἔϜι.
τōς τὺ Ϝάναχς, φεφύλαχσο, δίδοι δ' ἀρ(ε)τάν [τε καὶ ὄλβον.]

An epigram of four hexameter verses inscribed βουστροφηδόν on a small tile, broken at the bottom.

Vs. 1. **ἄγαλμα**: here used in its earlier and more general sense of 'pleasing gift, offering.'—Ϝ[**εκαβόλοι**]: or Ϝ[hεκαβόλοι], cf. Ϝhεκαδάμοε, no. 38.3.

Vs. 2. The first name, of which various restorations are possible, is in agreement with 'Εχέστροτος, and is either an epic patronymic or a designation of the gens or phratry to which 'Εχέστροτος (a Boeotian; note -στροτος 5) belonged.

Vs. 3. Here stood the subject of ἔπεμφσαν, the names of the donors. The form of which the final ον is preserved may be an adjective in agreement with, or a noun in apposition with, ἄγαλμα understood.

Vs. 4. **φεφύλαχσο**: Hom. πεφύλαξο, 65.—**δίδοι**: a rare imperative form which occurs in Pindar, and in another Boeotian and a Corinthian inscription, and is parallel to ἄγει, πίει. For the whole verse ending, compare those of Hom. Ar. 15 and 20.

38. Early vase inscriptions.

1. Probably from Tanagra. Sixth century B.C. Ἀρχ. Ἐφ. 1900.107.

Δ̄εμοθέρε̄ς hιαρὸν Ἀπόλōνος Καρυκε̄Fίō.

2. Thebes. Sixth century B.C. Ἀρχ. Ἐφ. 1900.107.

Ἱαρὸν τō Πυθίō ΓισFόδιϙος ἀνέθε̄κε.

3, 4. Tanagra. Sixth century B.C. IG VII.593, 606.

Ἐπὶ Fηεκαδάμοε ἐμί. Ἐπὶ Ὀκίβαε.

5. Uncertain origin. Probably fifth century B.C. IG VII. 3467. Schwyzer 441.

Μογέα δίδōτι ταῖ γυναικὶ δōρον Εὐχάρι τε̄ύτρε̄τιφάντō κότυλον, ὅς χ' ἅδαν πίε̄.

1) Cf. Paus. 9.20.3 ἔστιν... ἐν Τανάγρᾳ, καὶ ὅρος Κηρύκιον, ἔνθα Ἑρμῆν τεχθῆναι λέγουσι. But here the epithet Καρύκειος is applied to Apollo. Δ̄εμοθέρε̄ς is the same as Δαμοθέρσης found elsewhere, and, if the E is correctly read, the dedicator was an Athenian or Euboean.

3), 4) Examples of the early spelling οε and αε, 26, 30. For Fηεκα- see 52b. For ἐπί with dat. see 136.6.

5) Μογέα: masc. in -ᾱ. 105.1a.—τε̄ύτρε̄τιφάντō (see 94.7): ταῖ Εὐ-, daughter of Εὐτρητίφαντος. The first part of the name is identical with that of the Boeotian town which appears in Homer as Εὔτρησις. Cf. Εὐτρειτιδεῖες in a later Boeotian inscription. See 61.3.—ὅς: ὥς. 58a.

39. Thespiae. Early fourth century B.C. Platon-Feyel, BCH 62.149 ff.

Θεός· τύχα. | hιερὰ χρέματα Θεσπιέω|ν Διοπείθεος ἄρχοντος ἐν |
5 Ηεραίωι λέβε̄τες τριάκον||τα πέντε· ἐχῖνος· ὀβελίσσκω|ν δαρχ-
μαὶ τριάκοντα πέν|τε· χάλκια πλατέα πέντε· σκόφοι δοώδεκα·
10 ὑδρίαι hέν|δεκα· στάμνοι χάλκιωι τ||ρῖς· φιάλα· ἔπαρμα· κότος·
χάλκια· ποδανιπτῆρες hέξ· κρατε̄ρες τρῖς χάλκιοι· Fοι|νόχοια
15 χάλκια πέντε καὶ | δέκα· πελεκέες ὀκτό· ἄξιν||ος· hάμα· κόρτον
χάλκιον· hε̄μ|ιττα χαλκία· θράγανα διπλ|όα· κρατευταὶ τριπλόαι·
κρε|άγραι ὀκτό· τυροκνάσστιδες | τρῖς· Fαγάνω δύο· πούραυμα ||
20 φρυνοποπεῖον· λανπτερῶχ|οι σιδάριοι τρῖς· κλίναι πέν|τε· κλιν-

τε̄ρες πεντέκον|τα · δύγαστρον · ὑκτας · ἔπαρ|μα χάλκιον · τρεπέδδαι
25 Ꝺ Ꝺ Ꝺ · || μάχαιραι δέκα · Σίφαις λέβε̄τες | τρῖς, ὀβελίσκων δαρχ-
μαὶ τρῖς · ἐν Κρείσυι λέβε̄τε δύο, ὀβελίσκω|ν δαρχμάω δύο - - - -

Inventory of objects dedicated. Several of their names are
new and most of these of unknown meaning. So ἔπαρμα, ἡάμα (=
ἅμμα?), κόρτον, θράγανον, Ϝάγανον, ὑκτας, φρυνοποπεῖον. Dual
forms occur, δαρχμάω, Ϝαγάνω, λέβε̄τε, but always accompanied
by δύο. The spelling is of the transition period. Η ist still ℎ, but also
stands for ΗΕ in ἡένδεκα, ℎέξ, and ℎε̄μιττα (see 4.6). Ε still = ε
and the vowel η. But Ω is used, in some cases wrongly (χάλκιωι
nom. pl.). The υ is represented by V, also by Ο (σκόφοι, δοώδεκα,
perhaps also κόρτον and κότος), and once by ΟV (πούραυμα) so
common later.

40. Thebes. Middle of fourth century B.C. IG VII.2418.
Schwyzer 467. Ditt. Syll. 201. Tod 160.

[Τοὶ χρεί]ματα συνεβ[άλονθο ἐν τὸν πόλεμον | τὸν] ἐπο[λέμιον]
Βοιωτοὶ πε[ρὶ τῶ ἱαρῶ τῶ ἐμ Βελφοῖς | π]ὸτ τὼς ἀσεβίοντας τὸ
5 ἱαρὸ[ν τῶ Ἀπόλλωνος τῶ | Π]ουθίω. || Ἀριστίωνος ἄρχοντος ·
Ἀλυζῆοι - - - - - - - | πρισγε̄ες Χάροψ Δάδωνος, Ἀριστο - - - -
- - - - - | Ἀνακτοριέες τριάκοντα μνᾶς · πρι[σγε̄ες] - - - - - |
Φόρμω, Ἄρκος Τερε̄ος. | Βυζάντιοι χρουσίω Λαμψακανῶ στ[α-
10 τεῖρας] || ὀγδοέκοντα πέτταρας, ἀργυρίω Ἀτ[τικῶ δρα]|χμὰς
δεκαέξ · σύνεδροι Βυζαντίων [εἴνιξαν] | τὸ χρυσίον Κερχῖνος
Εἰροτίμω, Ἀγ - - - - - - | Δηλοπτίχω, Διωνύσιος Εἰραίωνος.
15 | Ἀθανόδωρος Διωνυσίω Τενέ[διος], || πρόξενος Βοιωτῶν, χει-
[λ]ίας δ[ραχμάς]. | Νικολάω ἄρχοντος · Ἀλυζ[ῆοι] ἄλλας τριά-
κοντα μνᾶς εἴ[νιξαν] · | πρισγεῖες Ἀλυζαίων Θεο - - - - - | [Ἀ]λε-
20 ξάνδρου, Δίων Πολυ[- - -] || [Ἀ]γεισινίκω ἄρχοντος · Βυζάντιοι
[συνεβά|λ]ονθο ἄλλως πεντακατίως στατεῖρα[ς χρυ|σ]ίως Λαμ-
ψακανὼς ἐν τὸν πόλεμον τὸν ὑ[πὲρ τῶ] | ἱαρῶ τῶ ἐμ Βελφοῖς ἐπο-
25 λέμιον Βοιωτ[οί] · | σύνεδροι εἴνιξαν Σῶσις Καρα[ι]ίχω, || [Π]αρ-
μενίσκος Πυράμου.

List of contributions for the Sacred War 355 ff. B.C. Note the
retention of the older spelling Ε beside ΕΙ, as πρισγε̄ες beside
πρισγεῖις, Att. αι in Ἀλυζαίων beside Ἀλυζῆοι, and Att. gen. sg.
in -ου beside -ω.

22. **τὸν ὑπὲρ** κτλ.: relative use of the article, unknown in the later Boeotian inscriptions. See **126**.—24. **εἴνιξαν: 144a**.

41. Temple of Apollo Ptous, near Acraephia. Between 312 and 304 B.C. IG VII.2723. Schwyzer 446. Solmsen-Fraenkel 16.

Βοιωτοὶ Ἀπόλλωνι Πτωίοι ἀνέθιαν ἄρχοντος Βοιωτοῖς Φιλο-κώμω Ἀ[ντ]ιγ[ενε]ιίω Θεισπιε[ῖος], | ἀφεδριάτευόντων Ἐμπεδο-[κ]λεῖος Ἀθανοκριτίω Ταναγρήω, Πούθωνος Α[ὐ]τομειδε[ίι]ω Ἐρχομενίω, | Ἱπποτίωνος Φαστυμειδοντίω Κορωνεῖος, ἘπιϜά[λ-τ]ιος Μαχωνίω Θειβήω, Νικίωνος Γ[ρ]υλ[ί]ωνος Πλαταεῖος, | Ἀριστοκλεῖος Ἀγασιήω Ἀνθαδονίω, Σάωνος Θιο[τ]ιμίω Θεισπι-εῖος, μαντευομένω Ὀνυμάστω Νικολαίω Θεισπιεῖος.

Dedication of a tripod to Apollo Ptous by the Boeotian league. This is one of a series of four belonging to the same period (IG VII.2723-2724b).

ἀφεδριατευόντων: 'those who serve as *ἀφεδριᾶται or official representatives at the dedication.' From ἑδριάω used like Att. ἱδρύω. Observe that in the case of the representative of Plataea the gen. sg. of the father's name is used, not the patron. adj. as in the case of the others. The same holds true in the other three dedications, and it is probable that this is not accidental, but that the Plataeans, so long associated politically with the Athenians, adopted the Attic usage at an early date.

42. Thespiae. About 230 B.C. Keramopoullos, Ἀρχ. Δελτ. 14.20 ff., πίναξ 2a. Feyel, BCH 60.181 ff., 405 ff. [ll. 1-9 fragmentary and omitted here].

10   ὁ μ[ι]σθωσάμενος πὰρ τᾶς ἀρχ[ᾶς τὸ]ν κᾶπον, ὃν ἀνέθεικε Σώ-στρατος ἱαρὸν | τῆς Μώσης, γαϜεργείσι Ϝέτε[α Ϝίκατ]ι· ἀρχι τῶ χρό[ν]ω ὅλας τᾶς μισθώσιος | ὅστις κα πεδὰ Νίκωνα ἄρχει · [τῶ δ'] ἐπὶ Νίκωνος ἐνιαυτῶ καταβαλεῖ τὰν μίσθωσιν | δραχμάων ΗΔΔ ▷ τὸ εἴμιτ[τον ΓΕ] ΔΤ τοῖ ταμίη. τῶν δὲ Ϝίκατι Ϝετέων καταβαλῖ | τοῖ ταμίη τὰν Μωσάων τὰμ μίσθ[ωσι]ν ἑκάστω τῶ 15   ἐνιαυτῶ ἐν τοῖ Ἀλαλκομενείοι μεινὶ || πρὸ τᾶς πέμπτας ἀπίοντος. ἐγγύως δὲ καταστάσι τῆ ἀρχῆ ἀξιοχρειέας [vacat] | τῶ μὲν ψεύδεος πάρχρειμα, ὅλας δὲ τᾶς μισθώσιος τριῶν ἀμεράων· κὴ ἐννέχυρον | δῶσι δύο ὀβολὼς ὑπέρ τε αὐτοσαυτῶ κὴ τῶν ἐγγύων ἑκάστω. ἠ δέ κα μεὶ καθιστάει | τὼς ἐγγύως, ἐπαμμισθώσι ἁ ἀρχά. ἠ δέ κα μῖον εὕρει ἐν τὰ Ϝίκατι Ϝέτεα, ἐν τὸ λεύκωμα | ἐσγραφείσετη ὑπὰ τᾶ[ς]

20 ἀρχᾶς αὐτὸς κὴ ὁ ἔγγυος τῶ ψεύδεος ἐπὶ τοῖ εἰμιολίοι. || ἡ δὲ κά
τις τῶν μισθωσαμένων μεὶ καταβάλλει τὰμ μίσθωσιν ἐν τοῖ γεγραμ-
μένοι | χρόνοι, ὁ ταμίας ὁ τᾶν Μ[ω]σάων ἐσγράψι αὐτὸν κὴ τὼς
ἐγγύως ἐπὶ τῇ μισθώσι τῇ ἀντὶ | ἐνιαυτῶ ἐπὶ τοῖ εἰμιολίοι, κὴ ἐπαμ-
μισθώσοντι τὸν κᾶπον ἐν τὰ περίσαα Ϝέτεα · | κὴ ἤ τί κα μῖον εὔ-
ρε[ι] ἐν τὸν λοιπὸν χρόνον, ἐν τὸ λεύκωμα ἐσγράψονθι αὐτὸν κὴ
τὼς | [ἐγ]γύως ἐφ᾽ εἰμιολίοι τοῖ μιονώματι παντὶ τῶν περισάων
25 Ϝετέων · ἡ δέ || κά τι ἐπιϜοικίξ[ε]ιτη, ἐπί κα δ[ι]εσσέλθει ὁ χρόνος,
ἀ[π]ίσετη λαβὼν ὅ κα ἐπιϜοικο|δομ[εί]σει. εἰ δέ τι κα δείει τέλος
ἐμφερέμεν ἐν τὰν πόλιν εἶ ἐν τὸ κοινὸν | Βοιωτῶν, ὕσι ὁ γ[αϜ]-
εργός · καταλίψι δὲ περὶ τὸ ἱαρὸν τῶ Μειλιχίω ἑκατὸν πόδας |
ἐμβαδόν. [ll. 29-32 omitted here].

From a long series of regulations for leases of land.

1 ff. 'The one who has rented from the board of officials the plantation (cultivated tract of land) which Sostratus dedicated to the Muses shall cultivate it for twenty years. The whole lease begins under the archon following Nikon. But for the year under the archon Nikon one shall pay down the rental of drachmas—, one half,—, to the treasurer.'—15 ff. 'He shall furnish trustworthy sureties to the board of officials,—in the case of a false declaration (on the part of the lessee as to his ability to pay) immediately, but for the whole lease within three days.'—17 ff. 'If he does not furnish sureties, the board of officials shall make a new lease. If (under the new lease) one receives less for the twenty years, the (original) lessee and the surety against false declaration shall be entered on the tablet for half as much again as the loss.' Similarly in l. 24, where the fuller εἰμιολίοι τοῖ μιονώματι.—ll. 22, 24. περίσαος: 'left over, remaining,' cpd. of -σαος = σοος.—25 f. If the lessee has built anything, when the rental period has elapsed, he may on leaving take with him whatever he has built (that is, the materials).' Cf. Ditt. Syll. 1097 ὅταν δὲ ὁ χρόνος ἐξίηι αὐτῶι τῆς δεκαετίας ἄπεισιν ἔχων τὰ ξύλα καὶ τὴν κέραμον καὶ τὰ θυρώματα.—26 ff. If there is any failure to pay the tax, the cultivator (the lessee) shall furnish it. (ὕσι = οἴσει). He shall leave free a space of a hundred feet around the shrine of Meilichios.'

43. Orchomenus. Between 222 and 200 B.C. IG VII.3172.

Inscr. Jurid. I, pp. 276 ff., 509 f. Schwyzer 523. Solmsen-Fraenkel
20. The sections of the text are given in the order in which they
were inscribed (cf. ll. 30 ff.), but the numbering of the original
publication is added in parentheses.

I
(D)   Τοὶ πολέμαρχοι τοὶ ἐπὶ Πολυκράτιος | ἄρχοντος Φιλόμειλος
      Φίλωνος, | Καφισόδωρος Διωνυσίω, ᾽Αθανόδω|ρος ῞Ιππωνος ἀνέ-
5
(106) γραψαν καθὼς || ἐποείσανθο τὰν ἀπόδοσιν τῶν δα|νείων τῶν Νικα-
II   ρέτας κὰτ τὸ ψά|φισμα τῶ δάμω.
(E)   (Μει)ν(ὸ)ς ᾽Αλαλκομενίω | Ϝικαστῇ κὴ ἕκτη, ἐπεψάφιδδε | Φι-
10   λόμειλος Φίλωνος, Καφισόδωρος || Διωνουσίω ἔλεξε · προβεβωλευ-
(111)
      μένον | εἶμεν αὐτῦ ποτὶ δᾶμον, ἐπιδεὶ ἐπεψα|φίττατο ὁ δᾶμος ἀπο-
      δόμεν Νικαρέτη⟨ι⟩ | Θίωνος τὸν ταμίαν τὸν προάρχοντα | τὰν τρί-
15
(116) ταν πετράμεινον ἀπὸ [τ]ᾶν ὑπερ||αμεριάων τᾶν ἰωσάων κὰτ τᾶς
      πόλιος, ὃ ἐ|πίθωσε αὐτὰν ἁ πόλις, ἀργουρίω δραχμὰς | μουρίας
      ὀκτακισχιλίας ὀκτακατίας τριά|κοντα τρῖς, κὴ τὼς πολεμάρχως
20
(121) ἀνελέσ|θη τάν τε σύνγραφον, ἃν ἔδωκαν οὖπὲρ || [ο]ὕτων τῶν χρει-
      μάτων κατ᾽ α[ὐ]τὺ αὐτῶ[ν] | κὴ ὁ ταμίας κὴ ὧν ποθείλετο Νικαρέ-
      τα δέκ[α], | κὴ τὰς ὑπεραμερίας διαγράψασθη τὰς [κὰτ] | τᾶς πό-
25   λιος τὰς ἐπὶ Ξενοκρίτω ἄρχοντος | ἐν Θεισπιῆς, κὴ οὖτα ϜεϜυκονο-
(126) μειόντων || τῶν πολεμάρχων κὴ τῶ ταμίαο ἀποδόν|τος τὰ χρείματα
      κὰτ τὸ ὁμόλογον τὸ πὰρ | Θιόφεστον Θιοδώρω Θεισπιεῖα τεθέν, |
30   δεδόχθη τῦ δάμυ · τὼς πολεμάρχως, | ἐπί κα τὸ ψάφισμα κούριον
(131) γένειτη, ἀγγρά||ψη ἐν στάλαν λιθίναν τό τε ψάφισμα οὖτο (II) |
      κὴ τὸ οὖπὲρ τᾶς ἀποδόσιος (III), κὰ(τ) ταὐτὰ δὲ κὴ | τὰς ὑπερα-
      μερίας τὰ(ς) κὰτ τᾶς πόλιος τὰς Νι|καρέτας (IV) κὴ τὸ ὅ[ν]ιουμα
35   τῶ γραμματεῖος τῶ δ[ι]|αγράψαντος αὐτὰς (V) κὴ τὰν σύγγραφον
(136) τὰν || τεθεῖσαν πὰρ Ϝιφιάδαν (VI) κὴ τὸ ἀντίγραφον ⟨κὴ | τὸ ἀντί-
      γραφον⟩ τῶ ὁμολόγω τῶ τεθέντος πὰρ Θιό|φεστον (VII) κὴ τὰν
      διαγραφὰν τῶν χρειμάτων ὧν ἔγραψαν αὐτῇ διὰ τρεπέδδας
40   (VIII), κὴ τὸ ἄλωμα | ἀπολογίτταστη ποτὶ κατόπ[τ]α[ς, π]όρον
(141) δ᾽ εἶμεν || ἀπὸ τῶν πολιτικῶν.
III
(F)   Δαματρίω νιουμεινίη | πετράτη, ἐπεψάφιδδε Κ[α]φισόδωρος Δι-
      ω|νουσίω, ᾽Αθανόδωρος ῞Ιππωνος ἔλεξε · προβε|[β]ωλευμένον εἶ-
      μεν αὐτῦ ποτὶ δᾶμον, ἐπιδεὶ, | παργενομένας Νικαρέτας Θίωνος
45
(146) Θεισπικᾶς || [κ]ὴ πραττώσας τὸ δάνειον τὰν πόλιν κὰτ τὰς οὔ-
      πε[ρ]|αμερία[ς] τὰς ἰώσας αὐτῇ, [ἀνα]γκάσ[θε]ν τὺ πολέμαρ]χυ κὴ
      ὁ ταμίας σουγχωρείσαντος τῶ δάμω δόμεν | [κ]ὰτ αὐ[τὺ] αὐ-

[τ]ῶν σούνγραφον πὸτ τῆ ούπαρχώση ούπε[ρ]|αμερίη, ἐ[ν τ]άν κα
50 ἐνενιχθείει ά ἀνφορά ἐν οὗτο, κ[ὴ] || κομίττ[ειτη] τὰ συνχωρειθέν-
(151) τα χρείματα, | δεδόχθη τῦ δάμυ· τὸν ταμίαν τὸν [π]ροάρχοντα |
[τὰν] τρίτα[ν] πετράμεινον ἀποδόμεν πεδὰ τῶν | πολεμάρχων Νι-
55 καρέτη ἀργ[υ]ρίω δραχμὰς μυρίας | [ὀκ]τακισχειλίας ὀκτακατία[ς]
(156) τριάκ[ο]ντα τρῖς Πολυ||κράτιος ἄρχοντος ἐν τῦ Δαματρίυ μεινὶ
κὴ τὰς ἐ[μ]πρᾶξις τὰς ἰώσας Νικα[ρέτη κὰτ] τᾶς πόλιος Ξεν[ο]|-
κρίτω ἄρχοντος ἐν Θεισπιῆς πάσας διαλιάνασ[θη] | τὼς πολεμάρ-
χως, κὴ τὰν σουνγραφάν, ἂν ἔχι κὰτ τ[ῶν] | πολεμάρχων κὴ τῶ
60 ταμίαο, ἀνελέσθη, πόρον [δ' εἶ]|||μεν ἐν οὗτο ἀπὸ τῶν τᾶς πόλιος
(161) ποθοδωμάτων πάντ[ων]. |
IV
(G)   Ξενοκρίτω, 'Αλαλκομενίω.—Νικαρέτα Θέωνος τᾶς π[ό]|λιος
'Ερχομενίων κὴ τῶ ἐγγύω Θίωνος Συννόμω· τὰ π|πάματα μούριη
65 ὀγδοείκοντα πέντε διού[ο] ὀβολίω· | κὴ τῶ τεθμίω Ϝίστωρ 'Αρισ-
(166) τόνικος Πραξιτέλιος· || Λιουκίσκω, Θιουίω, τὸ σουνάλλαγμα.—
Νικαρέτα Θίω|νος τᾶς πόλιος 'Ερχομενίων κὴ τῶ ἐγγούω Θίωνος |
Συννόμω· τὰ ππάματα δισχείλιη πεντακάτι[η]· | κὴ τῶ τεθμίω
Ϝίστωρ ὁ αὐτός· Λιουκίσκω, 'Ομολωῖω, | [τ]ὸ σουνάλλαγμα.—
70 Νικαρέτα Θίωνος τᾶς πόλι[ος || Ε]ρχομενίων κὴ τῶ ἐγγούω Θίω-
(171) νος Συννόμω· τὰ π|πάματα πετρακισχείλιη· κὴ τῶ τεθμίω
Ϝίστωρ | ὁ αὐτός· χρόνος ὁ αὐτός.—Νικαρέτα Θίωνος τᾶς πόλιος |
75 [Ε]ρχομενίων κὴ τῶ ἐγγούω Θίωνος Συννόμω· τὰ ππά|ματα
(176) χείλιη· κὴ τῶ τεθμίω Ϝίστωρ ὁ αὐτός· Λιουκίσκ[ω, || Θε]ιλου-
θίω, τὸ σουνάλλαγμα.
V
(H)   Διαγράψη τὰς ούπερ[α|μ]ερίας τὰς Νικαρέτας ἐν Θεισπιῆς τὰς
κὰτ τᾶς | [π]όλιος· τῶν τεθμοφουλάκων γραμματεὺς Σα.... |
VI
80   'Εδάνεισεν Νικαρέτα Θέωνος | Θεσπική, παρόντος αὐτῆι κυ-||
(A 3) ρίου τοῦ ἀνδρὸς Δεξίππου Ε[ὐ]|νομίδου, Καφισοδώρωι Δι[ο]|νυ-
σίου, Φιλομήλωι Φίλωνος, | 'Αθανοδώρωι "Ιππωνος, Πο[λυ]|κρί-
85 τωι Θάροπος καὶ ἐγγύοις || εἰς ἔκτεισιν τοῦ δανείου | Μνάσων
(8) Μέχγαο, Τελεσίας | Μέχγαο, Λασίππωι Ξενοτί|μου, Εὐάρει Εὐ-
90 χώρου, Περι|λάωι 'Αναξίωνος, Διονυσο||δώρωι Καφισοδώρου,
(13) Κωμί|ναι Τελεσίππου, 'Ονασίμωι | Θεογείτονος, Καφισοδώρωι |
95 Δαματρίχου, Νικοκλεῖ 'Αθα|νοδώρου 'Ορχομενίοις ἀργυ||ρίου
(18) δραχμὰς μυρίας ὀκτα|κισχειλίας ὀκτακοσίας τρι|άκοντα τρεῖς ἄτο-
κον ἐχ Θεσ|πιῶν εἰς τὰ Παμβοιώτια τὰ ἐ|π' 'Ονασίμου ἄρχοντος
100 Βοιωτοῖ[ς]. || ἀποδότωσαν δὲ τὸ δάνειον | οἱ δανεισάμενοι ἢ οἱ ἔγ-
(23) γυ|οι Νικαρέται ἐν τοῖς Πανβοι|ωτίοις πρὸ τῆς θυσίας ἐν ἡμέ|ραις

105
(28) τρισίν. ἐὰν δὲ μὴ ἀποδῶσ[ι,] ‖ πραχθήσονται κατὰ τὸν νό|μον·

[ἡ] δὲ πρᾶξις ἔστω ἔκ τε | αὐτῶν τῶν δανεισαμένων | καὶ ἐκ τῶν
110
(33) ἐγγύων, καὶ ἐξ ἑνὸ[ς] | καὶ ἐκ πλειόνων καὶ ἐκ πάν‖των καὶ ἐκ τῶν
ὑπαρχόντων | αὐτοῖς, πραττούσηι ὃν ἂν τρό|πον βούληται. ἡ δὲ
115 συγγραφὴ | κυρία ἔστω, κἂν ἄλλος ἐπι|φέρηι ὑπὲρ Νικαρέτας.
(38) Μάρ‖τυρες Ἀριστογείτων Ἁρμο|ξένου, Ἰθιούδικος Ἀθανίαο, |
120 Φιφιάδας Τιμοκλεῖος, Φαρ|σάλιος Εὐδίκου, Καλλέας Λυ|σιφάν-
(43) του, Θεόφεστος Θεοδώ‖ρου, Εὐξενίδας Φιλώνδου | Θεσπιεῖς. ἁ
VII σούγγραφος | πὰρ Φιφιάδαν Τιμοκλεῖος. |
(B) Ὀνασίμω ἄρχοντος Βοιωτοῖ[ς,] | μεινὸς Πανάμω, ὁμολογὰ ‖
125
(48) Νικαρέτη Θίωνος Θεισπικῆ, | παριόντος Νικαρέτη Δεξίπ|πω Εὐ-
130 νομίδαο τῶ ἀνδρὸς Θε[ι]‖σπιεῖος, κὴ τῆ πόλι Ἐρχομεν[ί]|ων·
(53) παρεῖαν οὑπὲρ τᾶς πόλ[ι]‖ος πολέμαρχοι Καφισόδω|ρος Διωνου-
135 σίω, Φιλόμειλος | Φίλωνος, Ἀθανόδωρος Ἵππω|νος· ἀποδόμεν
(58) τὰν πόλιν Ἐρ|χομενίων Νικαρέτη Θίωνος, ‖ ὃ ἐπίθωσαν οὑπὲρ
140 τᾶν οὑπε|ραμεριάων τᾶν ἐπὶ Ξενοκρί|τω ἄρχοντος ἐν Θεισπῆς,
(63) ἀρ|γουρίω δραχμὰς μουρίας ὀκτ[α]|κισχειλίας ὀκτακατίας τρ[ιά-]‖
κοντα τρῖς, ἔοχατον Ὀνασ[ί]‖μω ἄρχοντος ἐν τῦ Ἀλαλ[κο]|μενίοι
145 μεινί· σούγγραφον δὲ | γράψασθη τῶ ἀργουρίω τὼς | <τὼς> πολεμ-
(68) άρχως Ἐρχομενίων ‖ κὴ ἐγγούως, ὥς κα δοκιμάδδ[ει] | Νικα-
150 ρέτα, κὴ θέσθη μεσέγγ[υ]|ον πὰρ Φιφιάδαν Τιμοκλεῖος | Θεισπι-
(73) εῖα. ἐπὶ δέ κα κομίττε[ι]‖τη Νικαρέτα τὸ ἀργούριον ‖ πὰρ τᾶς πό-
λιος, ἐσλιανάτω Νικαρέτα τὰς οὑπερ|αμερίας, ἃς ἔχι κὰτ τᾶς πό-
λιος, τὰς ἐπὶ Ξενοκρίτω | ἄρχοντος ἐν Θεισπῆς πάσας, κὴ τὰν
σούγγραφον ἀπο|δότω Φιφιάδας τοῖς πολεμάρχυς κὴ τοῖ ταμίη
155 κὴ το[ῖς] | ἐγγούοις. ἠ δέ κα μεὶ ἀποδώει ἁ πόλις Νικαρέτη τὸ
(78) ἀρ‖γούριον ἐν τῦ γεγραμμένυ χρόνυ, τὰς μουρίας κὴ ὀκτ[α]‖κισ-
χειλίας ὀκτακατίας τριάκοντα τρῖς, ἀποδότω | τὰν σούγγραφον
κὴ τὰς οὑπεραμερίας τὰς κὰτ τᾶς | πόλιος, ἅπαν τὸ ἀργούριον τὸ
ἐν τῦ ὁμολό[γ]υ γεγραμ|μένον· (ἠ δέ κα) ἐν τῦ χρόνυ τῦ γεγραμ-
160
(83) μένυ μεὶ ἐθέλει κ[ομ]ίδδ[ε]‖σθη Νικαρέ[τ]α τὸ ἀργούριον, ἀπο-
δότω Φιφιάδας τὰν | σούγγραφον τοῖς πολεμάρχοις κὴ τοῖ ταμίη
κὴ τοῖς | ἐγγούοις, κὴ ποταποπισάτω Νικαρέτα τῆ πόλι Ἐρχο-|
μενίων κὴ τοῖς πολεμάρχοις κὴ τοῖ ταμίη κὴ τοῖς ἐγ|γούοις ἀρ-
165
(88) γουρίω δραχμὰς πεντακισμουρίας, κὴ τὴ ‖ οὑπεραμερίη ἄκουρύ-
νυ ἔνθω. Φίστορες Ἀριστογί|των Ἁρμοξένω, Ἰθούδικος Ἀθα-
νίαο, Φιφιάδας Τιμο[κλεῖ|ο]ς, Φαρσάλιος Εὐδίκω, Καλλέας
Λιουσιφάντω, Θιόφεισ|τος Θιοδώρω, Εὐξενίδας Φιλώνδαο

Θεισπιεῖε‹ι›ς. τὸ ὁμό|λογον πὰρ Θιόφειστον Θιοδώρω Θεισπιεῖα.

¹⁷⁰
(93) Διαγραφὰ || Νικαρέτη διὰ τραπέδδας τᾶς Πιστοκλεῖος ἐν Θεισπι|ῆς · Ἐπιτέλιος ἄρχοντος ἐν Θεισπιῆς, μεινὸς Ἀλαλκομε|νίω δευτέρω ἀμέρη ἐνακηδεκάτη, ἐπὶ τᾶς Πιστοκλεῖος | τραπέδδας Νικαρέτη παρεγράφει πὰρ Πολιουκρίτω Θάρο|πος Ἐρχομενίω τα-
¹⁷⁵
(98) μίαο οὑπὲρ τᾶς πόλιος τὸ σουνχωρει||θὲν τὰν οὑπεραμεριάων τᾶν ἐπὶ Ξενοκρίτω ἄρχοντος, | παριόντος πολεμάρχω Ἀθανοδώρω Ἵππωνος Ἐρχομενί[ω], | ἀργουρίω δραχμὴ μούρικ ὀκτακισχείλιη ὀκτακάτιη τριά|κοντα τρῖς.

Nicareta of Thespiae had lent various sums of money to the city of Orchomenus, for which she held against it certain notes, recorded in IV. When she appeared at Orchomenus to collect these (ll. 44 ff.), the city was unable to meet them, and an agreement was entered into according to which the city was to pay her the sum of 18,833 drachmas within a certain time and the polemarchs were to give her a personal contract for the payment. The text of the agreement (ὁμολογά) is given in VII, and of the contract (σούγγραφος), written in the κοινή, in VI. The sum of 18,833 drachmas is more than the total of the notes recorded in IV (17,585 dr., 2 obols), but probably less than they amounted to with the normal penalties for delayed payment. For the phrase ὃ ἐπίθωσε, ὃ ἐπίθωσαν (ll. 16, 135) 'which the city (they) persuaded her to accept,' implies some concession on her part. Finally the city passed a vote (III) to pay the amount and take up the notes and the contract. When this had been accomplished it passed a further vote (II) ordering all the documents to be inscribed in a specified order. This was done as stated in I, which serves as a heading to the whole inscription. Some of the typical financial terms recur in an inscription from Thisbe, SEG 3.342.

10 ff. **προβεβωλευμένον** κτλ.: 'that he had a probouleuma to present to the people, Whereas the people had voted that the treasurer in charge for the third period of four months should pay to Nicareta, in settlement of the notes of default which she held against the city, the sum which the city persuaded her (to accept), 18,833 drachmas, and that the polemarchs should take up the contract they gave for the money against themselves,

they and the treasurer and the ten whom Nicareta selected, and cancel the notes against the city (maturing) in the archonship of Xenocritus, and since the polemarchs had arranged these matters and the treasurer had paid the money according to the agreement deposited with Theophestus, be it voted by the people,' etc.

40-41. **νιουμεινίη** πετράτη: τετάρτη ἱσταμένου. On νιου- from νεο-, see **42**.5*a*.—46 ff. 'The polemarchs and the treasurer were obliged, with the assent of the people, to give a contract against themselves in addition to the existing note of default, until the levy for this purpose should be made and the amount agreed upon provided.' This is the only satisfactory interpretation of the most troublesome passage in the inscription, though one difficulty remains, the use of the singular οὐπεραμερίη where we should expect the plural.—49. ἐ[ν τ]άν: 'until,' originating in ἐν τὰν ἀμέραν. Cf. **136**.1.—**ἐν οὗτο**: 'for this purpose.' Cf. πόρον ἐν οὗτο ll. 59. 60.—**ἐνενιχθείει**, not ἐνενιχθεῖ, is declared certain by Baunack, Philol. 48.413, and agrees with uncontracted forms found elsewhere, as κουρωθείει (**151**.2).—50. **κομίττ[ειτη]**, not κομίττ[η], also after Baunack l.c.—56. **διαλιάνασ[θη]**: cf. ἐσλιανάτω l. 150, and **162**.10.

61 ff. The first date, archonship of Xenocritus, month of Alalcomenius, applies to the following notes (cf. ll. 23, 56, 136, 151) and is probably the time at which they fell due, while the date given at the end of each is the time of the loan (τὸ σουνάλλαγμα). Cf. Thalheim, Berl. Phil. Woch. 1893.267. The expression throughout is condensed. Ξενοκρίτω (ἄρχοντος), (μεινὸς) Ἀλαλκομενίω, Νικαρέτα Θέωνος (κατὰ) τᾶς πόλιος.

78 ff. The text of the contract is in the κοινή, though dialect forms are retained in some of the proper names. The names of the first two sureties are given by mistake in the nominative, but with the third the error is rectified.—113-114. **ἐπιφέρηι** 'presents it.'

154 ff. 'If the city fails to pay Nicareta in the time specified, it will have to pay the amount stated in the contract and the sum of the notes of default besides. But if Nicareta refuses to accept the amount named in the contract (as she might do in order to secure the exorbitant penalty for delay),

she forfeits both contract and notes and pays a heavy penalty.'
169/170. **διαγραφά Νικαρέτη** κτλ.: 'memorandum of payment to Nicareta (adnom. dat. 172) through the bank of Pistocles.' διαγραφά 'cancellation' (cf. διαγράψασθη l. 22), and so 'payment.' So ll. 172 ff., 'at the bank of Pistocles there was paid over to Nicareta by Polycritus the treasurer in behalf of the city the sum agreed upon of the notes of default' (part. gen.; cf. ἀπὸ τᾶν ὑπεραμεριάων ll. 14-15).

44. Lebadea. Third century B.C. IG VII.3083. Schwyzer 509.

Θιὸς τούχα ἀγα|θά. | Φαστίαο ἄρχοντος | Βοιωτῦς, ἐν δὲ Λεβα-||
5 δείη Δόρκωνος, Δωίλος | Ἰρανήω ἀντίθειτι τὸν | Φίδιον θεράποντα
10 Ἀν|δριχὸν τῦ Δὶ τῦ Βασιλεῖι | κὴ τῦ Τρεφωνίυ ἱαρὸν εἶ||μεν, παρ-
μείναντα πὰρ | τὰν ματέρα Ἀθανοδώ|ραν Φέτια δέκα, καθὼς ὁ |
πατεὶρ ποτέταξε· ἡ δέ κα | ἔτι δώει Ἀθανοδώρα, εἴσι [αὐτῆ] ||
15 Ἀνδριχὸς φόρον τὸν ἐν τῇ | θείχη γεγραμμένον· ἡ δέ τί | κα πάθει
Ἀθανοδώρα, παρμ|ενῖ Ἀνδριχὸς· τὸν περιττὸν | χρόνον πὰρ Δωί-
20 λον· [ἔ]πιτα ἰα||ρὸς ἔστω με[ὶ] ποθ[ί]κων μει|θενὶ μειθέν· μεὶ
ἐσσεῖμε|ν δὲ καταδουλίττασθη | Ἀνδριχὸν μειθενί· Ἀν|δριχὸν δὲ
25 λειτωργῖμεν || ἐν τῆς θοσίης τῶν θιῶν | <ων> οὔτων.

45. Lebadea. Second century B.C. IG VII.3080. Schwyzer 512.

[Σάων - - - - - - ἀντίθειτι τὸ Φίδιον | πη]δάριον Ἀθάνωνα τῦ Δὶ
τεῖ Βασιλεῖ κὴ τεῖ Τρεφωνίει ἱαρὸν εἶμεν τὸν πάν[τα] χρό]νον ἀπὸ
τᾶσδε τᾶς ἀμέρας, μεὶ προθίχοντα μείτε αὐτεῖ Σάωνι μείτε ἄλλει |
[μ]ειθενὶ κατὰ μειθένα τρόπον. ἡ δέ κά τις ἀντιποιείτη Ἀθάνωνος
5 εἴ ἄλλο τι ἀδικῖ || [κ]αθ' ὄντινα ὦν τρόπον, οὑπερδικιόνθω κὴ προΐ-
στάνθω τύ τε ἱαρεῖες κὴ τε[ὶ | ἱαρ]άρχη τὺ ἠὶ ἀντιτιουνχάνοντες
κὴ τῶν ἄλλων ὁ βειλόμενος. Φίστορε[ς] | . . . . λεις Σάωνος, Εὔβω-
λος Σωκράτιος, Νίκαργος κὴ Κράτων Εὐνοστίδ[αο].

46. Chaeronea. Second century B.C. IG VII.3303.

Καλλίκωνος ἀρχῶ μεινὸς Δαματρίω πεντεκηδεκάτη | Πούριππος
Προξένω ἀντίθειτι ἱαρὰν τὰν Φιδίαν θεράπη||[να]ν Ἀφροδιτίαν τῦ
Σαράπι, παραμείνασαν ἀσαυτῦ κὴ τῇ γου|[νη]κὶ αὐτῶ ἀγαθὴν ἅς
5 κα ζώωνθι, τὰν ἀνάθεσιν ποιόμε||[νος] διὰ τῶ σουνεδρίω κὰτ τὸν
νόμον· κὴ κατέβαλε τῦ ταμίη | [ἐ]πὶ τῶν ἱαρῶν τὸ γινιούμενον
δραχμὰς Φίκατι παραχρε[ῖ]μα.

47. Chaeronea: Second century B.C. IG VII.3352. Schwyzer 517.

'Αρχείνω ἀρχῶ μεινὸς Θουίω | πεντεκηδεκάτη Διουκλεῖς κὴ Κω-|
τίλα ἀντίθεντι τὰν Ϝιδίαν θρε|πτάν, ἦ ὄνιουμα Ζωπουρίνα, ἰαρ[ὰν]||
5 τεῖ Σεράπει, παραμείνασαν αὐτε|ῖς ἅς κα ζῶνθι ἀνενκλείτως, τὰν |
ἀνάθεσιν ποιούμενει διὰ τῶ σ[ο]||υνεδρίω κατὰ τὸν νόμον.

44-47. Manumission decrees, of which there are over one
hundred examples from Chaeronea alone, all of about the same
period. Even from the same year some are in dialect, some in
the κοινή, and some in a mixture of both. In those given here
κοινή influence shows itself in ἀγαθήν no. 46, in the ζ of ζώωνθι,
ζῶνθι nos. 46, 47 (vs. δώει no. 44), κατὰ τὸν νόμον no. 47 (vs. κὰτ
τὸν νόμον no. 46), παραμείνασαν nos. 46, 47 (vs. παρμείναντα no.
44), in προθίκοντα no. 45 (vs. ποθίκων no. 44), in ποιούμενει no. 47
(vs. ποιόμενος no. 46 = ποιιόμενος). Note ει for usual υ from
οι (30) in εἴσι = οἴσει. For θοσίης no. 44, see 24.

As in similar decrees from other parts of Greece, the act of
manumission takes the form of a dedication or sale (ἀπέδοτο at
Delphi, e.g., no. 55) to the divinity of the local shrine, thus
securing religious sanction and protection of the rights of the
slave who has purchased his freedom. Often the manumission
does not go into immediate effect, but is subject to various
conditions, such as remaining in service during the lifetime of
the master (nos. 46, 47) or for a term of years (no. 44), payment
of an annuity, etc. Cf. no. 55.

Phocian

Delphian

48. Delphi. Early sixth (or late seventh?) century B.C.
Schwyzer 317. Solmsen-Fraenkel 47. Tod 3. Homolle, Comptes
Rendus 1924, 149 ff. Daux, BCH 61.61 ff.

A [Κλέοβις καὶ Βί]τōν τὰν ματάρα
  [illegible]
B ἐάγαγον τοὶ δυιοί
  [Πολυ]μέδες ἐποίϜεh' 'Αργεῖος.

Inscribed on the bases of the statues of Cleobis and Biton,

which, as Herodotus (1.31) tells us, the Argives made and set up at Delphi. Delphian dialect (cf. especially ματάρα) except the artist's signature, which is in Argive.

For the words following ματάρα Homolle's σταδίōς as a reading is declared impossible by Daux, and with it his enticing restoration, namely σταδίōς [τετρόϙοντα πέντ]ε, goes by the board. Further, it is most unlikely that the E, the first letter of B, goes with the preceding, and we must return to the old reading ἐάγαγον with syllabic augment. In the following the favorite reading τōι δυγōι must be rejected (Daux, l.c.). The letters ΤΟΙΔΥΙΟΙ are best taken as τοὶ δυιοί = τοὶ δοιοί, with υ by influence of δύο. For the probable reading ἐποίϜēh' 'Αργεῖος see Buck, CP 20.139.

49. Delphi. Early fifth century B.C. GDI 1683 (with II, p. 722). Roberts 229. Schwyzer 320. Bourguet, BCH 49.25 ff.

> Τοὶ πεντεκαίδεκα | τὸν Λαβυαδᾶν ΤΟΝ[..?] | Θρασύμαχον
> 5 καὶ Καμ|ιρέα ἐπὶ Τριχᾶ ἄρχον||το, κἀπέδειξαν μηᾶ|ς δεκατέτορες
> καὶ | hēμιμναῖον κα|ὶ δραχμὰς πεντέ|κοντα καὶ Ϝέξ.

'The Fifteen of the Labyadae (cf. no. 52) - - - - held office and disbursed certain sums.' The construction and sense of the intervening clause are obscure.

50. Delphi. Fifth century B.C. Schwyzer 321. Solmsen-Fraenkel 48.

> Τὸν Ϝοῖνον μὲ φάρεν ἐς τοῦ δρ|όμου· αἰ δέ κα φάρēι, hιλαξά-
> στō | τὸν θεὸν hōι κα κεραίεται καὶ | μεταθυσάτō κἀποτεισάτō
> 5 πέν||τε δραχμάς· τούτου δὲ τōι κατα|γορέσαντι τὸ hέμισσον.

The inscription is on a wall connected with the stadium, where there were no doubt shrines of divinities. Prohibitions of the removal of the sacrificial meat are well known. Here we have a prohibition of the removal of the wine. 'If one does carry it off, one must propitiate the god for whom it is prepared (mixed), make an offering in its place,' etc.

51. Delphi. Late fifth century B.C. Schwyzer 322.

ἅδε Δελφοῖς Φασēλίτας τὸν | πέλανον διδόμεν, τὸ(ν) δαμόσ|ιον
ἑπτὰ δραχμὰς Δελφίδες δ|ύ' ὀδελός, τὸν δὲ Ϝίδιον τέτορε|ς ὀδελός.
Τιμοδίκō καὶ 'Ιστιαί|ō θεαρόντōν, 'Ερύλō ἄρχοντος.

1. ᾱδε certainly adv. 'in this way' (not for ἔαδε as taken by some), as clearly shown by Cret. ᾱδ' ἔϝαδε (no. 116). See 132.6—
2 ff. For πελανός, see no. 7 A 25 ff., note.—τὸ(ν) δαμόσιον—, τὸν δὲ ϝίδιον 'the public'—'the private', agreeing with πέλανον. Cf. no. 53.
52. Delphi. About 400 B.C. GDI 2561. Schwyzer 323. Solmsen-Fraenkel 49. Ionic alphabet, but with ϝ, and ᛒ = h (in contrast to H = η); lengthened o usually OY, but sometimes O.

A

[ὁ δὲ hόρκος] | ἔστω · ‟ταγε[υ]σέω δι[καίως κ]|ατὰ τοὺν νόμους τᾱς [π]ό[λι]|ος καὶ τοὺς τῶν Λαβυαδ[ᾶν] | πὲρ τῶν ἀπελλαίων καὶ
5 τᾱ||ν δαρατᾶν · καὶ τὰ χρήματα | συμπραξέω κἀποδειξέω [δ|ι]καίως τοῖς Λαβυάδαις [κ]|ωὖτε κλεψέω οὖτε [β]λα[ψ]έω | οὖτε τέχναι
10 οὖτε μαχαν[ᾶ||ι] τῶν τῶλ Λαβυαδᾶν χρημ[ά]|των · καὶ τὸς ταγοὺ[ς ἐπ]αξέ|ω τὸν hόρκον τοὺς [ἐν ν]έω[τ]|α κὰτ τὰ γεγραμμένα. hόρ-
15 κ|ος · hυπίσχομαι ποὶ τοῦ Δι||ὸς τοῦ πατρώιου · εὐορκέο|ντι μέμ μοι ἀγαθὰ εἴη, αἰ δ' | ἐφιορκέοιμι [ϝε]κών, τὰ κα|κὰ ἀντὶ τῶν ἀγαθῶν.‟|
20 Ἔδοξε Λαβυάδαις Βουκατ||ίου μηνὸς δεκάται ἐπὶ Κ[ά]||μπου ἐν τᾶι ἀλίαι σὺμ ψάφ|οις ἑκατὸν ὀγδοήκοντα | δυοῖν · τοὺς ταγοὺς
25 μὴ δέκ|εσθαι μήτε δαρατᾶν γάμε||λα μήτε παιδῆια μήτ' ἀπελ|λαῖα, αἰ μὴ τᾱς πατριᾶς ἐπ|αινεούσας καὶ πληθυόσα|ς ᾱς κα ἦι. αἰ δέ
30 τί κα πὰρ νό|μον κελεύσωντι, τῶν κελε||υσάντων ὁ κίνδυνος ἔστω. | τὰ δὲ ἀπελλαῖα ἄγεν 'Απέλ|λαις καὶ μὴ ἄλλαι ἀμέραι | μήτε ἄγεν
35 τοὺς ἄγοντας μ|ήτε τοὺς ταγοὺς δέκεσθα||ι · αἰ δέ κα [δ]έξωνται ἄλλαι | ἀμέραι ἢ 'Απέλλαις, ἀποτε|ισάτω ϝέκαστος δέκα δρα|χμάς ·
40 ὁ δὲ χρήζων καταγορ|εῖν τῶν δεξαμένων ἐπὶ τῶ||ν hυστέρων ταγῶν καταγο|ρείτω ἐν τᾶι ἀλίαι τᾶι με|τὰ Βουκάτια, αἴ κ' ἀμφιλλέ|γωντι
45 τοὶ ταγοὶ τοὶ δεξά|μενοι. ἄγεν δὲ τἀπελλαῖα || ἀντὶ ϝέτεος καὶ τὰς δαρά|τας φέρεν. hόστις δέ κα μὴ | ἄγηι τἀπελλαῖα ἢ τὰν δαρ|άταν
50 μὴ φέρηι, ἀμμόνιον κ|ατθέτω στατῆρα ἐπὶ ϝεκα||τέρωι, τῶι δὲ hυσ|τέρωι ϝέ|τει ἀγέτω τἀπελλαῖα καὶ | τὰν δαράταν φερέτω · αἰ δέ | κα
55 μὴ ἄγηι, μηκέτι δεκέσθ|ων ἀμμόνια, ἀλλ' ἢ ἀγέτω ἀπ||ελλαῖα ἢ ἀποτεισάτω ϝίκ|ατι δραχμὰς ἢ hυπογραφό|μενος τόκιομ φερέτω ·
60 καὶ | τὰν δαράταν τῶι hυστέρω|ι ϝέτει φερέτω ἢ ἀποτεισ||[άτω - - -.

B

5 [1-4 fragmentary. τ]||οἱ Λαβυάδα[ι Εὐκλείοι]|ς περὶ τᾶν δα[ρα-

τᾶν ἐπι]‖κρινόντων καὶ ['Απέλλα]|ις περὶ τῶν ἀπελ[λαίων, | π]αρ-
10 εόντες μὴ μεῖδ[ς he||ν]ὸς καὶ hεκατόν · τὰ[ν δὲ] | ψᾶφον φερόντων
ἀνδ[εξ]‖άμενοι ποὶ τδ 'Απόλλω[ν]|ος καὶ τοῦ Ποτειδᾶνος | τοῦ φρα-
15 τρίου καὶ τοῦ Δ||ιὸς πατρώιου δικαίως | οἰσεῖν κὰτ τὸν νόμους | τῶν
Δελφῶν · κήπευχέσθ|ω δικαίως τὰν ψᾶφον φέ|ροντι πόλλ' ἀγαθὰ
20 τοὺ[ς ‖ θ]εοὺς διδόμεν, αἱ δὲ ἀ[δ]‖ίκως, τὰ κακά. τοῦτα δὲ τ|οἱ τα-
25 γοὶ ἐπιτελεόντω|ν καὶ τῶι δεομένωι συν|αγόντων τοὺς Λαβυάδα‖ς ·
αἱ δέ κα μὴ ποιῶντι κὰ|[τ] τὰ γεγραμμένα ἢ μὴ το|[ὺ]ς ταγοὺς τὸν
30 hόρκον ἐ|παγάγωντι, ἀποτεισάτ|[ω] Ϝέκαστος ἐπὶ Ϝεκατέ‖|[ρ]ωι
δέκα δραχμάς. hόστ|[ι]ς δέ κα μὴ ὀμόσηι, μὴ τα||[γ]ευέτω · αἱ δέ κ'
35 ἀνώμοτο|ς ταγεύηι, πεντήκοντα | δραχμὰς ἀποτεισάτω. ‖ αἱ δέ κα
δέξωνται τοὶ [τ]‖αγοὶ ἢ γάμελα ἢ παιδῆι|α πὰρ τὰ γράμματα, ἀπο-
40 τ|εισάτω πεντήκοντα δρ|αχμὰς Ϝέκαστος τῶν δε||ξαμένων · αἱ δέ κα
μὴ ἀπο|τείσηι, ἄτιμος ἔστω ἐγ | Λαβυαδᾶν καὶ ἐπὶ τούτ|ωι καὶ ἐπὶ
45 ταῖς ἄλλαις | ζαμίαις, hέντε κ' ἀποτε||ίσηι. καὶ hδ̄ κα δέξωντα|ι ἢ
δαράταν ἢ ἀπελλαῖα | πὰρ τὰ γράμματα, μὴ ἔστ|ω Λαβυάδας
50 μηδὲ κοινα|νείτω τῶν κοινῶν χρημ||άτων μηδὲ τῶν θεμάτων. | αἱ
δέ τίς κα τῶν ταγῶν κ|αταγορῆι ποιῆσαί τι π|ὰρ τὰ γράμματα, ho
55 δὲ ἀν|τι[φ]ᾶι, τοὶ ταγοὶ ἐν τᾶι ‖ - - - - - - - - - - - - -

C

[ὀμ|νύτω ποὶ τοῦ 'Απόλλωνος κ|αὶ Ποτειδᾶνος τοῦ φρ]ατ[ρ|ίου
καὶ Διός, καὶ δικ]άζο[ν|τι μὲν δικαίως ἐπ]ευχέσ[θ|ω πόλλ' ἀγαθὰ
5 τ]οὺς θεοὺς [δ||ιδόμεν, αἱ δ' ἐ|φιορκέοι, κα|[κά · αἱ δέ κα μ]ὴ δικά-
ζηι hαι|[ρεθείς, ἀπ]οτεισάτω πέντ|[ε δραχμάς], ἄλλον δ' ἀνθελό|[με
10 νοι τ]ὰν δίκαν τελεόντ||[ων. hόσ]τις δέ κα πὰρ νόμον | [τι] ποιέοντα
τᾶι δίκαι hέ|ληι, τὸ ἥμισσον ἐχέτω. το|ὶ δὲ ταγοὶ τῶι καταγορέ-
15 ον|τι τὰν δίκαν ἐπιτελεόν||των · αἱ δὲ μή, τὸ διπλόν Ϝέκ|αστος ἀπο-
τεισάτω. hόστι|[ς] δέ κα ζαμίαν ὀφείληι. ἄτ|[ι]μος ἔστω, hέντε
20 κ' ἀποτεί|σηι. — Ηόδ' ὁ τεθμὸς πὲρ τῶ||ν ἐντοφήιων. μὴ πλέον
πέν|τε, καὶ τριάκοντα δραχμ[ᾶ]|ν ἐνθέμεν μήτε πριάμενο|[ν] μήτε
25 Ϝοίκω · τὰν δὲ παχεῖ|[α]ν χλαῖναν φαωτὰν εἶμεν. ‖ αἱ δέ τι τούτων
παρβάλλο|ιτο, ἀποτεισάτω πεντήκο|ντα δραχμάς, αἴ κα μὴ ἐξομ|ό-
30 σηι ἐπὶ τῶι σάματι μὴ πλ|έον ἐνθέμεν. στρῶμα δὲ hὲ||ν hυποβαλέ-
τω καὶ ποικεφ|άλαιον hὲν ποτθέτω · τὸν δ|ὲ νεκρὸν κεκαλυμμένον
35 φ|ερέτω σιγᾶι, κήν ταῖς στρ|οφαῖς μὴ καττιθέντων μη||[δ]αμεῖ,
μηδ' ὀτοτυζόντων ἐ|[χ]θὸς τᾶς Ϝοικίας, πρίγ κ' ἐ|πὶ τὸ σᾶμα hί-
κωντι, τηνεῖ | δ' ἔναγος ἔστω, hέντε κα ha | θιγάνα ποτθεθῆι. τῶν

40 δὲ π‖ρόστα τεθνακότων ἐν τοῖς | σαμάτεσσι μὴ θρηνεῖν μη|δ᾽ ὀτοτύ-
ζεν, ἀλλ᾽ ἀπίμεν Ϝο|ίκαδε ἕκαστον ἔχθω hομε|στίων καὶ πατραδελ-
45 φεῶν ‖ καὶ πενθερῶν κήσγόνων [κ]|αὶ γαμβρῶν. μηδὲ τᾶι hυσ[τ]|ε-
ραία(ι) μηδ᾽ ἐν ταῖς δεκάτ[α]|ις μηδ᾽ ἐν τοῖς ἐνιαυτοῖ[ς | μ]ήτ᾽ οἰ-
50 μώζεν μήτ᾽ ὀτοτύ[ζε‖ν]· αἰ δέ τι τούτων παρβ|άλλοιτο τῶν γε-
γραμ|μένων - - - - - - -

D

. . . . αχα...δ...|. . . . . . θοῖναι δὲ ταίδ|[ε νόμιμ]οι·
5 'Απέλλαι καὶ Β‖[ουκά]τια, Ηραῖα, Δαιδαφ‖[όρια], Ποιτρόπια,
Βυσίου | [μην]ὸς τὰν hεβδέμαν καὶ | [τ]ὰν hενάταν, κηΰκλει[α
10 κ]‖ἀρταμίτια καὶ Λάφρι[α κ]‖αὶ Θεοξένια καὶ Τελχίν‖ια καὶ Διοσ-
κουρῆια, Μεγ|αλάρτια καὶ Ηηράκλει[α], | καΐ κ᾽ αὐτὸς θύηι hια-
15 ρῆ[ι]‖ον καΐ κα λεχχοῖ παρῆι [κ]‖αΐ κα ξένοι Ϝοι παρέωντ‖ι hιαρῆια
θύοντες καΐ κ|α πενταμαριτεύων τύχη|ι· αἰ δέ τι τούτων παρβάλ-|
20 λοιτο τῶν γεγραμμένων, | θωεόντων τοί τε δαμιορ‖γοὶ καὶ τοὶ ἄλλοι
πάντε|ς Λαβυάδαι, πρασσόντων | δὲ τοὶ πεντεκαίδεκα. α[ἰ] | δέ κα
25 ἀμφιλλέγηι τᾶς θω|ιάσιος, ἐξομόσας τὸν νό‖[μιμ]ον hόρκον λελύ-
σθω. α‖[ἰ δ᾽ ἀ]λίαν ποιόντων ἄρχω‖[ν ἀ]πείη, ἀποτεισάτω ὀδε|λόν,
30 καὶ συγχέοι, ἀποτει|σάτω ὀδελόν. τοιάδε κῆν ‖ Φανατεῖ γέγραπται
ἐν [τ]‖ᾶι πέτραι ἔνδω· "τάδε Φά[ν]|οτος ἐπέδωκε τᾶι θυγατ|ρὶ
35 Βουζύγαι, τὰ hῆμιρρ[ή]‖νια κῆκ τᾶς δυωδεκατδο‖ς χίμαιραν καὶ
τήμπροναίαν δάρματα καὶ τὰ τῶι | Λυκείωι δάρματα καὶ τὰ|ν ἀγαί-
40 αν μόσχον." πάντων | καὶ Ϝιδίων καὶ δαμοσίω‖ν τὸμ προθύοντα
καὶ προ|μαντευόμενον παρέχεν | τὰ γεγραμμέ·:α Λαβυάδα|ις· τᾶι
45 δὲ θυσίαι Λαβυαδ‖ᾶν τὠπελλαίου μηνὸς τῶ‖ι Διονύσωι, Βουκατίοις|
τῶι Δὶ πατρωίωι καὶ τὠπ|όλλωνι τὰν ἀκρόθινα κα|ὶ συμπιπίσκεν
50 hαμεῖ το|ὺς Λαβυάδας· τὰς δ᾽ ἄλλας ‖ θοίνας κὰ[τ] τὰν hώραν
ἀπ|άγεσθαι.

Regulations of the phratry of the Labyadae.

A 3. **τοὺν νόμους**: τοὺς νόμους. So τὸν νόμους B 16, but usually
ς unassimilated. **97.1.—4. ἀπελλαίων**: 'victims for the 'Απέλλαι.'
Cf. ll. 44-46 where ἄγεν is used with ἀπελλαῖα, in contrast to
φέρεν with δαράτας. 'Απέλλαι is the name of the Delphian festival
corresponding to the Attic 'Απατούρια, at which children were
introduced into the phratries and offerings for the occasion were
made by the parents.—**5. δαρατᾶν**: 'cakes.' Ath. 3.110d, 114b

No. 52]   PHOCIAN INSCRIPTIONS   243

cites a δάρατον meaning 'unleavened bread' and says the word
was used by the Thessalians. The δαράται at the Delphian
festival were of two kinds (cf. l. 25), the γάμελα or cakes offered
in behalf of the newly married wives that were introduced into
the phratry by their husbands, and the παιδῆια offered for the
children that were introduced into the phratry by their parents.
—6. συμπραξέω κἀποδειξέω: 'I will collect and disburse.'
ἀποδείκνυμι, like Att. ἀποφαίνω, 'render account for, pay over.'
Cf. ἀπέδειξαν no. 49.—6/7 [κ]ωὔτε, new corrected reading. BCH
61.69. See 94.7.—10. τῶλ Λαβυαδᾶν: τῶν Λαβ-, elsewhere
unassimilated, as l. 3. 96.3.—11. 'I will impose the oath upon
the ταγοί for the next year.' Cf. B 27.

23 ff. 'The ταγοί are to receive neither, in the case of the
cakes (lit. of the cakes), the γάμελα or the παιδῆια, nor the
ἀπελλαῖα, unless the gens to which one belongs approves in full
session.' The approval of the gens (πατριά, as in Elis; πάτρα in
most Doric dialects) was a prerequisite to the introduction
into the phratry, which was the larger body including several
gentes.—30. ὁ: without h, as also A 38, C 19, but ho (demonst.)
B 53, hόδε C 19. Cf. ἆς A 28 beside hō B 45, hόστις A 46, B 30,
C 19. See 58a.—38 ff. 'Any one who wishes to accuse the ταγοί
of having received the offering at other than the stated times
shall bring the charge when their successors are in office.'—
45. ἀντὶ Ϝέτεος: 'by the year, annually.' 136.8.—56 'Or let him
sign a note (for the twenty drachmas) and pay interest.'

B 11-12. ἀνδεξάμενοι: 'undertaking, promising.' They swear
by the gods of the city, phratry, and gens.—23/24. 'The ταγοι
shall carry out these prescriptions and in case of need (so τῶί
δεομένωι, Vollgraff) convene the Labyadae.'—50. θεμάτων:
probably 'established rites, institutions,' though this meaning
of θέμα is not quotable. Cf. τεθμός = θεσμός 'law, ordinance,'
C 19.

C 1 ff. Oath of the person appointed to act as judge. The
missing conclusion of B must have been the provision for such
an appointment.—6 ff. 'If the one chosen fails to serve as
judge, he shall pay five drachmas, and (the ταγοί) shall bring the
case to issue by appointing another in his place. Whoever convicts
one guilty of an unlawful action shall receive half the fine' (cf.

no. 19.24/25).—19 ff. Law concerning funeral rites. Like the law of Iulis in Ceos (no. 8), this is directed against extravagance. —20 ff. 'One shall not expend more than thirty-five drachmas, either by purchase or (in articles taken) from the home.'— 23/24. 'The shroud shall be thick and of a light gray color.' For φαωτός = *φαιωτός, see 31, and, as used of mourning apparel, cf. φαιὰ ἱμάτια Polyb. 30.4, 5, and φαιὰ ἐσθής Ditt. Syll. 879.5— 25 ff. 'If one transgresses (παρβάλλω = παραβαίνω) any of these things, he shall pay fifty drachmas, unless he denies under oath at the tomb that he has spent more.'—29 ff. στρῶμα δὲ κτλ.: cf. no. 8.3/4.—31 ff. τὸν δὲ νεκρὸν κτλ.: cf. no. 8.10/11.—33 ff. κὴν ταῖς στροφαῖς κτλ.: 'they shall not set the corpse down anywhere at the turns of the road (but carry it straight on to the tomb without interruption), nor shall they make lamentations outside the house until they arrive at the tomb, but there there shall be a ceremony for the dead (? cf. ἐναγίζω) until the lid (?) is closed (cf. προστίθημι τὰς θύρας, etc.).' But the last part, from τηνεῖ on, is variously read and interpreted.—39 ff. 'There shall be no mourning for the former dead, but every one shall go home, except the members of the immediate family and the near relatives by blood or marriage.'—46 ff. 'There shall be no wailing or lamentation on the following days, nor on the tenth day, nor on the anniversaries.'—ἐνιαυτοῖς: See Glossary, and cf. τὰ ἐνιαύσια in the same sense at Ceos.

D 1 ff. Enumeration of the regular feasts. These are given in the order of their occurrence, as appears from the correspondence between many of them and the names of the months ('Απελλαῖος, Βουκάτιος, 'Ηραῖος, etc.).—5-7. 'Those which occur on the seventh and the ninth of the month Βύσιος.'—7/8. κηὕκλεια κάρταμίτια: καὶ Εὔκλεια καὶ 'Αρταμίτια.—12 ff. Feasts are also held 'if one sacrifices a victim for himself, if one assists (in the sacrifices for the purification of) a woman recently delivered of child, if there are strangers with him sacrificing victims, and if one is serving as πενταμαρίτας.' πενταμαρίτας is the name of some official appointed to serve five days (cf. Locr. πεντάμεροι, Halae), but nothing more is known about this office.—22. τοὶ πεντεκαί-δεκα: cf. no. 49.—26/27. 'If, when they hold an assembly, any official is absent.' ἄρχων nom. sg. ppl. 'one holding office.'—

29 ff. 'These things are written at Phanoteus on the inner side of the rock.' The ancient city of Phanoteus (Panopeus) was perhaps the original seat of the phratry of the Labyadae.—30. **Φανατεῖ**: cf. Φάνοτος ll. 30-31. Both Φανατεύς and Φανοτεύς occur in other inscriptions. See 46.—35. **τήμπροναίαν**: τὰ ἐμ Προναίαν. Cf. ἰαρήιον ἐμ Προναίαν of another inscription.—38. **τὰν ἀγαίαν μόσχον**: the 'admirable' or 'holy' calf (cf. glosses in Hesych., Et. M. and especially in the late Favor. Cam. ἀγαῖος· κατὰ τοὺς παλαιοὺς σεμνός, καλός, λαμπρός, κόσμιος).—38 ff. **πάντων** κτλ.: 'in the case of all undertakings, both private and public, for which one offers sacrifice or consults the oracle in advance, the one doing so shall furnish to the Labyadae the victims mentioned.' πάντων depends upon προθύοντα and προμαντευόμενον 'sacrificing etc. in advance of.'—47. **τὰν ἀκρόθινα** (ἀκρόθις = usual ἀκροθίνιον, as also in Pindar): sc. ταγοὺς παρέχεν 'the ταγοί shall furnish the first-fruits.'—48 f. **συμπιπίσκεν** κτλ.: 'invite the Labyadae to drink together.'—49 ff. **τὰς δ᾽ ἄλλας** κτλ.: 'the other feasts one shall carry out in accordance with the season.'

53. Delphi. Second quarter (?) fourth century B.C. P. Amundry, BCH 63.183 ff. Ll. 19-36 are omitted here.

Σ[κια]θίων |δά[μωι κα]ὶ ἀποίκοις · | τάδ[ε] ξύνθετα Δελ|φο[ῖς]
5 καὶ Σκιαθίο||ις · ἔ[δ]ωκαν προμαν|τεί[α]ν καὶ ἀτέλει|αν πά[ντ]ων
10 νόσφι π|ελαν[ō] · πελανὸν δ[ὲ] | τὸν μ[ὲν] δαμόσιον || στατῆ[ρ]α
αἰγιναῖ|ον, τὸν [δ]ὲ ἴδιον δύ|ο ὀδελώ · ἐς τὸ δέρμ|α τὸ δαμόσιον
15 δύο | ὀδελ[ώ], τὸ δὲ ἴδιον || ὀδελόν · αἴ κ᾽ ἐπὶ φρ|υκτώ παρίηι, τὸ
μὲ|ν δαμόσιον στ[α]τῆ|[ρ]α αἴ[γιναῖον, τόδ|ε ἴδιον] - - -

For πελανός see no. 7 A 25 ff., note.—For τὸν δαμόσιον, etc., see no. 51.—15/16 f. **αἴ κ᾽ἐπὶ φρυκτώ παρίηι**: 'if anyone presents himself for the (drawing of lots by means of) two beans.' The use of beans in drawing lots is recorded in Plut. Mor. 492 A, B, where φρυκτός is also used, and indicated by various glosses.

54. Delphi. Between 240 and 200 B.C. GDI 2653. Schwyzer 332.

Ἀγαθᾶι τύχαι. Δελφοὶ ἔδωκαν Νικάνδρωι | Ἀναξαγόρου Κολοφωνίωι, ἐπέων ποητᾶι, αὐ|τῶι καὶ ἐγγόνοις προξενίαν, προμαν-
5 τείαν, | ἀσυλίαν, προδικίαν, ἀτέλειαν πάντων, προε||δρίαν ἐν πάν-

τεσι τοῖς ἀγώνοις οἷς ἁ πόλις τί|θητι καὶ τἆλλα ὅσα καὶ τοῖς ἄλλοις
προξένοις καὶ | εὐεργέταις τᾶς πόλιος τῶν Δελφῶν· ἄρχοντος |
Νικοδάμου, βουλευόντων Ἀρίστωνος, Νικοδάμου, Πλεί|στωνος,
Ξένωνος, Ἐπιχαρίδα.

Proxeny decree in honor of the poet Nicander of Colophon,
whose writings included a prose work on Aetolia. At this time
the Aetolians were dominant in Delphi, and this shows itself
in the language of the inscriptions. See **279**. Note in l. 5 the
combination of Delph. πάντεσι with Aetol. ἀγώνοις.

55· Delphi. 186 B.C. GDI 2034. Schwyzer 335.

Ἄρχοντος [Ν]ικοβούλου μηνὸς Βουκατίου, ἐπὶ τοῖσδε ἀπέδοτο
Νεοπάτρα Ὀρθαίου | Δελφὶς τῶι Ἀπόλλωνι τῶι Πυθίωι σώματα
γυναικεῖα δύο αἷς ὀνόματα Ζωπύ|ρα, Σωσίχα, τιμᾶς ἀργυρίου μνᾶν
ἕξ, καθὼς ἐπίστευσαν Ζωπύρα, Σωσίχα τῶι | θεῶι τὰν ὠνάν,
5 ἐφ᾽ ὧιτε ἐλευθέρας εἶμεν καὶ ἀνεφάπτους ἀπὸ πάντων τὸμ || πάντα
βίον. βεβαιωτὴρ κατὰ τὸν νόμον· Δαμένης Ὀρέστα Δελφός. πα-
ραμε[ι]νάν|των δὲ Ζωπύρα, Σωσίχα παρὰ Νεοπάτραν ἄχρι κα ζώηι
Νεοπάτρα ποέουσαι | τὸ ποτιτασσόμενον πᾶν τὸ δυνατὸν ἀνεγκλή-
τως· εἰ δέ τί κα μὴ ποιέωντι | Ζωπύρα ἢ Σωσίχα τῶν ποτιτασσο-
μένων ὑπὸ Νεοπάτρας καθὼς | γέγραπται δυναταὶ οὖσαι, ἐξέστω
10 Νεοπάτραι κολάζειν καθώς || κα αὐτὰ δείληται καὶ ἄλλωι ὑπὲρ
Νεοπάτραν ἀζαμίοις ὄντοις καὶ ἀνυ|ποδίκοις πάσας δίκας καὶ
ζαμίας. εἰ δέ τί κα πάθηι Νεοπάτρα, ἐλεύθεραι | ἔστων Ζωπύρα
καὶ Σωσίχα κυριεύουσαι αὐτοσαυτᾶν καὶ ποέουσαι ὅ κα θέλων|τι,
καθὼς ἐπίστευσαν τῶι θεῶι τὰν ὠνάν. εἰ δέ τίς κα ἅπτηται Ζω-
πύρας | ἢ Σωσίχας ἐπεί κα τελευτάσηι Νεοπάτρα, βέβαιον παρε-
15 χέτω ὁ βεβαιωτὴρ τῶι || θεῶι τὰν ὠνὰν κατὰ τὸν νόμον. ὁμοίως δὲ
καὶ οἱ παρατυγχάνοντες κύριοι ἐόν|των συλέοντες ὡς ἐλευθέρας οὔ-
σας ἀζάμιοι ὄντες καὶ ἀνυπόδικοι | πάσας δίκας καὶ ζαμίας. εἰ δέ
τί κα ἀζετωθέωντι περὶ Νεοπάτραν πεπο|νηρευμέναι ἢ τῶν Νεοπά-
τρας ὑπαρχόντων τι, κύριοι ἐόντω οἱ ἐπίνομοι κολά|ζοντες αὐτὰς
20 καθ᾽ ὅτι κα αὐτοῖς δοκῆι ἀζάμιοι ὄντες καὶ ἀνυπόδικοι || πάσας
δίκας. μάρτυρες· τοὶ ἱερεῖς Ξένων, Ἄθαμβος, τῶν ἀρχόντων Εὐ-
κλείδας, | ἰδιῶται Ἱεροκλῆς, Χαρίξενος, Βάχχιος.

A typical Delphian manumission decree, of which there are
more than 1,600. See note to nos. 44-47. They show all varieties
of mixture of Delphian, Northwest Greek κοινή, and Attic

elements, e.g., in this inscription, 3 pl. imv. ἐόντω, ἐόντων, ἔστων. Nearly always at this time, the older αἰ, ἱαρός are replaced by εἰ, ἱερός, and τοί by οἱ, though τοί is frequently retained in the formal τοὶ ἱερεῖς beginning the list of witnesses.—17. ἀζετω-θέωντι κτλ.: 'are convicted of having done any wrong to Neopatra or her possessions.' Cf. ἐξελεγχθείησαν in another of the manumission decrees, and Hesych. ἄζετον· ἄπιστον, Σικελοί.

Exclusive of Delphi

56. Stiris. About 180 B.C. IG IX.i.32. GDI 1539. Ditt. Syll. 647. Schwyzer 353. Solmsen-Fraenkel 50.

A

[Θ]εὸς τύχαν ἀγα‖[θ]άν. στραταγέοντος | [τ]ῶν Φωκέων Ζευ-
5 ξίου, | [μ]ηνὸς ἑβδόμου, ὁμολο[γ‖ί]α τᾶ πόλει Στειρίων καὶ | [τᾶ]
πόλει Μεδεωνίων· συ[ν|ε]πολίτευσαν Στείριοι κα[ὶ | Μ]εδεώνιοι
10 ἔχοντες ἱερά, πό|[λι|ν], χώραν, λιμένας, πάντα || [ἐ]λεύθερα, ἐπὶ
τοῖσδε. εἶμεν | [τ]οὺς Μεδεωνίους πάντας | [Σ]τιρίους ἴσους καὶ
ὁμοίους, | καὶ συνεκλησιάζειν καὶ συ|ναρχοστατεῖσθαι μετὰ τᾶς ||
15 [πό]λιος τᾶς Στιρίων, καὶ δικά|[ζ]ειν τὰς δίκας τὰς ἐπὶ πόλι|[ο]ς
πάσας τοὺς ἐνικομένους | [τ]αῖς ἁλικίαις. ἱστάνθω δὲ κα[ὶ | ἱ]εροτα-
20 μίαν ἐκ τῶν Μεδεω‖|[ν]ίων ἕνα τὸν θυσέοντα τὰς | θυσίας τὰς πα-
τρίους Μεδεων|[ί]οις, ὅσαι ἐντὶ ἐν τῷ πολιτικῷ νόμ[ω, | μ]ετὰ τῶν
25 ἀρχόντων τῶν στα|[θ]έντων ἐν Στίρι· λανβανέτω || [δ]ὲ ὁ ἱεροτα-
μίας ἀρέσμιον, ὃ τ[οὶ | ἄ]ρχοντες ἐλάμβανον, ἡμι|[μ]ναῖον καὶ
τῶν χοῶν τὸ ἐπ[ι|β]αλὸν τῷ ἱεροταμίαι. συνδι|[κ]αξεῖ δὲ ὁ ἱεροτα-
30 μίας μετὰ || [τ]ῶν ἀρχόντων τὰς δίκας, ἃς | [τ]οὶ ἄρχοντες δικά-
ζοντι, καὶ ![κ]λαρωσῖ τὰ δικαστήρια, ἄ κα | δέη κλαρώειν, μετὰ τῶν
35 ἀ[ρ]‖χόντων. μὴ ἔστω δὲ ἐπάναγ‖|[κ]ες λειτουργεῖν τοὺς Μεδε-|
ωνίους ἐν Στίρι τὰς ἀρχάς, ὅσοι | γεγένηνται ἐν Μεδεῶνι ἄρ|χοντες,
40 ξενοδίκαι, πρακτῆρες, | δαμιουργοί, ἱερεῖς, ἱεράρχαι, καὶ || τᾶν
γυναικῶν ὅσαι ἱερητεύ|κατι, εἰ μή τις ἑκὼν ὑπομένοι · | ἱστάνθων
δὲ ἐκ τῶν ἀλειτου|ργήτων τῶν Μεδεωνίων κ|αὶ ἐκ τῶν Στιρίων·
δαμιουρ‖|[γ]εόντων δὲ καὶ τὰ ἐν Μεδε|[ῶνι ἱ]ερὰ καθὼς ὁ πολιτι-
45 κὸς νό|μος κελεύει. καὶ τὰν χ[ώ|ραν] τὰν Μεδεωνίαν εἶμεν |[π]ᾶσαν
50 Στιρίαν καὶ τὰν Στι‖|ρίαν Μεδεωνίαν κοινὰν π[ᾶ|σα]ν. κοινω-
νεόντω δὲ οἱ Μεδε|[ώ]νιοι τᾶν θυσιᾶν τᾶν ἐν Στί|[ρι] πασᾶν καὶ τοὶ

55 <τοὶ> Στίριοι τᾶν ἐν Με|δεῶνι πασᾶν. μὴ ἐξέστω δ||ὲ ἀποπολιτεύ-
σασται τού[ς] | Μεδεωνίους ἀπὸ τῶν Στιρί|[ω]ν μηδὲ τοὺς Στι-
ρίους ἀπὸ | [τ]ῶν Μεδε[ωνί]ων. ὁπότεροι | [δ]έ κα μὴ ἐμμείνωντι
60 ἐν τοῖ||[ς] γεγραμμένοις, ἀποτει|σάντων τοῖς ἐμμεινά[ν]||τοις ἀρ-
γυρίου τάλαν|τα δέκα.

B

[.......... π]οιεόντων · | [γ]ραψάντων δὲ τὰν ὁμ[ο]||λογίαν ἐν
5 στάλαν καὶ ἀν[αθέ]||ντων ἐν τὸ ἱερὸν τᾶς 'Α[θάν]||ας, θέστων δὲ
τὰν ὁμο[λογί]||αν καὶ παρὰ ἰδιώταν ἐσ[φρα]||γισμέναν. ἁ ὁμολογία
10 π[αρὰ] | Θράσωνα Λιλαιέα. μάρ[τυ]||ρες Θράσων Δαματρίου 'Ε|||λα-
τεύς, Εὐπαλίδας Θρά|σωνος Λιλαιεύς, Τιμο|κράτης 'Επινίκου Τι-
15 θορρε|ύς. δόντων δὲ τοὶ Στίριοι | τᾶ φατρία τῶν Μεδεωνί||ων ἐν
ἐτέοις τέτταροις | ἀργυρίου μνᾶς πέντε κα[ὶ | τ]όπον τὰν καλειμέ-
ναν | [Δ]α[μα]τρείαν.

Agreement establishing a συμπολιτεία or joint-citizenship
between the Stirians and Medeonians.

10. ἐλεύθερα 'free, open to all' (of both towns).—11 ff. τοὺς
κτλ.: 'all the Medeonians shall be Stirians with equal rights, and
shall join with the city of the Stirians in the assembly and in
appointing magistrates, and those who have arrived at proper
age shall try all cases which come before the state.'—18. ἰστάνθω:
Boeotian for ἰστάντω. So θέλωνθι in another Stirian inscription.
Cf. also κλαρωσῖ l. 32 with Boeot. ι for ει. See 231.—34 ff. μὴ
ἔστω κτλ.: 'those who have been officials in Medeon shall be
exempt from compulsory office holding in Stiris.'—40-41.
ἱερητεύκατι: 138.4.—55. ἀποπολιτεύσασται: στ = σθ as in
θέστων B 5. 85.1.

B 13 ff. The phratry of the Medeonians, in distinction from
the state, retained its own organization, and was to receive a
subsidy of money and land from the Stirians.

Locrian

57. Oeanthea (Galaxidi). Early fifth century B.C. IG IX.i.334.
GDI 1478. Roberts 231 and pp. 346 ff. Schwyzer 362. Ditt. Syll.
47. Solmsen-Fraenkel 44. Tod 24.

Ἐν Ναύπακτον κὰ τόνδε hἀπιϜοικία. ΛοϘρὸν τὸν Ηυποκνα-
μίδιον, ἐπ|εί κα Ναυπάκτιος γένεται, Ναυπάκτιον ἐόντα, hόπō
ξένον ὅσια λανχάν|ειν καὶ θύειν ἐξεῖμεν ἐπιτυχόντα, αἴ κα δείλε̄-
ται· αἴ κα δείλεται, θύειν καὶ λ|ανχάνειν κε̄ δάμō κε̄ Ϙοινάνōν αὐ-
5 τὸν καὶ τὸ γένος καταιϜεί. τέλος το||ὺς ἐπιϜοίϘους ΛοϘρō̄ν τō̄ν
Ηυποκναμιδίōν με̄ φάρειν ἐν ΛοϘροῖς τοῖ|ς Ηυποκναμιδίοις, φρίν
κ' αὖ τις ΛοϘρὸς γένεται τō̄ν Ηυποκναμιδίōν. αἰ | δείλε̄τ' ἀνχō-
ρεῖν, καταλείποντα ἐν τᾶι ἰστίαι παῖδα hε̄βατὰν ε̄̀ 'δελφεὸν ἐξ|εῖ-
μεν ἄνευ ἐνετε̄ρίōν· αἴ κα hυπ' ἀνάνκας ἀπελάōνται ἐ Ναυπάκτō
Λοϙ|ροὶ τοὶ Ηυποκναμίδιοι, ἐξεῖμεν ἀνχōρεῖν, hόπō Ϝέκαστος ἔν,
10 ἄνευ ἐ||ϝετε̄ρίōν. τέλος με̄ φάρειν μεδὲν hότι με̄ μετὰ ΛοϘρō̄ν τō̄ν
Ϝεσπαρί|ōν. — Α — "ΕνορϘον τοῖς ἐπιϜοίϘοις ἐν Ναύπακτον με̄
'ποστᾶμεν ἀ(π' 'Ο)ποντίōν | τέκναι καὶ μαχανᾶι μεδεμιᾶι ϜεϘόντας.
τὸν hόρϙον ἐξεῖμεν, αἴ κα δεί|λōνται, ἐπάγειν μετὰ τριάϘοντα Ϝέτεα
ἀπὸ τō̄ hόρϙō hεκατὸν ἄνδρας 'Ο|ποντίοις Ναυπακτίōν καὶ Ναυ-
15 πακτίοις 'Οποντίους. — Β — Hόσστις κα λιποτελέε̄||ι ἐγ Ναυ-
πάκτō τō̄ν ἐπιϜοίϘōν, ἀπὸ ΛοϘρō̄ν εἶμεν, ἔντε κ' ἀποτείσει τὰ
νό|μια Ναυπακτίοις. — Γ — Αἴ κα με̄ γένος ἐν τᾶι ἰστίαι ε̄̀ι ε̄̀
'χεπάμōν τō̄ν ἐπι|ϜοίϘōν ε̄̀ι ἐν Ναυπάκτōι, ΛοϘρō̄ν τō̄ν Ηυποκναμι-
δίōν τὸν ἐπάνχισ|τον κρατεῖν, ΛοϘρō̄ν hόπō κ' ε̄̀ι, αὐτὸν ἰόντα, αἴ
κ' ἀνε̄̀ρ ε̄̀ι ε̄̀ παῖς, τριō̄ν μ|ε̄νō̄ν· αἰ δὲ μέ, τοῖς Ναυπακτίοις νομίοις
20 χρε̄σται. — Δ — 'Ε Ναυπάκτō ἀνχōρέ||οντα ἐν ΛοϘρὺς τοὺς
Ηυποκναμιδίους ἐν Ναυπάκτōι καρῦξαι ἐν τά|ιγοραῖ, κε̄ν ΛοϘροῖς
τοῖ(ς)· Ηυποκναμιδίοις ἐν τᾶι πόλι, hō̄ κ' ε̄̀ι, καρῦξαι ἐν | τάγοραῖ.
— Ε — ΠερϘοθαριᾶν καὶ Μυσαχέōν ἐπεί κα Ναυπάκτι(ός τι)ς
γένετα|ι αὐτός, καὶ τὰ χρέματα τὲν Ναυπάκτōι τοῖς ἐν Ναυπάκτōι
χρε̄σται, | τὰ δ' ἐν ΛοϘροῖς τοῖς Ηυποκναμιδίοις χρέματα τοῖς
25 Ηυποκναμιδί||οις ||| νομίοις χρε̄σται, hόπōς ἀ πόλις Ϝεκάστōν νομί-
ζει ΛοϘρō̄ν τō̄ν Ηυποκν|αμιδίōν. αἴ τις hυπὸ τō̄ν νομίōν τō̄ν ἐπι-
ϜοίϘōν ἀνχōρέε̄ι ΠερϘοθαριᾶ|ν καὶ Μυσαχέōν, τοῖς αὐτō̄ν νομίοις
χρε̄σται κατὰ πόλιν Ϝεκάστους. | — F — Αἴ κ' ἀδελφεοὶ ἔōντι τō̄
30 'ν Ναύπακτον Ϝοικέοντος, hόπōς καὶ ΛοϘρō̄||ν τō̄ν Ηυποκναμιδίōν
Ϝεκάστōν νόμος ἐστί, αἴ κ' ἀποθάνει, τō̄ν χ|ρε̄μάτōν κρατεῖν τὸν
ἐπίϜοιϘον, τὸ κατιϙόμενον κρατεῖν. — Ζ — | Τοὺς ἐπιϜοίϘους ἐν
Ναύπακτον τὰν δίκαν πρόδιϜον hαρέσται πὸ τοὺς δ|ικαστε̄ρας,
hαρέσται καὶ δόμεν ἐν 'Οπόεντι κατὰ Ϝέος αὐταμαρόν. Λοϙ|ρō̄ν τō̄ν
35 Ηυποκναμιδίōν προστάταν καταστᾶσαι τὸν ΛοϘρō̄ν τōπιϜ||οίϘōι
καὶ τὸν ἐπιϜοίϘōν τō̄ι ΛοϘρō̄ι, hοίτινες κα 'πιατὲς ἔντιμοι <ες>

(ἔϙντι). — Η — Ηόσσ|τις κ' ἀπολίπε̄ι πατάρα καὶ τὸ μέρος τõν χρε̄μάτōν τō͂ι πατρί, ἐπεί κ' | ἀπογένε̄ται, ἐξεῖμεν ἀπολαχεῖν τὸν ἐπίϜοιϘον ἐν Ναύπακτον. | — Θ — Ηόσστις κα τὰ ϜεϜαδεϘόϝτα διαφθείρει τέχναι καὶ μαχαναῖ κα|ὶ μιᾶι, ηότι κα μὲ̄ ἀνφοτάροις

40 δοκέε̄ι, Ηοποντίōν τε χιλίōν πλέ̄θ||αι καὶ ΝαϜπακτίōν τõν ἐπιϜοίϘōν πλέ̄θαι, ἄτιμον εἶμεν καὶ χρέ̄|ματα παματοφαγεῖσται. τὸνκαλει- μένōι τὰν δίκαν δόμεν τὸν ἀρ|χόν, ἐν τριάϘοντ' ἀμάραις δόμεν, αἴ κα τριάκοντ' ἀμάραι λείπōντ|αι τᾶς ἀρχᾶς· αἴ κα μὲ̄ διδōι τō͂ι ἐνκα- λειμένōι τὰν δίκαν, ἄτιμ|ον εἶμεν καὶ χρέματα παματοφαγεῖσται,

45 τὸ μέρος μετὰ Ϝο||ικιατᾶν. διομόσαι ηόρϘον τὸν νόμιον. ἐν ὑδρίαν τὰν ψάφιξ|ξιν εἶμεν. καὶ τὸ θέθμιον τοῖς Ηυποκναμιδίοις ΛοϘροῖς ταὺ|τᾶ τέλεον εἶμεν Χαλειέοις τοῖς σὺν 'Αντιφάται Ϝοικέταις.

Law governing the relations between the Eastern Locrian colonists at Naupactus and the mother country. This does not refer to the founding of Naupactus, which was much earlier. Colonists are called ἄποικοι from the point of view of the mother country, but ἔποικοι as here (ἐπίϜοιϘοι) from the point of view of their new home. The Eastern Locrians are referred to ethnically as Hypocnemidians (of which Epicnemidians is an equivalent), politically as Opuntians, since Opus was the seat of government, the two terms standing in the same relation as Boeotian and Theban.

It is probable that one copy was set up at Opus, with another at Naupactus, and that the present tablet is still another copy, which with the addition of the last sentence, stating that similar relations are to subsist between colonists from Chaleion and the mother city, was set up at Chaleion, from which place it may easily have found its way to Galaxidi.

In both this and the following inscription double consonants (in part involving assimilation) are usually simplified in external combination (see **89**.7). So ἐ δάμο, ἐ λιμένος, etc., with assimilation of ἐκ (**100**); similarly ἐ Ναυπάκτō (once ἐγ Ναυπάκτō), in contrast to which ἐν Ναύπακτον, ἐν Ναυπάκτōι with original ἐν are always written out. Simplification of σσ in (no. 58) αἴ τι συλō͂ι, ἀνάτō συλēν, ἀδίκō συλēν = αἴ τις, etc., in view of which ηόπō ξένον (no. 57.2) = ηόπōς ξένον, though not quite parallel, is probable. No other Greek inscription has so many examples of Ϙ as no. 57, where it is uniformly employed before o or ρο. In no. 58 it is no longer used. In no. 57 lengthened ε is expressed by EI, lengthened o by O in the genitive singular, OV in the accusative plural. But in no. 58 always E and O. See **25d**. No. 57, beginning in l. 11, is divided into paragraphs by the letters Α-Θ.

No. 57 exhibits many instances of repetition (see l. 3, note), and some of omission of what is essential to clearness (e.g., the subject of ἀποθάνει l. 30), and in general the style of both inscriptions is crude and obscure.

1. 'The colony to Naupactus on the following terms.'— **hἀπιϝοιϰία**: hα ἐπιϝοιϰία. **94**.5.—**ϰὰ τõνδε**: **136**.5.—**Λοϙρὸν τὸν Ηυποϰναμίδιον** ϰτλ.: 'A Hypocnemidian Locrian, when he becomes a Naupactian, being a Naupactian, may as a ξένος share in the social and religious privileges (i.e., in the mother country) when he happens to be present, if he wishes. If he wishes, he may share in these privileges, both those of the people and those of the members of the societies, himself and his descendants forever. The colonists of the H. Locrians are not to pay taxes among the H. Locrians, until one becomes a H. Locrian again.' In ὅσια λανγάνειν ϰαὶ θύειν there is probably the same contrast as in ἱερὰ ϰαὶ ὅσια or Cretan θεῖνα ϰαὶ ἀνθρώπινα.—3. **αἴ ϰα δείλεται**: for the repetition cf. also ἔῐ ll. 16 f., δόμεν ll. 41 f., ϰαρῦξαι ἐν τάγορᾶι ll. 20 ff. —4. **ϰὲ δάμõ ϰὲϙοινάνõν**: ϰαὶ ἐϰ δήμου ϰαὶ ἐϰ ϰοινωνῶν. **94**.6, **100**.—7 ff. 'If a colonist wishes to return, he may do so without taxes of admission (to citizenship), provided he leaves behind in his house an adult son or brother. If the H. Locrians are driven from Naupactus by force, they may return without admission taxes to the town from which they each came. They are to pay no taxes except in common with the Western Locrians,' i.e., they are not to be subject to any special taxes as colonists.—**αἰ δείλετ'**: for subj. without ϰα (also in l. 26), see **174**.—9. **hόπõ ϝέϰαστος ἐν**: a 3 sg. ἦν is otherwise known only in Attic-Ionic, other dialects retaining the original ἦς. See **163**.3. Hence this is the 3 pl. ἦν agreeing with the logical subject they (cf. the preceding). Cf. Hom. ἔβαν οἰϰόνδε ἕϰαστος, etc.—11 ff. 'The colonists to Naupactus must take oath not to forsake the alliance with the Opuntians willingly by any device. If they wish they may impose the oath thirty years after this

oath, one hundred Naupactians upon the Opuntians and the
Opuntians upon the Naupactians.'—11. ἔνορϙον: used impersonally with the dative, like ἔνδικον in Cretan etc.—14 ff.
'Whoever of the colonists departs from Naupactus with unpaid
taxes shall lose his rights as a Locrian until he pays the Naupactians his lawful dues.' ἀποτείσει: or -ει? See 150*b*.—16 ff.
'If there is no family in the home, or heir to the property among
the colonists in Naupactus, the next of kin among the H.
Locrians shall inherit, from whatever place among the Locrians
he comes, and, if a man or boy, he shall go himself within three
months. Otherwise the laws of Naupactus shall be followed.'—
19 ff. 'If one returns from Naupactus to the H. Locrians, he
must have it announced in Naupactus in the market-place,
and among the H. Locrians in the city whence he comes.'—
22 ff. 'Whenever any of the Περϙοθαρίαι and the Μυσαχεῖς
(probably the names of two noble or priestly families, the first
obviously containing κοθαρός = καθαρός) becomes a Naupactian
himself, his property in Naupactus shall also be subject to the
laws in Naupactus, but his property among the H. Locrians
to the H. laws, as the law may be in the several cities of the
H. Locrians. If any of them, under the laws of the colonists,
return, they shall be subject to their own laws, each according
to the city of his origin.'—29 ff. 'If there are brothers of the one
who goes as a colonist to Naupactus, then, according to what
the law of the H. Locrians severally (i.e., in each city) is, if (one
of them) dies, the colonist shall inherit his share of the property,
shall inherit what belongs to him.' Note the double construction
with κρατεῖν according as the sense is partitive or not. But
many take TO as gen. sg. τõ in relative sense, though this use is
not otherwise attested in Locrian, and understand ἐστί with
κατιϙόμενον, translating 'which it is proper for him to inherit.'—
32 f. 'The colonists may bring suit before the judges with right
of precedence, they may bring suit and submit to suits against
themselves in Opus on the same day.' This provision is intended
to secure for the colonists the greatest expedition in their
litigation at Opus. **haρέσται** (i.e., ἑλέσθαι) **καὶ δόμεν** = λαβεῖν
καὶ δοῦναι (cf. Hdt. 5.83). δίκην λαβεῖν is usually 'to bring suit,'
as here, though sometimes the opposite, while δίκην δοῦναι is

usually 'to submit to suit' (e.g., Thuc. 1.28), as here, though
sometimes used of a magistrate, 'to grant trial,' as below, ll. 41 f.—
34 f. 'Whoever are in office for the year shall appoint from among
the H. Locrians a προστάτης, one of the Locrians for the colonist,
one of the colonists for the Locrian.' τὸν Λοϟρὸν Ηυποκναμιδίον
applies properly only to the appointment of the προστάτης for
the colonist, this being the important provision in continuation
of the preceding paragraph. Making the provision mutual was
an afterthought.—καπιατες without correction is to be read
κα 'πιατές, with hyphaeresis where we expect elision, from κα
and ἐπιατές, and adv. cpd. of Ϝέτος for which we should expect
ἐπιϜετές or ἐπιετές (intervocalic Ϝ is not always written, cf.
'Οπόεντι, δαμιουργούς). Some correct to 'πι(Ϝε)τές, but a by-form
with (Ϝ)ατ is possible. ΕΣ after ἔντιμοι is due to dittography
(cf. the ending of the preceding hοίτινες, 'πιατές). The omission
of ἔōντι may be the engraver's error, or simply ellipsis, such as
is not infrequent in a clause of this kind (Kühner-Gerth I,
p. 41, n. 2c).—36 f. 'A colonist to Naupactus who has left behind
a father and his portion of the property with the father, shall
inherit his share when (the father) dies.'—38 ff. 'Whoever
violates these statutes by any device in any point which is not
agreed to by both parties, the assembly of the Thousand in Opus
and the assembly of the colonists in Naupactus, shall be deprived
of civil rights and shall have his property confiscated.' For the
spelling ΝαϜπακτίον see 32.—παματοφαγεῖσται: 162.12.—41 ff.
'To the one who brings suit the magistrate shall grant trial
within thirty days, if thirty days of his magistracy remain.
If he does not grant trial to the one bringing suit he shall be
deprived of civil rights and have his property confiscated, his
real estate together with his servants. The customary oath
shall be taken. The voting shall be by ballot.' For μέρος 'real
estate', cf. the similar use of κλῆρος.—46 f. 'And this compact
for the H. Locrians shall hold good in the same terms for the
colonists from Chaleion under Antiphates.' See introductory
note.

58. Oeanthea. Early fifth century B.C. IG IX.i.333. GDI 1479.
Roberts 232 and pp. 354 ff. Schwyzer 363. Solmsen-Fraenkel 45.
Tod. 34.

A. Τὸν ξένον μὲ̄ ἁγε̄ν ἐ τᾶς Χαλείδος τὸν Οἰανθέα, μ|ε̄δὲ τὸν
Χαλειέα ἐ τᾶς Οἰανθίδος, με̄δὲ χρέματα αἴ τι συ|λο̄ι· τὸν δὲ συ-
λο̄ντα ἀνάτο̄ συλε̄ν. τὰ ξενικὰ ἐ θαλάσας ἁγε̄ν | ἄσυλον πλὰν ἐ
5 λιμένος το̄ κατὰ πόλιν. αἴ κ' ἀδίκο̄ συλο̄ι, τέ|τορες δραχμαί· αἰ
δὲ πλέον δέκ' ἁμαρᾶν ἔχοι τὸ σῦλον, hε̄|μιόλιον ὀφλέτο̄ Ϝότι συ-
λάσαι. αἰ μεταϜοικέοι πλέον με̄νὸς ε̄̇ | ὁ Χαλειεὺς ἐν Οἰανθέαι ε̄̇
'Ōιανθεὺς ἐν Χαλείοι, τᾶι ἐπιδαμίαι δίκαι χ|ρέστο̄. τὸν πρόξενον,
αἰ ψευδέα προξενέοι, διπλ|είοι θōιέστο̄.
10 B. Αἴ κ' ἀνδιχάζο̄ντι τοὶ ξενοδίκαι, ἐπο̄μότας hελέσ|το̄ ὁ ξένος
ὀπάγο̄ν τὰν δίκαν ἐχθὸς προξένο̄ | καὶ Ϝιδίο̄ ξένο̄ ἀριστίνδαν, ἐπὶ
μὲν ταῖς μναιαίαις καὶ πλέον πεντεκαίδεκ' ἄνδρας, ἐπὶ ταῖς | μειό-
15 νοις ἐννέ' ἄνδρας. αἴ κ' ὁ Ϝασστὸς ποὶ τὸν Ϝ||αστὸν δικάζεται κὰ
τᾶς συνβολᾶς, δαμιοργὸς hελέσται τὸ̄ς hορκō̄μότας ἀριστίνδαν τὰν
πε|ντορκίαν ὀμόσαντας. τὸ̄ς hορκō̄μότας τὸν αὐτὸ|ν hόρκον ὀμνύε̄ν,
πλε̄θὺν δὲ νικε̄ν.

The tablet consists of two documents inscribed by different
hands, as appears from forms of the letters and three vs. two dots
punctuation. The first, ending with χρέστο̄ l. 8, is a treaty between
Oeanthea and Chaleion of the kind known as σύμβολον or συμ-
βολά (the latter in l. 15). It is for the protection of foreigners,
that is citizens of other Greek states, visiting either city, from
reprisal at the hands of citizens of the other. Such reprisal or
seizure in enforcement of claims was freely employed, so far as
it was not specifically regulated by treaty. For graphic peculiarities see no. 57, introductory note.

1 ff. 'An Oeanthean shall not carry off a foreigner from Chaleian territory, nor a Chaleian from Oeanthean territory, nor his
property, in case one makes a seizure. But him who makes a
seizure himself one may seize with impunity. The property of a
foreigner one may carry off from the sea without being subject
to reprisal, except from the harbor of each city. If one makes
a seizure unlawfully, four drachmas (is the penalty); and if he
holds what has been seized for more than ten days, he shall owe
half as much again as the amount he seized. If a Chaleian sojourns
more than a month in Oeanthea or an Oeanthean in Chaleion,
he shall be subject to the local court.'

The second document consists of regulations of one of the two

cities, presumably Oeanthea, regarding the legal rights of foreigners.
'The proxenus who is false to his duty one shall fine double (the amount involved in each particular case). If the ξενοδίκαι (the judges in cases involving the rights of foreigners) are divided in opinion, the foreigner who is plaintiff (ὁπάγōν = ὁ ἐπάγων) shall choose jurors from the best citizens, but exclusive of his proxenus and private host (who would be prejudiced in his favor), fifteen men in cases involving a mina or more, nine men in cases involving less. If citizen proceeds against citizen under the terms of the treaty, the magistrates shall choose the jurors from the best citizens, after having sworn the quintuple oath (i.e., oath by five gods). The jurors shall take the same oath, and the majority shall decide.'

59. Probably from the neighborhood of Polis, east of Amphissa. Early fifth century B.C. Papadakis, 'Αρχ. 'Εφ. 1924.119 ff. Wilamowitz, Ber. Preuss. Akad. 1927.7 f. Solmsen-Fraenkel 46. Pezopoulos, Πολέμων 1.97 ff. Chatzis, 'Αρχ. 'Εφ. 1927/8.181 ff.

A. Τεθμὸς ὅδε περὶ τᾶς γᾶς βέβαιος ἔστō κὰτ τὸν | ἀνδαιθμὸν
πλακὸς 'Υλίας καὶ Λισκαρίας καὶ τōν ἀ|ποτόμōν καὶ τōν δαμοσίōν.
ἐπινομία δ' ἔστō γο|νεῦσιν καὶ παιδί· αἰ δὲ μὲ παῖς εἴε, κόραι· αἰ
5 δὲ μὲ κόρα εἴε, || ἀδελφεōι· αἰ δὲ μὲ ἀδελφεὸς εἴε, ἀνχιστέδαν ἐπι-
νεμέσθō κὰ τὸ | δίκαιον· αἰ δὲ μέ, τōι ἐπινόμōι (ὁμ)οίιōν. hότι δέ
κα φυτεύσεται |, ἄσυλος ἔστō. αἰ μὲ πολέμōι ἀνανκαζομένοις δόξ-
ξαι ἀν|δράσιν hενὶ κέκατον ἀριστίνδαν τōι πλέθει ἄνδρας δια|κα-
10 τίōς μεῖστον ἀξξιομάχōς ἐπιϜοίκōς ἐφάγεσθαι, hόστ||ις δὲ δαιθμὸν
ἐνφέροι ἒ ψᾶφον διαφέροι ἐν πρείγαι ἒ 'ν πόλι ἒ|'ν ἀποκλεσίαι, ἒ στά-
σιν ποιέοι περὶ γαδαισίας, αὐτὸς μὲ|ν Ϝερρέτō καὶ γενεὰ ἄματα πάν-
τα, χρέματα δὲ δαμιευόσθōν | καὶ Ϝοικία κατασκαπτέσθō κὰτ τὸν
ἀνδρεφονικὸν τετθμόν. ὅδε τετθμὸς ἰαρὸς ἔστō τō 'Απόλλōνος τō
15 Πυθίō καὶ τōν συνν||άōν· ἔμεν τōι τα]ῦτα παρβαίνοντι ἐξξόλειαν
αὐτōι καὶ γενεᾶι καὶ πα|μάτεσιν, τōι δ' εὐσεβέοντι hίλαος ἔστō.
ἀ δὲ γ[ᾶ τὸ μὲν ἔμισον] | (reverse side) τōν ὑπαπροσθι(δ)ίōν, τὸ
δ' ἔμισον τōν ἐπιϜοίκōν ἔστō. | τὸς κοίλōς μόρōς διαδόντō. ἀλλαγὰ
δὲ βέβαιο|ς ἔστō, ἀλαζέσθō δὲ ἀντὶ τō ἀρχō.

B. κομίζοιεν, ἀξιοδότας ἔστō τὰν αὐτō ὅιτινι χρεῖζοι.

C. αἰ δὲ τοὶ] δαμιοργοὶ κερδαίνοιεν ἄλλο | τōν γεγραμμένōν,

 hιαρὸν τõ 'Απόλλõ|νος ἐχέτõ ἄγαλμα δι' ἐννέα Fετ|έõν καὶ μὲ ποτι-
γράψαι κέρδος.

Like nos. 57, 58 this is a bronze tablet inscribed on both sides.
In contrast to no. 57 there is the boustrophedon writing, but
on the other hand no ?, so that the relative date is problematical.
There is some difference in the forms, notably in the dat. pl. of
cons. stems, ἀνδράσιν, etc., vs. -οις of nos. 57, 58. The reverse
side contains three lines which are a continuation of the ob-
verse, but above these a line concluding another law (B), and
below them three lines, to be read by turning upside down,
concluding still another decree (C).

A 1 ff. 'This law concerning the land shall be in force for the
partition of the plain of Hyla and Liscara, both the separate
lots (?) and the public.' 'Υλίας: adj. formed from the name of
the town attested by St. Byz. "Υλη . . . ἔστι καὶ πόλις Λοκρῶν τῶν
'Οζολῶν, and indirectly by Thuc. 3.101, where 'Υαῖοι should be
read "Υλιοι. Similarly Λισκαρίας adj. based on an unknown name
*Λίσκαρος or *Λίσκαρα.—ἀποτόμõν variously interpreted, but
probably the parts cut off (from the public domain).—ἀνδαιθμόν:
with δαιθμόν l. 10, see 164.4.

3 ff. 'The right of pasturage shall belong to the heads of families and to the son; if there is no son, to the daughter; if there
is no daughter, to the brother, if there is not brother, one shall
make the assignment to the next of kin according to what is
right; if not (if there is no next of kin), to the assignee from
among those of like family but outside the strict line of kin-
ship(?).' The letters following ἐπινόμõι are said by Pezopoulos
to be definitely OIION, for which it is difficult to find any
acceptable interpretation. But it is quite possible that the engraver with his eye on the last letters of the preceding word
ἐπιNOMOI neglected to add another OM, and that we may read
(ὀμ)οιιõν (for ' cf. ἰαρός l. 14), and understand 'like, similar'
persons as referring to collateral relatives, not within the limits
of technical kinship, the "ἔξω τῆς ἀγχιστείας" in the words of
Isaeus 11.7, etc. Cf. Pezopoulos, l.c., on such a possible use of
ὁμοῖος (but without the suggestion given above as to the reading).
—5. ἀνχιστέδαν: 133.7.—6. ἐπίνομος: here probably = κληρο-
νόμος, as in inscriptions of Delphi, etc.

6 ff. 'Whatever one plants, one shall be immune from its seizure. Except if under pressure of war the 101 men chosen from the best citizens, the majority, vote to introduce at least 200 colonists capable of bearing arms, whoever proposes partition or gives his vote for it in the council or in the assembly, or in the committee, or makes civil strife concerning partition of the land, he himself and his family shall be exiled for all time, his property confiscated, and his house destroyed just as under the law concerning murder.'—10. πρείγα: 'council' (of elders like the Spartan γερουσία). See 86.3.—12. Ϝερρέτō: 162.7.—δαμιευōσθōν: 140.4b. —15/16. The letters at the beginning of l. 16 are obscure, but πα|μάτεσιν is more probable than πά|ντεσιν.—17. ὑπαπροσθιδίōν: The fourth letter from the end is A, but, although the conglutinate -ιαῖος is common enough, it is less likely in such a derivative as this, and the correction is probable.—18 f. 'The valley portions they shall distribute. Exchange shall be allowed, but one must make the exchange in the presence of the magistrate.'

B. Conclusion of another law. '(If/when) they receive (?), one shall be entitled to give his share to whomever he wishes.'— τάν (Wilamowitz τᾶν) acc. sg. after the verbal notion implicit in ἀξιοδότας. Cf. τὰ μετέωρα φροντιστής, Plato.

C. 'If the demiurgi gain anything other than the amounts prescribed, it shall be held sacred to Apollo as an offering for a period of nine years, and one shall not enter it in addition as profit.' Otherwise Wilamowitz, followed by Pezopoulos, reading Ἐχέτō as an epithet of Apollo.

60. Tolophon. About middle of third century B.C. Wilhelm, Oest. Jhrh. 14.163 ff. Leaf, ABS 21.148 ff. Nikitskij, "AIAN-TEIA" in Žurn. min. nar. pr. 1913. Schwyzer 366. The text given here is mainly that of Nikitskij, which Wilhelm later recognized as an advance on his own. The side B, containing only proper names is omitted here.

Ἀγαθᾶι τ[ύχαι. | ἐ]πὶ τοῖσδε Αἰάντειοι καὶ ἁ πόλις Ναρυκαίων Λοκροῖς ἀνεδέξαντο τὰς κόρα[ς πέμψειν ἐν Ἴλιον. εἶμεν Αἰαντείους ἀσύλους | κ]αὶ ἀρυσίους καὶ πολέμου καὶ εἰρήνας καὶ ἐφ' αἵματι μὴ ἐπικωλύειν καὶ προδικία[ν αὐτοῖς διδόμεν αἴ τί κα ἀδικέωνται] |

καὶ αὐτᾶι τᾶι πόλει. ξενίων μὴ ἀπελαθῆμεν κατὰ ξενίας ἐλθόντα
5 ἀπὸ δαμοσίο[υ Ναρυκαίων· αἱ δέ κα ἀπελαθῆι, δεκαπέν||τ]ε
δραχμὰς τὸν ἄρχοντα ἀποτεῖσαι· αἱ δὲ δίκαι ἀλοίη, ὁ ἄρχων τριά-
κοντα δραχμὰ[ς ἀποτεισάτω· τῶν ἰδιωτᾶν τὸν συλλα]|βόντα κατὰ
ξενίαν ἀζάμιον εἶμεν. αἱ τῶν Αἰαντείων ῥυσιάζοι καταειδώς, τριά-
κο[ντα στατῆρας ἀποτεισάτω καὶ τοὶ ἄρ|χ]οντες τὰ ῥυσιαχθέντα
ἀμπράξαντες ἀποδόντω αὐθαμερὸν ἢ τᾶι ὑστεραίαι· εἰ δ[ὲ μὴ ἀμ-
πράξαιεν ἢ μὴ ἀποδοῖεν, τὸ δι|π]λοῦν ἀποτεισάντω. αἱ δὲ τῶν
Αἰαντείων καταδῆσαι ἀδίκως ἢ ἔρξαι, ἑκατὸν στατήρ[ας ἀποτει-
σάτω τᾶς ἀμέρας ἑκάστας] | καὶ τᾶς νυκτὸς ἄλλους ἑκάστας ἔντε
κα ἀφῆ. τροφεῖα τοῖς γονεῦσι τᾶν κορᾶν ἑκατέρ[ας μνᾶς ἐξ καθ'
10 ἔτος διδόμεν καὶ τοῖν] || κόραιν ἑκατέραι πεντεκαίδεκα μνᾶς ἐν
κόσμον καὶ τροφὰν παρέχειν ἔντε κα [ἐπανέλθωντι· τῶν Αἰαντείων
μὴ ἐᾶν πρα]θῆμεν ἐν πολεμίους ἀλόντα. οἰκίας Θήμωνος κατα-
καείσας ὁποίας κα τᾶι πόλε[ι Ναρυκαίων δόξαι, ἀνοικοδομηθῆμεν·]
| παντεῖ Λοκρῶν. Αἰαντείων εἴ τίς κα ἐλ Λοκροῖς οἰκεῖν δείληται,
ἀτέλειαν εἶμεν καθ[ὼς ἐν τᾶι πατρίδι· αἴ τις θύοι ἐν Ναρύκαι] |
θοίναν εἶμεν τοῖς Αἰαντείοις, εἶμεν πάντοις, καὶ τῶι ἱερεῖ τὰ δέρ-
ματα ἀποδιδόμεν καὶ τὰ [σκέλεα καὶ τἆλλα γέρεα· παναγυρίζειν] |
δὲ τοὺς Λοκροὺς πάντας τᾶι Λοκρίδι Αἰαντίαι ἐν Ναρύκαι· ἀγωνο-
θέτας δὲ εἶμεν Ναρυκα[ίους κατὰ τὰ πάτρια· ἐμ πολέμωι Αἰαντεί-] ||
15 ους παῖδας ὁμήρους μὴ δόμεν ἀέκοντας· ἐν τὰς κόρας | Ναρυκαίοις
ἀτέλειαν εἶμεν τᾶς ἐμ [πόλεμον ἱπποτροφίας καὶ εἰσφορᾶς·] | εἰ δέ
τίς κα ἀνακκάζηι τρέφειν ἵππους ἢ ὁμήρους παῖδας διδόμεν, τοὺς
Λοκροὺς τὰς δαπάνα[ς Ναρυκαίοις δόμεν. ἁ δὲ πόλις Ναρυ]|καίων
μὴ πεμψάτω ὅμηρα τῶν Αἰαντίων μηθένα. δίκαν τὸν ἄρχοντα
ἀμερᾶν τριῶ[ν τῶν Αἰαντείων τῶι ἐγκαλέσαντι] | καὶ ἐκκπρᾶξαι
δέχ' ἀμερᾶν τὸ κατὰ ξένον, μὴ ἀπογνῶμεν μάρτυρα παρεχόμεν[ον
ἀ]ξιόχρ[ειον· αἱ τίς κα ἀμφιλλέγηι τᾶς δίκας τᾶς] | πρότερον, τὰν
δίκαν εἶμεν ἐν τοῖς αὐτοῖς δικασταῖς· ἃ κα ἀλῶι τὸ μαρτυρ[ηθέν,
20 ἀτελὴ]ς ἔστω ἁ δίκα καὶ ὁ μαρτυρήσας ἐν ταῖ ἐφι||ορκίαι ἐχέστω
καὶ ἀποτεισάτω διπλόαν τὰν δίκαν· αἱ δέ κα μὴ πράξη ὁ ἄ[ρχων
- - - - - - - - - προει]|πάντω ὄντινα κα λάβη τῶν ἐκ τᾶς πόλιος ἐξ
ἇς κα τὸ ἔκκλημα ἢ ταῖ δί[και αἱρεῖσθαι πλουτίνδαν ἐκ τοῦ τέλεος
μὴ μεῖ]|ον τριακοντοδράχμου ἕνδεκα ἄνδρας, ἐν δὲ Ναρύκαι ἐξ
ἁπάντων [- - - - αἱ δέ κα δέ]|ηι δικάζειν, τοῖν κόραιν ἐπιδικῆσαι
τοῖν πρόσθ[ε]ν κὰτ τὸ δυ[νατόν - - - -, τοὺς ἄρχοντας Ναρυ]-|
καίων δίκαν δόμεν κὰτ ταὐτὰ καὶ ἐκπρᾶξαι. ὅρκος. ἐπὶ τ[ούτοις

ὑπισχόμεθα κατακολουθήσειν πάντοις τοῖς γεγραμμένοις ἐν ταῖ] ||
25 συνθήκαι καὶ ἐν τοῖς ὅρκοις· εὐορκεόντοις πολλ[ὰ ἀγαθὰ εἴη, ἐφι-
ορκεόντοις δὲ - - - -. ὀμόσαι ἄν]δρας πεντήκοντα πλουτίνδαν·
ὀμν[ύοντας ὅρκον τὸν νόμιμον - - - - - περὶ τᾶν] κορᾶν τᾶν
πεμφθεισᾶν [- - - - -

Terms under which the Αἰάντειοι (the Ajax clan) and the town
of Naryca (the reputed birthplace of Ajax) undertook for the
Locrians the duty of sending the maidens to Troy—namely the
enjoyment of common rights among the Locrians, from which
apparently they had previously been excluded. Naryca was in
Eastern Locris, but this inscription comes from some Western
Locrian temple, either one at Tolophon or that of Athena Ilias
in the nearby Physcus. The stone is broken in an irregular line
on the right and bottom, so that many of the restorations are
highly problematical conjectures. The dialect is mixed (e.g.,
both αἰ and εἰ), much the same as the Northwest Greek κοινή,
but with a touch of more special Locrian (so at least κατὰ ξενίας
l. 4 vs. κατὰ ξενίαν l. 6; 136.5).

2 ff. ʽThe Αἰάντειοι shall be immune from seizure and reprisal
both in war and peace, and one shall not interfere with them on
a charge of bloodshed (referring of course to Ajax's sacrilege),
and, if they are wronged in any way (?), priority of trial shall
be given to them and to the city. Anyone coming from the
public of Naryca shall not be excluded from the rights of hos-
pitality.'—3 f. [τῶν ἰδιωτᾶν, κτλ.: restoration and meaning very
uncertain.—6, 8. τῶν Αἰαντείων: partitive genitive as object
of the verb.—19. ἅ κα ἁλῶι τὸ μαρτυρ[ηθέν?] ʽin case what
is testified is (lit. convicted =) proved false.'(?)—23. ἐπιδικῆ-
σαι: probably ʽrender justice.'

Elean

61. Olympia. Before 580 B.C. GDI 1152. Inschr. v. Olympia 2.
Roberts 292 and pp. 364 ff. Schwyzer 409. Solmsen-Fraenkel 51.

ʼΑ Ϝράτρα τοῖς Ϝαλείοις. πατριὰν θαρρῆν καὶ γενεὰν καὶ ταὐτο͂. |
αἰ ζέ τις κατιαραύσειε, Ϝάρρῆν ὃρ Ϝαλείο͂· αἰ ζὲ μὲ ʼπιθεῖαν τὰ ζί-|
καια ὃρ μέγιστον τέλος ἔχοι καὶ τοὶ βασιλᾶες, ζέκα μναίς κα | ἀπο-
5 τίνοι Ϝέκαστος τὸν μέ ʼπιποεόντον καθυταὶς τοῖ Ζὶ ʼΟλυν||πίοι.

ἐπενπōι ζέ κ' Ἑλλανοζίκας καὶ τἆλλα ζίκαια ἐπενπ|έτō ἀ ζαμιορ-
γία· αἰ ζὲ μὲ 'νπōι, ζίφυιον ἀποτινέτō ἐν μαστρά|αι. αἰ ζέ
τις τὸν αἰτιαθέντα ζικαῖον ἱμάσκοι, ἐν ταῖ ζεκαμναίαι κ' ἐ|νέχο-
[ιτ]ο, αἰ Ϝειζὸς ἱμάσκοι. καὶ πατριᾶς ὁ γροφεὺς ταὐ[τ]ά κα
πάσκοι, | [αἴ τ]ιν' [ἀζ]ικέο[ι]. ὁ π[ί]ναξ ἱαρὸς Ὀλυνπίαι.

'The law of the Eleans (adnom. dat., 172). (An accused
man's) gens and family and his property shall be immune. If
any one brings a charge (against them), he shall be prosecuted
as in the case of (a charge against) a citizen of Elis. If he who
holds the highest office and the βασιλεῖς do not impose the fines,
let each of those who fail to impose them pay a penalty of ten
minae dedicated to Olympian Zeus. Let the Hellanodica enforce
this, and let the body of demiurgi enforce the other fines (which
they had neglected to impose). If he (the Hellanodica) does not
enforce this, let him pay double the penalty in his accounting.
If any one maltreats one who is accused in a matter involving
fines, let him be held to a fine of ten minae, if he does so wittingly.
And let the scribe of the gens suffer the same penalty if he
wrongs any one. This tablet sacred at Olympia.'

The numerous interpretations of this inscription have differed
fundamentally. According to that preferred here the object of
the decree is to do away with the liability which under primitive
conditions, such as survived longer in Elis than elsewhere, had
attached to the whole gens and family of an accused person,
also to prevent confiscation of his property and personal violence,
and to prescribe the manner in which penalties were to be
imposed.

1. πατριάν: like Delph. πατριά, Dor. πάτρα = γένος, while
γενεά is the immediate family.—θαρρῆν: 'be of good cheer,
without fear,' hence, as a technical term in Elean, 'be secure,
immune,' just as the Attic ἄδεια is in origin 'freedom from fear
(δέος).' It is used of persons and things. Cf. θ[άρρος] αὐτοῖ καὶ
χρēμάτοις in another inscription.—2. κατιαραύσειε: καθιερεύω,
but meaning first to 'utter an imprecation against some one' (cf.
κατεύχομαι), and then, since this was, or had been, the manner
of introducing a charge, simply κατηγορέω. Cf. κατιαραίων no. 65.5.
Like various other expressions in Elean, this reflects the essentially religious character of the legal procedure.—Ϝάρρēν = Ϝέρēν

No. 64]   ELEAN INSCRIPTIONS   261

(no. 63), cf. Locr. Ϝερρέτō (no. 59). 52, 162.7.—αἰ ζὲ μὲ κτλ.:
cf. no. 52 C 13-16. For ἐπενπōι, μαστράαι, ἱμάσκω, etc., see the
Glossary.

62. Olympia. Sixth century B.C. GDI 1149. Inschr. v. Olympia
9. Roberts 291 and pp. 362 ff. Schwyzer 413. Ditt. Syll. 9.
Solmsen-Fraenkel 52. Tod. 5.

Ἀ Ϝράτρα τοῖρ Ϝαλείοις καὶ τοῖς Ἐρ|Ϝαδίοις. συνμαχία κ' ἔα
ἑκατὸν Ϝέτεα, | ἄρχοι δέ κα τοῖ. αἰ δέ τι δέοι αἴτε Ϝέπος αἴτε Ϝ|άρ-
5 γον, συνέαν κ' ἀλάλοις τά τ' ἄλ(α) καὶ πὰ||ρ πολέμō. αἰ δὲ μὰ
συνέαν, τάλαντόν κ' | ἀργύρō ἀποτίνοιαν τοῖ Δὶ 'Ολυνπίοι τοὶ
καδαλέμενοι λατρειόμενον. αἰ δέ τιρ τὰ γ|ράφεα ταὶ καδαλέοιτο
10 αἴτε Ϝέτας αἴτε τ|ελεστὰ αἴτε δᾶμος, ἐν τἐπιάροι κ' ἐνέχ||οιτο τοῖ
'νταῦτ' ἐγραμένοι.

'The covenant of the Eleans and the Heraeans (of Arcadia).
There shall be an alliance for one hundred years, beginning with
the present year. If there shall be any need of word or deed, they
shall combine with one another both in other matters and in
war. If they do not combine, let those who violate (the agreement) pay a talent of silver consecrated to Olympian Zeus. If
any one violates these writings, whether private citizen, official,
or the state, let him be held in the penalty here written.'

63. Olympia. Sixth century B.C. GDI 1153. Inschr. v. Olympia
11. Roberts 294. Schwyzer 415.

Ἀ Ϝράτρα τοῖρ Χαλαδρίορ καὶ Δευ|καλίōνι· Χαλάδριον ἔμεν
5 αὐτὸν | καὶ γόνον Ϝισοπρόξενον, | Ϝισοδαμιοργόν· τὰν δὲ γᾶ[ν] ||
ἔχēν τὰν ἐν Πίσαι· αἰ δέ τις συλαίē, Ϝέρēν αὐτὸν | πὸ τὸν Δία, αἰ
μὲ δάμοι δοκέοι.

1. Χαλαδρίορ: confusion of acc. and dat. forms, as in another
inscription (Schwyzer 414).—5/6. Ϝέρēν κτλ.: 136.3.

64. Olympia. Sixth century B.C. GDI 1156. Inschr. v. Olympia 7. Roberts 296 and pp. 369 ff. Ziehen, Leges Sacrae 61.
Schwyzer 412.

κα θεαρὸς εἴē. αἰ δὲ βενέοι ἐν τίαροῖ, βοῖ κα θōάδοι καὶ κο-
θάρσι τελείαι, καὶ τὸν θεαρὸν ἐν τ|α(ὐ)ταῖ. αἰ δέ τις πὰρ τὸ γράφος
δικάδοι, ἀτελές κ' εἴē ἀ δίκα, ἀ δέ κα Ϝράτρα ἀ δαμοσία τελεία εἴ|ē
δικάδōσα· τōν δέ κα γραφέōν ὅτι δοκέοι καλιτέρōς ἔχēν πὸ τὸν θ(ε)όν,

ἐξαγρέōν καὶ ἐ|νποιον σὺν βōλαῖ (π)εντακατίōν ἀϜλανέōς καὶ
5 δάμοι πλēθύοντι δινάκοι· (δινά)κοι δέ κα (ἐ)ν τρίτ||ον, αἴ τι
ἐνποιοῖ αἴτ' ἐξαγρέοι.

This is the conclusion of an inscription which was begun on
another tablet not preserved.

'If he (some one previously mentioned) commits fornication(?)
in the sacred precinct, one shall make him expiate it by the
sacrifice of an ox and by complete purification, and the θεαρός
in the same way. If anyone pronounces judgment contrary to the
regulation, this judgment shall be void, but the decree of the
people shall be final in deciding. One may make any change in
the regulations which seems desirable in the sight of the god
(136.3), withdrawing or adding with the approval of the whole
council of the Five Hundred and the people in full assembly.
One may make changes three times, adding and withdrawing.'—
The restoration and interpretation of the last sentence, (δινά)κοι
κτλ., is uncertain. In l. 4 the adverb ἀϜλανέōς (see **55**) is used
loosely where we should expect an adjective in agreement with
βōλαῖ or πεντακατίōν.

65. Olympia. About middle of fourth century B.C. Schwyzer
424. Solmsen-Fraenkel 53.

Θεός· τύχα. ταίρ δὲ γενεαίρ μὰ φυγαδείημ μαδὲ κ|ὰτ ὁποῖον
τρόπον, μάτε ἐρσεναιτέραν μάτε θηλυτ|έραν, μάτε τὰ χρήματα
δαμοσιωμεν· αἰ δέ τιρ φυγαδ|είοι αἴτε τὰ χρήματα δαμοσιοία, φευ-
5 γέτω πὸτ τω Δ||ιὸρ τω̄λυμπίω αἵματορ, καὶ κατιαραίων ὁ δηλομη̄ρ |
ἀνάατορ ἤστω. ἐξη̄στω δέ, καί κα φυγαδεύαντι, τοῖ δ|ηλομένοι νο-
στίττην καὶ ἀττάμιον ἦμεν, ὅσσα κα ὔ|σταριν γένωνται τω̄ν περὶ
Πύρρωνα δαμιοργω̄ν. το|ὶρ δὲ ἐπ' ἄσιστα μὰ ἀποδόσσαι μάτε
10 ἐκπέμψαι τὰ χρ||ήματα τοῖρ φυγάδεσσι· αἰ δέ τι ταύτων πὰρ τὸ
γράμ|μα ποιέοι, ἀποτινέτω διπλ[ά]σιον τω̄ κα ἐκπέμπα κα|ὶ τω̄ κα
ἀποδω̄ται. αἰ δέ τιρ ἀδεαλτώhαιε τὰ στάλαν, | ὼρ ἀγαλματοφώραν
ἐόντα πάσχην.

'But one shall not exile the children (of an exile) either male
or female, under any circumstances, nor confiscate the property.
If any one exiles them or confiscates the property, he shall be
subject to trial before (in the name of) Olympian Zeus on a
capital charge, and any one who wishes may bring the charge

against him with impunity. And it shall be permitted, even in case they have exiled any, to any one who wishes to return and be free from punishment so far as concerns matters happening later than the time of the demiurgi under Pyrrhon. Those next of kin shall not sell or send off the property of the exiles, and if one does any of these things contrary to the regulation, he shall pay double the amount sent off and sold. If any one defaces the stele, he shall be punished like one guilty of sacrilege.'

Several times during the fourth century B.C. the oligarchy and democracy alternated in power in Elis, with resulting banishment and recall of exiles. It is probable that this decree belongs to the Macedonian period and perhaps refers to the exiles of 336 B.C. who were recalled in 335 B.C. Cf. Arrian 1.10.1 Ἠλεῖοι δὲ τοὺς φυγάδας σφῶν κατεδέξαντο, ὅτι ἐπιτήδειοι Ἀλεξάνδρῳ ἦσαν. It is a supplementary decree to another on the same subject, as is shown by δέ in the first sentence after the introductory formula, and the use of γενεαίρ without modifier, which must be understood from the preceding. On the dialect as compared with that of the earlier inscriptions, see **241**.

1. **γενεαίρ**: pl. of the collective γενεά 'offspring, family,' as in Mess. τὰν γυναῖκά τε καὶ τὰς γενεάς αὐτοῦ (GDI 4689.97).—4-5. **φευγέτω πὸτ τῶ Διὸρ** κτλ.: see **136**.3.—5. **δηλομήρ**: we expect δηλόμενορ. Probably an error, for which the existence of some such form as δηλοντήρ (cf. ἐθελοντήρ) may be responsible.— 6. **φυγαδεύαντι**: aor. subj. **151**.1.—12-13. **αἰ δέ τιρ ἀδεαλτώηαιε** κτλ.: cf. ἢν δέ τις [τὴν στήλην] ἀφαν[ίζηι ἢ τὰ γράμματα], πασχέτω ὡς ἱερόσυλος in an inscription of Iasus, GDI 5517. ἀδελτόω = ἀδηλόω, ἀφανίζω, is probably from *δεαλος (cf. δέαμαι, δῆλος), whence—perhaps through the medium of a verb δεάλλω— *δεαλτός, *δεαλτόω. According to another view, from δέλτος 'tablet' (cf. Cypr. δάλτος), so that the meaning would be 'make the stele ἄδελτος,' i.e., remove the tablet from the stele. For τὰ στάλαν see **96**.2.

66. Olympia. Late third or second century B.C. GDI 1172. Inschr. v. Olympia 39. Schwyzer 425.

Θεόρ · τύχα. | Ὑπὸ Ἑλλανοδικᾶν τῶν περὶ | Αἰσχύλον, Θυίω. |
5 ὅπωρ, ἐπεὶ Δαμοκράτηρ Ἁγήτορορ || Τενέδιορ, πεπολιτευκὼρ

παρ' ἀμὲ | αὐτόρ τε καὶ ὁ πατάρ, καὶ ἐστεφανωμέ|νορ τόν τε τῶν
Ὀλυμπίων ἀγῶνα καὶ | ἄλλοιρ καὶ πλείονερ, ἐπανιτακὼρ ἐν τὰν |
10 ἰδίαν τάν τε τῶ πατρὸρ θεαροδοκίαν δια||δέδεκται καὶ ὑποδέχεται
τοὶρ θεαροίρ, | ὁμοίωρ δὲ καὶ τοῖρ λοιποῖρ τοῖρ παρ' ἀμέων | τὰν
πᾶσαν χρείαν ἐκτενέωρ καὶ ἀπρο|φασίστωρ παρέχεται, φανερὰν
15 ποιέων | τὰν ἔχει εὔνοιαν ποτὶ τὰν πόλιν, καθὼρ || πλείονερ ἀπε-
μαρτύρεον τῶμ πολιτᾶν · | ὅπωρ δὲ καὶ ἀ πόλερ καταξίαιρ φαίνα-
ται | χάριτερ ἀνταποδιδῶσσα τοῖρ αὐτᾶρ | εὐεργέταιρ, ὑπάρχην
20 Δαμοκράτη πρό|ξενον καὶ εὐεργέταν δ' ἦ||μεν τᾶρ πόλιορ αὐτὸν καὶ
γένορ, καὶ τὰ | λοιπὰ τίμια ἦμεν αὐτοῖ ὅσσα καὶ τοῖρ ἄλ|λοιρ προ-
ξένοιρ καὶ εὐεργέταιρ ὑπάρχει παρὰ | τᾶρ πόλιορ. ἦμεν δὲ καὶ
ἀσφάλειαν καὶ πολέμω | καὶ εἰράναρ, καὶ γᾶρ καὶ βοικίαρ ἔγκτη-
25 σιν, καὶ || ἀτέλειαν, καὶ προεδρίαν ἐν τοῖρ Διονυσιακοῖρ | ἀγώνοιρ,
τᾶν τε θυσιᾶν καὶ τιμᾶν πασᾶν | μετέχην, καθὼρ καὶ τοὶ λοιποὶ
θεαροδόκοι | καὶ εὐεργέται μετέχοντι. δόμεν δὲ αὐτοῖ | καὶ Δαμο-
30 κράτη τὸν ταμίαν ξένια τὰ || μέγιστα ἐκ τῶν νόμων. τὸ δὲ ψάφισ-
μα | τὸ γεγονὸρ ἀπὸ τᾶρ βωλᾶρ γραφὲν ἐγ χάλκω|μα ἀνατεθᾶι
ἐν τὸ ἱαρὸν τῶ Διὸρ τῶ Ὀλυμπίω. | τὰν δὲ ἐπιμέλειαν τᾶρ ἀναθέ-
35 σιορ ποιήασσαι | Αἰσχίναν τὸν ἐπιμελητὰν τᾶν ἴππων. || περὶ δὲ
τῶ ἀποσταλάμεν τοῖρ Τενεδίοιρ | τὸ γεγονὸρ ψάφισμα ἐπιμέλειαν
ποιήαται | Νικόδρομορ ὁ βωλογράφορ, ὅπωρ δοθᾶι τοῖρ | θεαροῖρ
τοῖρ ἐμ Μίλητον ἀποστελλομέ|νοιρ ποτὶ τὰν θυσίαν καὶ τὸν
40 ἀγῶνα || τῶν Διδυμείων.

Proxeny decree in honor of Damocrates of Tenedos, who is
mentioned as one of the Olympian victors by Pausanias (6.17.1).
On the dialect as compared with that of the earlier inscriptions,
see 241. With ὑπὸ Ἑλλανοδικᾶν l. 2 for usual ἐπί with gen.,
compare Lac. hυπό with acc. in no. 71.66.

Northwest Greek κοινή

67. Thermum. About 270 B.C. IG IX².i.3. Schwyzer 381.
Ditt. Syll. 421.

A

ΣΥΝΘΗΚΑ ΚΑΙ ΣΥΜΜΑΧΙΑ ΑΙΤΩΛΟΙΣ ΚΑΙ ΑΚΑΡΝΑΝΟΙΣ

Ἀγαθᾶι τύχαι. Συνθήκα Αἰτωλοῖς καὶ Ἀκαρνάνοις ὁμόλογος.
εἰρήναν | εἶμεν καὶ φιλίαν ποτ' ἀλλάλους, φίλους ἐόντας καὶ συμ-
μάχους ἅμα|τα τὸμ πάντα χρόνον, ὅρια ἔχοντας τᾶς χώρας τὸν

Ἀχελῶιον ποταμ|ὸν ἄχρι εἰς θάλασσαν. τὰ μὲν ποτ' ἀῶ τοῦ Ἀχε-
5 λώιου ποταμοῦ Αἰτωλῶν εἶμεν, τὰ δὲ || ποθ' ἐσπέραν Ἀκαρνάνων
πλὰν τοῦ Πραντὸς καὶ τᾶς Δέμφιδος · ταύτας δὲ Ἀκαρνᾶν|ες
οὐκ ἀντιποιοῦνται. ὑπὲρ δὲ τῶν τερμόνων τοῦ Πραντός, εἰ μέγ κα
Στράτιοι καὶ Ἀγραῖ|οι συγχωρέωντι αὐτοὶ ποτ' αὐτούς, τοῦτο κύ-
ριον ἔστω, εἰ δὲ μή, Ἀκαρνᾶνες καὶ Αἰτωλοὶ | τερμαξάντω τὰμ
Πραντίδα χώραν, αἱρεθέντας ἑκατέρων δέκα πλὰν Στρατίων καὶ
Ἀγραί|ων · καθὼς δέ κα τερμάξωντι, τέλειον ἔστω. εἶμεν δὲ καὶ
10 ἐπιγαμίαν ποτ' ἀλλάλους καὶ γ||ᾶς ἔγκτησιν τῶι τε Αἰτωλῶι ἐν
Ἀκαρνανίαι καὶ τῶι Ἀκαρνᾶνι ἐν Αἰτωλίαι καὶ πολίταν εἶμε|ν τὸν
Αἰτωλὸν ἐν Ἀκαρνανίαι καὶ τὸν Ἀκαρνᾶνα ἐν Αἰτωλίαι ἴσογ καὶ
ὅμοιον. ἀναγραψάν|τω δὲ ταῦτα ἐν στάλαις χαλκέαις ἐπ' Ἀκτίωι
μὲν οἱ ἄρχοντες τῶν Ἀκαρνάνων, ἐν δὲ Θέρμ|ωι τοὶ ἄρχοντες τῶν
Αἰτωλῶν, ἐν Ὀλυμπίαι δὲ καὶ ἐν Δελφοῖς καὶ ἐν Δω(δ)ώναι κοι-
νᾶι ἑκάτ|εροι. ἐπὶ ἀρχόντων ἐμ μὲν Αἰτωλίαι στραταγέοντος Πολυ-
15 κρίτου Καλλιέος τὸ δεύτε||ρον, ἱππαρχέοντος Φίλωνος Πλευρωνίου,
γραμματεύοντος Νεοπτολέμου Ναυπακτίου, | ἐπιλεκταρχεόντων
Λαμέδωνος Καλυδωνίου, Ἀριστάρχου Ἐρταίου, Λέωνος Κα|φρέος,
Καλλία Καλλιέος, Τιμολόχου Ποτειδανιέος, Παμφαίδα Φυσκέος,
Σίμου | Φυταίεος, ταμιευόντων Κυδρίωνος Λυσιμαχέος, Δωριμάχου
Τριχονίου, Ἀρίστ|ωνος Δαιᾶνος, Ἀριστέα Ἱστωρίου, Ἀγήσωνος
20 Δεξιέος, Τιμάνδρου Ἐριναῖος, || Ἀγρίου Σωσθενέος · ἐν δὲ Ἀκαρ-
νανίαι στραταγῶν Βυνθάρου Οἰνιάδα, Ἐπι[λ]|άου Δηριέος, Ἀγή-
σωνος Στρατίου, Ἀλκέτα Φοιτιᾶνος, Ἀλκίνου Θυρρείου, Θέων|ος
Ἀνακτοριέος, Πολυκλέος Λευκαδίου, ἱππαρχέοντος Ἱππολάου
Οἰνιάδα, | γραμματεύοντος Περικλέος Οἰνιάδα, ταμία Ἀγελάου
Στρατικοῦ. | — Συμμαχία Αἰτωλοῖς καὶ Ἀκαρνάνοις ἅματα τὸμ
25 πάντα χρόνον. || εἴ τίς κα ἐμβάλληι εἰς τὰν Αἰτωλίαν ἐπὶ πολέμωι,
βοαθοεῖν τοὺς | Ἀκαρνᾶνας πεζοῖς μὲν χιλίοις, ἱππεῦσι δὲ ἑκατόν,
οὕς κα τοὶ ἄρχοντε|ς πέμπωντι, ἐν ἀμέραις ἕξ. καὶ εἴ τις ἐν Ἀκαρ-
νανίαν ἐμβάλλοι ἐπὶ πολέμωι, | βοαθοεῖν Αἰτωλοὺς πεζοῖς μὲν χι-
λίοις, ἱππέοις δὲ ἑκατόν, ἐν ἀμέραις ἕξ, οὕς | κα τοὶ ἄρχοντες πέμ-
30 πωντι. εἰ δὲ πλειόνων χρείαν ἔχοιεν ἅτεροι πότεροι, || βοαθοούντω
τρισχιλίοις ἑκάτεροι ἑκατέροις, ἐν ἀμέραις δέκα. τᾶς δὲ βοαθοίας
τ|ᾶς ἀποστελλομένας ἔστω τὸ τρίτομ μέρος ὁπλῖται. πεμπόντω δὲ
τὰμ βοάθιαν | ἐγ μὲν Ἀκαρνανίας οἱ στραταγοὶ τῶν Ἀκαρνάνων
καὶ οἱ σύνεδροι, ἐγ δὲ Αἰτωλίας | οἱ ἄρχοντες τῶν Αἰτωλῶν.
σιταρχούντω δὲ τοὺς ἀποστελλομένους στρατιώτ|ας ἑκάτεροι

τοὺς αὐτῶν ἀμερᾶν τριάκοντα· εἰ δὲ πλείονα χρόνον ἔχοιεν τᾶς
βοα||θοίας χρείαν οἱ μεταπεμψάμενοι τὰμ βοάθοιαν, διδόντω τὰς
35 σιταρχίας ἔστε κα | ἐν οἶκον ἀποστείλωντι τοὺς στρατιώτας. σι-
ταρχία δ᾽ ἔστω τοῦ πλείονος χρόν|ου τῶ[ι μὲν ἱππεῖ στα]τὴρ Κορίν-
θιος τᾶς ἀμέρας ἑκάστας, τῶι [δὲ] τὰμ πανοπλίαν ἔχο|[ντι ......
........], τῶι δὲ τὸ ἡμιθωράκιον ἐννέ᾽ ὀβολοί, ψιλῶι ἑπτ᾽ ὀβολοί.
ἀγείσθων | [39-42 fragmentary].

Treaty of alliance between the Aetolians and Acarnanians.
A fragment found at Olympia (Inschr. v. Olympia 40) has been
recognized as belonging to another copy deposited there. This
is an example of the mixed dialect current at this time in various
parts of Northwest Greece, which we call the Northwest Greek
κοινή. See **279**. Note, e.g., the retention of original ᾱ, κα, ποτί,
infin. in -μεν, 3 pl. imv. in -ντω, ξ in aor. (τερμαξάντω), but Att.
εἰ for αἰ, ου beside εο (e.g., ἀντιποιοῦνται but στραταγέοντος), οἱ
beside τοί, εἰς beside ἐν with acc. (εἰς τὰν Αἰτωλίαν but ἐν 'Ακαρνα-
νίαν), ἱππεῦσι beside ἱππέοις.

2/3, 24. **ἅματα τὸμ πάντα χρόνον**, a blend of the old formulaic ἅματα πάντα with the current τὸμ πάντα χρόνον.—16.
ἐπιλεταρχεόντων: this is the first reference to ἐπιλετάρχαι as
military officials in the Aetolian league. For the Achaean league,
cf. ἐπίλετοι, used of the citizen levies in contrast to the mercenaries, Polyb. 2.65, 5.91, 95, and ἐπιλετάρχης Plut. Arat. 32.

Laconian

68. Olympia. Sixth century B.C. IG V.i.1562. GDI 4405.
Inschr. v. Olympia 252. Roberts 261. Schwyzer 7.

[Δέξ]ο, Ϝάν[αξ] Κρονίδα [Ζ]εῦ 'Ολύνπιε, καλὸν ἄ[γ]αλμα
   ℎιλέϜο[ι θυ]μο͂ι το͂ι Λακεδαιμονίο[ις].

This is the inscription mentioned by Paus. 5.24.3, who repro-
duces it, eliminating the dialectal peculiarities, as follows:

Δέξο, ἄναξ Κρονίδα Ζεῦ 'Ολύμπιε, καλὸν ἄγαλμα
   ἱλάῳ θυμῷ τοῖς Λακεδαιμονίοις.

τοῖ Λακ. = τοῖς Λακ. (**97**.3), 'from the Lacedaemonians.' Cf.
Hom. δέξατό οἱ σκῆπτρον and Mel. 'Εκπℎάντοι δέξαι κτλ. (no.
114).

69. Delphi. Soon after 479 B.C. GDI 4406. Ditt. Syll. 31.
Roberts 259. Schwyzer 11. Solmsen-Fraenkel 21. Tod 19.

[Τ]ο[ίδε τὸν] | πόλεμον [ἐ]||πολ[έ]μεον · | Λακ[εδ]α[ι]μόν[ιοι], ||
5 'Αθ[α]ν[α]ῖ[ο]ι, | Κορίνθιοι, | Τεγεᾶτ[αι], | Σικυόνιοι, | Αἰγι-
10 νᾶται, || Μεγαρὲς, | 'Επιδαύριοι, | 'Ερχομένιοι, | Φλειάσιοι, |
15 Τροζάνιοι, || 'Ερμιονὲς, | Τιρύνθιοι, | Πλαταιὲς, | Θεσπιὲς, |
20 Μυκανὲς, || Κεῖοι, | Μάλιοι, | Τένιοι, | Νάξιοι, | 'Ερετριὲς, ||
25 Χαλκιδὲς, | Στυρὲς, | Γαλεῖοι, | Ποτειδιᾶται, | Λευκάδιοι, ||
30 Γανακτοριὲς, | Κύθνιοι, | Σίφνιοι, | 'Αμπρακιῶται, | Λεπρεᾶται.

The famous bronze serpent-column which once supported the
gold tripod set up at Delphi after the battle of Plataea. According
to Thucydides (1.132.3) and others, the Lacedaemonians, after
erasing the boastful epigram of Pausanias, inscribed simply the
names of the cities which had taken part in the war and had set
up the tripod. Note [ἐ]πολ[έ]μεον, for which the true Laconian
form would be ἐπολέμιον.

70. Found at Tegea. Fifth century B.C. IG V.ii.159. GDI
4598. Ditt. Syll. 1213. Schwyzer 57. Solmsen-Fraenkel 35.
Comparetti, Annuario 2.246 ff. Buck, CP 20.133 ff.

A   Ξουθίαι τῶι Φιλαχαίō διακάτι|αι μναῖ. αἴ κ᾽ αὐτὸς hίκε̄, ἀνελέσ-|
θō · αἰ δέ κ᾽ ἀποθάνει, τὸν τέκνōν | ἔμεν, ἐπεί κα πέντε Fέτεα ||
5 hε̄βόντι · αἰ δέ κα μὲ γενεὰ λ[ε]||ίπε̄ται, τὸν ἐπιδικατο̄ν ἔμεν · | δια-
γνο̄μεν δὲ τὸς Τεγεάτα[ς] | κὰ τὸν θεθμόν.

B   Ξουθίαι παρκαθέκα τῶι Φιλαχα|ιō τζετρακάτιαι μναῖ ἀργυρίō.
εἰ μ|έν κα ζόε̄, αὐτὸς ἀνελέσθō · αἰ δέ κ|α μὲ ζόε̄, τοὶ υἱοὶ ἀνελόσθō
5 τοὶ γνέ||σιοι, ἐπεί κα ἐβάσōντι πέντε Fέτε|α · εἰ δέ κα μὲ ζōντι,
ταὶ θυγατέρες | ἀνελόσθō ταὶ γνέσιαι · εἰ δέ κα μὲ | ζōντι, τοὶ
10 νόθοι ἀνελόσθō · εἰ δέ κα | μὲ νόθοι ζōντι, τοὶ ᾽ς ἄσιστα πόθικ||ες
ἀνελόσθō · εἰ δέ κ᾽ ἀνφιλέγōντ|(ι, τ)οὶ Τεγεᾶται διαγνόντō κὰ
τὸν θεθμόν.

Statements of two deposits of money made by a certain
Xuthias, son of Philachaeus, and the conditions for their future
disbursement. The place of deposit was without doubt the
temple of Athena Alea in Tegea, the Greek temples often being
used for such purposes. But the dialect is not Arcadian, and
must therefore represent that of a foreign depositor. The most
natural assumption is that Xuthias was from the neighboring

Laconia, and we are expressly informed (cf. Ath. 6.233) that the Spartans used to deposit money with the Arcadians to evade the law against holding private property. It has been suggested, partly on account of the names (Xuthias, Philachaeus), but mainly because of the retention of intervocalic σ (γνέσιοι, ἐβάσōντι), that Xuthias was not a Spartan proper, but an Achaean perioecus. But there is no good evidence that the perioeci differed in speech from the Spartans at this time, and the retention of intervocalic σ and of antevocalic ε (Fέτεα) is sufficiently explained by the fact that the document was intended for use outside of Laconia. See **59**.1, **275**.

A. 'For Xuthias the son of Philachaeus (are deposited) two hundred minae. If he comes in person, let him take it, but if he dies, it shall belong to his children five years after they reach the age of puberty. If no offspring survives, it shall belong to those designated by law as heirs. The Tegeans shall decide according to the law.' 2. The letters following αὐτός are so mutilated that no reading is certain. But the sense required is clear.

B. This was inscribed later than A, which was thereupon canceled, as shown by its mutilation. The Tegean engraver is responsible for the use of εἰ instead of αἰ, the subj. ζόε̄ (cf. **149**) in contrast to ἀποθάνει of A, the omission of h in υἰοί, ἐβάσōντι (cf. **58**d); and his blunder in writing τζετρακάτιαι was perhaps due to the Arcadian pronunciation (cf. **68**.3). It is also possible that in ll. 10-11 we should read, without correction, ἀνφιλέγōντοι, with Arc. -τοι = -ται (**139**.1). But the passive with μναῖ understood as subject is less natural than the corrected reading usually adopted.

71. Sparta. Fifth century B.C. IG V.i.213. GDI 4416. Roberts 264. Schwyzer 12. Solmsen-Fraenkel 22.

Δαμόνōν | ἀνέθε̄κε ᾿Αθαναία[ι] | Πολιάχōι
5   νικάhας | ταυτᾶ hᾶτ᾿ οὐδὲς || πέποκα τōν νῦν. |
Τάδε ἐνίκαhε Δαμ[όνōν] | τōι αὐτō̄ τεθρίππō[ι] | αὐτὸς ἀνιοχί-
10 ōν · | ἐν ΓαιαFόχō̄ τετράκι[ν] || καὶ ᾿Αθάναια τετ[ράκιν] | κε̄λευhύ-
νια τετ[ράκιν.] | καὶ Ποhοίδαια Δαμόνō[ν] | ἐνίκε̄ Hέλει, καὶ ho
15 κέλ[ε̄ξ | haμ]ᾶ, αὐτὸς ἀνιοχίōν || ἐνhε̄βόhαις hίπποις | hεπτάκιν ἐκ

τᾶν αὐτῶ | hίππον κὲκ τῶ αὐ[τ]ῶ [hίππō.] | καὶ Ποhοίδαια Δαμό-
20 νōν | [ἐ]νίκē Θευρίαι ὀκτά[κ]ι[ν] || αὐτὸς ἀνιοχίōν ἐν|hεβόhαις
hίπποις | ἐκ τᾶν αὐτῶ hίππον | κὲκ τῶ αὐτῶ hίππō. | κὲν Ἀριοντίας
25 ἐνίκē || Δαμόνōν ὀκτάκιν | αὐτὸς ἀνιοχίōν | ἐνhεβόhαις hίπποις |
30 ἐκ τᾶν αὐτῶ hίππον | κὲκ τῶ αὐτῶ hίππō, καὶ || ho κέλēξ ἐνίκē
h[αμᾶ]. | καὶ Ἐλευhύνια Δαμ[όνōν] | ἐνίκē αὐτὸς ἀνιοχίōν | ἐνhē-
35 βόhαις hίπποις | τετράκιν. || τάδε ἐνίκαhε Ἐνυμα[κρατίδ|ας]
πρᾶτ[ος π]αίδōν δόλ[ιχον | Λιθέ]hια καὶ κέλēξ μι[ᾶς | ἀμέρ]ας
40 hα[μᾶ] ἐν[ίκōν. | - - - || - - - - | - - - -] | δόλιχο[ν καὶ ho κέλēξ
45 μιᾶς] | ἀμέρας hαμᾶ ἐνίκōν. | καὶ Παρπαρόνια ἐνίκē || Ἐνυμακρατί-
δας παῖδας | στάδιον καὶ δίαυλον | καὶ δόλιχον καὶ ho κέ[λēξ] | μιᾶς
50 ἀμέρας hαμᾶ | ἐνίκē. καὶ Δαμόνōν || ἐνίκē παῖς ἰὸν ἐν | ΓαιαϜόχō
στάδιον καὶ | [δί]αυλον. | [κ]αὶ Δαμόνōν ἐνίκē | παῖς ἰὸν Λιθέhια ||
55 στάδιον καὶ δίαυλον. | καὶ Δαμόνōν ἐνίκē | παῖς ἰὸν Μαλεάτεια |
60 στάδιον καὶ δίαυλον. | καὶ Δαμόνōν ἐνίκē || παῖς ἰὸν Λιθέhια | στά-
διον καὶ δίαυλον. | καὶ Δαμόνōν ἐνίκē | παῖς ἰὸν Παρπαρόνια |
65 στάδιον καὶ δίαυλον, || καὶ Ἀθάναια στάδιον. | hυπὸ δὲ Ἐχεμένē
ἔφορο[ν] | τάδε ἐνίκē Δαμόνōν, | Ἀθάναια ἐνhεβόhαις | hίπποις
70 αὐτὸς ἀνιοχίōν || καὶ ho κέλēξ μιᾶς | ἀμέρας hαμᾶ ἐνίκē, καὶ | ho
hυιὸς στάδιον hαμᾶ | ἐνίκē. hυπὸ δὲ | Εὔιππον ἔφορον τάδε ||
75 ἐνίκē Δαμόνōν, Ἀθάναια | ἐνhεβόhαις hίπποις | αὐτὸς ἀνιοχίōν
80 καὶ | ho κέλēξ μιᾶς ἀμέρας | hαμᾶ ἐνίκē, καὶ ho hυιὸς || στάδιον
hαμᾶ ἐνίκē. | hυπὸ δὲ Ἀριστē̄ ἔφορον | τάδε ἐνίκē Δαμόνōν, | ἐν
85 ΓαιαϜόχō ἐνhεβόhαις | [h]ίπποις αὐτὸς ἀνιοχίōν || [κ]αὶ ho κέλēξ
μιᾶς ἀμέρας | [h]αμᾶ ἐνίκē, καὶ ho hυιὸς | στάδιον καὶ δίαυλον καὶ |
90 δόλιχον μιᾶς ἀμέρας | ἐνίκōν πάντες hαμᾶ. || hυπὸ δὲ Ἐχεμένē
ἔφορον | τάδε ἐνίκē Δαμόνōν, | ἐν ΓαιαϜόχō ἐνhεβόhαις | hίπποις
αὐτὸς ἀνιοχίōν, | [κ]αὶ ho hυιὸς στάδιον κ[αὶ - - -

Record of the victories of Damonon and his son.

3 ff. νικάhας κτλ.: 'Having won victories in such a manner as
never any one of those now living.'—7. 'With his own four-horse
chariot,' αὐτῶ reflexive as in ll. 16, 17, etc. 121.1-3.—9. 'In the
games of Poseidon,' with elliptical genitive as in εἰν Ἀίδαο, etc.
So ἐν Ἀριοντίας l. 24. ΓαιάϜοχος = Hom. γαιήοχος.—11, 31.
κέλευhύνια: καὶ Ἐλευσίνια (20, 59.1), games in honor of the
Eleusinian Demeter.—12, 18. Ποhοίδαια: Ποσειδώνια (49.1,
59.1, 61.4) celebrated at Helos in Laconia and Thuria in Messe-

nia.—15 ff. 'Seven times with colts from his own mares and his
own stallion.'—**ἐνhεβόhαις hίπποις**: ἐνηβώσαις 'being in ἤβη,
young mares.'—19. **Θευρίαι**: the usual form of the name is
Θουρία.—24. **'Αριοντία**: the name of some goddess or heroine
otherwise unknown.—35 ff. Victories won by 'Ενυμακρατίδας
(cf. l. 45). The name (cf. also 'Ενυμαντιάδας IG V.i.97.20, 280)
points to an ἔνυμα = ὄνυμα, ὄνομα, with an inherited *e*-grade
in the first syllable, which is seen in some of the cognate forms
of other languages, e.g. Old Prussian *emmens*, but was hitherto
unknown in Greek.—44, 63. **Παρπαρόνια**: Πάρπαρος is the name
of a mountain in Argolis where games were held.—49 ff. Victories
won by Damonon as a boy.—54, 60. **Λιθέhια**: games in honor of
Apollo Lithesius. —57. **Μαλεάτεια**: games in honor of Apollo
Maleates. Cf. Paus. 3.12.8.—66 ff. Victories won by Damonon
and his son at the same games.—66, 73, 81, 90. **hυπό** with acc.:
136.11.

72. Taenarum. Fifth to fourth centuries B.C. IG V.i.1232.
GDI 4591. Roberts 265*c*. Schwyzer 52.4). Transitional alphabet.
Η = h and once η.

5 'Ανέθεκε | τõι Ποhοιδᾶνι | Νίκōν | Νικαφορίδα || καὶ Λύhιππον |
   καὶ Νικαρχίδαν | καὶ ταύτᾶς πάντα. | ἔφορος | Εὐδαμίδας. ||
10 ἐπάκοε | Μενεχαρίδας | 'Ανδρομέδης.

73. Taenarum. Fifth to fourth centuries B.C. IG V.i.1231.
GDI 4592. Roberts 265*d*. Schwyzer 52,3). Transitional alphabet.
Η = h and η.

5 'Ανέθηκε | Αἰσχρίōν | 'Απειρότας | τõι Ποhοιδᾶ||νι 'Ηρακλήι-
   δαν | αὐτὸν καὶ | ταὐτõ. ἔφορος | Ηαγηhίστρατος. | ἐπάκō Πρυαῖος,||
10 'Επικύδη[ς].

Manumissions of slaves in the form of dedications to Poseidon.
ἐπάκοε, ἐπάκō: dual forms of ἐπάκοος 'witness.' ἐπάκō is the
contracted form, of which the uncontracted ἐπακόω occurs in
another inscription of the same class. ἐπάκοε is due to the analogy
of consonant stems, to which nouns in -οος are not infrequently
subject, e.g., Att. χοῦς (**112.**6), late νοῦς gen. sg. νοός, nom. pl.
νόες (after βοῦς, βοός, βόες).

74. Thalamae. Fourth century B.C. IG V.i.1317. GDI IV
p. 691. Schwyzer 54. Ionic alphabet, but Η = h as well as η.

Νικοσθενίδας τᾶι Παhιφᾶι | γεροντεύων ἀνέσηκε, | αὐτός τε καὶ
5 hο τῶ πατρὸς π|ατὴρ Νικοσθενίδας, προβειπ||άhας τᾶ σιῶ ποτ'
᾿Ανδρίαν συ|νεφορεύοντα ἀνι[σ]τάμεν | Νικοσθενίδαν ἐ[ν] τῶι
ἱ[ε]ρῶι, h|ὸν καὶ σὺν καλῶι χρῆσται.

From the shrine of Pasiphae at Thalamae, an oracle often
consulted by the Spartan officials. The name of the goddess
was Πασιφάα (Att. Πασιφάη), whence the contracted Πασιφᾶ,
like ᾿Αθηνᾶ, and here, with Lac. h for intervocalic σ, Παhιφᾶ.
Since Nicosthenidas the dedicator was a member of the Council
of Elders, his grandfather of the same name could not have been
living at the time. He was carrying out an injunction previously
laid upon the grandfather by the goddess, which for some reason
had been unfulfilled.

4 ff. **προβειπάhας** κτλ.: 'since the goddess had declared that
Nicosthenidas should set up in the shrine a statue in honor of An-
dreas his fellow-ephor, and that he would then consult the oracle
with success.' The construction ποτ' ᾿Ανδρίαν . . . ἀνιστά μεν is unusual, but other possible interpretations are equally difficult in
this respect.—**hὸν** κτλ.: infin. clause depending on προβειπάhας
'who would' = 'and that he would.' For χρῆσται = χρῆσθαι see **85**.1.

75. Sparta. Second century A.D. IG V.i. 296. Artemis Orthia
p. 318.

5 Νεικάγορος | Σωσιδάμου Εὐ|δάμω κάσεν | νικάσας κελ||οῖαν
καὶ μῶα|ν καὶ καθηρα|τόρειν καὶ μ|ῶαν καὶ ἀπὸ μ|ικιχιζομένων ||
10 μέχρι μελλειρο|νείας τοὺ(ς) Γααό|χους καὶ ᾿Ασάνεα | τὴν τῶν παί-
δων | πάλην ᾿Αρτέ|μιτι ᾿Ορθεία.

76. Sparta. Second century A.D. IG V.i. 279. Artemis Orthia
p. 318.

᾿Ονασικλείδας Φιλο|στράτου νεικάσας| κασσηρατόριν πρατο|παμ-
5 παίδων, ἀτρο||παμπαίδων, εἰρέ|νων δὲ κελοῖαν [᾿Αρτέμιτι κτλ.].

77. Sparta. Second century A.D. IG V.i.307. Artemis Orthia
p. 329.

Κλέανδρορ | ὁ καὶ Μῆνιρ | Καλλιστράτω | βουαγὸρ ἐπὶ ||
5 πατρονόμω | Γοργίππω τῶ (Γοργίππω) | νικάαρ μῶαν ᾿Αρτέ-|
μιτι Βωρσέα ἀνέση|κε.

78. Sparta. Second century A.D. IG V.i.289. Artemis Orthia
p. 321.

Εὐδόκιμορ (Εὐδοκίμω) κε|λοία καὶ Εὐδόκι|μορ Δαμοκράτεορ |
5 ὁ καὶ 'Αριστείδαρ κασ||σηρατόριο(ν) νεικάαν|τερ ἐπὶ 'Αλκάστω
βουαγοὶ | μικιχιδδομένων Φωρθέα.

Nos. 75-78 belong to a series, now over 130 in number, of dedication to Artemis Orthia by the victors in certain juvenile contests.
The fullest edition is in Artemis Orthia (= JHS, Supplementary
Report V). The object dedicated, the prize itself, was an iron
sickle, which was let into a socket, with which each of the
stone slabs is provided, some with several, even (no. 75) four.
Of the contests, one is called κασσηρατόριν, κατθηρατόριν, καθθηρατόριον, etc., i.e., καταθηρατόριον, not an actual chase of wild
beasts, but some athletic game call 'the hunt.' The μῶα, i.e.,
μοῦσα, was of course a musical contest. The word which is variously spelled κελοῖαν, κελῦαν, etc., probably from the root seen in
κέλαδος, κελαδέω, also denotes a musical contest. The βουαγόρ
was the 'leader of the βοῦαι (βοῦα· ἀγέλη παίδων Hesych.),' the
bands in which the Spartan boys were trained.—As was already
known from literary sources, an elaborate nomenclature applied
to the Spartan youth according to the successive years of their
training. The terms which occur in the inscriptions are as follows.
μικκιδδόμενος, μικκιχιδδόμενος, etc. (great variety of spellings),
derived from μικκός = μικρός (89.5a) or *μικκιχός with added
diminutive suffix (164.9), and probably denoting a ten-year-old
boy. πρατοπάμπαις 'in first year of full boyhood' (πάμπαιδος
occurs elsewhere). ἀτροπάμπαις 'in second year of full boyhood'
(ἀτρο- = ἀτερο-). μελλείρην (Plut., etc., but also implied by
μελλειρονεία no. 75) 'one about to be a εἴρην.' εἴρην 'ephebe.'
τριτίρην 'third-year ephebe.'—κάσεν, following a dative or genitive and meaning 'akin to,' belongs with κάσις 'brother' or
'sister,' κάσης· ἡλικιώτης, κάσιοι· οἱ ἐκ τῆς αὐτῆς ἀγέλης ἀδελφοί
τε καὶ ἀνεψιοί - - - Λάκωνες, Hesych., but the termination with
the invariable spelling -εν is unexplained.

A few of the dedications are in the κοινή, and a few show
Doric forms without specific Laconian coloring, e.g., νικάσας.
But most of them, like those given here, represent an artificial
revival of the local dialect, that is, artificial as regards its use
in inscriptions, but probably reflecting, though only crudely

and with great inconsistency in spelling (e.g., in the use of
σ = θ), the form of speech which still survived as a patois
among the Laconian peasants. Some of the peculiarities in spelling are not characteristic of Laconian especially, but of the
late period, e.g., ει = ῑ in νεικάαντερ etc., ω for ο in Βωρθέα,
final α for ᾱι in Βωρθέα etc.

Heraclean

79. The Heraclean Tables. End of fourth century B.C. IG
XIV.645. GDI 4629. Schwyzer 62. Solmsen-Fraenkel 23. Ionic
alphabet, but with Ϝ, and Ⱶ = h. Only Table I is given here.

I

Ἔφορος Ἀρίσταρχος Ἡρακλείδα· μῆς | Ἀπελλαῖος· ha πό-
λις καὶ τοὶ ὁρισταί, | Ϝε τρίπους Φιλώνυμος Ζωπυρίσκω, | πε καρυ-
5　κεῖον Ἀπολλώνιος Ἡρακλήτω, || αι πέλτα Δάζιμος Πύρρω, κν
θρῖναξ | Φιλώτας Ἱστιείω, με ἐπιστύλιον | Ἡρακλείδας Ζω-
πύρω, Διονύσωι. |
Ἀνέγραψαν τοὶ ὁρισταὶ τοὶ haιρεθέντες ἐπὶ τὼς χώρως τὼς
hιαρὼς τὼς τῶ Διονύσω, | Φιλώνυμος Ζωπυρίσκω, Ἀπολλώνιος
10　Ἡρακλήτω, Δάζιμος Πύρρω, Φιλώτας Ἱστιείω, || Ἡρακλείδας
Ζωπύρω, καθὰ [ὤρ]ιξαν καὶ ἐτέρμαξαν καὶ συνεμέτρησαν καὶ
ἐμέρι|ξαν τῶν Ἡρακλείων διακνόντων ἐν κατακλήτωι ἀλίαι.
Συνεμετρήσαμες δὲ ἀρξάμε|νοι ἀπὸ τῶ ἀντόμω τῶ hυπὲρ Παν-
δοσίας ἄγοντος τῶ διατάμνοντος τώς τε hιαρὼς χώ|ρως καὶ τὰν Ϝι-
δίαν γᾶν ἐπὶ τὸν ἄντομον τὸν ὁρίζοντα τώς τε τῶ Διονύσω χώρως
καὶ | τὸν Κωνέας hο Δίωνος ἐπαμώχη. κατετάμομες δὲ μερίδας
15　τέτορας· || τὰν μὲν πράταν μερίδα ἀπὸ τῶ ἀντόμω τῶ πὰρ τὰ
Ηρώιδεια ἄγοντος, | εὖρος ποτὶ τὰν τριακοντάπεδον τὰν διὰ τῶν
hιχρῶν χώρων ἄγωσαν, | μᾶκος δὲ ἄνωθα ἀπὸ τᾶν ἀποροᾶν ἄχρι ἐς
ποταμὸν τὸν Ἄκιριν, καὶ | ἐγένοντο μετριώμεναι ἐν ταύται τᾶι
μερείαι ἐρρηγείας μὲν δι|ακάτιαι μία σχοῖνοι, σκίρω δὲ καὶ ἀρρήκ-
20　τω καὶ δρυμῶ Ϝεξακάτιαι || τετρώκοντα Ϝὲξ σχοῖνοι ἡμίσχοι-
νον· τὰν δὲ δευτέραν μερίδα, εὖρος ἀπὸ | τᾶς τριακονταπέδω ἐπὶ
τὸν ἄντομον τὸν πρᾶτον, μᾶκος δὲ ἀπὸ τᾶν | ἀποροᾶν ἄχρι ἐς πο-
ταμόν, καὶ ἐγένοντο μετριώμεναι ἐν ταύται τᾶι με|ρείαι ἐρρηγείας
μὲν διακάτιαι hεβδεμήκοντα τρῖς σχοῖνοι, σκίρω δὲ | καὶ ἀρρήκτω

25 καὶ δρυμῶ πεντακάτιαι σχοῖνοι · || τὰν δὲ τρίταν μερίδα, εὖρος ἀπὸ
τῶ ἀντόμω τῶ πράτω τῶ πὰρ τὰν τρι|ακοντάπεδον ἄγοντος ἐπὶ τὸν
ἄντομον τὸν δεύτερον ἀπὸ τᾶς τρια|κονταπέδω, μᾶκος ἀπὸ τᾶν
ἀποροᾶν ἄχρι ἐς ποταμόν, καὶ ἐγέ|νοντο μετριώμεναι ἐν ταύται
τᾶι μερείαι ἐρρηγείας μὲν τριακάτιαι | δέκα δύο σχοῖνοι ἡμί-
30 σχοινον, σκίρω δὲ καὶ ἀρρήκτω καὶ δρυμῶ πεντα||κάτιαι τριάκοντα
ἡεπτὰ ἡμίσχοινον · τὰν δὲ τετάρταν μερίδα, εὖρος ἀπὸ | τῶ ἀντό-
μω τῶ δευτέρω ἀπὸ τᾶς τριακονταπέδω ἐπὶ τὸν ἄντομον τὸν |
ὁρίζοντα τάν τε ἡιαρὰν καὶ τὰν Ϝιδίαν γᾶν, μᾶκος δὲ ἀπὸ τᾶν ἀπο-
ροᾶν | ἄχρι ἐς ποταμόν, καὶ ἐγένοντο μετριώμεναι ἐν ταύται τᾶι
μερείαι ἐρρη|γείας μὲν τριακάτιαι ἡοκτὼ σχοῖνοι ἡμίσχοινον,
35 σκίρω δὲ καὶ ἀρρήκτω || καὶ δρυμῶ πεντακάτιαι τετρώκοντα μία
ἡμίσχοινον. |

Κεφαλὰ πάσας ἐρρηγείας χίλιαι ἡενενήκοντα πέντε σχοῖνοι,
σκί|ρω δὲ καὶ ἀρρήκτω καὶ δρυμῶ δισχίλιαι διακάτιαι Ϝίκατι
πέντε · | τὰν δὲ νᾶσον τὰν ποτιγεγενημέναν ἐς τὰν ἄρρηκτον γᾶν
συνεμε|τρήσαμες. ἀπὸ ταύτας τᾶς γᾶς ἀπολώλη ἐρρηγείας μὲν
40 τριακάτιαι || τρῖς σχοῖνοι ἡμίσχοινον, σκίρω δὲ καὶ ἀρρήκτω καὶ
δρυμῶ τετρα|κόσιαι τριάκοντα πέντε σχοῖνοι, ἐμ μὲν τᾶι πράται
μερείαι τᾶι | πὰρ τὰ Ηηρώιδεια ἐρρηγείας μὲν ἡεβδεμήκοντα Ϝὲξ
σχοῖνοι, σκί|ρω δὲ καὶ ἀρρήκτω καὶ δρυμῶ ἡεκατὸν ἡογδόηκοντα
πέντε σχοῖ|νοι, ἐν δὲ τᾶι τετάρται μερείαι τᾶι πὰρ τὰ Φιντία ἐρρη-
45 γείας μὲν || διακάτιαι Ϝίκατι ἡεππὰ σχοῖνοι ἡμίσχοινον, σκίρω δὲ
καὶ ἀρρή|κτω καὶ δρυμῶ διακάτιαι πεντήκοντα σχοῖνοι. Κεφαλὰ
πά|σας γᾶς ἡᾶς κατεσώισαμες τῶι Διονύσωι ἡεπτακάτιαι τριά-|
κοντα ἡοκτὼ σχοῖνοι ἡμίσχοινον · ταύταν τὰν γᾶν κατεσώισα|μες
50 ἐγδικαξάμενοι δίκας τριακοσταίας τοῖς τὰν ἡιαρὰν γᾶν Ϝι||δίαν
ποιόντασσιν. ἡαύτα ἐμισθώθη [ἡα γᾶ] κατὰ βίω | [ἡόσσα]ν ἡ[α]|-
μὲς κατεσώισαμες τριακατίων μεδίμνων τὸ Ϝέτος ἡέκαστον, | ἡα δὲ
πᾶσα γᾶ ἡα τῶ Διονύσω τετρακατίων δέκα μεδίμνων κάδ|διχος
τὸ Ϝέτος ἡέκαστον.

Ἐστάσαμες δὲ καὶ ὅρως ἐπὶ μὲν τᾶς | πλευριάδος ἄνω, ἡένα μὲν
55 ἐπὶ τῶ ἀντόμω τῶ πὰρ Πανδοσίαν || τῶ πὰρ τὰ Ηηρώιδεια τῶ ὁρί-
ζοντος τάν τε ἡιαρὰν γᾶν καὶ τὰν Ϝιδίαν | ἀνχωρίξαντες ἀπὸ τᾶν
ἀποροᾶν ἐς τὰν Ϝιδίαν γᾶν, ἡως μὴ καταλυ|μακωθῆς ἀδηλωθείη
καθὼς τοὶ ἔμπροσθα ὅροι, ἄλλον δὲ ἐπὶ τῶ ἀν|τόμω τῶ πὰρ τὰ
Φιντία ἄγοντος ἐστάσαμες πὰρ τὰν βυβλίαν καὶ | τὰν διώρυγα
60 ἀνχωρίξαντες ἡωσαύτως ἐς τὰν Ϝιδίαν γᾶν <ταν>. ἀλ||λως δὲ ἀντό-

ρως τούτοις ἐστάσαμες ἐπὶ τᾶς ἀμαξιτῶ τᾶς διὰ τῶ χα|ράδεος ἀγώ-
σας τᾶς πὰρ τὸν δρυμόν, τὰς μὲν στάλας ἐς τὰν ἱαρὰν | γᾶν, τὼς
δὲ ἀντόρως ἐς τὰν Ϝιδίαν γᾶν, καταλιπόντες Ϝικατίπεδον | ἄντομον.
ἐστάσαμες δὲ καὶ μεσσόρως, δύο μὲν ἐπὶ τᾶς ἱοδῶ τᾶς | ἀγώσας ἔκ
65 τε πόλιος καὶ ἐκ Πανδοσίας διὰ τῶν ἱαρῶν χώρων, δύο || δὲ ἐν
ταῖς ἱακροσκιρίαις · τούτως πάντας ἂν εὐθυωρείαν ὁμολό|γως ἀλ-
λάλοις, τὼς μὲν ἐς τὸ ἱαρὸν πλάγος τῶ ἀντόμω ἐπιγε|γραμμένως
"ἱαρὼς Διονύσω χώρων," τὼς δὲ ἐν τᾶι Ϝιδίαι γᾶι ἐπι|γεγραμμέ-
νως "ἀντόρως." ἱωσαύτως δὲ καὶ ἐπὶ τῶ ἀντόμω τῶ | πὰρ τὰ
70 Φιντία ἄγοντος ἐστάσαμες μεσσόρως, δύο μὲν ἐπὶ || τᾶς ἱοδῶ τᾶς
ἐκ πόλιος καὶ ἐκ Πανδοσίας ἀγώσας διὰ τῶν | ἱαρῶν χώρων, δύο
δὲ ἐπὶ τὰν ἱακροσκιριᾶν πὰρ τὰς τυρείας · | τούτως πάντας ὁμολό-
γως ἂν εὐθυωρείαν τοῖς ἐπὶ τᾶς ἱοδῶ | τᾶς διὰ τῶ χαράδεος ἀγώ-
σας πὰρ τὸν δρυμόν, τὼς μὲν ἐς τὸ ἱαρὸν | πλάγος ἐπιγεγραμμέ-
75 νως "ἱαρὼς Διονύσω χώρων," τὼς δὲ ἐς τὰν Ϝιδί||αν γᾶν ἐπιγε-
γραμμένως "ἀντόρως", ἀπέχοντας ἀπ' ἀλλάλων ἱως ἤ|μεν Ϝικα-
τίπεδον ἄντομον. ἐπὶ δὲ τᾶς τριακονταπέδω τᾶς διὰ τῶν ἱι|αρῶν
χώρων ἀγώσας ἐπὶ μὲν τᾶς πλευριάδος ἄνω δύο ἀπέχοντας ἀπ'
ἀλ|λάλων τριάκοντα πόδας, ἄλλως δὲ ἀντόρως τούτοις ἐπάξαμες
πὰρ | τὰν ἱοδὸν τὰν πὰρ τὸν δρυμὸν ἄγωσαν δύο ἀπέχοντας ἀπ'
80 ἀλλάλων || τριάκοντα πόδας · ἐν δὲ μέσσωι τῶι χώρωι ἐπὶ τᾶς τρια-
κονταπέδω τέ|τορας ἀπέχοντας ἀπ' ἀλλάλων ἧαι μὲν τριάκοντα
πόδας, ἧαι δὲ Ϝίκα|τι · ἐπὶ δὲ τῶ ἀντόμω τῶ πὰρ τὰν τριακοντά-
πεδον δύο ἀπέχοντας ἀπ' ἀλ|λάλων Ϝίκατι πόδας καὶ ἄλλως ἐπὶ τῶ
δευτέρω ἀντόμω ἀπέχοντας | ἀπ' ἀλλάλων Ϝίκατι πόδας · τούτως
85 πάντας ἀνεπιγρόφως ὁρίζοντας || τὰς μερείας τὰς ποτ' ἀλλάλως
τοῖς μεμισθωμένοις τὼς ἱαρὼς χώ|ρως. τὼς δὲ πάντας χώρως
τὼς τῶ Διονύσω τερμάζοντι τοί τε ἄντομοι | ἱό τε πὰρ τὰ Ἡρώι-
δεια ἄγων καὶ ἱο πὰρ τὰ Φιντία ἀπὸ τᾶν ἀποροᾶν ἄνω|θα ἄχρι ἐς
ποταμὸν τὸν Ἄκιριν. ἀριθμὸς ὅρων τῶν ἐστάσαμες τῶν μὲν | ἐπὶ
90 τῶ ἀντόμω τῶ πὰρ τὰ Ἡρώιδεια ἱεπτὰ σὺν τῶι ἐπὶ τᾶς πλευριά-
δος, || ἐπὶ δὲ τᾶς τριακονταπέδω ἱοκτὼ σὺν τῶι τετρώ‹ι›ρωι, ἐπὶ
δὲ τῶ ἀντόμω | τῶ τε πὰρ τὰν τριακοντάπεδον καὶ τῶ ἐχομένω δύο
ἐφ' ἑκατέρω, ἐπὶ δὲ τῶ | πὰρ τὰ Φιντία ἱεπτὰ σὺν τῶι πὰρ τὰν
βυβλίναν μασχάλαν καὶ πὰρ τὰν δι|ώρυγα. |
　　　　　Συνθήκα Διονύσω χώρων. ||
95 Ἐπὶ ἐφόρω Ἀριστίωνος, μηνὸς Ἀπελλαίω, ἱα πόλις καὶ τοὶ
πολιανόμοι, ἇς βότρυς Τίμαρ|χος Νίκωνος, Ϝε ἄνθεμον Ἀπολλώ-

νιος Ἀπολλωνίω, καὶ τοὶ ὁρισταὶ F̄ε τρίπους Φιλώνυ|μος Ζωπυρί-
σκω, π̄ε καρυκεῖον Ἀπολλώνιος Ἡρακλήτω, ᾱι πέλτα Δάζιμος
Πύρρω, | κ̄ν θρῖναξ Φιλώτας Ἱστιείω, μ̄ε ἐπιστύλιον Ἡρακλεί-
δας Ζωπύρω, μισθῶντι τὼς hι|αρὼς χώρως τὼς τῶ Διονύσω ἔχον-
100 τας hως ἔχοντι κατὰ βίω, καθὰ τοὶ Ἡρακλεῖοι διέ||γνον. τοὶ δὲ
μισθωσάμενοι καρπευσόνται τὸν ἀεὶ χρόνον, hᾶς κα πρωγγύως πο-
τάγων|τι καὶ τὸ μίσθωμα ἀποδιδῶντι πὰρ Fέτος ἀεὶ Πανάμω μη-
νὸς προτερείαι· καί κ' ἔμπροσθα | ἀποδίνωντι, ἀπαξόντι ἐς τὸν δα-
μόσιον ρογὸν καὶ παρμετρησόντι τοῖς σιταγέρταις τοῖς | ἐπὶ τῶν
Fετέων τῶι δαμοσίωι χοῖ μεστὼς τὼς χοῦς κριθᾶς κοθαρᾶς δοκί-
μας, hοίας κα hα γᾶ | φέρει· ποταξόντι δὲ πρωγγύως τοῖς πολια-
105 νόμοις τοῖς ἀεὶ ἐπὶ τῶν Fετέων ἔντασσιν πὰρ || πενταηετηρίδα, hώς
κα ἐθέλοντες τοὶ πολιανόμοι δέκωνται. καὶ αἴ τινί κα ἄλλωι |
παρδῶντι τὰν γᾶν, hάν κα αὐτοὶ μεμισθωσῶνται, ἢ ἀρτυσῶντι ἢ
ἀποδῶνται τὰν ἐ|πικαρπίαν, ἂν αὐτὰ τὰ παρηεξόνται πρωγγύως
hοι παρλαβόντες ἢ hοῖς κ' ἀρτύσει ἢ hοι πρι|άμενοι τὰν ἐπικαρπίαν,
ἂν hὰ καὶ hο ἐξ ἀρχᾶς μεμισθωμένος. hόστις δέ κα μὴ ποτάγει
πρωγγύ|ως ἢ μὴ τὸ μίσθωμα ἀποδιδῶι κὰτ τὰ γεγραμμένα, τό τε
110 μίσθωμα διπλεῖ ἀποτεισεῖ τὸ ἐπὶ τῶ Fέ||τεος καὶ τὸ ἀμπώλημα
τοῖς τε πολιανόμοις καὶ τοῖς σιταγέρταις τοῖς ἀεὶ ἐπὶ τῶ Fέτεος,
hόσσωι κα | μείονος ἀμμισθωθῆ πὰρ πέντε Fέτη τὰ πρᾶτα, hότι κα
τελέθει ψαφισθὲν hάμα πᾶν τῶι πράτωι | μισθώματι, καὶ τὰ ἐν
τᾶι γᾶι πεφυτευμένα καὶ οἰκοδομημένα πάντα τᾶς πόλιος ἐσσόνται.
Ἐργαξόν|ται δὲ κὰτ τάδε· hο μὲν τὸν πρᾶτον χῶρον μισθωσά-
μενος τὸν πὰρ τὸν ἄντομον τὸν hυπὲρ Πανδοσί|ας ἄγοντα τὸν πὰρ
τὰ Ἡρώιδα ἄχρι τᾶς τριακονταπέδω ἀμπέλων μὲν φυτευσεῖ μὴ
115 μεῖον ἢ δέκα || σχοίνως, ἐλαιᾶν δὲ φυτὰ ἐμβαλεῖ ἐς τὰν σχοῖνον
hεκάσταν μὴ μεῖον ἢ τέτορα ἐς τὰν | δυνατὰν γᾶν ἐλαίας ἔχεν· αἰ
δέ κα μὴ φᾶντι τοὶ μεμισθωμένοι δυνατὰν ἦμεν ἐλαίας ἔ|χεν, τοὶ
πολιανόμοι τοὶ ἀεὶ ἐπὶ τῶν Fετέων ἔντες καὶ αἴ τινάς κα ἄλλως
τοὶ πολιανόμοι ποθέ|λωνται ἀπὸ τῶ δάμω, ὀμόσαντες δοκιμαξόντι
καὶ ἀναγγελίοντι ἐν ἁλίαι θασάμενοι τὰν | γᾶν πὸτ τὰν τῶν ἐπι-
χωρίων. ἐπιμελησόνται δὲ καὶ τῶν hυπαρχόντων δενδρέων· αἰ δέ
120 τινά κα || γήραι ἢ ἀνέμωι ἐκπέτωντι, αὐτοὶ hεξόντι. ταῦτα δὲ πάντα
πεφυτευμένα παρηεξόντι καὶ ἐνδε|διωκότα, hόσσα ἐν τᾶι συνθήκαι
γεγράψαται, ἐν τῶι πέμπτωι καὶ δεκάτωι Fέτει ἀπὸ τῶ ποτεχεῖ
Fέ|τεος ἢ Ἀριστίων ἐφορεύει· αἰ δέ κα μὴ πεφυτεύκωντι κὰτ τὰ
γεγραμμένα, κατεδικάσθεν πὰρ μὲν τὰν | ἐλαίαν δέκα νόμως ἀργυ-

ρίω πὰρ τὸ φυτὸν ἑκάστον, πὰρ δὲ τὰς ἀμπέλως δύο μνᾶς ἀρ-
γυρίω πὰρ τὰν | σχοῖνον ἑκάσταν. τὼς δὲ πολιανόμως τὼς ἐπὶ τῶ
Ϝέτεος ποθελομένως μετ' αὐτοσαυτῶν ἀπὸ τῶ || δάμω μὴ μεῖον ἢ
125 δέκα ἄνδρας ἀμφίστασθαι, ἤ κα πεφυτεύκωντι πάντα κὰτ τὰν συν-
θήκαν, | καὶ τὼς πεφυτευκότας ἀνγράψαι ἐς δόγμα· ἀνγράφεν δὲ
ἡόσσα κα πεφυτεύκωντι· ἂν αὐτὰ δὲ τὰ | καὶ εἴ τινές κα μὴ πεφυ-
τεύκωντι κὰτ τὰν συνθήκαν, ἀνγραψάντω καὶ ἐπελάσθω τὰ ἐπιζά-
μι|α τὰ γεγραμμένα πὸτ τῶι ἄλλωι μισθώματι. αἰ δέ τίς κα ἐπιβῆι
ἢ νέμει ἢ φέρει τι τῶν ἐν τᾶι ἱαρᾶι | γᾶι ἢ τῶν δενδρέων τι κόπτηι
ἢ θραύηι ἢ πριῶι ἢ ἄλλο τι σίνηται, ἡο μεμισθωμένος ἐγδικαξῆ||-
130 ται ἡως πολίστων καὶ ἡότι κα λάβει αὐτὸς ἑξεῖ.

Τὰς δὲ τράφως τὰς διὰ τῶν χώρων ῥεώσας καὶ | τὼς ῥόως οὐ
κατασκαψόντι οὐδὲ διασκαψόντι τῶι ἡύδατι οὐδὲ ἐφερξόντι τὸ ἡύ-
δωρ οὐδ' ἀφερξόν|τι· ἀνκοθαρίοντι δὲ ἡοσσάκις κα δέωνται τὰ πὰρ
τὰ αὐτῶν χωρία ῥέοντα· οὐδὲ τὰς ἡοδὼς τὰς ἀπο|δεδειγμένας ἀρα-
σόντι οὐδὲ συνηερξόντι οὐδὲ κωλυσόντι πορεύεσθαι· ἡότι δέ κα
τούτων τι ποι|ῶντι πὰρ τὰν συνθήκαν, τοὶ πολιανόμοι τοὶ ἀὲς ἐπὶ τῶ
135 Ϝέτεος ἐπικαταβα(λί)οντι καὶ ζαμιωσόντι, || ἄχρι ἡῶ κα ἀφομοιώ-
σωντι κὰτ τὰν συνθήκαν. οὐ κοψεῖ δὲ τῶν δενδρέων οὐδὲ θραυσεῖ
οὐδὲ πριωσεῖ | οὐδὲ ἡῆς οὐδὲ ἡὲν οὐδὲ ἄλλος τήνωι. οὐδὲ γαιώνας
θησεῖ πὰρ τὼς ἡυπάρχοντας οὐδὲ σαρμευσεῖ, | αἰ μὴ ἡόσσα κα ἐν
αὐτᾶι τᾶι γᾶι ἡᾶι μεμίσθωται οἰκοδόμηται· οὐδὲ τοφιῶνας ἐν τᾶι
ἱαρᾶι γᾶι ποιησεῖ | οὐδὲ ἄλλον ἐασεῖ· αἰ δὲ μή, ἡυπόλογος ἐσσῆ-
ται ἡως τὰν ἱαρὰν γᾶν ἀδικίων. οἰκοδομησῆται δὲ καὶ οἰ|κίαν ἐν
τοῖς χώροις τούτοις, βοῶνα, μυχόν, ἀχύριον, τὸν μὲν βοῶνα τὸ μὲν
140 μᾶκος Ϝίκατι καὶ δυῶν πο||δῶν, τὸ δὲ εὖρος ἡοκτὼ καὶ δέκα ποδῶν,
τὸν δὲ ἀχύριον μὴ μεῖον τὸ μὲν μᾶκος ἡοκτὼ καὶ δέκα ποδῶν, | τὸ
δὲ εὖρος πέντε καὶ δέκα ποδῶν, τὸν δὲ μυχὸν πέντε καὶ δέκα πο-
δῶν παντᾶι. ταῦτα δὲ παρεξόντι οἰκο|δομημένα καὶ στεγόμενα καὶ
τεθυρωμένα ἐν τοῖς χρόνοις ἐν ἡοῖς καὶ τὰ δένδρεα δεῖ πεφυτευκῆ-
μεν· αἰ | δὲ μή, κατεδικάσθεν πὰρ μὲν τὸν βοῶνα Ϝὲξ μνᾶς ἀργυ-
ρίω, πὰρ δὲ τὸν ἀχύριον τέτορας μνᾶς ἀργυρίω, | πὰρ δὲ τὸν μυχὸν
τρὶς μνᾶς ἀργυρίω. τῶν δὲ ξύλων τῶν ἐν τοῖς δρυμοῖς οὐδὲ τῶν ἐν
145 τοῖς σκίροις οὐ πωλη||σόντι οὐδὲ κοψόντι οὐδὲ ἐμπρησόντι οὐδὲ
ἄλλον ἐασόντι· αἰ δὲ μή, ἡυπόλογοι ἐσσόνται κὰτ τὰς ῥήτρας | καὶ
κὰτ τὰν συνθήκαν. ἐς δὲ τὰ ἐποίκια χρησόντι ξύλοις ἐς τὰν οἰκο-
δομὰν ἡοῖς κα δήλωνται, καὶ ἐς τὰς | ἀμπέλως· τῶν δὲ ξηρῶν κο-
ψόντι ἡόσσα αὐτοῖς ποτ' οἰκίαν ἐς χρείαν· τοῖς δὲ σκίροις καὶ τοῖς

δρυμοῖς χρη|σόνται τοὶ μισθωσάμενοι ἀν τὰν αὐτῶ μερίδα ἕκασ-
τος. ὅσσαι δέ κα τᾶν ἀμπέλων ἢ τῶν δενδρέων ἀπο|γηράσωντι,
ἀποκαταοτασόντι τοὶ καρπιζόμενοι ἧως ἦμεν τὸν ἴσον ἀριθμὸν ἀεί.

150 Οὐχ ὑπογραψόνται || δὲ τὼς χώρως τούτως ἧοι μισθωσάμενοι
οὐδὲ τίμαμα ἧοισόντι οὔτε τῶν χώρων οὔτε τᾶς ἐπιοικοδο|μᾶς· αἰ
δὲ μή, ἧυπόλογος ἐσσῆται κὰτ τὰς ῥήτρας. αἰ δέ τίς κα τῶν καρ-
πιζομένων ἄτεκνος ἄφωνος ἀπο|θάνει, τᾶς πόλιος πᾶσαν τὰν ἐπι-
καρπίαν ἦμεν. αἰ δέ χ᾽ ὑπὸ πολέμω ἐγϜηληθίωντι ἧώστε μὴ
ἐξῆμεν | τὼς μεμισθωμένως καρπεύεσθαι, ἀνηεῶσθαι τὰν μίσθωσιν
καθά κα τοὶ Ηρακλεῖοι διαγνῶντι, καὶ μὴ | ἦμεν ἧυπολόγως μήτε
αὐτὼς μήτε τὼς πρωγγύως τῶν ἐν ταῖ συνθήκαι γεγραμμένων.

155 τὼς δὲ πρωγγύ||ως τὼς ἀεὶ γενομένως πεπρωγγευκῆμεν τῶν τε
μισθωμάτων καὶ τῶν ἐπιζαμιωμάτων καὶ τῶν ἀμ|πωλημάτων καὶ
τᾶν καταδικᾶν καὶ αὐτὼς καὶ τὰ χρήματα ἥ κα ἐπιμαρτυρήσωντι,
καὶ μὴ ἦμεν μήτε ἅρ|νησιν μήτε παλινδικίαν μηδὲ κατ᾽ ἄλλον μη-
δὲ ἕνα τρόπον τᾶι πόλι πράγματα παρέχεν μηδὲ τοῖς ἧυ|πὲρ τᾶς
πόλιος πρασσόντασσι· αἰ δὲ μή, ἀτελὲς ἦμεν.

Δεύτερος. Ηο δὲ τὸν δεύτερον μισθωσάμενος | καρπευσῆται
ἀπὸ τᾶς τριακονταπέδω τᾶς διὰ τῶν τετρώρων ἀγώσας ἐπὶ τὸν
160 ἄντομον τὸν πρᾶτον ἧόσ||σος κ᾽ εἶ καὶ πραξεῖ πάντα κὰτ τὰν συν-
θήκαν καὶ ἧυπόλογος ἐσσῆται καὶ αὐτὸς καὶ τοὶ πρώγγυοι, ἧότι
κα | μὴ πράξει κὰτ τὰν συνθήκαν.

Τρίτος. Ηο δὲ τὸν τρίτον χῶρον μισθωσάμενος καρπευσῆται
ἀπὸ τῶ ἀν|τόμω τῶ ἀνώτερον τᾶς τριακονταπέδω πὸτ τὸν ἄντομον
τὸν δεύτερον ἀπὸ τᾶς τριακονταπέδω καὶ | πραξεῖ πάντα κὰτ τὰν
συνθήκαν καὶ ἧυπόλογος ἐσσῆται καὶ αὐτὸς καὶ τοὶ πρώγγυοι,
ἧότι κα μὴ πρά|ξει κὰτ τὰν συνθήκαν.

Τέταρτος. Ηο δὲ τὸν τέταρτον χῶρον μισθωσάμενος πὰρ τε
165 τῶν πολιανό||μων τῶν ἐπὶ ᾽Αριστίωνος ἐφόρω καὶ τῶν ὁριστᾶν
καὶ πὰρ τῶν πολιανόμων τῶν ἐπὶ ᾽Αριστάρχω τῶ Ηρα|κλείδα
ἐφόρω h͞α ἄνθεμα Φιλωνύμω τῶ Φιλωνύμω, h͞α ἔμβολος Ηρα-
κλείδα τῶ Τιμοκράτιος καρπευ|σῆται ἀπὸ τῶ ἀντόμω τῶ τρίτω
ἀπὸ τᾶς τριακονταπέδω ἐπὶ τὸν ἄντομον τὸν ὁρίζοντα τώς τε τῶ
Διο|νύσω χώρως καὶ τὰ Φιντίας ἧο Κρατίνω παμωχεῖ. ἧο δὲ ἀν-
ηελόμενος ἐργαξῆται τὰ μὲν ἄλλα κὰτ τὰν | συνθήκαν, καθὼς κὰτ
τὼς λοιπὼς γέγραπται, τὰς δὲ ἀμπέλως τὰς ἧυπαρχώσας ἐργα-
170 ξῆται ἧως βέλτι||στα· ἧόσσαι δέ κα τᾶν ἀμπέλων ἀπογηράσκωντι,
ποτιφυτευσεῖ ἧώστε ἀεὶ ἧυπάρχεν τὸν ἴσον ἀριθμὸν τᾶν | σχοίνων

τὸν νῦν ὑπάρχοντα, Ϝίκατι τέτορας σχοίνως · αἱ δὲ μή, προκαδ-
δεδικάσθω δύο μνᾶς ἀργυρίω | πὰρ τὰν σχοῖνον ἑκάσταν. τὰς δὲ
ἐλαίας καὶ τὰς συκίας καὶ τὰ ἄλλα δένδρεα τὰ ἥμερα τὰ ὑπάρ-
χον|τα πάντα ἐν τᾶι μερίδι ταύται περισκαψεῖ καὶ ποτισκαψεῖ καὶ
περικοψεῖ τὰ δεόμενα, καὶ αἴ τινά κα γήραι ἢ | ἀνέμωι ἐκπέτωντι,
ἀποκαταστασεῖ μὴ μείω τὸν ἀριθμὸν τῶν ὑπαρχόντων · ποτιφυ-
175 τευσεῖ δὲ καὶ ἐλαίας || ἐν τᾶι ψιλᾶι ὁμολόγως ποιῶν τοῖς ὑπαρ-
χόντασσι δενδρέοις καὶ τὸν ἀριθμὸν τὸν ἵσον καθῶς καὶ ἐν τᾶι | ἄλ-
λαι συνθήκαι γέγραπται. ἥτι δέ κα μὴ πράξει ho ἀνhελόμενος
κὰτ τὰν συνθήκαν ἢ μὴ ἐν τοῖς χρό|νοις τοῖς γεγραμμένοις, ὑπό-
λογος ἐσσῆται τοῖς πολιανόμοις καὶ τοῖς σιταγέρταις τοῖς ἐπὶ τῶ
Ϝέτεος | καθὼς καὶ ἐν τᾶι ἄλλαι συνθήκαι γέγραπται. αἱ δέ κα τοὶ
πολιανόμοι τοὶ ἀεὶ ἐπὶ τῶν Ϝετέων ἔντες μὴ πρά|ξωντι πάντα κὰτ
τὰν συνθήκαν, αὐτοὶ ὑπόλογοι ἐσσόνται κὰτ τὰν συνθήκαν.
180 Ἐπὶ τούτοις ἐμισθώσαν||το τὰν μὲν πράταν μίσθωσιν ἀπὸ τῶν
τῶ Ηηρώιδα ‾με‾ κιβώτιον Βορμίων Φιλώτα πεντήκοντα ηεπτὰ
μεδί|μνων κάδδιχος · πρώγγυος τῶ σώματος ‾με‾ κιβώτιον Ἀρκὰς
Φιλώτα. τὰν δὲ δευτέραν μίσθωσιν ‾ηα‾ | ἔμβολος Δάμαρχος Φιλω-
νύμω τετρώκοντα μεδίμνων · πρώγγυος τῶ σώματος ..... Θεό-
δωρος Θε|οδώρω. τὰν δὲ τρίταν μίσθωσιν ‾Ϝε‾ γυῖον Πεισίας Λεον-
τίσκω τριάκοντα πέντε μεδίμνων · πρώγγυος | τῶ σώματος ‾κν‾
σφαιρωτῆρες Ἀριστόδαμος ...... τὰν δὲ τετάρταν μίσθωσιν
185 ‾αλ‾ λωτήριον || Φίλιππος Φιλίππω διακατίων ηεβδεμήκοντα ηοκτὼ
μεδίμνων · πρώγγυος τῶ σώματος ‾πε‾ καρυκεῖον | Ἀπολλώνιος
Ηηρακλήτω.|
      Γραμματεὺς ‾Ϝε‾ γυῖον Ἀριστόδαμος Συμμάχω · γαμέτρας Χαι-
ρέας Δάμωνος Νεαπολίτας.
      The lands which were the property of the temples of Dionysus
and Athena Polias having been encroached upon by private
parties, with a consequent diminution of their revenue, two
commissions were appointed to define and mark their boundaries,
survey them, and divide them into lots. Table I contains the
report of the commission dealing with the lands of Dionysus
(ll. 1-94), a statement of the regulations under which the lands
were offered for rental (ll. 95-179), and a list of those who took
leases, with their sureties and the amount of the rental (ll.
179-87). Table II contains a report of the commission on the
lands of Athena Polias.

On the 3 pl. fut. forms, as taken here, κοψόντι, καρπευσόνται, etc., see **141**b.

1-7. The groups of letters and names of objects which precede the name, as Ϝε τρίπους, etc. represent seals marking the tribe and family of the person.—11. **διαχνόντων**: = διαγνόντων in table II.9.66.—17. **ἀποροᾶν**: 'watersheds' (?). Schwyzer, Rh.M. 77.225 ff.—18 ff. **ἐρρηγείας** κτλ.: '201 σχοῖνοι of arable land, 646½ of brushwood, barren, and wooded, land.'—38. **νᾶσον**: 'alluvial land' as once an 'island.' Schwyzer, Rh.M. 77.231 ff.— 39. **ἀπολώλη**: 'had been lost,' i.e., by private encroachment. This land the commissioners restored to Dionysus, bringing suits against those who had appropriated it to private use (ll. 47 ff.).—49. **δίκας τριακοσταίας**: 'suits which had to be tried within thirty days.' Cf. no. 57.42 and the Attic δίκαι ἔμμηνοι.—56. 'Setting it (the boundary) back from the springs onto the private land, so that it should not be covered over with stones (which were washed down by the current) and made invisible, like the former boundaries.'—81. **ἧι μὲν . . . ἧι δὲ**: demonst. use of ὅς.—102. **ἀποδίνωντι**: 'thresh.'—104. **φέρει**: for φέρηι. 39. So usually, but also ἐπιβῆι, κόπτηι, θραύηι ll. 138-39, and ἀμμισθωθῆ l. 111.—105 ff. **καὶ αἴ τινί κα ἄλλωι** κτλ.: 'if they assign to another the land which they shall have leased, or devise it by will, or sell the harvest rights, those who take it over or those to whom it has been willed, or those who purchase the harvest rights, shall furnish sureties in the same manner as the one who leased it in the beginning.'— **μεμισθωσῶνται**: fut. perf. subj. 146.5.—108 ff. **hόστις δέ κα μὴ ποτάγει** κτλ.: 'whoever fails to fulfill his obligations shall pay not only double the rental for the year, but also, all together with the first rental, whatever rebate, namely the decrease allowed in re-leasing for the first five years, is determined by decree.' To insure leasing the land again it was generally necessary to offer it at a rental less than that originally fixed. The ἀμπώλημα is the 're-bargaining,' hence concretely the amount involved in it, the 'rebate.' Cf. also ll. 115 ff. 'be surety for the rentals, fines, rebates, and judgments.' hάμα l. 111 seems from its position to go with πᾶν as well as with τῶι πράτωι μισθώματι. For the whole situation, cf. from a Delian inscription, BCH 14.432, ἀνεμισθώσαμεν δὲ καὶ τῆς Χαριτείας τὸ μέρος, ὃ ἐμίσθωτο Μνησίμαχος οὐ καθιστάντος τοὺς ἐγγύους Μνησιμάχου, - - -· τὸ δὲ λοιπόν, ὅσωι ἔλαττον ηὗρεν ἡ γῆ ἀναμισθωθεῖσα, ὀφείλει Μνησίμαχος κτλ.—120. **ἐκπέτωντι**: ἔπετον, aor. of πίπτω, occurs also in Pindar and Alcaeus and is probably the form of all dialects except Attic-Ionic, where ἔπεσον shows a change of τ to σ which does not fall under the usual conditions (**61**) and is not certainly explained.—121. **γεγράψαται** fut. perf. **146.**5.—122. **κατεδικάσθεν**: 'have been condemned,' i.e., are hereby condemned in advance. Cf. προκαδ-δεδικάσθω l. 171.—128. **ἐπιβῆι**: 'trespasses,' from ἐπιβάω == ἐπιβαίνω.—130 ff. **τὰς δὲ τράφως** κτλ.: 'the ditches and canals which run through the lands they shall not dig deeper nor make a breach in for the water, nor shall they dam in or dam off the water.'—ἐφερξόντι, ἀφερξόντι, συνηερξόντι: these belong with Ion. ἀπέργω (Hom. also ἀποέργω), συνέργω, etc. from Ϝέργω, while Att. ἀπείργω etc. are from *ἐϜέργω with prothetic ε. The spiritus asper is found mainly as here, with the forms in ξ, e.g., Att. καθεῖρξα beside κατείργω.—136. **γαιῶνας**: 'mounds of earth.' **165.**4.—**σαρμευσεῖ**: meaning of σαρμεύω uncertain, perhaps 'make pits (storage pits).' Cf. Hesych. σαρμός· σωρὸς γῆς, καὶ κάλλυσμα. ἄλλοι ψάμμον, ἄλλοι χόρτον, and Et.M. σάρμα· χάσμα.—137. οἰκοδόμηται: perf. subj. of the same type as Cret. πέπᾱται (**151.**1). For lack of reduplication, as also in οἰκοδομημένα ll. 112, 141, cf. οἴκημαι etc. in Ionic (Hdt.) and later Attic.—**τοφιῶνας** 'burial places' (so, not 'tufa quarries') 6, **165.**4.—146. **ἐς δὲ τὰ ἐποίκια** κτλ.: 'But they shall use what wood they wish for the construction of the farm buildings,' i.e., the βοών, μυχός, etc.—149 ff. **οὐχ ὑπογραψόνται**: 'the lessees shall not mortgage the lands or make a payment (perhaps 'pay a fine') out of either the lands or the buildings thereon.' Note that when a stop is changed to an aspirate by a following h the latter is not written. So also αἰ δέ χ' ὑπὸ l. 152.

Argolic

80. Mycenae. Sixth century B.C. IG IV.492. Schwyzer 97. Solmsen-Fraenkel 28. Vollgraff, Mnemos. 57.221 f.

Φραhιαρίδας Μυ|κανέαθεν παρ' 'A|θαναίας ἐς πόλιος | ἱκέτας
5 ἔγεντο || ἐπ' 'Αντία καὶ Πυρ|Fία. εἶεν δὲ 'Αντί|ας καὶ Κίθιος
καἶσχρōν.

Very condensed and variously understood, but perhaps best (with Vollgraff, 1.c.) 'Phrasiaridas of Mycenae, (having been sent as) a suppliant, arrived from Athena from the citadel in the magistracy of Antias and Pyrrhias. (The reply?) Let Antias and Cithius and Aeschron be - - -.' Since the nature of the request is unknown, the meaning of the reply is obscure.— **ἔγεντο:** unthem. form = ἐγένετο, occurring in poets and here a formulaic expression.

81. Mycenae. Early fifth century B.C. IG IV.493. Schwyzer 98. Solmsen-Fraenkel 29.

Αἰ μὲ̄ δαμιοργία εἶε, τὸς ἱαρομνάμονας τὸς ἐς Περσε̄̃ το(ῖ)σι γονεῦσι κριτε̄̃ρας ἔμεν κὰ τὰ FεFρε̄μένα.

'If there is no body of demiurgi, the temple administrators to (the heroum of) Perseus shall judge between the parents according to what has been decreed.' This is only the conclusion of an inscription which must have been on the stone which once rested upon the base containing this line. Pausanias reports a heroum of Perseus on the road from Mycenae to Argos. It is probable that boys were employed in the cult and that disputes arose among the parents with regard to their appointment.

82. Argive Heraeum. Early fifth century B.C. IG IV.517. Schwyzer 96. Solmsen-Fraenkel 26.

[Η]α στάλα καὶ hο τελαμὸ̄ | [ἱ]αρὰ τᾶς Ηέρας τᾶς 'Αργε|[ί]ας.
5 ἱαρομνάμονες τοίδε · | ΠυρFαλίōν Δυμὰνς ἀFρέτευε, || 'Αλκαμένες Ηυλλεύς, | 'Αριστόδαμος Ηυρνάθιος, | 'Αμφίκριτος Πανφύλ|[λ]ας.

On the face of the stone, just below the inscription, is a rectangular cutting, with dowel holes, evidently intended for the reception of a tablet. This was the στάλα, while the τελαμό, properly 'support, pedestal,' refers to the whole stone in which the στάλα was set, and which would itself be called a στήλη in Attic. In several inscriptions from the region of the Euxine τελαμών is actually used as the equivalent of στήλη, e.g., ἀναγράψαντα τὸ ψάφισμα τοῦτο εἰς τελαμῶνα λευκοῦ λίθου ἀναθέμεν εἰς τὸ ἱερὸν τοῦ 'Απόλλωνος (GDI 3078, Mesembria). This use is doubtless of Megarian origin, and is closely allied to that seen here at Argos, though with complete loss of the original notion of 'support.'

The hieromnemones consist of a representative of each of four tribes, of which the Δυμᾶνες, whose representative presides, the Ὑλλεῖς, and the Πάμφυλοι, are the three tribes common to all Doric states, while the Ὑρνάθιοι are attested only for Argolis. Cf. Steph. Byz. s.v. Δυμᾶνες· φυλὴ Δωριέων. ἦσαν δέ τρεῖς, Ὑλλεῖς καὶ Πάμφυλοι καὶ Δυμᾶνες ἐξ Ἡρακλέους. καὶ προσετέθη ἡ Ὑρνηθία, ὡς Ἔφορος α'.

83. Argos. Sixth century B.C. Vollgraff, Mnemos. 57.206 ff. Boissevain, Mnemos. 58.13 ff. Schwyzer, Rh.M. 79.321 ff. Bourguet, Rev. Ét. Gr. 43.13 ff. SEG 11.314.

Ἐπὶ τōνδεōνέν δαμιοργόντōν τὰ ἐ|[ν] Ἀθαναίας ἐπ[ο]ιϜέθε τα-
δέν· τὰ ποιϜέ|ματα καὶ τὰ χρέματά τε καὶ τὸν ...... | .....
ἀ[νέθεν] ταῖ Ἀθαναίαι ταῖ Πολιάδι. ||

5 Συλεύς τε   τοῖσι χρέμασι τοῖσι χρε̄στερ-
  καὶ Ἐράτυιιος   ίιοισι τοῖσι τᾶς θιῶ μὲ χρέ-
  καὶ Πολύϙτōρ   [σ]θō Ϝηεδιέστας [ἐ]χθὸς
  καὶ Ἐξάκεστο[ς]   τō τεμένεος τō τᾶς Ἀ[θαν-]
  καὶ Ηαγι..   [αιίας] τᾶς Πολιάδος. δαμόσ-
10 καὶ Ἐρύϙο[ιρος]   ιον δὲ χ[ρ]όνσθō προ[τὶ τὰ
                                   ἱαρά]. αἱ δὲ σίναιτο, ἀφ[α]κεσ-
άσθō, ηοῖζ δὲ δαμιορ[γὸς ἐπ]α[να]νκασσάτō.
ηο δ' ἀμφίπολος μελεταινέτō τούτōν.

'When the following (namely the six listed in ll. 5-10, left column) were demiurgi, these things were made in the temple of Athena. The works and the treasures and the—they dedicated to Athena Polias. Syleus, etc. The treasures that are utensils of the goddess a private citizen shall not use outside the shrine of Athena Polias. But the state may use them for the sacred rites. If anyone injures them he shall make good the damage,— with how much, the demiurgos shall impose. The sacristan shall attend to these matters.'

1, 2. τōνδεōνέν, ταδέν (the latter occurring in another early Arg. inscription): 123.—7. Ϝηεδιέστας = ἰδιώτης, formed from *Ϝηέδιος beside *Ϝηίδιος in Arg. ηίδιος, usual Ϝίδιος, ἴδιος, after the analogy of τελέστας. Schwyzer, Rh.M. 79.323 ff.—10. δαμόσιον: Neut. sg. as collective with plural verb. So (Schwyzer) better than δαμοσίōν partitive gen. pl. (Vollgraff).—12. hoῖζ δέ: 97.4. 84. Argos. Sixth or early fifth century B.C. IG IV.554. Schwyzer 78. Solmsen-Fraenkel 24. Vollgraff, Mnemos. 58.29 ff.

[Θ]ēσαυρōν [τōν] τᾶς 'Αθαναίας αἴ τις ‹τις› | [ἒ τὰ]ν βōλὰν
τ[ὰν] ἀνφ' 'Αρίστōνα ἒ τὸν(ς) συναρτύοντας | [ἒ ἄ]λλον τινὰ τα-
μίαν εὐθύνοι τέλος ἔχōν ἒ δικάσ|[ζοι] ἒ δικάσζοιτο τōν γρασσμά-
5 τōν hένεκα τᾶς κατα||θέσιος ἒ τᾶς ἀλιάσσιος, τρέτō καὶ δαμευέσσθō
ἐνς | 'Αθαναίαν. ha δὲ βōλὰ ποτελάτō hἀντιτυχόνσα· αἱ | δέ κα
μέ, αὐτοὶ ἐνόχοι ἔντō ἐνς 'Αθαναίαν.

An act of indemnity for the management of the treasury of Athena, probably with reference to some specific irregularity which had occurred. Without such an act, persons who proposed or put to vote a proposition to use sacred funds for public purposes were liable to punishment. Cf. Thuc. 2.24, 8.15, Tod 51 B 11 ff.

'Concerning the treasures of Athena. If any magistrate calls to account the council under Ariston or his fellow ἀρτῦναι or any treasurer, or entertains or brings suit on account of the submission (to the assembly) of the proposals or on account of the action of the assembly, he shall be banished and his property be confiscated to treasury of Athena. The council which is in office shall enforce (the confiscation), otherwise they (the members of the council) shall themselves be liable to Athena.'

1. [θ]ēσαυρōν, κτλ.: gen. of the matter involved. 171.—Until the existence of a τιστις (cf. Lat. quisquis) is corroborated, it is better to assume simple dittography.—2. συναρτύοντας: the ἀρτῦναι as a body of Argive officials are mentioned by Thuc. 5.47.11.—3. τέλος ἔχōν: cf. El. ὃρ μέγιστον τέλος ἔχοι, no. 61.— 4 ff. τōν γρασσμάτōν hένεκα καταθέσιος κτλ.: 'on account of the deposition of written proposals (i.e., the formal introduction of a measure before the assembly) or the (consequent) act of the assembly.' This refers to some measure sanctioning the irregular use of the treasure. Those responsible for the introduction or passage of such a measure are to be immune from pro-

secution. For the order of words cf. Thuc. 1.57 τῆς Ποτιδαίας
ἕνεκα ἀποστάσεως. For γράσσμα = γράμμα, see **164**.4.

85. Argos. About 450 B.C. Ditt. Syll. 56. Schwyzer 83. Solmsen-
Fraenkel 27. Tod 33. SEG 11.316. Vollgraff, Verh. Kon. Ned.
Akad. Wet., Afd. Letterk., Nieuwe Reeks, Deel 51, no. 2.
[1, 2 fragmentary. τõι Τυλισίōι ἐξέ]μεν ξύλλεσθαι πλὰ[ν]
5 τ|[ὰ μέρε̄ τὰ Κνōσίōν συν]τέλλοντα ἐνς πόλιν. hότ[ι ‖ δέ κα ἐκ
δυσμεν]έōν hέλōμες συνανφότεροι, δα[σ|μō̄ι τō̄ν κὰτ γ]ᾶν τὸ τρίτον
μέρος ἔχεν πάντō̄ν, τ[õ|ν δὲ κὰτ] θάλασαν τὰ hέμισα ἔχεν πάντō̄ν.
τὰν δὲ [δ|εκ]άταν τὸνς Κνōσίονς ἔχεν, hότι χ' ἔλōμες κοι[ν|ᾶ]ι.
10 τō̄ν δὲ φαλύρōν τὰ μὲν καλλ(ι)στεῖα Πυθō̄δε ἀπ[ά]|‖γεν κοινᾶι
ἀμφοτέρονς, τὰ δ' ἄλλα τō̄ι "Α[ρει Κνōσ|]ō̄ι ἀντιθέμεν κοινᾶι ἀμφο-
τέρονς. ἐξ[αγō̄γὰν δ' ἒ]‖μεν Κνōσόθεν ἐνς Τυλισὸν κὲκ Τυλι[σō̄
Κνōσόνδ]|ε· α[ἰ] δὲ πέρανδε ἐξάγοι, τελίτō̄ hόσσα[περ hοι Κν]|ό̄-
15 σιοι· τὰ δ' ἐκ Τυλισō̄ ἐξαγέσθω hόπυ[ι κα λε̄ι. τō̄]|‖ιΠοσειδᾶνι
τō̄ι ἐν Ἰυτō̄ι τὸν Κνōσίō[ν ἰαρέα θύ]|εν. τᾶι Ἥραι ἐν Ἑραίōι θύεν
βō̄ν θέλει[αν ἀμφοτ]‖έρον[ς κ]οινᾶι, θύεν δὲ πρὸ Ϝακινθ[ίō̄ν - - - |
23 [lines 18-22 fragmentary or missing] χρέματα δὲ μὲ 'νπιπασ-
κέσθō̄ hο Κνōσιο[ς] | ἐν Τυλισō̄ι, hο δὲ Τυλίσιος ἐν Κνōσō̄ι hο
25 χρεῖζ[ō̄]‖|ν. μεδὲ χόρας ἀποτάμνεσθαι με̄δατέρονς με̄δ' ἄ[π]‖αν-
σαν ἀφαιρῖσθαι. ὅροι τᾶς γᾶς· Ηυõν ὅρος καὶ Α|ἰετοὶ κάρταμίτιον
καὶ τὸ τõ Ἀρχō̄ τέμενος κα[ὶ] | hο ποταμὸς κὲλ Λευκόπορον κά-
γάθοια, hᾶι hύδō̄|ρ ῥεῖ τõμβριον, καὶ Λᾶος. hῖ κα τō̄ι Μαχανεῖ
30 θύō̄μ‖ες τὸνς Ϝεξέκοντα τελέονς ὄϜινς, καὶ τᾶι Ἥραι | τὸ σκέλος
Ϝεκάστō̄ διδόμεν τõ Θύματος. αἰ δὲ συ|μπλέονες πόλιες ἐκ πολεμίōν
ἕλοιεν χρέματα, | hόπαι συγνοῖεν hοι Κνōσιοι καὶ τοὶ Ἀργεῖοι, |
35 hούτō̄ ἔμεν. τō̄ι "Αρει καὶ τἀφροδίται τὸν Κνōσι|‖ον ἰαρέα θύεν,
φέρεν δὲ τὸ σκέλος Ϝεκάστō̄. τὸν Ἀ|ρχὸν τὸ τέμενος ἔχεν τὸν
Ἀχάρναι. τοῖς θύονσι | ξένια παρέχεν τὸνς Κνōσίονς, τὸνς δ' Ἀρ-
γείονς τō̄ι χορō̄ι ἐν Τυλισō̄ι. αἴ κα καλε̄ι hο Κνōσιος πρ|εσγέαν,
40 hέπεσθαι hόπυι κα δέε̄ται· καί χ' ὁ Τυλίσ‖|ιος τὸν Κνōσιον, κατὰ
ταύτά. αἰ δὲ μὲ δοῖεν ξένι|α, βō̄λὰ ἐπαγέτō̄ ῥύτιον δέκα στατέρōν
αὐτίκα ἐ|πὶ κόσμος, κὲν Τυλισō̄ι κατὰ ταύτά hο Κνōσιος. hα στάλα
ἔσστα ἐπὶ Μελάντα βασιλέος. ἀϜρέτευ|ε Λυκōτάδας Ηυλλεύς. ἀλι-
45 αίαι ἔδοξε τᾶι τō̄ν ‖ ἰαρōν. ἀ(Ϝρέτευε) βō̄λᾶς Ἀρχίστρατος Λυκο-
φρονίδας. | τοὶ Τυλίσιοι ποὶ τὰν στάλαν ποιγραψάνσθō̄ τάδε· | αἴ
τις ἀφικνοῖτο Τυλισίōν ἐνς "Αργος, κατὰ ταύτά | σφιν ἔστō̄ hᾶιπερ
Κνōσίοις.

Treaty between the Cretan cities of Cnossus and Tylissus arranged under the auspices of Argos, which was regarded as the mother state. It was no doubt Tylissus which had appealed to Argos for support in safeguarding its independence against its powerful neighbor, and it is in favor of the weaker party that certain articles are framed (cf. ll. 14, 22 ff.) and Argive support granted (cf. ll. 37-38).

This is the official Argive draft, in the Argive alphabet and in the main in the Argive dialect. Only the characteristic Argive h = intervocalic σ is eliminated, not only in the Cretan name Κνόσιος (but cf. Κνōhίαν in the draft at Tylissus), but in βασιλέος of the dating (l. 43). Cf. 59.2, 275. There is a trace of the influence of preliminary Cretan in l. 33 hoι Κνόσιοι καὶ τοὶ ᾿Αργεῖοι (Cret. οἰ, Arg. τοί, 122).

A fragment found at Tylissus, containing another section of the same treaty (Schwyzer 84, revised text by Vollgraff, l.c.), is also in the Argive alphabet (Ͱ = λ, Ͱ = β, ⴱ = h, but once = η as in Cretan) and dialect, even having the Argive h = intervocalic σ, e.g., Κνōhίαν. The use of δυσμενέες for 'enemies,' which in literature is mainly poetical, is seen in both these inscriptions, and may be another Cretan element (cf. Law-Code VI.46), though not necessarily so. Likewise τέλλω = τελέω (l. 4, but τελίτō l. 13), as in Law-Code X.42 etc.

3. ξύλλεσθαι: σκύλλεσθαι 'plunder.' 87.—6 ff. Tylissus, being the party last named and the smaller of the two cities, is to be understood as the subject of ἔχεν. —9. φαλύρōν: λαφύρων. 88.— 13. τελίτō: τελείτω, cf. ἀφαιρῖσθαι l. 25, and 25c.—17. πρὸ Ϝαϙινθίōν: before the festival ῾Υακίνθια. 52c.—23 ff. 'The citizen of Cnossus may not acquire property in Tylissus, but any citizen of Tylissus who wishes may do so in Cnossus. Neither partly shall detach any part of the other's land or take it all away.' Both provisions are obviously for the protection of Tylissus.—ἐνπιπασκέσθō: 162.12.—28. κὲλ Λ-: καὶ ἐς Λ-, with crasis and assimilation (97.3).—28-29. 'where the rain-water flows, the torrent.'—29. hῖ: 25c.—30. Ἡέραι: written ⱵΡΑΙ; cf. 4.6.—36. τὸν: τὸ ἐν (94.2).—38 ff. 'If the Cnossian summon an embassy, (the Tylissian) shall conform for whatever purpose when it is required, and if the Tylissian (summons) the Cnossian,

he shall do likewise.'—39. καί χ' δ: καὶ αἴ κα ὁ.—41. 'The
council shall impose upon the κόσμοι a pledge of ten staters.'—
44-45. The document originally closed in l. 44, with the official
Argive dating. The rest, beginning ἁλιαίαι, is added in another
hand, and with a later dating, and empowers the Tylissians to
attach the provision of equal privileges with the Cnossians in
visiting Argos. ποιγραψάνσθō: 140.3*b*.

86. Cimolos. Fourth century B.C. IG XII.iii.1259. GDI 3277.
Schwyzer 85. Ditt. Syll. 261.

Θεός. | "Εκρινε ὁ δᾶμος ὁ τῶν | 'Αργείων κατὰ τὸ δόκη|μα τοῦ
5 συνεδρίου τῶν || 'Ελλάνων, ὁμολογη|σάντων Μα[λ]ίων καὶ | Κι-
μωλίων ἐμμενὲν | ἇι κα δικάσσαιεν τοὶ | 'Αργεῖοι π[ε]ρὶ τᾶν ||
10 [ν]άσων, Κιμωλίων | ἦμεν Πολύαιγαν, 'Ετη|ρείαν, Λιβείαν. ἐδί-|
κασσαν νικῆν Κιμωλί|[ο]υς. ἀρήτευε Λέων || [β]ωλᾶς σευτέρας,
15 Ποσίδα|ον γρο[φ]εὺς βωλᾶς, Πέριλ|λος Πεδίον.

Decision of the Argives in a dispute between Melos and
Cimolos.—15. σευτέρας: δευτέρας. 97.4.—Ποσίδαον, Πεδίον:
names of demes.

87. Argos. Third century B.C. Schwyzer 89.

Θεός. Πομάντιες ἀνέθεν | 'Απόλλωνι 'Αρισ[τ]εὺς Σφυρή|δας,
5 Φιλοκράτης Νατελιά|δας, γροφέ[ες] Αἰσχύλος 'Αραχνά||δας, Τρύ-
γης Αἰθωνίδας, καὶ κα|τεσκεύασσαν καὶ [ἤ]σσαντο [θείας] | ἐκ
μαντήας γᾶς ὀμφαλὸν καὶ τ[ὰ]|ν περίσταιν καὶ τὸ φάργμα καὶ
10 τὸν | βωμὸν προ[άγαγ]ον ποτ' ἀ[F]ῶ καὶ πέτ||τρινον ρόον καὶ τὰν
ἀ.... ραν | ὑπὲρ αὐτοῦ, καὶ θηαυρὸν ἐν τῶι μαν|τήωι κατεσκεύασ-
σαν τοῖς πελα|νοῖς κλαικτόν, καὶ τὰν ὁδὸν ἠργάσ|σαντο ἄπανσαν
15 καὶ ὀφρύαν πεδ' ἱα||ρὸν καὶ τὰν ἐπιπολάν, καὶ τὸνς βω|μὸνς ἐνς
τάξιν πεδάγαγον καὶ τ[ὸν]|ς κολοσσόνς, καὶ τὰν ἐπιπολὰν ὡ[μά]-|
λιξαν, καὶ τοῖχον [π]έτρινον πὰρ τὸ[ν] | - - - ἔθεν καὶ τὰνς θ[ύ-
20 ρα]νς τοῦ ναοῦ || ὠχύρωαν, [καὶ] λο[π]ίδας καὶ ἐπιχύ|[τ]αν ἀρ-
γυρέα ἔθεν καὶ θηαυρὸν ἐνς ἐ|[π]ο[ή]αντο [remainder frag-
mentary].

From the temple of the Pythian Apollo mentioned by Paus.
2.24.
2 ff. Σφυρήδας, Νατελιάδας, etc.: designations of the phratry or gens.—6 ff. 'Have had made and put in place, in accor-

dance with the divine oracle, the Omphalus of the Earth,
the colonnade, the enclosing wall, have moved the altar to
the east, have had made a stone conduit and the ... above it,
and in the oracle chamber a treasury, which can be locked, for
the monetary offerings; have constructed all the road, the ramp
leading to the shrine, and the surface area; have rearranged the
altars and the colossi, have leveled the surface, built a stone
wall by the ... , strengthened the doors of the temple, and
dedicated cups and a silver beaker.'—12/13. πελανοῖς: cf. no.
1 A 25 ff., note.—14. ὀφρύαν: here 'ramp.' Cf. the use of ὀφρύς
for 'embarkment', etc.

88. Troezen. Early second century B.C. IG IV.752 and p. 381.
Nikitskij, Hermes 38.406 ff. Schwyzer 104.

Εἰ δὲ δικάσαιτο, ἀποτεισάτω εἰ μὲν ἰδιώτας χιλίας δραχ[μάς],
5 εἰ δ[ὲ πόλις]‖| μυρίας, καὶ ἁ δίκα ἀτελὴς ἔστω. περὶ δὲ τῶν ἐρρυτι-
ασμένων ὑπὸ τᾶς πό|λιος ἢ ἀγμένων ἀπὸ τᾶς χώρας ἐν ταῖς ἀνε-
πιβασίαις· ἀπὸ τᾶγ κοινᾶ[ν] | πο[θ]όδων τᾶν ἐκ τῶν θυννείων
ἐπιλυθῆμεν τοὺς ἐρρυτιασμένους | στάσι ἀν' ὅ κα φέρηι ὁ λόγος
ὁ ταμία Φιλοκλέος, καὶ τοῖς σώμασιν τοῖς | ἀποπραχθεῖσιν ἀπὸ
10 τῶν πολεμάρχων, Ἀρτεμιδώρωι, Πύρρωι Θεο‖|δότωι, ἑκάστωι
δραχμὰς διακοσίας ἂν Τροζάνιοι νομίζοντι, καὶ τὰ | χωρία καὶ τὰς
οἰκίας ὅσσα ἐστὶ ἐρρυτιασμένα ὑπὸ τᾶς πόλιος ἀποδό|μεν τοῖς ἐρρυ-
τιασμένοις, ἐπιλύσαντας ἀπὸ τᾶγ κοινᾶν ποθόδων τοῖς | πεπεμμένοις
τι τῶν ἐρρυτιασμένων ὑπὸ τᾶς πόλιος. τὰς δ' ἐπιγαμίας | καὶ τὰς
ἐγκτάσεις ὑπάρχειν ἑκατέροις ποτ' ἀλλάλους εἰς ἄπαντα τὸ[ν ‖
15 χρόνον. ὅπ]ως δὲ τὰ συμφωνηθέντα κύρια ἦι. ἀποσ[τ]ειλάντω
πρεσβείας [ἀμφότ]εροι εἰς Ἀθάνας καὶ ἀξιούντω δόμεν αὐτοῖς
ἄνδρας τρεῖς, οἵτι[ν]ες π[α|ραγ]ενόμεν[οι] τὰ γεγονότα αὐτοῖς
ὁμόλογα ἐπικρίναντες ἀνα[θη]σοῦντ[αι| ἐν σ]τ[άλ]αις εἰς τὰ ἱερὰ
τό τε ἐγ Κα[λα]υ[ρείαι τ]οῦ Ποσειδᾶνος [καὶ τὸ ἐν Ἐπι|δ]α[ύ]-
ρ[ω]ι το[ῦ] Ἀσκλαπίου καὶ τὸ ἐν [Ἀθάναις] ἐν [ἀκ]ρο[π]όλει
τ[ᾶ]ς [Ἀθάνα]ς.

Agreement by Troezen with another city, probably Hermione,
in settlement of previous reprisals and certain other matters.
A part of the copy ordered set up at Epidaurus (l. 19) has been
found there (IG IV.²i.77). Influence of the κοινή appears in
the numerals διακόσιοι, χίλιοι, acc. pl. τρεῖς, and the use of σῶμα

as 'person' (as in papyri).—6. ἀνεπιβασία 'prohibition of traffic.'
—ἀπὸ τᾶγ κοινᾶν κτλ.: 'from the common proceeds of the tunny-fisheries those who have suffered by reprisal shall be recompensed by payment according to the account of the treasurer; and to those persons who were sold out by the polemarchs to each shall be given 200 drachmas in the coinage of Troezen.'—
13. πεπεμμένοις: 'to those who have worked on,' that is 'cultivated' any of the lands seized, from πένομαι (86.8).

89. Epidaurus. End of fifth century B.C. IG IV.²i.40/41. Ditt. Syll. 998. Schwyzer 108. Solmsen-Fraenkel 31. Alphabet transitional (form of the letters mostly Ionic, but ᗷ = h, never η, no Ω, gen. sg. O and OV).

[Τõι 'Απόλλōνι θύεν βõν ἔ|ρσενα καὶ hομονάοις βõ|ν ἔρσενα ·
5 ἐπὶ τõ βōμοῦ τõ] | 'Απόλλō[νος] τα[ῦτα] θ[ύεν κ]||αὶ καλαΐδα τᾶι
   Λατοῖ κα|ὶ τάρτάμιτι ἄλλαν, φερν|ὰν τõι θιõι κριθᾶν μέδι|μμνον,
10 σπυρõν hἐμίδιμμ|νον, οἴνου hἐμίτειαν κα||ὶ τὸ σσκέλος τοῦ βοὸς
   το|ῦ πράτου, τὸ δ' ἄτερον σκέ|λος τοὶ ἰαρομμνάμονες | φερόσθō ·
15 τοῦ δευτέρου β|οὸς τοῖς ἀοιδοῖς δόντō || τὸ σκέλος, τὸ δ' ἄτερον
   σκ|έλος τοῖς φρουροῖς δόν|τō καὶ τἐνδοσθίδια. |
20 Τõι 'Ασκλαπιõι θύεν βõ|ν ἔρσενα καὶ hομονάοις || βõν ἔρσενα
   καὶ hομονάα|ις βõν θέλειαν · ἐπὶ τοῦ β|õμοῦ τοῦ 'Ασκλαπιοῦ θύε|ν
25 ταῦτα καὶ καλαΐδα. ἀνθ|έντō τõι 'Ασκλαπιõι φερ||νὰν κριθᾶν μέ-
   διμμνον, σ|πυρõν hἐμίδιμμνον, οἴνυ|ου hἐμίτειαν · σκέλος τõ | πρά-
30 του βοὸς παρθέντō τ|[õι] θιõι, τὸ δ' ἄτερον τοὶ ἰ||[αρο]μνάμονες
   φ[ε]ρόσθō · τ|[οῦ δε]υτέρō τοῖς ἀοιδοῖ|[ς δόντō,] τὸ δ' ἄτερον
   το[ῖς | φρουροῖς δόντō καὶ τἐν|δοσθίδια.]

Regulations for sacrifices in the Asclepieum. For the frequent doubling of consonants see **89.2, 101.2**. For φερόσθō see **140.3b**.—
καλαῖς: 'hen' (from καλαϜίς, cf. καλέω 'call,' like Eng. hen to Lat. cano).—φερνά: here the gods' 'portion.'

90. Epidaurus. Late fourth century B.C. IG IV.²i.121. GDI 3339. Ditt. Syll. 1168. Herzog, Die Wunderheilungen von Epidaurus (Philol. Supplementband 22).

Θεός. Τύχα [ἀγ]αθά. | ['Ιά]ματα τοῦ 'Απόλλωνος καὶ τοῦ 'Ασκλαπιοῦ. |
[Κλ]εὼ πένθ' ἔτη ἐκύησε. αὔτα πέντ' ἐνιαυτοὺς ἤδη κυοῦσα ποὶ τὸν | [θε]ὸν ἱκέτις ἀφίκετο καὶ ἐνεκάθευδε ἐν τῶι ἀβάτωι. ὡς δὲ

5 τάχισ‖[τα] ἐξῆλθε ἐξ αὐτοῦ καὶ ἐκ τοῦ ἱαροῦ ἐγένετο, κόρον ἔτεκε,
ὃς εὐ|[θ]ὺς γενόμενος αὐτὸς ἀπὸ τᾶς κράνας ἐλοῦτο καὶ ἅμα τᾶι
ματρὶ | [π]εριῆρπε. τυχοῦσα δὲ τούτων ἐπὶ τὸ ἄνθεμα [ἐ]πεγρά-
ψατο· "οὐ μέγε|[θο]ς πίνακος θαυμαστέον, ἀλλὰ τὸ θεῖον, πένθ'
ἔτη ὡς ἐκύησε ἐγ γασ|[τρ]ὶ Κλεὼ βάρος, ἔστε | ἐγκατεκοιμάθη, καί
10 μιν ἔθηκε ὑγιῆ."—Τριετὴς ‖[φο]ρά. Ἰθμονίκα Πελλανὶς ἀφίκετο
εἰς τὸ ἱαρὸν ὑπὲρ γενεᾶς. ἐγ|[κοι]μαθεῖσα δὲ ὄψιν εἶδε· ἐδόκει αἰ-
τεῖσθαι τὸν θεὸν κυῆσαι κό|[ραν], τὸν δ' Ἀσκλαπιὸν φάμεν ἔγκυον
ἐσσεῖσθαι νιν καί, εἴ τι ἄλλο | α[ἰτ]οῖτο, καὶ τοῦτό οἱ ἐπιτελεῖν,
αὐτὰ δ' οὐθενὸς φάμεν ἔτι ποι|δ[εῖ]σθαι· ἔγκυος δὲ γενομένα ἐγ
15 γαστρὶ ἐφόρει τρία ἔτη, ἔστε πα‖ρέβαλε ποὶ τὸν θεὸν ἱκέτις ὑπὲρ
τοῦ τόκου. ἐγκατακοιμαθεῖσα | δὲ ὄψ[ι]ν εἶδε· ἐδόκει ἐπερωτῆν νιν
τὸν θεόν, εἰ οὐ γένοιτο αὐτᾶι | πάντ[α] ὅσσα αἰτήσαιτο καὶ ἔγκυος
εἴη, ὑπὲρ δὲ τόκου ποιθέμεν | νιν οὐθέν, καὶ ταῦτα πυνθανομένου
αὐτοῦ, εἴ τινος καὶ ἄλλου δέ|οιτ[ο], λέγειν, ὡς ποιησοῦντος καὶ
20 τοῦτο· ἐπεὶ δὲ νῦν ὑπὲρ τούτου ‖ παρείη ποτ' αὐτὸν ἱκέτις, καὶ τοῦ-
τό οἱ φάμεν ἐπιτελεῖν. μετὰ δὲ | τοῦτο σπουδᾶι ἐκ τοῦ ἀβάτου
ἐξελθοῦσα, ὡς ἔξω τοῦ ἱαροῦ ἦς, ἐτε|κε κό[ρ]αν.—Ἀνὴρ τοὺς τᾶς
·χηρὸς δακτύλους ἀκρατεῖς ἔχων πλὰν | ἑνὸς ἀ[φ]ίκετο ποὶ τὸν θεὸν
ἱκέτας. θεωρῶν δὲ τοὺς ἐν τῷ ἱαρῶι | [π]ίνακας ἀπίστει τοῖς ἰάμα-
25 σιν καὶ ὑποδιέσυρε τὰ ἐπιγράμμα‖[τ]α. ἐγκαθεύδων δὲ ὄψιν εἶδε·
ἐδόκει ὑπὸ τῶι ναῶι ἀστραγαλίζον|[τ]ος αὐτοῦ καὶ μέλλοντος βάλ-
λειν τῶι ἀστραγάλωι ἐπιφανέντα | [τ]ὸν θεὸν ἐφαλέσθαι ἐπὶ τὰν
χῆρα καὶ ἐκτεῖναί οὗ τοὺς δακτύλ|λους, ὡς δ' ἀποβαίη, δοκεῖν συγ-
κάμψας τὰν χῆρα καθ' ἕνα ἐκτείνειν | [τ]ῶν δακτύλων, ἐπεὶ δὲ
30 πάντας ἐξευθύναι, ἐπερωτῆν νιν τὸν θεὸν ‖ [ε]ἰ ἔτι ἀπιστησοῖ τοῖς
ἐπιγράμμασι τοῖς ἐπὶ τῶμ πινάκων τῶν | [κ]ατὰ τὸ [ἱ]ερόν, αὐτὸς
δ' οὐ φάμεν· "ὅτι τοίνυν ἔμπροσθεν ἀπίστεις | [α]ὐτο[ῖ]ς ο[ὐκ]
ἐοῦσιν ἀπίστοις, τὸ λοιπὸν ἔστω τοι" φάμεν "Ἄπιστος | ὄ[νομα]."
ἀμέρας δὲ γενομένας ὑγιὴς ἐξῆλθε.—Ἀμβροσία ἐξ Ἀθανᾶν | [ἀτε-
ρό]πτ[ι]λλος. αὕτα ἱκέτ[ις] ἦλθε ποὶ τὸν θεὸν. περιέρπουσα δὲ ‖
35 [κατὰ τ]ὸ [ἱα]ρὸν τῶν ἱαμάτων τινὰ διεγέλα ὡς ἀπίθανα καὶ ἀδύ-
να‖[τα ἐόν]τα χωλοὺς καὶ τυφλοὺς ὑγιεῖς γίνεσθαι ἐνύπνιον ἰδόν-|
[τας μό]νον. ἐγκαθεύδουσα δὲ ὄψιν εἶδε· ἐδόκει οἱ ὁ θεὸς ἐπιστὰς |
[εἰπεῖν] ὅτ[ι] ὑγιῆ μέν νιν ποιησοῖ, μισθὸμ μάντοι νιν δεησοῖ ἀν|-
40 [θέμεν ε]ἰς τὸ ἱαρὸν ὗν ἀργύρεον, ὑπόμναμα τᾶς ἀμαθίας· εἴπαν-‖
[τα δὲ ταῦτα] ἀνσχίσσαι οὗ τὸν ὀπτίλλον τὸν νοσοῦντα καὶ φάρμ[α|
κόν τι ἐγχέ]αι. ἀμέρας δὲ γενομένας [ὑ]γιὴς ἐξῆλθε.—Παῖς ἄφω-

νος. | [οὗτος ἀφίκ]ετο εἰς τὸ ἱαρὸν ὑ[πὲ]ρ φωνᾶς. ὡς δὲ προεθύσα-
το καὶ | [ἐπόησε τὰ] νομιζόμενα, μετὰ τοῦτο ὁ παῖς ὁ τῶι θεῶι πυρ-
φορῶν | [ἐκέλετο, πο]ὶ̀ τὸμ πατέρα τὸν τοῦ παιδὸς ποτιβλέψας,
45 ὑποδέκεσ||[σθαι αὐτὸν ἐ]νιαυτοῦ, τυχόντα ἐφ' ἃ πάρεστι, ἀποθυ-
σεῖν τὰ ἴατρα · | [ὁ δὲ παῖς ἐξ]απίνας "ὑποδέκομαι" ἔφα. ὁ δὲ πα-
τὴρ ἐκπλαγεὶς πάλιν | [ἐκέλετο αὐτ]ὸν εἰπεῖν. ὁ δ' ἔλεγε πάλιν καὶ
ἐκ τούτου ὑγιὴς ἐγέ|[νετο.—Πάνδαρ]ος Θεσσαλὸς στίγματα ἔχων
ἐν τῶι μετώπωι. οὗτος | [ἐγκαθεύδων ὄψ]ιν εἶδε · ἐδόκει αὐτοῦ
50 τ[αι]νίαι καταδῆσαι τὰ στί||[γματα ὁ θεὸς κα]ὶ̀ κέλεσθαι νιν, ἐπεί
[κα ἔξω] γένηται τοῦ ἀβάτου, | [ἀφελόμενον τὰν] ταινίαν ἀνθέμ[εν
εἰς τ]ὸν ναόν. ἁμέρας δὲ γενο|[μένας, ἐξανέστα] καὶ ἀφήλετο τὰ[ν
ται]νίαν καὶ τὸ μὲν πρόσωπον | [ἐκεκάθαρτο τῶ]ν στιγμάτ[ων,
τ]ὰν δ[ὲ τ]αινίαν ἀνέθηκε εἰς τὸν να||[ὸν ἔχουσαν τὰ γρ]άμματ[α]
55 τὰ ἐκ τοῦ μετώπου.—'Εχέδωρος τὰ Πανδά||[ρου στίγματα ἔλ]αβε
ποὶ τοῖς ὑπάρχουσιν. οὗτος λαβὼν πὰρ [Παν|δάρου χρήματα],
ὥστ' ἀνθέμεν τῶι θεῶι εἰς 'Επίδαυρον ὑπὲρ αὐ[τοῦ, | οὐκ] ἀπεδίδου
ταῦτα. ἐγκαθεύδων δὲ ὄψιν εἶδε · ἐδ όκει οἱ ὁ θε[ὸς] | ἐπιστὰς ἐπερω-
τῆν νιν, εἰ ἔχοι τινὰ χρήματα πὰρ Πανδάρου ἐ[ξ 'Α]||θηνᾶν ἄνθεμα
60 εἰς τὸ ἱαρὸν, αὐτὸς δ' οὐ φάμεν λελαβήκειν οὐθὲ[ν] || τοιοῦτον πὰρ
αὐτοῦ, ἀλλ' αἴ κα ὑγιῆ νιν ποιήσαι, ἀνθησεῖν οἱ εἰκό|να γραψάμενος·
μετὰ δὲ τοῦτο τὸν θεὸν τὰν τοῦ Πανδάρου ταινί|αν περιδῆσαι περὶ
τὰ στίγματά οὐ καὶ κέλεσθαί νιν, ἐπεί κα ἐξ|έλθηι ἐκ τοῦ ἀβάτου,
ἀφελόμενον τὰν ταινίαν ἀπονίψασθαι τὸ | πρόσωπον ἀπὸ τᾶς κρά-
65 νας καὶ ἐγκατοπτρίξασθαι εἰς τὸ ὕδωρ. ἁ||μέρας δὲ γενομένας
ἐξελθὼν ἐκ τοῦ ἀβάτου τὰν ταινίαν ἀφήλετο | τὰ γράματα οὐκ
ἔχουσαν, ἐγκαθιδὼν δὲ εἰς τὸ ὕδωρ ἑώρη τὸ αὐτοῦ | πρόσωπον ποὶ
τοῖς ἰδίοις στίγμασιν καὶ τὰ τοῦ Πανδάρου γρά|ματα λελαβηκός.—
Εὐφάνης 'Επιδαύριος παῖς. οὗτος λιθιῶν ἐνε[κά]||θευδε · ἔδοξε δὴ
70 αὐτῶι ὁ θεὸς ἐπιστὰς εἰπεῖν· "τί μοι δωσεῖς, αἴ τ[ύ]||κα ὑγιῆ
ποιήσω;" αὐτὸς δὲ φάμεν "δέκ' ἀστραγάλους", τὸν δὲ θεὸν γελά-|
σαντα φάμεν νιν παυσεῖν. ἁμέρας δὲ γενομένας ὑγιὴς ἐξῆλθε.— |
'Ανὴρ ἀφίκετο ποὶ τὸν θεὸν ἱκέτας ἀτερόπτιλος οὕτως, ὥστε τὰ |
βλέφαρα μόνον ἔχειν, ἐνεῖμεν δ' ἐν αὐτοῖς μηθέν, ἀλλὰ κενεὰ εἶ|μεν
ὅλως. ἔλεγον δή τινες τῶν ἐν τῶι ἱαρῶι τὰν εὐηθίαν αὐτοῦ τὸ ||
75 νομίζειν βλεψεῖσθαι ὅλως μηδεμίαν ὑπαρχὰν ἔχοντος ὀπτίλ|λου,|
ἀλλ' ἢ χώραμ μόνον. ἐγκαθ[εύδον]τι οὖν αὐτῶι ὄψις ἐφάνη · ἐδό-
κει τὸν θεὸν ἑψῆσαί τι φά[ρμακον, ἔπε]ιτα διαγαγόντα τὰ βλέφα|ρα
ἐγχέαι εἰς αὐτά. ἁμέρ[ας δὲ γενομέν]ας β (λ)έπων ἀμφοῖν ἐξῆλθε.

—Κώθων. σκευοφόρος εἰ[ς τὸ] ἰαρ[ὸν ἀνιών], ἐπεὶ ἐγένετο περὶ
80 τὸ δε‖καστάδιον, κατέπ[ε]τε. [ὡς δ' ἀ]νέστα, ἀνῶιξε τὸγ γυλιὸν
κα[ὶ ἐ]πεσκό|πει τὰ συντετριμμένα σ[κε]ύη. ὡς δ' εἶδε τὸγ κώθω-
να κατε[αγ]ό̄τα, | ἐξ οὗ ὁ δεσπότας εἴθιστ[ο π]ίνειν, ἐλυπεῖτο καὶ
συνετίθει [τὰ] ὄ|στρακα καθιζόμενος. ὁδοιπόρος οὖν τις ἰδὼν αὐ-
τόν, "τί, ὦ ἄθλι'," ἔ|φα, "συντίθησι τὸγ κώθωνα [μά]ταν; τοῦτον
85 γὰρ οὐδέ κα ὁ ἐν Ἐπιδαύ‖ρωι Ἀσκλαπιὸς ὑγιῆ ποιῆσαι δύναιτο."
ἀκούσας ταῦτα ὁ παῖς, συν|θεὶς τὰ ὄστρακα εἰς τὸγ γυλιόν, ἦρπε
εἰς τὸ ἱερόν. ἐπεὶ δ' ἀφίκε|το, ἀνῶιξε τὸγ γυλιὸν καὶ ἐξαῖρεν ὑγιῆ
τὸγ κώθωνα γεγενημέ|νον, καὶ τῶι δεσπόται ἡρμάνευσε τὰ πραχ-
θέντα καὶ λεχθέντα. ὡ|ς δὲ ἄκουσ', ἀνέθηκε τῶι θεῶι τὸγ κώθωνα.
90 — ‖ Αἰσχίνας ἐγκεκοιμισμένων ἤδη τῶν ἱκετᾶν ἐπὶ δένδρεόν τι
ἀμ|βὰς ὑπερέκυπτε εἰς τὸ ἄβατον. καταπετῶν οὖν ἀπὸ τοῦ δέν-
δρεος | περὶ σκόλοπάς τινας τοὺς ὀπτίλλους ἀμφέπαισε. κακῶς δὲ
δια|κείμενος καὶ τυφλὸς γεγενημένος καθικετεύσας τὸν θεὸν ἐν-|
95 εκάθευδε· καὶ ὑγιὴς ἐγένετο. — ‖ Εὔιππος λόγχαν ἔτη ἐφόρησε
ἓξ ἐν τᾶι γνάθωι. ἐγκοιτασθέντος | δ' αὐτοῦ ἐξελὼν τὰν λόγχαν ὁ
θεὸς εἰς τὰς χῆράς οἱ ἔδωκε. ἀμέρας | δὲ γενομένας ὑγιὴς ἐξῆρπε
τὰν λόγχαν ἐν ταῖς χερσὶν ἔχων. — | Ἀνὴρ Τορωναῖος δεμελέας.
οὗτος ἐγκαθεύδων ἐνύπνιον εἶδε· | ἐδόξε οἱ τὸν θεὸν τὰ στέρνα
100 μαχαίραι ἀνσχίσσαντα τὰς δεμε‖λέας ἐξελεῖν καὶ δόμεν οἱ ἐς τὰς
χεῖρας καὶ συνράψαι τὰ στή|θη. ἀμέρας δὲ γενομένας ἐξῆλθε τὰ
θηρία ἐν ταῖς χερσὶν ἔχων | καὶ ὑγιὴς ἐγένετο. κατέπιε δ' αὐτὰ
δολωθεὶς ὑπὸ ματρυιᾶς ἐγ κυ|κᾶνι ἐμβεβλημένας ἐκπιών. — |
Ἀνὴρ ἐν αἰδοίωι λίθον. οὗτος ἐνύπνιον εἶδε· ἐδόκει παιδὶ καλῶι ‖
105 συγγίνεσθαι. ἐξονειρώσσων δὲ τὸλ λίθον ἐγβάλλει καὶ ἀνελόμε|νος
ἐξῆλθεν ταῖς χερσὶν ἔχων. — | Ἑρμόδικος Λαμψακηνὸς ἀκρατὴς τοῦ
σώματος. τοῦτον ἐγκαθεύ|δοντα ἰάσατο καὶ ἐκελήσατο ἐξελθόντα
λίθον ἐνεγκεῖν εἰς τὸ | ἰαρὸν ὁπόσσον δύναιτο μέγισ[τ]ον. ὁ δὲ τὸμ
110 πρὸ τοῦ ἀβάτου κείμε‖νον ἤνικε. — | Νικάνωρ χωλός. τούτου καθ-
ημένου παῖς [τ]ις ὕπαρ τὸν σκίπωνα ἁρ|πάξας ἔφευγε. ὁ δὲ ἀστὰς
ἐδίωκε καὶ ἐκ τούτου ὑγιὴς ἐγένετο. — | Ἀνὴρ δάκτυλον ἰάθη ὑπὸ
ὄφιος. οὗτος τὸν τοῦ ποδὸς δάκτυλον ὑ|πό του ἀγρίου ἕλκεος δει-
115 νῶς διακείμενος μεθάμερα ὑπὸ τῶν θε‖ραπόντων ἐξενειχθεὶς ἐπὶ
ἑδράματός τινος καθῖζε. ὕπνου δέ νιν | λαβόντος ἐν τούτωι δράκων
ἐκ τοῦ ἀβάτου ἐξελθὼν τὸν δάκτυλον | ἰάσατο τᾶι γλώσσαι καὶ
τοῦτο ποιήσας εἰς τὸ ἄβατον ἀνεχώρησε | πάλιν. ἐξεγερθεὶς δέ, ὡς
ἦς ὑγιής, ἔφα ὄψιν ἰδεῖν, δοκεῖν νεανίσ|κον εὐπρεπῆ τὰμ μορφὰν

120 ἐπὶ τὸν δάκτυλον ἐπιπῆν φάρμακον.— ||'Ἀλκέτας 'Ἁλικός. οὗτος
τυφλὸς ἐὼν ἐνύπνιον εἶδε · ἐδόκει ὁ θεὸς ποτελθὼν τοῖς δα|κτύλοις
διάγειν τὰ ὄμματα, καὶ ἰδεῖν τὰ δένδρη πρᾶτον τὰ ἐν τῶι ἰαρῶι.
ἀμέρας δὲ γε|νομένας ὑγιὴς ἐξῆλθε.—'Ἡραιεὺς Μυτιληναῖος. οὗτος
οὐκ εἶχεν ἐν τᾶι κεφαλᾶι | τρίχας, ἐν δὲ τῶι γενείωι παμπόλλας.
αἰσχυνόμενος δὲ [ἄτε] καταγελάμενος ὑπ[ὸ] | τῶν ἄλλων ἐνεκάθ-
125 ευδε. τὸν δὲ ὁ θεὸς χρίσας φαρμάκωι τὰν κεφαλὰν ἐπόησε || τρί-
χας ἔχειν.—Θύσων 'Ἑρμιονεὺς παῖς ἀιδής, οὗ[τος] ὕπαρ ὑπὸ
κυνὸς τῶν | κατὰ τὸ ἰαρὸν θ[εραπ]ευόμενος τοὺς ὀπτίλλους ὑ[γιὴ]ς
ἀπῆλθε.

One of several stelae found in the Asclepieum recording the
cures effected. Cf. Paus. 2.27.3 στῆλαι δὲ εἱστήκεσαν ἐντὸς τοῦ
περιβόλου, τὸ μὲν ἀρχαῖον καὶ πλέονες, ἐπ' ἐμοῦ δὲ ἒξ λοιπαί. ταύταις
ἐγγεγραμμένα καὶ ἀνδρῶν καὶ γυναικῶν ἐστιν ὀνόματα ἀκεσθέντων
ὑπὸ τοῦ 'Ασκληπιοῦ, προσέτι δὲ καὶ νόσημα ὅ τι ἕκαστος ἐνόσησε καὶ
ὅπως ἰάθη· γέγραπται δὲ φωνῇ τῇ Δωρίδι.
The dialect shows considerable Attic influence, e.g., usually
εἰ rarely αἰ, contraction in ποιησοῦντος, etc., acc. pl. ἀκρατεῖς etc.
Secondary ō is always ου, and ē usually ει, but χηρός beside
χειρός, and ἀφήλετο (25c).—3. πενθ' ἔτη: 58c.—Cf. Paus. 2.27.1
οὐδὲ ἀποθνήσκουσιν οὐδὲ τίκτουσιν αἱ γυναῖκες σφίσιν ἐντὸς τοῦ
περιβόλου.—6. περιῆρπε: ἔρπω = εἶμι, 162.6.—7 ff. The words
on the votive offering form a rude epigram, hence the poetical
μιν, for which elsewhere νιν.—9/10. τριετὴς [φο]ρά: 'three year
gestation.'—43 ff. 'Then the boy who acted as torch-bearer for
the god, looking at the boy's father, bade him promise that he
(the boy), if he obtained what he was there for, would within
a year make the thank-offerings for his cure.'—66. ἑώρη: 280.—
74. ἔλεγον: probably error for ἐγέλαν; cf. διεγέλα l. 35.—75.
'When he had not even any rudiment of an eye, but only the
place for it,' i.e., the empty eye-socket.—98 f. δεμελέας: 'leeches.'
Cf. δεμβλεῖς· βδέλλαι Hesych.—102. αὐτά agrees in form with
θηρία, while with ἐμβεβλημένας we must understand δεμελέας.

Corinthian

91. Corinth. Early sixth century B.C. IG IV.358. GDI 3114.
Roberts 85. Schwyzer 124.

ΔϜΕνία τόδε [σᾶμα], τὸν ὄλεσε πόντος ἀναι[δές].

This and the following illustrate the Corinthian differentiation of ʙ = open ε or ē (η) and E= close ẹ corresponding to Attic spurious or genuine ει. See **28**. The epithaph forms a single hexameter. Cf. nos. 93-95.

92. Corinth. Early sixth century B.C. IG IV.210, 211, 219, 329. GDI 3119. Schwyzer 123.

a. Σιμίōν μ' ἀνέθ(ē)xε ΠοτΕδαϜōν[ι Ϝάναxτι]. ΠοτΕδ[άν].

b. Ϙυλōιδας μ' ἀνέθēxε Πο[τΕδάϜονι Ϝάναxτι]. ΠοτΕδάν.

c. -ōν μ' ἀνέθēxε ΠοτΕδᾶνι Ϝάν[αxτι]. ['Αμφι]τρίτα.

d. ΠεραΕόθεν hίϙομες.

From a large collection of pottery fragments found near Corinth. They are mostly votive offerings to Poseidon, and contain the name in both uncontracted and contracted forms, as ΠοτΕδαϜōνι and ΠοτΕδᾶνι, but in the nominative only the contracted ΠοτΕδάν. See **41**.4. For ΠεραΕόθεν (*d*), cf. Πείραιον Xen. Hellen. 4.5.1 ff. Probably ʙ in the first syllable is an error.

93. Corcyra. Early sixth century B.C. IG IX.i.867. GDI 3188. Roberts 98. Schwyzer 133, 1. Solmsen-Fraenkel 34*a*.

Ηυιοῦ ΤλασίαϜο Μενεκράτεος τόδε σᾶμα,
Οἰανθέος γενεάν· τόδε δ' αὐτōι δᾶμος ἐποίει·
ἒς γὰρ πρόξενϜος δάμου φίλος· ἀλλ' ἐνὶ πόντōι
ὄλετο, δαμόσιον δὲ καϙὸν ῥό[θιον πόρε κῦμα]
5 Πραξιμένες δ' αὐτōι γ[αία]ς ἀπὸ πατρίδος ἐνθὸν
σὺν δάμ[ō]ι τόδε σᾶμα κασιγνέτοιο πονέθē.

Monument of Menecrates. This and the two following are examples of metrical inscriptions composed in the epic style and with retention of several epic words, i.e., ἐνί, κασιγνέτοιο, στονό-Ϝε(σ)σαν, ἀϜυτάν (**32**) = αὐτήν, and inflectional forms, e.g., gen. sg. in -οιο and -ᾱϜο = -αο (**105**.2*b*), dat. pl. in -αισι, augmentless verb forms.

4. The restoration is that suggested by H. Frisk, Eranos 29.31 f.—6. **πονέθē**: transitive sense as in Homer.

94. Corcyra. Early sixth century B.C. IG IX.i.868. GDI 3189. Roberts 99. Tod 2. Schwyzer 133,2. Solmsen-Fraenkel 34*b*.

Σᾶμα τόδε 'Αρνιάδα· χαροπὸς τόνδ' ὄλε|σεν "Αρēς
βαρνάμενον παρὰ ναυσ|ὶν ἐπ' 'Αράθθοιο ϸhοϜαῖσι
πολλὸ|ν ἀριστεύ<τ>οντα κατὰ στονόϜεσαν ἀϜυτάν.

2. ϸhοϜαῖσι: cf. also Μhεί̄ξιος in another inscription of Corcyra.
See 76a.—3. ἀριστεύτοντα: error for ἀριστεύοντα or ἀριστεύϜοντα
(cf. 36).

95. Northern Acarnania (exact provenance unknown). Fifth
century B.C. IG IX.i.521. GDI 3175. Roberts 106. Schwyzer 140.

Προκλείδας τόδε σᾶμα κεκλ|έ̄σεται ἐνγὺς ὁδοῖο,
    ϸὸς περὶ τᾶς αὐτοῦ γᾶς | θάνε βαρνάμενος.

Προκλείδας: gen. sg. masc. in -ας. 105.2c.

96. Sicyon. Fifth century B.C. Orlandos, 'Ελληνικά 10.5 ff.

Τούτō̄ν δὲ κοινὰ ἔστō̄ τὸ ἐστιατόριον καὶ τὰ ὀρē̄ καὶ ϸο χαλκιόν |
καὶ τἆλα Ϝοικέουσίν γα καὶ τὰ τέλē̄ φέρουσιν· πō̄λē̄ν δὲ | μē̄δὲ συνα-
λάζεσθαι ἐξέστō̄. [There follows a list of 73 names].

The inscription has the characteristic X̄ = E, the san, but
the straight iota. The X̄ is used, like the Corinth. ʙ for ε and η
(μē̄δέ and η from εα in ὀρē̄, τέλē̄). But E for secondary ē̄, as at
Corinth (25d) in ΠΟΓΕΝ to be read πō̄λē̄ν rather than = Arg.
πωλέν. OV for secondary ō̄, as at Corinth (25d), in Ϝοικέουσιν,
φέρουσιν (for which see also 102).

97. Cleonae, found at Nemea. Sixth century B.C. Argive
alphabet, but Corinthian ꟻ = ē̄ (but not ε). AJA 1927, 433.
'Αρχ. 'Εφ. 1931, 103. SEG 11.290.

'Αρίστις με ἀνέθ|ε̄κε Δὶ Ϙρονίō̄νι Ϝά|νακτι πανκράτιο|ν νιϙō̄ν
τετράκις | ἐν Νεμέαι, Φείδō̄|νος Ϝhιὸς τō̄ Κλεō̄|ναίō̄.

Dedication by Aristis, son of Pheidon of Cleonae. The Corinthian ʙ is here used = η but not also = ε as at Corinth (cf.
ἀνΕθ̄ʙκΕ vs. Corinth. ανʙθ̄ɜκʙ no. 92b). Same practice in another archaic inscription of Cleonae (Schwyzer 129).—Ϝhιός:
52c.

Megarian

98. Selinus. Fifth century B.C. IG XIV.268. GDI 3046. Ditt.
Syll. 1122. Roberts 117. Schwyzer 166. Solmsen-Fraenkel 33.
Tod 37.

[Δι]ὰ τὸς θεὸς τό[σ]δε νικῶντι τοὶ Σελινόν[τιοι · | δι]ὰ τὸν Δία
νικῶμες καὶ διὰ τὸν Φόβον [καὶ] | δ[ιὰ] Ηἐρακλέα καὶ δι᾿ Ἀπόλ-
λōνα καὶ διὰ Π[οτ]∥ε[ιδᾶ]να καὶ διὰ Τυνδαρίδας καὶ δι᾿ Ἀθ[α]-∥
5 ν[ά]αν καὶ διὰ Μαλοφόρον καὶ διὰ Πασικ∣ρά∣τ]ειαν καὶ δι[ὰ] τὸς
ἄλλōς θεός, [δ]ιὰ δ[ὲ] Δία | μάλιστ[α]. φιλί[ας] δὲ γενομένας ἐν
χρυσ∣ἐō[ι] ἐλά[σα]ντα[ς, τὰ δ᾿] ὀνύματα ταῦτα κολ∣άψαντ[ας ἐς] τὸ
10 Ἀ[π]ολ[λ]όνιον καθθέμε∥ν, τὸ Διὸ[ς προ]γρά[ψα]ντες · τὸ δὲ χρυ-
σίον | ἐξέκ[οντα τ]αλάντōν ἔμεν.

The Selinuntians promise golden statues to the gods who
shall help them to victory. Instead of an express condition,
there is an enumeration of the gods who usually assist them,
the implication being that they will continue to do so.

1. 'Through the help of the following gods do the Selinuntians,
win victory. Through Zeus we conquer,' etc.—2. Φόβον: 'Ares'.
—5. Μαλοφόρον: 'Demeter.' Cf. Paus. 1.44.3 ἱερὸν Δήμητρος
Μαλοφόρου.—Πασικράτεια: 'Persephone.' Cf. Δέσποινα.—7 ff.
'(Resolved) when there is peace, making statues in gold and
engraving these names, to set them up in the temple of Apollo,
writing the name of Zeus first.'—προγράψαντες: nominative
carelessly written for accusative.

99. Decision of the Megarians. Epidaurus. Between 242 and
234 B.C. IG IV.926. GDI 3025. Ditt. Syll. 471. Schwyzer 157.

['Ε]πὶ στραταγ[οῦ τῶν Ἀ]χαιῶν Αἰγιαλεῦς, ἐν δ᾿ Ἐπιδαύρωι
ἐπ᾿ ἱαρεῦς | [το]ῦ Ἀσκλαπι[οῦ Δι]ονυσίου. κατὰ τάδε ἐκρίναν τοὶ
Μεγαρεῖς τοῖς | ['Επ]ιδαυρίοις καὶ Κορινθίοις περὶ τᾶς χώρας ἇς
ἀμφέλλεγον καὶ | [περ]ὶ τοῦ Σελλανύο[υ] καὶ τοῦ Σπιραίου, κατὰ
5 τὸν αἶνον τὸν τῶν Ἀ∥[χαι]ῶν δικαστήριον ἀποστείλαντες ἄνδρας
ἑκατὸν πεντήκοντα | [ἕνα] · καὶ ἐπελθόντων ἐπ᾿ αὐτὰν τὰν χώραν
τῶν δικαστᾶν καὶ κρινάν∣[των] Ἐπιδαυρίων εἶμεν τὰν χώραν, ἀντι-
λεγόντων δὲ τῶν Κορινθί∣[ων τῶ]ι τερμονισμῶι, πάλιν ἀπέστειλαν
τοὶ Μεγαρεῖς τοὺς τερμο∣ν[ιξ]οῦ[ν]τας ἐκ τῶν αὐτῶν δικαστᾶν
10 ἄνδρας τριάκοντα καὶ ἕνα κα∥[τὰ τ]ὸν αἶνον τὸν τῶν Ἀχαιῶν, οὗτοι
δὲ ἐπελθόντες ἐπὶ τὰν χώραν | ἐτερμόνιξαν κατὰ τάδε · ἀπὸ τᾶς
κορυφᾶς τοῦ Κορδυλείου ἐπὶ | [τ]ὰν κορυφὰν τοῦ Ἁλιείου · ἀπὸ τοῦ
Ἁλιείου ἐπὶ τὰν κορυφὰν τοῦ | [Κ]εραυνίου · ἀπὸ τοῦ Κεραυνίου
ἐπὶ τὰν κορυφὰν τοῦ Κορνιάτα · | ἀπὸ τᾶς κορυφᾶς τοῦ Κορνιάτα
15 ἐπὶ τὰν ὁδὸν ἐπὶ τὸν ῥάχιν τὸν τοῦ ∥ Κορνιάτα · ἀπὸ τοῦ ῥάχιος

τοῦ Κορνιάτα ἐπὶ τὸν ῥάχιν τὸν ἐπὶ ταῖ|ς Ἀνείαις ὑπὲρ τὰν Σκολ-
λείαν· ἀπὸ τοῦ ῥάχιος τοῦ ὑπὲρ τὰν Σκολ|λείαν ὑπὸ τᾶς Ἀνείας
ἐπὶ τὸν κορυφὸν τὸν ὑπὲρ τᾶς ὁδοῦ τᾶς ἀμα|ξιτοῦ [τᾶς κα]ταγού-
σας ἐπὶ τὸ Σπίαιον· ἀπὸ τοῦ κορυφοῦ τοῦ ὑπὲ|ρ τᾶς [ὁδοῦ] τᾶς
20 ἀμαξιτοῦ ἐπὶ τὸν κορυφὸν τὸν ἐπὶ τοῦ Φάγας· ἀπὸ || τοῦ κορυφοῦ
τοῦ ἐπὶ τοῦ Φάγας ἐπὶ τὸν κορυφὸν τὸν ἐπὶ τοῦ Αἰγι|πύρα[ς]· ἀπὸ
τοῦ κορυφοῦ τοῦ ἐπὶ τᾶς Αἰγιπύρας ἐπὶ τὸν κορυφὸν | τὸν τ[οῦ
Ἀρα]ίας· ἀπὸ τοῦ Ἀραίας ἐπὶ τὸν κορυφὸν τὸν ὑπὸ τᾶι Πέτρ|αι·
ἀπ[ὸ το]ῦ ὑπὸ τᾶι Πέτραι ἐπὶ τὸν κορυφὸν τὸν ἐπὶ τοῦ Σχοινοῦν-|
τος· ἀ[πὸ τ]οῦ κορυφοῦ τοῦ ὑπὲρ τοῦ Σχοινοῦντος ἐπὶ τὸν κορυ-
25 φὸν || τὸν κ[ατὰ τ]ὰν Εὐόργαν· ἀπὸ τοῦ κορυφοῦ τοῦ ὑπὲρ τᾶς
Εὐόργας [ἐπὶ] | τὸν ῥάχιν τὸν ὑπὲρ τᾶς Συκουσίας· ἀπὸ τοῦ ῥά-
χιος τοῦ ὑπὲρ τᾶς | Συ[κουσί]ας ἐπὶ τὸν κορυφὸν τὸν ὑπὲρ τᾶς
Πελλερίτιος· ἀπὸ τοῦ | κορυφοῦ τοῦ ὑπὲρ τᾶς Πελλερίτιος ἐπὶ τὸν
κορυφὸν τὸν τοῦ Π[αν|ίου]· ἀπὸ τοῦ Πανίου ἐπὶ τὸν ῥάχιν τὸν ὑπὲρ
30 τοῦ Ὀλ[κοῦ]· ἀπὸ τοῦ ῥά||[χιο]ς τ[οῦ] ὑπὲρ τοῦ Ὀλκοῦ ἐπὶ τὸν
ῥάχιν τὸν (ὑπὲρ) τοῦ Ἀπ[ολλ]ωνίου· ἀπὸ | τ[οῦ] ῥάχιος τοῦ ὑπὲρ
τοῦ Ἀπολλωνίου ἐπὶ τὸ Ἀπολλώνιον. δικασ||[ταὶ τ]οὶ κρίναντες
τοίδε. [There follow, ll. 32—99, the names of the arbitrators
and of those appointed to lay out the boundaries for them.]

Decision of the Megarians, appionted by the Achaean league
to arbitrate in a territorial dispute between Epidaurus and
Corinth.

1. **Αἰγιαλεῦς, ἰαρεῦς**: gen. sg. in -εῦς from -έος. 111.3.—
For the psilosis in ἐπ' ἰαρεῦς, see 58b.—3. **ἀμφέλλεγον**: 76.—
4. **Σπιραίου**: name of a harbor and promontory north of
Epidaurus, referred to by Thuc. 8.10.3 (with correction of
Πειραιόν to Σπίραιον) and Pliny, Nat. Hist. 4.18 (Spiraeum).—
αἶνον: αἶνος 'decree,' but distinct from a ψάφισμα. Cf. Delph.
μήτε κατὰ ψάφισμα μήτε κατ' αἶνον (GDI 2642.20).—19. **Φάγας**:
gen. sg. masc. in -ας. 105.2c. So Ἀραίας l. 22, but also the usual
form in Κορνιάτα ll. 13 ff. The confusion caused by the identity
with the feminine form is shown by τᾶς Αἰγιπύρας l. 21 beside
τοῦ Αἰγιπύρας l. 20.—32 ff. The list of names, arranged according
to the three Doric tribes, contains the characteristic forms
Θέδωρος, Θοκρίνης, etc. (42.5f).

Rhodian

100. Camirus. Sixth century B.C. IG XII.i.737. GDI 4140.
Schwyzer 272.

Σᾶμα τόζ' 'Ιδα|μενεὺς ποίη|σα hίνα κλέος | εἴη · ||
Ζεὺ δέ νιν ὅστις | πημαίνοι λειό|λη θείη.

τόζ' : τόδε. 62.2.—Ζεὺ δέ: Ζεὺς δέ. 97.4.—λειόλη: 'accursed.'
Cf. Hesych. λεώλης · τελείως ἐξώλης, and, for the first part of
the compound, λείως = τελείως in Archilochus, Hesych., etc.
101. Camirus. Sixth century B.C. IG XII.i.709. GDI 4127.
Schwyzer 273.

Εὐθυ[τ]ίδα | ἠμὶ λέσχα | τō Πραξσιόδō | τōὐφύλō ||τōὐφυλίδα.

λέσχα: 'grave.' The original meaning of the word (from
*λεχσκᾱ, cf. λέχος) was 'resting place,' whence either 'grave'
or the usual 'place of recreation, club.'—The last words are to
be read, with resolution of the crasis, τō Εὐφύλō, τō Εὐφυλίδα.
102. Camirus. Fourth (or third) century B.C. IG XII.i.694.
GDI 4118. Ditt. Syll. 339. Schwyzer 281. Solmsen-Fraenkel 42.

Ἔδοξε Καμιρεῦσι τὰς κτοίνας τὰς Καμιρέων τὰς | ἐν τᾶι νάσωι
καὶ τὰς ἐν τᾶι ἀπείρωι ἀναγράψαι πάσας | καὶ ἐχθέμειν ἐς τὸ ἱερὸν
τᾶς 'Αθαναίας ἐ στάλαι | λιθίναι χωρὶς Χαλκῆς · ἐξήμειν δὲ καὶ
5 Χαλκήταις || ἀναγραφήμειν, αἴ κα χρήιζωντι. ἐλέσθαι δὲ ἄνδρας |
τρεῖς αὐτίκα μάλα, οἵτινες ἐπιμεληθησεῦντι ταύ|τας τᾶς πράξιος
ὡς τάχιστα καὶ ἀποδωσεῦνται | τῶι χρήιζοντι ἐλαχίστου παρα-
σχεῖν τὰν στάλαν | καὶ τὰς κτοίνας ἀναγράψαι καὶ ἐγκολάψαι ἐν
10 τᾶι στά||λαι καὶ στάσαι ἐν τῶι ἱερῶι τᾶς 'Αθάνας καὶ περιβολι-
βῶ|σαι ὡς ἔχηι ὡς ἰσχυρότατα καὶ κάλλιστα. τὰ δὲ τε|λεύμενα ἐς
ταῦτα πάντα τὸν ταμίαν παρέχειν. | ἐγ δὲ ταυτᾶν τᾶν κτοινᾶν ἀπο-
15 δεικνύειν τοὺς | κτοινάτας μαστρὸν ἐν τῶι ἱερῶι τῶν ἁγιωτάτωι || ἐν
τᾶι κτοίναι κατὰ τὸν νόμον τὸν τῶν 'Ροδίων · | τούτοι δὲ συλλεγέ-
σθων ἐν Καμίρωι εἰς τὸ | ἱερὸν τᾶς 'Αθαναίας, ὄκκα τοὶ ἱεροποιοὶ
παραγγ[έλ|λ]ωντι, καὶ ἀθρεόντω τὰ ἱερὰ τὰ Καμιρέων [τὰ δα|μο]-
τελῆ πάντα, αἴ τι - - - - - -

The names of the κτοῖναι or demes of Camirus are to be
inscribed, both those on the island and those on the mainland.
For the latter cf., from the Periplus of Scylax, Χώρα ἡ 'Ροδίων
ἡ ἐν τῇ ἠπείρῳ.—The neighboring island of Χαλκῆ (see 42.2)

was under the control of Camirus at this time, yet evidently sustained a relation to it different from that of the other demes.— 6. ἐπιμεληθησεῦντι: 145.—8 ff. ἀποδωσεῦνται κτλ.: 'shall give out the contract to the one who is willing to furnish the stele at the lowest figure.'

103. Ialysus. Fourth (or third) century B.C. IG XII.i.677. GDI 4110. Ditt. Syll. 338. Schwyzer 284.

Ἔδοξε τοῖς μαστροῖς καὶ Ἰαλυσίοις, | Στράτης Ἀλκιμέδοντος εἶπε· | ὅπως τὸ ἱερὸν καὶ τὸ τέμενος | τᾶς Ἀλεκτρώνας εὐαγῆται
5 κα||τὰ τὰ πάτρια, ἐπιμεληθήμειν | τοὺς ἱεροταμίας ὅπως στάλαι | ἐργασθέωντι τρεῖς λίθου Λαρτ[ί]|ου καὶ ἀναγραφῇι ἐς τὰς στάλα|ς
10 τό τε ψάφισμα τόδε καὶ ἃ οὐχ ὅ||σιόν ἐντι ἐκ τῶν νόμων ἐσφέ|ρειν οὐδὲ ἐσοδοιπορεῖν ἐς τὸ τέ|μενος, καὶ τὰ ἐπιτίμια τῶ[ι] πράσ|σοντι
15 παρὰ τὸν νόμον· θέμειν δὲ | τὰς στάλας μίαμ μὲν ἐπὶ τᾶς ἐσό||δου τᾶς ἐκ πόλιος ποτιπορευομέ|νοις, μίαν δὲ ὑπὲρ τὸ ἱστιατόριον, | ἄλλαν δὲ ἐπὶ τᾶς καταβάσιος τᾶ[ς] | ἐξ Ἀχαίας πόλιος. |
20 Νόμος ἃ οὐχ ὅσιον ἐσίμειν οὐδὲ || ἐσφέρειν ἐς τὸ ἱερὸν καὶ τὸ τέ|μενος τᾶς Ἀλεκτρώνας. μὴ ἐσί|τω ἵππος, ὄνος, ἡμίονος, γῖνος |
25 μηδὲ ἄλλο λόφουρον μηθέν, μη|δὲ ἐσαγέτω ἐς τὸ τέμενος μη||θεὶς τούτων μηθέν, μηδὲ ὑποδή|ματα ἐσφερέτω μηδὲ ὕειον μη|θέν· ὅτι δέ κά τις παρὰ τὸν νόμον | ποιήσηι, τό τε ἱερὸν καὶ τὸ τέμενος | καθαιρέτω καὶ ἐπιρεζέτω, ἢ ἔνο||χος ἔστω τᾶι ἀσεβείαι· εἰ δέ κα | πρόβατα ἐσβάληι, ἀποτεισάτω ὑ|πὲρ ἑκάστου προβάτου ὀβολὸν |
35 ὁ ἐσβαλών· ποταγγελλέτω δὲ | τὸν τούτων τι ποιεῦντα ὁ χρήι||ζων ἐς τοὺς μαστρούς.

4. Ἀλεκτρώνας: a daughter of Helios and the nymph Rhodos, who was worshipped with divine honors by the Rhodians. Cf. Diod. 5.56, where the name appears as Ἠλεκτρυώνη.—7. λίθου Λαρτίου: also πέτρας Λαρτίας on another inscription, 'marble from Lartus,' a place in the neighborhood of Lindus.—10. ἐντι: pl. for sg. 163.10.—18. Ἀχαίας πόλιος: the name given to the acropolis of Ialysus. Cf. Ath. 8.360 ἐν τῇ Ἰαλυσῷ πόλιν ἰσχυροτάτην τὴν Ἀχαίαν καλουμένην.

104. Rhodian (?) inscription from Abu-Symbel in Egypt. Sixth century B.C. GDI 5261. Ditt. Syll. 1. Roberts 130. Schwyzer 301. Tod 4. The signatures added below (b-i) are omitted here.

a. Βασιλέος ἐλθόντος ἐς Ἐλεφαντίναν Ψα(μ)ματίχο | ταῦτα
ἔγραψαν, τοὶ σὺν Ψαμματίχδι τδι Θεοκλος | ἔπλεον. ἦλθον δὲ
Κέρκιος κατύπερθε, υἷς ὁ ποταμὸς | ἀνίη. ἀλογλοσος δ' ἦχε Πο-
5 τασιμπτό, Αἰγυπτίος δὲ Ἄμασις. || ἔγραφε δ' ἀμὲ Ἄρχον ἀμοι-
βίχο καὶ Πέλεϙος ὄυδάμο.

Inscribed on the legs of one of the colossal statues at Abu-
Symbel by Greek mercenaries who had taken part in an expedition up the Nile under Psammetichus II (594-589 B.C.). These
mercenaries were from Asia Minor and the adjacent islands.
Cf. Hdt. 2.154 and the names inscribed below, which include
two Ionians, from Teos and Colophon, and one Rhodian. The
main part of the inscription is clearly in Doric and may well
have been written by one of the Rhodian mercenaries.

a.3. **υἷς ὁ ποταμὸς ἀνίη**: 'as far as the river let them go
up.' For υἷς see 132.4.—5. **ἀμοιβίχο ὄυδάμο**: ὁ Ἀμοιβίχου, ὁ
Εὐδάμου. 94.1, 7.

106. Gela. Sixth century B.C. GDI 4247. Schwyzer 302.

Πασιάδαϝο τὸ | σᾶμα, Κράτες ἐ|ποίει.

Beginning of a hexameter. For Πασιάδαϝο see 105.2a.

106. Agrigentum. Second half of third century B.C. (before
210). IG XIV.952. GDI 4254. Schwyzer 307.

Ἐπὶ ἱεροθύτα | Νυμφοδώρου τοῦ Φίλωνος | παραπροστά(τα)
5 τᾶς βουλᾶς, | προεδρευούσας τᾶς φυλᾶς || τῶν Ὑλλέων, προαγο-
ροῦντος | Διοκλέος τοῦ Διοκλέος, | γραμματεύοντος Ἀδρανίωνος
Ἀλεξάνδρου, | ἀλίασμα ἔκτας διμήνου, Καρνείου ἐξήκο[ντ]ος
παντᾶι, | ὑπὲρ προξενίας Δημητρίωι Διοδότου Συρακοσίωι. ||
10 Ἔδοξε τᾶι ἀλίαι καθὰ καὶ τᾶι συ(ν)κλήτωι ρι'. ἐπειδὴ ἀνάγ|γελ-
λον οἱ πρεσβέες οἱ ἐς Ῥώμαν πορευθέντες, Πασίων | Πασίωνος
Κότητος καὶ Θεόδωρος Θεοδώρου Ξηνιάδα, | Δημήτριον Διοδότου
Συρακόσιον πολλὰς καὶ μεγάλας χρείας | παρεισχῆσθαι τῶι ἀμῶι
15 δάμωι καὶ μεγάλων ἀγαθῶν παραίτιο(ν) || γεγόνειν, τοῖς δὲ Ἀκρα-
γαντίνοις πάτριόν ἐστι καὶ ἐκ προγόνων | παραδεδομένον τιμεῖν
τοὺς ἀγαθοὺς ἄνδρας καὶ προϊσταμέ|νους τοῦ ἀμοῦ δάμου ταῖς κα-
ταξίοις τιμαῖς · | δεδόχθαι ἐπὶ ἀγαθᾶι τύχαι καὶ σωτηρίαι τοῦ δάμου
τῶν Ἀκραγαντίνων · | εἴμειν πρόξενον καὶ εὐεργέταν Δημήτριον
20 Διοδότου Συρακόσι||ον, ὅπω(ς) πᾶσι φανερὸν ἦ ὅτι ὁ δᾶμος τῶν
Ἀκραγαντίνων ἐπί|σταται χάριτας ἀπονέμειν καταξίας τοῖς εὐερ-

γετεῖν προαι|ρουμένοις αὐτόν. τὸ δὲ δόγμα τόδε κολάψαντας ἐς
χαλκώ|ματα δύο τὸ μὲν ἒν ἀναθέμειν εἰς τὸ βουλευτήριον, τὸ δὲ |
25 ἄλλο ἀποδόμειν Δημητρίωι Διοδότου Συρακοσίωι ὑπό||μναμα τᾶς
ποτὶ τὸν δᾶμον εὐνοίας· τοὺς δὲ ταμίας | ἐξοδιάξαι ἐς τὰ προγε-
γραμμένα ὅσον κα χρεία ᾖ, καὶ φέ|ρειν τὰν ἔξοδον διὰ τῶν ἀπολό-
γων. | ὁμογνώμονες τοῦ συνεδρίου πάντες.

Proxeny decree of Agrigentum in honor of Demetrius of
Syracuse. In view of l. 11 and of the fact that this inscription
was found at Rome, being evidently the copy given to Demetrius
(l. 24), it appears that he was resident in Rome, and his services
probably consisted in some dealings with the Roman senate in
behalf of Agrigentum.

8. ἀλίασμα κτλ.: 'decree in the sixth period of two months,
at the very end of the month Καρνεῖος.'—14. παρεισχῆσθαι:
εἴσχηκα, εἴσχημαι, for ἔσχηκα, ἔσχημαι, with ει after the analogy
of εἴληφα etc. (76), occur in several κοινή inscriptions.—15.
γεγόνειν: 147.2.

107. Rhegium. Second century B.C. IG XIV.612. GDI 4258.
Ditt. Syll. 715. Schwyzer 310.

Ἐπὶ πρυτάνιος Νικάνδρου τοῦ Νικοδάμου, βουλᾶς προστατέον-
τος Σωσιπόλιος τοῦ Δαματρίου, Χίωι Ἱππίου δυοδεκάται, ἔδοξε
τᾶι ἀλία | καθάπερ τᾶι ἐσκλήτωι καὶ τᾶι βουλᾶι· ἐπεὶ ὁ στρατα-
γὸς τῶν Ῥωμαίων Γναῖος Αὐφίδιος Τίτου υἱὸς εὔνους ὑπάρχει τᾶι
ἁμᾶ πόλει, ἄξιος φαινόμενος | τᾶς αὐτοῦ καλοκἀγαθίας, δεδόχθαι
Γναῖον Αὐφίδιον Τίτου υἱὸν στραταγὸν Ῥωμαίων στεφανῶσαι ἐν
τῶ ἀγῶνι τοῖς πρώτοις Ἀθανίοις ἐλαίας στεφά|νω καὶ πρόξενον
καὶ εὐεργέταν ποιῆσαι τοῦ δάμ(ο)υ τῶν Ῥηγίνων καὶ ἐγγόνους αὐ-
5 τοῦ, εὐνοίας ἕνεκεν ἃς ἔχων διατελεῖ εἰς τὸν δᾶμον τῶν Ῥηγί||νων.
τὰν δὲ βουλὰν τὸ ἀλίασμα κολαψαμέναν εἰς χαλκώματα δισσὰ τὸ
μὲν ἀναθέμειν εἰς τὸ βουλευτήριον, τὸ δὲ ἀποστεῖλαι Γναίω Αὐφιδίω.

Rhegium was a Chalcidian colony, and in the few early inscriptions the Ionic element predominates. But after its destruc-
tion by Dionysius of Syracuse in 387 B.C. and its subsequent
restoration, there were continual changes in its population.
Some of its new inhabitants must have been furnished by Gela
or Agrigentum, if we may judge by the language of this inscription
which is not merely Doric, but contains the Rhodian infin. -μειν

and the word ἀλίασμα, otherwise known only from inscriptions of Gela and Agrigentum.

1. χίωι: unexplained and probably an error of some kind.— 2. ἐσκλήτωι: refers to a small select body, probably mediating between the council and the assembly. Cf. Hesych. ἔσκλητος· ἡ τῶν ἐξόχων συνάθροισις ἐν Συρακούσαις. So also Corcyr. ἐπείσκλητος.

Coan

108. Cos. Middle fourth century B.C. Paton-Hicks 37. GDI 3636. Schwyzer 251A. Solmsen-Fraenkel 43. Herzog, Abh. Preuss. Akad. 1928. no. 6. pp. 6 ff. (revised text, followed here, with omission of the dots marking mutilated letters).

[The fragmentary first three lines omitted here.] [ἐ]ς
5 [ἀ]πο[καρ]υσσόντω, ἱεροποιοὶ δὲ καὶ τοὶ κάρυκες ἰόντω κ[α‖τ]ὰ
χ[ι]λ[ιασ]τύας, βοῦς δὲ ἐννῆ [ἐ]λᾶντι, βοῦν ἐξ ἐνάτας ἑκάστ[ας], |
[ἐ]ξ Α....έων καὶ Πασθεμιαδᾶν πράτων καὶ Ν[οσ]τιδᾶν· ἐς δὲ |
[τ]ὰν ἀ[γο]ρὰν ἐλάντω Πάμφυλοι πρᾶτοι, ἐν ἀγορᾶι συμμίσ‖[γ]ον-
ται· ὁ δὲ ἱερεὺς καθήσθω [παρὰ] τ[ὰ]ν τράπεζαν ἔχων τὰ[ν σ]‖το-
λὰν τὰν ἱεράν, τοὶ δὲ ἱερ[οποιοὶ ἑκατ]έρω τᾶς τραπέζας· Π[άμ-‖
10 φ]υλοι δὲ ἐπελάντω βοῦ[ς τρεῖς τού]ς καλλίστους, αἱ [μέγ κα]
τούτωγ κριθῆι τις· αἱ δὲ [μή, Ὑλλεῖς τρ]εῖς ἐλάντω, αἱ μ[έγ κα
τ|ο]ύτωγ κριθῆι τις· αἱ δὲ μ[ή, Δυμᾶνες τρ]εῖς τοὺς λοιπούς, αἱ
[μέ]‖γ κα τούτων κριθῆι τις· αἱ [δὲ μή, ἀτέρους] ἐλάντω ἐς τὰν
ἀ[γο|ρ]ὰν καὶ ἐπελάντω κατὰ τα[ὐτά, αἱ μ]έγ κα τούτωγ κριθῆι
15 τ[ις]· ‖ αἱ δὲ μή, τρίτον ἐπελάντω κατὰ τα[ὐτ]ά· αἱ δέ κα τούτων
κρι[θῆι] | μηδείς, ἐπικρινόντω βοῦν ἐκ χι[λιασ]τύος ἑκάστας·
ἐλά[σα]‖ντες δὲ τούτους συμμίσγον[ται τοῖ]ς ἄλλοις καὶ εὐθὺ
κ[ρίν?] |οντι καὶ εὔχονται καὶ ἀποκαρύ[σσο]ντι· ἔπειτα ἐπελᾶντ[ι
αὖ]‖τις κατὰ ταὐτά· θύεται δέ, αἱ μέγ κα ὑποκύψει, τᾶι Ἱστίαι·
20 θύ[ει] ‖ δὲ γερεαφόρος βασιλέων καὶ ἱερὰ παρέχει καὶ ἐπιθύει
ἱερὰ ἐξ [ἡ]‖μιέκτου· γέρη δὲ λαμβάνει τὸ δέρμα καὶ τὸ σκέλος,
ἱεροποι[οὶ] | δὲ σκέλος, τὰ δὲ ἄλλα κρέα τᾶς πόλιος· τὸν δὲ
κριθέντα τ[ῶι] | Ζηνὶ κάρυκες ἄγοντι ἐς ἀγοράν· ἐπεὶ δέ κα ἐν τᾶι
ἀγορᾶι ἔω[ν]‖τι, ἀγορεύει οὗ κα ἦι ὁ βοῦς ἢ ἄλλος ὑπὲρ κήνου ἐνδέ-
25 ξιο[ς]· ‖ "[Κώ]ιοις παρέχω τὸμ βοῦν, Κῶιοι δὲ τιμὰν ἀποδόντω
‹το› τᾶι Ἱστία[ι]·" | τιμώντω δὲ προστάται ὀμόσαντες παραχρῆ-

μα· ἐπεὶ δέ κα τι[μα|θῆ]ι, ἀναγορευέτω ὁ κῆρυξ ὁπόσσου κα τιμα-
θῆι· τουτῶ δὲ ἐλᾶντ[ι πα|ρ]ὰ τὰν Ἱστίαν τὰν Ἑταιρείαν καὶ θύοντι
(?)· ὁ δὲ ἱερεὺς στέπτει καὶ [ἐπι]|σπένδει κύλικα οἴνου κεκραμένου
30 πρὸ τοῦ βοός. ἔπειτα ἄγοντι τὸ[μ β|ο]ῦν καὶ τὸγ καυτὸν καὶ φθοίας
ἑπτὰ καὶ μέλι καὶ στέμμα· ἐξάγο[ντ|ε]ς δὲ καρύσσοντι εὐφαμίαν·
κηνεῖ δὲ ἐκδήσαντες τὸμ βοῦν κα[τ]|άρχονται θαλλῶι καὶ δάφναι·
τοὶ δὲ [κάρυκες κ]αρπῶντι τὸμ μὲγ χοῖ|[ρο]γ καὶ τὰ σπλάγχνα ἐπὶ
τοῦ βωμοῦ ἐπισπένδοντες μελίκρατον, ἔ[ντ|ερ]α δὲ ἐσπλύναντες
35 παρὰ τὸ[μ βωμὸν καρ]πῶντι· ἐπεὶ δέ κα καρπω[θῆι] || ἄποτα,
ἐπισπενδέτω μελίκρατον· ὁ δὲ [κᾶρ]υξ καρυσσέτω ἑορτάζε[ν Ζη-
ν]|ὸς Πολιέως ἐνιαύτια ὡραῖα ἑορτάν· [ἱερεὺς] δὲ τοῖς ἐντέροις
ἐπιθυέ[τω |θ]ύη καὶ τοὺς φθοίας καὶ σπονδὰς [ἄκρατο]ν καὶ κε-
κραμέναν καὶ στέ[μ]|μα· τουτῶ δὲ ἰόντω πὰρ τοὺς ἱαροποιὸς ἐς τὸ
οἴκημα τὸ δαμόσιον ἱα[ρ]|εὺς καὶ κάρυκες, ἱαροποιοὶ δὲ ξενίζοντι
40 τ[ὸν] ἱερῆ καὶ τὸς κάρυκας τα[ύ]|ταν τὰν νύκτα· ἐπεὶ δέ κα σπον-
δὰς π[οιή]σ[ω]νται, αἱρέσθω ὁ ἱαρεὺς [σ|φ]αγῆ τῶν ἱαροποιῶν
βοὸς τοῦ θυομένου τῶι Ζηνὶ τῶι Πολιῆι καὶ προα[γο|ρ]ευέτω
ἀγνεύεσθαι γυναικὸς καὶ ἀνδ[ρὸ]ς ἀντὶ νυκτός· τοὶ δὲ κάρυ[κε|ς]
αἱρείσθω σφαγῆ τοῦ βοὸς ὅγ κα χρήιζωντι ηὐτῶν καὶ προαγορευ-
έ[τω | ὅς κα δή]ληται τῶι αἱρεθέντι κατὰ ταὐτά. τᾶι αὐτᾶι ἀμέραι
45 Διονύσωι [Σκ]|υλλίται χοῖρος καὶ ἔριφος· τοῦ χοίρου οὐκ ἀπο-
φορά· θύει δὲ ἱερεὺς χ[αὶ ἱε|ρ]ὰ παρέχει· γέρη φέρει δέρμα, σκέλος.
Ἰκάδι· βοῦς ὁ κριθεὶς θύεται Ζηνὶ | [Πο]λιῆι· ἔνδορα ἐνδέρεται·
ἐφ' ἑστίαν θύεται ἀλφίτων ἡμίεκτον, ἄρτο[ι δ]ύο ἐξ ἡμιέκτου, ὁ
ἄτερος τυρώδης καὶ τὰ ἔνδορα· καὶ ἐπισπένδει ὁ ἱε[ρ]|εὺς τούτοις
οἴνου κρατῆρας τρεῖς· γέρη τοῦ βοὸς τῶι ἱερῆι δέρμα κ[αὶ σ|κέ]-
50 λος· ἱερὰ ἱερεὺς παρέχει· || καὶ χέλυος ἥμισυ καὶ κοιλίας ἥμ[ι|συ]·
θυαφόρωι δὲ τοῦ σκέλεος τοῦ τῶν ἱεροποιῶν δίδοται ἀκρίσχιον,
[κάρυ|ξι ν]ώτου δίκρεας, ὑπώμαια, αἱματίου ὀβελὸς τρικώλιος,
Νεστορίδαι[ς | δὲ] νώτου δίκρεας, ἰατροῖς κρέας, αὐλητᾶι κρέας,
χαλκέων καὶ κερα[μέ|ω]ν ἑκατέροις τὸ κεφάλαιο[ν· τὰ δὲ ἄλ]λα
55 κρέα τᾶς πόλιος· ταῦτα πάν[τα || οὐκ] ἀποφέρεται ἐκτὸς τᾶς π[ό-
λιος]. τᾶι αὐτᾶι ἀμέραι Ἀθαναίαι Πο[λι]|άδι ὄις κυεῦσα· θύει δὲ
ἱε[ρεὺς καὶ] ἱερὰ παρέχει· γέρη λαμβάνει δέ[ρ]|μα καὶ σκέλος.
ἐνάται με[τ' ἰκ]άδα Διονύσωι Σκυλλίται χοῖρος [καὶ] | ἔριφος·
τοῦ χοίρου οὐκ ἀποφορά· θύει ἱερεὺς καὶ ἱερὰ παρέχει· γέρη
[λ]|αμβάνει δέρμα καὶ σκέλος. ἑβδόμαι ἀνομένου ἐς Ἀλκηίδας
60 Δά[μ]||ατρι ὄις τέλεως καὶ τελέα κυεῦσα· τούτων οὐκ ἀποφορά·

κύλικες κ[αι|ν]αὶ δύο δίδονται· θύει ἱερεὺς [καὶ ἱερ]ὰ παρέχει·
γέρη δὲ οὔατα. ἔχκτ[αι Δι|ο]νύσωι Σκυλλίτα[ι χοῖρος καὶ ἔριφος·]
τοῦ χοίρου [ο]ὺκ [ἀποφορά· κτλ.]

Portion of a sacrificial calendar, enumerating the rites appropriate to each day of the year.

The dialect is somewhat mixed, with fluctuation between
earlier and later forms (e.g., ἱερός, ἱερεύς, but also the earlier
ἱαροποιοί beside ἱεροποιοί) and with some Ionic influence (τέλεως,
ἱρεύς, ἱαρεωσύνα). Generally ει, ου for secondary ē, but χῆνος,
δήλομαι, and old spelling E, O in αἱρέσθω (3 sg.) l. 40, vs. αἱρείσθω
(3 pl.) l. 43.

1-18. Selection of the ox for sacrifice to Zeus Polieus. After
the formal announcement and the arrival of the officials, they
(the tribes, each of them) drive in nine oxen, one from each
ninth (of the tribe). The Pamphyli first are to drive their oxen
to the agora and there they are united in a common herd (with
those of the other tribes, as they come in). When the priest
and the ἱεροποιοί have taken their place at the table, the Pamphyli are to drive up (ἐπελάντω 'drive up' for inspection) their
three finest oxen for selection. If none of these is chosen, the
Hylleis are to drive in three more, then the Dymanes, then,
if none has been chosen, (the same tribes in rotation) are to
drive up others, and again a third time. If still no choice has been
made (of the twenty-seven oxen driven up), they select an
additional ox from each χιλιαστύς (the third part of a tribe)
and unite these with the others. Then the choice is effected,
followed by vows and a proclamation of the choice.—**ἐλᾶντι**,
ἐλάντω, etc.: **159**.

18-22. The procedure is repeated and a sacrifice is made to
Histia. The main sacrifice, to which the preceding refers, is that
to Zeus Polieus as shown in l. 23.—19. **ὑποκύψει**: 'submits
tamely,' aor. subj. **150**.—20. **γερεαφόρος**: title occurring only
here and in an inscription from the neighboring small island of
Pserimos.—20/21. **ἐξ ἡμιέκτου**: cf. **136**.9.—24. **οὖ κα**, κτλ.:
the owner of the ox or another entitled to represent him (ἐνδέξιος
literally 'on the right').—30. **καυτόν**: 'burnt-offering,' in this
case a pig. Cf. χοῖρος προκατεύεται in another part of the calendar.

—35. ἄποτα: = ἄποινα 'without wine.' Cf. ἄποινος θυσία in schol. Hom.—42. ἀντὶ νυκτός: 'during the night.' 136.8.—43. ἡὐτῶν: = ἑαυτῶν 121.2. —47. ἔνδορα ἐνδέρεται: the reference is to certain parts of the victim which are wrapped up in the skin and made a special offering. Cf. Hesych. ἔνδρατα· τὰ ἐνδερόμενα σὺν τῇ κεφαλῇ καὶ τοῖς ποσίν.—50. χέλυος (new reading): here 'breast, chest' as in Hippocr.

Theran, Melian

109. Thera. Eighth (?) century B.C. IG XII.iii.536. GDI 4787. Schwyzer 214. Solmsen-Fraenkel 36.

a. Πheιδιπίδας ὦιπhε. *b.* Τιμαγόρας καὶ 'Ενπhέρης καὶ ἐγὡιπh[ομες]. *c.* "Ενπυλος τάδε—πόρνος. *d.* 'Ενπεδοκλῆς ἐνεϘόπτετο τάδε. *e.* Ϙὡρκε̄το μὰ τὸν 'Απόλω.

No. 109 belongs to a series of inscriptions cut in the solid rock and mostly of obscene content. Like the epitaphs in no. 110 and the Mel. no. 114, it belongs to the oldest period of the alphabet, when there were no signs for φ and χ, which were indicated by πh and κh or Ϙh, in consequence of which even θ was sometimes indicated by θh. Even at this early time F was completely lost, cf. Κλεαγόρας, 'Ορθοκλῆς, Λεονίδας, ἐποίε̄. ᗺ = h (also hε, hε̄) and = original η, but ε for ε̄ by contraction Θ = ω.—In no. 109*d, e* apparently a pun was intended in ἐνεϘόπτετο, which may be used in an obscene sense, and perhaps in Ϙὡρκε̄το which some wish to read Ϙὡρκ(h)ε̄το from ὀρχέομαι 'dance.'

110. Thera. Seventh century B.C. IG XII.iii.762. GDI 4808. Roberts 2. Schwyzer 215, 1).

a. 'Ρε̄κσάνωρ ἀρκhαγέτας, Προκλῆς, Κλεαγόρας, Περαιεύς.

b. "Αγλων, Περίλας, ΜάλεηϘος.

c. Λεοντίδας.

d. 'Ορθοκλῆς.

111. Thera. Sixth or early fifth century B.C. IG XII.iii. Suppl. 1324. Schwyzer 219. Solmsen-Fraenkel 37.

'Αγλο̄τέλης πράτισ|τος 'Αγορᾶν hικάδι |
Κα[ρ]νῆια θεὸν δεί|πν[ι]ξεν hο̄νιπαντίδα ||
καὶ Λακαρτο̄ς.

'Agloteles, son of Enipantidas and Lacarto, was the first to honor with a Carnean banquet the god (Apollo Carneus) on the twentieth of the month in which the Ἀγοραί were celebrated' (cf. Ἀγορήιοις no. 113). But the words from πράτιστος τὸ δείπνιξεν are variously interpreted. The inscription, up to the last two words, is metrical (two iambic trimeters), hence δείπνιξεν without augment and with the Att.-Ion. ν movable.

112. Thera. Fourth century B.C. IG XII.iii.436. GDI 4765. Ditt. Syll. 1032. Schwyzer 221. Solmsen-Fraenkel 38.

5 Οὖροι γᾶς | Θεῶν Ματρί. | Θεὸς ἀγαθᾶι τ|ύχαι ἀγαθοῦ δ||αίμονος
   θυσία | Ἀρχίνου· τῶι ἔτ|ει τῶι πρατίστ|ωι θύσοντι βοῦ|ν καὶ πυ-
10 ρῶν ἐγ || μεδίμνου καὶ | κριθᾶν ἐγ δύο μ|εδίμνων καὶ οἴνο|υ μετρη-
15 τὰν καὶ ἄλλα | ἐπάργματα ὧν αἱ ὧρ||αι φέρουσιν, μηνὸς Ἀρτε|μι-
   σίου πέμπται ἱσταμ|ένου καὶ μηνὸς Ὑακινθίο|υ πέμπται ἱσταμένου.

1 f. 'Boundaries of the land for the Mother of the Gods.' This was, doubtless, land dedicated to her service by Archinus, who also promises a sacrifice.—6 ff. 'In the very first year they shall offer an ox, a medimnus of wheat, etc.'—θύσοντι: instead of θυσέοντι (cf. no. 113), but with retention of the Doric ending, while φέρουσιν l. 15 is completely Attic, likewise Ἀρτεμισίου (cf. Ἀρταμιτίου no. 113).—ἐγ μεδίμνου, κτλ.: 136.9.

113. Thera. Fourth century B.C. IG XII.iii. 452. GDI 4772. Schwyzer 220.

Ἀρταμιτίο τετάρται | πεδ' ἰκάδα θυσέοντι | ἱαρόν, Ἀγορήιοις δὲ | [δ]εῖπνον καὶ ἱα[ρ]ὰ πρὸ τῶ σαμηίο.

'On the twenty-fourth of the month Artemisius they shall offer a sacrifice, and at the Agoreia (name of a festival) a banquet, and sacrifices in front of the image.'

114. Melos. Early sixth century B.C. IG XII.iii.1075. GDI 4871. Roberts 7. Schwyzer 207.

Παῖ Διός, Ἐκπhάντōι δέκσαι τόδ' ἀμενπhὲς ἄγαλμα
σοὶ γὰρ ἐπευχόμενον τοῦτ' ἐτέλεσσε γρόπhōν.

γρόπhōν (also γρόφōν in another inscription) = γράφων here 'carving.' 49.2. Ἐκπhάντōι: see no. 68, note.

Cyrenaean

115. Cyrene. Early fourth century B.C. Solmsen-Fraenkel 39.
SEG 9.1.no. 72 (with full bibliography of the extensive literature;
Oliverio, Documenti Antichi della Africa Italiana 2.14 ff., is the
latest full discussion, with the best photograph).

'Α]πόλλων ἔχρη[σε · | ἐς ἀ]εὶ καθαρμοῖς καὶ ἁγνηίαις κα[ὶ θε-|
ραπ]ηίαις χρειμένος τὰν Λεβύαν οἰκ[έν].

§ 1. [Αἴ] κα ἐπὶ τὰγ γᾶν ἢ ἐπὶ τὰμ πόλιν ἐπείηι νόσο[ς ἢ λι-||
5 μὸ]ς ἢ θάνατος, θύεν ἔμπροσθε τᾶμ πυλᾶν, [ἐναν|τίον] τῶ ἀποτρο-
παίω, τῶι 'Απόλλωνι τῶι ἀποτρό[π|ωι] χίμαρον ἐρυθρόν.

§ 2. [Κ]ᾶλον ἐν ἰαρῶι πεφυκός · αἴ κα τῶι θεῶι τὰν τιμὰ[ν |
10 ἐ]ρεῖσες, τῶι κάλωι χρησῆι καὶ ἐς ἰαρὰ καὶ ἐς βάβ[α||λα] καὶ ἐς
μιαρά. |

§ 3. 'Α[π]ὸ γυναικὸς ἀνὴρ τὰν νύκτα κοιμαθὲς θυσεῖ ὅ|[πυι κα]
δήληται · τὰν δὲ ἀμέραν κοιμαθὲς λωσάμεν[ος | θυσεῖ - - - - εἶτι,
ὅπυι κα δήλ[ητα]ι, πλὰν ἢ ἐς τ[ὸ | - - only a few letters legible
15 - - - - || - - -

§ 4. ['Α λ]εχώι ὄροφον μιανεῖ · τὸν μ[ὲν ὑπώροφον μιανεῖ, τὸν |
δ' ἐ]ξόροφον οὐ μιανεῖ, αἴ κα μὴ ὑπένθηι. ὁ δ' ἄ[νθρ|ω]πος, ὅ κα
ἔνδοι ἦι, αὐτὸς μὲν μιαρὸς τέντα[ι ἀμ|έρα]ς τρῖς, ἄλλον δὲ οὐ
20 μιανεῖ, οὐδὲ ὅπυι κα ἔνθ[ηι ο]||ὗτος ὁ ἄνθρωπος. |

§ 5. "Α κα μαντίων ὁσία παντὶ καὶ ἁγνῶι καὶ βαβάλω[ι] · |
πλὰν ἀπ' ἀνθρώπω Βάττω τῶ <τω> 'Αρχαγέτα καὶ | Τριτοπατέ-
ρων καὶ ἀπὸ 'Ονυμάστω τῶ Δελφῶι, | ἀπ' ἄλλω ὅπη ἄνθρωπος
25 ἔκαμε, οὐκ ὁσία ἁγνῶ[ι], || τῶν ἰαρῶν ὁσία παντί. |

§ 6. Αἴ κα ἐπὶ βωμῶι θύσηι ἰαρήιον ὅτι μὴ νόμος θύεν, τ[ὸ] |
ποτιπίαμμα ἀφελὲν ἀπὸ τῶ βωμῶ καὶ ἀποπλῦν|αι καὶ τὸ ἄλλο
λῦμα ἀνελὲν ἐκ τῶ ἰαρῶ, καὶ τὰν ἴκ|νυν ἀπὸ τῶ βωμῶ καὶ τὸ πῦρ
30 ἀφελέν ἐς καθαρόν · || καὶ τόκα δὴ ἀπονιψάμενος, καθάρας τὸ
ἰαρὸν καὶ | ζαμίαν θύσας βοτὸν τέλευν, τόκα δὴ θυέτω ὡς νομ|ο-
κώχιμος μέστα ἐς ἀδελφεῶν τέκνα. |

§ 7. Αἴ κα δεκατὸς ἦι ἄνθρωπος ἡβάτας, καθάρας α|[ὐ]τὸς
35 αὐτὸν αἵματι, καθαρεῖ τὸ ἰαρὸν καὶ πωλη||[θ]ὲς ἐν τᾶι ἀγοράι
ὁπόσσω κα πλείστω ἄξιος ἦ[ι], | προθυσεῖ πρὸ τᾶς δεκάτας ζαμίαν
βοτὸν τέλ|[ε]υν, οὐκ ἀπὸ τᾶς δεκάτας, καὶ τόκα δὴ θυσεῖ τὰν |
[δ]εκάταν καὶ ἀποισεῖ ἐς καθαρόν · αἰ δὲ μή, τῶν αὐ|[τ]ῶν δησῆ-
ται [σκ]οίκιον δὲ οἰσεῖ πᾶς ὁ θύων. ||

40 § 8. [Ἄ]νηβος αἰ μή τί κα ἑκὼν μιᾶι, ἀποχρεῖ καθάρασ|[θ]αι
αὐτὸν καὶ ζαμίας οὐ δεῖ· αἰ δέκα ἑκώμ μιᾶι, κα|[θ]αρεῖ τὸ ἱαρὸν
καὶ ζαμίαν προθυσεῖ βοτὸν τέλευν. |

§ 9. Αἴ κα χρήματα δεκατὰ ἦι, ἐκτιμάσας τὰ χρήματ|α, κα-
45 θαρεῖ τὸ ἱαρὸν καὶ τὰ χρήματα δίχα καὶ τόκα || [δ]ὴ προθυσεῖ
ζαμίαν βοτὸν τέλευν, οὐ τᾶς δεκάτ|[ας], καὶ τόκα δὴ θυσεῖ τὰν
δεκάταν καὶ ἀποισεῖ ἐς | [κα]θαρόν· αἰ δὲ μή, τῶν αὐτῶν δησεῖ.
τῶν δὲ χρημά|[τω]ν, ἅς κα δεκατὰ ἦι, ἐντόφιον οὐκ ἐνθησεῖ οὐδὲ
50 [ἧς ο]ὐδὲ ἕν, οὐδὲ χύτλα οἰσεῖ πρίν κα τῶι θεῶι ἀπο[δε||κατε]ύσει.
αἰ δέ κα χύτλα ἐνίκει ἢ ἐντόφια ἐνθῆι, κα|[θά]ρας τὸ Ἀπολλώνιον
ζαμίαν προθυσεῖ κατὰ τὰν | [ἀμα]ρτίαν βοτὸν τέλευν. |

§ 10. [Αἴ κ]α δεκατός ἐὼν ἄνθρωπος ἀποθάνηι, κατακομί-|
55 [ξα]ντες τὸν ἄνθρωπον, τᾶι μὲν πρατίσται ἀμέραι || [ἐπι]θησεῖ ὅ
τι κα δήληται ἐπὶ τὸ σᾶμα, δεύτερον δ|[ὲ ο]ὐδὲ ἕν, πρίγ κα ἀπο-
δεκατεύσει τῶι θεῶι, καὶ ο[ὐ]||δὲ θυ]σεῖ οὐδ' ἐπὶ τὸ σᾶμα εἶτι.
ἐκτιμασέντι δὲ οἵ[ω | κα πλ]είστω ἄξιος ἦς, κοινὸς ἐὼν τῶι θεῶι.
(κ)αθάρα[ς | δὲ τὸ] Ἀπολλώνιον καὶ τὰ χρήματα δίχα, προθύ-
60 [σα||ς αὐτὸ]ς ζαμίαν βοτὸν τέλευν, οὐκ ἀπὸ τᾶς δε(κ)ά[τ|ας, προ]-
βώμιον, θυσεῖ τὰν δεκάταν προβώμιον κ[α|ὶ ἀπο]ισεῖ ἐς καθαρόν.
αἰ δὲ μή, τῶν αὐτῶν δησεῖ. |

§ 11. [Αἴ κα ἀπ]οθάνηι δεκατὸς ἐὼν καὶ τὰ τέκνα καταλι-
65 [π|όμενα τ]ὰ μὲν ζῶι, τὰ δὲ ἀποθάνηι, ἐκτιμάσας τὰ [ἀ||πηλ-
λαγ]μένα, ὁπόσσω κα πλείστω ἄξια ἦι, καθάρα[ς τὸ | Ἀπολλώ]-
νιον καὶ τὰ χρήματα δίχα, προθυσεῖ ζαμ|ίαν | τὰν τῶ ἤ]βατᾶ προ-
βώμιον, καὶ τόκα δὴ θυσεῖ τὰν δε[κ|άταν προ]βώμιον. τὸν δὲ
ζοὸν καθάρας αὐτὸς αὐτ[ὸ|ν καθᾶρ]αι τὸ ἱαρὸν δίχα πωληθὲς ἐν
70 τᾶι ἀγοραῖ θ[υ||σεῖ τὰν τ[ῶ ἤβατᾶ ζαμίαν βοτὸν τέλευν καὶ
τόκ[α δὴ | θυσεῖ τὰ]ν δεκάταν καὶ | ἀποισεῖ ἐς καθαρόν· αἰ
[δὲ μ|ή, τῶν αὐτ]ῶν δησεῖ. |

§ 12. [Ἀρκτεῦε]ν ἐπεί κα ἄρξεται, θύεν κατὰ νόμον. [αἰ μέγ |
75 κα ἄρκος ἔν]θηι, τὸ λοιπὸν θυσεῖ ὁπόκα κα δήλη[ται· αἰ || δέ κα
μὴ ἔν]θηι, καθαρμὸς ἀποχρεῖ ὅπ[υι] τις τ[ὰν δεκέτ|ιν χαλάξει]·
καθᾶραι οὐ δεῖ, αἰ δέ κα δήλητ[αι, αἰ δέ κα μ|ή, κάθαρ]μα προ-
βώμιον οἰσεῖ ὅπυι τ[ις τὰν δεκέτιν χ|αλάξει· αἰ ἄ]νθρωπος δ'
80 ἐχάλαξε τ[ὰν παρθένον - - - | - - - -]ς μὲν ἐπ[ιθυσεῖ - - - || - - -
| - - - | - - - |

§ 13. [Νύμφ]αμ μ[ὲν αἴ κα ἔνθηι ἐς κοιτατή]ριον, ζ[αμίαν |
85 δεῖ] ἐς Ἄρτ[αμιν θύεν]· αὐτὰ δὲ οὐχ ὑπώροφ||[ος τῶι ἀνδρὶ

τένται οὐδὲ μιασεῖ, μέστα κα [ἐ|ς] "Αρτεμιν ἔνθηι. ἂ δέ κα ταῦτα
μὴ ποιήσα[ι|σ]α μιᾶι ἔκασσα, καθάραισα τὸ 'Αρταμίτιον ἐπ[ι |
θ]υσεῖ ζαμίαν βοτὸν τέλευν, καὶ τόκα δὴ εἶτ|[ι] τὸ κοιτατήριον·
90 αἰ δέ κα μὴ ἐκοῖσα μιᾶι, κα||[θ]αρεῖ τὸ ἱαρόν. |

§ 14. [Ν]ύμφαν δὲ τὸ νυμφήιον ἐς "Αρταμιν κατ[εν|θ]ὲν δεῖ,
ὁπόκα κα δήληται 'Αρτεμιτίοις, [ὥς κα | τ]άχιστα δὲ λώιον·
ἂ δέ κα μὴ κατένθηι, ἀ[ποθ|υ]σεῖ τᾶι 'Αρτάματι ἅ κ[α νομίζητ]αι
τοῖς ['Αρταμιτίοις || ὢ]ς μὴ κατελ ηλευ[θυῖα, καὶ τόκα δὴ καθαρεῖ
τὸ ἱαρ|ὸ]ν καὶ ἐπιθυσεῖ ζ[αμίαν βοτὸν τέλευν] |

§ 15. [Νύμφα ἐπεί κα διακορηθῆι, κάτε]ιτι τὸ νυμφήι[ον] | ἐς
"Αρταμιν [αὐτὰ] κ[αὶ τᾶι ἄρκωι δωσεῖ πόδας καὶ | τὰν κεφαλὰν
100 καὶ τὸ δέρμα· αἰ δέ κα μὴ κατ[έν]||θηι, πρὶν τεκὲν κάτειτι σὺμ
βοτῶι τελέωι· ἀ δ[ὲ] | κατίασσα ἀγνευσεῖ ἑβδέμαν καὶ ὀγδόαν |
καὶ ἠνάταν, καὶ ἀ μὴ κατεληλευθυῖα ἀγν|ευσεῖ ταύτας τὰς ἀμέρας·
αἰ δέ κα μιᾶι. καθα|ραμένα αὐτὰ καθαρεῖ τὸ ἱαρὸν καὶ ἐπιθυσ[εῖ] ||
105 ζαμίαν βοτὸν τέλευν. |

§ 16. Αἴ κα γυνὰ ἐγβάληι, αἰ μέγ κα διάδηλον ἦι, μ[ι]αίνονται
ὥσπερ ἀπὸ θανόντος, αἰ δέ κα μὴ | διάδηλον ἦι, μιαίνεται αὐτὰ ἀ
οἰκία καθάπε[ρ] | ἀπὸ λεχός. ||

110 § 17. 'Ικεσίων |

'Ικέσιος ἐπακτός· αἴ κα ἐπιπεμφθῆι ἐπὶ τὰν | οἰκίαν, 'αἰ μέγ
κα ἴσαι ἀφ' ὅτινός οἱ ἐπῆνθε, ὀ|νυμαξεῖ αὐτὸν προειπὼν τρῖς ἀμέ-
115 ρας· αἰ δ[έ] | κα τεθνάκηι ἔγγαιος ἢ ἄλλη πη ἀπολώλη[ι], || αἰ
μέγ κα ἴσαι τὸ ὄνυμα, ὀνυμαστὶ προερεῖ, αἰ | δέ κα μὴ ἴσαι
"ὦ ἄνθρωπε, αἴτε ἀνὴρ αἴτε γυνὰ | ἐσσί", κολοσὸς ποιήσαντα
ἔρσενα καὶ θήλεια[ν] | ἢ καλίνος ἢ γαΐνος, ὑποδεξάμενον παρτιθ-
120 [έ]|μεν τὸ μέρος πάντων· ἐπεὶ δέ κα ποιήσες τὰ || νομιζόμενα,
φέροντα ἐς ὕλαν ἀεργὸν ἐρε[ῖ]|σαι τὰς κολοσὸς καὶ τὰ μέρη· |

§ 18. 'Ικέσιος ἅτερος, τετελεσμένος ἢ ἀτελής. ἰσ|σάμενος ἐπὶ
δαμοσίωι ἱαρῶι, αἰ μέγ κα προ[φέ]||ρηται, ὁπόσσω κα προφέρηται,
125 οὕτως τελίσκ[ε]||σθαι· αἰ δέ κα μὴ προφέρηται, γᾶς καρπὸν θ[ύ]-|
εν καὶ σπονδὰν καθ' ἔτος ἀεί. αἰ δέ κα παρῆι ἐ[ς] | νέω, δὶς τόσσα.
αἰ δέ κα διαλίπηι τέκνον ἐπι[λα]||θόμενον καὶ οἱ προφέρηται, ὅ τι
κά οἱ μαντε[υ]|ομένωι ἀναιρεθῆι, τοῦτο ἀποτεισεῖ τῶι θεῶ<ι>
130 κ[αὶ] || θυσεῖ, αἰ μέγ κα ἴσαι, ἐπὶ τὸμ πατρῶιον, αἰ δὲ μή, [χρή]-
σασθαι.|

§ 19. 'Ικέσιος τρίτος, αὐτοφόνος· ἀφικετεύεν ἐς [τρι]||πολίαν
καὶ τριφυλίαν· ὡς δέ κα καταγγήλε[ι ἱκέ]|σθαι, ἴσσαντα ἐπὶ τῶι

135 ὡδῶι ἐπὶ νάκει λευκ[ῶι νί]||ζεν καὶ χρῖσαι καὶ ἐξίμεν ἐς τὰν δα-
μοσί[αν] | ὁδὸν καὶ σιγὲν πάντας, ἦ κα ἔξοι ἔωντι, [τὸ|ς] ὑποδεκο-
μένος τὸν προαγγελτ[ῆρα · ἐς τὸ ἰα|ρὸ]ν παρίμεν τὸν ἀφικτευ[ό]-
μενο[ν - - - - | - -] εων καὶ τὸς ἑπομένος [of the remaining lines
only a few letters are legible].

Ritual practices enjoined by the oracle of Apollo.
'Apollo proclaimed by oracle. Always practicing purifications
and holy acts and services they shall inhabit Libya.'—**χρείμενος**:
could be the Delphian form in this passage beginning Ἀπόλλων
ἔχρησε, but not necessarily so. See **158**.

§ 1. 'If disease or famine or death comes to the land or the
city, one shall sacrifice before the gates, facing the apotropaion,
a red goat to Apollo the averter of evil.'

§ 2. 'Timber grown in the sacred precinct. If you have deposited the price for the god, you may use the timber for things
sacred and profane and defiled.' —9. **ἐ]ρεῖσες** : probable reading.
Oliverio's π]οεῖσες = ποιῆοες l. 119 is to be rejected, for ει =
original η is unknown. ἐρείδω 'prop up, support', also 'make
firm, fix,' and below l. 120 probably 'deposit.' Here 'deposit'
or 'fix' = 'arrange for.'

§ 3. 'A man (purifying himself) from a woman, if he has
lain with her by night, he shall sacrifice wherever he wishes.
If he has lain (with her) by day, having washed himself, (he shall
sacrifice and) shall go wherever he wishes except into the - - - -.'
—13. The letters preceding ὅπυι κα δήληται are uncertain, but
εἴτι or κατεῖτι looks more probable than Oliverio's [μετ' ὀλίγ]ον τι.

§ 4. 'The woman in childbed will defile the house. The one
within the house she will defile, but the one outside the house
she will not defile, unless one comes inside. The person who is
inside shall himself be defiled for three days, but shall not defile
another, nor (any place) where this person comes.'—16. **ὄροφος**:
'roof' here = 'house', like Cret. στέγα.—18. **τένται**: = τέλεται =
ἔσεται. **72**.

§ 5. 'As to oracles, sanction (to consult them) belongs to
everyone, both the holy and the profane—except that (for those)
from the person Battus the Founder and the Ancestors and
Onumastus the Delphian (and) from any other person who died

(lit. from anyone else where a person died) there is no sanction for the holy. As to the shrines, sanction belongs to everyone.'— This is the most difficult paragraph and there has been no agreement in the interpretation. ἄ κα 'in case that' (cf. l. 93) properly requires a verb, but probably is here an abbreviated form of ἄ κα ἦι.—**μαντίων**: not from μάντις 'seer,' but from a *μάντιον = μαντεῖον, like ἱαρῶν l. 25 and Ἱκεσίων l. 110., gen. of matters or persons involved (**171**).—The passage ll. 22 ff. plainly refers to oracles of the dead (cf. νεκυομαντεῖον Hdt. 5.92, Paus. 9.30.6).— **22. τῶ‹τω›**: probably dittography. ἄνθρωπος points the contrast of oracles of deceased human beings to those of the gods.— **23. τῶ Δελφῶι**: cf. **38a.**—**24. ἔκαμε**: 'died.' Cf. Hom. βροτῶν εἴδωλα καμόντων.

§ 6. Regulations for one who has sacrificed a victim which it is not lawful to sacrifice.—**27. ποτιπίαμμα**: 'the fat that remains.' 164.4.—28/9 ἴκνυν. Cf. ἴκνυον· κονίαν, σμῆμα Hesych. Here 'ashes' ?—**31, 32. ὡς νομοκώχιμος μέστα ἐς ἀδελφεῶν τέκνα**: 'as bound by the law (which extends) up to the children of brothers.' νομοκώχιμος (or possibly νομωκώχιμος as Oliverio), parallel to κατοκώχιμος, is the probable reading. At the end of l. 31 there is no room after νομ for any more letters, so that the reading νόμ(ος) implies an abbreviation that is improbable.

§§ 7-11. Regulations for a δεκατός 'one subject to a tithe.'— **34/5 πωληθές κτλ.**: 'having been offered for sale in the market-place for whatever he is worth.'—**38, 46/7, 62, 72. ἀποισεῖ ἐς καθαρόν**: 'shall restore (things) to a state of purity.'—**39. [σκ]οίκιον**, some kind of receptacle, quotable from papyri, is the probable reading. Oliverio reads ἐποίκιον 'supellex' but this is not the sense of the word in CIGI 1730 (= IG IX.i.47) to which he refers.—**40, 41, 86, 89. μιᾶι**: 3 sg. aor. subj. (**144b, 151.**1) in pass. sense 'be defiled,' as also 3 sg. fut. μιασεῖ l. 85 vs. trans. μιανεῖ ll. 16-19.—**45. οὐ τᾶς δεκάτας**: = οὐκ ἀπὸ τᾶς δεκάτας ll. 36, 60.—**47. δησεῖ**: so certainly here (where Oliverio assumes omission of ται), and from the photograph probable in l. 62 (Oliverio δησειτ[αι]) and l. 72 (Oliverio δησεῖται, but no visible traces after ΕΙ).—48/9. Read οὐδὲ [ἧς ο]ὐδὲ ἕν after Tab. Heracl. 1.1.136. Calhoun, CP 29. 345.—53 ff. 'If the one subject to a tithe has died, after they have buried him, on the first day (the

heir) shall bring whatever he wishes to the grave, but afterwards
nothing until he has paid off the tithe to the god, and he shall not
make an offering or go to the grave. They shall evaluate (the
deceased δεκατός) for the most that he was worth, he being a
partner of the god (that is, in part indebted to him).'—57.
ἐκτιμασέντι: 42.5*e.*—65/6. ἐκτιμάσας κτλ.: '(the heir) having
evaluated the deceased (children) for the most they are worth.'

§ 12. This paragraph is wholly obscure without extensive
restorations. Those of Oliverio, repeated in SEG and with some
minor changes in the text above, are only plausible conjectures,
of which the critical ones are [ἄρκος] (the girl in the service of
Artemis, mentioned in l. 98), [ἀρκτεύε]ιν (should be rather
[ἀρκτεῦε]ν), and [δεκέτιν]. Even so, the sense is none too clear.

§§ 13-15. Regulations regarding a bride.—The restorations
in ll. 83/4 of the words before αὐτά and of διακορηθῆ in l. 97 are
of course uncertain.

§ 16. 'If a woman suffers a miscarriage or abortion, if it is
plain (that is, if the fetus is fully formed), (persons) are defiled
as from one dead, but if it is not plain the houshold itself is defiled
as from one in childbirth.'

§§ 17-19, with the heading 'About Suppliants.' The view of
Stukey, CP 32.32 ff., that the ἱκέσιοι were not suppliants but
supernatural beings, is not convincing. Although the text is
nearly perfect and the literal meaning generally clear, the
interpretation of the real situation is in part uncertain.

§ 17. 'Suppliant from abroad. If he has been sent to the home,
if (the master of the home) knows from whom he came to him,
he shall name this person, giving notice for three days. If he
(this person) has died within the land or has perished anywhere
else, if he (the master) knows the name he shall give notice by
name. But if he does not know, (then saying) "O person whether
thou art man or woman," having made figures male and female
of wood or clay, as host one shall place beside them the (proper)
portion of all (that is, the customary food and drink). When
you have done the things customary, bringing them to a virgin
forest deposit the figures and the portions.'

§ 18. 'Second suppliant, initiated or uninitiated. Having been
seated at the public shrine, if there is a declaration (by the

priest), for whatever amount is declared so it shall be fulfilled.
If there is no declaration, one shall sacrifice the fruit of the land
and a libation annually forever. If he presents himself anew,
then twice as much. If he leaves a child who has neglected it and
a declaration is made to him (the child), whatever is ordained
for him consulting the oracle this he shall pay to the god and
shall sacrifice, if he knows (where it is) on the ancestral tomb,—
if not, consult the oracle.'—126. αἰ δέ κα παρῆι: παρῆι is taken
by most commentators as 'omit' and so from πάρειμι, cpd. of
εἶμι in its use for 'pass by' (Hdt. 7.109, etc.). But from this one
expects παρείηι like ἐπείηι l. 4. As it stands, παρῆι belongs to the
cpd. of εἰμί. De Sanctis, Riv. fil. 55.206, so takes it.

19. 'Third suppliant, a homicide. One shall make intercession
to the tribunal of the three cities and the three tribes. When
one has announced that one is making supplication, having
seated (the suppliant) on the threshold, on a white fleece, one
shall wash and anoint him and go forth into the public road,
and they shall all keep silent, so long as they are outside, following
the announcer. The one for whom intercession is made shall
procede to the shrine - - and those following - - -'

Cretan

116. Drerus. Sixth century B.C. P. Demargne et H. van
Effenterre, BCH 61.333 ff., 62.194.

ˀΑδˀ ἔϜαδε πόλι· ἐπεί κα κοσμήσει δέκα Ϝετίōν τὸν ἀ|Ϝτὸν μὴ
κοσμέν· αἰ δὲ κοσμησίē, ὅπē δικασσίē, αὐτὸν ὀπῆλεν διπλεῖ κάϜτόν, |
θιὸς ὅλοι ὄν, ἄκρηστον ἤμεν, ἃς δόοι, κὄτι κοσμησίē μηδὲν ἤμην. |
ὁμόται δὲ κόσμος κὄι δάμιοι κὄι ἴκατι οἱ τᾶς πόλ[ιος].

As in other early Cretan inscriptions, ⊟ = η, but here beside E
which in some cases must also stand for η. Cf. ⊟ ⋀ E ⋔ beside
⊟ ⋀ ⊓ ⋔. We therefore transcribe ἤμēν beside ἤμην, and so
ὅπē, κοσμέν, κοσμησίē. ⋁ = λ in contrast to usual Cret. ⋀.

'Voted by the city as follows. When one shall have been
kosmos, the same one shall not be kosmos within ten years.
If he has become kosmos (within ten years), in whatever case
he pronounces judgment, he shall owe a double penalty and
himself—god destroy him—be without function as long as he

lives, and whatever he has done as kosmos shall be null and void. Jurors the kosmos and the damioi (those appointed from the people?) and the twenty of the city.'

1. **ᾄδ'**: 'in this manner, as follows' (**132**.6), confirming this interpretation of Delph. ἆδε in no. 51.—**πόλι**: for lack of article see 122*a*.—**κοσμησίε̄, δικακσίε̄**: 152.4.—The insertion between the first and second lines, just above κἀϜτόν, is obviously an imprecation thrown in. The letters are clear except for the third from the end, and that, despite the peculiar form that appears in the photograph, is probably the crooked iota and so taken by the editor. Read θιὸς ὄλοι ὄν, with 2. aor. act. (otherwise only attested in mid.) of ὄλλυμι and demonstrative use of ὅς.— 3. **ἄκρηστον**: = ἄχρηστον 'useless', here 'without right to function.'—4. **ἴκατι**: the absence of Ϝ, in contrast to ἔϜαδε, Ϝετίο̄ν, is strange, but seen also in ἰκάδι of another archaic inscription of Drerus.

117. Gortyn. Fifth century B.C. GDI 4991. Inscr. Jurid. I, pp. 352 ff. Schwyzer 179. Solmsen-Fraenkel 40.

 1 Θιοί. | Ὅς κ' ἐλευθέρο̄ι ε̄̓ δόλο̄ι μέλλε̄ι ἀν|πιμο̄λε̄ν, πρὸ δίκας μὲ̄
  ἄγεν. αἰ δ|έ κ' ἄγε̄ι, καταδικακσάτο̄ το̄ ἐλευθέρ|ο̄ δέκα στατε̄ρανς,
 5 το̄ δόλο̄ πέν||τε, ὅτι ἄγει, καὶ δικακσάτο̄ λαγάσαι | ἐν ταῖς τρισὶ
  ἀμέραις. αἰ [δέ] κα | μὲ̄ [λαγ]άσει, καταδικαδδέτο̄ το̄ μὲν | ἐλευ-
  θέρο̄ στατε̄ρα, το̄ δόλο̄ [δα]ρκν|ὰν τᾶς ἀμέρας Ϝεκάστας, πρίν κα
 10 λα||γάσει· το̄ δὲ κρόνο̄ τὸν δι[κ]αστ|ὰν ὀμνύντα κρίνεν. αἰ δ' ἀννί-
  οιτο | μὲ̄ ἄγεν, τὸν δικαστὰν ὀμνύντ|α κρ[ί]νεν, αἰ μὲ̄ ἀποπο̄νίοι
 15 μαῖτυς. | αἰ δέ κα μο̄λε̄ι ὁ μὲν ἐλεύθε[ρ]ον, || ὁ δ[ὲ δ]ο̄λον, κάρτο-
  νανς ε̄̓μεν | [ὅτερο]ί κ' ἐλεύθερον ἀποπο̄νίο̄ν|τι. αἰ δέ κ' ἀνπὶ δόλο̄ι
  μο̄λίο̄ντι | πόνιοντες Ϝὸν Ϝεκάτερος ε̄̓μ|εν, αἰ μέν κα μαῖτυς ἀποπο̄-
 20 νε̄ι, κ||ατὰ τὸν μαίτυρα δικάδδεν, αἰ | δέ κ' ε̄̓ ἀνποτέροις ἀποπο̄νί-
  ο̄ντι | ε̄̓ με̄δατέρο̄ι, τὸν δικαστὰν ὀ|μνύντα κρίνεν. ε̄̓ δέ κα νικαθε̄ι
 25 ὁ | ἔκο̄ν, [τ]ὸμ μὲν ἐλεύθερον λαγ||άσαι τᾶν πέ[ν]τ' ἀμερᾶν, τὸν δὲ
  δο̄|λ[ον] ἐς κε̄ρανς ἀποδόμε̄ν. αἰ δέ | κα μὲ̄ λαγάσει ε̄̓ μὲ̄ ἀποδο̄ι,
  δικακ|σάτο̄ νικε̄ν το̄ μὲν ἐλευθέρο̄ | πεντε̄κοντα στατε̄ρανς καὶ
 30 σ||τατε̄ρα τᾶς ἀμέρας Ϝεκάστ|ας, πρίν κα λαγάσει, το̄ δὲ δόλο̄ |
  δέκα στατε̄ρανς καὶ δαρκνὰν | τᾶς ἀμέρας Ϝεκάστας, πρίν κ' ἀ|πο-
 35 δο̄ι ἐς κε̄ρανς. ε̄̓ δέ κα καταδι||κάκσει ὁ δικαστάς, ἐνιαυτο̄ι π|ράδ-
  δεθθαι τὰ τρίτρα ε̄̓ μεῖον, | πλίον δέ μέ̄· το̄ δὲ κρόνο̄ τὸν δι|κανστὰ

40 ὀμνύντα κρίνεν. αἰ δέ | κα ναεύει ὁ δō̄λος ŏ̄ κα νικαθε̄͟|ι, καλίον ἀντὶ
μαιτύρον δυōν δ|ρομέōν ἐλευθέρōν ἀποδειξάτ|ō ἐπὶ τōͅ νᾱō͂ͅ ὅπε̄
κα ναεύει ε̄̆ α|ὐτὸς ε̄̆ ἄ(λ)λος πρὸ τούτō· αἰ δέ | κα με̆̀ καλε̄ͅ ε̄̆ με̆̀
45 δείξει, κατισ͟||[τάτ]ō̄ τὰ ἐ[γρα](μ)μένα. αἰ δέ κα με̄δ' | αὐτὸν
ἀποδō̄ι ἐν τōͅ ἐνιαυτōͅ, | τὰνς ἁπλόονς τ[ι]μὰνς ἐπικατ|αστασεῖ.
50 αἰ δέ κ' ἀποθάνε̄ι μ|ō̄λιομένας τᾱδ δί[κα]ς, τὰν ἁπλ||όον τιμὰν κα-
τ(α)στασεῖ. αἰ δ|έ κα κοσ[μ]ίον ἄγε̄ι ε̄̆ κοσμίοντο|ς ἄλλος, ε̄̆ κ'
ἀποστᾱι, μō̄λέν, καί κ|α νικαθε̄͂ι, κατιστάμεν ἀπ' [ᾱ̆]ς | [ἀμέρα]ς
55 ἄγαγε τὰ ἐγραμένα. || [τὸ]ν δὲ νενικαμένο[ν] κα[ὶ τὸν κα]-|||
II τακείμενον ἄγοντι ἄπατον | ε̄̆με̄ν.

Αἴ κα τὸν ἐλεύθερον ε̄̆ | τὰν ἐλευθέραν κάρτει οἴπε̄ι, ἑκα|τὸν
5 στατε̄͂ρανς καταστασεῖ· α͟||ἰ δέ κ' ἀπεταίρō, δέκα· αἰ δέ κ' ὁ δō͂λο|ς
τὸν ἐλεύθερον ε̄̆ τὰν ἐλευθέρα|ν, διπλεῖ καταστασεῖ· αἰ δέ κ' ἐλε|ύ-
θερος Ϝοικέα ε̄̆ Ϝοικέαν, πέντε | δαρκνάνς· αἰ δέ κα Ϝ[ο]ικεὺς Ϝοι-
10 κέα || ε̄̆ Ϝοικέαν, π[έν]τε στατε̄͂ρανς. | ἐνδοθιδίαν δō̄λαν αἰ κάρτει
δαμ|άσαιτο, δύο στατε̄͂ρανς κατασ|τασεῖ· αἰ δέ κα δεδαμν[α]μέ-
15 ναν πε|δ' ἀμέραν, [ὀ]δελόν, αἰ δέ κ' ἐν νυτ||τί, δύ' ὀδελόνς· ὀρκιō̄-
τέραν δ' ε̄̆|με̄ν τὰν δō̄λαν. αἴ κα τὰν ἐ|λευθέραν ἐπιπε̄ρε̄͂ται οἴπεν
20 ἀκε|ύοντος καδεστᾱ, δέκα στατε̄͂|ρανς καταστασεῖ, αἰ ἀποπō̄νίο||ι
μαῖτυς. αἰ κα τὰν ἐλευθέραν | μοικίον αἰλεθε̄͂ι ἐν πατρὸς ε̄̆ ἐν ἀ|δελ-
πιō͂ ε̄̆ ἐν τō̄ ἀνδρός, ἑκατὸν | στατε̄͂ρανς καταστασεῖ· αἰ δέ κ' ἐ|ν
25 ἄ(λ)λō̄, πεντε̄͂κοντα· αἰ δέ κα τὰν || τō̄ ἀπεταίρō, δέκα· αἰ δέ κ' ὁ
δō̄λος [τὰ]|ν ἐλευθέραν, διπλεῖ καταστασε|ῖ· αἰ δέ κα δō̄λος δō̄λō̄
30 πέν|τε. προϜειπάτō̄ δὲ ἀντὶ μαιτ|ύρον τριōν τοῖς καδεσταῖ|ς τō̄
ἐναιλεθέντος ἀλλύεθ|θαι ἐν ταῖς πέντ' ἀμέραις· | τō̄ δὲ δō̄λō̄ τōͅ
πάσται ἀντὶ | μαιτύρον δυōν. αἰ δέ κα μ|ε̆̀ ἀλλύσεται, ἐπὶ τοῖς ἑλόν-||
35 σι ε̄̆μεν κρε̄͂θθαι ὅπαι κα λε|ίōντι. αἰ δέ κα πονε̄ι δολō͂|σαθθαι, ὀμό-
40 σαι τὸν ἑλό|ντα τō̄ πεντε̄̄κονταστατέ|ρō καὶ πλίονος πέντον αὐ||τὸν
Ϝὶν αὐτōͅ Ϝέκαστον ἐπ|αριόμενον, τō̄ δ' ἀπεταίρō | τρίτον αὐτόν,
τō̄ δὲ Ϝοικέ|ος τὸν πάσταν ἄτερον αὐτ|ὸν μοικίοντ' ἑλέν, δολō͂σαθ-||
45 θαι δὲ με̆́.

Αἴ κ' ἀνε̆̀ρ [κα]ὶ [γυ]νὰ διακρ[ί]νōν[τ]αι, τὰ Ϝὰ α|ὐτᾱς ἔχεν, ἄτι
ἔκονσ' ε̄̆ιε π|ὰρ τὸν ἄνδρα, καὶ τō̄ καρπō͂ τ|ὰνν ε̄̆μίναν, αἴ κ' ε̄̆ι ἐς
50 τōν Ϝō͂||ν αὐτᾱς κρεμάτōν, κο̄τι | κ' ἐνυπάνει τὰν [ε̄̆μίνα]ν ἄτι |
κ' ε̄̆ι, καὶ πέντε στατε̄͂ρανς, αἴ κ' ὁ ἀ|νε̆̀ρ αἴτιος ε̄̆ι τᾱς κε̄[ρ]εύ-
55 σι|ος· α[ἰ] δὲ πō̄νίοι ὁ ἀνε̆̀ρ [αἴτι||ο]ς με̆̀ ε̄̆]με̄ν, τὸν δικαστὰν |||
III ὀμνύντα κρίνεν. αἰ δέ τι ἄλλ|ο πέροι τō̄ ἀνδρός, πέντε στ|ατε̄͂ρανς

5 καταστασεῖ κṓτι | κα πέρει αὐτόν, κṓτι κα παρ||έλει ἀποδότṓ
αὐτόν. ὂν δέ κ' | ἐκσαννέσεται δικάκσαι τ|ὰν γυναῖϰ' ἀπομόσαι τὰν
Ἄρ|τεμιν πὰρ 'Αμυκλαῖον πὰρ τὰν | Τοκσίαν. ὅτι δέ τίς κ' ἀπομο-||
10 σάνσαι παρέλει, πέντε στατ|ἔρανς καταστασεῖ καὶ τὸ κρ|έος αὐτόν.
αἰ δέ κ' ἀλλόττρι|ος συνεσάδδει, δέκα στ[ατ]ἔ|ρανς καταστασεῖ,
15 τṓ δὲ κρέ||ιος διπλεῖ ὅτι κ' ὁ δικαστὰς | ὀμόσει συνεσσάκσαι. | αἰ
ἀνὲρ ἀποθάνοι τέκνα κατ|αλιπṓν, αἴ κα λεῖ ἀ γυνά, τὰ Ϝὰ | αὐτᾶς
20 ἔκονσαν ὀπυίεθθα||ι κᾶτι κ' ὁ ἀνὲδ δṓι κατὰ τὰ ἐγ|ραμμένα ἀντὶ
μαιτύρṓν τρ|ιṑν δρομέṑν ἐλευθέρṑν· αἰ |δέ τι τṑν τέκνṑν πέροι, ἔν-
25 δι|κον ἔμεν. αἰ δέ κα ἄτεκνον || καταλίπει, τά τε Ϝὰ αὐτᾶς ἔκε|ν
κṓτι κ' ἐν[υ]πάνει [τ]ὰν ἐμ[ί]ν|αν κα[ὶ τ]ṑ καρπ[ṓ] τṑ ἔνδ[ο]θεν
π|εδὰ τṑν ἐπιβαλλόντ[ṑν] μοῖρα|ν λακὲ[ν] καί τί κ' ὁ ἀνὲδ δṓι ἀι
30 ἐγ||ραττει· αἰ δέ τι ἄλλο πέροι, ἔν|δικον ἔμεν. αἰ δὲ γυνὰ ἄτεκ|νος
ἀποθάνοι, τά τε Ϝὰ | αὐτᾶς τοῖς ἐπιβάλλονσι ἀπ|οδόμεν κṓτι ἐνύ-
35 πανε τὰν ἐ||μίναν καὶ τṓ καρπṓ, αἴ κ' ἔι ἐς | τṑν Ϝṑν αὐτᾶς, τὰν
ἐμίνα|ν. κόμιστρα αἴ κα λεῖ δόμεν | ἀνὲρ ἒ γυνά, ἒ Ϝεῖμα ἒ δυόδεκ|α
40 στατέρανς ἒ δυόδεκα στατ||έρṑν κρέος, πλίον δὲ μέ. αἴ κ|α Ϝοικέος
Ϝοικέα κριθεῖ δōō | ἒ ἀποθανόντος, τὰ Ϝὰ αὐτᾶ|ς ἔκεν· ἄλλο δ' αἴ
τι πέροι, ἔνδ|ικον ἔμεν.

45 Αἰ τέκοι γυνὰ κ||ε̄[ρ]ε[ύο]νσα, ἐπελεῦσαι τōι ἀ|νδρὶ ἐπὶ στέγαν
ἀντὶ μαιτ|ύρṑν τριṑν. αἰ δὲ μὲ δέκσαι|το, ἐπὶ τᾶι ματρὶ ἔμεν τὸ
50 τέκ|νον ἒ τράπεν ἒ ἀποθέμεν· ὀρκ||ιṓτέρōδ δ' ἔμεν τὸς καδεστ|ὰνς
καὶ τὸς μαίτυρανς, αἰ | ἐπέλευσαν. αἰ δὲ Ϝοικέα τέ|κοι κερεύονσα,
55 ἐπελεῦσαι | τōι πάσται τō ἀνδρός, ὃς ὄ||πυιε, ἀντὶ μαιτύρṑν [δυ]-
IV ōν. ||| αἰ δέ κα μὲ δέκσεται, ἐπὶ τōι | πάσται ἔμεν τὸ τέκνον τōι τ|ᾶς
5 Ϝοικέας. αἰ δὲ τōι αὐτōι αὖ|τιν ὀπυίοιτο πρὸ τō ἐνιαυτ||ṓ, τὸ παι-
δίον ἐπὶ τōι πάσται | ἔμεν τōι τō Ϝοικέος. κ̄ορκιό|τερον ἔμεν τὸν
ἐπελεύσαν|τα καὶ τὸς μαίτυρανς. γ|υνὰ κερεύονσ' αἰ ἀποβάλοι ||
10 παιδίον πρὶν ἐπελεῦσαι κα[τ]|ὰ τὰ ἐγραμμένα, ἐλευθέρṓ μ|ὲν κα-
ταστασεῖ πεντέκοντα | στατέρανς, δόλō πέντε καὶ Ϝίκατι, αἴ κα
15 νικαθε̄̂. ὂι δέ κα μ' ||εἴ[ε̄] τι(ς) στέγα ὅπυι ἐπελευσε|ῖ, ἒ αὐτὸν μὲ
ὀρεῖ, αἰ <αι> ἀποθ|είε̄ τὸ παιδίον, ἄπατον ἔμεν. | αἰ κύσαιτο καὶ
20 τέκοι Ϝοικ|έα μὲ ὀπυιομένα, ἐπὶ τōι τ[ō] || πατρὸς πάσται ἔμεν τὸ
τ|έκνον· αἰ δ' ὁ πατὲρ μὲ δṓοι, ἐ|πὶ τοῖς τṑν ἀδελπιṑν πάσ|ταις
ἔμεν.

25 Τὸν πατέρα τṑν | τέκνṑν καὶ τṑν κρεμάτṑν κ||αρτερὸν ἔμεν τᾶδ

δαίσιος | καὶ τὰν ματέρα τῶν Ϝῶν αὐ|τᾶς κρεμάτον. ἆς κα δόοντι, |
30 μὲ ἐπάνανκον ἔμεν δατε͂|θθαι· αἰ δέ τις ἀταθείε͂, ἀποδ||άτταθθαι
τῶι ἀταμένοι ἄ|ι ἔγρατται. ἒ δέ κ' ἀποθάνει τι(ς), | στέγανς μὲν
τὰνς ἐν πόλι κἄ|τι κ' ἐν ταῖ(ς) στέγαις ἐνε͂ι, αἷ|ς κα μὲ Ϝοικεὺς ἐν-
35 Ϝοικε͂ι ἐπ||ὶ κόραι Ϝοικίον, καὶ τὰ πρόβατα κα|ὶ καρτα[ί]ποδα, ἅ
κα μὲ Ϝοικέος ε͂ι, | ἐπὶ τοῖς υἱάσι ἔμεν, τὰ δ' ἄλ|λα κρέματα πάντα
40 δατε͂θθα|ι καλῶς, καὶ λανκάνεν τὸς μὲν || υἰὺνς ὁπόττοι κ' ἴοντι δύ|ο
μοίρανς Ϝέκαστον, τὰδ δ|ὲ θυγατέρανς ὁπότται κ' ἴον|τι μίαν μοῖ-
45 ραν Ϝεκάσταν. δ|ατε͂θ[θ]αι δὲ καὶ τὰ ματρ[ο͂]ια, ε͂ || κ' ἀποθα[νε͂]ι,
ἄιπε[ρ] τὰ [πατρο͂ι'] | ἔ[γραττ]αι. αἰ δὲ κρέματα μὲ εἴ|ε͂, στέγα δέ,
λακὲν τὰθ θ[υ]γατέ|ρας ἆι ἔγρατται. αἰ δέ κα λε͂|ι ὁ πατὲρ δο͂ὸς ἰὸν
50 δόμεν τᾶ||ι ὀπυιομέναι, δότο͂ κατὰ τ|ὰ ἐγραμμένα, πλίονα δὲ μέ. |
V ὀτείαι δὲ πρόθθ' ἔδο͂κε ἒ ἐπέσ|πενσε, ταῦτ' ἔκεν, ἄλλα δὲ μὲ ||| ἀπο-
λαν[κά]νεν. γυνὰ ὀ[τ]εία κ|ρέματα μὲ ἔκει ἒ [πα]τρὸδ δό|ντος ἒ
5 ἀ[δ]ελπιο͂ ἒ ἐπισπέν|σαντος ἒ ἀπολα[κ]όνσα ἄ||ι ὅκ' ὁ Αἰθ[α]λεύ(ς)
σταρτὸς ἐκόσ|μιον οἱ σὺν Κύ[λ]λο͂ι, ταύτ|ας μὲν ἀπολανκάνεν,
ταῖδ δὲ πρόθθα μὲ ἔ[ν]δικον ἔμ|εν.
10 Ἒ κ' ἀπ[ο]θάνει ἀνὲρ ἒ γυν||ά, αἰ μέν κ' ἔι τέκνα ἒ ἐς τέ|κνον
τέκνα ἒ ἐς τούτο͂ν τέ|κνα, τούτος ἔκε[ν] τὰ κρέμα|τα. αἰ δέ κα
15 μέτις ἔι τούτο͂|ν, ἀ<α>δελπιοὶ δὲ το͂ ἀποθανόν||τος κέκς ἀδε[λ]πιο͂ν
τέκν|α ἒ ἐς τούτο͂ν τέκνα, τούτ|ος ἔκεν τὰ κρέματα. αἰ δέ κα |μέτις
20 ἔι τούτο͂ν, ἀδευπιαὶ δ|ὲ το͂ ἀποθανόντος κὲς ταυτ||ᾶν τέκνα ἒ ἐς το͂ν
τέκνο͂ν τέ|κνα, τούτος ἔκεν τὰ κρέμα|τα. αἰ δέ κα μέτις ἔι τούτο͂ν, |
25 οἷς κ' ἐπιβάλλει ὅπο͂ κ' ἔι τὰ κρ|έματα, τούτος ἀναιλε͂θθα||ι. αἰ δὲ
μὲ εἶεν ἐπιβάλλοντε|ς, τᾶς Ϝοικίας οἵτινές κ' | ἴοντι ὁ κλᾶρος,
τούτονς ἔ|κεν τὰ κρέματα.
30 Αἰ δέ κ' οἱ | ἐπιβάλλοντες οἱ μὲν λεί||οντι δατε͂θθαι τὰ κρέματ|α,
οἱ δὲ μέ, δικάκσαι τὸν δι|καστὰν ἐπὶ τοῖλ λείονσι δ|ατε͂θθαι ἔμεν
35 τὰ κρέματα π|άντα, πρίν κα δάττονται. || αἰ δέ κα δικάκσαντος το͂
δ|ικαστᾶ κάρτει ἐνσείει ἒ ἄ|γει ἒ πέρει, δέκα στατε͂ραν|ς καταστα-
40 σεῖ καὶ το͂ κρέ|ιος διπλεῖ. τνατο͂ν δὲ καὶ καρ||πο͂ καὶ Ϝέμας κἀνπι-
δέμας κ|ἐπιπολαῖον κρεμάτον, αἴ κα μ|ὲ λείοντι δατε͂[θθαι - - τὸν
45 δ|ικαστ]ὰν ὀμνύντα κρῖνα|ι πορτὶ τὰ μο͂λιόμενα. [α]ὶ [δ]|| έ κα κρέ-
ματα δατιομένοι | μὲ συνγιγνο͂σκοντι ἀν|πὶ τὰν δαῖσιν, ὀνε͂ν τὰ κρέ-
50 μ|ατα κός κα πλεῖστον διδ|οῖ ἀποδόμενοι τᾶν τιμᾶν || δια[λ]ακόν-
το͂ν τὰν ἐπαβο|λάν Ϝέκαστος. δατιομέ|νοιδ δὲ κρέματα μαίτυρα|νς
VI παρέμεν δρομέανς ἐλε|υθέρονς τρίινς ἒ πλίανς. ||| θυγατρὶ δὲ διδο͂ι,
κατὰ τὰ αὐ|τά.

VI Ἄς κ' ὁ πατὲδ δόει, τὸν τὸ π|ατρὸς κρεμάτον πὰρ υἱέος | μὲ
5 ὀνε͂θθαι μεδὲ καταθίθ||εθθαι· ἄτι δέ κ' αὐτὸς πάσετ|αι ἒ ἀπολάκει
ἀποδιδόθθο͂, | αἴ κα λε͂ι. μεδὲ τὸν πατέρα τὰ το͂|ν τέκνον ἄτι κ' αὐ-
10 τοὶ πάσον|ται ἒ ἀπολάκοντι. μεδὲ τὰ τ||ᾶς γυναικὸς τὸν ἄνδρα
ἀπο|δόθαι μεδ' ἐπισπένσαι, μεδ' | υἱὺν τὰ τᾶς ματρός. αἰ δ|έ τις
πρίαιτο ἒ καταθεῖτο ἒ ἐ|πισπένσαιτο, ἀλλᾶι δ' ἔγρατ||[τα]ι, ἀι τάδε
15 τὰ γράμματα ἔγ||[ρατται, τὰ] μ[ὲ]ν κρέματα ἐπὶ τᾶι ματρὶ ἔμ|εν
20 κἐπὶ τᾶι γυναικί, ὁ δ' ἀπο|δόμενος ἒ καταθὲνς ἒ ἐπι||σπένσανς το͂ι
πριαμένο͂ι | ἒ καταθεμένο͂ι ἒ ἐπισπεν|σαμένο͂ι διπλεῖ καταστα|σεῖ
25 καὶ τί κ' ἄλλ' ἄτας ε͂ι, τὸ ἀπ|λόον· τον δὲ πρόθθα μὲ ἔν||δικον ἔμεν.
αἰ δέ κ' ὁ ἀντίμ|ολος ἀπομολε͂ι ἀνπὶ τὸ κρ|έος ο͂ι κ' ἀνπιμολίο͂ντι μ|ὲ
30 ἔμεν τᾶς ματ[ρ]ὸς ἒ τᾶ|ς γυναικός, μο͂λὲν ὄπε κ' ἐπ||ιβάλλει, πὰρ
το͂ι δικασταῖ | ἒ Ϝεκάστο͂ ἔγρατται. αἰ δέ κ' ἀ|ποθάνει μάτερ τέκνα
καταλιπό|νσα, τὸν πατέρα καρτερὸν ἔμεν | τον ματρο͂ίο͂ν, ἀποδόθαι
35 δὲ μὲ || μεδὲ καταθέμεν, αἴ κα μὲ τὰ τέκ|να ἐπαινέσει δρομέες ἰόν-
τες. | [α]ἰ δέ τις ἀλλᾶι πρίαιτο ἒ κατα|θεῖτο, τὰ μὲν κρέματα ἐπὶ
40 τοῖ|ς τέκνοις ἔμεν, το͂ι δὲ πριαμ||ένο͂ι ἒ καταθεμένο͂ι τὸν ἀποδ|όμενον
ἒ τὸν καταθέντα τὰν | διπλείαν καταστάσαι τᾶς τ|ιμᾶς, καὶ τί
45 κ' ἄλλ' ἄτας ε͂ι, τὸ ἀ|πλόον. αἰ δέ κ' ἄλλαν ὀπυίει, τὰ τ||έκνα [το͂]ν
[μ]ατρο͂ίο͂ν καρτερὸν|ς ἔμεν.

Αἴ κ' ἐδ δυσ[μενίανς] πε|ρα[θε͂ι κ]ἐκς ἀλλοπολίας ὑπ' ἀν|άνκας
50 ἐκόμενος κελο[μ]ένο͂ τι|ς λύσεται, ἐπὶ το͂ι ἀλλυσαμέν||ο͂ι ἔμεν, πρίν
κ' ἀποδο͂ι τὸ ἐπιβά|λλον. αἰ δέ κα μὲ ὁμολογίο͂ντ|ι ἀμπὶ τὰν πλε-
θὺν ἒ μὲ [κ]ελομέ|[ν]ο͂ αὐτο͂ [λ]ύσαθθαι, τὸν δικασ|τὰν ὀμνύντα
55 κρίνεν πορτὶ τὰ || μο͂λιόμενα. [τ]ο͂ ἐλευθέρο͂ τὸν | δε - - - -. [αἴ
VII κ' ὁ δο͂λος] ||| ἐπὶ τὰν ἐλευθέραν ἐλθὸν ὀπυίει, | ἐλεύθερ' ἔμεν τὰ
τέκνα. αἰ δέ κ' | ἀ ἐλευθέρα ἐπὶ τὸν δο͂λον, δο͂λ' ἔμ|εν τὰ τέκνα. αἰ
5 δέ κ' ἐς τᾶς αὐτ||ᾶς ματρὸς ἐλεύθερα καὶ δο͂λα | τέκνα γένεται, ἒ
κ' ἀποθάνει ἀ | μάτερ, αἴ κ' ε͂ι κρέματα, τὸνς ἐλε|υθέρονς ἔχεν. αἰ
10 δ' ἐλεύθεροι | μὲ ἐχσεῖεν, τὸνς ἐπιβάλλον|τανς ἀναιλε͂θαι. α[ἴ]
κ' ἐχς ἀγ|ορᾶς πρ[ι]άμενος δο͂λον μὲ π|εραιόσει τὰν Ϝεχσέκοντ'
15 ἀμ|ερᾶν, αἴ τινά κα πρόθ' ἀδικέ|χει ἒ ὕστερον. το͂ι πεπαμέν||ο͂ι
ἔνδικον ἔμεν.

Τὰμ πα|[τ]ρο͂ι[ο͂]κον ὀπυίεθαι ἀδελπι|ο͂ι τὸ πατρὸς τὸν ἰόντον
το͂ι | πρειγ[ί]στο͂ι. αἰ δέ κα πλίες πατ|ρο͂ιο͂κοι ἴο͂ντι κἀδελπι[ο]ὶ
20 το͂ πα||τρός, [τ]ο͂ι ἐπιπρειγίστο͂ι ὀπυί|εθαι. αἰ δέ κα μὲ ἴο͂ντι
ἀδελπιο͂|ὶ το͂ πατρός, υἱέεδ δὲ ἐχς ἀδελ|πιο͂ν, ὀπυίεθαι ἰο͂ι το͂ι [ἐ]ς

25 τõ π|ρειγίστο̄. αἰ δέ κα πλίες ἴοντ||ι πατρο̄ιο̄κοι κυίεες ἐκς ἀδε|λ-
πιõν, ἄλλōι ὀπυίεθαι τõι ἐπ|ὶ τõι ἐς [τ]õ πρει[γί]στο̄. μίαν δ' |
ἔκεν πατρōι[õ]κον τὸν ἐπιβάλ|λοντα, πλίαδ δὲ [μ]έ́.
30 ＊Αδ δέ κ' ἄν||õρος ἔ̄ι ὁ ἐπιβάλλōν ὀπυίεν ἔ̃ | ἁ πατρο̄ιο̄κος, [σ]τέ-
γαν μέν, αἴ | κ' ἔ̄ι, ἔκεν τὰν πατρο̄ιõκον, τᾶδ | δ' ἐπικαρπίας παν-
35 τὸς τὰν ἔμ|ίναν ἀπολανκάνεν τὸν ἐπιβ||άλλοντα ὀπυίεν. αἰ δέ
κ' ἀπό|δρομος ἰõν ὁ ἐπιβάλλōν ὀπυ|ίεν ἐβίōν ἐβίονσαν μὲ̀ λε̄̃ι
40 ὀπ|υίεν, ἐπὶ τᾶι πατρο̄ιόκōι ἔμε̄|ν τὰ κρέματα πάντα καὶ τὸν κ||αρ-
πόν, πρείν κ' ὀπυίε̄ι. αἰ δέ κα | δρομεὺς ἰõν ὁ ἐπιβάλλōν ἒ|βίονσαν
λείονσαν ὀπυίε|θαι μὲ̀ λε̄̃ι ὀπυίεν, μο̄λε̄̃ν τὸς | καδεστὰνς τὸς τᾶς
45 πατρο̄ι||όκō, ὁ δὲ [δ]ικα[σ]τ[ὰς] δικ[ακσά]||τō ὀπυίεν ἐν τοῖς δ[υ]οῖς
με̄̃|νσί. αἰ δέ κα μὲ̀ ὀπυίε̄ι ἀι ἔγρα|ται, τὰ κρέματα πάντ' ἔκον-
50 σα|ν, αἴ κ' ἔ̄ι ἄλλος, τõι ἐπιβάλλοντ||ι · αἰ δ' ἐπιβάλλōν μὲ̀ εἴε, τᾶς |
πυλᾶς τõν αἰτιόντōν ὅτιμ|ί κα λε̄̃ι ὀπυίεθαι. αἰ δέ κα τõ|ι ἐπι-
55 βάλλοντι ἐβίονσα μὲ̀ λε̄̃|ι ὀπυίεθαι ἔ̃ ἄνōρος ἔ̄ι ὁ ἐπιβ||άλ[λ]õν
VIII[κα]ὶ μ[ὲ̀ λ]ε̄̃[ι μέν]εν ||| ἁ πατρο̄ιο̄κος, στέγαμ μέν, | αἴ κ' ἔ̄ι ἐν
πόλι, τὰμ πατρο̄ιõκο|ν ἔκεν κἄτι κ' ἐνε̄̃ι ἐν τᾶι στέγ|αι, τõν δ' ἄλλōν
5 τὰν ἐμίναν δ||ιαλακόνσαν ἄλλōι ὀπυίεθαι τᾶς πυλᾶς τõν αἰτιόν-
τōν | ὅτιμί κα λε̄̃ι. ἀποδατε̄̃θαι δ|ὲ̀ τὸν κρεμάτōν ἴõι. αἰ δὲ μὲ̀ |
10 εἶεν ἐπιβάλλοντες τᾶι ‹παι› π||ατρο̄ιόκōι ἄ[ι ἔ]γρατται, τὰ κρ|έ-
ματα πάντ' ἔκ[ον]σαν τᾶς πυ|λᾶς ὀπυίεθ[α]ι ὅτιμί κα λε̄̃ι. | αἰ δὲ
15 τᾶς πυλ[ᾶ]ς μέτις λε|ίοι ὁ[π]υίεν, τὸς καδεστὰνς || τὸς τᾶς πατρο̄ιό-
κō Ϝείπαι κ|ατὰ [τὰν πυλ]ὰν ὅτι οὐ λ[ε̄̃ι ὁ]πυ|ίεν τις; καὶ μέν τίς
[κ' ὁ]πυίε̄ι, ἐ|ν ταῖς τριάκοντα ἔ̄ κα Ϝείπον|τι· αἰ δὲ μ(έ́), ἄλλōι
20 ὀπυίεθαι ὅτι||μί κα νύναται. αἰ δέ κα πατρὸ|ς δόντος ἔ̄ ἀδελ-
πιõ πατρο̄ιόκο|ς γένε̄ται, αἰ λείοντος ὀπ|υίεν ὄι ἔδōκαν μὲ̀ λείοι
25 ὀπυ|ίεθαι, αἴ κ' ἐστετέκνο̄ται, δια||λακόνσαν τõν κρεμάτōν ἄι
ἔ|γρατται [ἄλλ]ōι ὀπυίεθ[αι τᾶ]ς [π]|υ[λ]ᾶ[ς]. αἰ δὲ τέκνα μὲ̀
εἴε, πάντ' | ἔκονσαν τõι ἐπιβάλλον[τ]ι ὀπυ|ίεθαι, αἴ κ' ἔ̄ι, αἰ δὲ μέ́,
30 ἄι ἔγραττ||αι. ἀνὲ̀ρ αἰ ἀποθάνοι πατρο̄ι|όκōι τέκνα καταλιπόν, αἴ
κα [λ]ε̄̃ι, | ὀπυιέθō τᾶς πυλᾶς ὅτιμί κα ν|ύναται, ἀνάνκαι δὲ μέ́.
35 αἰ δὲ τέ|κνα μὲ̀ καταλίποι ὁ ἀποθανόν, || ὀπυίεθαι τõι ἐπιβάλ-
λοντι ἄ|ι ἔγρατται. αἰ δ' ὁ ἐπιβάλλōν τ|ὰν πατρο̄ιõκον ὀπυίεν μὲ̀
40 ἐπ|ίδαμος εἴε, ἁ δὲ πατρο̄ιõκος | ὄριμα εἴε, τõι ἐπιβάλλοντι ὀ||πυί-
εθαι ἄι ἔγρατται.

　　Πατρο̄ιõ|κον δ' ἔμεν, αἴ κα πατὲρ μὲ̀ ε̄̃ι ἔ̄ ἀ|δελπιὸς ἐς τõ αὐ[τõ]
πατρός. τὸν | δὲ κρεμάτō[ν κα]ρτερὸνς ἔμεν τ|ᾶς Ϝεργα[σ]ία[ς τὸς]
45 πάτρōανς, || [τ]ᾶς [δ' ἐπικαρ]πίας δια[λ]α[νκά]ν|εν [τ]ὰν ἐμίναν,

ᾶς κ' ἄ[ν]ōρ[ο]ς ἔι. | αἰ δ' ἀν[ό]ρōι ἰάτται μὲ εἴε ἐπι|ιβάλλōν, τὰν
50 πατρōιōκον καρ|τερὰν ἔμεν τōν τε κρεμάτōν κ||αὶ τō καρπō, κᾶς
κ' ἀν[ō]ρος ἔι, τ|ράπεθαι [π]ὰρ ται ματρί· αἰ δὲ μ|άτερ μὲ εἴε,
πὰρ τοῖς [μ]άτρōσι | τράπεθθα[ι]. αἰ δέ 'τις ὀπυίοι τὰ|ν πατρōιō-
55 κον, ἀλλᾶι δ' [ἔγ]ραττται, || πεύθεν [πορ]τὶ κόσμ[ο]ν ||| τὸνς ἐπι-
IX βά[λλοντανς.

'Ανὲρ αἰ | κ' ἀποθανὸν πα]τρōιōκον κα|ταλίπει, ἒ αὐ[τὰν ἒ πρὸ
5 αὐτᾶς τ|ονς πάτρōανς ἒ τὸ]νς μάτρōαν||ς καταθέμεν [ἒ ἀποδόθαι
τōν | κρεμάτōν καὶ] δικαίαν ἔμεν τ|ὰν ὀνὰν καὶ τὰν κα[τάθεσιν. αἰ |
δ' ἀλλᾶι πρί]αιτό τις κρέματα ἒ | καταθεῖτο τōν τᾶς πα[τρōιōκō,
10 τ]||ὰ [μ]ὲν [κρ]έματα ἐπὶ ται πατρōιōκ|ōι ἔμεν, ὁ δ' ἀποδόμενος ἒ
ϝατ|αθὲνς τōι πριαμένōι ἒ καταθε|μένōι, αἴ κα νικαθει, διπλεῖ κα-|
15 ταστασεῖ καὶ τί κ' ἀλλ' ἄτας ἔι, τ||ὸ ἀπλόον ἐπικαταστασεῖ, ἄ|ι
[τά]δε τὰ γ[ράμμ]ατ[α ἔγραττται, τ]||ō[ν δ]ὲ πρόθα μ[ὲ] ἔνδικον
ἔμεν. | αἰ δ' ὁ ἀντίμōλος ἀπομ[ōλ]ίο|ι ἀ[νπ]ὶ τὸ κρέος ōι κ' ἀνπιμō-
20 λί||ōντι μὲ τᾶς πατρōιōκō [ἔμ]ēν, | ὁ δ[ικ]αστὰς ὀμνὺς κρινέτō· αἰ |
δὲ νικάσαι μὲ τᾶς πατρ[ōι]ōκ|ō ἔμ[ē]ν, μōλēν ὀπē κ' ἐπιβάλλει, ἒ |
ϝεκάστō ἔγραττται.

25 Αἰ ἀν[δ]εχσ||άμ[ε]νος ἒ νενικαμένο[ς ἒ ἐνκ]||οιōτὰνς ὀπέλōν ἒ δια-
βαλόμε|νος ἒ διαϝειπάμενος ἀπο[θ]ά|νοι ἒ τούτōι ἄλλος, ἐπιμōλ|ēνν
30 ιō πρὸ τō ἐνιαυτō· ὁ δὲ δικα||στὰς δικαδδέτō πορτὶ τὰ [ἀ]ποπ|ōνιό-
μενα· αἰ μέν κα νίκας ἐπι|μōλει, ὁ δικαστὰς κō μνάμōν, | αἴ κα δōει
35 καὶ πολιατεύει, οἰ δὲ μ|αίτυρες οἰ ἐπιβάλλοντες, ἀνδοκ||ᾶδ (δ)ὲ κēν-
κοιōτὰν καὶ διαβολᾶς κ|αὶ διρέσιος μαίτυρες οἰ ἐπι|βάλλοντες ἀπο-
πōνιόντōν. ἒ δέ κ' ἀ|ποϝείποντι, δικαδδέτō ὁμόσ|αντα αὐτὸν καὶ
40 τὸνς μαίτυρ||ανς νικēν τὸ ἀπλόον. υἰὺς α|ί κ' ἀνδέκσεται, ᾶς κ' ὁ
πατὲ(δ) δōει, | αὐτὸν ἀτēθαι καὶ τὰ κρέματα | ἄτι κα πέπαται.
45 αἴ τίς κα πέρα|ι συναλ[λάκ]σει, ἒ ἐς πēρ[α]ν ἐπι||θέντι μὲ ἀποδιδōι,
αἰ μέν κ' ἀ|ποπōνίōντι μαίτυρες ἐβίοντ|ες τō ἑκατονστατερō καὶ
πλίο|νος τρέες, τō μείονος μέττ' ἐ|ς τὸ δεκαστάτερον δύο, τō μεί-||
50 ονος ἔνδ, δικαδδέτō πορ[τ]ὶ τὰ | ἀποπō[ν]ιόμενα. αἰ δὲ μαίτυρε|[ς]
μὲ ἀποπōνίοιεν, ἒ κ' ἔ[λ]θēι ὁ συ|ναλλάκσανς, ὁτερόν κ[α] κέλē-
Χ [τ]αι ὁ | μενπόμενος, ἒ ἀπομόσαι ἒ συν ||| [ll. 1-9, and most of
15 10-14, lacking] ματρὶ || δ' υἱὺν [ἒ ἄνδρα γυναικὶ δόμεν ἐ]|κατὸν
στα[τ]ēρα[νς] ἒ μεῖον, π|λίον δὲ μέ. αἰ δὲ πλία δοίē, αἰ | κα λείōντ'
20 οἰ ἐπιβάλλοντες, τ|ὸν ἄργυρον ἀποδόντες τὰ κρ||έματ' ἐκόντōν.
αἰ δέ τις ὀπέ|λōν ἄργυρον ἒ ἀταμένος ἒ μ|ōλιομένας δίκας δοίē, αἰ |

25 μὲ εἴε τὰ λοιπὰ ἄκσια τᾶς ἄ|τας, μεδὲν ἐς κρέος ἔμεν τὰν || δόσιν.

"Αντρō[π]ον μὲ ὀνέθα[ι] κατακείμενον, πρίν κ' ἀλλύσ|εται ὁ
καταθένς, μεδ' ἀμπίμō|λον, μεδὲ δέκσαθαι μεδ' ἐπισ|πένσαθαι
30 μεδὲ καταθέθαι. αἰ || δέ τις τουτōν τι Ϝέρκσαι, μεδ|ὲν ἐς κρέος
ἔμεν, αἰ ἀποπōνίο|ιεν δύο μαίτυρε(ς). |

"Ανπανσιν ἔμεν ὅπō κά τιλ λ|ε͂ι. ἀμπαίνεθαι δὲ κατ' ἀγορὰν ||
35 καταϜελμένōν τōμ πολιατᾶ|ν ἀπὸ τō λάō ō͂ ἀπαγορεύοντι. | ὁ δ' ἀμ-
πανάμενος δότō τᾶ|ι ἐταιρε͂ίαι τᾶι Ϝᾶι αὐτō ἰαρε͂|ιον καὶ πρόκοον
40 Ϝοίνō. καὶ || μέν κ' ἀνέλεται πάντα τὰ κρέ|ματα καὶ μὲ συννε͂ι γνέ-
σια τ|έκνα, τέλλεμ μὲν τὰ θῖνα καὶ | τὰ ἀντρόπινα τὰ τō ἀνπανα-
45 μέ|νō κἀναιλέθαι ἄιπερ τοῖς γ||νεσίοις ἔγρατται. αἰ [δ]έ κα μὲ |
λε͂ι τέλλεν ἄι ἔγρατται, τὰ κ[ρ]έ|ματα τὸνς ἐπιβάλλοντανς ἔκε|ν.
50 αἰ δέ κ' ε͂ι γνέσ[ι]α τέκνα τōι ἀν|παναμένōι, πεδὰ μὲν τōν ἐρσ||ένōν
XI τὸν ἀμπαντόν, ἄιπερ αἰ θ|έ[λε]ιαι ἀπὸ τōν ἀδελπιōν λανκά|νοντι ·
αἰ δέ κ' ἔρσενες μὲ ἴον|τι, θέλειαι δέ, [Ϝ]ισϜόμοιρον ἔ||||[μεν] τὸν
ἀνπαντὸν καὶ μὲ ἐ|πάνανκον ἔμεν τέλλεν τ[ὰ τ|ō ἀν]παναμένō καὶ τὰ
5 κρέμα|τ' ἀναιλ(ε͂)θαι ἄτι κα κατα[λίπε͂||ι ὁ ἀν]πανάμενος · πλίυι
δὲ τὸν | ἀνπαντὸμ μὲ ἐπικōρε͂ν. [αἰ δ' | ἀπο]θάνοι ὁ ἀνπαντὸς γνέ-
10 σια | τέκνα μὲ καταλιπόν, πὰρ τὸ[νς τ|ō ἀν]παναμένō ἐπιβάλλον-
ταν||ς ἀνκōρὲν τὰ κρέματα. αἰ δ[έ κα | λε͂ι] ὁ ἀνπανάμενος, ἀπο-
Ϝειπ|άθθō κατ' ἀγορὰν ἀπὸ τō λά[ō ō͂ | ἀπα]γορεύοντι καταϜελ-
15 μέν|ōν τōν πολιατᾶν · ἀνθέμε[ν δὲ || δέκ]α [σ]τατε͂ρανς ἐδ δικαστ|έ-
ριον, ὁ δὲ μνάμōν ὁ τō κσεν|ίō ἀποδότō τōι ἀπορρε͂θέντι. | γυνὰ δὲ
20 μὲ ἀμπαινέθθō μεδ' | ἄνεβος. κρέθαι δὲ τοῖδδε ἄ||ι τάδε τὰ γράμ-
ματ' ἔγραπσε, | τōν δὲ πρόθα ὅπαι τις ἔκει ε͂ ἀ|μπαντύι ε͂ πὰρ ἀμ-
παντō μὲ ἔτ' ἔ|νδικον ἔμεν.

25 "Αντρōπον ὅς κ' ἄγει πρὸ δίκας, || αἰεὶ ἐπιδέκεθαι. |

Τὸν δικαστάν, ὅτι μὲν κατὰ | μαίτυρανς ἔγρατται δικάδδ|εν ε͂
30 ἀπόμοτον, δικάδδε͂ν ἄι ἔ|γρατται, τōν δ' ἀλλōν ὀμνύντ||α κρίνεν
πορτὶ τὰ μōλιόμεν|α.

Αἴ κ' ἀποθάνει ἄργυρον | ὀπέλōν ε͂ νενικαμένος, αἰ μέ|ν κα λεί-
35 ōντι, οἷς κ' ἐπιβάλλει | ἀναιλέθαι τὰ κρέματα, τὰν ἄ||ιταν ὑπερ-
κατιστάμεν καὶ τὸ | ἀργύριον οἷς κ' ὀπέλει, ἐκόντ|ōν τὰ κρέματα ·
αἰ δέ κα μὲ λεί|ōντι, τὰ μὲν κρέματα ἐπὶ τοῖ|ς νικάσανσι ἔμεν ε͂ οἷς
40 κ' ὀ||πέλει τὸ ἀργύριον, ἄλλαν δὲ | μεδεμίαν ἄταν ἔμεν τοῖ|ς ἐπι-
βάλλονσι. ἀ[τ]έθαι δὲ ὑ|πὲρ μ[ὲ]ν τō [πα]τρὸς τὰ πατρō|ια, ὑπὲ(δ)
45 δὲ τᾶς ματρὸς τὰ μα||τρōια. |

Γυνὰ ἀνδρὸς ἄ κα κρίνεται, | ὁ δικαστὰς ὅρκον αἴ κα δικάκ|σει,
50 ἐν ταῖς Ϝίκατι ἀμέραις ἀ|πομοσάτō παριόντος τō δικα||στᾶ ὅτι
κ' ἐπικαλε͂ι. ΠροϜ[ε]ιπάτ|ō δὲ ὁ ἄρκōν τᾶ δίκας τᾶι γυνα|ικὶ καὶ
XII τō͂ι δικαστᾶι καὶ [τ]ō͂ι | μ[νά]μονι προτέταρτον ἀντὶ μ||||[αιτύρōν
ll. 1-15 lacking] ματρὶ υἰὐ‹ι›ς ἒ ἀ[ν]ὲρ γυναικὶ | κρέματα αἰ ἔδōκε,
ἆι ἔγρατ|το πρὸ τō͂νδε τōν γραμμάτōν, || μὲ ἔνδικον ἔμεν· τὸ δ'
20 ὕστε|ρον διδόμεν ἆι ἔγρατται. |
    Ταῖς πατρōιōκοις αἴ κα μὲ | ἴōντι ὀρπανοδικασταί, ἆ|ς κ' ἀνόροι
25 ἴōντι, κρ̄έθαι κατὰ | τὰ ἐγραμμένα. ὅπē͂ .. δέ κ' ἀ || πατρ[ōι]ō͂κος
μὲ ἰόντος ἐπι|βάλλοντος μēδ' ὀρπανοδικ|αστᾶν πὰρ τᾶι ματρὶ τρά-
30 πē|ται, τὸ; πάτρōα καὶ τὸμ μάτ|ρōα τὸνς ἐγραμμένονς τ||ὰ κρέ-
ματα καὶ τὰν ἐπικαρπί|αν ἀρτύεν ὅπαι κα (νύ)ναντι κά|λλιστα,
πρίν κ' ὀπυίεται. ὀπυί|εθαι δὲ δυōδεκαϜετία ἒ πρεί|γονα.

The famous Gortyn Law-Code. Although conveniently so
designated, it is not of course a complete code of laws, but a
series of regulations on various subjects, complete in itself,
as shown by the θιοί at the beginning and the unused space at
the end of the last column. The state of the alphabet (there are
no signs for φ and χ, which are not distinguished from π and κ.
See 4.1), the forms of the letters, and the direction of the writing
(βουστροφηδόν), are such as are usually characteristic of the sixth
century B.C., but the general style of the writing, precise and
regular, points to a later date. It is now generally believed that
the development of the alphabet was slower in Crete than elsewhere, and that the Code is of the fifth century B.C., probably
about the middle of it. There are also other inscriptions from
Gortyn containing regulations of a similar character but on
different subjects, one series of seven columns being known
sometimes as the Second Code (GDI 4998).

    Although a sign for η is lacking in the Law-Code, the ⊟ had
already been used with this value in an earlier period and н is
regularly so used in the inscriptions of the "North Wall",
which are not much later than the Law-Code. The infinitives
of contract verbs in -EN and the infinitives in -MEN are here
transcribed -ε͂ν and -με͂ν. See 25a.

    I.1-II.2. Disputes over the ownership of a slave or one alleged
to be a slave.

I.1 ff. 'Whoever is about to bring suit in relation to a free man or a slave, shall not make seizure before the trial. If he makes the seizure, (the judge) shall condemn him to a fine of ten staters in the case of a free man, five in case of a slave, because he seizes him, and shall decree that he release him within three days. But if he does not release him, (the judge) shall condemn him to a fine of a stater in the case of a free man, a drachma in the case of a slave, for each day until he releases him; and as to the time, the judge shall decide under oath.'—For the use of the genitive in τῶ ἐλευθέρō, τῶ δṓλō, see **171**. Similarly τῶ πεντēκονταστατέρō II.38. Observé the clear distinction in use, here and elsewhere, between διχάδδεν and χρίνεν. The former is used where the judge pronounces formal judgment according to the law and the evidence, the latter where he acts directly as arbiter. Cf. especially XI.26 ff.—11 ff. 'But if one denies making a seizure, the judge shall decide under oath, unless a witness testifies. If one party contends that a man is a free man, the other that he is a slave, those who testify that he is a free man shall be preferred. If they contend about a slave, each declaring that he is his, if a witness testifies, (the judge) shall declare judgment according to the witness, but if they testify for both or for neither, the judge shall decide under oath. In case the one in possession has been defeated, he shall release the free man within five days, and he shall surrender the slave. If he does not release (the free man) or surrender (the slave), (the judge) shall decree that (the plaintiff) have judgment (νιχē̃ν = Att. νιχᾶν) against him, in the case of the free man for fifty staters and a stater for each day until he releases him, in the case of the slave ten staters and a drachma for each day until he surrenders him. But at the end of a year after the judge has pronounced judgment, one may exact three times the amount (i.e., three times the original fines, instead of the accumulated fines for delay) or less, but not more. As to the time the judge shall decide under oath.'—The purpose of this last provision seems to be to prevent the accumulation of fines out of all proportion to the value of the slave.—τᾶν πέντ' ἀμερᾶν: gen. of time. **170.**—35. ἐνιαυτο̄ι: not 'year,' but 'anniversary.' See Glossary.—38 ff. 'If the slave on whose account one is defeated takes refuge in a temple, (the defeated party), summoning (the successful party) in the presence of two witnesses of age and free, shall point out (the slave) at the temple where he takes refuge, either himself or another for him; but if he does not make the summons or point him out, he shall pay what is written. If he does not even (referring back to ll. 34 ff.) surrender him (the slave) at the end of a year, he shall pay the simple fines in addition (to what is stated in ll. 34 ff.). If (the slave) dies while the suit is being tried, he shall pay the simple fine (i.e. without any additional fines for delay). If a member of the κόσμος (see Glossary) makes a seizure, or another (seizes the slave) of a member of the κόσμος, the case shall be tried after he (the official) has gone out of office, and, if defeated he shall pay what is written from the time when he made the seizure. But there shall be no penalty for seizing one condemned for debt or one who has mortgaged his person.'—The penalties fixed in ll. 47-50 and their relation to the provision in l. 36 are variously understood. Many take τιμάνς and τιμάν as referring to the value of the slave.

II.2-45. Rape and adultery.

II.2 ff. 'If one commits rape upon a free man or woman, he shall pay one hundred staters; but if upon (the son or daughter) of an ἀπέταιρος, ten.' The ἀπέταιρος, one who was not a member of a ἑταιρεία or society made up of citizens, occupied a social position midway between the ἐλεύθερος and the Ϝοικεύς. Possibly the ξένοι are meant.—11 ff. 'If one violates a household slave by force, he shall pay two staters, but if one that has already been violated, by day one obol, but if in the night two obols; and the slave shall have the preference in the oath.'—16 ff. 'If one attempts to have intercourse with a free woman who is under the guardianship of a relative (that is, with a young maiden), he shall pay ten staters if a witness testifies.'—28 ff. 'One shall announce before three witnesses to the relatives of the one caught (literally 'caught in,' i.e., in the house of the father, etc.) that he must be ransomed within five days; but to the master of a slave before two witnesses. But if he is not ransomed, it shall be in the power of the captors to do with him as they wish.'— 36 ff. 'If one declares that he has been the victim of a plot,

then the one who caught him shall swear, in a case involving
a fine of fifty staters or more, with four others (literally 'himself
as a fifth'), each calling down curses upon himself (if he testifies
falsely), but in the case of an ἀπέταιρος with two others, in a
case of a serf the master and one other, that he took him in
adultery and did not lay a plot.'

II.45-III.44. Rights of the wife in the case of divorce or death
of husband.

II.45 ff. 'If a man and wife are divorced, (the wife) shall have
her own property with which she came to her husband, and half
of the produce, if there is any from her own property, and half of
whatever she has woven within (the house), whatever there is,
and five staters, if the husband is the cause of the divorce. But
if the husband declares he is not the cause, the judge shall decide
under oath. But if she carries off anything else belonging to the
husband, she shall pay five staters, and whatever she carries off
and whatever she purloins this she shall return. But as regards
matters which she denies, (the judge) shall decree that she take the
oath of denial by Artemis, (proceeding) to the Amycleium to the
archer-goddess. If any one takes anything away from her after
she has taken the oath of denial, he shall pay five staters and the
thing itself. If a stranger helps her carry things off, he shall pay
ten staters and double the amount which the judge swears he
helped carry off.'—49. τὰνν ἐμίναν: 101.1.—50. κὄτι: here and
III.26, 34 = καὶ ὅτι, i.e., καὶ οὗτινος, gen. by attraction.—
III.14-15. κρέιος: χρήιος from χρήεος, gen. sg. with διπλεῖ.—
17 ff. 'If a man dies leaving children, if the wife wishes, she may
marry again holding her own property and whatever her husband
may have given her, according to what is written, in the presence
of three witnesses of age and free. But if she takes anything
belonging to the children, it shall be a matter for trial.'—27 ff.
'And of the produce in the house she shall share with the lawful
heirs.,— τὸν ἐπιβαλλόντον: ὁ ἐπιβάλλον, 'the heir at law,' a
short expression for ὃι ἐπιβάλλει (τὰ χρήματα); cf. V.21-22 οἷς κ'
ἐπιβάλλει.—37 ff. 'If man or wife wishes to make gifts, (it is
permitted), either clothing or twelve staters or something of the
value of twelve staters, but not more.'—κόμιστρα: perhaps a
technical term for certain kinds of gifts.

III.44-IV.23. Disposition of children born after divorce.

III.44 ff. 'If a divorced wife bears a child, she shall bring it to her husband at his house in the presence of three witnesses. If he does not receive it, the child shall be in the power of the mother either to bring up or to expose; and the relatives and witnesses shall have preference in the oath, as to whether they brought it.'—στέγαν: this is the regular word for 'house' in this inscription, Ϝοικία being 'household' (V.26) and Ϝοῖκος not occurring.— IV.14 ff. 'If the man has no house to which she shall bring (the child), or she does not see him, if she exposes the child, there shall be no penalty.'—ὅι δέ κα μ' εἴ[ε̄], κτλ.: this conforms to the reading of the stone, though the elision of the ε̄ of μέ̄ is difficult (or read μὲ̄'ί[ε̄] with aphaeresis?). For κα with the optative see **177**.

IV.23-VI.2. Partition of property among children and heirs-at-law.

IV.23 ff. 'The father shall be in control of the children and the division of the property, and the mother of her own property. So long as they live there need be no division. But if any one should be condemned to pay a fine, the one fined shall have his portion taken out and given him as is written.'—33 ff. αἷς κα κτλ.: 'which are not occupied by a serf residing in the country.'— 44 ff. 'And the property of the mother shall be divided, when she dies, in the same way as is prescribed for the property of the father.'—V.1 ff. 'Whatever woman has no property either by gift of father or brother or by promise or by inheritance, since the time when Cyllus and his colleagues of the σταρτός (subdivision of the tribe) of the Aethalians composed the κόσμος, these women shall share in the inheritance, but those (whose claims are) of prior date shall have no recourse.'—22 ff. 'If there is none of these, those to whom it falls according to the source of the property shall receive it. But if there are no heirs-at-law, those of the household who compose the κλᾶρος (i.e., the body of κλαρῶται or serfs attached to the estate) shall have the money.'—28 ff. 'If some of the heirs-at-law wish to divide the property, and others not, the judge shall decree that all the property belong to those wishing to divide, until they divide it. If any one, after the decision of the judge, enters in by force or drives or carries off anything, he shall pay ten staters and double the value of the object. In the matter of live stock, produce, clothing, ornaments, and furniture, if they do not wish to make a division, the judge shall decide with reference to the pleadings. If, when dividing the property, they do not agree as to the division, they shall sell the property, and, disposing of it to whoever offers the most, they shall receive each his share of the price.'— 34. δάττονται: aor. subj., cf. ἀποδάτταθθαι. 82, 151.1.—36. ἐνσείει: ἐνσ-είει (εἶμι). 151.3.—39. τνατὸν: θνητῶν = ζώων, as in Hdt. 2.68.—50. ἐπαβολά: also in a Boeot. inscr. (SEG 3.342, 15), ἐπη- Hesych.—VI.1. διδῶι: subj. without κα. 174.

VI.2-46. Sale and mortgage of family property.

VI.2 ff. 'As long as the father lives, one shall not purchase any of the father's property from the son, nor take a mortgage on it. But whatever (the son) himself has acquired or inherited, he may dispose of, if he wishes.'—14 f. ἀλλᾶι δ' ἔγραττai: 'and it is written otherwise' = 'otherwise than is written.' Cf. l. 37 and VIII.54.—ἆι τάδε τὰ γράμματα ἔγρατται: 'since the inscription of this law,' contrasted with τὸν δὲ πρόθθα, l. 24, 'in matters of previous date.' So in IX.15 and XI.19.— 25 ff. 'But if the opponent denies, with reference to the matter about which they are disputing, that it belongs to the mother or the wife, action shall be brought where it belongs, before the judge there where it is prescribed for each case.'

VI.46-VII.15. Repayment of ransom. Children of mixed marriages. Responsibility for the acts of a slave.

VI.46 ff. 'A ransomed person shall belong to the ransomer, until he pays what is proper.' The general sense is clear, but the restoration and precise interpretation are uncertain. Perhaps, with the reading of the text, 'if one is sold into hostile hands and some one, forced (to do so) upon his demanding it, ransoms him from his exile.'—51 ff. 'But if they do not agree about the amount, or on the ground that he did not demand to be ransomed.' etc.—55 ff. Something is certainly missing between the end of VI and the beginning of VII, either overlooked by the engraver in copying, or possibly added on the original substructure, which is not extant.—VII.1 ff. In the case of marriage between a male slave and a free woman, the status of the children depended on whether the slave went to live with the free woman, thus raising himself in a measure to her condition, or whether the woman went to live with the slave.—9. ἐκσεῖεν: εἶεν ἐξ αὐτᾶς.—10 ff. 'If one having purchased a slave from the market-place has not repudiated the purchase within sixty days, if the slave has wronged any one before or after, the one who has acquired him shall be liable.' The purchaser of a slave was allowed a certain time within which, upon discovering any faults, physical or otherwise, which had been concealed, he might repudiate the purchase. Not until the expiration of this period was the purchase binding, and the purchase liable for the acts of the slave. For the use of περαιόω, cf. also GDI 4998.vii αἴ κα μὴ περαιόσει ἢ κα πρίαται ἐν ταῖς τριάκοντ' ἀμέραις. But some take the meaning in both passages to be 'dispose of abroad.'

VII.15-IX.24. The heiress. Regulations for her marriage and the disposition of her property.

When, in default of sons, a daughter becomes the heiress (πατρδιῶκος, cf. πατροῦχος παρθένος Hdt. 6.57, Att. ἐπίκληρος), the choice of a husband, who becomes the virtual head of the family, is determined by fixed rules. The person so determined, the groom-elect, is known as ὁ ἐπιβάλλον ὀπυίεν (= ōι ἐπιβάλλει ὀπυίεν 'the one to whom it falls to marry') or simply ὁ ἐπιβάλλōν.

VII.15 ff. 'The heiress shall marry her father's brother, the oldest of those living. If there are several heiresses and father's brothers, they shall marry the next oldest. If there are no father's brothers, but sons of the brothers, she shall marry that one (who is the son) of the oldest. If there are several heiresses and sons of brothers, they shall marry the second (in order) after the son of the eldest (and so on).'—35 ff. 'If the groom-elect, being a minor, does not wish to marry (the heiress), though both are of marriageable age, all the property and the income shall belong to the heiress until he marries her.'—47 ff. 'If he does not marry her, as is written, she with all the property shall marry the next in succession, if there is another. But if there is no groom-elect, she may marry any one of the tribe she wishes, of those who ask for her hand.'—VIII.7-8. 'But they shall give him (the rejected groom-elect) his proper share of the property',— 20 ff. 'If one becomes an heiress after her father or brother has given her (in marriage), if she does not wish to remain married to the one to whom they gave her, although he is willing, then, if she has borne children, she may, dividing the property as is written, marry another of the tribe.'—24. ἐστετέχνὅται: perf. subj. like πέπᾱται etc., **151.**1.

IX.24-X.32. Various subjects.

IX.24 ff. 'If one dies who has gone surety or has lost a suit or owes money given as security or has been involved in fraud (?) or has made a promise (?), or another (stands in such relations) to him, one shall bring suit against said person before the end of the year. The judge shall render his decision according to the testimony. If the suit is with reference to a judgment won, the judge and the recorder, if he is alive and a citizen, and the heirs as witnesses, (shall give testimony), but in the case of surety and pledges and fraud (?) and promise (?), the heirs as witnesses shall give testimony. After they have testified, (the judge) shall decree that (the plaintiff), when he has taken oath himself and likewise the witnesses, has judgment for the simple amount. If a son has gone surety, while his father is living, he and the property which he possesses shall be subject to fine.'—26-27. The precise technical meaning of διαβαλόμενος and διαϜειπάμενος with the corresponding nouns διαβολᾶς, διϜέσιος ll. 35-36 is uncertain.—28-29. The third letter in l. 29 is obscure, but the most probable reading is ἐπιμϭλε͂νν ἰὅ, with νν as in τὰνν ἐμίναν II.48, and with ἰός used like ἐκεῖνος as in VIII.8.—43 ff. "If one has formed a partnership with another for a mercantile venture, in case he does not pay back the one who has contributed to a venture,' etc.—50. ἔνδ: for ἔνς (=εἶς) before following δ (**97.4**). —53. ὅτερόν κα κτλ.: 'whichever course the complainant demands, either to take oath of denial or —.' X 15.ff. 'Special legacies are not to exceed the value of 100 staters. If one makes a gift of greater value, the heirs, if they choose, may pay the 100 staters and keep the property.'—24. μεͅδὲν ἐς χρέος: 'to no purpose, invalid.'

X.33-XI.23. Adoption.

X.33 ff. 'Adoption may be made from whatever source any one wishes. The adoption shall be announced in the place of assembly, when the citizens are assembled, from the stone whence they make proclamations.'—41. συνν-ἑῑ: **101.**1.—42 ff. 'He shall perform the religious and social obligations of the one who adopted him.'—XI.10 ff. 'If the adopter wishes, he may renounce (the adopted son) in the place of assembly,' etc.—16. **ὁ δὲ μνά-μōν ὁ τō κσεν̄ίō**: 'the recorder who looks after the interests of strangers.'— 19 ff. 'These regulations (τοῖδδε) shall be followed from the time of the inscription of this law, but as regards matters of a previous date, in whatever way one holds (property), whether by virtue of adoption (i.e., of being the adopted son) or from the adopted son, there shall be no liability.'

XI.24-XII.35. Various supplementary regulations.

XI.24 f. 'If one seizes a man before the trial, any one may receive him (i.e., may offer the man an asylum).'—26 ff. 'The judge shall decide as is written whatever it is written that he shall decide according to witnesses or by oath of denial, but other matters he shall decide under oath according to the pleadings.' See note to I.11 ff.—31 ff. 'If one dies owing money or having lost a suit, those to whom it falls to receive the property, if they wish to pay the fine in his behalf and the money to those to whom he owes it, shall hold the property. But if not, the property shall belong to those who won the suit or those to whom he owes money, but the heirs shall not be subject to any further fine. The father's property shall pay the fine for the father, the mother's property for the mother.'—46 ff. 'When a woman is divorced from her husband, if the judge has decreed an oath, she shall take the oath of denial of whatever one charges within twenty days, in the presence of the judge.'—ὄτι: οὔτινος as in II.50.—XII.21 ff. 'The heiresses, if there are no ὀρφανοδικα-σταί, so long as they are under marriageable age, shall be treated according to what is written. In case the heiress, in default of a groom-elect or ὀρφανοδικασταί, is brought up with her mother, the father's brother and the mother's brother, those designated (above), shall manage the property and the income as best they can until she marries. She shall be married when twelve years of age or older.'

118. Gortyn. Third century B.C. GDI 5011. Ditt. Syll. 525.

[Θιοί. | τάδ' ἔϜαδε τ]ᾶι [πόλι] ψαφίδδονσι τρια|[κατίων πα]ριόν-των· νομίσματι χρῆτ|θαι τῶι καυχῶι τῶι ἔθηκαν ἁ πόλις· τὸδ ||

5 δ' ὀδελὸνς μὴ δέκετθαι τὸνς ἀργυρίος. | αἰ δέ τις δέκοιτο ἢ τὸ νόμι-
σμα μὴ λείοι | δέκετθαι ἢ καρπῶ ὠνίοι, ἀποτεισεῖ ἀρ|γύρω πέντε
10 στατῆρανς. πεύθεν δὲ | πορτὶ τὰν νεότα, τᾶς δὲ νεότας ὀμν||ύντες
κρινόντων οἱ ἑπτὰ κατ' ἀγοράν, | οἱ κα λάχωντι κλαρώμενοι. νικῆν
δ' ὄτε|ρά κ' οἱ πλίες ὁμόσοντι, καὶ πράξαντες | τὸν νικαθέντα τὰν
μὲν ἡμίναν [τῶι νι|κάσ]αντι δόντων, τὰν δ' ἡμίναν [τᾶι πόλι].

Decree of Gortyn regarding the use of bronze coinage.
3 ff. 'One shall make use of the bronze coin which the state
has established, and not accept the silver obols. If one accepts
them, or is unwilling to accept the (bronze) coin, or sells for
produce (i.e., trades by barter), he shall pay a fine of five silver
staters. Report shall be made to the body of young men, and of
this body the seven who are chosen by lot as supervisors of the
market shall decide under oath.'—ὠνίοι, πεύθεν: 162.15.—
νεότα, νεότας: 88a.

119. Hierapytna. Third or second century B.C. GDI 5041.

.... [ἑρπό]ντων δὲ οἱ Ἱεραπύτνιοι τοῖς Λυττίοις ἐς τὰ - - | ....
[οἱ δὲ] Λύττιοι τοῖς Ἱεραπυτνίοις ἐς τὰν εὐάμερον τὰν [τῶν Θευ-
δαισίων. ὁ δὲ κόσμος τῶν | Ἱεραπυτνί]ων ἑρπέτω Λυττοῖ ἐς τὸ
ἀρχεῖον· κατὰ ταὐτὰ δὲ καὶ ὁ τῶ[ν Λυττίων κόσμος ἑρπέτω ἐν
Ἱεραπύτναι ἐς] | τὸ ἀρχ[εῖον.] αἰ δὲ οἱ κόσμοι ἐλλίποιεν τὰν θυ-
σίαν τὰν ἠγραμμέναν, αἴ κα μή τι πόλε[μος κωλύσηι, ἀποτεισάν]-||
5 των ὁ κόσμος ἕκαστος ἀργυρίω στατῆρας ἑκατόν, οἱ μὲν Ἱεραπύ-
τνιοι τοῖς Λυττίοις τᾶι πόλει, [οἱ δὲ Λύττιοι τοῖς] | Ἱεραπυτνίοις
τᾶι πόλει. ὅτι δέ κα δόξηι ταῖς πόλεσιν ἐξελὲν ἢ ἐνθέμεν, ὅτι μὲν ἐξέ-
λοιμεν·μήτε ἔνθινον μή|τε ἔνορκον ἦμεν, ὅτι δὲ ἐγγράψαιμεν ἔνθινόν
τε ἦμεν καὶ ἔνορκον. εἰ δέ τί κα θεῶν ἱλέων ὄντων λάβω|μεν ἀπὸ
τῶν πολεμίων, λαγχανόντων κατὰ τὸ τέλος ἑκάτεροι. μὴ ἐξέστω
δὲ ἰδίαι μήτε πόλεμον ἐ|κφέρεσθαι χωρὶς μήτε εἰρήναν τίθεσθαι, αἴ
10 κα μὴ ἀμφοτέροις δόξηι. αἰ δέ τινές κα ἰδίαι ἐξενέγκωνται, || αὐτοὶ
καὶ διαπολεμόντων, καὶ μὴ ἔνορκοι ἔστων οἱ μὴ συμπολεμόντες.
στασάντων δὲ τὰς στάλας ἑκά|τεροι ἐν τοῖς ἰδίοις ἱεροῖς, οἱ μὲν
Ἱεραπύτνιοι Ὠλεροῖ ἐν τῶι ἱερῶι, τὰν δὲ ἐν Ἀπόλλωνι, οἱ δὲ Λύτ-
τιοι ἐν τῶι [ἱ]|ερῶι τ[ῶ Ἀπό]λλωνος καὶ ἐμ πόλει ἐν Ἀθαναίαι.
στατάντων δὲ καὶ κοινὰν στάλαν ἐν Γόρτυνι ἐν | τῶι ἱερῶι τῶ
........ι. Ὅρκος Λυκτίων. ὀμνύω τὰν Ἑστίαν καὶ Ζῆνα Ὀρά-
τριον καὶ τὰν Ἀθαναίαν Ὠλερίαν καὶ Ζῆνα | Μο[ννίτιον καὶ Ἥρ]αν

καὶ Ἀθαναίαν Πολιάδα καὶ Ἀπόλλωνα Πύτιον καὶ Λατὼ καὶ
15 Ἄρεα καὶ Ἀφροδίταν καὶ Κωρῆ||τας καὶ Νύμφας καὶ θεὸς πάντας
καὶ πάσας· ἦ μὰν ἐγὼ συμμαχησῶ τοῖς Ἱεραπυτνίοις τὸν πάντα
χρό|νον ἀπλ[όως] καὶ ἀδόλως, καὶ τὸν αὐτὸν φίλον καὶ ἐχθρὸν ἐξῶ,
καὶ πολεμησῶ ἀπὸ χώρας, υἴ κα καὶ ὁ Ἱεραπύτνιος, | καὶ τὸ δίκαιον
δωσῶ καὶ ἐμμενῶ ἐν τοῖς συνκειμένοις, ἐμμενόντων καὶ τῶν Ἱερα-
πυτνίων. ἐπιορκόντι μὲν | ἦμεν τὸς θεὸς ἐμμάνιας καὶ γίνεσθαι
πάντα τὰ ὑπεναντία, εὐορκῶσι δὲ τὸς θεὸς ἱλέος ἦμεν καὶ γίνεσθαι
πολ|λ<λ>ὰ κἀγαθά." Ὅρκος Ἱεραπυτνίων. "ὀμνύω τὰν Ἑστίαν
20 καὶ Ζῆνα Ὀράτριον καὶ Ἀθαναίαν Ὠλερίαν κα||[ὶ] Ζῆνα Μοννί-
τιον καὶ Ἥραν καὶ Ἀθαναίαν Πολιάδα καὶ Ἀπόλλωνα Πύτιον
καὶ Λατὼ καὶ Ἄρεα καὶ Ἀφροδί|ταν καὶ Κωρῆτας καὶ Νύμφας
καὶ θεὸς πάντας καὶ πάσας· ἦ μὰν ἐγὼ συμμαχησῶ τοῖς Λυκτί-
οις τὸν | πάντα χρόνον ἀπλόως καὶ ἀδόλως, καὶ τὸν αὐτὸν φίλον
καὶ ἐχθρὸν ἐξῶ, καὶ πολεμησῶ ἀπὸ χώρας, υἴ | κα καὶ ὁ Λύττιος,
καὶ τὸ δίκαιον δωσῶ καὶ ἐμμενῶ ἐν τοῖς συνκειμένοις, ἐμμενόν-
των καὶ Λυκτίων. ἐ|[π]ιορ[κό]ντι τὸς θεὸς ἐμμάνιας ἦμεν καὶ
25 γίνεσθαι πάντα τὰ ὑπεναντία, εὐορκῶσι δὲ τὸς θε||[ὸ]ς ἱλέος ἦμεν
καὶ γίνεσθαι πολλὰ κἀγαθά."

Treaty between Hierapytna and Lyttus. This illustrates the
mixed dialect sometimes known as East Cretan. See **273, 278**.
  1. **Λυττίοις**: note the interchange of assimilated and unassimilated forms, e.g., **Λυκτίων** l. 13. See **86** with 1.—17.
ἐπιορκόντι: see **42**.5*d*.
  120. Drerus. Late third or early second century B.C. GDI
4952. Ditt. Syll. 527. Schwyzer 193. Solmsen-Fraenkel 41.
Schwyzer, Rh. M. 77.237 ff. H. van Effenterre, BCH 61.327 ff.

Θεός τύχα. | ἀγαθᾶι τύχαι. | ἐπὶ τῶν Αἰθαλέ|ων κοσμιόν-
5 των || τῶν σὺγ Κυίαι καὶ | Κεφάλωι Πύρωι | Πίωι Βισίωνος, |
10 γραμματέος | δὲ Φιλίππου, || τάδε ὤμοσαν | ἀγελάοι παν|άζωστοι
15 ἑκα|τὸν ὀγδοή|κοντα· "Ὁμνύω || τὰν Ἑστίαν τὰν | ἐμ πρυτα-
νείωι | καὶ τὸν Δῆνα τὸν | Ἀγοραῖον καὶ τὸν Δῆ|να τὸν Ταλλαῖον ||
20 καὶ τὸν Ἀπέλλωνα | τὸν Δελφίνιον καὶ | τὰν Ἀθαναίαν τὰν |
25 Πολιοῦχον καὶ τὸν | Ἀπέλλωνα τὸμ Ποίτιον || καὶ τὰν Λατοῦν
καὶ τὰν | Ἄρτεμιν καὶ τὸν Ἄρεα | καὶ τὰν Ἀφορδίταν καὶ | τὸν
30 Ἑρμᾶν καὶ τὸν Ἅλιον | καὶ τὰν Βριτόμαρτιν || καὶ τὸμ Φοίνικα
καὶ τὰν | Ἀμφι[ώ]ναν καὶ τὰγ Γᾶν | καὶ τὸν Οὐρανὸν καὶ | ἥρωας

35 καὶ ἡρωάσσας | καὶ κράνας καὶ ποτα||μοὺς καὶ θεοὺς πάντας | καὶ
πάσας · μὴ μὰν ἐγώ | ποκα τοῖς Λυττίοις | καλῶς φρονησεῖν | μήτε
40 τέχναι μήτε μα||χανᾶι μήτε ἐν νυκτὶ | μήτε πεδ' ἀμέραν. καὶ | σπευ-
σίω ὅτι κα δύναμαι | κακὸν τᾶι πόλει τᾶι τῶν Λυττίων. ||| δικᾶν
45 δὲ καὶ πρ[αξί]||ων μηθὲν ἔνορκον | ἤμην. καὶ τέλομαι | φιλοδρήριος
50 καὶ | φιλοκνώσιος | καὶ μήτε τὰμ πό||λιν προδωσεῖν | τὰν τῶν Δρη-
55 ρίων | μήτε οὔρεια τὰ | τῶν Δρηρίων | μηδὲ τὰ τῶγ Κν[ω]|||σίων,
μηδὲ ἄν|δρας τοῖς πο|λεμίοις προδω|σεῖν μήτε Δρη|ρίους μήτε
60 Κνω||σίους, μηδὲ στά|σιος ἀρξεῖν καὶ | τῶι στασίζοντι | ἀντίος τέλο-
65 μαι, | μηδὲ συνωμοσί||ας συναξεῖν | μήτε ἐμ πόλει | μήτε ἔξοι τᾶς |
70 πόλεως μήτε | ἄλλωι συντέλε||σθαι · εἰ δέ τινάς | κα πύθωμαι συ-|
75 νομνύοντας, | ἐξαγγελίω τοῦ | κόσμου τοῖς πλί||ασιν. εἰ δὲ τάδε |
μὴ κατέχοιμι, | τούς (τ)έ μοι θεούς, | τοὺς ὤμοσα, ἐμ|μάνιας
80 ἤμη<ι>ν || πάντας τε καὶ πά|σας, καὶ κακίστω(ι) | ὀλέθρωι ἐξόλ-
85 λυ|σθαι αὐτός τε | καὶ χρήια τἀμά, || καὶ μήτε μοι γᾶν | καρπὸν
φέρειν ||| [μήτε γ]υναῖκας | [τίκτει]ν κατὰ φύ[σ]ιν μήτ]ε πάμα-
90 τα · || [εὐορκί]οντι δέ μοι | [τοὺς] θεούς, τοὺς | [ὤμοσα,] ἱλέους
95 ἤμεν || [καὶ πολ]λὰ κάγαθὰ | δι[δό]μ[ε]ν. ὀμνύω δὲ || τὸς αὐτὸς
θεούς · | ἦ μὰν ἐγὼ τὸγ κόσ|μον, αἴ κα μὴ ἐξορ|κίζοντι τὰν ἀγέ|λαν
100 τοὺς τόκα ἐ||γδυομένους τὸν | αὐτὸν ὅρκον, τόν|περ ἀμὲς ὀμωμό-|
105 καμες, ἐμβαλεῖν | ἐς τὰν βωλάν, ἂι || κα ἀποστάντι, | τοῦ μηνὸς
τοῦ Κο|μνοκαρίου ἢ τοῦ | Ἁλιαίου · ἁ δὲ β[ω]λὰ | πραξάντων
110 ἕκα||στον τὸν κοσμί|οντα στατῆρας | πεντακοσίους | ἀφ' ἅς κα
115 ἐμβάληι | ἀμέρας ἐν τριμήνωι · || αἱ δὲ λισσὸς εἴη<ι>, | ἀγγραψάν-
120 των | ἐς Δελφίνιον, | ὅσσα κα μὴ πρά|ξοντι χρήματα, || τοὔνομα
ἐπὶ πατρὸς | καὶ τὸ πλῆθος τοῦ ἀρ|γυρίου ἐξονομαίνον|τες · ὅτι δέ
125 κα πράξον|τι, ταῖς ἑταιρείαισιν || δασσάσθωσαν ταῖς | ἐμ πόλει
καὶ αἴ πεί | τινεν οὐρεύωντι Δρήριοι. ||| αἰ δὲ μὴ πρά[ξαι]|εν ἁ
130 βωλά, α[ὑτοὶ] || τὰ διπλόα ἀ[ποτει||σάντων · πρα[ξάν]|των δὲ οἱ
135 ἐρευταὶ | οἱ τῶν ἀνθρωπίνων | καὶ δασσάσθωσαν || ταῖς ἑταιρείαι-
σιν | κατὰ ταὐτά." ||
140 Τάδε ὑπομνάμα|τα τᾶς Δρηρίας χώρας | τᾶς ἀρχαίας τοῖς || ἐπι-
γινομένοις ἀζώ|στοις · τόν τε ὅρ|κον ὀμνύμεν | καὶ κατέχειν. | καὶ
145 οἱ Μιλάτιοι || ἐπεβώλευσαν | ἐν τᾶι νέαι νε|μονηίαι τᾶι πό|λει τᾶι
150 τῶν Δρηρίων ἕνεκα τᾶς | χώρας τᾶς ἁ||μᾶς, τᾶς ἀμφι|μαχόμεθα. |
155 Νικατὴρ | τᾶς ἀγέλας | . . . . || καὶ ἐλαίαν ἕ|καστον φυ-
160 τεύειν καὶ τεθραμ|μέναν ἀποδεῖ|ξαι · ὃς δέ κα μὴ || [φ]υτεύσει,
ἀπ|[ο]τεισεῖ στα|τῆρας πεν|τήκοντα.

Oath taken by the Drerian ephebi, promising loyalty to
Drerus and the allied Cnossus, but enmity to Lyttus. The
dialect shows a strong admixture of κοινή forms, but also retains
many of the Cretan characteristics. 3 ff. The same magistrates appear in another inscription of
Drerus, BCH 61.30, where the reading after Κεφάλωι is καὶ
Πύρου [κ]αὶ Πίου καὶ Βισίωνος.—11. ἀγελάοι: for ἀγελαῖοι (see
31) 'ephebi' members of the ἀγέλαι or bands in which the Cretan
youth were trained.—11/12. πανάζωστοι: cf. ἀζώστοις ll. 140/1,
'ungirded,' here an epithet of the ephebes.—45. δικᾶν δέ κτλ.:
'but nothing of lawsuits and executions shall be included in the
oath.'—97 ff. αἴ κα μὴ ἐξορκίξοντι κτλ.: 'unless they impose
the same oath upon the ἀγέλα, upon those who were then stripped'
(that is, became ephebes).—103. ἐμβαλεῖν: εἰσαγγελεῖν 'impeach.'
—104-5. ἆι κα ἀποστᾶντι: 'after they have gone out of office.'—
115. λισσός: metaphorical use, perhaps 'insolvent.'—127. τινεν:
τινες. 119.2a.—132-33. ἐ[ρ]ευταὶ οἱ τῶν ἀνθρωπίνων: 'the
collectors of public (in contrast to sacred) funds.' ἐρευταί =
ζητηταί, πράκτορες. Cf. ἐρεύω = ἐρευνάω Hesych., Eustath.—
146-7. νεμονηίαι: for νεομηνίαι. 88.

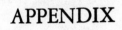

APPENDIX

SELECTED BIBLIOGRAPHY OF WORKS OF REFERENCE WITH THE ABBREVIATIONS EMPLOYED

PERIODICALS

Abh. Preuss. Akad. = Abhandlungen der preussischen Akademie der Wissenschaften.

ABS = Annual of the British School at Athens.

AJA = American Journal of Archaeology.

AJP = American Journal of Philology.

AM = Mitteilungen des deutschen archäologischen Instituts. Athenische Abteilung.

Annuario = Annuario della regia scuola archeologica di Atene.

'Αρχ. Δελτ. = 'Αρχαιολογικὸν Δελτίον.

'Αρχ. 'Εφ. = 'Αρχαιολογικὴ ἐφημερίς.

'Αθηνᾶ = 'Αθηνᾶ. Σύγγραμμα περιοδικὸν τῆς ἐν 'Αθήναις ἐπιστημονικῆς ἑταιρείας.

BCH = Bulletin de correspondance hellénique.

Ber. Preuss. Akad. = Sitzungsberichte der preussischen Akademie der Wissenschaften.

Ber. Sächs. Ges. = Berichte über die Verhandlungen der königlichen sächsischen Gesellschaft der Wissenschaften zu Leipzig. Philologisch-historische Classe.

Ber. Wien. Akad. = Sitzungsberichte der kaiserlichen Akademie der Wissenschaften in Wien. Philologisch-historische Classe.

(Berl.) Phil. Woch. = (Berliner) philologische Wochenschrift.

BzB = Bezzenberger's Beiträge zur Kunde der indogermanischen Sprachen.

CJ = Classical Journal.

Comptes Rendus = Comptes Rendus de l'Académie des inscriptions et belles-lettres.

CP = Classical Philology.

CQ = Classical Quarterly.

CR = Classical Review.

Diss. Argent. = Dissertationes philologicae Argentoratenses selectae.

Diss. Hall. = Dissertationes philologicae Halenses. Halle.

'Ελληνικά = 'Ελληνικά. 'Ιστορικὸν περιοδικόν.

Eranos = Eranos. Acta philologica Suecana.

Glotta = Glotta. Zeitschrift für griechische und lateinische Sprache.

Gött. Gel. Anz. = Göttingische gelehrte Anzeigen.

Gött. Nachr. = Nachrichten von der königlichen Gesellschaft der Wissenschaften zu Göttingen.

Hermes = Hermes. Zeitschrift für classische Philologie.

Hesperia.

IF = Indogermanische Forschungen.

IFAnz. = Anzeiger für indogermanische Sprach- und Altertumskunde.

JHS = Journal of Hellenic Studies.

Jb. arch. Inst. = Jahrb. des deutschen archäologischen Instituts.

Klio = Klio, Beiträge zur alten Geschichte.

KZ = Zeitschrift für vergleichende Sprachwissenschaft, begründet von A. Kuhn.

Mnemos. = Mnemosyne. Bibliotheca philologica Batava.

Mon. Antichi = Monumenti antichi pubblicati per cura della reale accademia dei Lincei.

MSL = Mémoires de la Société de linguistique.

Mus. Ital. = Museo italiano di antichità classica.

Neue Jb. = Neue Jahrbücher für das klassische Altertum, Geschichte und deutsche Literatur und für Pädagogik.

Oest. Jhrh. = Jahreshefte des oesterreichischen archäologischen Instituts in Wien.

Philol. = Philologus. Zeitschrift für das klassische Altertum.

Rev. Arch. = Revue archéologique.

Rev. de Phil. = Revue de philologie.

Rev. Ét. Gr. = Revue des études grecques.

Rh. M. = Rheinisches Museum für Philologie.

Riv. Fil. = Rivista di filologia.

TAPA = Transactions of the American Philological Association.

Wiener Stud. = Wiener Studien. Zeitschrift für klassische Philologie.

Woch. f. klass. Phil. = Wochenschrift für klassische Philologie.

TEXTS AND COMMENTARIES

Ditt. Or. = W. Dittenberger, Orientis Graeci inscriptiones selectae. Leipzig, 1903-5.

Ditt. Syll. = W. Dittenberger, Sylloge inscriptionum Graecarum. 3d ed. Leipzig, 1915-24.

Greek Inscr. Brit. Mus. = The Collection of Ancient Greek Inscriptions in the British Museum.

GDI = Collitz-Bechtel, Sammlung der griechischen Dialekt-Inschriften. Göttingen, 1884-1915.

Hoffmann = O. Hoffmann, Die griechischen Dialekte in ihrem historischen Zusammenhange mit den wichtigsten ihrer Quellen dargestellt. Göttingen.

    I. Der südachäische Dialekt [Arcadian and Cyprian]. 1891.

   II. Der nordachäische Dialekt [Thessalian and Lesbian]. 1893.

  III. Der ionische Dialekt, Quellen und Lautlehre. 1898.

IG = Inscriptiones Graecae consilio et auctoritate Academiae litterarum regiae Borussicae editae.

IV. Inscriptiones Argolidis, ed. M. Fraenkel. 1902.

IV.i². Inscriptiones Epidauri, ed. F. Hiller de Gaertringen. 1929.

V.i. Inscriptiones Laconiae et Messeniae, ed. W. Kolbe. 1913.

V.ii. Inscriptiones Arcadiae, ed. F. Hiller de Gaertringen. 1913.

VII. Inscriptiones Megaridis et Boeotiae, ed. W. Dittenberger. 1892.

IX.i. Inscriptiones Phocidis, Locridis, Aetoliae, Acarnaniae, insularum maris Ionii, ed. W. Dittenberger. 1897.

IX.i². Inscriptiones Aetoliae, ed. Guentherus Klaffenbach. 1932.

IX.ii. Inscriptiones Thessaliae, ed. O. Kern. 1908.

XI.ii. Inscriptiones Deli liberae, ed. F. Dürbach. 1912.

XI.iv. Inscriptiones Deli liberae, ed. P. Roussel. 1914.

XII.i. Inscriptiones Rhodi Chalces Carpathi cum Saro Casi, ed. F. Hiller de Gaertringen. 1895.

XII.ii. Inscriptiones Lesbi Nesi Tenedi, ed. W. Paton. 1899.

XII.iii. Inscriptiones Symes Teutlussae Teli Nisyri Astypalaeae Anaphes Therae et Therasiae Pholegandri Meli Cimoli, ed. F. Hiller de Gaertringen. 1898.

XII.iii. Supplementum, ed. F. Hiller de Gaertringen. 1894.

XII.v. Inscriptiones Cycladum, ed. F. Hiller de Gaertringen. 1903, 1909.

XII.vii. Inscriptiones Amorgi, ed. G. Delamarre. 1908.

XII.viii. Inscriptiones insularum maris Thracici, ed. C. Friedrich. 1909.

XII.ix. Inscriptiones Euboeae insulae, ed. E. Ziebarth. 1915.

XII. Supplementum, ed. F. Hiller de Gaertringen. 1939.

XIV. Inscriptiones Siciliae et Italiae, ed. G. Kaibel. 1890.

Inscr. Cret. = Inscriptiones Creticae, ed. N. Guarducci, I—IV. 1935+.

Inschr. v. Magnesia = O. Kern, Inschriften von Magnesia am Maeander. Berlin, 1900.

Inschr. v. Olympia = Dittenberger-Purgold, Inschriften von Olympia. Berlin, 1896.

Inschr. Jurid. = Dareste-Haussoullier-Reinach, Recueil des inscriptions juridiques grecques. Paris, 1895 ff.

Paton — Hicks = W. R. Paton and E. L. Hicks, The inscriptions of Cos. Oxford, 1891.

Roberts = E. S. Roberts, Introduction to Greek Epigraphy. Part I. Cambridge, 1887. Part II (with E. A. Gardner). Cambridge, 1905. All references are to Part I, unless II is added.

Schwyzer = E. Schwyzer, Dialectorum Graecarum exempla epigraphica potiora. Leipzig, 1923 (revised edition of Cauer's Delectus).

SEG = Supplementum Epigraphicum Graecum i—xii. Leyden, 1923+.

Solmsen-Fraenkel = F. Solmsen, Inscriptiones Graecae ad inlustrandas dialectos selectae. 4th ed. by E. Fraenkel. Leipzig, 1930.

Tod = Marcus Tod, A Selection of Greek Historical Inscriptions. 2d ed. Oxford, 1946, 1948.

Ziehen, Leges Sacrae = L. Ziehen, Leges Graecorum sacrae e titulis collectae. Leipzig 1906.

LEXICOGRAPHY

Bechtel, Personennamen = F. Bechtel, Die historischen Personennamen des Griechischen bis zur Kaiserzeit. Halle, 1917.

Fick-Bechtel = Die griechischen Personennamen nach ihrer Bildung erklärt und systematisch geordnet. 2d ed. by A. Fick and F. Bechtel. Göttingen, 1894.

Herwerden = H. van Herwerden, Lexicon Graecum suppletorium et dialecticum. 2d ed. Leyden, 1910.

LS = Liddell and Scott's Greek—English Lexicon. 9th ed. Oxford, 1940.

Pape = W. Pape, Wörterbuch der griechischen Eigennamen. 3d ed. Braunschweig, 1884.

Searles = Helen M. Searles, Lexicographical Study of the Greek Inscriptions. Chicago, 1898.

GREEK GRAMMARS

Kretschmer, Sprache (in Gercke und Norden, Einleitung in die Altertumswissenschaft). 3d ed. Leipzig, 1923.

Kühner-Blass = Kühner's Ausführliche Grammatik der griechischen Sprache. 3d ed. Part I, revised by Blass. 2 vols. Hannover, 1890-92.

Kühner-Gerth = Kühner's Ausführliche Grammatik der griechischen Sprache. 3d ed. Part II, revised by Gerth. 2 vols. Hannover, 1898-1904.

Lejeune, Traité de phonétique grecque. Paris 1947.

Meillet, Aperçu d'une histoire de la langue grecque. 3rd ed. Paris, 1930.

Schwyzer, Gr. Gram. = E. Schwyzer, Griechische Grammatik, 2 vols. München, 1939-50. (vol. 3, Index, by D.G. Georgacas, 1952).

Smyth = H. W. Smyth, Greek Grammar for Colleges. New York, 1920.

GREEK DIALECTS [1]

Ahrens = H. L. Ahrens, De Graecae linguae dialectis. 2 vols. Göttingen, 1839-43.

Bechtel = F. Bechtel, Die griechischen Dialekte. 3 vols. Berlin.
  I. Der lesbische, thessalische, böotische, arkadische und kyprische Dialekt. 1921.
  II. Die westgriechischen Dialekte. 1923.
  III. Der ionische Dialekt. 1924.

---

[1] A list of the numerous monographs on special dialects is omitted. The majority of these are now antiquated.

Hoffmann = Hoffmann, Die griechischen Dialekte. 3 vols. See above, p. 338.

Meister = R. Meister, Die griechischen Dialekte. 2 vols. Göttingen.
I. Asiatisch-Äolisch, Böotisch, Thessalisch. 1882.
II. Eleisch, Arkadisch, Kyprisch. 1889.

Thumb-Kieckers = A. Thumb, Handbuch der griechischen Dialekte. 2te Auflage von E. Kieckers. Heidelberg, 1932.

NOTES AND REFERENCES [1]

1. Interrelation of the dialects. Ahrens I, 1 ff. Collitz, Die Verwandtschaftsverhältnisse der griechischen Dialekte mit besonderer Rücksicht auf die thessalische Mundart, 1885. Smyth, The Dialects of North Greece, AJP 7.421 ff., 1887. Hoffmann, De mixtis Graecae linguae dialectis, 1888. Hoffmann I, 1 ff., 1891. Solmsen, Thessaliotis und Pelasgiotis, Rh. M. 58.598 ff., 1903. Id., Eigennamen als Zeugen der Stammesmischung in Boeotien, Rh. M. 59.481 ff., 1904. Meister, Dorer und Achäer I, 1904. Thumb, Dialektforschung und Stammesgeschichte, Neue Jb. 1905, 385 ff. Buck, The Interrelations of the Greek Dialects, CP 2. 241 ff., 1907. Kretschmer, Zur Geschichte der griechischen Dialekte, Glotta 1.4 ff., 1907. Fick, Äoler und Achäer, KZ 44.1 ff., 1911. Debrunner, Die Besiedelung des alten Griechenland, Neue Jb. 1918, 433 ff. Meillet, Aperçu 72 ff., 1930. Kretschmer, Sprache (Gercke und Norden, Einleitung³) 75 ff., 1927. Buck, CP 21.16 ff., 1926. Debrunner in Ebert, Reallexikon der Vorgeschichte IV, 510 ff. Kretschmer, Glotta 28.231 ff., 30.84 ff. Thumb-Kieckers 47 ff. Schwyzer, Gr. Gram. 1.75 ff. A. Tovar, Primitive geographical expansion of Ionic, Emerita 12 (1944) 245 ff.

3. Although, for reasons stated in the Note, a detailed treatment of the literary dialects is excluded from the plan of this book, the following summaries for those other than Homeric, later Ionic, or Attic, may be of service. They are arranged with references to the appropriate sections of the grammar.

ALCAEUS AND SAPPHO

Texts: Diehl, Anthologia Lyrica. Lobel, Sappho. Lobel, Alcaeus.

The language of Alcaeus and Sappho is substantially their native Lesbian, the characteristics of which, summarized in **201-3, 206-7**, are nearly all represented in the texts. Epic influence shows itself in the use of ν movable, a few cases of lack of augment, the occasional σ beside σσ (**82, 83**), -δειροι beside -δέραι, etc. (**54**), a few occurrences of gen. sg. -āο, gen. sg. -οιο, ἄνερος, etc., as well as in various other matters of prosody and phraseology. The texts contain many cases of hyper-Aeolic αι, some of hyper-Aeolic ρρ, etc.; also the spelling σδ = ζ, which is late (**84**), and various other corruptions.

The papyrus fragments, and likewise the quotations in late authors,

---

[1] Except for the few following, those previously given (in the "Introduction") are not repeated here. Any important corrections or additions have been incorporated in the main text, and the references, with others later, may be found in Schwyzer, Griechische Grammatik.

scholiasts, grammarians, so far as these latter have not been further corrupted in transmission, reflect the current Alexandrian text. This latter very probably goes back to a redaction by earlier grammarians from Aeolic Asia Minor (some such are known by name), who were familiar with the Aeolic of their time, say the late fourth or early third century B.C. This hypothesis receives support from the treatment of final ηι, ωι, ᾱι, which in some of the Oxyrhynchus texts, and likewise in the verses of Balbilla (a woman of Hadrian's time who imitated the Sappho of her copy), appear as η, ω, but αι, a differentiation which accords neither with contemporaneous practice nor with that of the poets' time, but agrees with that of some Lesbian inscriptions of the late fourth century (38). Cf. Kehrhahn, KZ 46.296 ff., Bechtel 1.45.

5. στρότος, βροχέως, ἄμβροτε, τρόπην, χόλαισι, ἐμμορμένον = εἱμαρμένον, ὄρπετον (cf. ἁρπετόν Hesych., from weak grade of ἕρπω) = ἑρπετόν, σπολέω (cf. σπόλεισα· σταλεῖσα Hesych.). So τετορταῖος in Theocritus.—
6. ὀν, ὀνία, ὀνίαρος, κόθαρος.—8. φᾶμα,. etc., generally. But also hyper-Aeolic αι = ᾱ, due to the regular correspondence of αισ to ᾱς from ανς (see below, to 77.3, 78). So nom. sg. Αἰολίδαις, Κρονίδαις, βορίαις (similar forms in Balbilla and the grammarians), further ἐπέραισε, ἐπτόαισ' beside ἐπτόασεν (from πτοάω = πτοέω, 161.2a), μέμναισ', ὄμναισαι, φαισθ', 3 sg. φαῖσι (cf. regular 3 pl. φαῖσι), all these before σ, more doubtful μέμναιμ', μαχαίταν. (Some other cases in Diehl's text are without MS. authority and due to a wrong theory of αι = η; cf. CP 10. 215 ff.).—9.2. χρύσιον, πορφυρίαν, χάλκιαι, κυνίαισι, συκίαν, βορίαις, τίωι, but generally ε (θέοισιν, ἔων, etc.).—13.1. ἴρος.—13.3a. ἄτερος.—17. αἱμιόνοις, αἱμιθέων.—18a. κέρναις.—19.1. ζάβαις, ζάδηλος, ζακρυόεις, etc. = δια-.—19.2, 4. πέρροχος, περρέχοισ', περεθήκαο (cf. περρεθήκατο Hesych.), πὲρ ἀτιμίας (cf. πέρρ ἀπάλω Theocr.), πορφύρον, πορφύρα, ἀργύρα; Περράμω, Περάμοιο.—22 with b. ἀπύ, ὔμοι, ὑπίσσω, ὔσδων.—25. η, ω, as κῆνος, ἦχεν, infin. -ην, gen. sg. -ω, ὤρανος (but also ὄρανος, the explanation of which is uncertain). —31. Ἄλκαος, Φωκάας, πόας, λαχόην, πόησαι, etc.—35 with a. αὔως, ναύω, ναύοις, δεύοντος, ἐπιδεύης, χευάτω, αὐάταν, αὐάδην.—38. Regularly -ᾱι, but frequently (in some papyrus texts, always) -η, -ω. See above.— 41.2. φάος, σάος, μάομαι, περεθήκαο.—41.3. ἀελίω and ἀλίω.—41.4. gen. pl. -ᾱν, Ποσείδᾱν, but πεδάορον, Ἀίδαο.—42.1. εὐάνθεα etc., but ἦρος. κείσαι, but οἴχηι, πότηι.—42.3. ἦχεν, ἤλπετο, κῆνος, infin. -ην, but ὤκεες, ἔγχεε, καγχέεται.—42.4. φίλει, κατάγρει.—42.5, 6. ὀνκαλέοντες, ἔων, gen. sg. -εος, etc.—43. ἰππήων, βασίληες, etc.—44.3. gen. sg. -ω, gen. sg. αἴδως, αὔδως, acc. sg. νῶν beside νόον.—44.4. ἰμέροεν, νιφόεντος, etc. ο + ει, χαύνοις.—47. φᾶμι, not φαῖμι. For 3 sg. φαῖσι, see above, to 8. For δοκίμοιμι the better reading is δοκίμωμι. Forms like γέλαιμι, ἴσταιμι, etc., quoted by the grammarians (cf. Hdn. 2.825), are not confirmed even for the Alexandrian text.—49.2. χρέτος, χρέτησαι.

52. Initial ϝ before a vowel is so written or implied by the meter for the pronominal Ϝοῖσι, Ϝόν, Ϝέθεν, but generally ignored, as εἴπην, ἴδοισαν, ἴδμεν, ἔργον, etc., without preventing elision or causing position length.— 53. Intervocalic ϝ lost, as κλέος, ῥόαι, etc., πάις (as in Homer), παῖδος. (But see above, to 35).—54. From νϝ etc., ϝ lost without lengthening of the preceding vowel, μόνος, κάλος, κόρα, δέραι, περάτων, ἴσος. But also ποικιλόδειροι, περάτων, and ἴσος with first syllable long, probably due to epic influence, likewise ἔννεκα (also Theocr.) with hyper-Aeolic νν (cf. 54b) = Hom. εἴνεκα. —55. βρόδα, βροδοδάκτυλος, βραδίναν, βράκεα.—57. Psilosis.—67. πτόλις, probably epic.—68.2 with a. πέμπε, πήλυι, κασπολέιδε. —74. ἀέρρει, ἐγέρρην, ἰμέρρει, παρορίννει.—75. βόλλομαι, μελλιχόμειδε. 76. ἄμμες, ὔμμες, ἔμμεναι, ἔμματα, σελάννα, φάεννος, ἐράνναν, ἰλλάεντι, χέρρας. But once with λ δισχελίοις.—77.1, 79. κτένναις, γένναto, ἄγγελλαι, ἀέρρατε, συνέρραισα. But hyper-Aeolic ρρ in θόρρακες, better θώρακες.

—77.3. παῖσα, Μοῖσα, πλήθοισα, λίποισα, μειδιάσαισα, μίγεισα, etc., 3 pl. ἀπυκρύπτοισι, φαῖσι, ἴεισι, ἐπιρρόμβεισι, etc.—78. acc. pl. -αις, -οις, nom. sg. m. pple. οἴκεις, μέδεις (= μεδέων).—80. κόρσαι, χέρσω.—82, 83. Usually σσ, but also σ (epic influence), μέσσον, μέσοι, ὅσσος, ὅσα, ἔσσο, τέλεσσαι, τέλεσον, πόδεσσιν, γυναίκεσσιν, etc., ἄνδρεσι, ἄμμεσιν, στήθεσιν, etc.—84. ὕσδων, πέσδων, μέσδον, etc.—89.4. κάλημμι, etc., νόημμα, πεποιημ-μέναις, κλᾶμμα, ἀροτρώμμεν, δίννηντες, διννάεις. Cf. also below, to 101.1.— 89.8. ἔσλος, μάσλης.—94.1. ὤνηρ, τῶμον.—94.3. κώττι.—94.6. κἀπί, κἄμματα, κἀλέφαις, κάν, etc. (α uniformly in pap. texts), but also κῆν, κῆκ.—94.7. κωὐκί, κωὔτε.—95-99. κὰτ τό, κὰμ μέν, κὰκ κεφάλας, κάββαλε, etc., πὰρ δὲ, πὲρ μὲν, πὲρ κεφάλας, περσκόπεισα, ἀπ πατέρων.—101.1. ὀννώρινε, ἀσύνετος, ἀσυννέτημμι.—102. ν movable frequent (epic influence).—103. Recessive accent, attested by the grammarians, also shown in papyrus texts (so far as the accent is written at all), as κόθαρον, gen. pl. λύγραν, παίσαν, μερίμναν, etc., likewise Ζεῦς (for Ζεύς). 104. Voc. sg. Δίκᾰ, gen. pl. -ᾶν, dat. pl. -αισι(ν) but ταῖς, acc. pl. -αις. —105. Gen. sg. once -ᾱο (epic).—106. Gen. sg. -ω, rarely -οιο (epic), dat. pl. -οισι(ν) but τοῖς, acc. pl. -οις.—107.3. πόδεσσιν, etc.—108.2. Acc. sg. ἀβλάβην, ἐμφέρην, etc., dat. sg. Διννομένηι, voc. sg. μελλιχόμειδε (cf. -ᾱ in Δίκα).—109.2. πόλιος and πόληος (epic).—111. βασίληες, τοκήων, etc. (above, to 43). But Ἄρευς, gen. Ἄρευος, acc. Ἄρευα (Hom. Ἄρης, Ἄρηος) with ευ extended from nominative.—114. ἴα.—116. Gen. πέμπων, δέκων.—118.3c. Gen. ἔμεθεν, σέθεν, ϝέθεν.—119. ἄμμες, ὔμμες, ἄμμι(ν), ὔμμι(ν), and ἄμμεσιν.—121.1. ἐμ' αὔται, ἐμ' αὔτωι.—125. κῆνος.—128. Dat. sg. τίωι, dat. pl. τίοισιν = Hom. τέω, etc.—129.2. ὄττινες, ὄττινας, gen. sg. ὄττω, dat. pl. ὄτοισι.—ὄππα, ὄππατα, ὄπποσε.—130. τέουτος = τοιοῦτος.—132.4. πήλυι, ἄλλυι, τύιδε, ἔνδυς.—132.5. πάνται.—132.11. ὄτα, πότα, ὄπποτα, ἄλλοτα.—133.6. αἴ.—134.1, 2. αἰ, κε, κεν.—135. ὀν, ἀπύ, ὑπά, εἰς, πεδά. 138.1. τίθησθα etc.—138.1a. -ης, -ηις?—138.5. σύναχθεν, etc., but ἐστάθησαν (epic).—143. ἐκάλεσσα, χαλάσσομεν.—146.1. ὑπαδεδρόμακε.— 147.2. τεθνάκην.—147.3. λελάθων, ἐκγεγόνων, etc.—150. χαλάσσομεν.— 153. ἔχην etc.—154.2. ἔμμεναι.—155.2. μεθύσθην, τελέσθην.—157. κά-λημμι, φίλησθα, φορήμεθα, ἐπόημμεν, εὐωχήμενος, ἐπιρρόμβεισι, χόλαισι, ἐπαίνεντες, πολέμεντι, δίννηντες (cf. a), οἴκεις, μέδεις.—157b. βόα, ἄγρει. τίμαι, βόα(ι) ὄπταις, χαύνοις, ὀνκαλέοντες, ποτεόνται.—159. ἀδικήει, ποθήω.— 161.2. ὄρημμι, ποτέονται beside ἀμφιπόταται, ἐκπεποταμένα.—161.2a. ἐξεπόνασαν, ἐπτόασεν (and ἐπτόαισ', above, to 8; cf. ἐπτοάθης Eur.).— 161.3. δοκίμωμι = δοκιμάζω.—162.2. ἄγρει.—162.8. ἐζώομεν.—163.3. ἦς.—163.8. ἔσσα and ἔοισα.—164.1. βασιλήιος, πεμπεβόηα.—164.2. ἰλλάεις = ἴλαος, like Hom. μεσήεις = μέσος.—164.4. ὄππα = ὄμμα.

ALCMAN

Text: Diehl, Anthologica Lyrica.

The language of Alcman agrees with Laconian in its general Doric features, and in several others that were not general Doric, as η, ω, not ει, ου (25), infin. -ην (153.2), acc. pl. -ως (106), ἐνθ- = ἐλθ- (72), κάρρων (80), etc. But some of the special Laconian peculiarities were ignored. So certainly the change of intervocalic σ (59.1), of which there is no trace. So probably the Lac. δδ = ζ (84), which occurs only in one MS of one passage (Diehl no. 100). Alcman probably wrote ζ, for which σδ, frequent in the texts, was a late spelling. The σ for θ (64) was much later than Alcman's time, but is frequent in the texts especially in certain words, as σιοί = θεοί. The ι for ε in this and some other forms represents a Laconian pronunciation (9.5), but one that is ignored in the spelling of the majority of forms (ὀρέων, αἰνέοντι, etc.), and very likely by Alcman himself. In the matter of spelling, σιοί may owe its ι as well as the σ to the redaction of grammarians.

The most conspicuous Lesbian feature in Alcman, as also in other lyric poetry, is the use of Lesbian participial forms like ἔχοισα, λιποῖσα, θεῖσα, etc. (**77**.3). Such forms are so frequent in Alcman as to indicate that his practice was uniform in this class and that exceptions in the text are to be suspected, not only καμοῦσιν with its Att.-Ion. ου, but also λαβῶσ' (Diehl no. 28), which, though good Laconian, rests on an emendation. It was only the Lesbian participial form that was adopted, not the general Lesbian treatment of vowel + νσ, which is not attested for other categories, not even the analogous Μοῖσα as in Pindar, but Μῶσα, and never in third plural forms. κλεννά (Diehl no. 1.44) is a Lesbian form (**76**), which may go back to the poet. Forms that are Lesbian, but also current in epic, as infin. -μεναι, dat. pl. παίδεσσι, etc., may be grouped with other examples of epic influence. Such are the frequent use of ν movable (**102**), σ beside σσ, as τόσσος, τόσος (**82**), γούνατα, δουρί (**54**), the latter wrongly emended to δωρί (Diehl no. 77; but Lac. δορϝί or δορί), πρότι (**135**.6), 3 pl. ἔχουσιν, εὕδουσιν.

8. ά, δᾶμος, ἀμέρα, etc.—**9**.5. σιοί, ἡμισίων, σιειδής, ἀργύριον, παγχρύσιος, but τέο, ἐπέων, αἰνέοντι, etc.—**13**.1. ἱαρός, also ἐπίασε (cf. Theocr. πιάξας), as in late Att. = ἐπίεσε.—**13**.3. ὄκα, etc., γα.—**25**. η, ω, as κῆνος, χηρός, ἦμεν, ὠρανόν, Μῶσα, gen. sg. -ω, acc. pl. -ως (but some cases of ει, ου left in text).—**41**.1. ὁρῆς, ποτήσθω.—**41**.2. φῶς, 3 sg. opt. νικῷ.—**41**.3. ἄλιον.—**41**.4. Ἀλκμάων, Ἀλκμάν, παιᾶνα, gen. pl. -ᾶν.—**42**.1. ἔπη, ἄνθη, ἦρ.—**42**.5. uncontracted εο, εω, or ιο, ιω.

52. ϝάνακτι, ϝέθεν, ϝάδη, etc. (ϝ written in some sources but mostly restored).—**53**. δάϝιον, αὐειρομέναι, but φῶς, ἄλιον, etc.—**61**. ἐντί, etc., τύ.—**64**. σιοί, παρσένος, σαλασσο-, σάλλει, etc.—**68**. βλῆρ = δέλεαρ. γλέπω, γλέφαρον = βλέπω, βλέφαρον.—**72**. ἐνθοῖσα, κέντο.—**76**. ἦμεν, ἀμές, χηρός, etc., but κλεννά (Lesb.).—**77**.3. Lesb. partic. forms ἔχοισα, φέροισα, λιποῖσα, ἐνθοῖσα, λυθεῖσα, etc.—**80**. κάρρων.—**82**, **83**. τόσσος, τόσος, ἐδάσσατο, ἐσσαμέναι, παίδεσσι, etc.—**84**. Usually ζ or late σδ, as μάσδων, etc., once δδ, καθαρίδδην.—**94**.2, 6. κὴν, κηπί, κώπώραν.—**95**, **99**. κά(τ) τάν. καβαίνων.—**102**. ν movable frequent.

104. Gen. pl. -ᾶν, dat. pl. -αισι, -αις.—**106**. Gen. sg. -ω, acc. pl. -ως, dat. pl. -οισι(ν), -οις.—**107**. Nom. sg. μάκαρς, like Cret. μαίτυρς. Dat. pl. παίδεσσι, etc.—**118**. Gen. τέο, ϝέθεν. Dat. μοι, τοι, τίν. Acc. ἐμέ, σέ, τέ, τύ, νίν.—**119**. ἀμές, ἀμέων, etc.—**120**. ἀμός, ϝα, σφεά, σφοῖς, σφετέρως.—**122**. Nom. pl. ταί.—**125**. κῆνος.—**132**.2. αὐτεῖ.—**132**.8. ὦτ'.—**132**.11. ὄκα, ποκα, τόκα, also ὄκκα.—**134**.1. αἰ.—**134**.2. κα (ἄν in Diehl no. 81, but improbable).—**135**. ἐς, πεδά, προτί.—**138**.3. παρήσομες, ὑμνέωμες.—**138**.4. αἰνέοντι, ἐντί (εὕδουσιν, ἔχουσιν epic, if genuine).—**138**.5. ἐπέβαν.—**142**. ἁρμόξατο.—**142**a. ὀνίχων.—**153**.1. φαίνην, etc. (mostly corrected from -εν or -ειν).—**154**. ἦμεν, etc., ἔδμεναι.—**163**.3. ἧς.—**163**.8. παρέντων. —Note also aor. ἔγεντο, as in Hesiod, Sappho, etc., likewise κέντο = κέλτο.

PINDAR AND BACCHYLIDES

Cf. Schöne, Leipziger Studien für klass. Phil. 19.181 ff. Texts: Pindar, Schroeder; Bacchylides, Blass-Suess.

The retention of original ᾱ = Att.-Ion. η, together with ᾱ from ᾱο ᾱω = Att.-Ion. εω, ω, is the most conspicuous characteristic of the choral lyric, and the only non-Att.-Ion. feature which prevails with any approach to consistency (even this not complete) and persists in the choruses of Attic tragedy. The weight of ᾱ-forms is further increased by the choice of Att.-Ion. ᾱ, not Dor. η, from αε (νικᾶν = Dor. νικῆν, etc.).

Of the general Doric characteristics (cf. **223**), which are common to

the West Greek dialects and partly to Boeotian and Thessalian, only a
few appear frequently, some occasionally, and others not at all. Thus
Pindar, who uses much more Doric than Bacchylides (or Simonides), has
usually 3d pl. -οντι, infin. -μεν = -ναι, frequently ξ in forms like κατεφάμιξεν, τύ beside σύ, τίν beside σοι, rarely τόκα beside τότε (and only ὅτε,
πότε), and never κα, πρᾶτος, (ϝ)ίκατι, 3 sg. ἧς, 1 pl. -μες, but only the Att.-
Ion. ἄν (or Aeol. κε(ν)), πρῶτος, εἴκοσι, ἦν, -μεν.
   Aeolic features, occurring also in Homer, are κε(ν) = ἄν, the double
nasals in ἄμμες, etc., κλεεννός (both P. and B.), perf. pple. with ντ (πεφρί-
χοντας etc.). Specific Lesbian, in Pindar regularly Μοῖσα, φέροισα, etc.,
frequently 3 pl. -οισι (in B. only Μοῖσα beside Μοῦσα).
   Pindar has a few cases of ἐν with acc., sometimes attributed to his
native Boeotian. But Delphian influence is perhaps more probable.
There is no clear evidence that the poet's language was affected by his
local dialect.
   8. ᾱ most consistently in broad categories which could have only ᾱ
in Doric, as the endings of ᾱ-nouns of the first declension, non-present
tenses and derivatives of verbs in -αω, suffix -τᾱς, -τᾱτος, personal endings
-μαν, -σθαν. In individual words Doric ᾱ usually retained, as μάτηρ,
ἁδύς, φάμᾱ, but occasionally Att.-Ion. η (at least in our texts, and need
not be rejected), as φήμᾱ (B.), which, though a hybrid form, is not
stylistically offensive beside genuine Doric ἥβᾱ.
   13. Non-Doric ἱερός (but σκιαρός), Ἄρτεμις, ὅτε, ποτε, τότε, rarely
τόκα, never κα, γα.—25. ει, ου, not η, ω.—41.1. Att.-Ion. ᾱ, not Dor. η,
as νικᾶν, νικᾶι, τιμᾶι, συλᾶται, etc.—41.2. τιμῶντες, etc.—φάος, σαόφρων
(B.) and σώφρων.—41.3. ἀέλιος, ἅλιος.—41.4. Gen. sg. masc. -ᾱ, sometimes
-ᾱο (P.), gen. pl. -ᾱν, ᾱς, Ποσειδᾱων, Ποσειδᾱν,.λᾱός (but Μενέλᾱς, etc.),
νᾱός, ᾱώς, ξυνᾱονες, ξυνᾱων, ὁπᾱων, κοινᾱνι, etc.—42.1. ἔτεα, βέλεα, etc.,
rarely -η. κέαρ, ἔαρ, ἦρος (P.).—42.3, 4. τρεῖς, φιλεῖ, etc.—42.5. εο or
ευ, as gen. sg. -εος, -ευς, φιλέοντα, φιλεῦντας.—42.6. φιλέων, etc.—43.
βασιλῆες, etc., also Ἀχιλλέος, etc.—49.2, 4. τράφω, τράχω, τάμνω.—52.
Former ϝ mostly ignored in prosody, but sometimes effective, especially
in the case of reflexive οἱ.—53. Once ἀυάταν for ἀ(ϝ)άταν.—54. μόνος,
κόρα, ὅρος and less commonly μοῦνος, κούρα, οὖρος.—61. ἐφίητι, φέροντι,
etc. (beside Lesb. or Ion. σ-forms, see below, to 138.4), τύ (beside σύ),
but εἴκοσι, Ποσειδάν (once perhaps Ποτειδᾱνος).—68.2. φήρ.—76. Lesb.
ἄμμες, etc., κλεεννός, κελεδεννός.—77.3. Lesb. Μοῖσα, in Pindar regularly
φέροισα, etc., and frequently 3 pl. -οισι.—82, 83. ὅσσος, ὅσος, τελέσσαι,
τελέσαι, etc.—89.7. ἐσλός (P.).—88. γλέφαρον.—94. κήν, κῆκ, χῶτι, etc.—
95. ἄν frequent, rarely παρ, κατ, περ, as πὰρ ποδός, πὰρ χειρός, πάρφρων,
κἀν νόμον, πέροδος, περ' αὐτᾱς.—102. ν movable frequent.
   105-6. Gen. sg. masc. -ᾱ, sometimes -ᾱο, gen. pl. -ᾱν, dat. pl. -αις,
-αισι.—106. Gen. sg. -ου, also frequently Hom. -οιο, dat. pl. -οις, -οισι.—
107.3. πόδεσσι, etc. frequent.—109.1. -ις, -ιος, etc.—111. -ευς, -ῆος, and
-έος.—114-5. πρῶτος, not Dor. πρᾱτος, εἴκοσι, not Dor. (ϝ)ίκατι.—118.
ἐγώ, ἐγών, τύ and σύ; gen. σέο, σέθεν; dat. ἐμοί, μοι, σοί, τοι, τίν, οἱ, ἱν (?);
acc. ἐμέ, με, σε, ἕ, νιν.—120. τεός, ἑός, and σός, ὅς; ἁμός, ὑμός, σφός, and
ἁμέτερος, etc.—122. ταί, τοί, and αἱ, οἱ.—126. Art. as rel. frequent.—
132.11. ὅτε, ποτε, τότε, rarely τόκα.—134.1. εἰ, never αἰ.—134.2. ἄν and
κε, κεν, never κα.—135.4. ἐς, εἰς, and rarely ἐν in Pindar.—135.5. πεδά
beside usual μετά.—135.6. ποτί beside πρός.—136.7. ἀμφί frequent.—
138.2. ἐφίητι, but τίθησι, δίδωσι.—138.3. -μεν, not -μες.—138.4. In Pindar
ἐντί, φαντί, φέροντι, etc. usually, but also Lesb. -οισι(ν). In B. usually
-ουσι(ν), rarely -οντι.—138.5. ἔβαν, τίθεν, φάνεν, etc.—142. κατεφάμιξεν,
παιάνιξαν, etc. (beside forms with σσ, σ).—142a. ὄρνιχες.—147.2. γεγάκειν,
κεχλάδειν.—147.3. πεφρίκοντας, κεχλάδοντας.—153.1. -ειν.—154. -μεν,
also -μεναι, -ναι.—161.2a. πονάω.—162.7. ἴσᾱμι = οἶδα.—163. 3 pl. in

Pindar ἐντί, once εἰσίν, in B. εἰσί. 3 sg. imperf. ἦν, not ἧς.—**164**.4. τεθμός, τέθμιος.—**162**.12. πᾶμα, πέπαται.

Cf. Magnien, Le syracusain littérair, et l'idylle XV de Théocrite, MSL 21.49 ff. A. S. F. Gow, Theocritus edited with introduction and commentary (1950) pp. LXXI ff.

The Sicilian literary Doric that appears in the scanty fragments of Epicharmus and Sophron and in the corrupt texts of other Sicilian and Italiot writers, but is best known from Theocritus, is based mainly on the Doric of Syracuse, though most of its characteristics are common to other Doric dialects. Its striking difference from the language of Pindar is due not so much to Sicilian peculiarities, though there are some, as to its much more thoroughgoing adherence to Doric.

Theocritus imitated various literary dialects, the epic (XII, XXII), the Lesbian lyric (XXVIII-XXX), the mild Doric of the choral lyric (XVI-XVIII, XXIV). But most of the poems are in the fuller Doric, based mainly on the Sicilian Doric of Epicharmus and Sophron and of his native Syracuse, but with many epic forms (ἄν, κε, εἰ, ν movable, gen. sg. -οιο, ἄμμες, ἐπέεσσι, etc.) and the Lesb. Μοῖσα, ἔχοισα, etc. It is to these poems that the following summary applies.

8. ᾱ regularly. Rarely Att.-Ion. η, as in Hom. phrase βίην καὶ κάρτος. Hyper-Doric ᾱ in ἄμισυς (but this in a Lesbian poem), other cases doubtful. —**13.** Epic ἱερός (ἱαρός in Epich., Sophron), but σκιαρός, κα, γα, ὅκα, etc.—**25.** η and ει, mostly ω but also ου, with great fluctuation in MSS., e.g. ἦνθε, ἦμεν, εἰμές, gen. sg. -ω, κώρα, κούρα.—**41**.1 ὁρῆτε etc.—**41**.2. Normal Dor. ω in ὁρῶν, σιγῶντι, πειρώμενοι, etc. Hyper-Dor. ᾱ in 2 sg. aor. ἐπάξα, ἐκτάσα of some MSS.—**41**.4. ἄς, gen. sg. -ᾱ, also epic -ᾱο, gen. pl. -ᾶν, etc.—**42**.1. ἄνθεα, etc., but 2 sg. mid. -ηι from -εαι.—**42**.3, 4. εὐμενέες, φιλέει, etc., but usually contraction.—**42**.5. εο or ευ, gen. -εος, -ευς, ἐόντα, εὖντα, etc.— **42**.6. ἑών, φιλέων, but fut. δοκῶ, ἀξῶ, etc.—**43**. βασιλῆος, etc. (also -εος).— **44**.3. ἄθρως = ἄθροος, gen. sg. -ω.—**52, 53**. No ϝ.—**54**. κώρα (κούρα), μώνα and κόρα, μόνα.—**61**. εἴκατι, τύ, πλατίον, τίθητι, ἐντί, etc.—**72**. ἦνθον, βέντιστος.—**77**.3. Lesb. Μοῖσα, ἔχοισα, etc.— **82, 83**. ὅσσος, ὅσος, ἔσσεται, etc.—**84**. ζ and σδ.—**89**.5a. μικκός.—**94**. κήν, κῆς, χώνήρ, etc.—**95**. ἄν, πάρ, πέρ, κάτ, πότ.—**102**. ν movable frequent.—**104-5**. Gen. sg. masc. -ᾱ (rarely epic -ᾱο), gen. pl. -ᾶν, dat. pl. -αις, -αισι(ν), acc. pl. -ᾱς frequent.— **106**. Gen. sg. -ω (and epic -οιο), dat. pl. -οις, -οισι(ν), acc. pl. -ως, sometimes -ος.—**107**.3. πάντεσσι, etc., also epic ἔπεσσι(ν).—**111**. βασιλῆος, etc. (and -εος).—**114, 116**. πρᾶτος, τέτορες, εἴκατι (cf. Heracl. ϝείκατι).—**118**. Nom. τύ; gen. ἐμεῦς, μευ, τεῦς, τευ, σέθεν; dat. ἐμίν, μοι, τίν, τοι, οἱ; acc. τύ, τέ, τίν, νιν.—**119**. Lesb. ἄμμες, ὔμμες, etc.—**120**. τεός, ἑός, ἀμός.— **122**. τοί, ταί, and οἱ, αἱ.—**125**. τῆνος.—**129**.2 ὅττι.—**132**.2. τηνεῖ.—**132**.5. πᾶι, παντᾶι.—**132**.7. πῆ, ὅπη, τῆδε.—**132**.8. ὦ, τηνῶ, τηνῶθε.—**132**.11. ὅκα, πόκα, τόκα, ὅκκα.—**133**.4. ἔνδοι.—**134**.1. αἱ and εἱ.—**134**.2. κα, ἄν, and κε(ν).—**135**.6. ποτί, rarely πρός.

138. 2 sg. συρίσδες etc., beside usual -εις. 3 sg. τίθητι, προίητι. 1 pl. λέγομες, etc. 3 pl. ἐντί, φαντί, λέγοντι, etc.—**141**. ἐσσεῖται and ἔσσεται, οἰσεῦμες and οἴσεται, etc.—**142**. χαρίξηι, ἐργαξῆι, θεσπίξασα, etc.—**142a**. κλαίξ.—**143**. γελάσσαι.—**147**.1. δεδοίκω, πεποίθεις, πεφύκει, etc.—**153**. -ειν (or -ην) and -εν.—**154**. θέμεν, ἦμεν, etc.—**157**. Once ποθόρημι with Lesb. type.—**159**. πεινᾶντι, γελᾶντι, παρελᾶντι, (ὀπτάντες Epich.).—**161**.2. ποθορεῦσα, συλεύμενος.—**161**.2a. ἐξεπόνασεν.—**162**.6, 7. ἴσᾱμι = οἶδα. λέω = θέλω.—**163**. ἐντί, ἧς.

4. Kirchoff, Studien zur Geschichte des griechischen Alphabets, 4th ed. Roberts, Introduction to Greek Epigraphy, I. Rehm, Die Schrift des griechischen Kreises, in Müller's Handbuch der Altertumswissenschaft VI.6.191 f. Hiller v. Gaertringen in Ebert, Reallexicon der Vorgeschichte II.357 ff. Falkner, Zur Frühgeschichte des griechischen Alphabets, in Brandenstein's Frühgeschichte und Sprachwissenschaft 110 ff.

Facsimiles of archaic inscriptions in Roberts, and Roehl, Imagines inscriptionum graecarum antiquissimarum. Photographs in Kern, Inscriptiones Graecae.

Kirchoff's map needs some revision in detail, e.g., Rhodes should be colored red. Cf. Wiedemann, Klio 8.523 ff., 9.364.

The Phoenician alphabet, now known from about 1000 B.C., was adopted and adapted to Greek speech. The significant innovation, one common to all the local alphabets, was the use of Phoenician consonant signs to express the five Greek vowels. The increase from 22 to 23 letters is due to the fact that the Phoenician wau is represented by two letters, (1) the Ϝ, based on a variant form, but with the original consonantal value and position in the alphabet, (2) the Y corresponding to the usual Phoenician form, but given vowel value and placed at the end of the alphabet. The four Phoenician signs for sibilants were taken over, but without stabilization in use (Ϻ or M = σ, I and Ξ with varying values).

The origin of the supplementary letters, Φ, X, Ψ, has been widely discussed, without decisive results. But it is generally agreed that both X and Ψ have originally guttural value, and it is highly probable that the Ψ is based on a form of the Phoenician kaph (it agrees precisely with the kaph-form of the earliest Phoenician inscription), the source of K.

In view of the agreement in the use of the Phoenician consonant signs to express the vowels we can scarcely escape the conclusion that the adaptation was made at some particular time and place. For the time estimates have varied by several centuries, but the probability is that it should be placed sometime in the course of the ninth century B.C. The earliest records were very likely on perishable material, such as merchants' accounts on papyrus. Some interval must have elapsed between the original adaptation and the time of the earliest inscriptions on pottery or stone. The Dipylon vase, on which is inscribed the earliest known Attic inscription (with the only example of the reclining alpha, like the Phoenician aleph but already with the supplementary X) is now ascribed to the first half of the eighth century B.C., and somewhat later but still in that century the inscribed sherds from Hymettus and some from Corinth and elsewhere. The scrawls on the rocks at Thera, though undateable, are clearly among the oldest specimens of Greek writing. As to the place of origin, one can say no more than that one naturally thinks of some one of the islands most accessible to Phoenician commerce.

The belief that the Greek alphabet must have had its birth at a given time and place does not exclude the possibility that, under continued familiarity with the Phoenician alphabet in other places, some of the variant letter forms in local alphabets may be based on Phoenician variants.

Some of the striking variants in letter forms are the following:

A. ⟑ ("reclining alpha") Athens (Dipylon vase). ⋈ ("four-barred alpha") usual in Boeotia, occasional elsewhere as in Locris (so no. 57), etc.

B. ⟩ Crete. Ϝ, ⟩, ⟨ Thera. ⌐ Corinth. Ϝ, ⌐ Argos. ⋈ Selinus, Melos.

Γ. Γ, ⌐, Λ, <, C, / (this last in Ach. colonies).

E. Ε frequent in Boeotia. Ɓ Corinth, Corcyra, Acarnania, Cleonae, Megara. Ⴟ Sicyon.

F. ⅂, Ϻ Crete. Ͷ Pamphylia and some Cretan towns (see **51***b*). ꓩ Chalcis, Corcyra, Thessaly, Boeotia, Ε frequent in Boeotia, sometimes elsewhere.

H. 日 early, ▯ Cnidus. ⊢ (source of ⌞, ʿ) Heraclea, rarely Cumae. Elis, Sicyon, Epidaurus.

Θ. ⊗, ⊕, ⊙ Rarely Θ, ⦶, 日.

I. Ϩ, ʅ, ʔ Athens (Dipylon vase), Crete, Thera, etc. Ƹ Corinth.

Λ. L Athens (but Γ Dipylon vase), Chalcis, Boeotia, East Locris (also Crete, no. 116). Γ Crete, Thera, Melos, Naxos, Corinth, Corcyra, West Locris, Elis, Thessaly.

M. Early ᴍ. Ↄ Mantinea.

Ξ. ⵏ Argos, Amorgos. 日 Etruscan abcdaria. ▯ Naxos (probably; see no. 6). ⧗ Pamphylia.

O. Ω Delos, Paros Thasos Siphnos. C Melos, Cnidus.

Π. Γ, ꟼ Thera, Boeotia, etc. C Crete.

M (san) = σ. Crete, Thera, Melos, Sicinos, Corinth, Corcyra, Sicyon, Argolis (also Ƹ), Locris (once beside Ƹ in no. 59), Ͷ = $\underline{\sigma}$ Mantinea.

T = σσ Halicarnassus, Teos, Ephesus, Erythrae, Cyzicus, Naucratis, Selinus. Ψ = σσ Pamphylia.

Σ. Ϩ Athens, Euboea, Boeotia, Elis, etc. ʓ Laconia, Abu-Symbol.

X. + Locris, Phocis, Thessaly, Boeotia, Arcadia, Selinus.

Ψ = ψ. Ж Locris. Arcadia. ⧗ Elis, Laconia. Ψ = ξ Melos, Thera.

GLOSSARY AND INDEX

In the alphabetical arrangement the presence of Ϝ is ignored, in order to obviate the separation of the many forms which occur with and without it. Thus (Ϝ)ίκατι, i.e., Ϝίκατι or ίκατι, and να(Ϝ)ός in the position of ναός. Ϙ stands in the position of κ.

For inflectional forms the conventional captions (nom. sg., 1 sg. pres. indic.) are sometimes substituted, and in these the transcription which we have employed for forms occurring in the epichoric alphabets is frequently replaced by the more familiar spelling, e.g., ε̄, ō, h, by η, ω ', or Cret. π, κ, by φ, χ. But the precise form occurring is sometimes retained as a caption, or added, or given separately with a cross-reference. Brevity and convenience in each case have been preferred to consistency.

The references are: numbers in bold faced type, to the sections of the Grammar; otherwise to the numbers of the inscriptions.

ά = ἀ. **58**a
ἀϜάταται Lac. **53**
ἀβέλιος Cret. = ἥλιος. **41**.3, **54**
ἀβλοπία Cret. = ἀβλαβία. **49**.3, **66**
ἀγαῖος Delph. No. 52 D 38, note
ἄγαλμα. No. 37, note
ἀγαλματοφώρ El. = ἱερόσυλος.**107**.1
Ϝάγανον Boeot., meaning? No. 39
ἄγαρρις West Ion. 'assembly.' **49**.2, **80** with a
'ΑγασιλέϜō Eub. = 'Αγασίλεω.**41**.4, **53**
ἀγγροφά Epid. **49**.2
ἀγέλαι Cret., 'bands' in which the Cretan youth were trained
ἀγελάοι Cret., 'ephebi.' **31**, no. **120**.11, note
ἄγερσις East Ion., 'assembly.' **49**.2
'Αγλαο-, 'Αγλω-. **41**.2
ἀγνέω = ἄγω. **162**.1
ἀγορά Delph., Thess. = ἐκκλησία
ἀγορανομέω Thess., 'preside over the assembly,' like Att. ἐπιστατέω. See preceding. In other states the ἀγορανόμοι were officers in charge of the 'market' etc.
ἀγόρασσις Boeot. **164**.3
ἀγρέω Lesb., El., ἀνγρέω Thess. (**58**c) = αἱρέω. **162**.2
ἀγχιστέδαν Locr. **133**.7

ἄδε, ἄδε 'in this way.' **132**.6
ἀδεαλτώhαιε El., from ἀδεαλτόω = ἀδηλόω, ἀφανίζω. **59**.3, **152**.4, no. **65**.12, note
ἀδελφεός = ἀδελφός. **164**.9
ἀδευπιαί Cret. = ἀδελφαί. **71**, **164**.9
ἀδηλόω Heracl. 'make invisible'
ἀδηνέως 'without fraud, plainly.' Chian ἀδηνέως γεγωνέοντες 'calling out plainly,' no. 4 B. Cf. Hesych. ἀδηνέως · ἀδόλως, ἁπλῶς, χωρὶς βουλῆς
ἄδος, ὁ Ion. 'decree.' See ἀνδάνω
ἀέλιος = ἥλιος. **41**.3
ἀζαθός Cypr. = ἀγαθός. **62**.2
ἀζετόω Delph. 'convict.' No. 55.17, note
ἄζωστος Cret. 'ungirded,' epithet of the ephebes. No. **120**.11/12, note
"Αθαββος Delph. = "Αθαμβος **69**.3
αἱ West Greek, Aeol. = εἰ. **134**.1, 2c
ἄι = ἦ adv. **132**.5
ἄι Lesb., ἀί Arc., αἰί Ion., ἀίν Thess. = ἀεί. **133**.6
ἀίδασμος Ion. **133**.6
αἰϜεί Cypr., Phoc. = ἀεί. **53**, **133**.6
αἰλέω Cret. = αἱρέω. **12**
αἶλος Cypr. = ἄλλος. **74** b
αἰλότρια El. = ἀλλότρια. **74** b

αἱμάτιον Coan, etc. 'coagulated blood and meat, sausage-meat.' Cf. Hesych. αἱμάτια· ἀλλάντια
αἱμίονος Lesb. = ἡμίονος. 17
αἵμισυς Lesb. = ἥμισυς. 17, 61.5
ἀίν Thess. = ἀεί. 133.6
αἶνος 'decree.' No. 99.4, note
αἱρεθές Ther. = αἱρεθείς. 78
αἶσα 'share.' 191
αἰσιμνάτας, αἰσιμνῶντες Meg. = αἰσυμνήτης, etc. 20, 258
ἀκεύω Cret. 'take care of, act as guardian.' Cf. ἀκεύει· τηρεῖ. Κύπριοι Hesych.
Ϝακίνθια Arg. = Ὑακίνθια. 52 c
ἀκκόρ late Lac. = ἀσκός. 86.3 b
ἀκρατής Ion. = ἄκυρος. Cf. καρτερός
ἀκρόθις Delph. = ἀκροθίνιον. No. 52 D 47, note
ἄκρος Corcyr. = ἄκρος. 58 c
ηακροσκιρίαι Heracl. 'heights covered with brushwood.' 58 c
ἀϜλανέōς El. 'wholly, in full.' 55, no. 64.4, note
ἁλία 'assembly.' (1) Delph. (no. 52), used for the meeting of the phratry; (2) Acarn., Corcyr., Heracl., Gela, Agrig., Rheg. = ἐκκλησία. 55
ἁλιαία 'assembly.' Arc., Arg., Mycen, Nemea
ἁλίασμα 'decree.' Gela, Agrig., Rheg.
ἁλίασσις Arg. 'act of the ἁλιαία.' 164.3
ἁλιασταί Arc., in form = Att. ἡλιασταί, but title of Tegean officials who enforced penalties etc. (no. 19.23)
ἄλινσις Epid. 'stuccoing.' 77.3 a
ἄλιος Dor., ἅλιος Lesb. = ἥλιος. 41.3
Ϝαλίσκομαι Thess. = ἁλίσκομαι. 52 c, 89.1
ἄλλα Lesb. 'elsewhere.' 132.6
ἀλλάζω Locr. = ἀλλάσσω. 84 a
ἀλλᾶι Cret., Corcyr. 'otherwise.' 132.5
ἀλλεῖ 132.2
ἄλλη 'elsewhere.' 132.7
ἀλλοπολία Cret. = ἀλλοδημία. Cf. Cret. πόλις = δῆμος
ἀλλότερρος Lesb. = ἀλλότριος. 19.2
ἀλλόττριος Cret. 89.2
ἄλλυ Arc. = ἄλλο. 22
ἄλλυι Lesb. 'elsewhere.' 132.4
ἀλλύω Cret. = ἀναλύω 'ransom'

ἄλϜον Cypr. Sicil. ἅλος (ἀ), Arc. ἅλων (ἀ) 'plot of cultivated land, plantation.' Cf. Att. ἅλως, Hom. ἀλωή. No. 23.9, note
ἀλοργής Ion. 167
ἄλωμα Boeot. = ἀνάλωμα. 164.8
ηαμᾶ Lac. 132.6
ηάμα Boeot. = ἅμμα (?). No. 39
ἀμάρα Locr., Delph. = ἡμέρα. 12, 58 b
Ἀμάριος Ach. 12
ἀμβόλιμος 'adjourned.' Arg.
ἀμβρ[ό]την Lesb. = ἁμαρτεῖν. 5, 49.2a
ἀμεῖ Delph. = ὁμοῦ. 132.2
ἀμέν late Cret. = ἡμεῖς. 119.2a
ἀμέρα with lenis. 58b
ἀμές, ἀμές. 57, 58b, 76, 119
ἀμιθρέω Ion. = ἀριθμέω. 88
ἄμμες, ἄμμε Lesb., ἀμμέ Thess. = ἡμεῖς, ἡμέας. 76, 119
ἀμμόνιον Delph. 'penalty for delay.' From ἀναμένω. Cf. Hom. καμμονίη = καταμονή
ἀμοιϜά Corinth. = ἀμοιβή. 51a
ἀμπ- in early Cretan words, see under ἀμφ-
ἀμπείση Arc., aor. subj. of ἀναπείθω. No. 22.60, note
ἀμπελωργικός Heracl. 167
ἀμπώλημα Heracl. 'rebate.' Heracl. Tab. I.108 ff., note
ἀμφαίνομαι Cret. (e.g. ἀμπαίνεθαι, ἀμπανάμενος, ἀνπανάμενος, ἄμπαντος, ἄνπαντος) 'adopt'
ἄμφανσις Cret. (ἄνπανσιν) 'adoption' (act of). 77.3a
ἀμφαντύς Cret. (ἀνπαντύι) 'adoption' (condition of, i.e. state of being an adopted son)
ἀμφεικάς 'day after the twentieth.' Coan, Ther.
ἀμφί. 136.7
ἀμφίδημα Cret. 'ornament,' gen. sg. ἀνπιδέμᾱς. 112.5
Ἀμφικτίονες, -κτύονες. 20
ἀμφιλλέγω, ἀμφίλλογος. 76a
ἀμφιμωλέω, ἀμφίμωλος Cret., see μωλέω
ἀμφίσταμαι Heracl. 'investigate.' Cf. Hesych. ἀμφίστασθαι· ἐξετάζειν
ἀν = ἀνά. 95
ἄν Arc. = ἃ ἄν. 58d
ηάν Arc. = ἄν. 58d
ἀνάατορ El., see ἄνατος
Ϝάναξ = ἄναξ. 52
ἀνασκηθής Arc., see ἀσκηθής

ἄνατος 'immune from punishment.' El. ἀνάατορ, Locr. adv. ἀνάτō(ς). 53
ἀνδάνω = δοκέω 'be approved, voted.' 162.3
ἀνδιχάζω Locr. 'be of divided opinion.' Cf. Hdt. 6.109 δίχα γίγνονται αἱ γνῶμαι
ἀνδρεφονικός Locr. = ἀνδρο-. 167
ἀνδρήιος Cret.; ἀνδρήος Delph. 164.1
ἀνέθεαν, ἀνέθιαν = ἀνέθεσαν. 9.2, 138.5
ἀνεκκλήτως Delph. = ἀνεγκλήτως. 69.3
ἀνελόσθō Lac. = ἀνελέσθων. 140.3b
ἀνεπίγροφος Heracl. = -γραφος. 49.2
ἀνέσηκε Lac. = ἀνέθηκε, 64
ἄνευν Epid. = ἄνευ. 133.6
ἄνευς El. = ἄνευ. 133.6, 136.4
ἀνηεῶσθαι Heracl., from ἀνίημι. 146.3
ἀνηρίθευτος Ion. = ἀνερίθευτος 'not venal.' 167a
ἀνιοχίω Lac. = ἡνιοχέω. 9.8
ἄνις Mess., etc. 133.6
ἀννίομαι Cret. = ἀρνέομαι. 86.5
ἀνοσίjα Cypr. 'impiety.' No. 23.29
ἀνπ- in early Cretan words, see under ἀμφ-
ἀνταποδιδῶσσα El. = -διδοῦσα. 89.4
ἀντί. 136.8
ἀντίγροφον Cret., Anaph. = ἀντίγραφον. 49.2
ἀντίμολος Cret. 'opponent, defendant,' see μωλέω
ἀντιτυγχάνω Arg., Boeot., Delph., Lac. = παρατυγχάνω 'happen to be present,' or 'in office' (so nos. 45, 84)
ἄντομος Heracl. 'road, path'
ἄντορος Heracl. 'counter-boundary'
ἀντρῆιον Cret. = ἀνδρεῖον. 62.2
ἄντρōπος Cret., Pamph. = ἄνθρωπος. 66
ἀνφόταρος Locr. = ἀμφότερος. 12
ἀνώγω Cypr. 191
ἄνωθα Heracl. = ἄνωθεν. 133.1
ἀνωθεοίη Ion. 157c
ἄνōρος Cret., Thess. = ἄωρος
ἀξιάω Lesb. (ἀξιάσει) = ἀξιόω. 161.5. ἀξιῶι Calym. 159a
ἀξιοδότας Locr. No. 59b, note
αὀτός East Ion. = αὐτός. 33
ἀπ Thess. = ἀπό. 95

ἀπαγορεύω Cret. 'proclaim'
ἄπατος Cret. = ἄνατος, used impersonally, e.g., ἄγοντι ἄπατον ἔμεν 'there shall be no fine for the one who seizes.' 53
'Απείλōν Cypr. = 'Απόλλων. 49.3, 74b
ἀπελάōνται Locr. 159
ἀπελευθερίζω Delph., Thess. = ἀπελευθερόω. 161.4. Thess. ἀπελευθερεσθένσα, 18, 77.3
ἀπέλλα. Lac. = ἐκκλησία. Cf. 'Απελλαῖος, name of a month. 'Απέλλαι Delph., name of a festival corresponding to the Attic 'Απατούρια
ἀπελλαῖα Delph. 'victims for the 'Απέλλαι'
ἀπέλλω Lesb. = ἀπειλέω. 75
'Απέλλων = 'Απόλλων. 49.3
ἀπεσσούα Lac. 145b
ἀπέταιρος Cret. 'one who is not a member of a ἑταιρεία.' 117.II.5, note
ἀπεχομίνος Arc. = -μένους. 10
"Απλουν Thess. = 'Απόλλων. 49.3
ἀποδεδόανθι Boeot. = -δεδώκασι. 138.4, 146.1
ἀποδείγνυσθαι Eretr. = -δείκνυσθαι. 66
ἀποδόσσαι El. = ἀποδόσθαι. 85.2
ἀπόδρομος Cret. 'a minor.' See δρομεύς
ἀποϜελέω El. = ἀπειλέω. 75
ἀπολιήνω Boeot. 162.10
ἀπολογίτταστη Boeot. = ἀπολογίσασθαι 82, 85.1, 142
ἀπομωλέω Cret. 'contend in denial, deny.' See μωλέω
ἀποπιπράσκω 'sell,' Lesb., Ion., etc.
ἀποστράψαι Delph. = ἀποστρέψαι. 49.2
ἀποτίνοιαν El. = ἀποτίνοιεν. 12a
ἄποτος Coan = ἄοινος. No. 108.35, note
ἀποφορά Coan 'carrying off'
ἀποφωνέω Cret. (ἀποπōνίοι, etc.) 'bear witness.' See φωνέω
ἀππασάμενος Boeot. = ἀνακτησάμενος. 69.4, 162.12
ἀππεισάτου Thess. = ἀποτεισάτω. 68.2
ἀπύ Arc., Cypr., Lesb., Thess. = ἀπό. 22
ἀπυδίει Arc. = ἀποδέει. 9.5
ἀπυδόας Arc. = ἀποδούς 144

ἀπυδόσμιος Arc. 'for sale.' No. 18.28, note
ἀπυδοσμός Arc. = ἀπόδοσις 'payment.' 164.4.
ἀπυλιῶναι Arc. 'smooth out, settle (?).' 162.10
ἀπυϲεδομίν[ος] Arc. = ἀποδεδομένους. 10, 68.3a
ἀπυτείω Arc. See τίνω
ἀπύω Arc. 'summon' = poet. ἠπύω, 191
ἀπώμοτος Cret. 'under oath of denial'
ἄρατρον Cret. = ἄροτρον 161.5
ἀράω Heracl. (ἀράσοντι) = ἀρόω. 161.5
Ϝαργάναι Delph. = Ἐργάνη. 12
Ϝάργον El. = ἔργον. 12
ἀργύριος Lesb. = ἀργύρεος. 164.6. Lesb. ἄργυρα, 19.4, Thess. ἀργύρος. 19.3
ἀρέσμιον Phoc. 'fee, perquisite.' From ἀρέσκω
 hαρέσται Locr. = ἐλέσθαι. 12, 85.1
Ϝαρήν Cret. = ἀρήν (Att. inscr.), nom. of ἀρνός. 52
ἀϜρέτευε, ἀρήτευε Arg. 55 with b
Ἀρίσταιχνος Coan. 69a
ἀριστίνδαν Locr. 133.7
ἀρνηάς 'ewe.' Lesb.
hάρνησις Heracl. = ἄρνησις. 58d
ἀρρέντερος Arc. = ἄρρην. 80, 165.1
ἄρρηκτος 'unplowed.' Heracl.
Ϝάρρω El. 12, 162.7
ἄρσην. 49.2, 80
Ἄρταμις = Ἄρτεμις. 13.2
Ἀρταμίτιός = Ἀρτεμίσιος. 61.3
Ἀρτεμίρια Eretr. = Ἀρτεμίσια. 60.3
ἀρτύω Heracl. 'devise by will.' Cf. Hesych. ἄρτυμα· διαθήκη, and ἀρτῦναι· διαθεῖναι. In Cretan (no. 117.XII.32) 'manage.' In Arcadian 'arrange, prepare.' Cf. the official titles Arg. ἀρτῦναι (no. 85.2, note), Epid. ἀρτῦνοι, Ther. ἀρτυτήρ
ἀρχιδαυχναφορέω Thess., see δαύχνα
ἀρχιττολιαρχέω Thess. 'be the first ptoliarch.' See ττολίαρχοι
Ἀρχοκράτης Rhod. = Ἀρχεκράτης. 167
ἀρχός Boeot., Cret., Ion., Locr. = ἄρχων 'magistrate'
ἇς = ἕως. 41.4, 45.4, 132.12

ἀσαυτός reflex. pron. 121.4
ἄσιστα El., Lac. = ἄγχιστα. 113.3. Lac. τοὶ ἄσιστα πόθικες, El. τοῖρ ἐπ' ἄσιστα 'those next of kin.' Cf. Cret. οἱ ἐπ' ἄνχιστα πεπαμένοι 'the nearest owners,' Locr. ἐπάνχιστος 'next of kin'
Ἀσκαλαπιός Thess. = Ἀσκληπιός. 48
ἀσκηθής Arc., used of animals 'without blemish'
ἀστάς Epid. = ἀναστάς. Cf. 77.2
Ἀστο- Thess. = Ἀριστο-. 88b
Ϝαστός = ἀστός. 52
ἄτα Cret. 'penalty, fine.' 53
ἀταγία Thess. No. 35.6, note
ἀτάω Cret. (ἀταμένοι, ἀταθείε) 'fine. 53
ἄτε Lac. (hᾶτ'). 132.6
ἀτελέν Cypr. = ἀτελῆ. 108.2
ἀτερόπτιλος (and -ιλλος) Epic., see ὀπτίλος
ἄτερος = ἕτερος. 13.3
Ἀτθόνειτος Thess. = Ἀφθόνητος. 86.2
ἄτι Cret. = ἄτινα. 129.3
ἀτροπάμπαις Lac. Nos. 75-78, note
ἀττάμιος El. = ἀζήμιος. 84
ἀυάδης Lesb. = ἀηδής. 35
αὐάτα Lesb. = ἄτη. 35a, 53
αὖθι Arc. 133.1a
αὖθιν Rheg. = αὖθις. 133.6
Αὐκλίεια Arc. 9.5, 33a
αὔληρα Dor. 55a
αὔρηκτος Lesb. = ἄρρηκτος. 55a
αὐσαυτός, αὐσωτός Delph., reflex. pron. 121.4
αὖσος Cret. = ἄλσος. 71
αὐταμαρόν Locr. = αὐθημερόν. 12, 58b, 133.6
αὐταμέριν Cret. = αὐθημερόν. 133.6
αὐταμερόν = αὐθημερόν. 133.6
ἀϜυτάν Corcyr. = αὐτήν. 32
ἀϜυτάρ Att. = αὐτάρ. 32, 50
αὐταυτός reflex. pron. 121.4
αὐτεῖ, Boeot. αὐτῖ. 132.2
αὐτεῖς Boeot. = αὐτοῖς. 30
αὖτιν Cret.; αὖτις Arc., Ion. = αὖθις. 133.6
αὐτός 121.3, 4, 125.2
αὐτοσαυτός reflex. pron. 121.4
αὐτούτα, αὐτώντα Sicil. = ἑαυτοῦ, ἑαυτῶν. 121.4
αὔφιτα Cret. = ἄλφιτα. 75
αὔως Lesb. = ἕως. 35
ἀφακεσάσθō Arg. 58c

ἀφεδριατεύω Boeot. 'serve as ἀφε-δριάτας or official dedicator.' No. 41, note

ἀφερξόντι Heracl. 'shut off' (water by damming). No. 79.130 ff.,note

ἀφεώσθω Arc., from ἀφίημι. 146.3

ἀφικνέμένων Orop. = ἀφικνουμένων. 158

Ἀφορδίτα Cret. = 'Αφροδίτη. 70.1

ἀφφάνω Cret. = ἀμφάνω. 69.3

ἄφωνος Heracl. 'intestate'

ἄχι Dor. 'where.' 132.6

ἀχύριος Heracl. 'building to hold chaff.' Cf. Hesych. ἄχυρος· ὁ ἀχυρών. ἀχυροδόκη· ἀποθήκη τῶν ἀχύρων

ἀψευδήων Arc. 149, 159

ἀ(Ϝ)ώς Dor. etc. = ἕως. 35, 41.4

βάβᾱλος Cyren. = βέβηλος. 46.1

Βαδρόμιος Coan, Rhod. = Βοηδρομιών. 44.2

βαθοέω Lesb. = βοηθέω. 44.2

βανά Boeot. = γυνή. 68.1

βάρναμαι = μάρναμαι. 88

βασιλᾶες El. = βασιλῆες. 15

βασιλεύς official title in many states. In some the chief magistrate; in others restricted to religious functions, like the ἄρχων βασιλεύς at Athens, e.g., at Chios (no. 4 C) and Miletus; βασιλεῖς an official body, e.g., in Mytilene (no. 26) and Elis (no. 61)

βάω, βέω (cf. 161.2) Dor. = βαίνω. Heracl. ἐπιβῆι, Cyren. παρβεῶντα, also ἐκβῶντας Thuc. 5.77

βέβαιος Locr. = κύριος

βεβαιωτήρ Delph. = -τής. 164.5

βείλομαι Boeot. = βούλομαι. 49.3, 68.2, 75

βέλλομαι Thess. = βούλομαι. 49.3, 68.2, 75. 3 pl. subj. βέλλουνθειν, 27, 139.2

Βέλφαιον Thess. = *Δέλφαιον, Δελφίνιον. 68.2

Βελφοί Lesb., Boeot. = Δελφοί. 68.2

βενέω El. = βινέω. 18b

βέντιστος Dor. = βέλτιστος. 72

βεττόν Lac. = *Ϝεστόν. 86.4

βέφυρα Boeot. = γέφυρα. 68.2

βίδεοι, βίδυοι Lac., title of officials. 51

βίετος Cret. = βίοτος. 167

βλῆρ = δέλεαρ. 42.1, 68.1

βόα(ι) Lab. 41a 157b, 159

βοαθοέω, βοαθέω = βοηθέω. 44.2, 45

βοαθός, βοηθός = -θόος. 45

βοιηθέω = βοηθέω. 31a

βοικίαρ El. = οἰκίας. 51

βόλιμος Delph., Epid. = μόλιβος. 88

βόλλα Lesb. = βουλή. 75

βολλεύω Lesb. = βουλεύω

Βολόεντα Cret. 44.4, 51

βόλομαι Arc., Cypr., Ion. = βούλομαι. 75b

Βόρθιος Cret. = Ὄρθιος. 51

βοῦα, βουαγόρ Lac. Nos. 75-78, note

βουσός Arc. 'cattle run.' 45

βοών Heracl. 'cow-shed.' 165.4

βροχύς Boeot., Thess., Arc. = βραχύς. 5

βυβλία Heracl. 'papyrus marsh.' τὰν βυβλίαν no. 79.Ι.58 = τὰν βυβλίναν μασχάλαν 92

βύβλινος Heracl., see preceding

βυβλίον = βιβλίον. 20

βωθέω Ion. = βοηθέω. 44.2, 45

βωλά Boeot., Cret., Arg., etc. = βουλή. 25, 75

Βωρθέα, Βωρσέα Lac. = 'Ορθία. 51, 64

βῶς Dor. = βοῦς. 37.1

γά W. Grk., Boeot. = γέ. 13.3

γαεργός Boeot.; γαϜεργόρ Lac. = γεωργός. 167

ΓαιάϜοχος Lac. = γαιήοχος. 53

γαιών Heracl. 'heap of earth, mound.' 165.4

γάμελα Delph. = γαμήλια 'wedding cakes.' 164.10

γεγράβανται Arg. = γεγράφαται. 66, 139.2

γεγράψαται Heracl. 146.5

γεγωνέω Chian 'call aloud.' 184

-γελᾶ, γελᾶντι 159

γενεά 'family, offspring,' also in plural 'descendants.' No. 61, 65

γερεαφόρος Coan, title of a priestly official. γερηφόρος occurs also in Pserimos near Calymna

γερουσία, Lac. γερωhία (59.1), title of the council at Sparta and some other places (as Ephesus, Andania, Dyme in Achaea)

γίνομαι = γίγνομαι, 86.10

γῖνος Rhod. = γίννος

γίνυμαι Boeot., Thess. = γίγνομαι. 86.10, 162.4

γινώσκω = γιγνώσκω. 86.10
γλάσσα Ion. = γλῶσσα. 49.5
γλέπω Dor. = βλέπω. 88
γλέφαρον Dor. = βλέφαρον. 88
γνῶμαν El. = γνῶμεν. 12a
γνώμη, γνώμα 'opinion, declaration' of an official body, frequent in Ionic and Doric
γνοσία Arc. = γνῶσις. 164.10
γράθμα Arg. = γράμμα. 164.4
γραμματίδδω Boeot. = γραμματεύω. 84, 161.4
γραμματιστάς = γραμματεύς 161.4
γράσσμα Arg. = γράμμα. 164.4
γραφής Arc. = γραφεύς. 111.4
γράφος El., Arc. = γράμμα. 241
γροφά, γροφεύς, etc. = γραφή etc. 49.2
γυμμνικός Arg. 89.2
γυμνάδδομαι Lac. 84
Γυνόππαστος Boeot. 69.4

δαιθμός = δασμός. 164.4
δαῖσις Cret. 'division'
δακκύλιος Boeot. = δακτύλιος. 87
δάλτος Cypr. = δέλτος. 49.3
Δαλφοῖς = Δελφοῖς. 12b
δαμέτας Carpath. = δημότης. 167
δαμιεργέντων Cyren. 42.5e
*δαμιοϜοργός, δαμιεργός, δαμιοργός, title of high officials, eponymous in many places. 167
δαμιόμεν Cret. 157c
δαμιοργόντōν Arg. 42.5d
δαμιωέμεν, δαμιώοντες Boeot. = ζημιοῦν, etc. 159
Δαμοκρέτω Lesb. = Δημοκρίτου. 18
δαμοσιοία El. = δημοσιοίη. 15, 157c
δαμοσιῶμεν El. = δημοσιοῦν. 157c
δαμοτέλην Lesb. = -τελῆ, 108.2
δαράτα Delph. 'a ceremonial cake.' No. 52 A 5, note
δαρκνά Cret., see δαρχνά
δάρμα Delph. = δέρμα. 12
δαρχμά = δραχμή. 49.2a. δαρχμάω, dual Boeot. 104.9
δαρχνά Cret. (δαρκνά) = δραχμή. 49.2a, 69a
δάτταθθαι, δάττōνται Cret. = δάσασθαι, δάσωνται. 82
δαύχνα Thess., Cypr. = δάφνη. 68.4a
δέατοι Arc. = δοκῇ. 139.1, 151.1, 191
δείλομαι = βούλομαι. 49.3, 68.1, 75
δείμενος Boeot. = δεόμενος. 158

δέκεθαι Cret. = δέχεσθαι. 66, 85.3
δέκνυμι Ion. = δείκνυμι. 49.1
δέκο Arc. = δέκα. 6, 114.10, 116a
δέκομαι = δέχομαι. 66
δέκοτος Arc., Lesb. = δέκατος. 6, 114.10, 116a
δέκων Lesb., Chian, gen. pl. of δέκα. 116
δέλλω Arc. = βάλλω. 49.3, 68.1
δεμελεῖς Epid. 'leeches.' No. 90. 98, note
δενδρύω 'dive under water.' Epid.
ΔϜενίας Corinth. = Δεινίας. 28, 54d
δέρϜα Arc. = δέρη. 54
δέρεθρον Arc. = βάραθρον. 68.3
Δεύς Boeot., Lac., Rhod. = Ζεύς. 84
δεύω Lesb., Thess. = δέω 'want.' 35
δέφυρα Cret. = γέφυρα. 68.2
δήλομαι = βούλομαι. 49.3, 68.1, 75. El. δηλομήρ, no. 65.5, note
δημορίων Orop. = δημοσίων. 60.3
Δῆνα Cret. = Ζῆνα. 84. 112.1
διακνόντων Heracl. = διαγνόντων. 66
διάλαμψις = διάληψις 'distinction,' in late Lesb., Cret., etc. Cf. And., Thess. λάμψομαι = λήψομαι, as also in Hdt. -λᾱμψις, like late -ληψις
διαλιήνω Boeot. 162.10
διατελόντι Arg. 42.5d
Διδύμοιυν Arc. = Διδύμοιν. 106.7
διέ Thess. = διά. 7
διεγέλα Epid. 159
διεσαφείμενος Thess. 158
Δι(Ϝ)ει- = Διΐ-. 112.2
διὲ κί Thess. = διότι. 68.4, 131
διηκόσιοι Ion. = διακόσιοι. 117.2
δικάδδω Cret., El. = δικάζω. 84
δίκαια El. 'legal penalties, fines.' ζίκαια, 62.2
δικάσζω Arg. = δικάζω. 89.1
δικάσκοποι officials at Mytilene 'inspectors of justice'
δικαστήρ Locr., Pamph. = -τής. 164.5
δικάως Lesb. = δικαίως. 31
δίκνυμι Cret. = δείκνυμι. 49.1
δίκρεος Cos, Chios 'double portion of flesh, a double cut'
δινάκω El. 'change, amend.' Cf. δίνω
δίννηντες Lesb. 89.4, 156a
Διόζοτος Boeot., Thess. = Διόδοτος. 166.2

διορθωτήρ Corcyr. = -τής. **164**.5
διούο Boeot. = δύο. **24**
διπλεῖ Cret., Heracl. **132**.2
διπλεῖος Locr., Cret. = διπλός
δίρεσις Cret. = διάρρησις in form. No. **117.IX.26** ff., note
δίφυιος, ζίφυιος, El. = διπλάσιος. **62**.2
δίωρος Arc. 'having two boundaries.' **54***c*
δόγμα 'decree,' usually that of a league, council, or selected body, as distinguished from the decree by popular vote, the ψήφισμα
δοϜέναι Cypr. = δοῦναι. **154** 1
δόκημα Arg. = δόγμα. No. **87**
δοκιμάδδω Boeot. = δοκιμάζω. **84**
δοκιμόω Lesb., Ion. := δοκιμάζω. **161**.3
Δολφοί Coan. **49**.3
δουλίζω Boeot., Phoc. = δουλόω. **161**.4
δούρραντα Thess. = δωρούντα. **89**.4, **162**.1*a*
δοώδεκα Boeot. = δυώδεκα. **24**
δρίφος Syrac. = δίφρος. **70**.2
δρομεύς Cret. 'one who is of age.' Boys under seventeen were not allowed to enter the gymnasia, which the Cretans called δρόμοι, and so were termed ἀπόδρομοι.
δυϜάνω Cypr. = δίδωμι. **162**.5
δύγαστρον Boeot. = ζύγαστρον. **84**
δύε Lac. := δύο. **114**.2
δυεῖν = δυοῖν. **114**.2
δύο, plural forms δυῶν, δυοῖς, δύας. **114**.2
δυόδεκα, δυώδεκα = δώδεκα. **115**
δυωδεκαῖς, δωδεκαῖς Delph. = Ion. δωδεκηἰς 'sacrifice consisting of twelve victims'
δώκω Cypr. = δίδωμι. **162**.5
δώλα, δῶλος Dor. = δούλη, δοῦλος. **25***f*
δῶμα 'temple.' **191**
δωός Cret. = ζωός. **84**
δώω Boeot., Cret. = ζώω. **84**.1, **162**.8

έ Locr. := ἐκ. **100**
ἔα El. = εἴη. **15**, **31**
ϜεϜαδεκότα Locr. **146**.1, **162**.3
ἔασσα = οὖσα. **163**.8
ἑβδεμαῖος Epid. = ἑβδομαῖος. **114**.7
ἑβδεμήκοντα Delph., Heracl. = ἑβδομήκοντα. **114**.7

ἔβδεμος = ἕβδομος, **48**, **114**.7
ἐβολάσετυ Pamph. **162**.2*a*
ἔγγροφος Cret. = ἔγγραφος. **49**.2
ἐγδοτήρ Argol., Lac.; ἐσδοτήρ Att. 'one who lets the contract.' **164**.5
ἔγεντο = ἐγένετο. No. **80**, note
ἐγϜηληθίωντι Heracl. **75**, **151**.2
ἐγκαθιδών Epid. **58***c*
ἔγκτασις = ἔγκτησις **162**.12*a*
ἔγραμμαι Cret., El. = γέγραμμαι. **137**
ἔγρασφεν := ἔγραψεν. **87**
ἔγρατται Cret. = γέγραπται. **86**.2, **137**
ἐγρύϜαι Calymn. **144***b*, **151**.1
Ἐδάλιον = Ἰδάλιον. **10**
ϜΗεδιέστας Arg. := ἰδιώτης. **52***b*, No. **83**.7, note
ἐδούκαεμ Thess., ἐδώκαιν Delph. = ἔδωκαν. **138**.5
ἔδραμα Epid. = ἔδρα. Cf. the rare ἔδρασμα
ἔθεν Epid. = οὗ, gen. 3 pers. pron. **118**.3
εἶ = οὗ adv. **132**.2
Ϝειζός El. = εἰδώς. **62**.2
εἰχ Arc. = εἰ. **134**.2*a*
Ϝείκατι Heracl. = εἴκοσι. **116**
εἴκοιστος Lesb. = εἰκοστός. **20***a*, **77**.2, **116** with *a*
εἰλύτα Boeot.; ἐλλύτα Ther. 'a kind of cake'
εἴλω εἰλέω. **75**
εἱμάτιον, εἱματισμός = ἱμάτιον, etc. **25***e*
εἴμειν Rhod. = εἶναι. **163**.7. εἴμμειν **89**.4
εἴμεν = εἶναι. **163**.7
εἶν Eub., Chian = εἶναι. **160**
εἴνατος Ion. = ἔνατος. **54**
εἴνεκα Ion. = ἕνεκα. **54**
εἴνιξαν Boeot. = ἤνεγκαν. **144***a*
Ϝειπ- (Cret. Ϝείπōντι, etc.) = εἰπ-. **52**
εἴρην Lac., also τριτίρενες. Nos. **75**–**78**, note
εἴρηται Ion. = εἰρέαται. **43**, **139**.2
εἴσχημαι := ἔσχημαι. No. **106.14**, note
ϜΗεκαδάμοε Boeot. **30**, **46**, **52***b*
ἔκασσα Cyren. = ἑκοῦσα. **163**.8*a*
Ϝέκαστος, ἕκαστος. **52***b*
Ϝεκατέρη. **132**.7
ἑκατέρω Coan, adv. 'on each side of.' **132**.8*a*
Ϝεκέδαμος Thess. **46**, **52***b*
ἔκκλημα Locr. = ἔγκλημα. **69**.3

Ϝεϙόντας Locr. = ἑκόντας. 52
ἡεκοτόν Arc. = ἑκατόν. 6, 116*a*
117
ἐκπέτωντι Heracl. = ἐκπέσωσι. No.
79.120, note
ἔκτεισις, not ἔκτισις. 28*a*
ἐκτιμασέντι Cyren. 42.5*e*
ἐλάτω, ἐλάντω Coan 159
ἐλαύθερος late Delph. = ἐλεύθερος. 33*a*
ἔλεξε = εἶπε. So regularly in Boeotian and Thessalian decrees, where Attic and most dialects have εἶπε. Also Argive.
ἡελέσται Locr. = ἑλέσθαι. 85.1
ἐλέστειν Thess. = ἑλέσθαι. 85.1, 156
Ἐλευθενναῖος Cret. = Ἐλευθερναῖος. 86.5
Ἐλευhύνια Lac. = Ἐλευσίνια. 20, 59.1
ἐλλευθερία Delph. 89.4
ἐλούθερος Cret. = ἐλεύθερος. 33*a*
ἐμέθεν Dor. = ἐμοῦ. 118.3
ἐμέος Dor. = ἐμοῦ. 118.3
ἐμετρίωμες Heracl. = ἐμετροῦμεν. 9.6, 42.5*b*
ἐμίν W. Grk. = ἐμοί. 118.4
ἔμμανις 'wroth.' Cret.
ἔμμεν Thess. = εἶναι. 163.7
ἔμμεναι Lesb. = εἶναι. 154.2, 163.7
ἔμμι Lesb., ἐμμί Thess. = εἰμί. 76
ἔμπαν Dor. = ἔμπης. 133.6
ἔμπασις = ἔγκτησις. 162.12
ἔμπροσθα Heracl. 133.1
ἐμφανιξόντας Arg. 42.5*d*, 142
ἐμφανίσσω Thess. = ἐμφανίζω. 84*a*
ἐν = εἰς. 135.4
? ἔναγος Delph. 'ceremony for the dead.' Cf. ἐναγίζω. No. 52 C 38, note
ἡένατος Delph., Ther. = ἔνατος. 58*c*, 114.9
ἐνδεδιωκότα Heracl. = ἐμβεβιωκότα 'alive.' 68.1
ἐνδειγνύμενος Ther. = ἐνδεικνύμενος. 66
ἐνδέρω, ἔνδορα Coan. No. 108.47, note
ἐνδεύω Lesb. = ἐνδέω 'want.' 35
ἐνδικάζομαι, Arc. ἰνδικάζομαι (10), 'be subjected to suit.' No. 19.34, note
ἔνδικος Cret., ἴνδικος Arc. (10), used impersonally with dative of the person who is 'liable to, or has right to, trial.' No. 19.34, note

ἐνδοθίδιος Cret. 'belonging within.' 165.2
ἔνδοι 'within.' 133.4
ἔνδορα Coan. See ἐνδέρω
ἐνδόσε Ceos = εἴσω. 133.4
ἐνδοσθίδια Epid. 'entrails.' 165.2
ἔνδυς Delph. 'within.' 132.4, 133.4
ἔνδω Delph. 'within.' 132.8*a*, 133.4
ἐνενιχθεῖει Boeot. = εἰσενεγχθῆ. 144*a*, 151.2, no. 43.49, note
ἐνετέρια Locr. 'taxes of admission' (to citizenship). From ἐνίημι, like Att. εἰσιτήρια from εἴσειμι
ἐνεφανίσσοεν Thess. = ἐνεφάνιζον. 84*a*, 138.5
ἐνηἑβόhαις Lac. from ἐνηβάω. 41.2, 59.1
ἐνθαῦθα Att. (inscr.) = ἐνταῦθα. 65
ἐνθαῦτα Ion. = ἐνταῦθα. 65
ἐνθεῖν = ἐλθεῖν. 72
ἔνθινος, from ἔνθα. Meg.
ἔνθῖνος Cret. = ἔνθεος. 164.10
ἔνθω Boeot = ἔστων. 138.4, 163.6
ἐνιαύτιος Coan, Delph. = ἐνιαύσιος. 61.3
ἐνιαυτός (1) 'end of the year, anniversary,' (2) 'year.' For the former and more original meaning, which the word sometimes has in Homer, cf. Delph. no. 52 C 47, Cret. no. 117 I 35, IV 4
ἐνκοιόταί Cret., sc. δαρχναί 'money given as security.' Cf. Hesych. κοῖον· ἐνέχυρον, κοιάζει· ἐνεχυράζει. Deriv. of κεῖμαι
ἡεννέα Heracl. = ἐννέα. 58*c*, 114.9
ἔννεκα Lesb. = ἔνεκα. 54*b*
ἐννῆ = ἐννέα. 42.1, 114.9
ἔνοτος Lesb. = ἔνατος. 6, 114.9, 116.9
ἐνπίδες Meg. = ἐλπίδες. 72
ἐνπιπάσκομαι 'acquire' Arg. 162.12
ἔνς Cret. = εἰς, 114.1
ἔνσα Thess. = οὖσα. 77.3, 163.8
ἐντάδε Argol. = ἐνθάδε. 65
ἐν τάν Boeot. 'until.' 136.1, no. 43.49, note
ἔντασις Thess. = ἔγκτησις. 163.12
ἔντασσιν Heracl. = οὖσιν. 107.3, 163.8
ἐνταῦτα El. = ἐνταῦθα. 65
ἔντε Locr., ἡέντε Delph. = ἔστε, ἕως. 58*c*, 132.11, 135.4
ἔντες Heracl. = ὄντες. 163.8
ἐντί = εἰσί. 163.2

ἔντιμος Locr. 'in office.' Cf. Plat. Rep. 528 C

ἐντιτός 'liable to suit' Cret. Cf. ἐντιτόν· ἔνδικον Hesych.

ἐντοῦθα Cumae = ἐνταῦθα. 65, 124 ἐντῦθα Orop. 34a

ἐντοφήια Delph. = ἐντάφια 'funeral rites.' Cyren. ἐντόφιον 'burial gift.' Cf. Hesych. ταφήια· ἐντάφια, εἰς ταφὴν ἐνθέντα ἱμάτια. 6, 164.1

ἔντω = ἔστων. 163.6

Ἐνυμακρατίδας Lac. = Ὀνυμα-. No. 71.35, note

ἐνυφαίνω Cret. (ἐνυπάνει), 'weave within' (the house)

Ϝέξ = ἕξ. 52b, 114.6

ἐξαγρέω El. = ἐξαιρέω. 162.2

ἐξάν = ἐξῆς. 133.6

ἐξαντίαι Arc. 'over against, near by.' No. 22.13, note

ἐξαρχίδιος Cret. 165.2

ἔξει Lac. = ἔξω. 133.5

ἐξεικάττιοι Thess. = ἐξακόσιοι. 19.3, 117.2

ἐξελαύνοια Arc. 152.1

ἐξερρύᾱ Epid. 144b

ἐξήκοιστος Lesb. = ἐξηκοστός. 116 with a

ἐξξανακάδεν Thess. = ἐξαναγκάζειν. 69.3, 84, 89.1

ἔξοι = ἔξω. 133.5

ἐξόμεινον Thess. = ἐξάμηνον. 6

ἐξορύξε Cypr. 'expropriate.' No. 23.12, note

ἔξος = ἔξω. 133.5

ἐξς Ion. 101.2

Ϝέος Locr. = ἑαυτοῦ. 118.3

ἐπ Thess., Boeot. = ἐπί. 95

ἐπαβολά Cret., Boeot. 'share.' 167a

ἐπάκοε, ἐπάκō, ἐπακόω Lac., dual of ἐπάκοος. Nos. 72, 73, note

ἐπάνακκον = ἐπάναγκες. 69.3

ἐπανιτάω El. 'return.' Cf. ἰτητέον = ἰτέον, and Hesych. εἰταχεῖν· ἐληλυθέναι

ἐπάνχιστος Locr. 'next of kin.' See ἄσιστα

ἐπαπύλογος Arc. 'in defense.' No. 22.34, note

ἔπαργμα Ther. = ἄπαργμα 'offering.' Cf. Att. (inscr.) ἐπαρχή beside ἀπαρχή

ἔπαρμα Boeot., meaning? No. 39

ἐπαρεώμενοι Cyren. 42.5b, 161.2

ἔπειτε, ἔπειτεν Ion. = Att. ἔπειτα. 132.11

ἐπελάω = ἐπελαύνω. 159. Coan ἐπελάντω 'drive up,' but Heracl. ἐπελάσθω and Arc. ἐπελασάσθων mean 'collect, enforce' (fines). Cf. also Arg. ποτελάτō 'enforce,' Ion. ἐνηλάσιον 'rental'

ἐπελευσεῖ (fut.), ἐπέλευσαν (aor.) Cret. 'bring.' 162.15

ἐπεμπάω El. (ἐπενπōι, ἐπενπέτō) 'enforce'; also ἐμπάω (μὲ 'νπōι). No. 61

ἔπερος 'sheep' (literally 'wooly') Lesb.

ἐπές Arc. 'with reference to.' 136. 12

ἐπεστάκοντα Thess. = ἐφεστηκότα. 58b, 147.3

ἔπετον Dor., etc. = ἔπεσον, aor. of πίπτω. See no. 79.120, note

ἐπεχεῖ Delph., ἐπεχές Arg. = ἐφεξῆς. 132.2

ἐπηρειάζω = Att. ἐπηρεάζω. No. 19.46, note

ἐπί Boeot. = ἐπεί. 29

Ϝέπιϳα Cypr. = ἔπεα. 9.3

ἐπίαρον El. = *ἐφίερον 'sacred penalty'

ἐπιατές ('πιατές) Locr. 'for the year.' No. 57.35; note

ἐπιβάλλων Cret., short expression for ὧι ἐπιβάλλει. Sometimes = ὧι ἐπιβάλλει (τά χρήματα), i.e., 'heir-at-law'; sometimes ὧι ἐπιβάλλει (ὀπυίεν), i.e., 'groom-elect'

ἐπιβῆι Heracl., see βάω

ἐπιδεί Boeot. = ἐπειδή. 29

ἐπιδημέωριν Eretr. = ἐπιδημῶσιν. 60.3

ἐπιδικατοί Lac. = οἷς ἐπιδικάζεται 'those to whom property is adjudged by law, heirs-at-law.' No. 70. For -ατός cf. θαυματός beside θαυμαστός

ἐπιζημίωμα Heracl. = ἐπιζήμιον 'penalty.' 164.10

ἐπιζύγιον Arc. = ὑποζύγιον

ἐπιθεῖαν El. = ἐπιθεῖεν. 12a

ἐπιθιάνε Arc. = ἐπιθιγγάνῃ. 62.3

ἐπίθωσε Boeot. 161.3

ἐπικαταβάλλω Heracl. = ἐπιβάλλω 'impose upon'

ἐπίλεκτοι, ἐπιλεκτάρχαι. No. 67. 16, note

ἐπιμεμηνάκαντι Arg. 138.4, 146.1

ἐπιϜοικία Locr. = ἐποικία

ἐπιοικοδομά Heracl., collective, used of the buildings belonging to the land. No. 79.150, note

ἐπίϜοικος Locr. = ἔποικος
ἐπιπῆν Epid. = καταπάσσειν. Cf. Hesych. πῆ καὶ πῆν ἐπὶ τοῦ καταπασσε καὶ καταπάσσειν
ἐπιπηράω Cret. (ἐπιπέρεται) = πειράω
ἐπίποκος 'unshorn' Coan. (also LXX)
ἐπιπόλαια χρήματα Cret. 'movable property.' Cf. Harpocration ἐπίπλα· τὴν οἵον ἐπιπόλαιον κτῆσιν καὶ μεταχομίζεσθαι δυναμένην
ἐπιπρείγιστος Cret. 'the next oldest.' See πρείγιστος
ἐπισκεάζω Corcyr. = ἐπισκευάζω 36
ἐπισπένδω Cret. 'solemnly promise.' Cf. Lat. spondeo. ἐπέσπενσε, 77.3
ἐπιτάδευμα Cret.
ἐπιχύτας Arg. = ἐπίχυσις 'beaker.' No. 87
ἐποίϜεhε Arg. 53, 59.2
ἐποίϜεσε Boeot. 53
ἐποίκια, τά Heracl. 'farm buildings'
ἐποισε͂ Arc., aor. subj. to fut. οἴσω. No. 18.21, note
Ϝέπος =ἔπος. 52
ἔππασις Boeot. = ἔγκτησις. 69.4, 162.12
hεπτάκιν Lac. = ἑπτάκις. 133.6
ἐπῶλον Arg. 42.5d
ἐπōμόται Locr. 'jurors'
ἐρανεσταί Ach. = -ισταί. 18b
Ϝέργον = ἔργον. 52
ἐρευταί Cret. = ζητηταί 'collectors.' No. 120.132, note
ϜεϜρεμένα Arg. = εἰρημένα. 55
ἐϜρετάσατυ Cypr., see Ϝρετάω
Ἑρμώνοσσα Chian = -ασσα. 46.1
ἐροτός Boeot., Thess. = ἐρατός. 5
ἐρουτᾶι Thes. 41.1a, 157b, 159
ἔρπω 'go, come.' 162.6
ἐρρηγεῖα Heracl. = ἐρρωγυῖα. 49.5, 146.3, 148
Ϝέρρω El., Locr. = ἔρρω := φεύγω. 52. 162.7
ἐρσεναίτερος El. := ἄρρην. 49.2, 80, 165.1
ἔρσην = ἄρρην. 49.2, 80
Ἔρχομενός Arc., Boeot. = Ὀρχομενός, 46.1
ἐς = ἐκ. 100 with a
ἔσγονος = ἔκγονος. 100
ἐσδέλλω Arc. = ἐκβάλλω. 49.3, 68.1, 100

ἐσδοκά 'contract' Arc., in form = ἐκδοχή (cf. 66, 100)
ἐσδοτήρ Arc., see ἐγδοτήρ
ἐσκεθῆν Arc., *ἐκσχεθεῖν 'keep out, exclude.' 65, no. 21.50, note
ἐσκηδεκάτη Boeot. = ἐκκαιδεκάτη. 114.6
ἔσκλητος Sicil., title of a select official body. 100a, no. 107.2, note
ἐσλιήνω Boeot. 162.10
ἐσλός, ἔσλος = ἐσθλός. 89.8
Ϝεσπάριος Locr. = ἑσπέριος. 21, 52d
ἐσπεράω Arc. = ἐκπεράω 'transgress' 100
ἐσπράτται Cret. = ἐκπράκται. 86.1
ἐσπρεμμίττω Cret. = ἐκπρεμνίζω. 84, 86.7
ἐς Boeot. = ἐξ. 100
ἔσσα = οὖσα. 163.8
ἐσσάμενος Arg. 144c
ἔσσομαι = ἔσομαι. 83
ἔστε 'until.' 132.12, 135.4
ἔστεισις Arc. = ἔκτεισις. 28a
ἔστελλα Lesb., Thess. = ἔστειλα. 79
ἑταιρήα Cyren. 164.1
ἔταλον Lesb., ἔτελον Coan 'yearling.' 49.3
ἐτάξαιν Thess. = ἔταξαν. 138.5
Ϝέτας El. = ἔτης 'private citizen'
Ϝέτος = ἔτος. 52. Cret. Ϝέτεθθι, 81b. Arc. dat. sg. ἔτι, 9.5
ἔτος = ἔτος. 58c
ἐττά Cret. = ἑπτά. 86.2
ἔττε Boeot. = ἔστε. 86.4
εὐάμερος, ἁ Cret. = ἑορτή
Εὐβάλκης Lac. 36
εὐεργετές Thess. = εὐεργετέων. 78, 157
εὐθυορϜία Arc. 54c
εὖιδε Lesb. := εἶδε. 35a
ϜεϜυκονομειόντων Boeot. = ᾠκονομηκότων. 146.1, 147.3
Ϝευμένας Cret. = Ϝελμένας 'assembled.' 71, 75
εὖνοα = εὔνοια. 31
εὐϜρετάσατυ Cypr., see Ϝρετάω
εὐσαβέοι El. = εὐσεβέοι. 12a
εὐσχάμενος = εὐξάμενος. 87
εὐτοῦ Thess. = ἑαυτῷ. 121.2, no. 32.16, note
Εὔτρητις Boeot. = Εὔτρησις. 61.3
εὐχωλά Arc.-Cypr. 'prayer of imprecation.' 191
ἔφαβος pseudo-dial. = ἔφηβος. 280
ἐφακέομαι Delph. 'repair.' 58c

360 THE GREEK DIALECTS

ἐφάνγρενθειν Thess. = ἐφαιροῦνται, κατηγοροῦνται. 27, 58, 139.2, 157, 162.2, no. 32.41, note
ἐφερξόντι Heracl. 'shut in' (water by damming). No. 79.130 ff., note
ἐφθορκώς Arc. = ἐφθαρκώς. 5
ἐφιορκέω = ἐπιορκέω. 58c
ἐφορευωκότων Cyren. 161.3
ἐχεπάμο̄ν Locr. 'heir.' 162.12
ἐχθός, ἔχθω, ἔχθοι = ἐκτός. 66, 133.3
ἐψαφίττατο Boeot. = ἐψηφίσατο. 82, 142
ἔωκα = εἶκα. 49.5, 146.3
Γέχω (cf. Lat. veho), Cypr., Pamph. 53

ζά Lesb. = διά. 19.1
ζᾶ Cypr. = γῆ. 62.4
ζαμιοργία El. 'the body of demiurgi.' 62.2, 167
ζαν Cypr., see no. 23.10, note
ζέλλω Arc. = βάλλω. 68.3
ζέρεθρον Arc. = βάραθρον. 68.3
Ζῆνα, Ζηνός, etc. 37.1, 112.1
ζίχαια El., see δίχαια
ζίφυιος El., see δίφυιος
Ζόννυσος Lesb. = Διόνυσος. 19.1
ζτεραῖον Arc. No. 16, note
ζώω, Boeot. δώω. 162.8

ἤ Boeot. = αἰ. 134.1
ἔ Cypr. = εἰ. 134.1
ἤ 'when, where,' etc. 132.7
ἤγραμμαι Cret. = γέγραμμαι. 137
Γῆμα Cret. = εἶμα. Gen. sg. Γήμᾶς. 112.5
ἤμεν, ἤμειν, ἤμην = εἶναι. 25, 76, 154.3-5, 163.7
ἤμην 1 sg. imperf. mid. of εἰμί. 163.9
ἠμί = εἰμί. 25, 76
ῆεμίδιμμνον Epid. = ἡμέδιμνον. 88a, 89.2
ἠμίνα Cret. 'the half.' 164.10
ῆεμιρρήνιον Delph., probably 'half-grown sheep,' i.e. such as are midway between lambs and full-grown sheep. 55a
ἤμισσον, Boeot. εἴμιττον, ῆέμιττα. 81. ἤμισον. 89.6
ἡμίτεια Epid. 61.5, 164.10
ἠμιτυέκτο̄ Cret. = ἡμιέκτου. 61.5
ἤμυσυ = ἤμισυ. 20
ἤν Ion. = ἐάν. 134.2b
ἤν = ἦσαν. 163.4
ἤναι Arc. = εἶναι. 154.1, 163.7

ἤνατος Cret., Arg. = ἔνατος. 54, 114.9
ἤνεικα, ἤνικα = ἤνεγκα. 49.1, 144a
ἤνται Mess. = ὦσι. 151.1, 163.9
Γηρόντων, Γέροντι Cret., fr. Γέρδω. 86.6
ῆς = ἤν. 163.3
ῆς Heracl. = εἰς. 114.1
ἤσσαντο Arg. 144c
ἤστω El. = ἔστω. 163.5
ἤται Delph. = ᾖ. 151.1, 163.9
ἤτω = ἔστω. 163.5
ἡὐτῶν Coan = ἑαυτῶν. 121.2
ἤχοι Orop. = ὅπου. 132.3
ἠώς Ion. = ἔως. 41.4b

θάλαθθα Cret. = θάλαττα. 81a
θάλαττα. 81. θάλλαττα. 89.4
Θαρῆς Ther. 42.2, 80
θαρρέω El. = θαρσέω, θαρρέω, but in technical sense of 'be secure, immune.' So θάρρος 'security, immunity.' 80, no. 61.1, note
Θε- Meg., etc. = Θεο-. 42.5f
θεαρός, Arc. θεαορός = θεωρός. 41.4. θεαρόντο̄ν Delph. 42.5d
θέθμιον = θέσμιον. 65, 164.4
θεθμός = θεσμός. 65, 164.4
θείκα Boeot. = διαθήκη 'will'
Θεισπιεύς Boeot. 9.4a
Θεόζοτος Boeot., Thess. = Θεόδοτος. 166.2
θεομοιρία Coan = θεοῦ μοῖρα 'the part consecrated to the god'
Θεόρδοτος Thess.=Θεόσδοτος. 60.4, 166.2
θεορός, θευρός = θεωρός. 41.4a
θέρσος = θάρσος. 49.2
θέστων Phoc. = θέσθων. 85.1
θηαυρός Arg. = θησαυρός. 59.2
θηκαῖον 'burial place' Coan (ὅρος τῶν θηκαίων)
θηλύτερος El. = θῆλυς. 165.1
θιαωρία Boeot. = θεωρία. 41.4
θιγάνα Delph. 'lid, cover' (?). Cf. Hesych. θίγωνος· κιβωτοῦ. See no. 52 C 33 ff., note
θιθέμενος Cret. = τιθέμενος. 65
θῖνος Cret. = θεῖος. 164.10
Θιοκορμίδας Lac. 60.4
Θιόππαστος Boeot. 69.4
θιός = θεός. 9. θιός Arg. 56
Θιόφειστος Boeot. 68.2
Θο- Meg., etc. = Θεο-. 42.5f
θοσία Boeot. = θυσία. 24
θράγανον Boeot., meaning? No. 39
θύρδα Arc. = θύραζε. 133.2

θύρωτον Epid. = *θύρωτρον. 70.3
θύσθεν Arc. 89.8, 133.1
θυφλός Cumae = τυφλός. 65
θύχα Cret. = τύχη. 65
θωάδδω El. (θōάδοι) 'impose a fine.' See following
θω(ι)άω 'impose a fine.' Locr. θōιέστō, Att. θōᾶν, Delph. θωεόντων. 161.2. Cf. Att. θω(ι)ά, Ion. θωιή (37.2), Delph. θωίασις

Ία Lesb., Thess., Boeot. = μία. 114.1
Ιαθθα Cret. = οὖσα. 81a, 163.8
Ιαρειάδδω Boeot. 'serve as priest.' 84
Ιαρές Cyren. = ἱερεῖς. 111.3
Ιαρήιον = ἱερεῖον. 164.1
Ιαρόμαος, official title, El. Cf. Hesych. ἱερόμας· τῶν ἱερῶν ἐπιμελούμενος.
Ιαρο(μ)μνάμονες, see ἱερομνήμων
Ιαρός, ἱαρός = ἱερός. 13.1, 58b
Ιασσα = ἰοῦσα. 163.8a
ἰjατήρ Cypr. = ἰατρός. 56, 164.5
ἴατρα, τά Epid. 'perquisites for healing.' 165.3
Ιαττα Cret. = οὖσα. 81, 163.8
ἴγγυος Arc. = ἔγγυος. 10
ἰγκεχηρήκοι Arc., 3 sg. perf. opt. from verb = Att. ἐγχειρέω. 10, 25
ἴδδιος Thess. = ἴδιος. 19.3, 58c
ἰδέ Cypr. 'then, and.' 134.6
Fίδιος, Arg. hίδιος = ἴδιος. 52b, 58c
Ιέρεως Mil. = ἱερεύς. 43, 111.5
Ιέρηα = ἱέρεια. 28b
Ιερήι(ι)ον = ἱερεῖον 37.2, 164.1
Ιερής Arc.; ἰjερές Cypr. = ἱερεύς. 111.4. Arc. dat. sg. ἱερῖ 9.5
Ιερητεύω = ἱερατεύω. 167. ἱερητεύκατι Phoc., 138.4
Ιεριτεύω, ἱαριτεύω = ἱερατεύω. 167. ἱαριτευωκότων Cyren. 161.3
Ιεροθυτέω Arc., Phoc., Rhod., etc., 'be ἱεροθύτης.' Arc. ἱεροθυτές, 78, 157
Ιεροθύτης (-ας) official title. Sometimes applied to priestly attendants, sometimes to priestly officials of high rank, who were even, in some places, the eponymous officers
Ιερομνήμων, -μνάμων title of certain superior officials, primarily in charge of religious matters, 'sacred commissioners, ministers of religion,' also delegated to the Amphictionic council. Arc. ἱιε-

ρομνάμονσι, 77.1a. Mycen., Epid. ἰαρο(μ)μνάμονες, 58b, 89.2
Ιεροποιός title of officials in charge of religious matters, sometimes regular magistrates, sometimes extraordinary commissioners
Ιερός, ἱερός. 58b
Ιερωτεύω = ἱερατεύω. 167
Ιθθάντες Cret. 82b, 162.9
Ιθύς Ion., Boeot. (also lit. Dor.) = εὐθύς. As in lit. Ion., so also inscriptional ἰθύς (Ephesus), ἴθυνα (Chios), though εὔθυνος, εὐθύνω also occur. Proper names in 'Ιθυ- are Ionic and Boeotian.
Ικάς = εἰκάς. 116. Ther. hικάδι, 58c
(F)ικαστός Boeot. = εἰκοστός. 116 with a
(F)ίκατι = εἴκοσι. 52, 61.2, 116
Fικατίδειος, ὁ Heracl., name of a particular (twenty-foot) road
Fικατίπεδος Heracl. 'twenty feet wide,' used with ἄντομος
Ικέτας Arg = ἱκέτης 58d
Ικμαμένος Cypr. 'stricken' (in battle), 'hit' Denom. from *ἱκμᾶ. Cf. ἴκταρ 'at one blow, at once,' Hesych. ἰκτέα· ἀκόντιον, Lat. īcō
Ικοστός Thess. = εἰκοστός. 116
ἴκω = Ἀth.ἥκω, in most, perhaps all, other dialects, e.g. (beside Homer and lit. Doric) Corinth. hίφομες, Delph. hίκωντι, Arc. hίκοντι
ἴλαος, ἴλεος, ἴληος (Lac. hίλεFος) = ἴλεως. 49.5, 53. Arc. ἴλαος 58d
hιλαξάστō Delph., from ἱλάσκομαι. 85.1
hίλεFος Lac., see ἴλαος
Ιμάσκω El., probably 'maltreat,' related to ἱμάς, ἱμάσσω
Ιμάτιον Att. 25e
Ιμπασις, ἴνπασις Arc. = ἔγκτησις. 10, 162.12
Ιν Arc.-Cypr. = ἐν. 10, 135.4
Fιν = οἱ dat. 3 pers. pron. 118.4.
Fιν αὐτōι Cret. = ἑαυτῷ. 121.1
Ινάγω Arc. = εἰσάγω. 10
Ιναλίνω Cypr. 'write upon.' 10. Cf. Hesych. ἀλίνειν· ἀλείφειν, and ἀλειπτήριον· γραφεῖον. Κύπριοι
Ινδικάζομαι Arc., see ἐνδικάζομαι
Ινδικος Arc., see ἔνδικος
Ινμενφής, ἴνμονφος Arc. 'blameworthy, impious.' 10
Ινπολά Arc. = ἐμπολή. 10
Ινφαίνω Arc. 'inform' in legal sense. Cf. εἰσφαίνω Ath. 75 A

ἰνφορβίω, ἰνφορβισμός Arc. No. 18, note
ἰός Cret. = ἐκεῖνος. 114.1
hϜιός = υἱός. 52c
ἰουιῶ Boeot. = υἱοῦ. 24
'Ἱππέδαμος Rhod. = 'Ἱππόδαμος. 167
ἱππότας Boeot. (as in Hom., Hdt.) = ἱππεύς
ἰράνα, etc. = εἰρήνη. 8c, 58c
ἴρεια Lesb. = ἱέρεια 'priestess.' 13.1
ἴρευς Lesb. = ἱερεύς. 13.1
ἰρητεύω Lesb. = ἱερατεύω. 13.1, 167
ἰρος Lesb., ἱρός, ἱρός Ion. = ἱερός. 13.1
ἴσαμι Dor. = οἶδα. 162.9. Subj. Cret. ἴσαντι, Cyren. ἴσᾱι. 151.1
ἰσόθι Arc. 'within the distance of.' 133.1a, no. 22.13, note
Ϝίσος, ϜίσϜος, ἴσος = ἴσος. 50b, 52, 54, 58c. Lesb. ἰσσοθέοισι, 54b
ἴσσατο, ἥσατο, ἰσσάμενος, etc. 144c
ἰστία, ἰστία = ἑστία. 11
ἰστιατόριον Rhod. = ἑστιατόριον 'banquet-hall.' Cf. Hesych. ἰστιατόρια· δειπνητήριον. 11
Ϝίστωρ Boeot. 'witness.' 52d
ἴττω Boeot. = ἴστω. 86.4
ἰών Boeot. = ἐγών. 62.3, 118.2

κα W. Grk., Boeot. = κε, ἄν. 134.2
κά = κατά. 89.7, 95
κά Arc.-Cypr. = κάς = καί. 97.2, 134.3
καδαλέομαι El. = καταδηλέομαι 'injure, violate.' καδαλέμενος, καζαλέμενος. 89.7, 158
κάδδιξ, gen. κάδδιχος, Heracl., Mess., a measure. Cf. Hesych. κάδδιχον· ἡμίεκτον, and Lac. κάδδιχος 'urn' (Plut. Lyc. 12)
καθεστάκατι Delph. 138.4
κακριθέε Arc. = κατακριθῇ. 89.7, 151.2
καλαῖς Epid. 'hen.' No. 89, note
καλείμενος = καλούμενος. 158
καλλίτερος El. = καλλίων
καλλύ[σμα]τα Ceos 'sweepings.' Cf. Hesych. σάρματα· καλλύσματα
καλϜός Boeot. = καλός. 54
κάρζα Lesb. = καρδία. 19.1
καρπόω 'offer,' especially 'a burnt offering,' in Smyrna, Thera, Athens, as often in the Septua-

gint. Cf. Hesych. καρπωθέντα· τὰ ἐπὶ βωμοῦ καθαγισθέντα. = κάρπωμα· θυσία. Coan καρπῶντι, 159
κάρρων = κρείττων. 80, 113.1
καρταῖπος, pl. καρταίποδα, Cret. 'large cattle,' in contrast to πρόβατα used of sheep and goats. Cf. καρταίπους 'bull' in Pindar.
καρτερός Ion., Cret. = κρατερός, in meaning often = κύριος 'valid.' Cf. also Ion. ἀκρατής 'invalid,' κρατεῖν 'be valid,' Cret. κάρτων q.v. 49.2a
κάρτος = κράτος. 49.2a
κάρτων Cret. = κρείττων, in meaning = κυριώτερος, as κάρτονανς ἔμεν 'shall prevail, be of greater authority.' Cf. καρτερός. 49.2a, 81, 113.1
ΚαρυκεϜίο Boeot. = Κηρυκείου. 53, 164.1
κάς Arc.-Cypr. = καί. 134.3
κασίγνητος Lesb., Cypr.; Thess. κατίγν[ειτος] 191
-κάσιοι Arc. = -κόσιοι. 116a, 117.2
κασσηρατόριν, καθθηρατόριν, καθθηρατόριον Lac. 'the hunt,' name of an athletic game. 45.6, 64, Nos. 75-78, note
κάτ = κατά. 95
καταγελάμενος Epid. 159
καταγρέω Lesb. = καθαιρέω 'convict, condemn.' 162.2
καταδουλίττασται Boeot. = -δουλίσασθαι. Cf. 82, 85.1, 142
καταϜελμένον Cret. 'assembled.' 75
καταθένς Cret. = καταθείς. 78
καταιϜεί Locr. 53
κατακείμενος Cret. 'one whose person is mortgaged' passive of κατατίθημι 'mortgage,' mid. 'take a mortgage'
κατάκλητος Heracl. 'summoned.' κατάκλητος ἁλία = Att. σύγκλητος ἐκκλησία
καταλλάσσω Arc., intrans. 'act otherwise'
καταλοβεύς Cret., Epid. = *καταλαβεύς 'support.' 49.3
καταλυμακόω Heracl. 'cover over with stones.' Cf. Hesych. λύμακες· πέτραι. -λυμακωθής, 78
κατάπερ = καθάπερ. 57a. Also for καττάπερ. 126
κάταρϜος Arc. = κατάρατος. 54

κατατίθημι Cret., Mess. = ὑποτίθη-
μι 'mortgage,' mid. 'take a mortgage'
κατέθιjαν Cypr. = κατέθεσαν. 138.
5
κατείρων Lesb. = καθιεροῦν. 13.1,
155.3
κατενθόντας, κατηνθηκότι Arc. =
κατελθόντας, κατεληλουθότι. 72,
146.1
κατέϜοργον Cypr., aor. οἱ κατείργω. 5
κατιαραίω El. (κατιαραῖον, κατιαραύσειε). 12a, 161.1, no. 61.2,
note
κατίγν[ειτος] Thess., see κασίγνητος
-κάτιοι = -κόσιοι. 61.2, 116a,
117.2
κατιστάμεν Cret. 57a
κατοικείουνθι Thess. = κατοικῶσι.
138.4, 159
κατόπερ Ion. beside κατάπερ = καθάπερ
καττάπερ = καθάπερ. 126
κατύ Arc. = κατά. 22
καυχός Cret. = χαλκός. 65, 71
κε = ἄν. 134.2
κεῖνος = ἐκεῖνος. 125.1
κεκλεβώς Mess. 66
κέλευθος Arc. 'road.' 191
κέλεξ Lac. = κέλης 142a
κέντο Dor. = κέλτο. 72
κεραίω = κεράννυμι. 229
κέρναν Lesb. = κιρνάναι. 18a, 155.
3
Κέτιον = Κίτιον. 10
κή Boeot. = καί. 26
κῆνος = ἐκεῖνος. 125.1
κέρευσις Cret. = χήρευσις 'divorce'
κεφάλωμα 164.9
Κιάριον Thess. = Κιέριον 12
κιξαλλεύω Ion. 'act as highwayman'
κιξάλλης Ion. 'highwayman.' Used
with ληιστής in no. 3 B 19, as in
Democr. fr. 260 ed. Diels. Probably of Carian or Lycian origin
κίς Thess. = τίς. 68.4, 131
κίων, ἁ Thess., often used instead
of στάλλα = στήλη
κλαικτός Argol., Mess. = κλειστός.
142a
κλάιξ Argol., Mess. = κλείς. 142a
κλᾶρος Cret. 'the body of κλαρῶται
or serfs attached to the estate'
-κλέας, personal names in. 166.1

-κλέϜες, -κλέης, -κλῆς, personal
names in. 108.1a
κλέϜος Phoc. 53
Κλευάς Thess. 35a
κλίνη Naples, Cumae 'niche in a
tomb.' No. 11
Κνωσός. 89.4b
κοθαρός = καθαρός. 6
κόθαρσις El. = κάθαρσις. 6
κοινάν, κοινανέω = κοινών, κοινω-
νέω, 41.4. κοινανόντι Arg. 42.5d
κοινάω Thess., Dor. = κοινόω.
161.5
κόμιστρα, τά Cret. 'gifts.' 165.3
κομιττάμενοι Boeot. = κομισά-
μενοι. 142
κόρϜα = κόρη. 54
κορζία Cypr. = καρδία. 5, 19.1
κόρτον Boeot. = κύρτος (?) 24, no.
39
κοσμέω (-ίω) Cret. 'be a member
of the κόσμος.' See following.
κοσμόντες, 42.5d
κόσμος Cret. 'the body of chief
magistrates' (collective; a single
member was called κοσμίων, see
preceding); also used of a single
member of this body, with pl.
κόσμοι
κότερος Ion. = πότερος. 68.4
κότος Boeot. = κύτος. 24, no. 39
κοτύλεα Coan = κοτύλη. 71b
κούρη = κόρη. 54
κραμάσαι Epid. = κρεμάσαι. 12c
κράνα = κρήνη. 8c
κράναιυν Arc. = κρήναιν. 104.10
κρατόντες Cret. = κρατοῦντες, 42.5d
κρέννω Thess. = κρίνω. 18. 74
κρέτος = κράτος. 49.2
κρίννω Lesb. = κρίνω. 74. Aor.
ἔκριννα, 77.1
κριτήρ Argol. = κριτής. 164.5
κρόμπος Arc. No. 20.9 ff., note
κτέννω Arc. = κτείνω. 74
κτοίνα Rhod., a territorial division
similar to the Attic deme. Cf.
κτίζω, κτίσις
κτοινάτας, κτοινέτας Rhod. 'member of the κτοίνα.' 167
κυεδσα, κυεεῦσα Coan, 42.5
κυκάν Epid. = κυκεών. 41.4
ϙύϜνυς Chalcid. 22d, 24a
κυμερέναι Cypr. = κυβερνᾶν. 8,8
157
κυνία Lesb. 9.2
κῦρρον Thess. = κύριον. 19.3
κωμέτας Arg. 167

κώρα Cret. = κόρη. 25, 54
κώς Ion. = πῶς. 68.4

Λᾱ- from Λᾱο-. 41.4, 45.3
λαββάνω Delph. = λαμβάνω. 69.3
λάβωισιν Chian = λάβωσιν. 77.3
λhαβών Aegin. = λαβών. 76a
λαγαίω Cret. 'release;' aor. λαγάσαι. Cf. ἀπολάγαξις, 142a
λάζομαι Meg., Boeot. (λάδδουσθη,
ὑπολάδδουνθη), Ion. λάζυμαι =
λαμβάνω
Λαππαίων Cret. 69.3
Λάρισα. 89.4b
λᾶς, Cret. gen. λᾶō. 112.4
Λασαῖος Thess. = Λαρισαῖος. 88b,
no. 32.19, note
λατραι[όμενον], λατρειόμενον El. =
λατρευόμενον 'consecrated.' 12a,
161.1
λαφυροπώλιον Arc. 'sale of booty.'
No. 19.9 ff., note
λειτορεύω Thess. = ἱερατεύω. Cf.
Hesych. λείτορες· ἱέρειαι, and
λητῆρες· ἱεροὶ στεφανοφόροι. Ἀθα-
μᾶνες. Related to Att. λειτουργέω
(39)
λείω, see λέω
λειόλης Rhod. 'accursed.' No. 101,
note
λεχχοῖ Delph., see λεχώι
λελάβηκα Arc., Ion., Epid. 137,
146.1
Λέντιχος Cyren. 42.5e
λέσχα Rhod. 'grave.' No. 101,
note
Λεσχαῖος Thess., epithet of Apollo.
No. 30, note
Λεττίναιος Thess.=Λεπτίναιος. 86.2
λεύσσω 'behold.' 191
λευτον Arc., meaning? No. 18.3
note
λεχώι Cyren., gen. sg. λεχός Cyren.,
dat. sg. λεχχοῖ Delph. 63, 111.5a.
λέω, Cret. λείω = θέλω. 162.12
-λιήνω (= -λεαίνω) Boeot. 'cancel.'
162.10
λίθιος Thess. = λίθινος. 164.6
λιμήν Thess. = ἀγορά 'market-
place' (Thess. ἀγορά = ἐκκλησία).
So also Cypr. (Hesych.) and Ion.
(GDI 5545.25)
λίνινος Boeot. = λίνεος. 164.6
λιποτελέω Locr., 'leave taxes unpaid.' Cf. λιποστρατία, etc.
λισσός Cret. 'insolvent' (?). No.
120.115, note

λοπίς Arg., some kind of shallow
vessel. Cf. λοπάς and λεπίς
Λόφριον Aetol. 5
Λύττος Cret. = Λύκτος. 86.1
λωτήριον Arg., Heracl. = λουτή-
ριον. 44.4

μά El. = μή. 15
μά Thess. = δέ. 134.4
μαίτυρες Cret., Epid. = μάρτυρες.
71a
μάν El. = μέν. 12a
μαντήα, μαντῆον Arg. 164.1
μάντοι Epid. = μέντοι. 12c
μάσλης Lesb. = μάσθλης. 89.8
μαστράα El., μαστρεία Mess. 'accounting.' Cf. Hesych. μαστρίαι·
αἱ τῶν ἀρχόντων εὔθυναι. 12a, 31
μαστρός title of an official at
Delphi, Rhodes, Pelene. Cf.
Delph. κατάμαστρος, Mess. ὑπό-
μαστρος 'subject to fine'
ματάρα Delph. = μητέρα. 12
μέδιμμνον Epid. 89.2
μέζων Arc., Ion. = μείζων. 113.1
μεθάμερα Epid. = μεθ' ἁμέραν.
Adverb formed like ὑπερκέφαλα
from ὑπέρ κεφαλάν
μεί Boeot., Thess. = μή. 16
μhειάλ[αν] Pamph. = μεγάλην.
62.3, 76a
μειννός, μεινός Thess. = μηνός.
77.1, 112.3
Μhείξιος Corcyr. 76a
μείς = μήν. 112.3
μείστον Locr. 'at least.' 113.3
μεμισθωσώνται Heracl. 146.5
Μέννει Boeot. = Μένης. 89.5.
108.2
Μενοκράτης Cret. = Μενεκράτης.
167
μέντον = μέντοι. No. 32.38, note
μερεία Heracl. = μερίς
μέρος Locr. 'real estate.' No. 57.44,
note
μές Thess. 'until.' 132.12
μεσακόθεν Arc. 65, 133.1
μεσέγγουος Boeot., adj. 'with a
third party.' Cf. μεσεγγυάω LS
μεσόμνη Att. = μεσόδμη. 87
μέσποδι Thess. 'until.' 132.12
μέσσορος Heracl. 'intermediate
boundary'
μέστα Cret., Cyren. 'until.' Arc.
μέστε. 132.12
μεταϜοικέω Locr. = μετοικέω. 53
μέτερρος Lesb. = μέτριος. 19.2

μετριώμεναι Heracl. = μετρού-
μεναι. 42.5*b*
μέττ' ές Cret. 'until.' 86.4, 132.12
μέττος Boeot., Cret. = μέσος. 82
μεύς El. = μήν. 112.3
μηδαμεῖ Delph. = μηδαμοῦ. 132.2
μηδεία Lesb. = μηδεμία. 114.1
μηδεπόθι Arc. 133.1*a*
μηθείς = μηδείς. 66
μῆννος Lesb. = μηνός. 77.1, 112.3
μής Heracl. = μήν. 112.3
μιᾶι 3 sg. aor. subj., Cyren. 144*b*,
   151.1, no. 115.40, note
μικκιχιδδόμενος Lac. 89.5*a*, nos.
   75-78, note
μικκός. 89.5*a*
Μίντων Arg. = Μίλτων. 72
Μίργος Eretr. = Μίσγος. 60.4
μιστός Cret. = μισθός. 85.1
μναμμεῖον Thess. = μνημεῖον. 89.4
Μνασσᾶ Thess. = Μνασία. 19.3
μοῖσα Lesb. = μοῦσα. 77.3
μοιχέω Cret. (μοιχίδν, etc.) = Dor.
   μοιχάω = μοιχεύω. 161.2
μοῦνος Ion. = μόνος. 54
μυχός Heracl. 'storehouse, granary'
μῶα Lac. = μοῦσα. Cf. 59.1
μωλέω Cret. (μōλέν, μωλέν, etc.)
   'contend' (in law). So also Cret.
   ἀμφιμωλέω, ἀμφίμωλος, ἀντίμω-
   λος, ἀπομωλέω, adv. ἀμωλεί. Cf.
   Hesych. μωλήσεται· μαχήσεται.
   Related to Hom. μῶλος 'contest.'
   Cf. ἀγωνίζομαι as a law-term in
   Attic
μῶσα = μοῦσα. 77.3

ναεύω Cret. 'take refuge in a temple'
νακόρος, see νεωκόρος
να(F)ός = νεώς. 41.4, 53, 54*d*
ναποῖαι, see νεωποίης
ναῦος Lesb. = νεώς. 35, 54*d*
ναῦσσον name of a tax, Coan, also
   (spelled with T) at Cyzicus
νεί Arc. = νή, ναί. 134.7
νεμονηία Cret. = νεομηνία. 89
νεότας Cret. 'an official body of
   young men,' gen. νεότας, acc.
   νεότα. 88*a*
νεωκόρος Ion., Delph. ναοκόρος,
   Delph., Epid., Coan νακόρος (41.4
   45.3), custodian of the temple,
   sacristan.' In some places the
   office became one of considerable
   rank and honor

νεωποίης Ion., Coan ναποῖαι. 31.
   41.4. Cf. also Ion. νεωποιός,
   Boeot. ναποιός. Title of officials
   in general charge of the affairs
   of the temple
νήατος Arc. = νέατος. No. 20.10 ff.,
   note
νικάηας, νικάαρ Lac. = νικάσας.
   59.1, 60.2
νίν = ἔ. 118.5
νιουμεινία, νιουμείνιος, νιυμείνιος Boeot.
   = νουμηνία, νουμήνιος. 42.5*a*
νόμαιος Ion. = νόμιμος. 164.10
νόμιος Locr. = νόμιμος. 164.10
νόμος Heracl., a coin. Cf. Lat.
   nummus
νοσσιά, etc. 42.5*f*
νοστίττω El. = *νοστίζω, νοστέω.
   84
νυ Cypr., Boeot. 134.5
νύναμαι Cret. = δύναμαι. 88
νυττί Cret. = νυκτί. 86.1

ξεῖνος, ξῆνος, ξένϜος = ξένος. 54
ξέννος Lesb. = ξένος. 54*b*
ξενοδίκαι Locr., Phoc., title of
   judges in cases involving the
   rights of ξένοι. ξενοδίκης is used
   by a late writer to translate the
   Latin *praetor peregrinus*
ξύλεα Coan = ξύλα. 71*b*
ξύλλεσθαι Arg., in form = σκύλλεσθαι (87), but meaning 'pillage'
   (cf. σκῦλον)
ξύν = σύν. 135.7
ξῦνός Ion. = κοινός. 135.7

ὁ = ὁ. 58*a*
Ὄαξος = Ϝάξος. 51*a*
ὀβελλός Boeot., ὀβελλός Thess. =
   ὀβολός. 49.3, 68.1, 89.4
ὀγδοίης, ὀγδοιήκοντα. 31*a*
ὄγδοος, ὄγδοϜος. 114.8
ὀγδῶι Ion. = ὀγδόη. 44.2
ὀγδώκοντα Ion. = ὀγδοήκοντα. 44.2
ὀδελός = ὀβολός. 49.3, 68.1
ὀείγω Lesb. = οἴγω. 49.1
ὄζος Cret. = ὅσος. 82
ὀθθάκιν Cret. = ὁσάκις. 81*a*, 133.6
ὄθι Arc. 132.1*a*
ὄθμα Lesb. = ὄμμα. 164.4
Ϝοι = οἱ dat. 3 pers. pron. 118.4
Ϝοικιάτας = οἰκέτης. 167
οἰκείη Arg. 157*c*
Ϝοικεύς Cret. = οἰκέτης. 167
οἰκιστήρ = -τής. Cyren. 164.5
Ϝοῖκος = οἶκος. 52

Ϝοίκω Delph. = οἴκοθεν. 132.8
Ϝοῖνος = οἶνος. 52
οἰϜος Cypr. = οἶος 'alone.' 53. 191
οἰρών Cypr. (ἰν τὸιρῶνι) 'district.'
Cf. οἰρῶν 'boundary line,' Hesych.
οἰς Delph. = οἶ. 132.3
hοισόντι Heracl. = οἴσοντι. 58d
οἴϝω Cret. (οἴπεν, οἴπει), Ther.
(οἴπηε, etc.), Lac. (Hesych.)
'have sexual intercourse'
ὅκα, also ὅκκα = ὅτε. 132.11
ὀκοῖος Ion. = ὀποῖος. 68.4
hοκτακάτιοι Heracl. = ὀκτακόσιοι.
58c, 117.2
ὀκτάκιν Lac. = ὀκτάκις. 133.6
ὀκτό Lesb. = ὀκτώ. 114.8
ὀκττώ Ephes. 89.1
hοκτώ Heracl. = ὀκτώ. 58c, 114.8
ὀκτωκόσιοι Lesb. = ὀκτακόσιοι,
117.2
ὄλετρος Cret. = ὄλεθρος. 63
ὀλίος = ὀλίγος. 62.3
Ὀλυππίχην = Ὀλυμπίχην. 69.3
ὀμιώμεθα Lac. 42.5b
ὀμολογά, ἀ, ὀμόλογον, τό Boeot. =
ὀμολογία
ὀμονόεντες Lesb. = ὀμονοοῦντες.
44.4, 157
ὀν Lesb., Thess., Cypr. = ἀνά. 6
ὀνάλα, ὀνάλουμα Thess. = ἀνάλωμα.
164.10
ὀνγράψειν Thess. = ἀναγράψαι. 27,
156
ὄνδικος Arc. = ἀνάδικος. 6
ὄνε Thess. = ὅδε. 123
ὀνεθείκαεν Thess. = ἀνέθηκαν. 138.5
ὀνί Arc. = ὅδε. 123
ὄνιουμα Boeot. = ὄνομα. 22c, 24
ὄννα Lesb. = ὠνή. 25f
ὄννιθα Cret. = ὄρνιθα. 86.5
ὄνυ Arc.-Cypr. = ὅδε. 123
ὄνυμα = ὄνομα. 22c
ὅπαι. 132.5
ὅπει. 132.2
ὀπειδεί Thess. = ἐπειδή. 132.7
ὀπέρ Boeot., Arc. = ὑπέρ. 24
ὅπη. 132.7
ὅπι Cypr. No. 23.29, note
ὀπιδδόμενος Lac. = ὀπιζόμενος. 84
Ὀπόεντι, Ὀποντίους, Ηοποντίον
Locr. = Ὀποῦντι, Ὀπουντίους,
etc. 44.4, 58d
ὀπόθι Arc. 133.1a
ὀπόταρος El. = ὀπότερος. 12
ὀπόττος Boeot., ὀπόττος Cret. =
ὀπόσος. 82

ὄππα Lesb. 129.2, 132.6
ὄππα Lesb. = ὄμμα. 164.4
ὄππως Lesb. 129.2
ὀπτίλος Dor. = ὀφθαλμός. Occurs
in Epidaurian (-ίλος and -ίλλος,
no. 90 passim), as Laconian in
Plut. Lyc. 11, and in the writings
of Archytas and Phintias. ὀπ-τ-
ίλος (cf. ὀπ-τήρ etc.) like ναυ-τ-
ίλος beside ναύ-της
ὀπτό El. = ὀκτώ. 114.8
ὀπύ Arc. = ὑπό. 22, 24
ὄπυι. 132.4
ὄπυς Rhod. 132.4
ὄπω Dor. (Cret. ὄπō, Lac. hόπō) =
ὁπόθεν. 132.8
ὄπωρ Eretr., ὄπωρ El. = ὅπως.
60.1, 3, 97a
ὄρβος Corcyr. = ὅρος. 51
ὄρεγμα, measure of length, Heracl.
ὀρκίζω = ὀρκόω. 161.4
ὀρκιότερος Cret. 'having preference
in the oath'
hορκōμόται Locr., Arc. 'jurors'
ὄρνιξ = ὄρνις. 142a
ὄρϜος Corcyr., ὅρος Heracl., ὦρος
Arg. = ὅρος. 54, 58c
ὄροφος 'house' Cyren. No. 115.16,
note
ὀρτή Ion. = ἑορτή. 42.5f
ὀρύξε Cypr., see ἐξορύξε
ὀρφανοδικασταί Cret. (ὀρπανοδικα-
σταί) 'officers appointed to look
after the affairs of orphans or
minors.' Cf. Att. ὀρφανοφύλακες
Ϝός Cret. = ὅς. 120.3, 121.1
ὀσέοι Arc. = ὅτεῳ. 68.3, 128,
129.2
ὅσια Arc., Locr. = ὅσια. 58e
ὀστροφά Thess. = ἀναστροφή. 77.2,
no. 33.20, note
ὅτα Lesb. = ὅτε. 13.3, 132.11
ὀτεῖος Cret. = ὀποῖος, ὅστις. 68.1,
130
ὄτερος Cret. = ὀπότερος. 127
Ϝότι Locr., error for hότι. 129.2a
ὅτιμι Cret. = ὅτινι. 128, 129.2
ὄττις, etc. Lesb. = ὅτις, etc. 129.2
ὄττος Cret. = ὅσος. 82
οὐδές Lac. = οὐδείς. 114.1
οὐθαμεῖ Epid. = οὐδαμοῦ. 132.2
οὐθείς = οὐδείς. 66
οὖλος Ion. = ὅλος. 54
οὐρεῖον, ὠρεῖον Cret. 'guard-
house.' From οὖρος 'watcher,'
like Att. φρούριον from φρουρός
οὐρεύω Cret. 'watch'

 οὖρος Ion. = ὅρος. 54
οὖτο, οὖτα, etc., Boeot. = τοῦτο, ταῦτα, etc. 124
ὀφέλλω Arc., Hom. = ὀφείλω. 73a
ὀφήλω Arc., Arg., Cret. = ὀφείλω. 75; aorist and perfect, Att. ὦφλον, ὤφληκα 'be condemned to pay a fine, be adjudged guilty.' So Arc. aor. infin. ὀφλέν, perf. [Ϝō]φλέασι, Ϝōφλēκόσι. 52a, 138.4, 146.1
ὀφέλōμα Cret. = ὀφείλημα. 167
ὀφρύς Arg. 'ramp.' No. 87.14, note

παῖ, παι 132.5
παιδιχός Lac. = παιδικός. 164.9
παιρίν Eretr. = παισίν. 60.3
παῖς = υἱός, or, sometimes, θυγάτηρ. Lesb., Boeot., Cypr., Locr., Ion. Cf. παῖς, κόρα 'son, daughter' in no. 59.4
παῖσα Cyren. = πᾶσα. 77.3
πᾶμα = κτῆμα. 162.12
παματοφαγεῖσται 'be confiscated' Locr. 162.12
παμωχέω Heracl. 'possess.' Cf. Hesych. παμῶχος· ὁ κύριος. 'Ιταλοί, and παμωχίων· κεκτημένος. 162.12
παναγορία Arc. = πανήγυρις. 164.10
Παναγόρσιος Arc., name of a month
πανάγορσις Arc. = πανήγυρις. 5, 49.2, 80a
πανάζωστοι Cret. No. 120.11, note
Πάναμμος Thess. = Πάνημος, name of a month
πάνσα Arc., Arg., Cret., Thess. = πᾶσα. 77.3
παντᾶι Heracl., Lesb. πάνται. 132.5
παντεῖ Locr. 132.2
πανῶνιος Cypr. 'wholly salable.' No. 23.10, note
πάομαι = κτάομαι. 162.12
Πάονι Arc. 41.4
πάρ El. = περί. 12, 95
πάρ = παρά. 95
παρά with acc. for dat. 136.2
παραμαξεύω Arc. 'drive in a wagon off (the highroad).' Cf. ἐπαμαξεύω, καθαμαξεύω. No. 18.23, note
παραπροστάτας Agrig. 'an adjunct προστάτας' or presiding officer of the council. Cf. παραπρυτάνεις in Teos
παρβάλλω Delph. = παραβαίνω 'transgress'

παρβεῶντας Cyren. 42.5b, 161.2
πάρδειχμα Epid. = παράδειγμα. 66
παρεῖαν Boeot. = παρῆσαν. 138.5
παρεῖς Boeot. = παρῆν. 163.3
παρετάζω Arc. 'examine into' (cf. ἐξετάζω) and so 'approve.' παρετάξωνσι (no. 19.28), 142. παρ-ͱεταξαμένος (no. 18.20), 173
παρῖς Boeot. = παρῆν. 16a
παρκαθέκα Lac. = παρακαταθήκη
ΠασιάδαϜο Gela. 105.2a
πάσκω El. = πάσχω. 66
πασσυδιάζω Lesb. 'assemble'. 96.2
πασσυδίηι Ion. = πανσυδίηι. 96.2
πάστας Cret. 'owner.' 162.12
παστάς = παραστάς. 89.8
πατάρα Locr. = πατέρα. 12
πάτρα Arc., Dor. = γένος 'gens.' Ion. πάτρη also, rarely, in this sense
πατριά Delph., El. = γένος 'gens,' as in Hdt. 1.200
πατροῖōκος Cret. = ἐπίκληρος 'heiress.' 117.VII.15 ff., note
πέ Arc. = πεδά, μετά. 95, 135.5
πεδά = μετά. 135.5
Πεδαγείτνιος = Μετα-. 135.5
πεδάϜοικοι Arg. = μέτοικοι. 53, 135.5
πεδίjα Cypr. = πεδίον
πεῖ, πει = ποῦ, που. 132.2
Πειλεστροτίδας Boeot. 68.2
πεῖσαι Thess. = τεῖσαι. 68.2
πείσει Cypr. = τείσει. 68.2b
πελανός. No. 7.A.25 ff., note
πέλεθρον = πλέθρον. 48
πέλεκυ Cypr., used of a sum of money equal to 10 minae. No. 23.15, note
πελτοφόρας Boeot. = πελταστής
πέμπε Lesb., Thess. = πέντε. 68.2, 114.5
πέμποτος Arc. = πέμπτος. 114.5
πενταͱετηρίς Heracl. = πενταετηρίς. 58c
πενταμαριτεύω Delph. 12. no. 52 D 16, note
πεντάμεροι, title of officials, Locr. (Halae). See preceding
πεντηκόντων Chian = gen. pl. of πεντήκοντα. 116
πεντορκία Locr. 'quintuple oath, oath sworn by five gods.' 58d
πέντος Cret., Amorg. = πέμπτος. 86.2, 114.5
πεπείστειν Thess. = πεπεῖσθαι. 85.1, 156

πεπεμμένος Troez. **86**.8, no. **88**.13, note

πεποιόντεισσι Boeot. = πεποιηκόσι. **9**.4*a*, **146**.1

περ = περί. **91***a*

περαιόω Cret. 'set aside, repudiate' (the purchase of a slave). No. 117.VII.10, note

πέρανδε Arc. 'abroad'

περιβολιβόω Rhod. 'fasten round with lead.' **88**

περίδρομοι, officials at Mytilene 'clerks of the court'

περίσαος 'left over, remaining.' No. **42**.22

περιωρεσία Sicil. Dor. **18***b*

Περ9οθαρίαι Locr. **6**, **95**

πέροδος Delph. = περίοδος. Cf. **95**

Πέρραμος Lesb. = Πρίαμος. **19**.2

περτ' Pamph. = πρός. **135**.6

πέσσυρες Lesb. = τέτταρες. **68**.2, **114**.4

πεστάντες Thess. = περιστάντες. **89**.8

Πεταγείτνιος = Μετα-. **135**.5

πέτευρον Orop., Delos, πετεύριον Erythrae 'notice-board.' **135**.5*a*

Πετθαλός Thess. = Θεσσαλός. **65**, **68**.2, **81***c*

πετράμεινον Boeot. = τετράμηνον. **68**.2

πέτρατος Boeot. = τέταρτος. **49**.2*a*, **68**.2, **114**.4

πετροετηρίς Thess. = τετρα-. **5**, **68**.2

πέτταρες, πετταράκοντα Boeot. = τέτταρες, τετταράκοκτα. **68**.2, **114**.4, **116**

πέττρινος Arg. **89**.2

πεύθω Cret. **162**.15

πεφειράκοντες Thess. = τεθηρακότες. **68**.2, **147**.3

πεφυτευκῆμεν Heracl. **147**.2

πήλυι Lesb. = τῆλε. **68**.2, **132**.4

πέποκα Lac. = πώποτε. **132**.7, 11

πίσυρες Hom. = τέτταρες. **11**, **68**.2, **114**.4

πιτεύω 'irrigate,' ἀπίτευτα 'un-irrigated.' Boeot.

πλάγος Heracl. 'side'

πλαθύοντα El. = πληθύοντα. **15**

πλάν Dor., etc. = πλήν

πλέες Lesb. = πλέονες. **113**.2

πλευριάς, -άδος Heracl. = πλευρά

πλέθα, ἁ Locr.; Boeot. πλείθα 'assembly'

πλῆθος (1) 'amount,' (2) 'majority.' (3) frequently 'people, assembly.' Arc. dat. sg. πλήθι **9**.5

πληθύς = πλῆθος, as in Homer. Cret. 'the amount,' Locr. 'the majority'

πλίες Cret. = πλέες = πλέονες. **9**.4, **42**.7, **113**.2

πλίυι Cret. = πλέον. **113**.2, **132**.4

πλός Arc. = πλέον. **42**.5*g*, **113**.2

πλουτίνδαν Locr. **133**.7

ποεῖ, ποήσω, etc. = ποιεῖ, etc. **31**

πόεστι Arc. = πρόσεστι. **59**.4*a*

ποεχόμενον Cypr. = προσεχόμενον 'adjacent to.' Cf. προσεχής. **59**.4

πόθικες Lac. = προσήκοντες. For stem πόθικ- to ποθίκω, cf. προίξ, προικός

ποθίκω Boeot. = προσήκω. Cf. ἵκω

πόθοδος = πρόσοδος. Cf. ποτί = πρός

ποθόδωμα Boeot., Epir. = πρόσοδος. **164**.10

ποί = πρός. **135**.6

ποιγραψάνσθō Arg. **77**.2, **135**.6. **140**.3*b*

ποιεῖνται, ποιείμενος. **158**

ποιενσι Arc. = ποιοῦσι. **77**.3, **157**

ποιϜέω = ποιέω. **53**; Argol. ποιϜέσανς. **78**.3

ποιήασσαι El. = ποιήσασθαι. **59**.3, **85**.2

ποιήαται El. = ποιήσηται. **59**.3, **151**.1

ποικεφάλαιον Delph. = προσκεφάλαιον. **135**.6

ποιὸν, ποιόντος, ποιόντων, etc. **42**.5*d*

Ποίτιος Cret. = Πύθιος. **30***a*

πόκα = πότε. **132**.11

πὸκ κί Thess. = ὅτι. **68**.4, **131**

πόλερ El. = πόλις. **18***b*

πολιανόμοι Heracl., title of municipal magistrates in charge of public buildings, streets, etc., like Roman aediles. Called ἀστυνόμοι at Athens, Rhodes, etc.

πολιάτας Dor. = πολίτης. **167**

πολιᾶχος Lac. = πολιοῦχος. **167**

πόλις = δῆμος. Especially frequent in decrees of Phocis, Locris, Thessaly, and other parts of Northwest Greece, and notably in Crete, where it is almost constant

πόλῑς Lesb. nom. pl. **109**.3

πόλιστος Heracl. = πλεῖστος. **113**.2, ἡως πολίστων = ὡς πλείστων

πολιτήα = πολιτεία. 28*b*
πόλλιος Thess. = πόλιος (πόλεως). 19.3
Ποhοιδάν, Ποhοίδαια Lac. = Ποσειδῶν, Ποσειδώνια. 41.4, 49.1, 59.1, 61.5
ποππάν Cret. = πομπήν. 69.3
πορθιέα Arc. 'passage, path' (?). No. 20.9, note
πόρνοψ Boeot., Lesb. = πάρνοψ. 5
πορτί Cret. = πρός. 70.1, 135.6
πός Arc.-Cypr. = πρός. 135.6 with *a*
Ποσειδάν, Ποσοιδᾶν, Ποhοιδάν, ΠοτΕδάϜōνι, Ποτειδάν, etc. 41.4, 49.1, 59.1, 61.4
πότ = ποτί, πρός. 95
ποταποπισάτω Boeot. = προσαποτεισάτω. 68.2
ΠοτΕδά(Ϝ)ōν, Ποτειδάν, see Ποσειδάν
ποτελάτō Arg. 'enforce.' 159
ποτεχεῖ Heracl., ποτεχές Ach. = προσεχῶς. 132.2
ποτί = πρός. 61.4, 135.6
ποτικλαίγω Heracl. 'be close to, adjacent to.' 142*a*
ποτιπίαμμα Cyren. 86.8, 164.4
ποτισκάπτω Heracl. = *προσσκάπτω 'dig up to, heap earth upon'
ππάματα Boeot. = κτήματα 69.4, 162.12
πράδδω Cret. = πράττω. 84*a*
πρασσόντασσι Heracl. 107.3
πράτιστος. 114.1
πρατοπάμπαις Lac. Nos. 75-78, note
πρᾶτος W. Grk., Boeot. = πρῶτος. 114.1
πρείγα Locr. = γερουσία. 86.3
πρείγυς, πρειγευτάς, πρεγγευτάς, πρείγων, πρείγιστος Cret. = πρέσβυς, etc. 68.1, 86.3 with *a*
πρεισβεία Thess. = πρεσβεία. 86.3
πρεσγέα, πρεσβήα Arg. 86.3, 164.1
πρήγιστος Cret., πρηγιστεύω Coan. 86.3*a*
πρήξοισιν Chian = πρήξωσιν. 77.3, 150
πρήσσω Ion. = πράττω. Cf. 8, 81
πρήττω Eub. = πράττω. 81
πρῆχμα Chian = πρῆγμα, πρᾶγμα. 66
πρισγεῖες Boeot. = πρέσβεις. 68.1, 86.3
πριῶι, πριωσεῖ Heracl. 159*a*, 161.3

προαγορέω Agrig. 'be προάγορος, presiding officer of the ἁλία'
προαγρημμένω Lesb. = προαιρουμένου. 89.4, 157*a*, 162.2
προάνγρεσις Thess. = προαίρεσις. 162.2
πρόβατα 'sheep' in Attic, but 'cattle' in a wide sense, domestic quadrupeds, large (kine), or small (sheep and goats), in Ionic and in Arcadian (no. 18. 14 ff.); in Cretan, used of small cattle in contrast to καρταίποδα (no. 117.IV.36)
προβειπάhας Lac. = προειπάσας. 51, 59.1
πρόθθα Cret. = πρόσθεν. 133.1
προξεννιοῦν Thess. = προξενιῶν. 19.3, 41.4*c*
πρόξενϜος Corcyr., πρόξηνος Cret. = πρόξενος. 54
πρόσθα Dor. = πρόσθεν. 133.1
προσθαγενής Arc. (προσσθαγενές). No. 17.33 ff., note
προσθίδιος El. (προστιζίōν). 165.2
προσμέτρεις Lesb. = προσμετρέων. 157
προσπερμεία 'sprinkling with seed' Coan
πρόστα Delph., πρόστεν Thess. = πρόσθεν. 85.1, 133.1
προστάτης. (1) As at Athens, one who looks after the rights of aliens. So in no. 57.34. (2) The chief magistrate of a city or state. (3) προστάται = Att. πρυτάνεις. So in Cos, Calymna, Cnidus, etc.
[προστί]θησ[θον] Lesb. = προστιθέσθων. 157*a*
προσφάγιον Ceos = πρόσφαγμα 'sacrifice'
πρότανις Lesb. (rarely Att.) = πρύτανις. The more usual prefix προ- replaces here the related but uncommon πρυ-.
προτεράσιος 'of the previous time.' Delph.
προτερεία Heracl. = προτεραία 'the day before.' 46.2
προτηνί Boeot. 'formerly.' 123, 136.1
προτί = πρός. 135.6
πρυτανήιον = πρυτανεῖον. 164.1
πρωγγυεύω Heracl. 'be surety'
πρώγγυος Heracl. 44.4
πτόλεμος = πόλεμος. 67

370 THE GREEK DIALECTS

πτόλις Cypr., etc. = πόλις. 67
Πύρϝος, ΠυρϝΙας, ΠυρϝαλΙōν 54e
πῦς Dor. = ποῖ. 132.4
Πύτιος = Πύθιος. 66
πῶ Dor., etc. 132.8

Ϝρῆσις Arc. 'declaration.' 55
ῥήτρα, El. Ϝρᾱτρα, Cypr. Ϝρέτα, originally 'saying'. (Cf. ῥήτκρ, etc.) but in various dialects also used of a 'formal agreement, compact, decree, law.' Cf. Heracl. κὰτ τὰς ῥήτρας καὶ κὰτ τὰν συνθήκαν 'according to the laws and the compact,' Photius ῥῆτραι· Ταραντῖνοι δὲ νόμους καὶ οἷον ψηφίσματα, and LS s.v. II. So El. Ϝρᾱτρα 'law, covenant' Cypr. Ϝρέτα 'compact,' Ϝρετάω 'promise.' 15, 55, 70.3
ῥηχμός Arg. = ῥηγμός. 66
phoϝαῖσι Corcyr. 53, 76a
ῥογός Heracl. 'granary.' Cf. Hesych. ῥογοί· σιροὶ σιτικοί, σιτοβολῶνες, and Pollux 9.45 σιτοβόλια· ταῦτα δὲ ῥογοὺς Σικελιῶται ὠνόμαζον
ῥόϝος Cypr. 53
ῥόπτον Epid. = ῥόπτρον. 70.3
ῥύτιον, ῥυτιάζω Argol. = ῥύσιον, ῥυσιάζω. 61.3

σά Meg. = τίνα. 128
σαδράπας = σατράπης. Still other variations in the transcription of the Persian word (χšaθ'apāvā) are seen in ἐξαιθραπεύοντος, ἐξσατραπεύοντος, ἐξατράπης
Σακρέτης, etc. 41.2
Σαλαμōνα El. = Σαλμώνη. 48
σαρμεύω Heracl. No. 79.136, note
Σαυγένεις, Σαυκράτεις Boeot. 41.2
σελάνα Dor. etc., σελάννα Lesb. = σελήνη. 76
Σελινόεντι, Σελινόντιοι. 44.4
σιός Lac. =θεός. 64 σίν=θεόν 42.5g
σις Cypr., σις Arc. = τις. 68.3, 128
σιταγέρται Heracl. 'receivers and inspectors of grain.' So ἀγέρται οἱ ἀπό σιτωνίας at Tauromenium, σιτοφύλακες at Athens, Tauromenium, etc., σιτῶναι at Athens, Delos, etc.
σίτηριν Eretr. = σίτησιν. 60.3
σκευᾱōν El. = σκευέων. 12a
-σκευω- Meg., Cret. ἐπεσκεύωσαν, etc. 161.3

σκόφος Boeot. = σκύφος. 24
σπάδιον Arg. = στάδιον. 88
σπέλλω Lesb., Thess. σπόλος. 68.2a
σποϝδδάν Cret. = σπουδήν. 32, 89.4
σπυρός Coan, Epid., Syrac., Ther., Cyren. = πυρός
στάλα Dor., etc.; στάλλα Lesb., Thess. = στήλη. 75
σταρέστω Delph., fr. aor. of στέρομαι. 49.2
σταρτός Cret., a subdivision of the tribe. 49.2a
στέγα Cret. 'house.' No. 117.III. 46, note
στέγασσις Epid. 164.3
στέπτω Coan = στέφω. 66
στεφανίζω = -όω. 161.4
στεφάνοι Lesb. 157b
στεφανῶι. 159a
στεφών Ion. 'ridge.' 165.4
στοίχεις Lesb. = στοιχέων. 78, 157
στονόϝεσαν Corcyr. 164.2
στορπά, στορπάος Arc. = ἀστραπή. ἀστραπαῖος. 5, 31
στραταγός (Lesb. στρότ-), title of the chief magistrate of the Achaean and Aetolian Leagues, also at times of others, as the Arcadians, Thessalians, Phocians etc.; also of local magistrates in Mytilene (no. 26), Eresus, Tegea (no. 19), etc; under Macedonian rule = provincial 'governor', in Roman times 'prefect' (no. 107).
στρατήα Arg. 164.1
στρότος, στρόταγος=στρατός, etc. 5
στροφά Delph. 'turn of the road.' No. 52 C 33 f.
στυμέον Arc. 22b
σύββολον Delph. = σύμβολον. 69.3
σύγγραφος, ἁ Arc., Boeot., Mess., σύγγροφος (49.2) Delph., Argol. = συγγραφή 'contract'
συγχέαι Ion. 144
συκία Lesb. 9.2
συλαίē El. 157c
συμβόλικτρον ἁ Arc. No. 20.26, note
συμπιπίσκω Delph. 'invite to drink together'
συναρτύω Arg. 'belong to the body of ἀρτύναι.' No. 84.2, note
συναρχοστατέω Phoc. 'join in appointing magistrates'

συνδαυχναφόροι Thess. 'fellow δαφνηφόροι.' See δαύχνα
συνhερξόντι Heracl. 'enclose, cut
off' (the roads). No. 79.130 ff.,
note
συνεσσάδδω Cret. = συν-εκ-σάττω
'assist in carrying off.' Cf. χρήματα ἐκσκευάζειν Strabo. 84a
συνκλείς, -εῖτος Thess. = σύγκλητος ἐκκλησία. 164.10
σφάδδω Boeot., σφάζω Ion. =
σφάττω. 84a
σφεις Arc. = σφίσι. 119.4
σφηνόπους Ceos 'having wedge-
shaped feet'
σφυχή = ψυχή. 87
σῶς, σω-, Σω-. 41.2

ταγά Thess. 'time when there is a
ταγός,' hence 'time of war.' No.
35, note
ταγεύω Delph., Thess. 'hold the
office of ταγός'
ταγός official title, Cypr., Delph.,
Thess. In Thessaly applied to
(1) a military leader of the united
Thessalians appointed only in
time of war (cf. no. 35, note),
(2) city officials like the ἄρχοντες
of many places (nos. 32-34). At
Delphi, officials of the phratry
of the Labyadae (no. 52)
ταί = αἱ. 122
ταῖ El. = τάδε. 122
ταιννί, ταῖννυ Arc. = ταῖσδε. 97.1,
123
ταῖς Lesb., El. = τός. 78
τάμνω = τέμνω. 49.4
τᾶμον Thess. 'of the present time.'
Cf. Hom. τῆμος 'then.'
τάνε Thess. = τάδε. 123
τανί Boeot. = τήνδε. 122
ταννί, τανί Arc. = τῆσδε, τῶνδε,
τάσδε. 97.1, 123
τάνυ Arc. = τάδε. 123
ταοτα East Ion. = ταῦτα. 33
ταυτᾶ Lac. 132.6
ταὐτᾶ Locr. 'likewise.' 132.6
ταῦται = αὖται. 124
ταυτέ El. 132.7
ταύτων El. = τούτων. 124
τε͞δε. 132.7
τεθμός τετθμός, τέθμιος = θεσμός,
θέσμιος. 164.4
τεῖδε. 132.2
τειμά, τειμή = τιμή. 21
τείω Arc., see τίνω

τέκνα Locr. = τέχνη. 66
τελαμό͞ Arg. 'support.' 89.9, no.
82, note
τέλειος, τέλεος (1) 'perfect, unblemished,' (2) frequently = κύριος 'valid' (examples in Arg.,
Delph., Locr., Aetol., El., Ach.),
ἀγορά (ἀλιαία, etc.) τέλειος = Att.
ἐκκλησία κυρία
τελεστά El. 'official.' Cf. τέλος 'office.' 105.1a
τελεστήρ Argol. 'priest.' 164.5
τέλεστρα, τά Ion., Coan 'expenses
of inauguration.' 165.3
τελεσφορέντες Cyren. 42.5e
τέλεως Coan = τέλειος. 43, 276
τέλλω Arg., Cret. (as also in poetry) = τελέω
τέλομαι Cret. = ἔσομαι. No. 120.
46, 63, 69/70
τένται Cyren. = τέλεται = ἔσεται.
72
τέος Dor. = σοῦ. 118.3
τεός Dor., Lesb., τιός Boeot. =
σός. 120.2
τέουτος Lesb. = τοιοῦτος. 130
τέρτος Lesb. = τρίτος. 18a
τέρχνιϳα (or τρέχνιϳα) Cypr.
'shrubs, trees.' Cf. Hesych.
τέρχνεα· φυτὰ νέα and τρέχνος·
στέλεχος, κλάδος, φυτόν, βλάστημα
τέσσαρες, τέσσερες. 81, 114.4
τεσσερακόντων Chian, gen. pl. of
τεσσεράκοντα. 116
τεταρτεύς Coan, a measure, like
ἑκτεύς
τέταρτος, τέτρατος. 49.2a, 114.4
τετθμός, see τεθμός
τετίμο͞νται El. 161.3
τέτορες W. Grk. = τέτταρες. 54e,
114.4. Acc. pl., 107.4
τέτορτος Arc. = τέταρτος. 5, 114.4
τετράκιν Lac. = τετράκις. 133.6
τετράϳοντα, τετρώκοντα = τετταράκοντα. 116
τέτρωρον Heracl. 'group of four
boundary stones.' 41.2
τε͞δε. 132.7
Τήιοι Ion. 37.2
Τῆνα, Ττῆνα Cret. = Ζῆνα. 84,
112.1
τηνεῖ 125.1, 132.2
τῆνος = ἐκεῖνος. 125.1
τίθηντι Mess. = τιθῶσι. 151.1
τίμαι Lesb. 41.1a, 157b, 159
Τιμακλῆς, Τιμακράτης, Τιμάναξ =
Τιμοκλῆς, etc. 167

τιμασία Arc. = τίμησις. 164.10
τιματήρ Cyren. = -τής. 164.5
τιμόστον El. 140.4b, 161.3
τίν Dor. = σοί. 118.4
τίνω, fut. τείσω, aor. ἔτεισα (not
τίσω, ἔτῖσα), in Attic and elsewhere, 28a. πείσω, ἔπεισα, 68.1, 2.
Arc. new present τείω in ἀπυτειέ-
τω (no. 19.43)
τιούχα Boeot. = τύχη. 24
τιρ El. = τις. 60.1
τίτας 'magistrate who collects
fines,' τᾶς τιτύϝος 'fine,' τιτου-
έσθō (33a) 'impose a fine.' Cret.
τίωι, etc. Lesb. 9.2
ΤλασίαϝΟ Corcyr. 105.2a
τνατός Cret. = θνητός. 66
τόζ' Rhod. = τόδε. 62.2
τοί = οἱ. 122
τοῖ El. = τόδε. 122
τοιί Boeot. = οἴδε. 122
τοίνεος Thess. = τοῦδε. 123
τόχα = τότε. 132.11
τόκιος or τόκιον Delph. = τόκος
'interest'
τομάς Arc. = τόμος, τομή 'section
of land'
τόνε Thess. = τόδε. 123
τōτο = τοῦτο. 34a
τού Boeot. = σύ. 61.5
τοῦννεουν Thess. = τῶνδε. 123
τοῦτα, τούτας, τούτēι = ταῦτα, etc.
124
τουτεῖ. 132.2
τοῦτοι = οὗτοι. 124
τουτώ. 132.8
τοφιών Heracl. = ταφεών 'burial-
place.' 6, 165.4
τρακάδι Thess. = τριακάδι. 19.4
τράφη Amorg. = τάφρη. 70.2
τράφος Heracl. = τάφρος. 70.2
τρέες Cret. = τρεῖς. 42.3
τρέπεδδα Boeot. = τράπεζα. 18,
84
τρέω Arg. = φεύγω in legal sense.
No. 84.5
τρῆς Ther. = τρεῖς. 25, 114.3
τριάκοιστος Lesb. = τριακοστός.
116 with a
τριακοντάπεδος (sc. ὁδός) Heracl.
'a road thirty feet wide'
τριηκόσιοι Ion. 117.2
τρίινς Cret. 114.3
τρικώλιος Coan = τρίκωλος. ὀβε-
λὸς τρικώλιος 'three-pronged fork'
τριπανάγορσις Arc. See πανάγορσις
τρῖς = τρεῖς. 114.3

τρίτρα, τά Cret. 'the threefold
amount.' 165.3
ττολίαρχοι Thess. (Phalanna), for
πτολίαρχοι. 67, 86.2. City officials. Cf. the πολιτάρχαι of Thessa-
lonica (Acts 17.6) and other Macedonian towns (Ditt. Syll. 318)
Τροφώνιος Boeot. = Τρεφώνιος.
46.1
τύ Dor. = σύ, σέ. 61.5, 118.2,5
τύ, τῦς Boeot. = τοί, τοῖς. 30
τυῖ Boeot. = τοίδε. 122
τυῖδε Lesb. 132.4
τύμος Corcyr. = τύμβος
τυρεία Heracl. 'cheese-press'
τωινί, τῶινυ Arc. = τῷδε. 123
τωνί Arc. = τοῦδε. 123

ὑ Cypr. = ἐπί. 135.8
ὑϝαίς Cypr. 'forever.' 133.6
Ὑβρέστας Thess. = Ὑβρίστας. 18
ὕγγεμος Cypr. 135.7
ὑδαρέστερον Lesb. 'less pure.' Used
with χέρναν of mixing water and
wine, and so applied also to the
debasement of coinage. No. 25,
note
ὑδρία Locr. = ὑδρία. 58d
υἱ Cret.; υἱς Rhod. = οἱ. 132.4
ϝυκία Boeot. = οἰκία. 30
ὐκτας Boeot., meaning? No. 39
ἡυλōρέοντος Thess., from ὑλωρέω
'be ὑλωρός,' the official in charge
of the public forests (cf. Arist.
Pol. 6.8.6). 157b, 167
ὑμέν late Cret. = ὑμεῖς. 119.2a
ὑμμές, ὑμέ = ὑμεῖς, ὑμέας. 119.2, 5
ὕμμες, etc. Lesb. = ὑμεῖς etc. 119
ὅμοιος, Arc., Lesb. = ὅμοιος. 22b
ὐνέθεκε Cypr. = ἀνέθηκε. 22
ὐνέθυσε Arc. = ἀνέθηκε. 22, no. 15,
note
ὐνιερόσει Arc. 152.4
ὑός, ὑύς = υἱός, υἱύς. 31
ὑπ Thess. = ὑπό. 95
ὑπά or ὑπα = ὑπό. 135.3
ὑπαπροσθίδιος Locr. 'a previous
citizen,' in contrast to a colonist.
135.3, 165.2
ὕπαρ Pamph. = ὕπερ. 12
ὑπεραμερία (also οὐ-, ὁ-) Boeot.
'note of default'
ὑποδεδρόμακε Lesb. 146.1
ὑπό El., Lac. = ἐπί with gen. in
expressions of dating. 136.11
ὑποδιασύρω Epid. = διασύρω 'ri-
dicule'

ὑππρὸ τᾶς Thess. 'just previously.'
136.1, 10. No. 32.43, note
hυπύ Cumae = ὑπό. 22d
ὕς Arg. = οἶ. 132.4
ὕσταριν El. = ὕστερον 12, 133.6
ὑστερομειννία Thess., οὑστερομειν-
νία Boeot. = Att. ἔνη καὶ νέα 'the
last day of the month.' Formed as
a pendant to νεομηνία
ὕσωπος Ceos = ὕσσωπος. Semitic
loan-word, hence variation in
spelling
ὑχέρον Cypr. = ἐπιχείρου. 135.8
ὕφαμμα = ὕφασμα. 86.8, 164.4

φάλυρον Arg. = λάφυρον. 88
Φανατεύς, Φανοτεύς Delph. 46.1
φάος. 41.2
φαρθένος Arc. = παρθένος. 65
φάρξις Epid. = φράξις. 49.2a
φάρχμα Epid. = φράγμα. 49.2a, 66
φάρω Locr., El., Delph. = φέρω. 12
φατρία, φάτρα = φρατρία. 70.3
φαωτός Delph. 'light-gray.' 31,
no. 52 C 24, note
φερνά Epid. = φερνή, but meaning
'portion' (for the god)
φερόσθō Epid. 140.3b
Φετταλός Boeot. = Θεσσαλός. 68.2
φεῶν Dodona = θεῶν. 68.5
φήρ Lesb. = θήρ. 68.2
φθέραι Arc. = φθεῖραι 80, 89.7
φθέρρω Lesb. = φθείρω. 74
φθήρω Arc. = φθείρω. 25, 74
φίντατος Dor. = φίλτατος. 72
Φίντων, Φιντίας = Φίλτων, Φιλτίας. 72
φοινικήια Ion. = γράμματα. Cf.
Hdt. 5.58. 164.1
φονές Arc. = φονεύς. 111.4
φράττω Boeot. = φράζω. 84a
φρήταρχος Naples = φρατρίαρχος.
70.3
φρίν Locr. = πρίν. 66
φρονέοι Cypr. = φρονέωσι. 59.4
φροντίδδω, φροντίττω Cret. = φρον-
τίζω. 84
φρυκτός 'bean for drawing lots.'
No. 53.15/16, note
φρυνοποπεῖον Boeot. meaning?
No. 39
φυγαδείω El. = φυγαδεύω. 161.1.
Aor. subj. φυγαδεύαντι, 151.1

φύοντες Dodona = θύοντες. 68.5
φωνέω Cret. (πόνίοι, etc.) 'declare,
bear witness.' Cf. ἀποφωνέω
(ἀποπόνίοι, etc.) in same sense

χάλκιος Lesb. = χάλκεος. 9.2,
164.6
χάραδος Heracl. = χαράδρα 'ravine'
Cf. Hom. χέραδος
χαρίϜετταν Boeot. = χαρίεσσαν.
53, 164.2
χείλιοι, χέλλιοι, χήλιοι 76, 117.3,
Att. χίλιοι 25e
ΧελιδϜόν Aetol. 54f
χέλυος 'breast, chest' Coan. no.
108.50, note
χερρ- Lesb. = χειρ-. 76
χηρ- = χειρ-. 25, 76
χραι(δ)δω El. = χρήζω. 84
χραύζομαι Cypr. = following
χραύομαι Cypr. 'border on.' 191
χρῆα Arc. = χρέα. 43
χρηέομαι, forms of. 162.13
χρήμενος, χρείμενος. 158
χρηίζω, χρήζω 'wish.' 162.14
χρύσιος Lesb. = χρύσεος. 9.2.
164.6

ψάφιγμα, ψάφιμμα Cret. = ψήφισμα. 86.9, 142a
ψαφίδδω Boeot., Cret. = ψηφίζω.
84
ψάφιξις Aetol., ψάφιξξις Locr. =
ψήφισις 'act of voting.' Locr. ἐν
ὑδρίαν τὰν ψάφιξξιν εἶμεν (no.
57.45) = Att. ψηφίζεσθαι ἐς ὑδρίαν. 89.1, 142a
ψήφιζμα = ψήφισμα. 60.4

ὦ Dor. etc. = ὅθεν 132.8
ὠβά Lac., a division of the people.
Cf. ὠάς· τὰς κώμας and ὠγή·
κώμη Hesych. (β and γ = Ϝ. 51
with a)
ὦν = οὖν. 25f
ὠνέω Cret. 162.15
ὠραῖα Coan 'festivals celebrated at
a fixed date.' Cf. Hesych. ὠραῖα
. . . τάσσεται . . . ἐπὶ τῶν καθ' ὥραν
συντελουμένων ἱερῶν.—ὠραία ἡμέρα. ἡ ἑορτή
ὦρος Cret., Arg. = ὅρος. 54
ὄτι Cret. = οὕτινος. 129.3

CHARTS

Chart I exhibits, in a form which may be easily surveyed, the distribution of many important peculiarities common to several dialects.

The presence of a given peculiarity is indicated by a cross opposite the name of the dialect and beneath a caption which, is sufficient to identify the phenomenon, though not always to define it, and should always be interpreted in the light of the section of the Grammar to which reference is made. The cross is sometimes surrounded by a circle as an intimation of some reservation, the nature of which will be understood from the section referred to.

Chart II is condensation, showing the most striking isoglosses.

CHART I

	η from ᾱ (8)	λεώς (41.4)	ἡμείς (119.2,5)	ἔθηκεν (102)	ἔθεσαν (138.5)	εἰ (134.1)	ἄν (134.2)	Infin. in -ναι (154.1)	ἰν = ἐν (10)	gen. sg. -ᾱυ (22)	πός = πρός (135.6)	σίς = τις (68.3)	κάς = καί (134.3)	ὀνυ = ὅδε (123)	dat. w. ἀπό, etc. (136.1)	ἐμμί, στάλλα, etc. (74-79)	ἰα = μία (114.1)	antevoc. ι > ι̯ (19)	καλέσσαι (143)	φερέμεν (155.1)	ρε = ρι (18)	πέμπε (68.2)	perf. pple in -ουν (147.3)	patr. adj. = gen. sg (168)	ἀγρέω, ἀγνρέω = αἰρέω (162.3)	πόδεσσι (107.3)	δέχοτος (6)	ὀν (ὐν) = ἀνά (6)	ἀπό = ἀπύ (22)	φίλημι (157)	ορ, ρο = αρ, ρα (5)	πεδά (135.5)	(125.?)
Attic	+	+	+	+	+	+	+	+																									
Ionic (E.C.W. — E.C.W.)	+	+	+	+	+	+	+	+																									
Arcadian				+	+	+	+	+	+	+	⊙	⊙	+	+														+	+	+	+	+	+
Cyprian								+	+	+	+	+	+	+	+	+												+	+	+	+		
Lesbian																+	+	+	+		+	+	+	+	+	+	+	+	+	+	+	+	+
Thessalian																+	+	+		+	+	+	+	+	+	+		+	+	+	+		
Boeotian																+		+	+	⊙	+	+	+			+					+	+	+
Phocian																										+							
Locrian																										⊙							+
Elean																									+	⊙				⊙			+
Laconian																																	+
Heraclean																																	
Megarian																																⊙	
Corinthian																										⊙							
Argolic																										⊙					⊙	+	
Rhodian																																	⊙
Coan																									⊙								⊙
Theran / Cyrenaean																										⊙					⊙	+	
Cretan								⊙																							⊙	+	

1	2	3	4	5	6	7	8	9	10	11	12	13	14	15	16	17	18	19	20		
+	+	+	+	+	+	+	+	+	+	+	+	+	+							δίδωτι	**61**.1
+	⊙	+	⊙	+			+	+	+		+	+	+							(ϝ)ίκατι	**116**
+	+	+		+			+	+	+	+	+	+	+				+			τριακάτιοι, -κάσιοι	**61**.2, **117**.2
+	+	+	+	⊙	+	+	+	+	⊙	+	⊙	+				⊙				ξ in aor., etc.	**142**
	+	+	+	+	+	+	+	+	+	+	+	+	+							τοί	**122**
+	+	+	+	+	+	+	+	+	+		+	+	⊙							ίαρός	**13**.1
	+	+	+	+	+	+		+			+	+	⊙							Ἄρταμις	**13**.2
+	+	+	+	+	+	+	+	+	+	+	+	+								κα, τόκα	**13**.3, **132**.11
+	+	+	+	+	+	+	+	+			+	+								πρᾶτος	**114**.1
+	+	+	+	+	+	+	+			+	+	+								ὅπει	**132**.2
⊙	+	+		+	+	+	+	+			+									1 pl. -μες	**223**a
+	+	+	+	+	+	+	+			+										fut. -σέω	**141**
+		+		+		+	+			+	+									τέτορες	**114**.4
				+		+					+									τετρώκοντα	**116**
+	+	+	+	+	+	+	+		+		+	⊙								αἴ τίς κα	**179**
		+	+	+	+	+	+			+										τῆνος	**125**
⊙				⊙			+			⊙	+									αὐτοσαυτός	**121**.4
+	+		+																	fut. pass. w. act. end.	**145**
+	+	+	+	+				+	+			⊙								adv. in -ν = -ς	**133**.6
+					+			+												Ἀπέλλων	**49**.3
+	+				+			+												λέω, λείω = θέλω	**162**.11
						+			+	+	+	+								masc. -ᾱ, gen. -ᾱς	**105**.1a, 2c
							+		+	+	+	+			+	+				ἐν = εἰς	**135**.4
⊙	⊙							+		+	+	+								καλείμενος	**158**
								+		+	+									φάρω	**12**
								+		+										πάντοις	**107**.3
								⊙		+	+	⊙	⊙	⊙			⊙			στ = σθ	**85**.1
										+			+	⊙		+				dat. sg. -οι	**106**.2
										+		⊙								acc. pl. -ες	**107**.4
											+	+	+	+						Ἱπποκλέας	**166**.1
									+		+	+	+	+				+		Φιλώνδας, -όνδας	**164**.8
												+	+							ει = η	**16**
												+	+							φέρονθι	**139**.2
												+	+							γίνυμαι	**162**.4
			+									+	+							ἔλεξε = εἶπε	Glossary

CHART II

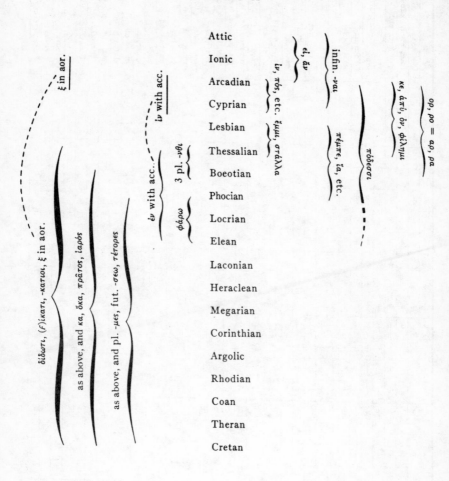

Attic

Ionic

Arcadian

Cyprian

Lesbian

Thessalian

Boeotian

Phocian

Locrian

Elean

Laconian

Heraclean

Megarian

Corinthian

Argolic

Rhodian

Coan

Theran

Cretan

ξ in aor.

ἐν with acc.

δίδωτι, (ϝ)ίκατι, -κατιοι, ξ in aor.

as above, and κα, ὄκα, πρᾶτος, ιαρός

as above, and pl. -μες, fut. -σεω, τέτορες

ἐν with acc.

3 pl. -νθι

φάρω

εἰ, ἄν

infin. -ναι

ἰν, πός, etc.; ἔμμι, στάλλα

πέμπε, ἰα, etc.

πόδεσσι

op, ρο = αρ, ρα

κε, ἀπύ, ὀν, φίλημι